Praise for Peter Cozzens's

THE EARTH IS WEEPING

"A valuable panoramic view. . . . Treachery on such an epic scale can bear many retellings, and this account stands out for its impressive detail and scope."
—*The Washington Post*

"Scorching vividness. . . . Crisp, muscular prose that offers clear pictures of men at war. A sweeping work of narrative history that synthesizes the work of countless historians. . . . [*The Earth Is Weeping*] recognizes fragments of nobility and humanity amid epic tragedy. . . . Without implying any false equivalence, Cozzens emphasizes history's tangled complexity."
— *San Francisco Chronicle*

"Scores of fascinating characters. . . . Vivid descriptions of ordinary people on both sides. . . . A sweeping, sharp and stylish history of the Indian Wars."
—*Minneapolis Star Tribune*

"Unlikely to be surpassed. . . . For those wishing to learn the story of the Indian Wars of the American West, this is the book to turn to."
—*The Weekly Standard*

"An evenhanded and smoothly written volume that is no less ambitious in scope than *Bury My Heart at Wounded Knee*."
—*The American Scholar*

"Sets a new standard for Western Indian Wars history."
—*True West*

"A striking and thorough explanation. . . . This is a history book, but it is also a present-tense book, full of ironies about how we're not so different from nineteenth-century Westerners." —*Big Sky Journal*

"In his exceptional book, Cozzens in no way ignores injustices done to Indians, but he insists we not ignore the white perspective, either. In short, the author achieves what he set out to do—bringing historical balance to the story of the Indian Wars."
—*Wild West*

PETER COZZENS

THE EARTH IS WEEPING

Peter Cozzens is the author or editor of seventeen acclaimed books on the American Civil War and the Indian Wars of the American West, and is a member of the advisory council of the Lincoln Prize. He is also a retired Foreign Service officer. He was awarded the American Foreign Service Association's highest honor, the William R. Rivkin Award, given annually to one Foreign Service officer for exemplary moral courage, integrity, and constructive dissent. Cozzens lives in Kensington, Maryland, with his wife.

www.petercozzens.net

THE EARTH IS WEEPING

✳

THE EPIC STORY
OF THE INDIAN WARS FOR
THE AMERICAN WEST

PETER COZZENS

VINTAGE BOOKS
A Division of Penguin Random House LLC
New York

The Library of Congress has cataloged the Knopf edition as follows:
Names: Cozzens, Peter, [date] author.
Title: The earth is weeping : the epic story of the Indian wars
for the American West / by Peter Cozzens.
Description: First edition. New York : Alfred A. Knopf, 2016.
Includes bibliographical references.
Identifiers: LCCN 2015044077
Subjects: LCSH: Indians of North America—Wars—1866–1895. |
West (U.S.)—History—1860–1890.
Classification: LCC E83.866 .C69 2016 | DDC 978/.02—dc23
LC record available at http://lccn.loc.gov/2015044077

Vintage Books Trade Paperback ISBN: 978-0-307-94818-2
eBook ISBN: 978-0-307-95805-1

Author photograph by Antonia Feldman
Maps by Mapping Specialists, Ltd.
Book design by Maggie Hinders

www.vintagebooks.com

Printed in the United States of America
10   9

For Antonia

If the lands of the white man are taken, civilization justifies him in resisting the invader. Civilization does more than this: it brands him a coward and a slave if he submits to the wrong. If the savage resists, civilization, with the Ten Commandments in one hand and the sword in the other, demands his immediate extermination.

—Report of the Indian Peace Commissioners, 1868[1]

I remember that the white men were coming to fight us and take away our land, and I thought it was not right. We are humans too and God created us all alike, and I was going to do the best I could to defend my nation. So I started on the warpath when I was sixteen years old.

—FIRE THUNDER, CHEYENNE WARRIOR[2]

We have heard much talk of the treachery of the Indian. In treachery, broken pledges on the part of high officials, lies, thievery, slaughter of defenseless women and children, and every crime in the catalogue of man's inhumanity to man the Indian was a mere amateur compared to the "noble white man."

—LIEUTENANT BRITTON DAVIS, U.S. ARMY[3]

CONTENTS

MAPS

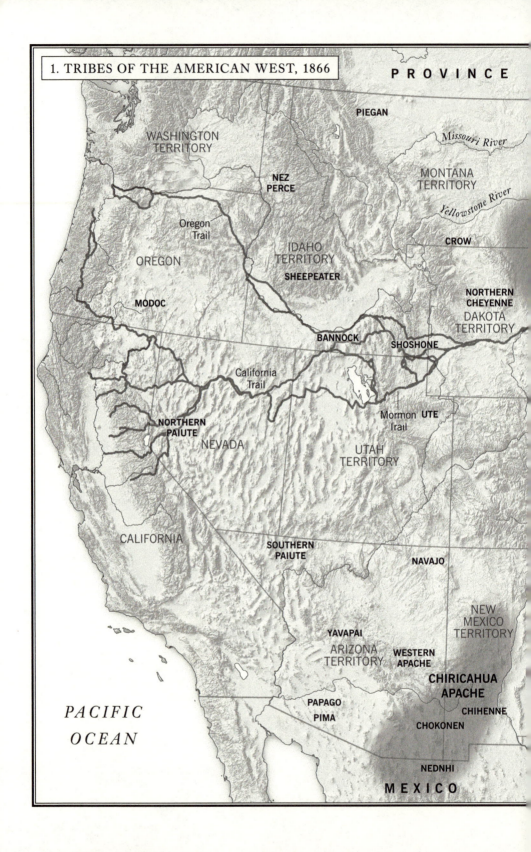

1. TRIBES OF THE AMERICAN WEST, 1866

PROVINCE

PIEGAN

Missouri River

MONTANA
TERRITORY

Yellowstone River

WASHINGTON
TERRITORY

NEZ
PERCE

Oregon
Trail

OREGON

IDAHO
TERRITORY

SHEEPEATER

CROW

MODOC

NORTHERN
CHEYENNE

DAKOTA
TERRITORY

BANNOCK

SHOSHONE

California
Trail

Mormon
Trail

UTE

NORTHERN
PAIUTE

NEVADA

UTAH
TERRITORY

CALIFORNIA

SOUTHERN
PAIUTE

NAVAJO

NEW
MEXICO
TERRITORY

YAVAPAI

ARIZONA
TERRITORY

WESTERN
APACHE

CHIRICAHUA
APACHE

PAPAGO

PIMA

CHIHENNE

CHOKONEN

PACIFIC

OCEAN

NEDNHI

MEXICO

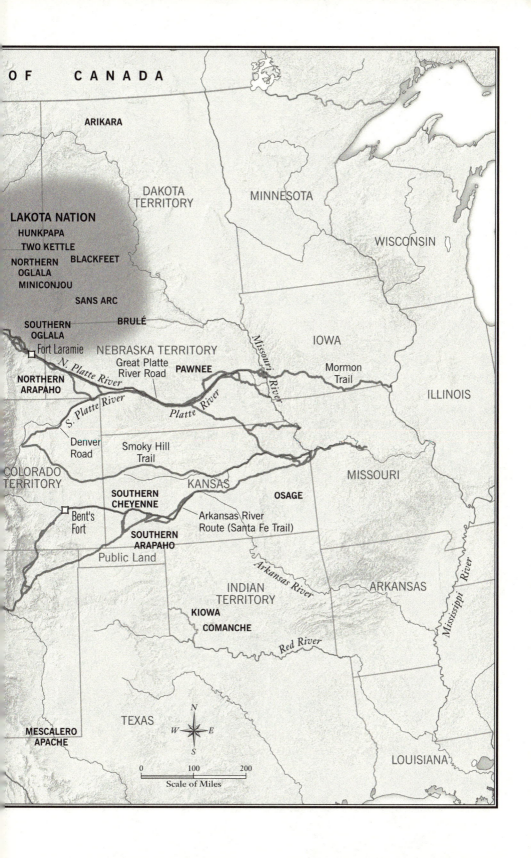

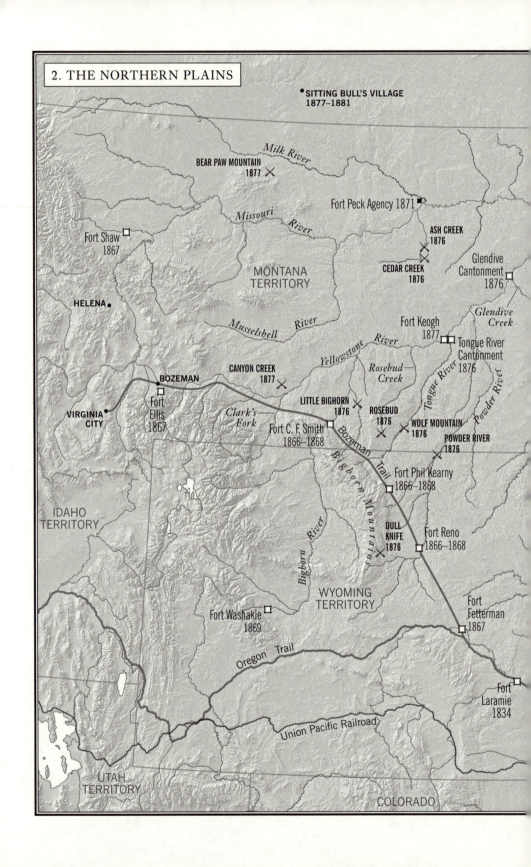

2. THE NORTHERN PLAINS

• SITTING BULL'S VILLAGE
1877–1881

BEAR PAW MOUNTAIN
1877 ✕

Milk River

Fort Peck Agency 1871 ■

ASH CREEK
1876 ✕

Missouri *River*

Fort Shaw 1867 ▫

CEDAR CREEK
1876

Glendive
Cantonment
1876 ▫

MONTANA
TERRITORY

Glendive
Creek

HELENA •

Musselshell *River*

Fort Keogh
1877 ▫

Tongue River
Cantonment
1876

Yellowstone *River*

CANYON CREEK
1877 ✕

Rosebud
Creek

Tongue River

Powder River

BOZEMAN

LITTLE BIGHORN
1876 ✕

ROSEBUD
1876 ✕

WOLF MOUNTAIN
1876 ✕

POWDER RIVER
1876 ✕

VIRGINIA
CITY •

Fort
Ellis
1867 ▫

Clark's
Fork

Fort C. F. Smith
1866–1868

Bozeman Trail

Fort Phil Kearny
1866–1868 ▫

IDAHO
TERRITORY

Bighorn River

Bighorn Mountains

DULL
KNIFE
1876 ✕

Fort Reno
1866–1868 ▫

WYOMING
TERRITORY

Fort Washakie
1869 ▫

Fort
Fetterman
1867 ▫

Oregon Trail

Fort
Laramie
1834

Union Pacific Railroad

UTAH
TERRITORY

COLORADO

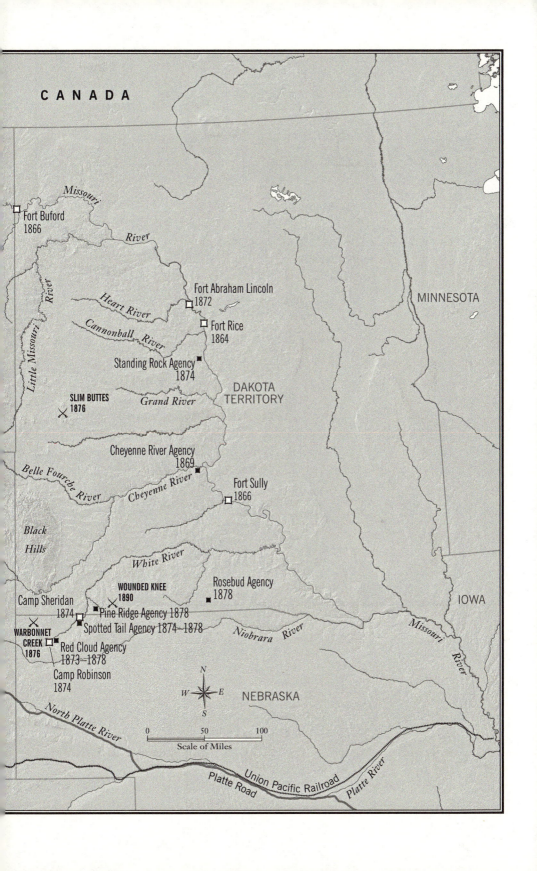

CANADA

Missouri

Fort Buford
1866

River

Little Missouri River

Heart River

Fort Abraham Lincoln
1872

MINNESOTA

Cannonball River

Fort Rice
1864

Standing Rock Agency
1874

DAKOTA
TERRITORY

SLIM BUTTES
1876

Grand River

Cheyenne River Agency
1869

Belle Fourche River

Cheyenne River

Fort Sully
1866

*Black
Hills*

White River

WOUNDED KNEE
1890

Rosebud Agency
1878

Camp Sheridan
1874

Pine Ridge Agency 1878

WARBONNET
CREEK
1876

Spotted Tail Agency 1874–1878

Red Cloud Agency
1873–1878

Niobrara River

Missouri River

IOWA

Camp Robinson
1874

N
W   E
S

NEBRASKA

North Platte River

0   50   100

Scale of Miles

Platte Road   Union Pacific Railroad   *Platte River*

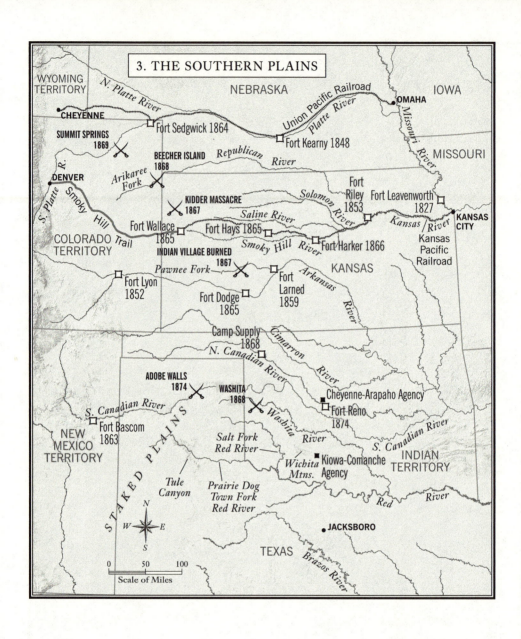

3. THE SOUTHERN PLAINS

WYOMING TERRITORY

N. Platte River

NEBRASKA

IOWA

CHEYENNE

Union Pacific Railroad

OMAHA

Fort Sedgwick 1864

Platte River

Missouri River

MISSOURI

SUMMIT SPRINGS 1869

Fort Kearny 1848

BEECHER ISLAND 1868

Republican River

DENVER

Arikaree Fork

S. Platte R.

Smoky Hill Trail

KIDDER MASSACRE 1867

Saline River

Solomon River

Fort Riley 1853

Fort Leavenworth 1827

KANSAS CITY

COLORADO TERRITORY

Fort Wallace 1865

Fort Hays 1865

Fort Harker 1866

Smoky Hill River

Kansas River

Kansas Pacific Railroad

INDIAN VILLAGE BURNED 1867

Pawnee Fork

KANSAS

Fort Lyon 1852

Fort Dodge 1865

Fort Larned 1859

Arkansas River

Camp Supply 1868

N. Canadian River

Cimarron River

ADOBE WALLS 1874

WASHITA 1868

Washita River

Cheyenne-Arapaho Agency

Fort Reno 1874

NEW MEXICO TERRITORY

Fort Bascom 1863

S. Canadian River

Salt Fork Red River

Wichita Mtns.

Kiowa-Comanche Agency

S. Canadian River

INDIAN TERRITORY

STAKED PLAINS

Tule Canyon

Prairie Dog Town Fork Red River

Red River

N
W E
S

JACKSBORO

TEXAS

Brazos River

0   50   100
Scale of Miles

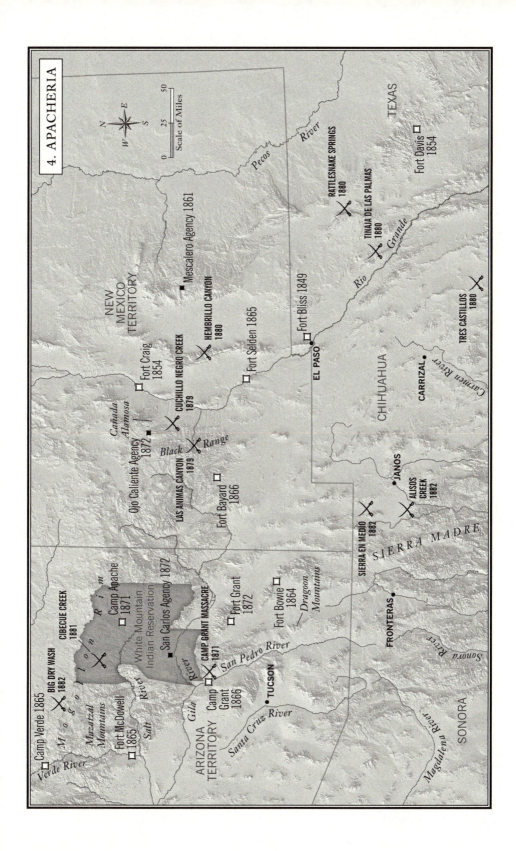

4. APACHERIA

Scale of Miles
0   25   50

TEXAS

Pecos River

RATTLESNAKE SPRINGS 1880

TINAJA DE LAS PALMAS 1880

Fort Davis 1854

Mescalero Agency 1861

NEW MEXICO TERRITORY

HEMBRILLO CANYON 1880

Rio Grande

Fort Bliss 1849

Fort Selden 1865

Fort Craig 1854

CUCHILLO NEGRO CREEK 1879

EL PASO

TRES CASTILLOS 1880

Cañada Alamosa 1872

Ojo Caliente Agency

LAS ANIMAS CANYON 1879

Black Range

Fort Bayard 1866

CHIHUAHUA

Carmen River

CARRIZAL

JANOS

ALISOS CREEK 1882

Camp Verde 1865

BIG DRY WASH 1882

CIBECUE CREEK 1881

Mogollon Rim

Camp Apache 1871

White Mountain Indian Reservation

San Carlos Agency 1872

Fort Grant 1872

Fort Bowie 1864

Dragoon Mountains

SIERRA EN MEDIO 1882

SIERRA MADRE

FRONTERAS

Mazatzal Mountains

Fort McDowell 1865

Salt River

Gila River

CAMP GRANT MASSACRE 1871

Camp Grant 1866

San Pedro River

TUCSON

ARIZONA TERRITORY

Santa Cruz River

Sonora River

SONORA

Magdalena River

Verde River

CHRONOLOGY

1862 AUGUST–DECEMBER · Dakota (Sioux) Uprising, Minnesota.

1864 NOVEMBER 29 · Sand Creek Massacre, Colorado.

1865 JUNE 27 · General Sherman assumes command of the Military Division of the Missouri.

    OCTOBER · Little Arkansas River Treaties negotiated with Southern Plains tribes.

1866 JULY · Red Cloud's War on Bozeman Trail, Montana Territory, begins.

    DECEMBER 21 · Fetterman Fight, Montana Territory.

1867 APRIL 19 · General Hancock burns Pawnee Fork villages in Kansas, initiating Hancock's War.

    JULY 1 · Kidder Massacre, Kansas.

    AUGUST 1 · Hayfield Fight, Montana Territory.

    AUGUST 2 · Wagon Box Fight, Montana Territory.

1868 FEBRUARY 29 · General Sheridan assumes command of the Department of the Missouri.

    SEPTEMBER 17–19 · Battle of Beecher Island, Colorado.

    NOVEMBER 4 · Chief Red Cloud signs Fort Laramie Treaty, ending Red Cloud's War.

    NOVEMBER 27 · Battle of the Washita, Indian Territory.

1869 JULY 11 · Battle of Summit Springs, Kansas.

    SUMMER · Sitting Bull elected head chief of non-reservation Lakotas.

1870 JANUARY 23 · Massacre of a Piegan village on the Marias River, Montana Territory.

1871 APRIL 30 · Camp Grant Massacre, Arizona Territory.

    OCTOBER · Colonel Mackenzie's first campaign on the Staked Plain, Texas.

1872   SEPTEMBER 28 · Battle of the North Fork of the Red River, Texas.

NOVEMBER 29 · Clash on Lost River, Oregon, beginning Modoc War.

DECEMBER 28 · Battle of Salt River Canyon, Arizona Territory.

1873   APRIL 11 · Modocs assassinate General Canby.

AUGUST 4 AND 11 · Custer skirmishes with Sitting Bull's Lakota coalition.

OCTOBER 3 · Modoc Captain Jack is hanged.

1874   JUNE 8 · Apache chief Cochise dies.

JUNE 27 · Battle of Adobe Walls, Indian Territory.

JULY–AUGUST · Custer discovers gold in the Black Hills.

SEPTEMBER 28 · Battle of Palo Duro Canyon, Texas.

NOVEMBER 8 · Battle of McClellan Creek, Texas.

1875   APRIL 23 · Slaughter of Southern Cheyennes at Sappa Creek, Kansas.

NOVEMBER 3 · President Grant convenes secret White House meeting to plan strategy for provoking war with the Lakotas.

1876   MARCH 17 · Battle of Powder River, Montana Territory.

EARLY JUNE · Lakotas and Northern Cheyennes hold joint Sun Dance at Deer Medicine Rocks, Montana Territory.

JUNE 17 · Battle of the Rosebud, Montana Territory.

JUNE 25 · Battle of the Little Bighorn, Montana Territory.

SEPTEMBER 9 · Battle of Slim Buttes, Dakota Territory.

SEPTEMBER · Reservation Lakota chiefs relinquish the Unceded Indian Territory.

OCTOBER 21 · Battle of Cedar Creek, Montana Territory.

NOVEMBER 25 · Destruction of Dull Knife's Northern Cheyenne village on the Red Fork of the Powder River, Wyoming Territory.

1877   JANUARY 8 · Battle of Wolf Mountain, Montana Territory.

MAY 6 · Crazy Horse surrenders at Fort Robinson, Nebraska.

MAY 7 · Sitting Bull enters Canada.

JUNE 17 · Battle of White Bird Canyon, Idaho Territory, first clash of the Nez Perce War.

JULY 11–12 · Battle of the Clearwater, Idaho Territory.

AUGUST 9–10 · Battle of the Big Hole, Montana Territory.

SEPTEMBER 5 · Crazy Horse is killed at Fort Robinson.

SEPTEMBER 30–OCTOBER 5 · Battle of Bear Paw Mountain, Montana Territory, and the surrender of Nez Perce chief Joseph.

1878   SEPTEMBER 9 · Northern Cheyenne exodus begins.

1879   JANUARY 9 · Northern Cheyenne outbreak from Fort Robinson.

MARCH 25 · Chief Little Wolf surrenders, ending Northern Cheyenne exodus.

SEPTEMBER 29–OCTOBER 5 · Battle of Milk Creek, Colorado.

1880   AUGUST 6 · Battle of Rattlesnake Springs, Texas.

OCTOBER 15 · Apache chief Victorio killed at Tres Castillos, Chihuahua, Mexico.

1881   JULY 20 · Sitting Bull surrenders at Fort Buford, Dakota Territory.

AUGUST 30 · Battle of Cibecue Creek, Arizona Territory.

1882   JULY 17 · Battle of Big Dry Wash, Arizona Territory.

1883   MAY–JUNE · Crook's Sierra Madre Campaign, Mexico.

MAY 10 · Sitting Bull becomes an "agency Indian" on the Great Sioux Reservation.

1885   MAY 17 · Geronimo breaks out of White Mountain Reservation, Arizona Territory.

1886   MARCH 25–27 · Crook and Geronimo meet at Cañon des los Embudos, Sonora, Mexico.

SEPTEMBER 3 · Geronimo surrenders to General Miles at Skeleton Canyon, Arizona Territory.

SEPTEMBER 8 · Chiricahua Apaches removed from Arizona Territory.

1889   JUNE · Sioux Land Commission breaks up the Great Sioux Reservation.

1890   DECEMBER 15 · Sitting Bull is killed on the Standing Rock Reservation, North Dakota.

DECEMBER 29 · Tragedy at Wounded Knee Creek, Pine Ridge Reservation, South Dakota.

1891   JANUARY 15 · Brulé and Oglala Lakotas surrender at Pine Ridge Agency, South Dakota.

THE EARTH
IS WEEPING

———•———

OUR CHILDREN
SOMETIMES BEHAVE BADLY

PATRONS OF P. T. BARNUM'S American Museum in April 1863 were in for a treat. For twenty-five cents, they could gaze upon eleven Plains Indian chiefs just arrived in New York City from a visit to the "Great Father" President Abraham Lincoln. These were not the "random beggars or drunken red men from Eastern reservations" that Barnum normally presented to the public, *The New York Times* assured readers. They were Cheyennes, Arapahos, Kiowas, and Comanches— "roamers of the remotest valleys of the Rocky Mountains." Barnum promised three dramatic performances daily, but the engagement was strictly limited. "Come now, or you're too late," trumpeted the great showman. "They are longing for their green fields and wild forest homes, and must be seen now or not at all."[1]

Barnum teased New Yorkers with extravagant previews. He rode through the streets of Manhattan with the Indians in an oversized carriage preceded by a marching band. The great showman and the chiefs made stops at schools, where children performed calisthenics and sang songs for them. Newspapers responded with amused derision, but the Indians captivated the public. Crowds flocked to the four-tier theater of Barnum's Broadway Street gallery to see staged "pow-wows." The Indians said little, but their painted faces, long braids, buckskin scalp shirts, and scalp-trimmed leggings delighted show goers. At the final curtain call on April 18, Chief Lean Bear of the Southern Cheyennes bade New Yorkers farewell on behalf of the delegation.[2]

✳

Chief Lean Bear was a member of the Council of Forty-Four, the governing body of the Cheyenne people. Council chiefs were peace-makers, enjoined by tribal custom never to permit passion to displace reason and to always act on behalf of the tribe's best interests, which in 1863 most elder Cheyenne chiefs construed as friendly relations with the mushrooming white population in the Territory of Colorado that crowded their already diminished hunting lands. But official Washington was troubled. Confederate agents were rumored to be circulating among the Plains Indians, trying to incite them to war. To counter the threat (which was in fact baseless) and smooth over differences with the tribes, the Indian Bureau had arranged for Lean Bear and ten other chiefs to visit the Great Father. The Indian agent Samuel G. Colley and their white interpreter accompanied them.

On the morning of March 26, 1863, two weeks before the opening of their New York extravaganza, the Indians, their agent, and their interpreter had filed into the East Room of the White House through a murmuring throng of cabinet secretaries, foreign diplomats, and distinguished curiosity seekers. "Maintaining that dignity or stolidity characteristic of the stoics of the woods," a Washington journalist told his readers, "they quietly seated themselves on the carpet in a semi-circle, and with an air of recognition to the destiny of greatness to be gazed at, seemed quite satisfied with the brilliancy of their own adornings and colorings."[3]

After a fifteen-minute wait, President Lincoln strode into the room and asked the chiefs if they had anything to say. Lean Bear arose. As the crowd of dignitaries pressed closer, Lean Bear momentarily lost his composure. The chief stammered that he had much to say but was so nervous that he needed a chair. Two chairs were brought, and Lincoln sat down opposite the chief. Cradling his long-stem pipe, Lean Bear spoke, hesitantly at first, but with a growing eloquence. He told Lincoln that his invitation had traveled a long way to reach them and the chiefs had traveled far to hear his counsel. He had no pockets in which to hide the Great Father's words but would treasure them in his heart and faithfully carry them back to his people.

Lean Bear addressed Lincoln as an equal. The president, he said, lived in splendor with a finer lodge, yet he, Lean Bear, was like the president, a great chief at home. The Great Father must counsel his white children to abstain from acts of violence so that both Indians and whites might travel safely across the plains. Lean Bear deplored the white man's war then raging in the East and prayed for its end. He closed with a reminder to Lincoln that as chiefs of their peoples he and the other Indian leaders must return home, and Lean Bear asked the president to expedite their departure.[4]

Then Lincoln spoke. He began with good-humored but marked condescension, telling the chiefs of wonders beyond their imagination, of "pale-faced people" in the room who had come from distant countries, of the earth being a "great, round ball teeming with whites." He called for a globe and had a professor show them the ocean and the continents, the many countries populated with whites, and finally the broad swath of beige representing the Great Plains of the United States.

The geography lesson over, Lincoln turned somber. "You have asked for my advice . . . I can only say that I can see no way in which your race is to become as numerous and prosperous as the white race excepting living as they do, by the cultivation of the earth. It is the object of this government," continued Lincoln, "to be on terms of peace with you and with all our red brethren . . . and if our children should sometimes behave badly and violate treaties, it is against our wish. You know," he added, "it is not always possible for any father to have his children do precisely as he wishes them to do." Lincoln said an officer called the commissioner of Indian affairs would see to their early return west. The chiefs were given bronzed-copper peace medals and papers signed by Lincoln attesting to their friendship with the government, after which Lean Bear thanked the president and the council concluded.[5]

The chiefs' stay in Washington did not end with the White House meeting, however. As if the journey east had not sufficed to demonstrate the power of the white people, for ten days the commissioner of Indian affairs insisted on shuffling the delegation from one government building and army fortification to another. Then Agent Colley accepted P. T. Barnum's invitation to New York. By the time the Indians boarded a train for Denver on April 30, 1863, they had been in the white cities nearly a month.[6]

*

President Lincoln's peace pledge rang hollow in the Territory of Colorado, where Governor John Evans's idea of interracial amity was to confine the Cheyennes on a small and arid reservation. Although they had signed a treaty three years earlier agreeing to accept reservation life,

Lean Bear and the other peace chiefs were powerless to compel their people to relinquish their freedom. Cheyenne hunting parties ranged over eastern Colorado and the unsettled western Kansas plains as they had always done. They harmed no whites; indeed, the Cheyennes considered themselves at peace with their white neighbors, but Coloradans nonetheless found their presence intolerable. Governor Evans and the military district commander, Colonel John Chivington, who had political ambitions of his own in Colorado, took dubious reports of cattle theft by hungry Cheyennes as an excuse to declare war on the tribe. In early April 1864, Chivington ordered cavalry to fan out into western Kansas and to kill Cheyennes "whenever and wherever found."

Lean Bear and his fellow peace chief Black Kettle had passed the winter and early spring quietly near Fort Larned, Kansas, where they traded buffalo robes. Now tribal runners brought word of the imminent danger. Recalling their hunting parties, Lean Bear and Black Kettle started their people northward to find protection in numbers among Cheyenne bands gathering on the Smoky Hill River. But the army found them first.

On the night of May 15, 1864, Lean Bear and Black Kettle camped on a muddy, cottonwood-fringed stream three miles short of the Smoky Hill. At dawn, hunting parties fanned out onto the open plain in search of buffalo. Before long, they were back, pounding their ponies to the lodge of the camp crier. They had spotted four columns of mounted soldiers on the horizon, and the troops had cannon. As the crier awakened the village, Lean Bear rode forward with a small escort to meet the soldiers. His medal from President Lincoln rested on his breast in plain view, and in his hand he carried the peace papers from Washington. From atop a low rise, Lean Bear saw the troopers at the same time they saw him. Their commander ordered his eighty-four men and two mountain howitzers into a battle line. Behind Lean Bear, four hundred warriors from the village assembled warily.[7]

Lean Bear rode forward, and a sergeant cantered toward him. All must have seemed well to the chief. After all, he and the Great Father had pledged mutual peace. Dignitaries from around the globe had greeted him at the White House. Army officers in the forts around Washington had been gracious and respectful. The people of New York City had honored him. He had his medal and peace papers to prove that he was the white man's friend. But the Great Plains was a world unto itself.

Lean Bear was just thirty feet from the soldiers when they opened fire. The chief was dead before he hit the ground. After the smoke cleared, several troops broke ranks and pumped more bullets into his corpse. As Lincoln had cautioned Lean Bear, his children sometimes behaved badly.[8]

*

A newspaperman once asked George Crook, one of the preeminent generals in the West, how he felt about his job. It was a hard thing, he replied, to be forced to do battle with Indians who more often than not were in the right. "I do not wonder, and you will not either, that when Indians see their wives and children starving and their last source of supplies cut off, they go to war. And then we are sent out there to kill them. It is an outrage. All tribes tell the same story. They are surrounded on all sides, the game is destroyed or driven away, they are left to starve, and there remains but one thing for them to do—fight while they can. Our treatment of the Indian is an outrage."[9]

That a general would offer such a candid and forceful public defense of the Indians seems implausible because it contradicts an enduring myth: that the regular army was the implacable foe of the Indian.

No epoch in American history, in fact, is more deeply steeped in myth than the era of the Indian Wars of the American West. For 125 years, much of both popular and academic history, film, and fiction has depicted the period as an absolute struggle between good and evil, reversing the roles of heroes and villains as necessary to accommodate a changing national conscience.

In the first eighty years following the tragedy at Wounded Knee, which marked the end of Indian resistance, the nation romanticized Indian fighters and white settlers and vilified or trivialized the Indians who resisted them. The army appeared as the shining knights of an enlightened government dedicated to conquering the wilderness and to "civilizing" the West and its Native American inhabitants.

In 1970, the story reversed itself, and the pendulum swung to the opposite extreme. Americans were developing an acute sense of the countless wrongs done the Indians. Dee Brown's elegantly written and passionately wrought *Bury My Heart at Wounded Knee* and, later that same year, the film *Little Big Man* shaped a new saga that articulated the nation's feelings of guilt. In the public mind, the government and the army of the latter decades of the nineteenth century became seen as willful exterminators of the Native peoples of the West. (In fact, the government's response to what was commonly called the "Indian problem" was inconsistent, and although massacres occurred and treaties were broken, the federal government never contemplated genocide. That the Indian way of life must be eradicated if the Indian were to survive, however, was taken for granted.)

Bury My Heart at Wounded Knee still deeply influences the way Americans perceive the Indian Wars and has remained the standard popular work on the era. It is at once ironic and unique that so crucial a period of our history remains largely defined by a work that made no attempt at historical balance. Dee Brown gave as the stated purpose of his book the presentation of "the conquest of the American West as the victims experienced it," hence the book's subtitle, *An Indian History of the American West*. Brown's definition of victims was severely circumscribed. Several tribes, most notably the Shoshones, Crows, and Pawnees, cast their fate with the whites. *Bury My Heart at Wounded Knee* dismissed these tribes as "mercenaries" with no attempt to understand them or explain their motives. These Indians, like the army and the government, became cardboard cutouts, mere foils for the "victims" in the story.

Such a one-sided approach to the study of history ultimately serves no good purpose; it is impossible to judge honestly the true injustice done the Indians, or the army's real role in those tragic times, without a thorough and nuanced understanding of the white perspective as well as that of the Indians. What I have sought to do in this book, then, is bring historical balance to the story of the Indian Wars. I hesitate to use the word "restore" when speaking of balance, because it is the pendulum swings that have defined society's understanding of the subject since the closing of the military frontier in 1891.

Of inestimable benefit to my work has been the wealth of Indian primary sources that have become available since the publication of *Bury My Heart at Wounded Knee*. They have enabled me to tell the story equally through the words of Indian and white participants and, through a deeper understanding of all parties to the conflict, better address the many myths, misconceptions, and falsehoods surrounding the Indian Wars.

A myth as enduring as that of an army inherently antagonistic toward the Indians is that of united Indian resistance to white encroachment.

No tribe famous for fighting the government was ever united for war or peace. Intense factionalism ruled, each tribe having its war and peace factions that struggled for dominance and clashed, sometimes violently, with one another. One of the most committed advocates of peaceful accommodation with the whites paid for his convictions with his life; a disgruntled member of the tribe's war faction poisoned him.

Unanimity existed only among tribes that accepted the white invasion. Influential chiefs such as Washakie of the Shoshones saw the government as guarantors of his people's survival against more powerful tribal enemies. The Shoshones, Crows, and Pawnees all proved invaluable army allies in war, following the adage that the enemy of my enemy is my friend.

Not only did the Indians fail to unite in opposing the westward expansion of "civilization," but they also continued to make war on one another. There was no sense of "Indianness" until it was too late, and then it came but dimly through a millennial faith that brought only bloodshed, horror, and broken hopes.

Intertribal conflict was in part the consequence of a fact that has never been appreciated but that will become apparent as this book unfolds: that the wars between Indians and the government for the northern plains, the seat of the bloodiest and longest struggles, represented a displacement of one immigrant people by another, rather than the destruction of a deeply rooted way of life. A decade after Lean Bear's murder, an army officer asked a Cheyenne chief why his tribe preyed on their Crow neighbors. He responded, "We stole the hunting grounds of the Crows because they were the best. We wanted more room."[10] That was a sentiment that the Coloradans determined to rid their territory of the Cheyennes could readily appreciate.

PART ONE

CHAPTER I

THE PLAINS AFLAME

PRESIDENT LINCOLN vastly understated the case when he told Lean Bear that his white children sometimes behaved badly. In the two and a half centuries between the settlement of the Jamestown colony in Virginia and Lincoln's cautionary words to the Cheyenne chief, a relentlessly expansionist white population had driven the Indians westward without regard to treaty obligations or, sometimes, even simple humanity. The government of the young American Republic had not intended to exterminate the Indians. Nor had the founding fathers simply coveted Indian land. They had also wanted to "enlighten and refine" the Indian, to lead him from "savagery" to Christianity, and to bestow on him the blessings of agriculture and the domestic arts—in other words, to destroy an incompatible Indian way of life by civilizing rather than by killing the Indians.

The "civilized" Indians would not live on their homeland, which the federal government meant to purchase from them at the best possible price by means of treaties negotiated on the legal premise that tribes held title to their land and possessed sufficient sovereignty to transfer title to the true sovereign; that is to say, the United States. The federal government also pledged never to deprive the Indians of their land without their consent or to make war on them without congressional authorization. To prevent settlers or individual states from infringing on Indian rights, in 1790 Congress enacted the first of six statutes collectively known as the Nonintercourse Act, which prohibited the purchase of Indian land without federal approval and carried stiff punishments for crimes committed against Indians.

Not surprisingly, the punishment provision of the law quickly proved toothless. President George Washington attempted to intercede on behalf of the Indians, to whom, he insisted, full legal protection must be afforded, but his admonitions meant nothing to land-hungry whites living beyond the government's reach. In order to prevent a mutual slaughter, Washington sent troops to the nation's frontier. Once sucked into the fray, the small American army spent two decades and nearly all its limited resources in wresting the Old Northwest from powerful Indian confederations in undeclared wars. That set a dismal precedent; henceforth, treaties would be a mere legal veneer to conceal wholesale landgrabs that Congress tried to palliate with cash annuities and gifts of merchandise.

After George Washington, no president lost much sleep over Indian rights. Indeed, the executive branch led the way in divesting the Indians of their homelands. In 1817, President James Monroe told General Andrew Jackson that "the savage requires a greater extent of territory to sustain it than is compatible with the progress and just claims of civilized life, and must yield to it." As president in the 1830s, Jackson took Monroe's injunction to its harsh but logical extreme. With the authority granted him under the Removal Act of 1830, and by employing varying degrees of duress, Jackson swept the roving tribes of the Old Northwest beyond the Mississippi River. When southerners pressured him to open Indian lands in Alabama and Georgia, Jackson also uprooted the so-called Five Civilized Tribes—the Choctaws, Chickasaws, Creeks, Cherokees, and Seminoles—and resettled them west of the Mississippi River in Indian Territory, an unsustainably large tract spreading over several future states, which was gradually reduced to comprise solely present-day Oklahoma. Most of the "civilized" Indians went peaceably, but it took two long and bloody conflicts for the army to dislodge the Seminoles from their Florida strongholds, and a handful ultimately were allowed to remain.[1]

Jackson never doubted the justice of his actions, and he truly believed that once beyond the Mississippi River the Indians would be forever free from white usurpation. Fur trappers, traders, and missionaries would be permitted to pass through the Indians' new home and venture out onto the Great Plains, or into the mountains beyond, but there assuredly would be no further upheaval because army explorers had reported the Great Plains as unsuited to white settlement, and the public took them at their word.

But already there were pressures on the periphery. A burgeoning fur trade on the Missouri River expanded white contact with the western tribes. Also, the removal treaties bound the federal government to protect the relocated tribes not only from acquisitive whites but also from hostile Plains Indians, who had no desire to share their domain with newcomers, be they Indian or white. Meanwhile, white Missourians and Arkansans demanded protection from the dispossessed Indians in the event they found their new land somewhat less than the Eden they had been promised (which they did). The government's answer was to build a chain of nine forts from Minnesota southward to northwest Louisiana between 1817 and 1842, creating a tantalizing abstraction known as the Permanent Indian Frontier.

*

Of the 275,000 Indians whose homelands lay outside Indian Territory and beyond the newly constituted military barrier, the government cared little and knew even less.[2] White conceptions of the Indians of the American West were simplistic and tended toward extremes; Indians were either noble and heroic or barbaric and loathsome. But when the "Permanent Indian Frontier" crumbled less than a decade after its creation, a cataclysmic chain of events suddenly brought whites and Indians face-to-face west of the Mississippi.

The first crack in the permanent frontier appeared in 1841. Lured by the promise of fertile land in California and the Oregon Country, a few lumbering caravans of white-topped prairie schooners ventured tentatively onto the plains. The trickle soon became a torrent, and the rutted wagon road thus created along the shifting sands of the dreary Platte River became etched in the nation's psyche as the Oregon Trail.

Then came the annexation of Texas in 1845, and a year later the United States and Britain settled a contentious dispute over the Oregon boundary. In early 1848, the War with Mexico ended in the Treaty of Guadalupe Hidalgo, by which Mexico ceded California, the Great Basin, and the Southwest, as well as its claims to Texas, recognizing the Rio Grande as the international border. In just three years, the United States had grown by nearly a million square miles and become a continental nation. Expansionist orators exhorted Americans to fulfill the nation's Manifest Destiny by emigrating to Texas, California, or the Pacific Northwest. (No one as yet considered the Great Plains other than a vast and tedious obstruction.) In August 1848, gold was discovered in California's American River. The following year saw a mass migration unequaled in the young nation's history. Within a decade, there were more whites in California than there were Indians in the entire West. Genocidal gold seekers decimated California's peaceable small tribes, and the growth of white settlements in the newly organized Oregon Territory alarmed the stronger northwestern tribes.

As yet there had been no open conflict with the Indians in the West, but the peace was tenuous, warned the commissioner of Indian affairs. The Indians, he said, had abstained from attacking emigrant trains out of an expectation of reward from the government and not from fear, because they had not felt "our power and know nothing of our greatness and resources."[3]

They would not feel that power for some time to come; the government lacked anything resembling a coherent Indian policy, and the small regular army needed time to build forts in the West. In any case, the commissioner of Indian affairs need not have feared any great, concerted resistance to the white deluge. For one thing, the Indians did not perceive the white onslaught for the apocalyptic threat to their way of life that it was. But even if they had, the Indians of the American West had no common identity—no sense of "Indianness"—and were too busy fighting one another to give their undivided attention to the new threat.

And this was their Achilles' heel. Only in the Pacific Northwest were the Indians able to unite against the sudden and vigorous white expansion. Few tribes in the West proved able to maintain the internal unity necessary to oppose the white advance. Nearly every tribe broke into two factions, one advocating peaceful accommodation with the whites and adopting white ways, the other holding fast to the traditional ways, resisting the government's enticements to go peaceably onto reservations. The government grew adept at exploiting these rivalries, giving the army a potent fifth column in its battles to bring the "hostile" Indians to heel. The army would also come to benefit immeasurably from the intertribal warfare that lay at the very foundation of the culture of the Indians of the West. That the army needed Indian allies in order to prevail would prove axiomatic.

In the relations between tribes, there was nothing subtle; outsiders were either allies or enemies. The most intense intertribal conflict occurred on the northern plains, where warfare was fluid and continuous, as tribes struggled to conquer or protect hunting grounds. Tribes everywhere in the West survived and prospered by entering into alliances; those that went it alone suffered horribly. Open battles were rare; wars normally took the form of endless small raids and counter-raids that chipped away at the loser's domain.

On the Great Plains, the foundation of the Indian way of life was the American bison, commonly known as the buffalo. Buffalo meat was a staple. From the hide, the Indians fashioned robes for warmth and trade, containers for transport and storage, and skins for the distinctive conical tipi—also known as a lodge. No part of the animal was wasted. Not only did the buffalo undergird the economy, but it also shaped the Plains Indians' religion and culture.

Well before the first American ventured beyond the Mississippi River, the European gifts of horses, guns, and disease had radically altered Plains and Rocky Mountain Indians' cultures. In the sixteenth century, the Spaniards had introduced the horse to the New World. As the Spanish frontier pushed into the present-day southwestern United States, horses fell into the hands of Indians. Afterward, through theft and barter, the horse culture spread rapidly from tribe to tribe. In 1630, no tribe was mounted; by 1750, all of the Plains tribes and most of the Rocky Mountain Indians rode horses. The horse did not create the buffalo culture, but it made hunting infinitely easier. Horses also increased the frequency and fury of intertribal clashes, because warriors were able to range over distances previously unimaginable on foot. The gun, introduced to the Indians by French trappers and traders, made the hostile encounters far more deadly. White man's diseases were deadlier yet, decimating western tribes just as they had ravaged those east of the Mississippi. No one knows precisely how many succumbed, but in 1849 alone cholera carried off half the Indian population of the southern plains.[4]

A grand irony of the Great Plains is that none of the tribes with which the army would clash were native to the lands they claimed. All had been caught up in a vast migration, precipitated by the white settlement of the East. This Indian exodus had begun in the late seventeenth century and was far from over when the Oregon Trail opened in 1843. As the dislocated Indians spilled onto the plains, they jockeyed with native tribes for the choicest hunting lands. In a very real sense, then—and this cannot be overemphasized—the wars that were to come between the Indians and the government for the Great Plains, the seat of the longest and bloodiest struggles, would represent a clash of emigrant peoples. A way of life was lost, but it had not been of long duration.

The most powerful newcomers before the whites spilled onto the plains were the Sioux, formerly a woodlands people of the present-day upper Midwest. As it shifted west, the Sioux nation separated into three divisions: the Dakotas, a semisedentary people who clung to the Minnesota River; the Nakotas, who settled east of the Missouri River; and the Lakotas, who wrestled their way onto the northern plains. The Lakotas were the true horse-and-buffalo Sioux of popular imagination, and they constituted nearly half the Sioux nation. The Lakotas in turn divided into seven tribes: the Oglalas, Brulés, Miniconjous, Two Kettles, Hunkpapas, Blackfeet, and Sans Arcs, of which the Oglalas and the Brulés were the largest. In fact, these two tribes alone outnumbered all the non-Lakota Indians on the northern plains.

In their westward march across present-day Nebraska and the Dakotas during the early nineteenth century, the Lakotas gradually allied themselves with the Cheyennes and the Arapahos, who had been pushed onto the northern plains in advance of the Lakotas and had already forged an enduring bond, albeit an odd coupling. Their languages were mutually unintelligible, an impediment they overcame with a sophisticated sign language, and their characters could not have been more dissimilar. The Arapahos tended to be a kindly and accommodating people, whereas the Cheyennes evolved into fearsome warriors. The first contact between the Lakotas and the Cheyenne-Arapaho combination was hostile, because they competed for the game-rich Black Hills country. "Peace would be made," a Cheyenne chief recounted. "They would hold out the pipe to us and say, 'Let us be good friends,' but time and again treacherously broke their promises." Not until the 1840s did the Lakotas keep their word. By then, many of the Cheyennes and Arapahos, fed up with the duplicity of the Lakotas and lured by white traders, had migrated south, forming the Southern Cheyenne and Southern Arapaho tribes and leaving the Lakotas the undisputed suzerains of the northern plains.

The Lakotas and the Cheyennes and Arapahos who remained on the northern plains had the same tribal enemies—the badly outnumbered but hard-fighting Crows of present-day central Montana and northern Wyoming and the semi-agricultural Pawnees who dwelled along the Platte River in Nebraska. The basis of the rivalry was both a relentless drive by the Lakota–Northern Cheyenne–Northern Arapaho alliance to expand their hunting lands and the warrior culture common to all Plains tribes. Geographically separated from each other, the Crows and the Pawnees never formed an alliance, but being badly in need of friends—or enemies of their enemies conceived of as friends—both tribes instead eventually cast their fate with the whites.[5]

Similar jostling had occurred on the southern plains. The Kiowas, expelled from the Black Hills by the Lakotas, had retreated southward into the country known as Comancheria, where they first fought and then concluded an alliance with the Comanches. The uncontested lords of the southern plains and the most accomplished horsemen in the West, the Comanches were a fierce and cruel people who roamed and raided at will from the Arkansas River deep into Texas. They warred sporadically with Mexico but got along well enough with the Americans until settlers threatened their hunting grounds. The Republic of Texas treated the Comanches even worse than had the Mexican government, pursuing a policy of betrayal and brutality that culminated in the slaughter of a Comanche peace delegation. The Comanches afterward counted Texans as their bitterest enemies, and they regarded depredations against Texas settlers as both just retribution for the murder of their peace chiefs and good sport.

The Southern Arapahos and Southern Cheyennes availed themselves of their proximity to Comancheria to raid Comanche and Kiowa horse herds until 1840, when the four tribes concluded a permanent peace, forming a potentially potent combination to contest the advancing whites.[6]

*

All but the most dull-witted federal official understood that the quiet along the overland roads, which had so pleasantly surprised the commissioner of Indian affairs in 1849, was temporary. As emigrants depleted timber, grass, and game at an alarming rate, Indians along the travel routes were reduced to near starvation. Recognizing that the Indians must eventually either stand and fight, ally themselves with the whites, or perish, the government accepted three responsibilities: to provide military protection to the emigrant roads and to the burgeoning white settlements; to extinguish Indian land titles; and to develop a humane policy to provide for the divested Indians. That the government would meet its responsibilities looked doubtful. The small frontier army had barely enough men to defend its small forts, much less protect emigrants. Negotiation appeared the only viable short-term strategy, and to treat with the Indians, the Bureau of Indian Affairs called on Tom Fitzpatrick, a former mountain man turned Indian agent. Enjoying the implicit trust of the Plains tribes, Fitzpatrick had proven more capable than any other agent of performing the herculean duties of the office as it was then defined. As the federal government's representative to one or more tribes, an Indian agent was required to work to prevent conflict between settlers and Indians, cooperate with the military as needed to keep the peace, and distribute government annuities honestly and promptly.

In 1851, Fitzpatrick assembled ten thousand Northern Plains Indians at Fort Laramie for a council of unsurpassed magnitude. The chiefs signed an agreement called the Fort Laramie Treaty—which, as was nearly always the case, the Indians understood only dimly, if at all—and then joyously accepted gifts for their people from the Great Father. Two years later, Fitzpatrick concluded a similar accord at Fort Atkinson with the Southern Plains tribes. The dual treaties were models of brevity, their provisions seemingly unambiguous. The Indians were to refrain from warring among themselves or against Americans; to accept formal tribal boundaries; to permit the government to build roads and forts in their territories (it already had); and to not molest pioneers transiting their country. In exchange, the government promised to shield the Indians from white despoilers of their lands (which it lacked either the capacity or the will to do) and to pay the tribes annuities for fifty years (which the Senate subsequently slashed to ten years).

Fitzpatrick had done his job, but he condemned the treaties as mere temporizing. "The policy must be either an army or an annuity," he argued with uncommon prescience. "Either an inducement must be offered to them greater than the gains of plunder, or a force must be at hand able to restrain them and check their depredations. Any compromise between the two systems will only be liable to all the miseries of failure." Fitzpatrick also disapproved of the custom of extinguishing Indian title for the simple reason, he said, that the Plains Indians held no title beyond a "vagabond right," amounting to the privilege of occupancy by conquest. Few Indians would have argued with him, and none seriously considered halting raids on tribal foes simply because the government willed it. Nor would they accept tribal boundaries. "You have split my land and I don't like it," declared a Lakota chief. "These lands once belonged to the Kiowas and the Crows, but we whipped these nations out of them, and in this we did what the white men do when they want the lands of the Indians."[7]

Despite the treaties, conflict often arose between the army and the Indians, though seldom purposely. Sometimes it resulted from a single rash or foolish act committed by hot-blooded young warriors or blundering junior army officers. Such was the case on the northern plains in August 1854, when John L. Grattan, a cocky lieutenant fresh from West Point who had boasted that he could crush the entire Lakota people with a handful of infantry and a howitzer, picked a fight with the peaceable Brulé chief Conquering Bear over an emigrant's stray cow that a warrior had butchered. Conquering Bear offered to make restitution, but Grattan instead fired on his village. When the smoke cleared, Conquering Bear lay mortally wounded, and Grattan and twenty-nine soldiers were dead.

Grattan's foolhardy act had constituted naked aggression. Certainly it was provocation enough for the Brulés to declare open war on the whites. Nonetheless, the Brulés demonstrated remarkable restraint. A war party attacked a stagecoach and killed three passengers; otherwise, emigrant trains continued to pass through the Brulé country unimpeded. But that did not satisfy the War Department, which refused to concede that Grattan's foolish actions had precipitated the clash. Determined to avenge what it called the Grattan Massacre, the War Department ordered Colonel William S. Harney to administer the Indians a sound "thrashing." He did so two years later, obliterating a Brulé camp near Blue Water Creek in the Nebraska Territory in September 1856, killing half of the warriors and taking most of the women and children captive. The humbled Brulé chiefs surrendered the perpetrators of the stagecoach raid, among whom was a daring war leader named Spotted Tail. Held at Fort Leavenworth for a year, Spotted Tail found the white man's power so impressive that he became a lifelong peace advocate, or—as some Lakotas put it—he returned from incarceration "fat, soft, and supine." Beefy he might have been, but Spotted Tail was hardly supine, and he would rise meteorically to a position of unparalleled power over the Brulé tribe.

For a decade, the specter of Harney "the Butcher" haunted the entire Lakota nation. There was much loud talk in council lodges but no action—just a gnawing hunger for revenge. Harney empathized with the Indians. Taking no pleasure in his victory over the Brulés, he reminded Washington that "the Indians had been simply defending their rights."[8]

In the spirit of injustice engendered by the "Grattan Massacre," the government also decided that the Cheyennes, who had caused emigrants no real trouble and had no intention of doing so, nonetheless merited punishment. An army attack on an unsuspecting Cheyenne village on the Solomon River in the Kansas Territory in the summer of 1857 killed few warriors but scored a psychological victory, teaching them, according to the Cheyenne Indian agent, the futility of opposing the white man.

It was a bad moment for the Cheyennes to concede defeat. The year after the Solomon River fight, white prospectors found gold in present-day eastern Colorado. Almost overnight, the city of Denver sprang up. Miners and farmers elbowed their way onto Cheyenne and Arapaho hunting grounds, overrunning most of the huge tract promised the tribes under the Treaty of Fort Laramie negotiated by Tom Fitzpatrick a decade earlier. In February 1861, ten Cheyenne and Arapaho chiefs— Black Kettle and Lean Bear among them—signed the Fort Wise Treaty, which committed their tribes to live on a pitifully small reservation on the arid plains of southeastern Colorado Territory. Although most Cheyennes and Arapahos disavowed the chiefs' pledges and continued to inhabit their traditional hunting grounds, they committed no acts of violence. None of the Indians could foresee the horrible consequences their passive resistance would soon engender.

Meanwhile, farther south, efforts to subdue the Kiowas and the Comanches proved worse than useless. Neither tribe molested the emigrant trails, but they continued to attack Texas settlements. That Texas now constituted part of the United States was of no consequence to them. When regular army protection proved wanting, the Texas Rangers took the lead in whipping the Comanches in three engagements that inflamed the Indians, who not only visited unprecedented devastation on the Texas and Mexican frontiers but also struck at westbound travelers.

The military was largely powerless to stop them. Much of the antebellum frontier army's limited resources were devoted to quashing Indian uprisings in the Pacific Northwest that dragged on for three bloody years. At the conclusion of the last war in 1858, the vanquished

Indians signed treaties that fixed their reservation boundaries. The herding of the Pacific Northwest tribes onto carefully prescribed tracts and the Fort Wise Treaty three years later were the first steps in what was gradually to become known as the policy of concentration. Indians would be removed from land that whites wanted or had already taken and relocated as far as possible from the contaminating influence of the invaders. Then would begin the noble experiment of converting the Indians into Christian farmers. Of course, because most Indians were not interested in the blessings the white man wished to bestow, government attempts at concentration usually meant war.[9]

The whites were coming now, in numbers incomprehensible to the Indians. They assaulted Indian lands from every direction. Settlers rolled in from the east, while miners poked at the periphery of the Indian country from the west, north, and south and simply overran it when new mineral strikes were made. In westerners' parlance, Indians who resisted the onslaught were to be "rounded up" and rendered harmless on reservation land too miserable to interest the whites. It would be a grand encirclement and a slow strangulation that would require three decades to choke the life out of recalcitrant Indians.

*

During the tumultuous 1850s, only the Southwest remained quiet. The vast region, which embraced not only present-day Arizona and New Mexico but also northern Mexico, was called Apacheria after its dominant Indian occupants, the Apaches. Far from being a distinct tribe, the Apaches were a loose conglomeration of bands divided into two great divisions, the Eastern and the Western.[10] Two groups of the Western Division—the Western Apaches and the Chiricahuas, neither of which had much use for the other—would cause the government the greatest difficulties.

By the time the first Americans ventured into Apacheria in the 1820s, the Western Apaches and the Chiricahua Apaches had been at war, first with Spaniards and then with Mexicans and their Indian collaborators, for nearly two centuries. Confounding troops, laying waste to haciendas, and levying tribute on towns, the Apaches rendered the Mexican presence in Apacheria tenuous at best. The Apaches initially greeted Americans warmly as fellow enemies of the Mexicans, but tension quickly mounted after the United States obtained much of

Apacheria under the Gadsden Purchase Treaty of 1853, which obligated Washington to prevent Apache raids into Mexico. This the Apaches could not comprehend. The Mexicans remained their enemies and had been the enemies of the Americans; why, then, should they cease raiding south of the border as long as they behaved themselves north of it?

Then, in 1860, prospectors discovered gold in the mountainous western reaches of the Territory of New Mexico, the heart of the Chihenne (Eastern Chiricahua Apache) homeland. When the Chihenne chief Mangas Coloradas attempted to broker a peaceful accommodation, prospectors horsewhipped him, whereupon he declared war on the Americans. Even more egregious was the mistreatment accorded Cochise, chief of the Chokonens (Central Chiricahuas), who was on friendly terms with settlers in his desert homeland in present-day southeastern Arizona. George H. Bascom, another blundering lieutenant cut from the same West Point mold as Grattan, squandered the goodwill in February 1861 when he arrested Cochise and several of his warriors under the mistaken impression that the chief had kidnapped a boy from a distant ranch. Cochise escaped and took hostages of his own. After several days of fruitless parleying, Cochise killed his hostages, and Bascom hanged the Chiricahuas, including Cochise's brother. With that, Arizona exploded in an orgy of violence.

And then, in the spring of 1861, the regular army vanished from the frontier. Indians puzzled over the abrupt departure of the soldiers. The Chiricahuas, concluding they had beaten the army, stepped up their depredations. But the Plains Indians hesitated and in so doing missed a brief, unique opportunity to slow the white tide.

The Plains Indians' moment to strike passed, and soon new soldiers came—westerners who thought no more of shooting an Indian than they did a deer. They were a tougher caliber of men than the regulars, and there were far more of them. Fifteen thousand volunteers, drawn from the nearly three million eventually raised by the federal government to combat the Southern rebellion, saw duty in the West during the Civil War, double the strength of the antebellum frontier regular army. Most hailed from California, which was to be expected, because the state's population stood at nearly half a million and continued to climb. In fact, the Civil War caused no drop in emigration to the West. On the contrary, despite the momentous upheaval that absorbed the energies and resources of the North and the South, mineral strikes throughout the West enticed whites in ever greater numbers into previously undisturbed Indian lands.

Indeed, despite the seemingly endless need for more troops to defeat the Confederacy, the Lincoln administration encouraged people to hit the trails west. In 1862, Congress passed the Homestead Act. Beginning January 1, 1863, any U.S. citizen or intended citizen, including free slaves and female heads of household, would receive title to 160 acres of federal land west of the Mississippi River, provided the claimant had improved the property, had resided on it for five consecutive years, and had never taken up arms against the United States. Families looking for a fresh start farming on the prairie filled the emigrant roads, already swollen with fortune seekers, and the pressure on Indian lands intensified.

The population boom led to the creation of six territories between 1861 and 1864: Nevada, Idaho, Arizona, Montana, Dakota, and Colorado, which grew the fastest of them all. A direct road to Denver was laid. Called the Smoky Hill Trail, it ran through prime Indian hunting ground. Soon stagecoach and telegraph lines crisscrossed the Indian country, while the states of Nebraska and Kansas pushed their borders deeper onto the plains. Although their anger at the white interlopers mounted, the Southern Plains tribes kept the peace, even as the circle of their world grew smaller.

Despite the quiet on the southern plains, there was enough violence elsewhere for two volunteer generals, James H. Carleton and Patrick E. Connor, to achieve fame in the Civil War West. In July 1862, part of Carleton's "California Column" drove several hundred Chiricahua warriors under Cochise and Mangas Coloradas from Apache Pass, a strategic defile in the heart of Chokonen country. Mangas Coloradas was wounded in the encounter; six months later, a Carleton subordinate lured the chief into camp under a flag of truce and then murdered him. Despite the twin blows, the Chiricahuas were hardly beaten; on the contrary, after Carleton left, Cochise redoubled his effort to depopulate southeastern Arizona.

Continuing east, Carleton vanquished the small Mescalero Apache tribe of the New Mexico Territory. Next he crushed the powerful Navajo nation, which had been engaged with New Mexicans in a long war of raids and retaliation, in a scorched-earth campaign led by his old friend the legendary frontiersman Kit Carson. While Carleton waged war in the Southwest, General Connor cleared the travel routes between California and Utah and then decimated a renegade Shoshone band that had made war on Rocky Mountain gold miners.[11]

*

While the Southwest bled and the Rocky Mountains trembled, relative calm prevailed on the northern plains until 1863, when warfare erupted on an unprecedented scale. The cause was indirect—a brutal uprising of the Dakota Sioux, whose once ample Minnesota reservation had shrunk to a sliver of land along the Minnesota River while the white population of the state had soared. Predatory traders plied the Dakotas with liquor and separated them from their annuity money, and missionaries harassed them. Nearby farmers prospered, while hunger and hopelessness stalked the reservation. On August 17, 1862, young warriors returning empty-handed from a hunt murdered six settlers. There was no premeditation, but there was also no containing a decade of accumulated rage. Faced with certain government retaliation, the chiefs chose to fight, and Dakota war parties butchered hundreds of settlers before Union troops drove them onto the plains and into the arms of their Nakota kinsmen. In pitched battles in 1863 and 1864, the army crippled the Dakotas and the Nakotas, who—less a small number who escaped to Canada or joined the Lakotas—afterward submitted to reservation life.

The Minnesota uprising also sent shock waves across the relatively quiescent southern plains. Coloradans, already uneasy at sharing the territory with the Southern Cheyennes and Arapahos, were horrified. They construed the slightest Indian offense—there had been precious few, and those that did occur consisted of bloodless horse and cattle raids—as portending a similar massacre on their soil. Preemptive strikes against the tribes made sense to many Coloradans, including the military district commander, Colonel John Chivington. Indeed, it was Chivington's policy of preemptive war that had cost Lean Bear his life. After Lean Bear was murdered, Chief Black Kettle had restrained the warriors from wiping out the small army detachment responsible for the atrocity. But neither he nor any other chief could long prevent wrathful warriors from retaliating against the overland routes and isolated ranches in southern Nebraska and western Kansas. No longer merely stock-stealing enterprises, their raids were now grim and gory affairs, replete with rape and butchery. Although most attacks in the summer of 1864 were perpetrated by the Dog Soldiers—an unfailingly belligerent Cheyenne band—young men from Black Kettle's band were also guilty of some of the more notorious atrocities.

In August, Governor Evans and Colonel Chivington recruited a short-term regiment, the Third Colorado Cavalry, composed of rowdies, ruffians, and gutter trash eager to kill Indians. Before they could act, Black Kettle sued for peace. Evans had invited friendly Indians to separate themselves from the hostiles, and now Black Kettle was doing just that, but the public clamored for revenge. Evans passed the problem to Chivington, whose principal concern was ensuring that his Colorado cavalrymen saw action before their enlistment expired. At daybreak on November 29, Chivington swept down on Black Kettle's unsuspecting village at Sand Creek. As Chivington deployed for the attack, Black Kettle raised first the American flag and then a white flag over his tipi. But Chivington wasn't interested in displays of patriotism or truces. He wanted no prisoners taken, and none were. Two hundred Cheyennes, two-thirds of them women and children, were massacred in a manner reminiscent of the Minnesota uprising. They "were scalped, their brains knocked out," an army interpreter later testified. "The [Coloradans] used their knives, ripped open women, clubbed little children, knocked them in the head with their guns, beat their brains out, and mutilated their bodies in every sense of the word." Black Kettle, however, escaped along with his wife, who somehow survived nine wounds. Wanting only to avoid the inevitable cycle of war and retribution, he took the survivors well south of the Arkansas River. Meanwhile, Colonel Chivington and the "Bloody Third" rode into Denver to a hero's welcome.[12]

As Indian fury over the Sand Creek Massacre scorched the snow-covered southern plains, Southern Cheyenne, Arapaho, and Lakota chiefs agreed to "raise the battle-axe until death." That meant not a fight to the finish, as the ominous words suggested, but rather a massive raid followed by a return to customary pursuits like hunting buffalo and sparring with enemy tribes. In January and February 1865, warriors ravaged the Platte River Road and threw Denver into a panic. Then the allied tribes headed north to the Black Hills to escape retribution and recount their exploits to their northern kinsmen, who in turn staged a "war" of their own. As many as three thousand warriors, constituting the largest war party the Great Plains had ever seen, attacked Platte Bridge Station, a strategic but weakly garrisoned military post, mangling a cavalry detachment and ambushing a wagon train. With that, the Indians considered the soldiers sufficiently chastised, and they scattered for the fall buffalo hunt.

In the army's view, however, the conflict had scarcely begun. In February, the War Department created a sprawling new geographic command called the Military Division of the Missouri to encompass the Great Plains, Texas, and the Rocky Mountains. Headquarters were in St. Louis, Missouri. The division commander, the bombastic but capable major general John Pope, had fashioned plans for a concerted offensive in the early spring of 1865 before Indian ponies recovered from the harsh plains winter and raids resumed on the emigrant routes. Three expeditions were to strike the recalcitrant Plains tribes simultaneously. Pope predicated his strategy on two premises: that Civil War veterans would be available in large numbers for duty in the West, and that he would have authority to deal with hostile tribes as he saw fit.

Pope's was a fine plan, but it was not to be. With the end of the Civil War in April 1865, Union volunteers expected to go home, and they no sooner arrived in the West than they deserted. The second pillar of Pope's plan—civilian support—eroded before the campaign had even begun. Simply put, after Sand Creek the government had no stomach for a fight. Instead, Congress authorized Governor Newton Edmunds of the Dakota Territory to negotiate a new treaty with the Lakotas and appointed a commission to negotiate a lasting peace on the southern plains. The War Department also wavered. In the end, only one of Pope's three columns took the field. Commanded by General Connor, the expedition marched on the Black Hills in August 1865. Connor's operation was a fiasco. Men deserted in droves, and in a pair of inept encounters with the Lakotas and the Cheyennes, two of Connor's columns barely escaped annihilation. That ended, at least for the moment, the military's effort to win a peace.[13]

*

Seldom had government policy toward the Plains Indians been consistent or even coherent. So it was in the autumn of 1865, when Governor Edmunds invited to his peace conference the very Indians then battling Connor. That none of them came was of little concern to Edmunds. Because his sole reason for seeking a treaty was to make the Dakota Territory appear safe to prospective settlers, in October he collected the signatures of some dissipated chiefs of "stay-around-the-fort" bands and proclaimed peace on the northern plains. For reasons known only to himself, the commissioner of Indian affairs endorsed Edmunds's fiction.

Something more closely approximating a real treaty was concluded at a grand peace council with the southern tribes on the Little Arkansas River in October 1865. Repudiating Chivington's "great wrongs," the commissioners convinced the Indians that their interests would best be served by accepting a reservation that encompassed much of southwestern Kansas, nearly all the Texas Panhandle, and a large part of Indian Territory—another step on the road to concentration, another tightening of the circle.

Generous on paper, the treaty proved an empty gesture. Texas refused to relinquish any portion of the panhandle, and Kansas refused to sanction a reservation within its boundaries. The only portion of the proposed reservation that the federal government controlled lay within Indian Territory. The Treaty of the Little Arkansas, General Pope sneered, was not worth the paper it was printed on.[14]

But that was no longer a matter of Pope's concern. In late June 1865, he relinquished command of the Military Division of the Missouri to Major General William T. Sherman. Second only to Ulysses S. Grant in the pantheon of Northern war heroes, Sherman brought to the job a profound love of the West, where, he wrote to a friend, his "heart has always been." It was an odd sentiment, considering that the West had nearly killed him. As a San Francisco bank manager before the Civil War, Sherman had suffered from anxiety and acute asthma brought on by the city's belligerent business climate. But locals had appreciated his West Point background, and during the vigilante days of 1856 they elected him to a brief stint as major general of the California militia. When Sherman assumed command of the Military Division of the Missouri nine years later at the age of forty-five, his furrowed face, gray-streaked stubble beard, and unkempt close-cropped hair gave him more the appearance of an aged prospector than a potent general in the prime of life.

Sherman held contradictory opinions of the Indian. On the one hand, he felt pity for "the poor devil [who] naturally wriggles against his doom" and anger at "whites looking for gold [who] kill Indians just as they would kill bears and pay no regard for treaties." He objected, however, to the Indians' "sloth" and believed that they must be treated as recalcitrant children in need of "discipline." When discipline failed, then total war became necessary, with an outcome unpleasant to contemplate. Addressing a class of graduating West Pointers, Sherman could only advise them to help achieve the "inevitable result" as humanely as possible.[15]

Inevitable, perhaps. But war was something Sherman could ill-afford in 1866. Union volunteers were mustering out far faster than regular forces could reestablish themselves on the frontier. Congress was determined to maintain the smallest possible standing army, and Sherman found himself with fewer than twelve thousand troops, scarcely sufficient to patrol the emigrant roads. Before stepping down, General Pope had promulgated strict rules compelling civilians to travel only on these main routes and to band together in trains of sufficient size to defend themselves. Although the orders were difficult to enforce, westerners applauded their intent, and Sherman renewed them.

The frontier army in 1866 thus found itself in the dual role of gatekeeper and guardian of the westering population of a nation suddenly delivered from internecine war and bursting with energy. During one six-week period, more than six thousand wagons passed through Nebraska headed west. Emigrants scoured the land along the travel routes like locusts until there was not a stick of wood with which to kindle a fire; even buffalo chips were at a premium. Along the Platte River Road, telegraph poles became more plentiful than trees. Isolated ranches offered inviting targets to Indian raiders or, as one officer observed, to white marauders masquerading as Indians. Dismissive of the risks, the governor of Kansas organized the state-sponsored Immigrant Society to lure settlers to western Kansas, and thanks to the Homestead Act there was no dearth of takers; in the decade following the Civil War, the populations of Kansas and Nebraska grew threefold.

Sherman pinned his hopes for a permanent peace not on the army but rather on the transcontinental railroad, then under construction. The rapid westward progress of the Union Pacific astounded him; by late 1866, track had reached the north bank of the Platte opposite Fort Kearny (meanwhile, beyond his jurisdiction, the Central Pacific was slowly pushing east into the Sierra Nevada mountain range). Sherman proposed to accord the Union Pacific "all the protection and encouragement" within his power to give. That, however, would require troops Sherman did not yet have. As he told Grant in August, "We are in no condition to punish the Indians this year, for our troops are barely able to hold the long thin lines that are traveled by daily stages and small parties of emigrants . . . All I ask is comparative quiet this year, for by next year we can have new cavalry enlisted, equipped, and mounted, and ready to go and visit the Indians where they live."[16]

But a Janus-faced Indian policy and an uncompromising Oglala war leader named Red Cloud were about to deny Sherman the tranquillity he so badly needed.

CHAPTER 2

RED CLOUD'S WAR

RED CLOUD abhorred liquor, "the water that makes men crazy." Alcoholism killed his Brulé father three decades before Lieutenant Grattan fired the ill-conceived volley that touched off war with the Lakotas. Fatherless at age four, his family name disgraced, Red Cloud went to the Platte River country in 1825 to live with his mother's Northern Oglala band, whose chief was her brother, the affable Old Smoke. Initially ostracized, Red Cloud compensated for his dubious lineage with superior war skills.

Brave and charismatic, Red Cloud built a considerable following while still in his twenties, but he was quick to anger and had a cruel streak that cost him the respect of many Lakotas. Some also considered him a murderer for having shot a rival chief during a brawl. When Old Smoke died around 1850, his son formally succeeded him as chief, but by then Red Cloud had cemented his position as a war leader, and he became de facto chief in times of trouble.[1]

Between 1861 and 1862, the Northern Oglala and Miniconjou Lakotas and their Cheyenne and Arapaho allies fought a final, all-out war with the Crows for control of the Powder River country. By the terms of the Fort Laramie Treaty, the land belonged to the Crows, but the 150-mile-wide tract between the Bighorn Mountains and the Black Hills was prime hunting ground, and their enemies meant to have it. That they succeeded was largely due to Red Cloud. Now forty-three years old, he had entered the second stage of a great fighting man's life—that of strategist. Red Cloud set general objectives and organized large war parties but delegated their conduct to younger men of merit, including a strange and silent twenty-two-year-old Oglala warrior named Crazy Horse.

With the defeat of the Crows, the allied tribes thought they had found a home far from grasping whites, but in 1862 gold was discovered in southwestern Montana Territory. A year later, the frontier entrepreneur John Bozeman blazed a trail to the diggings along the eastern base of the Bighorn Mountains, straight through the heart of the newly won hunting grounds. White travelers so thoroughly depleted buffalo and antelope herds that the Northern Oglalas nearly starved during the winter of 1865–1866.

The crucial question for the government as spring 1866 approached was whether the Indians would move against the Bozeman Trail. Most high officials, including General Sherman, assumed that the winter of hunger would render them pliable, but to make certain the Indians remained quiet, Sherman ordered two posts built on the Bozeman Trail, which were to be named Fort Phil Kearny and Fort C. F. Smith. The forts would belong to the Department of the Platte, commanded by Brigadier General Philip St. George Cooke, a doddering regular army officer shelved during the Civil War.[2]

While Sherman arranged to occupy the Bozeman Trail, in early June 1866 the Indian Bureau convened a peace council at Fort Laramie to negotiate the Indians' permission for whites to travel over the Bozeman Trail unmolested. All the principal Northern Oglala and Miniconjou chiefs were present, but Red Cloud spoke loudest. His opposite at the Fort Laramie talks was Edward B. Taylor. An Indian Bureau representative for whom deceit was a perfectly acceptable negotiating tool, Taylor assured Red Cloud that the government would forbid travelers to despoil the Bozeman country, which a subordinate called an impossible promise, "well calculated to deceive the Indians." Taylor also assured the chiefs that the Great Father had no wish to garrison soldiers on the Bozeman.

The lie held until June 13, when the Second Battalion, Eighteenth U.S. Infantry, commanded by Colonel Henry B. Carrington, marched into Fort Laramie en route to the Bozeman Trail to build and garrison the two planned forts. When Red Cloud saw the soldiers, he exploded, haranguing the peace commission for "treating the assembled chiefs as children" and pretending to negotiate for rights in a country they intended to conquer. Accusing the government of bad faith, he vowed to expel the army. "The Great Father sends us presents and wants us to sell him the road," declared Red Cloud wrathfully, "but the White Chief goes with soldiers to steal the road before Indians say Yes or No." He and his adherents returned north to prevent white soldiers from stealing from them the land that they had only recently stolen from the Crows. Meanwhile, Taylor secured the agreement of several stay-around-the-fort chiefs with no claim to the country and then telegraphed Washington that a cordial peace had been obtained. Throughout the remainder of 1866, he would feed the Interior Department a steady stream of misinformation and lies that blinded the government to the dangers on the Bozeman Trail.[3]

*

Colonel Henry B. Carrington fought well from behind a desk. He owed his rank to political connections and spent the Civil War on staff assignments. Little about him inspired confidence as a combat leader. Just five feet four inches tall, Carrington was an elitist who once called a subordinate illiterate because the man had attended public schools. Yet while Carrington's Yale Law School degree and bookishness might have served him well in Washington parlors, they counted for nothing with the combat veterans he commanded. Sherman, however, was not worried and encouraged officers' wives to accompany "Carrington's Overland Circus." In early July, this procession of seven hundred troops; three hundred women, children, and civilian contractors; and 226-mule-drawn wagons set out for the Bighorn region laden with everything except sufficient ammunition for sustained combat.[4]

On July 15, Carrington selected a grassy valley just south of the junction of the Bozeman Trail and Big Piney Creek as the site of the future Fort Kearny. From the construction camps, the blue snow-fringed Bighorn Mountains on the western horizon seemed close enough to touch. Strategically, the site was sound; it lay in the heart of the Northern Oglala hunting lands. But from a tactical standpoint, it left much to be desired. High ground dominated the valley on three sides. Two miles to the north, the Bozeman Trail passed behind a long elevation called Lodge Trail Ridge. West of the fort, a low ridge that Colonel Carrington christened the Sullivant Hills in honor of his wife's maiden name blocked the view to a pinery five miles distant that provided the wood Carrington needed to build the stockade. That alone should have caused the colonel to reconsider the location. He found it inconceivable, however, that a large force of hostile Indians might lurk amid forests and hills "too lovely to define, too picturesque to imitate." But they were there, a delegation of Cheyenne peace chiefs warned Carrington on July 16—thousands of them under Red Cloud's banner. Whether because he disbelieved their warning, doubted their motives, or was just plain overconfident, Carrington declined their offer of a hundred warriors; he had, he assured the chiefs, men enough of his own.

The next morning, Red Cloud struck the Bozeman, and in the flight of an arrow it became a ghost trail, devoid of white travelers. Then the Indians turned their attention to the unfinished fort itself, and the picturesque landscape took on a menacing aspect. During the day, warriors watched the soldiers from Lodge Trail Ridge. After nightfall, Indian campfires burned uncomfortably close. War parties rose from the earth and thundered down the Sullivant Hills, corralling wood trains and keeping the troops in a constant state of alarm. Anyone who became separated from his companions or ventured out alone was as good as dead. Carrington's inexperience, a seemingly trivial matter in the hopeful atmosphere of early summer, now paralyzed the command, such as it was; Carrington had no cavalry, and most of the enlisted men were raw recruits, carrying outmoded muzzle-loading Springfield rifled muskets. Few men could shoot straight because Carrington scheduled no target practice; he considered finishing Fort Kearny before winter more important than basic training. Carrington had the added responsibility of constructing Fort C. F. Smith, and so, on August 9, he sent two companies under Captain Nathaniel C. Kinney through the loose Indian cordon ninety miles up the Bozeman Trail to build the post. While the men labored, Captain Kinney settled into a long drunk, leaving to the wolves the bodies of soldiers killed beyond the gates.

Carrington's greatest handicap was not untrained soldiers or inebriated subordinates but a high command in denial. Taylor's sham treaty and repeated assurances of Indian goodwill led General Cooke to ignore Carrington's pleas for more men and ammunition. Cooke reported none of the latter's concerns up the chain, and in late August, as warriors flocked to Red Cloud's banner, an uninformed Sherman assured General Grant that all was well on the Bozeman Trail. Meanwhile, Red Cloud's star was ascendant; the Northern Cheyenne and Arapaho war factions stood with him, while the Miniconjou, Sans Arc, and Hunkpapa Lakotas all contributed large parties to the war effort. Even a handful of Crows switched sides. By September 1, 1866, at least fifteen hundred warriors had congregated in Red Cloud's Tongue River valley encampment. Time was running out for Carrington.[5]

*

On October 31, Carrington dedicated Fort Kearny. The colonel might have been an unknown quantity as a combat officer, but he was certainly a fine engineer. He had constructed a seventeen-acre marvel of frontier-army engineering enclosed within a thirty-nine-hundred-foot-long wall of eight-foot-high pine logs. There were firing platforms and loopholes for rifles and two blockhouses. Awesome to behold, the defenses seemed excessive to a visiting army inspector, who censured Carrington for "[thinking] only of building his post."

General Cooke also wanted Carrington to show some combat initiative, urging him to attack Red Cloud when winter came. Carrington resisted. In letter after letter, he had made clear to Cooke the obstacles he faced. His 308 officers and men were stretched thin guarding the post's wood and hay trains and escorting army wagons on the Bozeman Trail. Morale was low, and the troops were poorly clad. Talk of an offensive was nonsense. Discontented subordinate officers eager for action compounded Carrington's woes, particularly Captain William Judd Fetterman, who complained of being "afflicted with an incompetent commanding officer." Fetterman also purportedly boasted that under proper leadership—meaning himself—"a company of regulars could whip a thousand, and a regiment could whip the whole array of hostile tribes."[6]

Fed up with a prodding department commander and sniping subordinates, in early December Carrington vowed to strike back the next time the Indians raided the daily wood trains. He finally had reinforcements—fifty cavalry recruits who could hardly mount their horses—and decided to test them and their commander, Lieutenant Horatio S. Bingham. Unbeknownst to Carrington, the Indians were planning a surprise of their own. Using decoys, they wanted to lure soldiers from the fort into an ambush behind Lodge Trail Ridge. It was a timeworn Indian tactic, but one unfamiliar to Carrington and his officers. At daybreak on December 6, one hundred warriors perhaps led by the young Crazy Horse (the evidence of his presence is inconclusive) gathered along the pinery road. Red Cloud took up a station on a ridge to direct the decoys with flags and mirrors.

The wood train left Fort Kearny on schedule. When the wagons were three miles out, the decoys struck. Carrington countered with a pincer movement that misfired because Lieutenant Bingham disobeyed orders and chased Indian decoys into an ambush. Most of his caval-rymen escaped, but a panic-stricken Bingham simply threw away his pistol and awaited his end. A search party later found him sprawled naked over a tree stump with fifty arrows protruding from his body. Afterward, Captain Fetterman grumbled that "the fight was a failure and that Carrington was not fit to conduct one." Carrington might have agreed; in any event, he staged no more attacks. Instead, he began feverishly to drill his men.[7]

*

When the great blow fell on Fort Kearny two weeks later, it was led by Miniconjous, not Red Cloud, on behalf of a recently deceased Mini-conjou chief with a score to settle. Many years earlier, drunken soldiers had looted and defecated in his lodge. Before dying, the chief told his friends to avenge the indignity with an attack on the white intruders.

Because the decoy-and-ambush tactic had nearly succeeded on December 6, the Miniconjous chose to repeat it. Once again, a small band would attack the wood train and then retreat in apparent disarray when troops rode to relieve it. Mounted decoys would linger to lure the soldiers over Lodge Trail Ridge to a lower, abutting ridge along which the Bozeman Trail ran north to Peno Creek. There the main force would spring the trap.[8]

*

December 21 dawned gray and cold. The ground was bare, but the smell of coming snow hung heavy in the air. The Cheyennes, Arapa-hos, and Oglalas, all under Red Cloud's general supervision, hid in a lightly timbered gully west of the Bozeman Trail ridge. The Minicon-jous took position in a bald ravine to the east. At 10:00 a.m., the wood train rolled out of Fort Kearny. An hour later, it came under attack.[9]

At 11:00 a.m., Captain Fetterman led forty-nine infantrymen out of the fort. On cue, the Indian decoys appeared. Everyone's blood was up. A warrior yelled in English, "You sons of bitches come out and fight us!" Two well-armed civilians with personal grudges against the Lako-tas rode with the soldiers. A captain who was about to transfer out also joined the detachment in order to have "one more chance to bring in the scalp of Red Cloud himself." Carrington, meanwhile, told Lieuten-

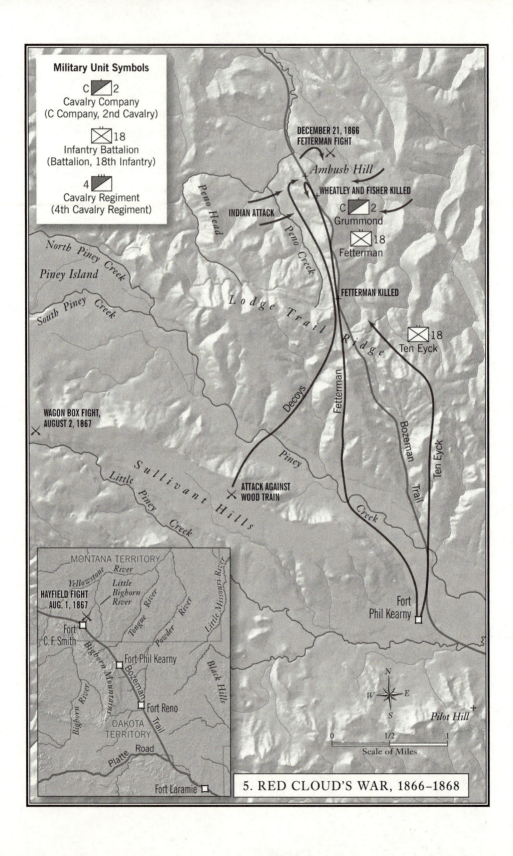

Military Unit Symbols

C ⊠ 2
Cavalry Company
(C Company, 2nd Cavalry)

⊠ 18
Infantry Battalion
(Battalion, 18th Infantry)

4
Cavalry Regiment
(4th Cavalry Regiment)

North Piney Creek

Piney Island

South Piney Creek

DECEMBER 21, 1866
FETTERMAN FIGHT

Ambush Hill

WHEATLEY AND FISHER KILLED

Peno Head

INDIAN ATTACK

C ⊠ 2
Grummond

Peno Creek

⊠ 18
Fetterman

FETTERMAN KILLED

L o d g e   T r a i l

R i d g e

⊠ 18
Ten Eyck

WAGON BOX FIGHT,
AUGUST 2, 1867

Decoys

Fetterman

Bozeman Trail

Ten Eyck

Little

S u l l i v a n t   H i l l s

Piney

ATTACK AGAINST
WOOD TRAIN

Creek

Piney   Creek

MONTANA TERRITORY

Yellowstone River

Little Bighorn River

HAYFIELD FIGHT
AUG. 1, 1867

Fort
C. F. Smith

Tongue River

Powder River

Little Missouri River

Fort Phil Kearny

Bighorn Mountains

Bighorn River

Bozeman Trail

Fort Reno

Black Hills

DAKOTA
TERRITORY

Platte   Road

Fort Laramie

Fort
Phil Kearny

N
W   E
S

Pilot Hill

0   1/2   1
Scale of Miles

5. RED CLOUD'S WAR, 1866–1868

ant George W. Grummond, an alcoholic and impetuous member of the anti-Carrington clique, to take twenty-seven cavalrymen and "report to Captain Fetterman, implicitly obey orders, and never leave him."

The decoys rode leisurely over Lodge Trail Ridge, taunting the soldiers to make haste. Carrington had ordered Fetterman not to go beyond the ridge, and for a moment the troops paused atop the ridge, appearing from the fort like so many flyspecks on the horizon. Then they vanished down the far side of Lodge Trail Ridge, beyond which, four miles north of Fort Kearny, between fifteen hundred and two thousand warriors, most armed only with bows and arrows, lances, and war clubs, waited expectantly. What happened next is conjectural. Fetterman apparently tried to hold Grummond back, but the impulsive lieutenant spurred after the decoys, chasing them for a mile and a half until the ridge dropped away and the Bozeman Trail crossed Peno Creek. There hundreds of mounted warriors suddenly thundered out of the ravines, enveloping Grummond's and Fetterman's commands in a matter of minutes. Grummond led his cavalrymen back up the ridge in a doomed effort to rejoin Fetterman. Knowing the hopelessness of trying to outrun the Indians, the two civilian volunteers dismounted behind a rock outcrop and opened a stinging fire with their repeating rifles. They would die surrounded by scores of empty shell casings and several pools of blood. Fetterman's infantrymen, meanwhile, struggled with their muzzle-loaders against the circling warriors. So great was the hail of arrows into the small blue cluster that the Indians were more at risk from friendly fire than from the soldiers' bullets. A Cheyenne warrior who saw an arrow fly across the ridge and pierce a Lakota's brain said there were so many arrows lying about that a man had no need to use his own but could simply pick up all he needed.

Resistance from the infantry might have been minimal; the young Oglala chief American Horse said that many soldiers appeared to be paralyzed with fear. It soon turned into the sort of close-order combat the Lakotas called "stirring gravy." As infantrymen fell with arrow wounds, dismounted warriors descended upon them, first counting coup and then smashing their skulls with war clubs. American Horse landed Fetterman a disabling blow and then cut his throat, while the officer who had bragged about taking Red Cloud's scalp shot himself in the temple.

The infantry and the cavalry fought and died apart. Grummond fell early, decapitating a warrior with his sword before a blow from a war club dropped the lieutenant. The Indians said his troopers kept together, leading their horses up the ridge until they became too hard to handle. The sixteen-year-old Cheyenne warrior Fire Thunder, who was in his first fight, tried briefly to catch an animal, "but then I thought it was a good day to die and so I just went ahead fighting. I wasn't after horses—I was after white men." As the temperature fell and the hillsides grew icy, "we were told to crawl onto the soldiers," Fire Thunder said. "When we got closer someone hollered: 'Let's go! This is a good day to die. At home our women are hungry.' Then we all jumped up and went for them."[10]

The Indians did a thorough job in the forty minutes of combat; no soldier survived. A relief party from the fort later counted eighty-one nude and mutilated corpses. "Some had the top of their skulls cut off and their brains taken out, others their arms cut out of their sockets," said a member of the detail. Indeed, Fetterman's men were pincushions for the Indians' fury. One hundred sixty-five arrows protruded from a single body. "We walked on top of their internals and did not know it, in the high grass," another man said. "[We] picked them up, that is, their internals, and did not know the soldiers they belonged to. So you see, the cavalryman got an infantryman's guts, and an infantryman got a cavalryman's guts."

December 21 was the winter solstice, and darkness came at 4:00 p.m. In the gathering twilight, the relief party loaded all the corpses they could find and then brought them in, the post surgeon said, in the same fashion as "hogs brought to market." Thirty-one dead remained frozen on the field. Over the objections of his officers, Carrington, who had no intention of letting the Indians think him too timid to recover his own dead, led a detachment out the next night to gather up the bodies overlooked by the relief party. There were no Indians left to impress, however. Satisfied that they had achieved a great victory in the battle of "a Hundred in the Hand," the warriors returned to the Tongue River valley for the winter.[11]

✳

News of the Fetterman "massacre" staggered the nation and hugely embarrassed the army. Cooke removed Carrington, Grant removed Cooke, and Sherman fumed, telling Grant, "We must act with vindictive earnestness against the Sioux, even to their extermination, men, women, and children." He ordered the new Department of the Platte commander, Colonel Christopher C. Augur, to prepare a summer offensive.

But Sherman's plans collided with a formidable peace offensive inspired by the findings of an investigative body gotten up by Congress in the aftermath of Sand Creek. Named after its chairman, Senator James R. Doolittle, the committee published its report in January 1867. After nearly two years of investigating, the Doolittle Committee concluded that disease, drink, intertribal warfare, the "aggressions of lawless whites," and the "steady and resistless white emigration into their hunting lands" were endangering the very existence of the Plains tribes. After fustigating the dishonest agents and profiteering whiskey traders who preyed on friendly Indians, and the double-talking emissaries who confused and angered Indians of hostile or uncertain disposition, the committee went on to recommend that the tribes be moved far from the travel routes and white settlements and then consolidated on isolated reservations, where warriors could be made over into self-sufficient Christian farmers. Although hardly a novel concept, the Doolittle blueprint would drive federal Indian policy for the next fifteen years.

The western press railed against the "same wishy-washy namby-pamby course that is ever pursued by the government," but Congress and the Interior Department sided with Doolittle. In February 1867, President Andrew Johnson signed legislation creating a commission to determine how to end the war with Red Cloud without recourse to force of arms. Sherman reluctantly put his plans on hold.

Like General Sherman, Red Cloud labored under heavy constraints. The allied tribes had been unable to decide on a target for the summer, and when Red Cloud failed to broker a consensus, the Indians split into two groups. In July 1867, between five hundred and eight hundred Cheyennes set out to attack Fort Smith, while Red Cloud led a thousand Lakotas to renew the battle against Fort Kearny.

Unbeknownst to the Indians, they faced a markedly stronger foe than they had in 1866. Colonel Augur had bolstered Forts Kearny and Smith with reinforcements, with new breech-loading rifles that boosted the soldiers' rate of fire and confidence, and with new commanders. At Fort Smith, troop confidence was qualified, however; expressing the consensus view, the post surgeon said the new commander, Lieutenant Colonel Luther P. Bradley, was an "arbitrary self-important old bachelor that no one liked; he knew nothing about fighting Indians." Fort Kearny fared better. Its new commander was Lieutenant Colonel John E. Smith, a serious-minded soldier with a superb Civil War combat record whom the men esteemed. At long last, Fort Kearny had a fighting man in charge.[12]

*

The Cheyennes drew first blood that summer. With the garrison having trebled (a development Indian scouts easily divined), an attack against Fort Smith was out of the question. Two and a half miles northeast of the fort, however, there was an exposed outpost in a hay field where contract workers had improvised a small corral in which to assemble if attacked. On the night of July 31, a friendly Crow warned the hay cutters that the next morning "the whole face of the earth will be covered with Indians." Ignoring him, they went to work as usual. While they cut and bundled, the army detail of twenty-two soldiers passed the time playing cards and pitching horseshoes. At noon, a rifle crack from a lookout signaled trouble. As hundreds of mounted Cheyennes filed into the hay field, the soldiers and contractors withdrew into the log corral. Everyone took cover except the lieutenant, who cursed the men for cowards until an Indian sniper shot him through the temple. The teamster and former Union officer Al Colvin took charge. His orders were succinct and vivid. "Keep down and out of sight. Save your ammunition . . . and save the last shot for yourself." The firepower of the soldiers' new breech-loading rifled muskets and the civilians' repeating rifles stunned the warriors. After two attacks failed, the Indians set fire to the hay and then advanced behind the sheet of flames, which receded twenty feet short of the corral. Firing blindly through the smoke, the defenders squeezed off enough shots to blunt the assault. The Indians made a final push from the south on foot. Anticipating their move, Colvin concentrated his forces and told the men to blast away at close range with their shotguns. Colvin personally killed a Lakota chief, who fell too near to the corral for warriors to retrieve his corpse. From high bluffs beyond the creek, the Indians wailed for their lost leader.

The fight raged for four hours. When the shooting started, Colonel Bradley had slammed the fort's gates shut and forbidden anyone to go out. As the afternoon progressed, he had a change of heart and dispatched reinforcements. The rescuers brought along two cannon.

Indians dreaded these "medicine guns," and they quit the field after the first shots.

At least twenty Indians died in the Hayfield Fight. The whites lost three killed and three wounded. To make the Indians think twice about attacking again, Bradley ordered the head of the Lakota chief Colvin had killed stuck to a pole outside the front gate of Fort Smith.[13]

Ninety miles down the Bozeman Trail, Red Cloud rode against Fort Phil Kearny as nominal leader of a loose assemblage of warriors stirred by the summer Sun Dance ceremony. Their target was Fort Kearny's exposed outpost, the old pinery. There, an oblong corral of fourteen small, flimsy wagon boxes (standard army wagons with their running gear removed) of doubtful defensive value was the rallying point for the woodcutters and the infantry company guarding them. Repeating the ruse that had drawn out Fetterman, on the clear and hot morning of August 2 a decoy party scattered the occupants of the wood camps. The soldiers, however, refused to be lured into the open. Together with four civilians, the two officers and twenty-six enlisted men lay down inside the wagon boxes to fire through crudely bored holes or crouched behind barrels, bundles of clothing, or anything else that might stop a bullet. Captain James Powell gave just one order: "Men, here they come. Take your places and shoot to kill." Nothing more was needed. The men understood their predicament. Veterans looped their shoe-laces over one foot and their rifle trigger. Should the Indians overrun their defenses, the old soldiers would blow their own brains out.

From a hilltop a mile away, Red Cloud and the senior war leaders and elder chiefs watched the battle begin badly for the Indians. The army mule herd proved too tempting to resist, and two hundred warriors galloped onto the plateau prematurely to round it up. When the main party—perhaps under Crazy Horse—swept toward the corral from the southwest, they found the resistance stronger than expected. "After we had commenced firing, a great number of Indians rode within 150 yards and sitting on their ponies, waited for us to draw ramrods for reloading, as they supposed we were yet using the old muzzleloaders," remembered a private. "Instead of drawing ramrods and losing precious time, we simply threw open the breechblocks of our new rifles to eject the empty shell and slapped in fresh ones. This puzzled the Indians, who withdrew out of range." Red Cloud later called the soldiers' breechloaders "much-talk guns."

The Indians' reluctance to press home the attack against the constant fire of the new rifles was in keeping with their aversion to heavy casualties, but it cost them the battle. Every defender who left an account agreed that the action would have been over in ten minutes had the Indians kept coming. Instead, the warriors circled the corral from a safe distance, yelling menacingly while hiding on the far side of their ponies and loosing arrows from under the animals' necks. It was a fearsome but harmless spectacle, because most arrows flew wildly. But the soldiers' aim was scarcely better. Fast-moving Indians were a hard target, and no one could see more than a few yards through the smoke. Besides, raising one's head above the wagon boxes to shoot was a risky proposition. The deadliest fire came from Indian snipers, one of whom killed a lieutenant who stood up during the attack. When a soldier implored him to get down, the lieutenant barked, "I know how to fight Indians," and then promptly collapsed with a bullet in the head.

The Indians made their second onrush on foot, darting serpentine toward the wagons and throwing themselves behind folds in the ground between rushes. It came no closer than the first. Leading a third assault, Red Cloud's nephew fell in the first volley. Mounted warriors south of the corral kept a respectful distance until the attack broke up. They made a final, halfhearted approach and then left. Captain Powell had seven killed and four wounded. The Indians suffered roughly a dozen dead and thirty wounded. Some warriors claimed victory because they had made off with two hundred mules; the more honest preferred not to speak of the day.

Although the Hayfield and Wagon Box Fights boosted army morale, strategically they were meaningless. The army still lacked the means to take the offensive, and the Indians continued to raid the Bozeman Trail with impunity. Having experienced only tactical setbacks, costly though they were, Red Cloud and his fellow chiefs remained adamant that the Bozeman forts be abandoned or there would be no peace.[14]

*

The commander of Fort Smith was quite willing to accommodate Red Cloud. "The only way that peace can be made with the Indians is giving up this country," Colonel Bradley wrote to his fiancée on September 5, 1867. "It is the best hunting ground they have, and I do not see that we need it for ten or twenty years at least . . . So, for the sake of economy, if not for the sake of humanity, it were better to withdraw even at the expense of our pride." Lacking the forces necessary to occupy the Reconstruction South, guard the Union Pacific Railroad, and defend the Bozeman Trail simultaneously, the government also was willing to capitulate. No help could be expected from a Congress determined to retrench after the staggering cost of the Civil War. The arguments of peace advocates that it was cheaper, easier on the national conscience, and more effective to feed than to fight the Indians won broad support in both chambers. Rapid progress on the Union Pacific also made acceptance of Red Cloud's terms palatable. By the spring of 1868, track had been laid to Ogden, Utah, permitting safe travel to the Montana goldfields. Grant ordered General Sherman to abandon the Bozeman Trail forts.[15]

In April, peace commissioners invited Red Cloud to Fort Laramie to sign a treaty. (Six months earlier, the commissioners had concluded a treaty with the Southern Plains tribes at Medicine Lodge Creek, securing safe passage for whites traveling west to Colorado.) Breathtaking in its scope, this second treaty signed at Fort Laramie (not to be confused with the 1851 Fort Laramie Treaty) constituted the government's blueprint of the Lakota future. Laden with technical jargon, it confused even white officials, but it met Red Cloud's demand. Not only would the government close the Bozeman Trail; it would also grant the Lakotas an immense expanse. Present-day South Dakota west of the Missouri River would become the Great Sioux Reservation, for the "absolute and undisturbed use and occupation" of the Lakotas. There the government would build schools and provide rations and annuities for thirty years; in exchange, the Indians were expected to become tillers of the soil—in other words, "civilized." The proposed treaty also granted the Lakotas hunting rights above the North Platte River (roughly the northern half of Nebraska) and along the Republican River in northwestern Kansas "so long as the buffalo may range thereon in such numbers as to justify the chase." Finally, the Fort Laramie Treaty of 1868 contained a vaguely worded clause designating the land north of the North Platte River from the western limit of the reservation to the Bighorn Mountains as Unceded Indian Territory. Although undefined, the northern boundary of the tract came to be understood, by the government at least, as the Yellowstone River. In its totality, the Unceded Indian Territory roughly encompassed present-day northeastern Wyoming and southeastern Montana. What little clarity the clause contained was found in the provision that no whites would be permitted to settle in the Unceded Indian Territory without Indian permission. Whether Lakotas who wished to live off the hunt rather than the government dole might reside there was left unclear. In any case, the Lakota lands were to be inviolate; the peace permanent.

After burning Forts Kearny and Smith and laying in the winter supply of meat, Red Cloud arrived at Fort Laramie on November 4, leading a procession of 125 Lakota chiefs and headmen, ample proof of the high standing he enjoyed. And by governmental anointment, he was now head chief of the Lakotas. The distinguished members of the Peace Commission were gone, and it fell to the post commander to conclude matters with the Lakotas. He was no match for Red Cloud, who dominated the proceedings. Emphasizing that his people had no intention of becoming farmers, Red Cloud said he had come to Fort Laramie not because the Great Father's representatives had summoned him but because he wanted ammunition with which to fight the Crows. Nonetheless, he would make peace. With great ceremony, Red Cloud washed his hands with dust from the floor, placed his mark on the treaty, shook hands all around, and then made a long speech. He might have trouble controlling his young warriors, but he promised to honor the treaty as long as the white man did.

Red Cloud left, however, without fully understanding its terms. He believed the Oglalas could settle permanently in the Unceded Indian Territory and continue to trade at Fort Laramie as they had for two decades. Nor did he know that the treaty nurtured the seed of dispossession. By accepting fixed boundaries, Red Cloud had effectively agreed to relinquish his freedom whenever the government saw fit.[16]

Red Cloud had won his war. Whether he would prevail in peace, only time would tell.

———◆———

CHAPTER 3

WARRIOR AND SOLDIER

A FTER RED CLOUD'S WAR, no sane army officer would have repeated Captain Fetterman's boast that a company of regulars
could whip a thousand Indians. From objects of scorn, warriors became
enemies worthy of the highest respect. Officers compared their own
second-rate soldiery with Indian combatants and came away amazed.
Colonel Richard I. Dodge, who spent three decades studying Indians
when not fighting them, concluded that they made "the finest soldiers
in the world."

The Indians had not suddenly become superb fighters when the
whites appeared in the West; tribes had long battled one another over
hunting grounds or horses. Indeed, fighting was a cultural imperative, and men owed their place in society to their prowess as warriors.
Although each tribe had its unique customs or character—the impetuous Comanches, for instance, thought their Kiowa allies deliberated too
much before acting, and the Cheyennes considered their Arapaho allies
too accommodating—the patterns of tribal government and warfare
among the Rocky Mountain and Plains tribes were strikingly similar.
Fathers raised their sons to aspire to great martial deeds, and training
for a warrior's life began early. At age five or six, boys were made to
run long distances and to swim streams and were regularly deprived
of food, water, and sleep—all with a view to toughening their bodies.
Between the ages of seven and ten, boys received their first bow and
arrows and were taught to shoot first for distance and then for accuracy.
By the time a boy reached adolescence, his riding skills were unparalleled; he was, to again quote Colonel Dodge, not only the finest soldier
but also "the best rough rider and natural horseman in the world."[1]

Boys participated in their first raiding party at age fourteen or fifteen in the role of mascot or menial. By age eighteen, a young man was expected to have counted coup, stolen a horse, and taken a scalp. At age twenty, he had perhaps shown enough ability to lead a small war or raiding party. By twenty-five, he might be a subchief. If he had been successful, he could expect to have won many war honors and stolen many horses and perhaps even have two lodges (tipis) with a wife and children in each. (Between six and eight people typically lived in a lodge.) In most tribes, a warrior's career ended between the ages of thirty-five and forty, or after he had a son old enough to take his place. (If a man came into early middle age childless, he adopted a son from a fellow warrior who had more than one fighting-age son.) This system of forced early retirement ensured a fighting force that was young and vigorous. A retired warrior became a counselor to young warriors, a trainer of boys, or, if his career had been distinguished and his medicine powerful, a council chief or senior war leader (like Red Cloud) responsible for planning strategy and guiding large encounters. Although warriors often boasted of a desire to die in battle, a long life brought no shame. On the contrary, tribal elders imparted wisdom and restrained the young warriors when necessary, their services so valued that they were expected to keep out of harm's way themselves except when the village was under attack.[2]

Warriors earned honors on a graded scale that varied only slightly from tribe to tribe. Counting coup, which meant touching an enemy, usually with a long and ornate rod called a coup stick, ranked first among war honors. In the absence of a coup stick, any handheld object would do; the less lethal the object, the greater the honor. Touching a live, armed enemy without trying to kill him rated higher than counting coup on a dead man. The number of coups that could be counted on a corpse varied, but the first coup carried the greatest weight. Warriors also counted coups on women, children, prisoners, and stolen horses. Lesser war honors included the capture of a shield or gun and the taking of a scalp, which served several purposes. Most important, a fresh scalp afforded a warrior incontrovertible proof that he had killed someone. If taken without friendly casualties, enemy scalps became objects of celebration in a boisterous village ceremony called the victory or scalp dance. Warriors adorned their war shirts and leggings with scalps or tied them to a pony's bridle before battle.

Although scalps were most often taken off the dead, scalping in and of itself was not intended to kill. Unless grievously wounded, victims often survived the ordeal, particularly if they were Indians. Indian men wore their hair long, which made taking the scalp of an enemy warrior relatively swift and simple. Grasping a tuft or braid in one hand, with the other a warrior made a two- or three-inch-wide cut around the base of the skull, usually with a butcher knife. A quick jerk tore away the skin and hair with a "report like a popgun." White victims required more work, and warriors sometimes had to scalp the entire head to get enough hair to justify the effort. Indian scalps counted more than those of whites, whom most Indians considered inferior opponents. At the Fetterman Fight, warriors contemptuously tossed the scalps of soldiers on the ground beside their victims.

The mutilation of enemy dead was a common Plains Indian practice in which both sexes indulged. Westerners considered it conclusive proof that Indians were irredeemable savages; for their part, the Indians believed that disfiguring an enemy's corpse protected the killer from the dead man's spirit in the afterlife.

War honors were a requisite for admission into warrior societies, to which young warriors aspired, and competition between these fraternities of fighting men was spirited. Each sought to strike the first blow of the annual raiding season. The Lumpwood and Fox warrior societies of the Crows extended the competition to the domestic front, occasionally stealing one another's wives from their own villages as if they were horses. (Surprisingly, no fatalities seem to have arisen from the practice.) Warrior societies did not necessarily fight as a unit, but when they did, the consequences could be catastrophic. A string of sharp reverses or a single shattering defeat might wipe out the entire group. In battle, society officers were expected to scorn danger and sometimes to court it, which meant opportunities for promotion were high.[3]

War honors were inextricably linked to sex. They were the surest way to win a girl's heart, making them excellent motivators for young men to fight hard. A Crow man, for instance, could not marry until he had turned twenty-five or counted coup, and a married Crow male with no coup to his credit was denied the important privilege of "painting his woman's face." Among the Cheyennes, young men could not even court girls until they had demonstrated their courage in battle or on raids. Mothers grilled their daughters' suitors on their war records and dismissed as a coward any man found wanting. Cheyenne women had a song for men who wavered in battle. "If you are afraid when you charge," the song went, "turn back. The Desert Women will eat you." In other words, women would slander them so mercilessly that death became preferable. "It was hard to go into a fight, and [we] were often afraid," confessed the Cheyenne warrior John Stands in Timber, "but it was worse to turn back and face the women." Fear of ridicule notwithstanding, no warrior would risk battle without the protection of his sacred power, commonly translated as "medicine," upon the strength of which his courage, competence, and very survival were believed to depend.

The search for medicine began in youth with a vision quest, also known as a medicine dream. Repairing to a lonesome and dangerous place, a vision seeker spent a prescribed period—normally four days and nights—without food or water, praying for a helper from nature or the bird or animal kingdom to visit him. Apparitions addressed the vision seeker in parables, which were interpreted by a spiritual adviser, usually a medicine man, for a fee, or through lifelong contemplation. A creature or element of nature revealed in a vision became a man's medicine. In combat, a warrior emulated the ways of his helper (the swiftness of an eagle, the cunning of a fox) and carried in a small neck bag tokens reflective of his vision. He painted the vision symbolically on his shield, clothing, horse, and lodge and harnessed its power by means of a unique and sacred collection of items gathered in a large medicine bundle. Warriors unable to obtain medicine in vision quests sometimes sought spiritual power through self-torture. As a last recourse, a warrior could purchase medicine from a medicine man or share in the medicine of a friend or family member. Indians, however, considered medicine gotten from a third party to be relatively weak. Warriors flocked to men with proven medicine in the hope of sharing in its power or benefiting from the possessor's divinely bestowed gifts.[4]

Warriors esteemed guns as their most cherished possessions and went to great lengths to get the latest repeating rifles, the legendary lever-action Winchester being a favorite. Few, however, could afford them. Most had to make do with old muzzle-loading muskets of doubtful utility or captured single-shot army rifles. Moreover, ammunition for any rifle was hard to come by. Improvident soldiers occasionally sold cartridges to Indians, only to have the bullets shot at them when hostilities erupted. With few exceptions, warriors lacked the requisite knowledge or tools to repair broken weapons, and it was difficult to find accommodating white gunsmiths.

Thus, many had to rely on the bow and arrow. Not that the traditional Indian weapon was a liability; army officers were astonished at the striking force of arrows, even when employed by a relative novice. One young lieutenant learned from his Indian scouts how to fire an arrow into a buffalo with such force that the tip came out the other side. "The power of the bow may be better understood," he explained, "when I tell you that the most powerful Colt revolver will not send a ball through a buffalo." When used by Indians trained with the bow from boyhood, the effect was even more astonishing. "I have seen a bow throw an arrow 500 yards," added the lieutenant, and "once found a man's skull transfixed to a tree by an arrow which had gone completely through the bones and imbedded itself so deep in the wood as to sustain the weight of the head." Colonel Dodge, one of the army's closest students of Indian arms and tactics, found the rate of fire of a bow and arrows remarkable. A warrior, observed the colonel, "will grasp five to ten arrows in his left hand and discharge them so rapidly that the last will be on its flight before the first has touched the ground." Warriors normally carried twenty arrows in their quivers; they scrounged more on the battlefield when they ran out. War clubs and long, brightly painted lances rounded out a warrior's offensive arsenal.

To defend themselves, warriors carried small buffalo-hide shields that Colonel Dodge judged "as impenetrable as iron and . . . almost perfect protection against the very best rifle." Believing that the greatest protection came from shields infused with sacred power, a warrior painted his with sacred symbols and appended feathers and enemy scalps and prayed over it until its medicine was perfect. A shield of proven worth was highly esteemed, guarded closely, and passed from generation to generation.[5]

Whenever possible, warriors went into battle fortified by devotional exercises. Some fought in their best war dress, not because they believed the clothes would enhance their skills, explained a Cheyenne, but in order to look their best when going to meet the Great Spirit. Weather permitting, however, warriors typically fought only in their breechcloths; doing so enabled them to move faster and, the Indians believed, optimized the power of their medicine. Warriors painted themselves and their horses with sacred colors for protection or with symbols meant to advertise past exploits. The total effect of a painted warrior and horse terrified not only soldiers but also enemy warriors. Properly painted and blessed by his personal sacred ritual, a warrior supposed himself safe from harm. On the other hand, a warrior caught spiritually unprepared for battle felt so vulnerable that he would often flee at the first opportunity. Medicine cut both ways.[6]

The Indians of the American West might have been among the best soldiers man for man in the world, but their tactics, developed over decades of intertribal warfare, were poorly suited to open combat against a disciplined regular army unit. Seen from a soldier's perspective, Indian formations often appeared invincible. Masses of Indians surrounded their war leader, united in a ragged but formidable line that charged without apparent order and at a signal scattered like leaves before a storm, only to regroup and dash at army flanks until, said Colonel Dodge, "the plain is alive with flying, circling horsemen, each lying flat on his horse or hanging to the side to escape the shots of the pursuing enemy or rush upon the enemy in a living mass of a charging, yelling terror."

The rush, however, nearly always came up short. Loath to drive home an attack unless certain of winning, Indians preferred to lay traps and bait the enemy with decoy warriors, a tactic that hardly ever worked (the Fetterman Fight being a rare exception). Not only was the ploy obvious to all but the most inexperienced foe, but aspiring warriors also commonly ruined the surprise by charging early in order to count first coup.

The Indians had a singular concept of battlefield victory. If many men won war honors, they counted as a triumph an encounter that the army might consider a tactical draw. Regardless of the outcome, if a war leader or great warrior died, a battle was reckoned a calamity, particularly if the medicine of the dead was thought to have been strong. The fall of one such man might suffice to break up an Indian attack or end a battle. Indians also feared artillery. A few cannon shots invariably dispersed them.

Esteemed though they were, war chiefs had only limited influence. They agreed among themselves in a general way on what they hoped to accomplish in battle. Each subchief then gathered his followers around him and outlined the plan, and things proceeded from there. Once the shooting started, war chiefs signaled their men in several ways, sometimes by holding a flag or a lance or a gun or a robe tilted in a particular direction, by using mirrors flashed from high ground, or with the shrill notes of an eagle-bone war whistle. Ordinarily, warriors heeded their advice, but obedience was discretionary in nearly every matter except bringing off the dead and the wounded, an obligation that made army counts of Indian losses rough estimates at best. Warriors practiced long and hard at rescuing a fallen man while at a gallop. "To this drill," Colonel Dodge observed, "is owed the fact that nearly every official report of a fight with Indians has a statement in effect as follows: 'Indian casualties unknown; several were seen to fall from their horses.'"[7]

The army was apparently unaware that some warriors went into battle intending to die, be it to gain glory at any price or to end the pain of a terminal illness or personal tragedy. The Indians called them "suicide warriors." Their preferred manner of passing was to repeatedly charge an enemy unarmed until killed. Although they contributed nothing positive to a fight, to die a suicide warrior was nonetheless considered highly honorable, and no one tried to stop a man bent on ending his life thusly. Fortunately for the war strength of the tribe, there were relatively few suicide warriors.

The suicide warrior was the extreme manifestation of the Indian axiom that in warfare and raiding a warrior remained an individual. He was always, in a sense, his own man. He answered to his supernatural helpers and conducted himself in accordance with their teaching. He developed a close allegiance to his warrior society and fought under its rules and obligations, which in the case of some societies included fighting to the death no matter what the odds. Standing above all this, however, was his responsibility to protect his people, whether from tribal enemies or the army. As the 1860's drew to a close, soldiers seemed to most Indians the lesser of the two threats.[8]

*

Red Cloud's War had revealed a regular army woefully unprepared for its Indian-fighting mission. The army's problems, however, were of no interest to westerners, who expected General Sherman to punish the Indians whenever and wherever they caused trouble. If Sherman was not up to the job, argued the western press, then western volunteers should be recalled to federal service to do it for him. Perhaps, editors speculated, Sherman was at heart just another weak-willed appeaser.

The badgering got the better of Sherman. Smarting at the loss of the Bozeman Trail forts, in late 1868 he blasted his critics with an open challenge:

In the last two years I have done as much as any reasonable man could hope for, and if any man be incredulous, let him enlist, and he will soon find out if he don't earn his pay. It is a physical impossibility for the small army [that] Congress maintains, to guard the exposed settlements any more than we can catch all the pickpockets in our cities. Clamor on the subject against me is simply folly. We do our duty according to our means.

Those means not only were sorely limited but also were fast shrinking. Even as the Indian Wars intensified, Congress—intent on paying down the massive national debt incurred during the Civil War—repeatedly reduced the rolls of the regular army. From an authorized strength of fifty-four thousand men in 1866, the army would plummet to just twenty-five thousand by 1874. Reconstruction duties siphoned off a third of the army and sucked the institution into partisan politics. As Southern states were readmitted to the Union, their representatives made common cause with the budget balancers in order to emasculate their blue-coated former oppressors, and the frontier army became a skeleton force.

Declining numbers were not the army's only problem. Gone were the sober and purposeful volunteers who had restored the Union. In their place was a decidedly inferior brand of soldier. Not all were "bummers and loafers," as the New York *Sun* alleged. There were also a disproportionately large number of urban poor, criminals, drunkards, and perverts. Few soldiers were well educated, and many were illiterate. Unskilled laborers in search of a steady job flocked to recruiting depots, usually to desert when better-paying work became available. One-third of the frontier army consisted of recent immigrants, mostly German and Irish, some of whom had seen service in European armies and proved an asset, and sprinkled among the American undesirables were good men who had fallen on hard times. Nevertheless, as one general observed, while the army had a greatly improved rifle, "I rather think we have a much less intelligent soldier to use it."[9]

Incentives to enlist were few. By the 1870s, regulars earned just ten dollars a month, three dollars less than had Civil War volunteers a decade earlier. Promotion to the noncommissioned ranks offered a modest increase in salary and, after thirty years, a small pension, but only 1 percent of enlisted men stayed the course. Surprisingly, in view of the army's need for quality recruits, after the Civil War the minimum age for enlistees was raised from eighteen to twenty-one, a requirement that was strictly enforced.

A new recruit received his initiation to army life at one of four large recruiting depots, where he was given a cursory physical examination, an ill-fitting uniform, poor food, and no training. Until assigned to a regiment, recruits bided their time in menial labor. Any relief a recruit might have felt at leaving the recruiting depot for service in the West usually ended the moment he saw his duty station, which more often than not was an isolated, barely habitable wreck, such as Fort Garland, Colorado, which a visiting journalist found to consist of a mere handful of flat-roofed and squat redbrick and adobe buildings, "altogether dispiriting in their unmitigated ugliness." Things weren't much better in Texas. When a regular cavalry regiment reoccupied Fort Duncan after the Civil War, the barracks were overrun with bats. The troopers drove out the creatures with their sabers, but the "nauseating odor" of guano lingered for months.[10]

General Sherman knew that most of his soldiers lived in squalor. His 1866 inspection report of the posts in the Military Division of the Missouri read like marginalia in a tenement owner's ledger. The general found Fort Laramie, Wyoming, to be "a mixture of all sorts of houses of every conceivable pattern and promiscuously scattered about, the two principal buildings so damaged and so rickety that on a windy night the soldiers sleep on the parade [ground]." Of Fort Sedgwick, Colorado, a post first built of sod, Sherman conjectured, "Surely, had the Southern planters put their Negros in such hovels, a sample would have been exhibited as illustrative of the cruelty and inhumanity of the man-masters." There was little, however, that Sherman could do to relieve the meanness of the frontier soldier's surroundings. The army budget was simply too small and the number of posts too great to make any but rudimentary improvements.[11]

Once he was settled into his quarters, a soldier's life assumed a numbing routine. Bugle calls regulated the day's activities, few of which had much to do with soldiering. The men built telegraph lines and roads, cleared lands, erected and repaired the buildings on post, cut wood, and burned brush—everything, grumbled an officer, "except what they are supposed to have enlisted to perform." With funding tight, only a fortunate few received more than a handful of rounds annually for training. Not until the early 1880s did the army encourage target practice, and replacements routinely took the field having never fired a rifle or ridden a horse. In combat, the consequence could be down-right embarrassing. In his first Indian fight, a new lieutenant winced at his men's atrocious marksmanship as they fired several hundred mercy shots at a severely wounded horse less than one hundred yards away without hitting it.

Not only were soldiers poorly trained, but they were also poorly uni-formed. Clad in woolen navy-blue blouses and sky-blue trousers, the troops roasted in the summer and, because their overcoats were too thin, froze in the winter. Footwear was so crude that the right shoe could hardly be distinguished from the left. Regulation hats fell to pieces quickly, forcing many soldiers to buy civilian headwear out of their meager salaries. Shirts were blue, gray, or checked as suited the wearer. Cavalrymen wore loose handkerchiefs knotted under the neck. Most either padded the seats of their trousers with canvas or donned canvas pants or corduroy breeches for greater comfort, and some wore Indian moccasins instead of regulation boots. A visiting English war correspondent thought the casually dressed frontier soldiers bore "a suspicious resemblance to banditti."[12]

Until 1874, the army employed a hodgepodge of weapons. The ponderous Civil War–era muzzle-loading Springfield rifled musket remained the standard infantry weapon just long enough to ensure the rapid slaughter of Captain Fetterman's command. By the end of 1867, most infantrymen carried Springfields altered to fire a metallic car-tridge loaded at the breech; these were the weapons that so stunned the Lakotas at the Wagon Box and Hayfield Fights. In 1873, the army settled on the .45-caliber Springfield as the standard infantry weapon and replaced the cap-and-ball Colt and Remington revolvers popu-lar during the Civil War with the Colt .45 single-action revolver (the famed "Peacemaker"). Cavalry regiments were armed with revolvers and either the single-shot Sharps carbine or the seven-shot Spencer. They were also issued sabers, which were seldom carried on campaign, because officers realized that before a trooper could get close enough to an Indian to use a saber, he would be bristling with arrows. Soldiers groused about not being well armed, but few were good enough marks-men to do justice to the weapons they were issued.

Endless isolation and mind-numbing manual labor caused enlisted men to sink into "a plodding, sullen sort of existence." Good food might have helped morale, but army rations were as monotonous as a soldier's day, the mainstays of the garrison menus being hash, baked beans, a watery meat stew called slumgullion, coarse bread, and stringy beef from range cattle. Soldiers supplemented their diets with produce grown in post and company gardens. In the field, troops subsisted largely on bacon and surplus Civil War hardtack (biscuits).

All but the most righteous soldiers sooner or later succumbed to one or more of the three moral scourges of the military frontier: drinking, whoring, and gambling. Until 1877, when President Rutherford B. Hayes yielded to abstinence advocates and forbade the sale of alcohol on military posts, soldiers could buy liquor from the post trader, whose licensed establishment served as general store, bar, and social club, where at least a modicum of control could be exercised over the men. But as soon as prohibition took effect on posts, soldiers switched their patronage to "hog ranches," seedy off-post establishments that offered up rotgut whiskey and cheap prostitutes. Soldiers in need of sex also frequented the lodges of promiscuous Indian women or patronized the quarters of authorized camp laundresses, who sometimes supplemented their legitimate earnings with prostitution. The consequences were predictable. A future general said venereal disease was so pervasive at frontier posts that "it was a common saying that post surgeons had nothing to do but confine laundresses and treat the clap."[13]

Noncommissioned officers (NCOs), whose duty it was to keep the men in line, instead frequently facilitated vice. The story was told of a cavalry first sergeant who superintended an orgy for his troops at a hog ranch. In order that they might more easily service his troopers, the sergeant had the prostitutes strip nude and then posture themselves atop a round table at which the men were drinking. At Camp Grant, Arizona, the sergeants ran an illegal gambling racket, profiting handsomely as bankers at payday barracks poker games. For all their shortcomings, however, NCOs were the backbone of the frontier army. More often than not, company commanders gave their first sergeants a free hand. Good NCOs were a godsend to officers, and the tough but paternalistic Irish or German first sergeant became a stereotype in his own time. On the other hand, if left unsupervised, a bad NCO could wreak havoc on a company. Brutal sergeants inflicted punishments forbidden by regulation. It was not uncommon at frontier posts to see soldiers staked to the ground under the burning sun, bound spread-eagle to wagon wheels, or suspended from trees by their thumbs. Disgusted at the rampant sadism, one department commander admonished officers to rein in tyrannical NCOs, who "will cause more discontent and trouble in a company than the best company commanders can allay."

For a general to find it necessary to lecture lieutenants and captains on their basic duties would be unthinkable in today's army or, for that matter, during most of the history of the U.S. Army. But the frontier officer was a special breed. Talent there was; many fine generals of the early twentieth century began their careers as junior officers in the West. But even the most dedicated officer found it hard to keep motivated among the rogues' gallery of bickering, backbiting mediocrities, drunks, and martinets in epaulets that plagued the army. At its best, the officer corps was a fractious lot, with generals and colonels nourishing grudges against one another born of perceived or real slights during the Civil War and lower-ranking officers squaring off according to age and experience.[14]

For former Civil War officers of all ranks, the transition to the small postwar army was hard. Regular army officers had held commands during the war based on their volunteer rank or brevet (honorary commissions nominally bestowed for exceptional service), rather than their substantially lower regular army grade. After the war, they tumbled in rank. George Armstrong Custer, for instance, fell from a major general of volunteers to a regular army captain on staff duty until his mentor Major General Philip H. Sheridan arranged his promotion to lieutenant colonel in the newly formed Seventh Cavalry. In the closing months of the war, George Crook had been a major general of volunteers commanding an eight-thousand-man army corps. Afterward, he reverted to lieutenant colonel in a frontier regiment that barely mustered five hundred men. To salve their wounded pride, officers wore the rank of their highest brevet grade and were addressed in official correspondence by their volunteer rank until Congress prohibited both practices in 1870.

Those demoted faced a long road back. An officer's time in grade grew as the size of the army shrank, so that a new second lieutenant could expect to serve twenty-five years before making major and, if he lasted that long, thirty-seven years before reaching the rank of colonel. In 1877, the *Army and Navy Journal* predicted that within a decade "there will not be one-fourth part of the present field officers in the Army physically capable of supporting the hardships of an active campaign. They will be worn-out old men."[15]

And often dissipated. Watching the long hours of idleness in garrison take its toll on his brother officers, a future general wrote, "There was much guard duty to be done, but drill hours were few, and the study of the art of war was not the fashion. Naturally, cards, billiards, and liquor attracted many; the last even more so because of the hardships of intermittent campaigning." Officers took their gambling seriously. When one lieutenant's poker cronies caught him cheating at cards, they slapped charges of conduct unbecoming of an officer against him. Unable to persuade his fellow gamblers—who were no more honest than he—to drop the charges, the ostracized lieutenant committed suicide.

Both gambling and alcoholism were as prevalent among officers as they were among enlisted men. The sorry sight of inebriated officers stumbling to and from their quarters undoubtedly hurt unit morale. Few drunken officers, however, were punished for dereliction of duty or unbecoming conduct, and some were promoted in spite of their excessive drinking. A party of Montana gold prospectors who stopped at Fort C. F. Smith in October 1866, during the opening days of Red Cloud's War, were shocked to find the commanding officer, Captain Nathaniel C. Kinney, "beastly drunk." It was not that they had caught him at a bad moment. "The citizens told us that he had been in that condition for weeks. There is one thing certain, that he did not draw a sober breath during the few days that we remained there."[16]

What could a soldier condemned to squalor, boredom, low pay, brutality, and duty under drunken officers do? He could desert, and thousands did. The turnover in the First Cavalry was typical. Of the 1,288 recruits the regiment received during a three-year period, 928 deserted—some individually, others in groups. During the winter of 1867, the Seventh Cavalry lost hundreds to desertion. NCOs could not be relied on to stem the flow; on the contrary, they sometimes were the instigators, and one Seventh Cavalry officer later recalled a company first sergeant who, after evening roll call, told thirty men to saddle their horses for detached service. When they had put the post well behind them, the sergeant halted the detachment, told the men they were deserters, bade them good-bye, and then set off for the mining country. Two or three returned to report the deception, but the rest followed the first sergeant to the gold mines.

Men often went "over the hill" for reasons having little to do with army life. Some had enlisted simply to get a free ride to the goldfields. Others were "vicious vagabonds" who jumped from regiment to regiment under assumed names. Many deserted to make better money in the West, where laborers were few and wages generally much higher than in the East. Spring was the preferred season to skip out, preferably just after payday, because railroad construction resumed when the ground thawed and travel to the mining regions or new towns became easier. Deserters ran little risk of capture, and those caught faced comparatively light punishment. During the Civil War, desertion was punishable by death, but in the postwar West the army was less concerned about losing men to desertion than about losing the weapons and equipment the deserters usually took with them.[17]

*

One class of soldiers seldom deserted, drank to excess, or posed disciplinary problems—the men of the regular army's four black regiments: the Ninth and Tenth Cavalry and the Twenty-Fourth and Twenty-Fifth Infantry. Generally speaking, black men enlisted for loftier purposes than whites. For most white recruits, the army was a temporary refuge until something better turned up. For black recruits, nearly all of whom were illiterate ex-slaves, the army offered both a career and a chance to demonstrate the potential of their race. "The ambition to be all that soldiers should be is not confined to a few of these sons of an unfortunate race. They are possessed of the notion that the colored people of the whole country are more or less affected by their conduct in the army," observed the white chaplain of a black regiment. "This is the bottom secret of their patient toil."

Black regiments were led by white officers. Notwithstanding the racism of the time, the officers and their men commonly developed a deep mutual esteem. Officers whose white units fought alongside black troops could admire their fighting ability and esprit de corps without granting racial equality. Observing the Tenth Cavalry in action, the captain of a white regiment conceded "the colored race is a valuable military asset." But, he added by way of backhanded praise, they "must be officered by whites else they are of no account." Of course, black regiments were far more often targets of bigotry than of praise. White enlisted men resented taking orders from black sergeants, and senior officers sometimes set poor examples, such as the colonel who refused to allow the "nigger troops" of the Tenth Cavalry to form near his white regiment on parade.

The entire system was rigged against black soldiers. The Quartermaster Corps shortchanged black regiments in both quality and quantity of supplies, equipment, and horses. The War Department relegated black regiments to service in particularly disagreeable sectors of the frontier, especially Texas, where civilians harassed, insulted, menaced, and sometimes murdered black soldiers. The killers invariably escaped punishment.

Comanches and Southern Cheyennes called the black troopers of the Tenth Cavalry Buffalo Soldiers, either out of respect for the regiment's fighting ability or because the Indians thought the soldiers' dark curly hair resembled a buffalo's coat. The black cavalrymen accepted the name with pride, and it eventually became a generic term for all black soldiers. Indians were loath to fight the Buffalo Soldiers, said a journalist in a position to know, "because of the penchant which the darkies have for taking their hair"—in short, for retaliation in kind.

The Indians understood the low status of blacks in the white man's world. During a battle with the Buffalo Soldiers, Ute warriors taunted their opponents with an improvised jingle:

> Soldiers with black faces,
> You ride into battle behind the white soldiers;
> But you can't take off your black faces,
> And the white-faced soldiers make you ride behind them.[18]

But whether campaigning alone, alongside, or behind white troops, black soldiers consistently fought with courage and competence against the Indians, a claim few white units could make.

✳

A small and mediocre army was the primary but by no means the only hindrance to General Sherman and his subordinates. They were also hampered by an unwieldy command structure and their own failure to develop a doctrine for fighting an unconventional foe. In 1866, the War Department divided the West into two military divisions roughly separated by the Continental Divide—the Military Division of the Pacific and Sherman's sprawling Military Division of the Missouri, which encompassed the present-day states of Arkansas, Iowa, Texas, Kansas, Colorado, Oklahoma, Nebraska, Wyoming, Utah, Montana, North and South Dakota, and the eastern half of Idaho. Needless to say, most of the fighting was expected to take place in Sherman's division. The military divisions were subdivided into departments comprising two or more states or territories. It was a tidy arrangement for administrative purposes, but with the Indians making war where they pleased, conflicts were seldom confined to a single department. Against an elusive and constantly moving enemy, department commanders found it difficult to coordinate their efforts, and orders from division to department headquarters were frequently "overtaken by events" before they reached their intended recipients.

The basic army strategy, an Indian commissioner explained to Red Cloud, was for "the Great Father to put war-houses all through the Indian country," an approach of limited effectiveness given the small size of the frontier army. Few "war-house" commanders had enough men to garrison their posts adequately, much less pursue hostile Indians. Almost every senior officer, Sherman included, believed that consolidating forces in a few strategically located posts was sounder policy. Settlers and local governments, however, expected protection everywhere and wanted soldiers close at hand, and in Washington their voices drowned out the protests of the generals. The consequence was a policy of dispersal for defense and temporary concentration for offensive operations, an approach compromised not only by the small number of available troops but also by a comparative lack of mobility. Indian ponies thrived on prairie grasses and could survive on cottonwood bark. Warriors were raised to endure deprivation; a bit of dried buffalo meat might last them several days. But army horses needed grain, and soldiers needed regular rations. "In too many cases," lamented a veteran officer, "expeditions against Indians have been like dogs fastened by a chain: within the length of the chain irresistible, beyond it powerless. The chain was the wagon train and supplies."[19]

Senior officers disagreed sharply on which arm of the service was better suited to fight Indians. Cavalry commanders naturally advocated the mounted arm as most capable of chasing down fast-riding warriors. The trouble was, without regular forage, cavalry mounts broke down quickly. Besides, critics asserted, frontier cavalrymen were really no more than mounted infantry; they rode to the battlefield and then dismounted to fight, losing a quarter of their strength before a shot was fired, because one in every four men had to remain behind the firing line to hold the horses. Colonel Nelson A. Miles presented the infantryman's case to Congress. "I believe that a body of infantry troops can walk down any band of Indians in four months. The first thirty days the cavalry will make a much longer distance, but after that time the horses begin to get poor and weak and give out, and the infantry grow stronger. The longer they march the stronger they get."

Neither the cavalry nor the infantry had much chance of finding Indians without Indian scouts. Colonel Carrington had understood this. Before setting out for the Bozeman Trail, he had tried to recruit Winnebago and Crow Indians in order to have "a few soldiers who knew the Indian styles of warfare, and were up to their tricks." Enthusiastic Crow chiefs had offered him 250 warriors, but the army denied Carrington the necessary funds. The presence at Fort Phil Kearny of Crow Indians who knew the Lakota manner of making war might well have averted the Fetterman debacle (as might the warriors that the Cheyenne peace chiefs had offered Carrington).

After Red Cloud's War, the army incorporated friendly Indians into field operations. Already a battalion of Pawnees, regularly enlisted, uniformed, and well armed, had blunted Cheyenne and Lakota raids on the Union Pacific Railroad. A commissioner of Indian affairs suggested the army organize a paramilitary force of three thousand young warriors from friendly tribes to "rush to the scene of actual or threatened troubles." But the War Department never warmed to the idea; too many Washington desk officers mistrusted Indians, and the Pawnee experiment was never repeated. Instead, the army came to rely upon Indian scouts to help soldiers find and fight an enemy raised in a culture of war making. Competent frontier officers knew they stood no chance of winning without them.[20]

—◆—

CHAPTER 4

HANCOCK'S WAR

MAJOR GENERAL Winfield Scott Hancock came to the West in the autumn of 1866 with a reputation as one of the premier Union generals in the Civil War. General Grant considered him to have been his finest corps commander, but he was the wrong man to command the Department of the Missouri. Hancock knew nothing about Indians and had no interest in learning, a grievous deficiency in a general whose department embraced the Smoky Hill and Arkansas River routes, two of the three emigrant roads across the plains.

A year earlier, General Pope had contended that the Treaty of the Little Arkansas, by which the Southern Plains tribes had agreed to accept large reservations well removed from the emigrant routes, was not worth the paper it had been printed on. Confounding Pope's prediction, Black Kettle and other Southern Cheyenne and Southern Arapaho peace chiefs had abided by its terms. But the continued onrush of settlers compromised the chiefs' limited influence over the warrior societies. The powerful Dog Soldier band of the Southern Cheyennes was particularly restive, and with good cause. Their western Kansas hunting grounds had come under siege after the 1865 reopening of the Smoky Hill Trail. Not only were the endless wagon trains once again tearing up their land, but a new rail line called the Union Pacific Railroad Eastern Division was also then snaking its way west alongside the Smoky Hill Trail; already its tracks crept into central Kansas. More perilous to the Dog Soldiers' way of life than the railroad were the clusters of sod shanties, clapboard shacks, and walled tents that mushroomed along the line. Soon the buffalo ranges were speckled with these crude precursors of cities and towns. Not having signed the Little Arkansas Treaty, the Dog Soldier chiefs felt no obligation to relocate south of the Arkansas River; even the chiefs who signed the treaty thought it gave their people hunting rights along the Smoky Hill. Besides, the western Kansas reservation that the peace commissioners had promised the Indians had not materialized. During the winter of 1866–1867, Northern Oglalas and Cheyennes came south to boast of their victories on the Bozeman Trail. Why, the warlike northerners asked their southern kinsmen, did they not also rise up against the white trespassers?

With so many sources of instability threatening the peace, Hancock's position demanded patience and forbearance, neither of which he applied to the task. On the basis of a handful of minor raids in 1866, some of which were likely the handiwork of white desperadoes, the general accepted the dubious claims of westerners and credulous subordinates that the Indians were planning a general war in the spring of 1867. One of the principal purveyors of bogus claims was Kansas's governor, Samuel J. Crawford, who had organized an immigrant company to populate sparsely settled western Kansas, and to entice prospective settlers, he needed the security that a strong military presence provided; the Indian bogeyman was the surest way to obtain a large force.

In March 1867, Hancock proposed a major expedition into western Kansas. Publicly, he maintained that it would fight only if provoked; privately, however, Hancock told Sherman that he hoped the Cheyennes would refuse his demands and precipitate a war, "as some punishment seems to be necessary." General Sherman knew better. His autumn 1866 tour had revealed that accusations of Indian depredations were trumped up. Yet Sherman's eagerness to avenge the Fetterman disaster got the better of him, and he gave Hancock his full support. When Red Cloud renewed the war in the North in the spring of 1867, Sherman obtained a special appropriation from Congress to fund Hancock's expedition. If he couldn't beat Red Cloud, he could at least make Indians somewhere suffer.

*

In this poisoned environment, Hancock arrived at Fort Larned, Kansas, in early April, ostensibly to confer with the Southern Cheyenne chiefs. He brought with him fourteen hundred troops, the largest force assembled on the plains to that date, including the entire Seventh Cavalry. Hancock's first field order belied the protestations of peace he made to the chiefs. "We go prepared for war, and will make it, if a proper occasion presents," he announced to his officers. "No insolence will be tolerated from any Indians whom we may encounter. We wish to show them that the government is ready and able to punish them if they are hostile." Assuredly, it never occurred to Hancock to explore the causes of Indian disaffection.[1]

Hancock met first with the chiefs of the Dog Soldiers and their Southern Oglala allies, whose villages rested on the Pawnee Fork of the Arkansas River, thirty-five miles west of Fort Larned. The chiefs had braved a brutal early April blizzard to keep their appointment with Hancock, hobbling into the general's camp on half-starved ponies at sunset on April 12. Overriding the objections of the Cheyenne agent Major Edward W. Wynkoop, who had tried to make him understand that the Cheyennes, believing that only the sacred power of the sun could guarantee honesty and wisdom in council, never held nocturnal parleys, Hancock ordered an immediate conference. There he delivered a disjointed harangue that bewildered both the interpreters and the chiefs. That only five chiefs had answered his summons infuriated the general; he had "a great deal to say to the Indians" and wanted to say it only once. "Tomorrow I am going to your camp," Hancock told them. "I have heard that a great many Indians want to fight. Very well; we are here, and we come prepared for war." Tall Bull of the Dog Soldiers spoke for the chiefs: "You sent for us, we came here. We never did the white man any harm; we don't intend to . . . You say you are going to the village tomorrow. If you go, I shall have no more to say to you there than here." In other words, keep away from the village. Hancock concluded the council with a bitter non sequitur: he would exterminate the entire Cheyenne tribe should a single war party ever so much as set a pony hoof on the Union Pacific Railroad Eastern Division. The surgeon of the Seventh Cavalry found Hancock's behavior reprehensible. It was the general who was "insolent," he averred, not the Indians; Hancock had "talked to those Indian warriors and orators as a cross schoolmaster would to his refractory scholars." Before leaving, the chiefs begged Major Wynkoop to dissuade Hancock from marching on the village, but Hancock, who wanted to intimidate the Cheyennes with the thunderous might of his command, ignored Wynkoop.[2]

At daybreak on April 13, Hancock set out for the Pawnee Fork villages. Dog Soldier scouts hung on the column's flanks and reported Hancock's progress to the chiefs while other warriors set prairie fires to delay the general, though none fired a single shot at the soldiers. Late in the afternoon, Chief Pawnee Killer of the Southern Oglalas emerged from the smoke to promise the chiefs would parley with the general the next morning. Hancock took him at his word and halted for the night. The morning of April 14 came and went with no sign of the chiefs. Wynkoop's reminder that Indians carried no watches and reckoned time more loosely than whites failed to impress Hancock, and he angrily resumed the march. By now, the Cheyenne women and children had packed up and fled. The chiefs were also alarmed; perhaps another Sand Creek was in the offing. The Cheyenne warrior Roman Nose offered a solution: he would ride out and kill Hancock.

Roman Nose was not one to be taken lightly. Strong and hot-tempered, he was the most admired warrior on the southern plains, with a reputation for courage and daring so great that Major Wynkoop assumed him to be a chief. But Roman Nose, knowing that his volatility might endanger his people, had consistently refused a chieftainship. The only man capable of restraining him when angered was Chief Bull Bear of the Dog Soldiers. A giant of a man, standing six feet six inches tall, Bull Bear at heart was a peacemaker, but the present situation demanded preparedness, and so he and the other Cheyenne and Oglala chiefs rode out to meet Hancock accompanied by three hundred warriors.

Startled by a martial display that "was not part of the program," Hancock hastily deployed his fourteen hundred men in line of battle. Cavalrymen unslung their carbines, and the artillerymen loaded and primed their cannon. With everyone wondering whether the mutual show of force would end in bloodshed, Wynkoop rode forward to calm the chiefs and lead them and Roman Nose to an impromptu parley with Hancock midway between the lines.

"It was blowing a gale," Hancock said, and everyone had to shout to be heard. Addressing Roman Nose, the general demanded to know the Indians' intentions. Although a great warrior, Roman Nose was not entitled to speak on behalf of the chiefs, but he answered anyway. "We don't want war," he said. "If we did we would not come so close to your big guns." As Roman Nose spoke, women and children streamed onto the prairie. Hancock insisted the chiefs halt the flight, at which point Roman Nose suggested the chiefs return to the villages while he remained behind to kill Hancock. Roman Nose then touched the general lightly with his coup stick—a preliminary to dispatching him with a war club, which he would have done had Chief Bull Bear not grabbed his pony's bridle and led him away. Unaware of how close he had come to death, Hancock closed the council. The chiefs departed, and the line of warriors receded into the horizon. Bull Bear's quick reflexes had averted a battle that might very well have degenerated into a second Sand Creek. That night, the Indian men took the most reasonable course of action; they decamped with the remaining women and children, heading north in small parties to foil pursuit. In their haste, the Indians left their lodges standing.

When dawn revealed the villages deserted, a near-apoplectic Hancock ordered the lodges and their contents burned and the Seventh Cavalry to give chase. Together, Wynkoop and Hancock's second-in-command prevailed upon the general to spare the villages until the cavalry reported in; the Indians' flight, they said, was perfectly understandable, given the massacre at Sand Creek, which the army establishment had condemned. Destroying the villages, Wynkoop warned, would provoke "an Indian outbreak of a most serious nature."[3]

✳

Hancock had entrusted the pursuit to an officer equally inexperienced in plains warfare—Lieutenant Colonel George Armstrong Custer, acting commander of the Seventh Cavalry. Custer was twenty-seven years old, a bold and impetuous young officer whom fortune had favored with uncanny consistency. Handsome in a delicate way, slim and muscular, and blond and freckled, Custer sported a full mustache and curly, shoulder-length hair, which he sometimes trimmed for field service. His moods ran to extremes; normally the most jovial of companions, Custer sometimes sank unpredictably into what his wife called "long silences," periods of brooding solitude during which he spurned all company. The son of an Ohio farmer and blacksmith, Custer, whose friends and family called him Autie and who also answered to his middle name, had spent much of his boyhood with his half sister and her husband in Monroe, Michigan. As a West Point cadet, he never let studies interfere with fun, graduating last in the class of 1861. He was fortunate to have graduated at all; just prior to shedding his cadet gray for the army blue, Custer had been court-martialed for refereeing rather than breaking up a fight between two cadets while cadet officer of the day. Dismissal was the normal punishment for such a transgression, but with the country at war Custer received only a reprimand. From that day forward, he was a young man in a hurry. Within months, he was a captain and aide-de-camp to the commander of the Army of the Potomac, George B. McClellan, who became quite fond of the "gallant boy, undeterred by fatigue, unconscious of fear, but his head always clear in danger." A year later, Custer commanded a cavalry brigade at Gettysburg and then met Major General Philip H. Sheridan, with whom he established a lifelong bond of mutual loyalty and respect. Under Sheridan, Custer led a cavalry division through the 1864 Shenandoah Valley Campaign from one stunning victory to another. He knew instinctively when to charge, when to hold fast, and when to retire. After Appomattox, Sheridan wrote to Custer's wife, Libbie, "There is scarcely an individual who has contributed more to bring about this desirable result than your gallant husband."

The beautiful and intelligent Elizabeth "Libbie" Bacon, daughter of a distinguished Monroe, Michigan, judge, was a dynamo in her own right. Her father initially disapproved of her courtship with Custer; he thought her passionate young suitor of little account and dubious morality (Custer had apparently bedded four of the town's most desirable girls before turning his attention to Libbie), and he forbade Libbie to see Custer until he obtained a general's star. Custer got his star, and the couple wed in February 1864, becoming as inseparable as the exigencies of war permitted, and their correspondence when separated steamed with sexual innuendo. Though their relationship was tumultuous, Libbie's devotion to Autie was complete. "I was never an admirer of a submissive wife," she told a friend, "but I wish to look to my husband as superior in judgment and experience and to be guided by him in all things."[4]

After the Civil War, however, it was Custer who needed guidance. Like other officers who held volunteer ranks or brevets higher than their regular army rank, he plummeted in grade, in Custer's case from major general to captain, and seriously considered resigning his commission until Sheridan obtained a lieutenant colonelcy for him in the new Seventh Cavalry. Although Custer preferred a military career to civilian endeavors, the frontier army baffled and angered him. No longer did he command ardent volunteers; the soldiers of the Seventh Cavalry were as mediocre, undisciplined, and prone to desert as those of any other regular unit, the officers little better.

Custer's first mission with the Seventh Cavalry nearly proved his last. The second morning on the trail of the Pawnee Fork fugitives, he left his regiment to hunt for antelope. Coming upon his first buffalo, Custer "fairly yelled with excitement and delight"—that is, until the buffalo gored his mount. Drawing his revolver to shoot the buffalo, he accidentally killed his horse. Custer had no idea where he was; in the thrill of the chase, he had "lost all reckoning." After walking blindly for five miles, he spotted a dust cloud on the horizon. "A hasty examination soon convinced me that the dust was produced by one of three causes: white men, Indians, or buffaloes. Two to one in my favor at any rate." Custer sat down and waited until, the dust lifting, he descried a cavalry guidon. Custer's famous luck had apparently followed him to the plains.[5]

Pressing on with the Seventh Cavalry to the Smoky Hill, Custer found the route in shambles, with three of every four stage stations either abandoned or burned. Two terrified men still on duty told him that Indians had raided a nearby station and killed its three occupants. Without bothering to confirm their story, Custer sent a dispatch to Hancock blaming the Pawnee Fork bands. That was the news Hancock had hoped for. On the morning of April 19, over the strenuous objections of Wynkoop and some of his own officers, he burned the villages. Custer, meanwhile, had given the matter a bit more thought. The men who reported the raid had gotten the story secondhand from a passing stagecoach driver who could not say what Indians were responsible or if the guilty parties were even Indians. After belatedly ordering a reconnaissance, which revealed that the trail of the Pawnee Fork villagers had crossed the Smoky Hill River forty miles west of the westernmost destroyed station and ran due north, Custer penned a second dispatch absolving the Pawnee Fork bands, which left Hancock unmoved; the smoldering villages, the general insisted, had at a minimum harbored "a nest of conspirators."

Agent Wynkoop was inconsolable. "I know of no overt act that the Cheyennes have committed to cause them to be thus punished," he wrote to the Indian Department. "This whole matter is horrible in the extreme, and these same Indians of my agency have actually been forced into war."[6]

＊

From the charred remains of the Pawnee Fork villages, Hancock marched east to meet with the Kiowa chiefs at Fort Dodge and tried to put a stop to their incessant raids on the Texas frontier. Once again, Hancock's ignorance of Indians was on full display. Bungling the talks badly, he unwittingly became a player in an internal Kiowa power struggle. The head chief had died that winter, and there were two contenders for his position: Kicking Bird and Satanta. Kicking Bird was young for a chief, just thirty-two years old, soft-spoken, and slightly built. He advocated peaceful accommodation with the whites—Texans excluded. Satanta was nearing fifty. A blustering braggart, he led the Kiowa war faction and was infamous on the Texas frontier as a killer and kidnapper. When speaking to army officers, he masked his animosity behind a facade of flowery words and false promises. Ostentatious in the extreme, Satanta often painted his lodge, his entire body, and his horse the sacred color red.

Hancock met first with Kicking Bird. The commander of Fort Dodge vouchsafed Kicking Bird's "reliability," and Hancock took a fairly conciliatory line, telling the chief that the peace would hold so long as the Kiowas remained south of the Arkansas River emigrant route and committed no depredations. On April 29, six days after Kicking Bird's visit, Satanta swaggered into Hancock's office at his oratorical best, mixing reassurances with friendly counsel and forcefully asserting his preeminence among Kiowa chiefs. Satanta cautioned Hancock not to trust Kicking Bird, whose "speeches amount to nothing." The Cheyennes, Arapahos, Comanches, Kiowas, Apaches, and some Lakotas, Satanta said, "knew me to be the best man, and sent information that they wanted nothing but peace."

A credulous Hancock extended Satanta a singular honor: he presented him with a blue major general's coat, complete with gold shoulder straps and insignia of rank. The Indians understood the army hierarchy and knew that major generals were rare on the plains. Consequently, Satanta accepted the coat as conclusive proof that the whites considered him the head chief of the Kiowas. With the gift of a uniform, Hancock had diminished the influence of the peaceable Kicking Bird and enhanced that of the hostile Satanta.[7]

His business with the Kiowas concluded, on May 2 Hancock marched to Fort Hays. There he unexpectedly found the Seventh Cavalry, paralyzed by want of forage. Hancock ordered Custer to take the field as soon as supplies arrived and then repaired to his headquarters at Fort Leavenworth, confident he had reached an understanding with the Kiowas. Satanta, on the other hand, took great pleasure in having duped the general. After the Kiowa Sun Dance in early June, Satanta decided to have some fun at the army's expense. Decked out in his new uniform, he took a war party to Fort Dodge, shot a cavalryman full of arrows, and then ran off with an army horse herd. After leading the animals across the Arkansas River, Satanta paused on the far bank, tipped his hat to the pursuing troops, wheeled, and disappeared.[8]

∗

As Major Wynkoop had feared, Hancock's destruction of the Pawnee Fork villages infuriated not only the Dog Soldiers and their Southern Oglala friends but also nearly the entire Southern Cheyenne tribe. No sooner had Hancock broken up his command than war parties battered the Smoky Hill Trail and the Platte River Road, attacking stagecoaches, burning stage stations, and butchering at least a hundred settlers. Dead bodies were seen floating along the Platte River, and war parties ambushed work parties on the Union Pacific Eastern Division, slowing construction to a crawl. Dog Soldiers even prowled near the gates of Fort Wallace, the westernmost army post on the Smoky Hill.[9]

At Fort Hays, Custer grew morose and petulant. His failure to find Indians in April galled him, and nature reproached him with battering storms. Week after soggy week, the Seventh Cavalry lay idle waiting for supply trains. Desertions soared. Doleful letters from Libbie at Fort Riley disturbed Custer, and he meted out severe punishments for trivial infractions of discipline. When six men slipped out briefly to buy fruits and vegetables, Custer ordered their heads shaved and then marched them through camp in disgrace, a punishment that one captain considered "atrocious" because scurvy was rampant in the regiment.

On June 1, after the rains stopped and supplies arrived, Custer began a halfhearted search of western Kansas, evidently more interested in seeing Libbie than in finding Indians. Custer suggested she come to Fort Wallace, where he expected to put in after the expedition. "I will send a squadron there to meet you," he wrote. "I am on a roving commission, going nowhere in particular, but where I please." Detaching a squadron in mid-campaign to escort his wife to a post too dangerous for dependent families seems not to have struck him as odd.

Custer's preoccupation with Libbie's welfare soon precipitated a needless tragedy. On June 17, Custer met with General Sherman, who was in the area on another inspection tour. Sherman explicitly ordered Custer to scout the forks of the Republican River (the heart of

Dog Soldier country) and then repair with the regiment to Fort Sedg-wick on the Platte River Road for further instructions and for sup-plies. Instead, Custer dispatched Major Joel Elliott to Fort Sedgwick to check for new orders and sent the regimental wagon train to Fort Wallace for supplies—and to fetch Libbie, who he supposed would be there. A day after Major Elliott returned to Custer's camp, Sherman telegraphed Fort Sedgwick with orders for Custer to make Fort Wal-lace his new base of operations. The post commander at Fort Sedgwick entrusted their delivery to Lieutenant Lyman Kidder and a ten-man escort guided by a Lakota scout.[10]

Kidder never reached Custer. On July 1, a dozen Oglala hunters spotted the soldiers a mile north of a Dog Soldier and Oglala camp on Beaver Creek. It was a sultry day, and most of the Dog Soldiers were lounging in the shade of their lodges when the Oglalas galloped into the village, shouting for the Dog Soldiers to grab their ponies. As the Indians drew near, Kidder waved his men into a shallow ravine. There the soldiers dismounted, sealing their fate. Mounted Dog Soldiers cir-cled them, while Oglalas crept unseen through the tall grass toward the ravine. The fight lasted less than ten minutes. Warriors stripped and scalped the corpses, pulverized their skulls with rocks and war clubs, sliced off their noses, and slashed the sinews of their arms and legs to cripple them in the hereafter. The Oglalas also scalped Kidder's Lakota guide, who had begged for mercy from his tribesmen. As a sign of con-tempt, they left his scalp beside his body.

Eleven days later, circling buzzards and a horrible stench led Custer to what remained of the Kidder detachment. "We could not even dis-tinguish the officer from his men," he reported. "Each body was pierced by from twenty to fifty arrows, and the arrows were found as the savage demons had left them, bristling in the bodies." The army called the engagement the Kidder Massacre.[11]

On July 13, the Seventh Cavalry finally limped into Fort Wallace; it would be weeks before the regiment was fit to take the field again.

While the Seventh rested, Custer began a journey toward a court-martial and disgrace. Ostensibly to secure supplies, he set out on the evening of July 15 for Fort Harker, 141 miles east of Fort Wallace, with a small escort. From Fort Harker, he intended to push on to Fort Riley to rejoin Libbie. Custer's sudden leave-taking had been prompted by an anonymous letter suggesting he "look after his wife a little closer." Not only had Libbie not acted on his wish that she come to Fort Wallace, but she had also been much in the company of Lieutenant Thomas B. Weir, a handsome and charming young alcoholic. Their relationship might have been sexual; at the very least, the two flirted openly.[12]

Custer drove his troopers across the Kansas plains without regard for men or horses. Indians ambushed six soldiers whom Custer had sent out to retrieve an errant mare; when they failed to return, Custer refused to send out a search party. One of the men was killed, and another wounded. Later, as the horses gave out, dismounted troopers were shoved into wagon-wheeled ambulances. Pausing neither for rest nor meals, Custer reached Fort Harker in fifty-five hours. He awakened the district commander in the dead of night and told the groggy colonel that he was going on to Fort Riley by train. Learning the next morning of Custer's unauthorized dash across Kansas, the now wide-awake officer ordered his arrest and, with Hancock's support, preferred charges against him.

Libbie was not distressed by her husband's predicament. On the contrary, she reveled in his devotion to her. "When he ran the risk of a court-martial in leaving [Fort] Wallace, he did it expecting the consequences," she told a friend. "We are quite determined not to live apart again, even if he leaves the army otherwise so delightful for us." He did leave the army, but not by choice. On October 11, a court-martial found Custer guilty of "absence without leave from his command" and "conduct to the prejudice of good order and military discipline" and sentenced him to a one-year suspension without pay. So ended Custer's first Indian campaign.[13]

*

Custer's headlong peregrinations in western Kansas proved worse than futile. The ease with which the Indians evaded the Seventh Cavalry encouraged them not only to intensify their raids on the Smoky Hill Trail and Union Pacific Eastern Division but also to strike the other emigrant routes. Pressure for a solution mounted in the western press, and General Sherman reluctantly acceded to the Kansas governor's demand that he federalize a regiment of Kansas volunteers.

The only force that had proven able to best the Oglalas and the Cheyennes was Major Frank North's Pawnee Battalion. North's command was an experiment in recruiting friendly Indians as soldiers that paid handsome dividends. Uniformed in regulation blue and well armed, the two hundred warriors of the Pawnee Battalion protected Union Pacific work crews far more effectively than the army. They marched and drilled as cavalry but fought in the loose formations of Plains warriors. In early August, a Pawnee company attacked a large Cheyenne war party that was plundering a derailed freight train, killing by North's estimate seventeen warriors. Cheyenne sources disputed the numbers, but the blow kept their war parties away from the railroad.

And then, in late August, the Indian raids abruptly ended. It was not pressure from the Pawnees that brought quiet but rather Cheyenne religion. A messenger had made the rounds of the Cheyenne camps with a summons from Stone Forehead, guardian of the Sacred Medicine Arrows. The chiefs were to bring their bands to the Cimarron River. The time had come to renew the Sacred Medicine Arrows, a ceremony the Cheyennes believed essential to their very survival as a people. After their Cheyenne allies left them, the Southern Oglala war parties dispersed for the autumn buffalo hunt. The Northern Cheyennes were unable to slip past the cordon of forts along the Platte, but all the Southern Cheyennes attended the Sacred Medicine Arrows renewal. One item of business preceded the ceremony—what to do about a new, and entirely unexpected, government peace offer.[14]

The Cheyenne council might well have greeted the offer with amusement; certainly it would have perceived it as a sign of weakness. General Hancock had ridden boldly forward in the early spring supremely confident of his ability to impose his will on the tribe. He had destroyed the Dog Soldiers' village and that of their good friends the Southern Oglalas, after which the Indians had ridden rings around the soldiers with the greatest of ease. Having failed to conquer a peace, the Great Father was now pleading with the Indians to talk.

CHAPTER 5

THE LAST TREATY

T HE LATEST government olive branch was the fifth to be proffered the Plains tribes in the sixteen years since Tom Fitzpatrick's
grand council with the northern tribes had produced the Fort Laramie Treaty of 1851. Both that agreement and the Fort Atkinson Treaty
with the Southern Plains Indians in 1853 had been meant to induce
the Indians to recognize tribal boundaries and stay clear of the emigrant roads—both necessary precursors to concentrating the Indians
on reservations. The treaties had failed on the first count but largely
succeeded on the second. They had also begun the insidious process of
splitting the tribes into war and peace factions. Eight years after Fort
Atkinson, the government had induced ten Cheyenne and Arapaho
chiefs to sign the Fort Wise Treaty, committing their tribes to live
on a pathetic, desolate little reservation in southeastern Colorado—an
early attempt at extreme concentration. Most Southern Cheyennes and
Arapahos disavowed the treaty, widening the breach between tribal war
and peace factions. In 1865, Newton Edmunds negotiated his burlesque
of a treaty with Lakota nonentities, which accomplished nothing. Then
came the Treaty of the Little Arkansas that same year, intended to right
the wrongs of Sand Creek and again persuade the Indians to keep off
the travel routes and gradually congregate on large reservations. The
treaty had brought the Indians no closer to reservations, but it had at
least obtained peace until General Hancock stirred up the Indians on
the southern plains.

This fifth peace effort was the brainchild of John B. Henderson,
chairman of the Senate Committee on Indian Affairs. The Henderson

bill authorized the president to appoint a peace commission to negotiate a "permanent" treaty with Plains Indian tribes "at war with the United States." It contained the usual beatific language about remodeling the Indians into the red counterpart of the white man, but its immediate purpose was the same as that behind the Treaty of the Little Arkansas: to confine the Indians on reservations well removed from the travel routes and settlements.

The Henderson bill occasioned little debate. The Civil War had ended more than two years earlier, but scant progress had been made in clearing the plains for the whites who flooded the West in ever swelling numbers. The last thing the government wanted was to provoke yet another Indian conflict or a repetition of the "Chivington Process." And so, on July 20, 1867, President Andrew Johnson signed the Henderson bill into law.[1]

Sherman laughed at the legislation. "Of course I don't believe in such things for commissions cannot come into contact with the fighting Indians, and to talk with the old ones is the same old senseless twaddle," he told General Grant. Nevertheless, Sherman conceded, he was "partially reconciled by delay." Army contracts were in disarray, and future expeditions could be expected to cost even more than had Hancock's. "It may be that we had better dally along this year," he concluded, "and hurry up the railroad, and try to be better prepared next year."

Cooperating with meddlesome civilians was one thing, but Sherman was mortified to find himself appointed chairman of the Peace Commission, and he quickly passed the gavel to the commissioner of Indian affairs, Nathaniel G. Taylor. Other members of the commission included Samuel F. Tappan, who had led the military investigation of the Sand Creek Massacre; the former brigadier general John B. Sanborn, something of an expert on Indian affairs; Brigadier General Alfred H. Terry, a fair-minded man with no experience in Indian matters; and the still vigorous major general William S. Harney, called out of retirement.

The Peace Commission got off to a rocky start. In early September, the commissioners traveled up the Missouri River with instructions to gather all the Northern Plains tribes together for a conference. Low waters forced them to turn back, and they succeeded only in meeting with a delegation of friendly Northern Cheyennes and the Brulé Lakotas of Chief Spotted Tail, whom they warned not to molest the Union Pacific Railroad, then pushing its way westward across Nebraska. Sherman might have yielded the commission chairmanship, but he did most of the talking, and it was blunt. Advising the Indian conferees that they could no more stop the locomotive than they could the rising and setting of the sun, he promised them that the commissioners would return in November, at which time the chiefs could either come to terms or find themselves "swept away" by the army, a rather silly threat because none of the Indians with whom the commission met had caused any trouble. Sherman neglected to tell the gathered chiefs the reason for the adjournment, which was that Red Cloud, with whom they most wanted to talk, had refused to meet until after the Bozeman Trail forts were closed. There Sherman's participation in the Peace Commission ended. President Andrew Johnson summoned him to Washington to offer him the position of secretary of war. Sherman, who had no use for either politics or the nation's capital, declined: he was a soldier and would serve only under General Grant.[2]

The commissioners, less Sherman, continued on to the southern plains, where prospects appeared mixed. They knew they would be negotiating at a legal disadvantage. Article II of the 1865 Treaty of the Little Arkansas, one of the few clauses the Indians understood, gave them the right to live on the "unsettled lands" between the Arkansas and the Platte Rivers (southern Nebraska and western Kansas). The crux of the problem was that the Indians expected the unsettled lands to remain that way; Nebraskans and Kansans did not. On the plus side, the Kiowas, Kiowa-Apaches (a small tribe long affiliated with the Kiowas), the Southern Arapahos, and a large portion of the Comanches had agreed to a council in October at Medicine Lodge Creek, near a favorite Kiowa Sun Dance site sixty miles south of Fort Larned. The Southern Cheyennes, however, were noncommittal. Roman Nose, of all people, urged patience with the tribe: the commissioners must "keep a strong heart" and wait while Chief Stone Forehead and the Southern Cheyenne council considered the invitation.

Chief Satanta of the Kiowas, on the other hand, looked forward to the peace council as a grand forum in which to parade his presumption to tribal leadership. And he gained himself a bit of advance publicity. Attired in his major general's uniform, Satanta rode into Fort Larned in early October with an insouciant offer to protect the commissioners from the Cheyennes, after which he and the press corps all became gloriously drunk. The convivial party included the future explorer and adventurer Henry Morton Stanley, then an obscure stringer for a St.

Louis newspaper. In spite of the free liquor and adulation, Satanta was eager to get away from Fort Larned because, as he said over his cups in broken English, the post "stinks too much of white man."

At least twenty-five hundred Indians greeted the Peace Commission and its escort of four companies of the Seventh Cavalry (less Custer) when they arrived at Medicine Lodge Creek on October 14. Black Kettle and his sixty lodges represented the Cheyennes. Stone Forehead had ordered him to act as intermediary for the tribe, with a threat to kill his ponies if the beleaguered chief refused.[3]

When the Medicine Lodge Creek council finally convened on October 19, Senator Henderson struck a conciliatory tone, pledging to compensate the Indians for Sand Creek and bestow on them "comfortable homes upon our richest agricultural land." Satanta was unimpressed. "This building of homes for us is all nonsense," he said. "We don't want you to build any for us. We would all die. My country is small enough already. If you build us houses, the land will be smaller. Why do you insist on this?"

"Satanta's speech produced a rather blank look upon the face of the peace commissioners," observed Henry Morton Stanley, who added, "Satanta has a knack of saying boldly what he needs, regardless of what anybody thinks." And Satanta made good copy. To the public, he become known as the Orator of the Plains.

Smoldering at the attention bestowed on Satanta, Kicking Bird fixed his gaze on Commissioner Taylor's top hat and said nothing. As the council adjourned, Taylor made him a gift of it. That evening, the Kiowa chief marched back and forth in front of the council tent wearing the hat, telling his tribesmen that he was "walking in the white man's way." When he wearied of the burlesque, Kicking Bird stomped the hat shapeless. While Kicking Bird paced outside, a bareheaded Taylor drafted a treaty to present to the Kiowa, Comanche, and Arapaho chiefs the next morning. Its premise was simple: the buffalo would eventually become extinct, leaving the Indians no alternative but to settle down and farm.[4]

The second day of the council, October 20, nearly slid into mayhem. "Civilized" Osage Indians had entered camp during the night and sold whiskey to young Kiowa and Comanche warriors, who now sat unsteadily on horseback scowling while their chiefs unanimously rejected the peace terms. The Comanche chief Ten Bears wanted nothing to do with reservation life. "I was born upon the prairies, where the wind blew free, and there was nothing to break the light of the sun. I live like my fathers before me, and like them, I live happy." Before Senator Henderson could reply, Satanta and Ten Bears fell to arguing. Ten Bears berated the Kiowas for their womanly way of talking matters to death; Satanta retorted that the Comanches were creatures of impulse who made senseless raids. Their warriors scuffled, and the interpreters barely succeeded in restoring order before anyone was hurt.

Henderson implored the Indians to reconsider their position. The buffalo would perish before the onrush of settlers, and the Great Father wanted to give the Indians good land while it was still available. In desperation, Henderson promised the Indians hunting rights south of the Arkansas River on land outside the boundaries of the proposed reservation, an unauthorized concession. At nightfall, Taylor adjourned the council, telling the chiefs to come prepared to sign the treaty in the morning.

The document that Henderson handed the chiefs on October 21 was a grandiloquent guarantee of eternal harmony between Indians and whites that offered the Indians houses, farm implements, and schools—the very things they had rejected in council. And it boxed them in. The Comanches and the Kiowas were to share a 2.9-million-acre tract in Indian Territory comprising the southwestern half of present-day Oklahoma. It was good land in traditional Comanche territory, but it represented only a fraction of the country that had been Comancheria at its apex. In exchange for accepting that which they deplored, the Indians were to "withdraw all opposition" to the building of forts and railroads in their country and refrain from molesting travelers. In the end, it was not Henderson's words that swayed the Indians but the lure of gifts piled high in wagons arrayed within sight of the council ground. There had been too much talk, said Kicking Bird, it was time for the commissioners to hand out presents; the white men could have their paper. He, Satanta, Ten Bears, and sixteen other Comanche and Kiowa chiefs placed an X on the document.

How much of the treaty the Indians understood is impossible to say. Henry Morton Stanley thought they had no idea what they had signed. The treaty began, "From this day forward," which Stanley said really meant, "Until the white man wanted more land." Certainly no one who understood Plains Indians could expect them to surrender their way of life so easily.[5]

Toward evening, dark clouds gathered over the council ground. A hard wind blew over the plains, and cold raindrops pelted the tents and lodges. Out of the storm came Black Kettle and three Cheyenne chiefs. Speaking for the tribal council, the peaceably inclined chief Little Robe said his people needed four or five more nights to complete the Sacred Medicine Arrow ceremony. Taylor agreed to wait four days—and no more.

The deadline came and went, but the commission remained. Some of the Comanches and Kiowas left. The warrior societies, however, stayed to help the Seventh Cavalry protect the commission from the Cheyennes, should they arrive. Exasperated at the Cheyennes' non-appearance, the Arapaho chief Little Raven carped about the tribe's treachery until he grew tiresome to the commissioners. He wanted a reservation near Fort Lyon, anything to put distance between his people and the Cheyennes, who, he said, were always dragging the Arapahos into war. Commissioner Taylor praised Little Raven as "the noblest work of God—an honest man," but otherwise ignored him. The circle was closing, and Indian alliances were crumbling.

On the morning of October 27, Indian criers announced that Cheyennes were near. Black Kettle told the commissioners the warriors would come in shooting, but they should not worry; that was the traditional Cheyenne greeting of friendship. No one took any chances, however. The soldiers stood in front of their tents, weapons at the ready. A group of Comanche warriors armed with lances stood watch over the council tent. Little Raven and Satanta also assembled their warriors to help the soldiers defend the commissioners. Not entirely trusting in his own assurances, Black Kettle galloped out of camp to meet his tribesmen. General Harney walked to the near bank of Medicine Lodge Creek in his dress uniform and waited. The other commissioners huddled behind him.

At noon, the Cheyennes appeared, riding parallel to the creek in a long graceful column four abreast. Directly opposite the Peace Commission camp, the warriors wheeled into four lines. A bugle sounded, and the first rank kicked their ponies. They splashed across the creek and galloped toward the commissioners, yelling and firing pistols in the air. A few feet in front of General Harney, the warriors pulled their reins hard. Their ponies slid into a squat, and their riders dismounted. Surrounding the commissioners, the warriors laughed and shook hands with everyone. The remaining ranks followed suit.[6]

The peace council held on October 28, 1867, was brief. Senator Henderson apologized for the army's "grievous error" in destroying the Pawnee Fork villages. He offered the Cheyennes shared hunting rights with the Kiowas and the Comanches and repeated what he had told the Comanches and the Kiowas: that the whites were many, the Indians few; that the buffalo were vanishing and settlers were overrunning the plains. The Cheyennes must choose a reservation soon, Henderson said, farming was their only hope. The Missouri senator received the same answer from the Cheyennes as he initially had from the Comanches and the Kiowas: they wanted none of the white man's largesse.

A tall, handsome council chief named Buffalo Chip spoke for the Cheyennes. Reiterating their claim to western Kansas, he said, "You think you are doing a great deal for us by giving these presents to us, but if you gave us all the goods you could give, yet we would prefer our own life. You give us presents and then take our lands; that produces war. I have said all."[7]

Henderson found himself face-to-face with failure. His colleagues suggested an adjournment to consider Buffalo Chip's words, but the senator wanted to push ahead. He called Buffalo Chip and an interpreter aside, beyond hearing of the newspapermen and other commissioners. When the men returned to the council, Henderson announced that he and Buffalo Chip had reached an understanding. The Cheyennes would be permitted to hunt between the Arkansas and the Platte Rivers as provided for in the Little Arkansas Treaty, so long as they kept at least ten miles from railroads and settlements. In exchange, the Cheyennes and the Arapahos were expected to take up permanent homes once the buffalo were gone, which, Henderson reiterated, would be soon. The Cheyenne-Arapaho Reservation would be a 4.3-million-acre tract in Indian Territory (Little Raven's plea for a separate home for the Arapahos was ignored). Other terms were the same as those offered the Kiowas and the Comanches.

Henderson's compromise solved nothing. Rapid settlement of western Kansas made it nearly impossible for the Cheyennes to keep ten miles away from whites and still have room enough to hunt. Unable to imagine a future devoid of buffalo, the Cheyenne chiefs accepted the treaty, as did Little Raven in the interest of avoiding strife.

Henderson withheld the final text from the Cheyennes, the Arapahos, and the press. He had not made the promised changes to the treaty, which meant that his guarantee of off-reservation hunting rights would not appear on the document submitted to the Senate for ratification.

Henderson, however, did not hold a monopoly on deceit. The Cheyennes were also opaque. Roman Nose, the only man able to control the young warriors, had begged off from the council on the pretext of a slight illness. More important, Stone Forehead had also declined the invitation; he wanted no part of the white man's empty words. Without the blessing of the keeper of the Sacred Medicine Arrows, the treaty had no standing with the Cheyennes.

Ignorant of Cheyenne ways, the peace commissioners were guardedly optimistic that they had laid the basis for a lasting peace. But one astute cavalry captain knew better. "The Cheyennes have no idea what they are giving up. The treaty amounts to nothing, and we will certainly have another war sooner or later with the Cheyennes, and probably with the other Indians, in consequence of the misunderstandings of the terms." A mixed-blood interpreter took a longer view, and what he saw bode ill for his mother's people. "This was, in a way, the most important treaty ever signed by the Cheyennes," he later wrote, "and it marked the beginning of the end of the Cheyenne as a free and independent warrior and hunter."[8]

In every conceivable sense, Medicine Lodge Creek had been a catastrophe for the Indians. The peace council had spotlighted both their fractiousness and their inability to appreciate the ever-growing threat the whites presented to their way of life. The Comanches and the Kiowas had bickered, the Cheyennes had fallen out among themselves, and their critical alliance with the Arapahos had cracked. Observing the discord, Senator Henderson had sublimated his good intentions in favor of a cynical manipulation of the Indians. Whether the treaty would advance the government objective of concentrating the Indians on reservations without the need for army coercion remained to be seen.

*

Reading of the Medicine Lodge Creek proceedings, General Sherman could only despair of a peace purchased with paper. So long as treaties permitted the Cheyennes and the Arapahos to roam north of the Arkansas River, he regarded war as inevitable. In his mind's eye, Sherman clearly saw the noose tighten around the Indians' necks. The westward march of land surveys and settlements, railroads, and mail routes had already carved out large sections of the Indians' western Kansas hunting grounds, leaving only small and scattered tracts with fast-diminishing game. Mining communities rolled eastward off the Rocky Mountains. Of course the buffalo would disappear, and the Indians would either adapt to the white man's ways or perish. But in the meantime, with few available troops, Sherman recognized that the army could do little to prevent clashes between Indians and settlers or to pursue and punish fast-moving war parties should war commence. So long as the Indian signatories of the Medicine Lodge Treaty behaved, Sherman intended to play a waiting game. Defending the railroads remained his first priority.

The task would be easier with the arrival at Fort Leavenworth, Kansas, of the newly appointed commander of the Department of the Missouri, Major General Philip H. Sheridan. President Johnson intended frontier duty to be punishment for Sheridan, who as military governor of Texas and Louisiana had enforced congressional Reconstruction laws too vigorously to suit the lenient president. The South's gain was the Indian's loss. With Sherman and Sheridan working together in the West under the overall command of Grant, the Plains tribes were now confronted with the triumvirate that had won the Civil War.

Sheridan's solution to the Indian problem, formed while fighting Indians in the Pacific Northwest as a young officer in the 1850s, was simple and immutable: Indians were best lifted from "barbarism" by "practical supervision coupled with a firm control and mild discipline." But Sheridan had a singular notion of what constituted mild discipline, having hanged warriors randomly during an Indian uprising in Oregon for the "salutary effect" it would have on fellow tribesmen. That he kept an Indian mistress had not deterred Sheridan from waging war without remorse against her people. Like Sherman, he was a proponent of total war, which he also often waged against his fellow officers over perceived slights.[9]

In the spring of 1868, General Sherman kept Sheridan on a tight leash. Although the Southern Plains tribes had ample cause for complaint when annuities, arms, and ammunition promised at Medicine Lodge Creek did not materialize, they kept the peace. But trouble was brewing all the same. Whiskey bought with buffalo robes inflamed the young warriors. The entire adult male population of some Cheyenne and Arapaho villages was often roaring drunk. And drunk or sober, the young men had to follow the cultural imperative to fight. When spring came, they renewed their customary raids on the Pawnees in Nebraska and the Kaws in eastern Kansas. The Dog Soldiers were also ready to do battle, but not for honors or horses; they intended to hold on to their hunting grounds in the Smoky Hill River and Republican River country of westernmost Kansas, peaceably if possible, but by war if the whites intruded, and they gained potential reinforcements in May when Southern Cheyenne and Arapaho bands from below the Arkansas River ventured north to join the Dog Soldiers on the summer hunt. It was their right, Senator Henderson had told them, so long as they kept west of Kansas settlements. To Sheridan, who might not have been privy to Henderson's double-dealing, such a large concentration of Indians portended war. On Sheridan's southern flank, it was already a reality: the Kiowas and the Comanches were back to killing Texans, as if Medicine Lodge Creek had been but a playful lark between raiding seasons.

Sheridan did nothing to gain the Indians' confidence. On the contrary, he went out of his way to antagonize them. When Cheyenne and Arapaho peace chiefs complained to him about the many unfulfilled promises of the Medicine Lodge Treaty—arms and annuities had not been delivered, and those few who were inclined to walk the white man's road had no idea where it lay, because Congress had not yet opened the reservations—the pugilistic general interpreted their reasonable grievances as "insolence." As the council broke up, the Indian agent asked Sheridan for permission to issue the guns to the Indians when they arrived. "Yes," Sheridan said, "give them arms, and if they go to war the soldiers will kill them like men." To which a Cheyenne chief retorted, "Let your soldiers grow long hair, so that we can have some honor in killing them."[10]

Shortly after that encounter, Sheridan engaged as spies three capable squaw men, as frontiersmen with Indian wives were known, under the command of Lieutenant Frederick H. Beecher, a well-educated and courageous young officer who drank too much.

Beecher's agents found no signs of unrest among the Indians, and the lieutenant's first reports to Sheridan were hopeful. He absolved the Indians of responsibility for the minor depredations that had occurred, instead blaming them on white desperadoes. Sheridan was pleased at the prospect of "averting trouble till the favorite war season of the Indians was over." In other words, Sheridan believed war with the Southern Cheyennes and Arapahos would come; he and Sherman simply wanted it at a time and place of their choosing.[11]

A harmless Cheyenne scrimmage with the Kaws in eastern Kansas upset their calculations, however. The governor of Kansas was willing to let the incident pass, but his nervous constituents inundated Washington with baseless claims of impending raids on the border settlements. That prompted the Indian Bureau to suspend delivery of arms and ammunition to the Indians. Neither the Southern Cheyennes nor the Dog Soldiers needed guns; Lieutenant Beecher's spies had found them already armed to the teeth. But the delay rankled them as a matter of principle. Circumstances were ripe for a violent clash.

It came in early August, when a Dog Soldier war party, beaten in a skirmish with the Pawnees and liquored up on whiskey bought from ranchers on the Solomon River, ran into a posse, which opened fire on them. No one was hurt, but the inebriated Indians immediately exploded with pent-up rage, killing fourteen white men, raping several women, and kidnapping two children in lightning raids. As word of the violence spread through the Cheyenne villages, tribal discipline disintegrated. Dog Soldier chiefs lost control of their warriors. War parties struck isolated farms and ranches, waylaid wagon trains and stagecoaches, and ran off cattle from central Kansas to eastern Colorado. Nearly two hundred warriors prowled the outskirts of Denver. In Kansas, panic-stricken settlers streamed east from the outlying settlements, some with only the clothes on their backs.

The devastation galvanized Generals Sherman and Sheridan into action. Sherman ordered his aggressive subordinate to drive the Cheyennes from Kansas, a prospect that delighted Sheridan, who also wanted to hang the guilty parties, kill their ponies, and destroy their villages.[12]

The nation responded to the outbreaks in the usual fashion. The western press demanded the extermination of all Indians who could even remotely be considered hostile; eastern humanitarians urged restraint in order to safeguard the innocent. The *Army and Navy Journal* labeled the latest raids simply "one more chapter in the old volume," the result of alternately feeding and fighting the tribes. "We go to them Janus-faced. One of our hands holds the rifle and the other the peace-pipe, and we blaze away with both instruments at the same time. The chief consequence is a great smoke—and there it ends."[13]

*

There would be no peace pipe while Sheridan was in command. The Indians might be unbeatable during the summer and the fall, when their ponies were strong, but they could at least be kept on the run and, with the right men, perhaps hurt a bit. In view of the need to use his troops to protect the railroad, not to mention their conspicuous record of incompetence in tracking Indians, Sheridan directed his inspector general, Major George A. "Sandy" Forsyth, to recruit a fifty-man ranger force of "first class frontiersmen" to hunt down the hostiles. Forsyth welcomed the assignment. He had passed the Civil War largely on staff duty with Sheridan. Now he hungered to see action of any sort.

Qualified recruits were easy to come by. Thousands of Civil War combat veterans had flocked to the frontier to make a fresh start; for those whom prosperity passed over, a chance to earn steady pay with a rifle was inviting. Kansans who had lost loved ones in Indian raids enlisted eagerly; they called themselves the Solomon Avengers. Forsyth accepted Lieutenant Beecher as his second-in-command on the condition he stay sober.

On August 29, 1868, Forsyth set out for the Solomon River, elated with his "field command and roving commission." Carrying Spencer repeating rifles and Colt revolvers and not much else, his scouts traveled light but well armed. After several days of gentle meandering over the plains, on September 11 Forsyth's men picked up a war party's fresh trail leading toward the Arikaree Fork of the Republican River in Colorado Territory. Thrilled at the discovery, the captain drove his company with a single-minded intensity, pounding the plains for thirty to forty miles a day. What had begun as a faint path gradually widened into a broad, heavily trodden road, obviously made by a large Indian village on the move. On the afternoon of September 16, Forsyth made camp alongside the parched Arikaree Fork. The horses were blown; the men down to their last rations. That evening, Forsyth's guide, an experienced plainsman, cautioned the major against riding into a trap. Affecting an air of bravado, Forsyth not only dismissed the guide's counsel but also chose a terrible bivouac site. The only remotely defensible position was a small sandbar a few dozen yards behind the men that rose a mere three feet above narrow threads of turbid, sluggish water. A bit of shrubby undergrowth punctuated with stunted willows and cottonwood trees offered the only cover on the island.

The night was full of strange forebodings. Signal arrows shot across the horizon, and campfires flickered on the distant hills. Coyotes, or Indians impersonating coyotes, howled unseen in the dark. Forsyth's confidence deserted him. Feeling "restless, anxious, and wakeful," he rose repeatedly to visit his sentries or to confer with his subordinates. The major was ready to listen.[14]

*

All summer long, the Sacred Medicine Arrows had spread their blessing over the Dog Soldiers' country. Vast herds of buffalo populated the
headwaters of the Republican River. Scattered for the summer hunt,
the Dog Soldier camps now came together in a single village under the
leadership of Tall Bull and Bull Bear. Roman Nose was there, as was
Pawnee Killer and his Southern Oglalas. Twelve miles northeast of the
village, Major Forsyth walked his fretful beat.

At daybreak on September 17, the Indians attacked from a ridge
north of Forsyth's camp but not as the war chiefs had planned. To
maintain the element of surprise, Tall Bull had admonished the warriors to fight as a single unit, and he ordered Dog Soldier *akicitas* (tribal
police) to lash anyone who disobeyed. As usual, the eagerness of youth
upset the equation. Before dawn, eight warriors charged the scouts'
horses and awakened the camp. When Tall Bull and the main body
came up, the scouts were armed and ready. Not so their commanding officer. The sight of several hundred charging Indians paralyzed
Major Forsyth, who recovered his senses only after someone suggested
that he withdraw to the island. Few of the men, however, waited for
the command. Scurrying like scared quail, they scattered over the
island.[15]

Tying their horses to bushes, the scouts entrenched using knives, tin
cups, or more often than not their bare hands. They worked their Spencer carbines fast and frantically, some men lying prone, others jumping up and dropping down with each shot. Dust and smoke blocked
their view. The scouts failed to hit a single Indian, but the rapid volleys
blunted the attack, and the Indians retreated. In their place, Cheyenne
marksmen crept to within a few yards of the island. Hidden in tall buffalo grass, they gunned down a dozen men, including Major Forsyth.
A bullet tore into his right thigh, ranging upward until it lodged just
under the skin. A second round shattered his left leg below the knee.
The expedition's army medical officer was also hit. But the hardest
blow to Forsyth was the death of Lieutenant Beecher. "He half staggered, half dragged himself to where I lay," Forsyth noted, "and calmly
lying down, said quietly, 'I have my death wound, I am shot in the
side and dying.'" In an adjacent sand pit, the medical officer slumped,
insensible, his oozing brain tracing a ghastly trail down his shirt. The
wounded could expect little help. Besides mortally wounding the sur-

geon, the Indians had killed all the company's horses and seized the pack mules carrying the medical equipment.

At 2:00 p.m., the Indians attacked again. Conspicuous in the charge was a middle-aged Cheyenne widow. Still in mourning, she sought death in battle as a suicide warrior. Four times she rushed the island, singing her death song. Finally, losing heart, she returned to the ridge, where hundreds of women and children had congregated to watch the battle. As the fourth assault sputtered out, an exasperated war chief invoked the widow's exploits to harangue his warriors, crying, "What are you men doing? You are letting a woman get the best of you." The shamed warriors charged the island two more times. The scouts' Spencer rifles broke up each assault.

Roman Nose had been absent from the attacks, not venturing from the village until mid-afternoon. The great warrior was inconsolable; the medicine upon which he relied for success in battle had been broken by an act that its strictures forbade. "At the Lakota camp the other day something was done that I was told must not be done," he told Tall Bull. "The bread I ate was taken out of the frying pan with something made of iron. This is what keeps me from making a charge. If I go into this fight, I shall certainly be killed." As Roman Nose spoke of his broken medicine, a war leader galloped angrily to his side. "Well, here is Roman Nose, the man that we depend on, sitting behind this hill. Do you not see your men falling out there? All those people fighting out there feel that they belong to you, and here you are behind this hill." Reluctantly, Roman Nose prepared for battle. He unpacked his war bag, painted his face, offered his warbonnet to the sacred spirits and mother earth, and then, taking his place at the head of the Indian formation, charged with the reckless abandon of one whose fate was preordained. He swept over the riverbank and almost trampled two or three scouts before a bullet caught him in the small of the back. Returning to the bluff, Roman Nose dismounted and then stretched himself out on the ground, mortally wounded. After he was hit, there were no more charges.

A cold rain fell during the night. Two scouts slipped through the Indian lines and began a forty-five-mile trek to Fort Wallace for help. The situation on the island was grim. Twenty-one of the fifty-two defenders were either dead or wounded. All were hungry, their rations having been packed on the runaway mules. The survivors sliced steaks from the dead horses and strengthened their rifle pits. For four days, the Indians harassed the scouts but mounted no serious attacks. They left on September 22. Tormented by hunger and searing heat, burdened with wounded, and lacking horses to move them, Forsyth's scouts held on, hoped for a relief force to find them, and subsisted on putrefied horse meat. "My God," a scout scribbled in his diary, "have you deserted us?"[16]

It appeared so. On the morning of September 25, a scout combing the prairie for snakes, prairie dogs, or anything edible abruptly froze and then cried, "Indians!" Back in the rifle pits, the men seized their rifles for a last stand. The unknown horsemen drew nearer. And then their dark faces and blue uniforms came into focus: It was Company H, Tenth U.S. Cavalry, a unit of Buffalo Soldiers under the command of Captain Louis H. Carpenter.

"Oh the unspeakable joy!" recalled a scout. "Shouts of joy and tears of gladness were freely commingled." The "haggard, wolfish look on the countenances" of the scouts disturbed Carpenter, but he was most concerned about his friend Major Forsyth, who was lucid but slipping fast. Blood poisoning had set in, and Carpenter's surgeon said the major would not have lived a day longer without medical care. The surgeon also had to restrain the Buffalo Soldiers, who with the best of intentions had given their rations to the starving men. "If the doctor had not arrived in time," said a black trooper, "we would have killed them by feeding them to death." As it was, Forsyth's company had suffered six dead and fifteen wounded. The Indians, who said they lost nine warriors, resumed their raiding. They called the action "the Place Where Roman Nose was killed." The army named it the Battle of Beecher Island.[17]

*

Although Beecher Island was militarily insignificant, the encounter at least ended well for the scouts. The army, on the other hand, was about to stumble badly. The ability of Forsyth's scouts to hold their own against a huge force of Indians awakened hope in General Sheridan that the army might be able to contribute something meaningful toward pacifying western Kansas. A properly orchestrated strike against known Southern Cheyennes and Arapaho villages on the Cimarron River might compel the war parties to withdraw to protect their families. Sheridan, however, operated under a false premise. The

Cimarron River villages belonged to Black Kettle, Little Raven, and other peace chiefs. Some of their young men had joined the war parties, which consisted primarily of Dog Soldiers, but for the most part the peace chiefs had managed to restrain their warriors.

Sheridan assigned the mission to Lieutenant Colonel Alfred Sully, commander of the District of the Upper Arkansas. Although Sully lacked the killer instinct Sheridan expected of subordinates, he had compiled a creditable record fighting Indians in the Dakota Territory during the Civil War. But Sully had become oddly passive in the field. On September 7, he headed south from Fort Dodge with nine troops of the Seventh Cavalry, Major Joel Elliott commanding, and three infantry companies—just over five hundred men in all. The foray bordered on the comical. Sully rode with undisguised dread in a two-wheeled ambulance. On September 10, the expedition reached the Cimarron River, only to find the Cheyenne and Arapaho villages gone. The next morning, a war party carried off two troopers from Sully's rear guard. When the rear-guard commander gave chase, Sully had him arrested; he wanted no second Fetterman disaster on his record.

The nonsense continued for five more days. Army wagons foundered in quicksand. Rations ran short. Indians nipped at Sully's flanks. Tired of the "interminable sand hills," the dispirited colonel turned back. Warriors rode alongside the column just out of range, thumbing their noses and slapping their buttocks. Major Elliott summed up the experience for a friend. "I had the honor to command the cavalry on that expedition, and if that was *fighting*, then Indian wars must be a huge joke."[18]

Generals Sherman and Sheridan were not laughing. Raids on the Smoky Hill dragged on into October. Already seventy-nine civilians were dead, thirteen women had been raped, over a thousand head of stock had been stolen, countless farms, stage buildings, and rolling stock had been destroyed, and travel had been brought to a standstill. It was time for army retaliation on an unprecedented scale—a "predatory war," as Sherman put it, to drive the Cheyennes and the Arapahos to surrender or starvation. The bloody summer had brought about in him a brutal metamorphosis. No longer did he pity Indians brought to the brink of starvation by congressional dawdling. "The more I see of these Indians, the more I become convinced that they all have to be killed or be maintained as a species of paupers," he told his brother Senator John Sherman. "Their attempts at civilization are simply ridiculous."[19]

But General Sherman was officially still a peace commissioner. As such, he was duty-bound to protect the nonbelligerent bands. Sherman's solution, with Indian Bureau concurrence, was to move the Cheyenne-Arapaho Agency to Fort Cobb, an abandoned army post on the Washita River in Indian Territory, and assign a favorite subordinate, Colonel William B. Hazen, who also happened to be a bitter foe of Sheridan's, the job of segregating peaceful Indians from the "hostiles." Tacitly excusing their sanguinary indiscretions in Texas for reasons known only to himself, Sherman instructed Hazen to issue the Kiowas and the Comanches the annuities due them under the Medicine Lodge Treaty and to keep the tribes out of the impending war. As for the Cheyennes and the Arapahos, Sherman told Hazen he "proposed to give them enough of war to satisfy them to their heart's content."[20]

Sheridan would bear the cudgel, attacking their villages during the dead of winter, a time when war ponies were gaunt and warriors unsuspecting. Black Kettle did not have to be privy to Sherman's plans to know what danger the winter might bring. It is said that when he learned of the summer raids on the Saline River settlements, he tore off his clothes and pulled out clumps of hair in grief. Experience had taught the long-suffering peace chief that white retribution was often blind and unrelenting.[21]

———•••———

CHAPTER 6

OF GARRYOWEN IN GLORY

To GEORGE ARMSTRONG CUSTER, the sorry events of 1868 on the southern plains, where the Medicine Lodge Treaty had proven bankrupt and the army impotent, were merely newspaper headlines. Suspension from duty in October 1867 had worked no hardship on the irrepressible young lieutenant colonel. While the Seventh Cavalry thrashed about under the uncertain hand of Colonel Sully, Custer had passed a "most agreeable" autumn in Monroe, Michigan, with Libbie. The chance of a reprieve seemed remote. In June, Grant had turned down Sheridan's request to restore him to duty. And so Custer was greatly surprised in late September to receive a telegram from Sheridan ordering him to return to his post; the military situation had turned sufficiently grim for Grant to have relented. While Custer rode the rails to Kansas with "unbounded gratification," Sheridan enjoyed a good cigar in peace knowing, as he told his staff, that "Custer had never failed him." And neither, it appeared, would Sherman, who promised to support unconditionally whatever actions Sheridan might take in his winter war against the Southern Cheyennes and Arapahos, "even if it ends in [their] utter annihilation."

Sheridan expected no trouble in finding Indians; it was the arctic-like winter weather that worried him. The Southern Cheyennes and Arapahos traditionally made their winter camps just east of the Texas Panhandle, in an area of abundant game and sheltering rivers that Sheridan called an "Indian Paradise." And so it seemed to the Indians, who were certain that the same brutal weather that kept them rooted to their tipis would keep the soldiers in their forts. They had no under-

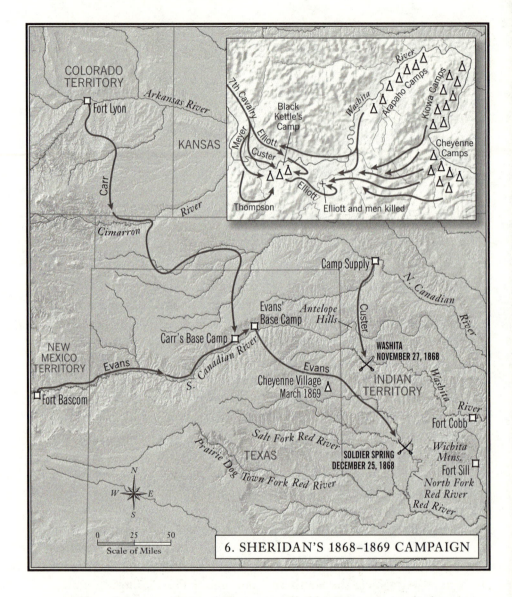

6. SHERIDAN'S 1868–1869 CAMPAIGN

standing of the man General Sherman called his "persevering little ter-
rier dog," nor of his intention to throw everything he had against them
and against nature.

There was nothing subtle in Sheridan's plan. Beginning in mid-
November, three columns would converge on the Indians. Major
Eugene Carr would march southeast from Colorado Territory and
Major Andrew W. Evans would march east from New Mexico Terri-
tory with several hundred men each. They would act as "beaters," driv-

ing any "straggling bands" into the path of the main strike force under Sully, who would march due south from Fort Dodge, Kansas, toward the principal Indian villages. Sheridan gave Sully eleven companies of the Seventh Cavalry under Custer, five companies of infantry, and a generous complement of teamsters—a total of seventeen hundred men. Sheridan also expected the newly recruited and federalized Nineteenth Kansas Cavalry to join Sully on the march. That would swell the command to nearly twenty-seven hundred. A small contingent of Osage warriors, bitter enemies of the Cheyennes, were recruited as guides. As ranking officer, Sully would command the expedition, but Sheridan counted on Custer to deliver a victory. While Custer whipped the Seventh Cavalry into shape, Sully built a temporary depot, which he named Camp Supply, in what Sheridan acknowledged to be a "most suitable place" midway between Fort Dodge and the likely location of the Indian villages.[1]

That was the last compliment Sheridan was to pay Sully. Having only reluctantly appointed Sully to command the expedition, Sheridan now traveled to Camp Supply to oversee operations. It was good that he did, because Sully and Custer were barely on speaking terms. Six days earlier, when the Seventh Cavalry had chanced upon the fresh trail of a large Cheyenne war party headed for the Kansas settlements, Sully had enraged Custer by vetoing as too risky his proposal to follow the war party's back trail to their villages. Siding with Custer, Sheridan sent Sully back to Kansas to shuffle papers.

With Sully gone, Sheridan wrote to a friend, "everybody here is as cheerful as the birds in early spring." No one had heard from the Nineteenth Kansas Cavalry, which, unbeknownst to Sheridan, had become lost in a blizzard, but the general was unconcerned by the Kansans' absence. On November 22, he turned Custer and the Seventh Cavalry loose to find and destroy the "hostile" Indian villages, presumed to be on the Washita River. That suited Custer just fine. Not even the blizzard that dumped a foot of snow on Camp Supply that night could dampen Custer's enthusiasm for the hunt. He considered the snow, which was still falling fast and hard when he bade Sheridan farewell, his best ally; he could move in it, while the heavily laden Indian villages could not. Given another week of winter squalls, he promised to return with "satisfactory evidence that my command had met the Indians."[2]

The Southern Cheyennes and Arapahos welcomed the wall of snow as a sure obstacle to the army, and they also took comfort in numbers.

Nearly the entire Southern Arapaho and Cheyenne tribes (less the Dog Soldiers, who clung to western Kansas) were camped together. Several Kiowa, Kiowa-Apache, and Comanche villages also lay just downriver. All told, some six thousand Indians wintered on the Washita.

Two miles upstream from their tribesmen, Black Kettle's village of fifty-three lodges stood in sorrowful isolation. Whether by choice or because the council chiefs might have banished Black Kettle, after Sand Creek he and his three hundred followers always wintered alone. Their present campsite, resting behind a half-mile loop in the Washita River, was a good one, even if it was remote. A thick fringe of timber along the steep banks acted as a windbreak and provided ample wood for lodge poles and fuel for fires. Grass for the ponies was plentiful. A chain of red-shale ridges and bluffs paralleled the river a mile to the north of the village.

Black Kettle, however, was not at home. Braving the blizzard, he and an Arapaho friend had traveled eighty grueling miles to Fort Cobb to ask Colonel Hazen to protect them. Black Kettle was entirely honest. Confessing that he had been unable to restrain all his warriors, the chief nevertheless believed he could keep the young men off the warpath if Hazen permitted his band to camp at Fort Cobb. But the colonel had nothing to offer the Cheyennes and the Arapahos. The Great Father had made Hazen a peace emissary only to the Comanches and the Kiowas; he had no control over the "great war chief" General Sheridan; it was with him that they must reach terms. And they must also stay away from Fort Cobb. Their hearts frozen by Hazen's cold words, Black Kettle and his friend turned homeward.[3]

While Black Kettle pleaded for peace, the 844 officers and men of the Seventh Cavalry pounded toward the Washita. On November 25, they reached the South Canadian River, where Custer made plans to find the Indian back trail that Sully had forbidden him to follow two weeks earlier. The next morning, he sent Major Joel Elliott (who had laughed at Sully's conduct of the autumn campaign) east along the north bank of the river with three companies, while he prepared to scout the south bank with the main body. Elliott had hardly left when Custer received word that the major had found the fresh trail of a large war party heading southeast and was giving chase. The game was on.

Custer traveled light through deep and unbroken snow. The troopers carried only their weapons, a hundred rounds of ammunition, a small ration of coffee and hard bread, and a bit of forage. Four ambulances and two light wagons with extra ammunition and rations struggled along behind the column. At 9:00 p.m., Custer met up with Elliott, and the reunited Seventh Cavalry entered the Washita valley. The night was cold and clear. The telltale sound of horseshoes crunching the crusted snow carried far. Just after midnight, Custer crawled to the crest of a ridge overlooking the Washita River, faintly visible a mile off. Blackness engulfed the far bank. But the distant barking of dogs and crying of infants betrayed Custer's prey. For a moment, his conscience panged him. "Savages though they were and justly outlawed, I could not but regret that a war such as we were engaged in . . . would possibly prevent discrimination."[4]

Nevertheless, Custer hastily outlined a battle plan. There was no time to reconnoiter, he told his officers. To preserve the element of surprise, they must strike at dawn. Custer intended to engulf the village with four widely separated columns. Major Elliott would strike the village from the north. Captain William Thompson would splash across the Washita to a hillcrest south of the encampment. Captain Edward Myers would attack due east. Custer, with the largest column, would attack from the northwest, straight into the village. The four commands were to push off when they heard the regimental band strike up "Garryowen," the Seventh Cavalry's marching song. Speed was essential; the columns, Custer emphasized, were "to go in with a rush." Captain Thompson ventured a question: "Suppose we find more Indians there than we can handle?" To which Custer replied, "All I am afraid of is we won't find half enough. There are not Indians enough in the country to whip the 7th Cavalry."[5]

*

Black Kettle rode slowly into his village at sunset on November 26, his pony exhausted by the six-day journey from Fort Cobb. Later in the evening, warriors from Black Kettle's band left the war party that Major Elliott was pursuing and slipped into their lodges, leaving behind an implicating trail.

A strange paralysis gripped Black Kettle's village. A Cheyenne warrior who had fallen behind the war party after his pony went lame thought he had seen soldiers on the horizon. A friend told him the objects must have been buffalo, suggesting that perhaps the warrior's conscience troubled him for having disobeyed Black Kettle and gone on the warpath. The chastened warrior told no one else of his sighting. Later some passing Kiowas warned the Cheyennes that they had seen a wide trail heading toward the Washita. The Cheyennes laughed at them. As the night deepened, Black Kettle called together the village elders for coffee and counsel, telling them that Sheridan was already in the field and that Hazen could not help the Cheyennes. Black Kettle's wife implored them to break camp at once, but the men decided to wait until dawn to move. Inexplicably, Black Kettle neglected to send out wolves (scouts) to keep a lookout for soldiers. After the council, Black Kettle's wife unburdened herself to a woman friend. "I don't like this delay. We could have moved long ago. It seems we are crazy and deaf and cannot hear."

Four long hours remained until daybreak. Shivering in their saddles in subzero cold, the soldiers were in a foul mood. Near dawn, Custer's officers saw a light shoot above the eastern horizon, which in their benumbed state they mistook for a rocket. The light hovered over Black Kettle's village. It was the morning star—in Plains Indian religion, the god of fire and light.[6]

Black Kettle rose early on November 27, his village still slumbering. A lone woman emerged from her tipi. Wading the icy Washita to retrieve her husband's ponies, she saw charging cavalry bear down on the pony herd; splashing back across the river, she ran through camp screaming the news. Black Kettle fired a shot of alarm. Telling the women and children to save themselves, he lifted his wife onto his pony, climbed behind, and then galloped toward the protection of the timber and steep banks of the Washita. Soldiers blocked his path and opened fire. A bullet struck Black Kettle in the back, and he slipped dead from his pony, facedown into the frigid water. Beside him lay his wife, also shot dead.

As planned, Custer struck the village first. Riding stirrup to stirrup with him was his reliable chief of scouts, twenty-six-year-old Ben Clark, married to a Cheyenne girl, and Captain Louis H. Hamilton, the popular and capable grandson of Alexander Hamilton. A single shot struck Hamilton in the chest, killing him instantly. Custer galloped on, shooting an Indian at point-blank range. Then he and Clark drew off from the column and climbed a lone knoll three hundred yards south of the village to watch the unfolding action.[7]

The village was a swirling cauldron of confusion. Gunfire, screaming women and children, yelping dogs, and horses' pounding hooves rent the brittle morning cold. Cheyennes spilled from their lodges, some wrapped only in blankets. A Cheyenne girl helped mothers shepherd barefoot children behind the steep banks of the Washita. Razor-sharp ice cut their feet, and the water ran red with blood. But the river offered no refuge. Sharpshooters in bushes on the north bank and troopers emerging from the village subjected the Indians to a murderous cross fire. The death songs of Cheyenne women punctuated the racket.

Riding from the knoll to the river, Ben Clark spotted twenty warriors, women, and children huddled behind a caved-in section of the north bank. A hail of bullets from the sharpshooters put a quick end to them. And then Clark witnessed "a terrible example of a Cheyenne mother's despair." The last surviving woman stepped into the open holding a baby at arm's length and brandishing a long knife in her other hand. Mistaking the light-skinned infant for a white captive, a sharpshooter yelled, "Kill that squaw. She's murdering a white child." Before a gun could be fired, said Clark, "the mother, with one stroke of her knife, disemboweled the child [and] drove the knife to the hilt in her own breast and was dead. A trooper poked his carbine over the bank and shot her through the head, but it was a needless cruelty."[8]

Cruelty was the order of the day in Custer's command. The Osage guides—"bloodthirsty wretches," Clark called them—committed most of the atrocities. They had held back during the charge for fear the soldiers might mistake them for Cheyennes. But after the village was cleared (which took just ten minutes), they fell upon the dead, severing heads and slashing women's breasts. The Osage chief had lost his wife to a Cheyenne raiding party the year before. The first corpse he encountered had already been scalped, so he cut off the head and smashed it against the frozen ground. Soldiers were also guilty of outrages. Two Cheyenne women witnessed a trooper shoot down a pregnant woman and then slice open her stomach and pull out the fetus. At least one soldier took a scalp. Captain Myers's men fired on fleeing women and children until Custer, informed by Ben Clark of the breach of orders, put a stop to it.

Captains Myers and Thompson had botched their assignments. They failed to close the circle east of Black Kettle's village, and many noncombatants passed through the gap between their commands. Warriors crouched in ravines or behind trees covered the escape of these women, children, and elderly. It was then that Major Elliott caught sight of another group of dismounted Indians plodding east. He shouted for volunteers to catch them. Seventeen men, including Sergeant Major Walter Kennedy, answered Elliott's call. As his detachment set off, Elliott waved to an officer and said, "Here goes for a brevet or a coffin."

Elliott got a coffin. He overtook the party after killing two warriors who tried to shield their escape. Elliott told Kennedy to take the prisoners to the village and then started after yet another group. The sergeant major did not get far. Four Arapahos killed him when he paused to allow a Cheyenne woman to bind her children's bleeding feet. Meanwhile, a mile east of Black Kettle's village, Elliott blundered into a large party of warriors galloping toward the village from downriver. The troopers turned loose their horses and then lay down in a small circle, feet to the center. For an hour, perhaps longer, Elliott held the Indians at bay. Unable to overcome the soldiers while on horseback, the warriors dismounted and crawled toward them. As the Indians edged closer, the troopers held their carbines above the tall grass that protruded from the snow and fired blindly. A mounted Arapaho warrior darted into the soldiers' circle, counting coup until a bullet knocked him to the ground. His deed spurred scores of warriors to follow him, and they soon overwhelmed Elliott's detachment. After the warriors moved off, vengeful Cheyenne women hacked apart the corpses.

Lieutenant Edward S. Godfrey, leading a platoon after fleeing Cheyennes on the north bank of the Washita, nearly shared Elliott's fate. Brought to a halt by a tall promontory, Godfrey crept to the top to discover that he was now the pursued; not only was the valley beyond blanketed with tipis, but hundreds of mounted warriors also were riding toward him. Godfrey hastened to report his discovery to Custer. "Big village?" stammered Custer. "What's that?" Godfrey had also heard rapid firing from down the south bank. Might it be Elliott? Custer dismissed the notion; Captain Myers, he said, "had been fighting down there all morning and probably would have reported it."[9]

Matters seemingly more urgent than Elliott's whereabouts demanded Custer's attention. Prisoners confirmed Godfrey's report of vast Indian encampments downstream. As the afternoon wore on, growing numbers of well-armed Cheyenne, Arapaho, and even Kiowa warriors from the lower villages gathered atop high ground bordering the valley floor. "The hills appeared to be alive with them," marveled Ben Clark.

The Indians had turned the tables on Custer. "For from being the surrounding party," he later confessed, "we now found ourselves surrounded and occupying the position of defenders of the village."

Although Custer still enjoyed numerical superiority, his supply of ammunition was running dangerously low, and Indians now stood between the ammunition wagons and Black Kettle's village.

Suddenly the wagons bounced down the hills north of the river with warriors in close pursuit and lurched into camp "in the nick of time," said an officer. With cartridge boxes full, the Seventh Cavalry carried out grim orders from Custer: they were to burn the village and kill the eight hundred captured ponies. The sad business of slaughtering the pony herd took two chaotic hours. Wounded animals broke free and ran about, bleeding, until they dropped. The river ran red, prompting the Cheyennes to call that tragic day the Battle of the Red Moon.

Thick smoke rose from the valley floor where Black Kettle's village had stood. Near sundown, the Seventh Cavalry band struck up "Ain't I Glad to Get out of the Wilderness" and rode onto the snow-packed rolling land north of the Washita River in close marching order. Then they started downriver, as if to attack the other villages. It was a ruse, and it worked. The warriors retreated to protect their families, who were already hastily packing up. After moving slowly down the valley for several miles, Custer briskly countermarched the regiment and made for Camp Supply.

The number of Indian casualties at the Battle of the Washita remains uncertain. Custer brought away fifty-three Cheyenne women and children, eight of whom were wounded. He claimed to have killed 103 warriors, or slightly more fighting men than a village the size of Black Kettle's could possibly have held, but never offered the source of his inflated numbers. The captives later said that 18 warriors had been killed and 16 women and 9 children had died at the Washita. In Custer's defense, some of the women had apparently wielded weapons. Cheyenne wounded were likely more than double the number of dead, for a probable total of 125 Indian casualties. Whatever the true count, Custer was satisfied. In a private dispatch to Sheridan, he crowed, "We have cleaned Black Kettle and his band out so thoroughly that they can neither fight, dress, sleep, eat, nor ride without sponging upon their friends."[10]

Given that Custer had the advantages of surprise and at least an eight-to-one numerical edge over Black Kettle's warriors, his own losses of twenty-two killed (including Elliott and his seventeen men, whose fate was unknown to Custer) and thirteen wounded were hardly a cause for celebration. Nor could Custer's well-choreographed, triumphal march into Camp Supply—the band playing "Garryowen" and Black Kettle's scalp dangling from an Osage lance—conceal the anger many Seventh Cavalry officers felt at Custer's decision not to search for Major Elliott. Custer advanced a hopeful theory: Elliott was simply lost and would find his way into Camp Supply. Sheridan found that "a very unsatisfactory view of the matter," but he balanced Custer's lame conjecture against the winter blow his protégé had dealt Cheyenne complacency.

Custer's decision not to search for Elliott and his men laid the basis for bitter and lasting factionalism within the officer corps of the Seventh Cavalry. Captain Frederick W. Benteen, a capable but choleric officer who disliked Custer intensely, used Elliott's death to fan the flames of dissension. After the battle, Benteen asked Ben Clark to testify that Custer had "knowingly let Elliott go to his doom without trying to save him." When Clark refused, Benteen wrote a florid letter to a friend accusing Custer of having abandoned Elliott. It appeared anonymously in *The New York Times*, and Custer threatened to horsewhip the author. But when Benteen confessed authorship, he dropped the matter.[11]

Although the officers of the Seventh Cavalry were bitterly divided over Custer's handling of Elliott's disappearance, they did agree on one thing: the desirability of their female Cheyenne captives. While the Osages held a boisterous scalp dance within view of the terrified women the night after the battle, Cheyenne survivors said Custer and his officers appeared among them to select bedmates. Custer, the captives said, chose the beautiful nineteen-year-old Monahsetah, daughter of Chief Little Rock, killed with his friend Black Kettle. As other Cheyennes drifted in to surrender, the officers of the Seventh Cavalry picked out more sexual partners. The Cheyenne accounts are plausible. Custer's unbridled sexual appetite was well established, and a company commander boasted in a letter to his brother that the officers had ninety Cheyenne females from which to choose; "some of them," he added, "are very pretty." As for himself, "I have one that is quite intelligent. It is usual for officers to have two or three lounging around."[12]

*

While the officers of the Seventh Cavalry bickered and fornicated in the relative isolation of Camp Supply, much of the American public waxed indignant over their actions at the Washita. From high places came demands for "an immediate and unconditional end to the war policy." It was not only eastern humanitarians who protested the destruction of Black Kettle's village. Calling the fallen Black Kettle "as good a friend of the United States as I am," the tough old general Harney accused the army of having provoked an Indian war. Edward W. Wynkoop, on leave at the time of the Washita, resigned as Cheyenne-Arapaho agent in protest over Custer's "wrong and disgraceful" attack, which he equated with Sand Creek.

Before the Washita Campaign began, General Sherman had promised to shield Sheridan from public and political criticism, a pledge he now made good with a vigorous verbal counterattack that, unfortunately, was built on a lie. In the immediate aftermath of the affair, Custer had reported recovering two white children from Black Kettle's camp. That, Sherman assured General Grant, was proof positive that there had been hostiles in Black Kettle's village. But the children existed only in Custer's imagination. Although Sheridan knew the truth, he nonetheless repeated the fiction in his own report to Sherman, who thus unwittingly perpetuated it.[13]

The legitimacy of Custer's attack on Black Kettle's village was open to honest debate, but allegations that Custer had perpetrated a massacre were unjust. His surprise assault was consistent with Sherman and Sheridan's strategy of total war. Black Kettle was unquestionably a man of peace—even Sherman acknowledged as much—but his camp did harbor warriors guilty of raiding in Kansas. Unlike Sand Creek, where soldiers were encouraged to kill women and children, Custer took pains to spare noncombatants. Innocent lives were lost, and acts of cruelty occurred, but a massacre is defined as the indiscriminate killing of a large number of helpless and unresisting people, and such was neither Custer's intent nor the outcome of the lopsided Battle of the Washita.

*

Not surprisingly, the Battle of the Washita threw the Southern Plains tribes into an uproar. Nearly all the Southern Cheyenne and Arapaho tribes fled west. Custer's attack also frightened the Kiowas, half of whom, mostly followers of Satanta, quit Fort Cobb and fell in with the Cheyennes and the Arapahos near Sweetwater Creek on the Texas Panhandle. There was much talk of war, but relatives of the captive

Cheyenne women prevailed on the chiefs not to retaliate. For the time being, the Cheyennes and the Arapahos would keep to their Sweetwater Creek camp. Reconsidering their decision to run, Satanta and his Kiowas opted to return to Fort Cobb and Hazen's protection.[14]

Satanta's return put him on a collision course with a new expedition under General Sheridan. The bulldog general viewed the Washita as merely the first phase of his winter campaign. On December 7, 1868, he started south from Camp Supply with fifteen hundred troops drawn from the Seventh Cavalry and the tardy Nineteenth Kansas Cavalry. Although Custer retained nominal command, Sheridan in fact directed operations, intending first to find Major Elliott and then to fight any hostile Indians who might turn up. Black Kettle's unusually cooperative sister accompanied them as a guide.[15]

Sheridan pressed on to the Washita battlefield through a violent snowstorm and arctic cold. There scouts found the stone-cold chalk-white bodies of Elliott and his men. In an abandoned Cheyenne village downstream, Sheridan and Custer made a soul-chilling discovery. Beside the remains of a campfire lay the body of a young white woman with two bullet holes in her scalped and crushed head. Crumpled beside her was a dead child, evidently slammed against a tree. Enraged Cheyennes had killed them both. A Kansas volunteer recognized the pair as twenty-one-year-old Clara Blinn and her two-year-old son, seized by an Arapaho war party that summer. Sheridan had known of Clara Blinn's captivity—in early November, Clara's father had appealed to the general to save his daughter and grandchild—but knew not whom to blame. Black Kettle's sister filled in the blanks, in a manner of speaking. To protect her people, she pinned the crime on Satanta. Sheridan not only bought the story but even embellished it, writing to Sherman that "the poor woman had been reserved to gratify the brutal lust of the chief, Satanta." Here was a clear score for Sheridan to settle with the Kiowas.[16]

For six miserable days, through snow and sleet, Sheridan followed a broad Indian trail from the Washita River toward Fort Cobb. When Satanta learned of Sheridan's approach, he prevailed upon Colonel Hazen to intervene. On December 17, a Kiowa delegation bearing a white flag gave Sheridan a message from Hazen asking the general to call off his attack. All the Indians around Fort Cobb were friendly, insisted Hazen, and had "not been on the warpath this season." Hazen suggested Sheridan question Satanta for information on the location of the hostile Cheyennes and Arapahos.

William T. Sherman, commanding general of the U.S. Army from 1869 to 1883. "We must act," he said in 1867, "with vindictive earnestness against the Sioux, even to their extermination, men, women, and children."

Red Cloud of the Oglala Lakota posing at a photographer's studio in Washington, D.C., in 1880. His fighting ability made him a Lakota leader; the U.S. government made him a chief.

Captain William J. Fetterman purportedly boasted that under proper leadership "a company of Regulars could whip a thousand, and a regiment could whip the whole army of hostile tribes." On December 21, 1866, the Indians proved him wrong.

Troopers of the Tenth U.S. Cavalry, one of four black regiments known as Buffalo Soldiers. Although black soldiers were excellent fighting men and—unlike white soldiers—seldom deserted, the War Department often relegated black units to service in particularly disagreeable sectors of the frontier.

A Plains Indian village in winter, the season in which Indians were most vulnerable to attack. Army strikes on winter encampments nearly always succeeded.

On a winter campaign, arctic temperatures and fierce plains blizzards were often a more dangerous enemy than hostile Indians.

The loss of a pony herd crippled an Indian village and its warriors. Securing the herd was a mission for the cavalry or Indian scouts.

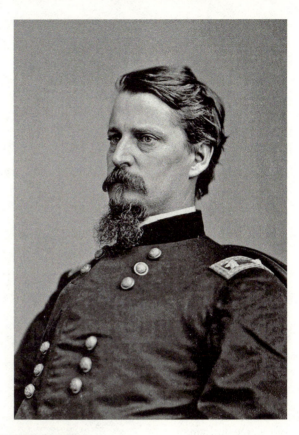

Winfield S. Hancock. His ignorance of Indian ways and blind arrogance precipitated the first post–Civil War conflict with the Southern Plains tribes.

Kiowa Chief Satanta, the Orator of the Southern Plains, was a swaggering braggart and constant terror to Texas settlers.

RIGHT George Armstrong Custer and his bride, Elizabeth Bacon "Libbie" Custer, shortly after their marriage in 1864. He was twenty-four years old, she twenty-one when they wed. Theirs was a passionate but tumultuous relationship.

BELOW Custer discovers the corpses of Lieutenant Lyman Kidder's detachment, July 12, 1868. "Each body," said Custer, "was pierced by from twenty to fifty arrows."

LEFT Philip H. Sheridan as a major general during the Civil War. A Comanche chief is said to have told Sheridan, "Me good Injun," to which Sheridan reputedly replied, "The only good Indians I ever saw were dead."

BELOW The Battle of Beecher Island, September 17, 1868, one of the hardest-fought engagements of the Indian Wars

ABOVE Custer leads the charge into
Black Kettle's village at the Battle of the
Washita, November 27, 1868.

RIGHT The caustic and critical Ranald S.
Mackenzie was the army's premier cavalry
commander. In the Civil War a shell
fragment sliced off the first two fingers of
his right hand. His Fourth Cavalrymen
labeled him Three Finger Jack. The
Indians called him Bad Hand.

An incredulous Sheridan thought Hazen's letter "a pretty good joke." By "trickery and double dealing," Sheridan believed, the Kiowa chiefs had deceived Hazen into writing the letter. Yet as much as he wanted to fight the Kiowas, Sheridan felt compelled to honor the promise of Sherman's protégé. He met with Satanta and Lone Wolf, also an influential Kiowa chief, and insisted that Satanta's people prove their pacific intentions by accompanying the troops to Fort Cobb. The chiefs agreed and sent runners to bring them in. When two days passed with no sign of Satanta's village, Sheridan "put on the screws." He arrested Satanta and Lone Wolf, with a promise to hang them if the Kiowas did not surrender within forty-eight hours.

Hazen leaped to the chiefs' defense. Satanta and Lone Wolf could not possibly have been at the Washita, he assured Sherman, because they had passed the night before the battle at his tent at Fort Cobb. They had decamped because Custer's attack spooked them, insisted Hazen, and had been returning to Fort Cobb when Sheridan's approach rendered the Kiowas "as uncontrollable as a herd of scared buffalo."[17]

Sheridan and Hazen had only their reputations at stake in the stand-off; Lone Wolf and Satanta's lives, on the other hand, hung in the balance. Confined to a well-guarded tent, Satanta was the picture of despair. A cavalry officer watched him "wrap his blanket around himself, swing back and forth, and chant the most doleful and monotonous death song. Stooping over, he would scoop up sand and dirt and put them into his mouth. Then he would go around and . . . shading his eyes with his hand, would sweep the horizon to discover if possible the approach of his people."

Satanta survived. On the afternoon of December 20, a large party of warriors rode into Fort Cobb; before dawn on the twenty-first, nearly the entire tribe had come in. Reluctantly, Sheridan released Satanta and Lone Wolf. He always regretted that "the two manacled wretches thus saved their necks," the more so because "for some years afterward their devilish propensities led them into Texas, where both engaged in the most horrible butcheries."[18]

No sooner had the Kiowa chiefs slipped the noose than Sheridan learned that Major Carr's winter expedition had turned back to Fort Lyon after a month of battling panhandle blizzards without seeing a single Indian. Major Evans, however, had better news to report. On Christmas Day, he decimated a Comanche village of sixty lodges at Soldier Spring, near the Wichita Mountains. Although very few of the Comanches in that unfortunate band had been guilty of raiding—even in Texas—Sheridan crowed to Sherman that Evans's "victory" had given the final blow to the backbone of the Indian rebellion. It was typical Sheridan hyperbole, and misplaced at that, but his winter campaign had nevertheless achieved considerable success. The Cheyennes might have eluded him, but the Kiowas were under his thumb, as were about one-third of the Comanches. In fact, Sheridan suddenly found himself with more Indians at Fort Cobb than he could feed. To prevent a hunger-driven Indian stampede, Sheridan began work on a combined Kiowa-Comanche agency and new post called Fort Sill built on salubrious land farther south.[19]

Next, Sheridan turned his attention to the Cheyennes and the Arapahos. First he tried diplomacy of a sort, demanding that the chiefs surrender unconditionally or face unrelenting war. Sheridan thought the Washita captives were his trump card, but his ultimatum largely fell on deaf ears. Speaking for the last time with anything approaching unanimity, the Cheyenne and Arapaho chiefs pleaded that their ponies were too weak and Fort Cobb too distant for a winter journey. Sheridan gave the Indians time to reconsider their decision—and the Arapaho peace chief Little Raven availed himself of the hiatus to surrender—but the Cheyennes remained obdurate. Sheridan's patience ran out. Spring was near. War ponies would grow fat on the new grass, and raids on the Kansas settlements would resume. On March 2, 1869, he sent Custer with the Seventh Cavalry and the Nineteenth Kansas Cavalry to deal the hostiles "such treatment as past conduct and existing circumstance demanded."[20]

Sheridan would not be on hand for Custer's return. On March 4, Ulysses S. Grant became the eighteenth president of the United States. Sherman succeeded him as commanding general of the army, and Sheridan, in turn, won a third star and command of the Military Division of the Missouri, with headquarters in Chicago. His promotion, however, held little interest for soldiers struggling to survive the winter. Custer's expedition set out poorly provisioned, the commissary having failed to deliver the beef cattle Custer intended to drive along with him. Troops exhausted their rations in two weeks. Hunting was futile, because the trail toward the Staked Plain led through a sandy wasteland barren of game. Only the rapid decline in their animals, which the soldiers ate, saved the men from starvation.

Unlike the Kansas volunteers, the troopers of the Seventh Cavalry were accustomed to Custer's hard marches, and it came as no surprise to them that he pressed on. Consistent with the proverbial "Custer's

Luck," on the afternoon of March 15, while riding alone with his orderly and Osage guides several miles ahead of the troops, Custer found Stone Forehead's village on Sweetwater Creek. Prepared for any contingency, the Sweet Medicine chief met Black Kettle's killer under heavy escort, his hands and face painted red, the ceremonial color of both war and peace. Stone Forehead invited Custer to the Sacred Arrow Lodge, telling the colonel that he did so in order to reassure his people that the troops intended them no harm. Stone Forehead's unspoken reason for holding council with Custer was to invoke the power of the Sacred Medicine Arrows to divine the flaxen-haired colonel's true purpose.

Accompanied only by his adjutant and trusting in his knowledge of sign language, Custer followed Stone Forehead into the Cheyenne village. Custer's intentions were decidedly belligerent. When he met Stone Forehead, a member of the chief's escort had let slip that there were large Cheyenne camps close by, some of which Custer mistakenly thought belonged to the "mischievous, blood-thirsty" Dog Soldiers. Here "was the opportunity we had been seeking," Custer mused, "to administer a well-merited punishment to the worst of all Indians." Custer intended to talk until his troops came up, after which he would attack all the Cheyenne villages. But as he neared the Sacred Arrow Lodge, Custer learned there were two young white female captives in the village, both of whom had been seized in Kansas that autumn. "Of course it was then out of the question to assume a hostile attitude, [because] the opening of the attack would have been the signal for their murder."[21]

The ensuing council ceremonies mystified Custer, and the significance of his seat beneath the Sacred Medicine Arrows escaped him. Lost also to Custer was the meaning of a Cheyenne medicine man's "petition or prayer to the Great Spirit," which in fact was an invocation for divine help to kill Custer should his words prove false. To drive home the point, after Custer smoked the sacred pipe, Stone Forehead emptied the ashes on the colonel's boots, a curse to hasten Custer's demise if he ever again made war on the Cheyennes. Custer was aware only that he had obtained Stone Forehead's promise to release the white women.

Emerging from the lodge, Custer beheld a plain blanketed with hundreds of whooping warriors, armed and painted for battle. Beyond them, in a dismounted line of battle, stood the Seventh Cavalry and the Nineteenth Kansas Volunteer Cavalry. The Kansans cast a ragged shadow. Their faces were black with campfire smoke, their eyes sunk deep. A burning desire to avenge murdered friends and family had kept them going. When Custer's adjutant ordered them into camp, the troops were stunned. Ignorant of the two female captives in the village, the Kansans dispersed believing the Cheyennes had faced down Custer.[22]

Two days later, Custer redeemed himself to the Kansans. The chiefs had yet to make good their promise to turn over the women. A group of young warriors were in Custer's camp, ostensibly to entertain the soldiers with feats of horsemanship, but in reality under orders from Stone Forehead to distract Custer while the village slipped away. When an officer reported the ruse, Custer acted swiftly, directing his men to disarm and seize the Indians. Most of the warriors escaped, but Custer snared four of them and then presented an ultimatum to the Cheyenne chiefs: surrender the white women or watch your men hang.

After three days of wrangling, the Cheyennes capitulated, and the two women entered Custer's lines, terrified, emaciated, and nearly naked. Their story was brutally familiar to the Kansans. They had been gang-raped by the warriors, beaten without provocation by the Cheyenne women, and passed from hand to hand by purchase or as gambling winnings. In retaliation, Custer duplicitously refused to release the captive men until the Cheyennes surrendered. His bad faith astonished the chiefs, one of whom later attested, "Sometimes [Custer] would talk good and sometimes bad to them; they could not understand him. He told them he wanted them to follow him on to Camp Supply; but he talked so strangely to them they would not trust him."

In late March 1869, Custer started home well satisfied with himself. In an ebullient report to Sheridan, he enumerated his achievements: "We have penetrated every haunt frequented by the five tribes which were lately hostile. We now know their accustomed routes and hiding places. We have taught the Indians that they are safe from us at no place and at no season, and that the white man can endure the inclemencies of winter better than the Indian."[23]

The advent of spring, however, rendered Custer's fanfaronade meaningless, for with better weather the tactical advantage shifted to the Indians. A few Arapaho holdouts surrendered, but most of the Southern Cheyennes remained at large, trying to keep as far from white men as possible.

✻

In a private letter written from Fort Sill, the post commander, Colonel Benjamin H. Grierson, no friend of Sheridan's, offered a bleak appraisal of the winter campaign, which he called a "grand fizzle" that had cost the lives of more soldiers than Indians (leaving out the innocent women and children) and had served chiefly to get Sheridan his third star. Although Grierson's vitriol contained an element of truth, Sheridan's campaign forever shattered the tenuous bonds of Cheyenne tribal unity.

At Stone Forehead's behest, in early May 1869 the Southern Cheyennes and Dog Soldiers assembled to decide their future. Instead of the traditional search for consensus, the meeting pitted Chief Little Robe, who had come from the Fort Sill Agency for the occasion, and the Dog Soldier chief Tall Bull against each other. As spokesman of the peace faction, Little Robe, once a highly respected Dog Soldier warrior himself, presented Tall Bull with a startling ultimatum that no single chief had the authority to issue: Tall Bull could either accept reservation life in Indian Territory or go home. The Dog Soldiers then decided upon the unthinkable; not only would they leave Indian Territory, but they would also abandon their beloved Republican River valley.

Why the Dog Soldiers chose to quit their country without a struggle is not known. Probably they judged the growing number of settlers rolling toward their border, the rapidly advancing railroad, and a suddenly competent army simply too much to resist without suffering Black Kettle's fate. Whatever the reason, reservation life was out of the question. The Dog Soldiers had always been free, pronounced Tall Bull, and they would remain so or die fighting. Their destination would be the Black Hills, where they would join forces with the Oglalas. With that, the momentous tribal council meeting broke up. Two hundred Dog Soldier warriors and their families repaired to the Republican River to hold the spring buffalo hunt and, according to a well-informed army officer, "make a last big strike" before relinquishing their homeland. Little Robe returned to the reservation. Stone Forehead opted for the middle ground; he would remain on the Texas Panhandle with his two hundred lodges and wait to see what happened to Tall Bull and Little Robe.[24]

The wait was short. No sooner had the Dog Soldiers reached the Republican River than they collided with Major Carr's Fifth Cavalry. Smarting over his dismal winter performance, Carr was out to make a fresh start in the Department of the Platte under a new commander, the quietly competent colonel Christopher C. Augur. On May 13, along the banks of Beaver Creek, Carr attacked the Dog Soldier village, killing twenty-five warriors at a cost of three dead and four wounded. He briefly pursued the Indians into Nebraska before they scattered and the trail ran out.[25]

The Dog Soldiers retaliated with a month of bloody raids. Augur again unleashed Carr, with instructions to engage any Dog Soldiers in the Republican River country who did not surrender unconditionally. Riding under Carr's command was the Fifth Cavalry, Major Frank North's Pawnee Battalion, and, as chief guide, a handsome, well-spoken twenty-three-year-old buffalo hunter and army scout named William F. "Buffalo Bill" Cody. For a month, the Dog Soldiers eluded Carr, constantly shifting their camps and traveling in small groups. On July 10, they reached Summit Springs, near the South Platte River in eastern Colorado. Most wanted to cross the South Platte into the Lakota country at once. Tall Bull, however, judged the water too high and decided to wait two days for it to recede.

Tall Bull had erred—fatally. The next day, Buffalo Bill and the Pawnees discovered the Dog Soldier village nestled in a treeless valley. It was a hot and smoky afternoon; warriors had been out that morning burning grass to erase their trail. Now they idled about their lodges. Three miles away, Carr concentrated his force for a charge. To the Pawnees went the honor of leading the assault on their bitter enemies. Within twenty minutes, the village was theirs. The Pawnees galloped after the fleeing Cheyennes, shooting and yelling, while the cavalry fanned out around the abandoned lodges. Organized resistance was impossible. Dog Soldiers fought singly or in small clusters to buy time for their women and children to escape. Over the din came Tall Bull's voice: "All of you that are on foot and cannot get away follow me." With two of his three wives, his little daughter, and a handful of mostly elderly followers, Tall Bull made for a ravine, but not before shooting two captive white women. At the edge of the ravine, Tall Bull killed his horse and staked his dog rope in the ground; he would defend that spot to the death. A gunshot wound in the head ended his stand. The only Cheyennes to leave the ravine alive were Tall Bull's eldest wife and their daughter, who were fortunate enough to surrender to North himself before the major's Pawnee scouts got them.

The Pawnees did most of the killing at Summit Springs, and they killed without mercy. The Cheyennes expected as much. "I do not belittle the Pawnees for their killing of women or children because as far back as any of us could remember the Cheyenne and Sioux slaughtered every male, female, and child they could run across of the Pawnee tribe," said a Dog Soldier survivor. "Each tribe hated the other with a deadly passion and savage hearts [that] know only total war." Sherman and Sheridan's notion of total war paled beside that of the Plains Indians.

Carr achieved complete victory at Summit Springs. He reported fifty-two Cheyennes killed (sexes and ages unspecified), an unknown number wounded, and seventeen women and children captured. No soldiers died, and only one was wounded, barely scratched by an arrow. Carr burned eighty-six lodges and captured 450 ponies. Remnants of Tall Bull's village reached the Lakota camps in the Black Hills, but the Dog Soldiers as a band had ceased to exist. In those twenty terrifying minutes at Summit Springs, their world ended. For all their truculence, the Dog Soldiers had not sought war with the whites. Tall Bull had spoken truthfully when he told General Hancock in 1867 that the Dog Soldiers wanted only to live unmolested in their Republican River home. When the Union Pacific Railroad began its inexorable way toward their country, bringing thousands of settlers and driving off the buffalo, the Dog Soldiers had fought to save their country and their way of life the only way they knew how—with horrific raids calculated to terrorize the whites into keeping away. Few whites understood the Dog Soldiers' behavior, and fewer still could excuse the atrocities. The Dog Soldiers were likewise unable to comprehend the social and economic forces that impelled the whites to take their country. Nevertheless, it was a brutal fate that decreed the Dog Soldiers' annihilation after they had given up the struggle.

The possibility that the Dog Soldiers had acted from desperation and dread seems never to have occurred to Major Carr either. In the debris of the abandoned Dog Soldier village, he found letters from government officials that he jokingly told a fellow officer "certify to the high character of certain Indians, whom must have greatly degenerated since they were written." One of the letters was from their former Indian agent, the fair-minded Edward W. Wynkoop, emphasizing that Tall Bull was peaceably disposed and disinclined to fight "unless forced to do so by imprudent acts of white men."[26]

Wynkoop's words of warning had been written on the wind.

CHAPTER 7

THE BLOODY POLICY OF PEACE

WITH CUSTER's dubious triumphs and Carr's unequivocal victories on the Republican River, Sheridan's 1868–1869 campaign had achieved its objectives: western Kansas and southern Nebraska were cleared of hostile Indians, the travel routes were secured, and the perpetrators of the 1868 Kansas raids had been punished (as had the innocent among Black Kettle's people). The Southern Plains tribes had learned that winter was no longer their ally and that soldiers, when coupled with their Pawnee and Osage auxiliaries, were enemies to be feared, the more so as the Indian shield had shattered. The Arapahos had abandoned their alliance with the hopelessly factionalized Southern Cheyennes. The Dog Soldiers had been eliminated. And the Kiowas and the Comanches had gone their own way, collecting rations on their reservation and depredating in Texas.

*

Sheridan's victories, ironically, came at a time when the federal government was poorly prepared to deal with the defeated tribes. Preoccupied with the bitter politics of Reconstruction, neither the outgoing president, Andrew Johnson, nor Congress had been able to fashion an Indian policy, "leaving things," as General Sherman put it, "to caprice and the haphazard."

The army, the Washington bureaucracy, and Congress all stepped clumsily into the vacuum. Army leaders advocated the return of the Bureau of Indian Affairs to the War Department (its home before the creation of the Interior Department), which, they said, would put an end to the interdepartmental bickering that the Indians exploited. A perspicacious colonel offered an apt analogy: the army was the "stern but henpecked father"; the Indian Bureau, the "indulgent mother"; and the Indians the "recalcitrant children" who profited from the contention between their parents. Western public opinion, Congress, and all the peace commissioners except the commissioner of Indian affairs, Nathaniel G. Taylor, were for restoring the Indian Bureau to the War Department, and in December 1868 the House passed a transfer bill.[1]

The Bureau of Indian Affairs loudly protested. Commissioner Taylor called the House measure "tantamount to perpetual war" and warned that army stewardship would carry "demoralization and disease" to the Indians. Taylor, however, was on shaky ground when he claimed moral superiority over the army; the Indian Bureau stank of corruption. A popular story told of a chief who described his agent to General Sherman thusly: "Our agent great man. When he comes he brings everything in a little bag, when he goes it takes two steamboats to carry away his things." Agents regularly connived with contractors and Indian traders to cheat the Indians out of their annuity goods, reselling them and submitting false vouchers to cover their tracks. Not surprisingly, the Indian Bureau had few defenders. The public and the press called the shadowy consortium of civilian swindlers, crooked politicians, and malfeasant officials the "Indian Ring" and despised their illicit dealings.

Also wading into the drifting waters of Indian affairs were the eastern humanitarians with their high-minded vision of a conciliatory Indian policy. They railed against government neglect of its treaty obligations and demanded that Congress appoint honest agents capable of controlling frontier rapacity. The Religious Society of Friends (the Quakers) petitioned Congress more gently, but with the same intent.[2]

The election of Ulysses S. Grant as president in November 1868 seemingly boded well for the army. After all, as commanding general he had defended Sherman and Sheridan's hardfisted approach to the Indian problem and decried civilian meddling. But President-elect Grant was not General Grant, and to the surprise of the generals he welcomed ideas from the reformers, particularly the Quakers. Embracing their suggestion that religious men replace spoilsmen as agents, Grant gave the Quakers control over the two most critical—and difficult— Indian Bureau field operations: the Northern Indian Superintendency, comprising six agencies in Nebraska, and the Central Superintendency, which embraced Kansas and the "uncivilized" portion of Indian Territory (that is to say, the Southern Cheyenne and Southern Arapaho, and the Kiowa and Comanche agencies). The apportionment of these superintendencies to the Society of Friends became known as Grant's Quaker Policy. To run the remaining superintendencies and agencies in the West, Grant selected honest and reliable army officers.

Grant also wanted to establish independent oversight of the Indian Bureau. To achieve it, he persuaded Congress to create the Board of Indian Commissioners. Composed of wealthy philanthropists, the board was given wide authority to scrutinize the operations of the Indian Bureau in Washington and in the field. And then Grant did something even more remarkable: he appointed an Indian to be commissioner of Indian affairs.

The new commissioner was Ely S. Parker, a full-blooded Seneca Iroquois sachem from upstate New York and a civil engineer who had risen to the rank of brevet brigadier general on Grant's staff during the Civil War. Parker was a man of proven integrity. Although he subscribed to the prevailing view that the Indians' future lay in acculturation, he nonetheless could be counted on to make it as painless as possible. In June 1869, Parker instructed his staff on their duties under the Grant administration: Indian agents and their superintendents were to assemble Indians in their jurisdictions on permanent reservations, get them started on the road to civilization, and above all treat them with kindness and patience. Indians who refused to settle on reservations would be turned over to military control, however, and treated as "friendly or hostile as circumstances might justify."

Grant saw no humane alternative to his administration's carrot-and-stick body of principles that the press labeled the "Peace Policy" and its concomitant policies of concentrating the Indians on reservations far from whites and of consolidating small reservations into larger ones populated by two or more tribes, which meant that tribes promised exclusive homes stood to lose them regardless of treaty guarantees.

While not the exclusively military approach the generals had hoped for, the Peace Policy at least gave the army an influential and clearly defined role in Indian affairs. Phil Sheridan interpreted Parker's instructions to suit his purposes, telling his commanders that all Indians off their reservations should be presumed hostile.[3]

The Peace Policy began promisingly, from the government perspective at least; no one, Parker included, cared what the western tribes thought of the administration's plan for bottling them up and dismantling their cultures. Indian agents and army officers worked in relative harmony. There were sporadic Indian clashes during the autumn of 1869, but none rose to the level of open warfare, and a general peace appeared within reach. That is, until an inebriated major in the Montana Territory violently upset the Grant administration's careful calculations.

*

The Peace Policy had little meaning in the wilds of northern Montana, home to the Piegan Indians, a small tribe belonging to the Blackfoot Confederacy. There were no neatly drawn reservation borders, no easy distinction between friendly and unfriendly Indians, and precious little cooperation between the army and the Indian agents. Everything was blurred and ambiguous. The whites were split. Settlers and miners crowding the Piegan country exaggerated the Indian threat and wanted the Piegans exterminated; dealers in whiskey and guns wanted their Indian customers protected. The Piegans were also divided. The band of Chief Heavy Runner favored peace; that of Mountain Chief talked of war but limited its activities to horse stealing and avenging tribesmen murdered by white ruffians.

The army did not know quite what to make of the situation. The district commander, Colonel Philippe Régis de Trobriand, held an exaggerated view of the Piegan threat, and he badly wanted to punish Mountain Chief. De Trobriand's reports drew an uncertain response from Sherman and Sheridan. Both feared that a misstep might bring on another public firestorm like that following the Washita, and Sheridan told de Trobriand to forgo preemptive military operations against Mountain Chief if any danger of molesting friendly Indians existed. The risk was real—Heavy Runner and Mountain Chief's bands were camped near each other on the Marias River, a hundred miles southeast of present-day Glacier National Park—but de Trobriand felt certain that with competent scouts he could isolate Mountain Chief's camp and destroy it. Taking de Trobriand at his word, Sheridan gave him permission to strike, suggesting Major Eugene M. Baker, who had done good service under him in the Civil War and had been brevetted for "zeal in actions against Indians," as the right man to lead the attack. Unfortunately, Baker also had a zeal for the bottle.

On January 19, 1870, an apparently drunk major Baker set out with six cavalry companies and explicit orders to leave Heavy Runner's people alone. Two scouts accompanied him to make sure he hit the right target—Joe Kipp, a close friend of Heavy Runner's, and Joe Cobell, the husband of Mountain Chief's sister. Cobell, however, would prove keener on protecting his brother-in-law than on doing his assigned duty.

At dawn on January 23, Baker found a Piegan village of thirty-seven lodges nestled in a timbered bottom of the Marias River valley. Baker deployed his men dismounted in a semicircle along bluffs overlooking the village. It was intensely cold and deathly still. Smallpox had struck the camp, and the sick and listless Piegans neglected to post guards. The only Piegan up and about was a seventeen-year-old warrior named Bear Head who had risen early to retrieve his horse, which he had left on the bluffs. Trudging upward, he came face-to-face with the soldiers. Major Baker grabbed Bear Head and motioned to him to keep quiet. At that moment, Joe Kipp stumbled through the snow toward Baker, yelling that the village was that of Heavy Runner, not Mountain Chief. Furious that Kipp's shouting had alerted the village, Baker ordered the scout arrested. It made no difference whose camp it was, Baker told Kipp; a Piegan was a Piegan, and he intended to attack. Heavy Runner, who had heard Kipp's cry, rushed toward the soldiers waving a safe-conduct pass from the Indian Bureau. Joe Cobell shot the chief dead, whereupon Baker barked the command "Open fire; continue as long as there is any resistance."

There was no resistance, but the soldiers fired anyway, and Baker made no effort to stop them. In thirty minutes of madness, women and children were shot or burned alive in their lodges. Bear Head said Baker laughed as he walked through the smoldering wreckage and gazed upon the charred corpses. Near sunset, a wicked windstorm blew over the bluffs and swirled into the valley. The temperature hovered at thirty degrees below zero. Fires crackled in the woods, and some time after dark the pony herd stampeded. Nerves frayed as the night deepened. Two young Piegan men made a dash for freedom and were recaptured and brought before a spiteful lieutenant, who ordered the escapees killed. As the troopers readied their carbines, the officer growled, "No, don't use your guns. Get axes and kill them one at a time." Obediently, the soldiers dragged the prisoners aside and hacked them to death.

Baker reported 173 Piegans killed and 140 captured at the cost of one man dead. He claimed that nearly all the Indian casualties had been warriors, when in fact he had murdered 90 women and 50 children. Sheridan accepted Baker's report at face value and lavishly praised him to Sherman for meting out "well-merited punishment." Sherman, who was skeptical of Baker's body count, told Sheridan to brace himself for "the cries of those who think the Indians are so harmless."

Those cries came loud and fast. Piegan survivors told an Indian Bureau investigator that all but fifteen of those killed had been women, children, and the elderly. The agent was careful to qualify this information as the Indian version of events, but Vincent Colyer, the secretary of the Board of Indian Commissioners, published it as established fact. Condemnation of the army resounded in both chambers of Congress and in the eastern press, which demanded courts-martial of all involved in "this shocking massacre."[4]

The criticism unhinged Sheridan. He babbled about past Indian atrocities, dwelling on the salacious—raped women, castrated men, and skull-crushed infants. That the Piegans were guilty of no such crimes was irrelevant to Sheridan. In a bizarre bit of logical gymnastics, he declared that because Colyer had defended the Piegans and because the Piegans were Indians, Colyer clearly wanted crimes against settlers to continue. As for the women who had been killed, Sheridan said that they probably deserved it because everyone knew that Indian females fought harder than Indian men. Sheridan's irrational outbursts and his defense of morally reprehensible conduct made the general a hero on the frontier. East of the Missouri River, however, they tarnished his reputation badly. The Marias Massacre—for that is what it was, with more innocent Indians gunned down in cold blood on the Marias River than at Sand Creek—also massacred army hopes of gaining control of Indian affairs. The 1870 army appropriations bill ended the practice of filling Indian agencies with army officers by vacating the commission of any officer who held a civilian position. The Marias Massacre provided the excuse, but aye votes came mostly from congressmen more concerned about regaining patronage jobs than preventing Indian deaths.

President Grant outmaneuvered them on the patronage front. "Gentlemen," he told the bill's sponsors, "you have defeated my plan of Indian management; but you shall not succeed in your purposes, for I will divide these appointments up between the religious churches, with which you dare not contend." The president had checkmated Congress, and the Peace Policy, though bloodied, survived substantially unchanged.[5]

But a far more profound change was in the wind. Shortly before the Marias Massacre shook the nation's conscience, Commissioner Parker had taken aim at what he considered one of the most pernicious aspects of government Indian policy—the treaty system, the foundation of relations between Indians and the government since the birth of the Republic. Having labored hard to protect the rights of the Senecas, he knew whereof he spoke. Parker reasoned as follows: Treaties involved compacts between sovereign powers with the authority to compel compliance, and Indian tribes were not sovereign nations because their leaders lacked such authority. Rather, Parker held the Indians to be wards of the government with "mere possessory title" to the land they claimed. Treaties, he argued, gave tribes a false notion of independence. "It is time," Parker concluded, "that this idea should be dispelled, and the government cease the cruel farce of thus dealing with its helpless and ignorant wards." President Grant and the Board of Indian Commissioners agreed.[6]

The practical effect of the end of the treaty system was to give the executive branch a freer hand in negotiating with the Indians. Agreements reached with wards of the government did not require Senate ratification, as had treaties. Henceforth, peace commissioners would be answerable for their actions only to the president, his cabinet, and public opinion.

*

Chief Red Cloud hardly considered himself "helpless and ignorant." After all, it was he who had expelled the army from the Bighorn Mountain country, and "his" war had been the only thing approaching an Indian victory on the plains. Red Cloud's surprise and indignation can only be imagined when he and his warriors came to Fort Leavenworth in the spring of 1869 to trade there as they always had, only to learn that the treaty Red Cloud had signed obligated his people to take both their persons and their business to a reservation that would be designated for them on the Missouri River. Red Cloud had also expected the army to abandon Fort Fetterman, built on the North Platte River in 1867 as a staging ground for operations on the Bozeman Trail, but the fort still stood.

It was a moment fraught with danger and a watershed in Red Cloud's relations with the white man. Clearly the terms of the 1868 Fort Laramie Treaty had been misrepresented to him. He had ample cause to renew his war and a thousand angry warriors at his side to fight for him. But the fire in Red Cloud had subsided. Life in the Unceded Indian Territory was proving hard. Game was scarce, and the winter had been harsh. Rather than make war, he wanted to go to Washington and present his grievances to the Great Father. Although he now spoke merely for the Oglalas—and only a portion of the tribe at that—Red Cloud's fateful decision represented the first step toward Indian capitulation on the northern plains. By not consulting with the other Lakota tribes, he underscored their lack of unity. Red Cloud's forbearance in the face of government chicanery set in motion the wheels of white conquest of the northern plains. Though they would sometimes slow, or temporarily reverse their bloody course, there could be no stopping them. General Sherman urged President Grant to turn Red Cloud down, but Grant rejected his old friend's counsel, preferring to overawe Red Cloud with a carefully orchestrated visit to Washington than risk another war with him.

On June 1, Red Cloud and fifteen Oglala subchiefs arrived in Washington. There, in the alien bustle of the nation's capital, they encountered Red Cloud's rival Spotted Tail and his headmen. The Brulés were furious with the Great Father. They had resettled voluntarily on the Missouri River, for which act the government was quick to recognize Spotted Tail as head chief of the "friendly" Lakotas. Spotted Tail, however, hated the new agency; the country was devoid of game, and he wanted to return to his old Nebraska hunting grounds. Coincidentally, the Grant administration brought Spotted Tail to Washington to persuade him not to quit his agency on the Missouri River at the very same time it intended to coax Red Cloud into accepting one. Commissioner Parker had expected trouble between the two chiefs, but they put aside old differences in the interest of presenting a united front before the Great Father.

Red Cloud proved as formidable a foe in the offices of Washington bureaucrats as he had on the field of battle. He met first with Secretary of the Interior Jacob D. Cox, whose vague promise to "try to do everything that is right" if the Lakotas kept the peace left him cold. "The Great Father may be good and kind, but I cannot see it," Red Cloud told Cox. "[He] has left me nothing but an island. Our nation is melting away like the snow on the side of the hills where the sun is warm, while your people are like the blades of grass in spring when summer is coming." Red Cloud's terms were firm. They included the removal of Fort Fetterman, the barring of whites from the Black Hills and the Bighorn Mountains, trading privileges for the Oglalas at Fort Laramie, and no reservation on the Missouri River. The eastern press delighted in Red Cloud's "plain, bold words," calling them an eloquent expression of the government's "faithlessness and gross swindling" that precipitated Indian wars.[7]

The greatly anticipated grand council with the Great Father was a bust, because Grant categorically refused to dismantle Fort Fetterman. Negotiations went downhill from there. And then Red Cloud pulled out his trump card. When Cox read Red Cloud the terms of the treaty, the chief said he had never signed any such document and had no intention of complying with it. A chagrined Cox assured Red Cloud the peace commissioners had been honest men. "I do not say the Commissioners lied," the chief countered, "but the interpreters were wrong. The object of the whites was to crush the Indians down to nothing. I will not take the paper with me. It is all lies." The council adjourned. Believing the Great Father had cheated them yet again, that night in their hotel several of the Oglalas and Brulés contemplated suicide. With great reluctance, Red Cloud agreed to another meeting.

While the Lakotas talked of taking their lives, Cox and Parker huddled with Grant. For the sake of peace, they agreed to yield. The next morning, Cox told Red Cloud that his people could live near Fort Laramie. Although it was merely a tactical retreat, the government had accommodated Red Cloud for the second time in two years. Washington also permitted Spotted Tail to resettle the Brulés in northwest Nebraska.

It took much cajolery on his part, but Red Cloud eventually mustered most of the Oglalas—and a considerable number of Northern Cheyennes and Northern Arapahos—at the new Red Cloud Agency. But there were five Lakota tribes beyond Red Cloud's reach: the Hunkpapas, Sans Arcs, Blackfeet, Two Kettles, and Miniconjous. The guiding spirit of the non-reservation Lakotas was a revered Hunkpapa war chief and holy man named Sitting Bull. His followers were joined by disaffected Oglalas, who had gravitated to a modest, enigmatic warrior of unsurpassed skill and growing fame named Crazy Horse. These Lakotas had no interest in the Peace Policy or in any other government offers; they intended to live the traditional nomadic life or perish in the attempt.

*

Ely Parker would not have to concern himself with these free-roaming Lakotas. In January 1871, a former chairman of the Board of Indian Commissioners falsely accused him of defrauding the government in the purchase of Indian supplies. It was a personal vendetta, and a congressional committee cleared Parker of wrongdoing. Nevertheless, he resigned in disgust in August 1871.

Parker at least had the satisfaction of seeing the treaty system abolished during his tenure. It died with a whimper, buried in a single statement in an obscure clause of the Indian appropriation act: "Hereafter no Indian nation or tribe within the United States shall be acknowledged or recognized as an independent nation, tribe, or power with whom the United States may contract a treaty." Indians were now legal wards of the government.

The nation paid scant notice to the matter. What remained hotly contentious, however, was the Peace Policy itself. Grant left no doubt about where he stood. "When I said 'Let us have peace,' I meant it," he proclaimed in June 1871. "I don't like riding over and shooting these poor savages. I want to conciliate them and make them peaceful citizens. You can't thrash people so that they will love you. Even though they are Indians, you make enemies friends by kindness."[8]

The eastern press exalted the Peace Policy. "In his inaugural address, General Grant said 'Let Us Have Peace'—and WE HAVE HAD PEACE," proclaimed a Maine daily. The Peace Policy had wrought "marvels," gushed *The Philadelphia Post*. "There are no more armed warriors, stung to deeds of murder and outrage by the robberies of unprincipled politicians acting as agents. The nomadic tribes are settling on reservations, exchanging the scalping knife for the plow, and from the [Quakers] forgetting barbarity." The *New-York Tribune* predicted an imminent "end of our Indian wars and the hatchet buried from Oregon to Texas." The dawn of a brighter day in the West had seemingly broken at last.[9]

Unless you happened to be a frontier Texan. The Comanches and the Kiowas struck deep into the Lone Star State, rolling the thin line of frontier settlements back nearly 150 miles. They ran off tens of thou-

sands of horses and head of cattle, ransomed captive women and children, and tortured and killed when it suited them. Eastern newspapers
might speak confidently of Indians burying metaphorical war hatchets,
but the only war hatchets Texans knew were real, and the Indians were
burying them with alarming frequency in the skulls of settlers.

*

There had been a glimmer of hope in the spring of 1868 when the
Kiowas and the Comanches came to Fort Cobb, Indian Territory, their
designated agency under the Medicine Lodge Treaty, to receive promised rations and presents. The Kiowas and the Comanches were not
happy that Fort Cobb was in Wichita Indian country rather than their
homeland, but they were willing to give the Great Father a chance—
that is, until they were greeted by a clerk with empty storerooms and
news that the Indian agent had resigned. Furious and hungry, the Indians ransacked the agency and then renewed their raids on Texas settlements with greater frequency and ferocity.

Texans rightly blamed Grant's Peace Policy for the upsurge in depredations. The Peace Policy prohibited troops from entering the Kiowa-
Comanche Reservation without a request from the agent, which meant
that the Indians had simply to slip back across the reservation boundary ahead of pursuing soldiers, an easy enough feat. Observing them
depredate with impunity, a Dallas editor fumed that only in Texas did
the federal government hold American life and property so cheap and
the "privileges of barbarous savages" so dear.

Once safely on the reservation, the Indians expected no trouble from
their new agent, Lawrie Tatum, a bald and burly middle-aged Quaker
farmer from Iowa. They had greeted him with disdain. The only part
of the white man's road that interested him, Satanta told Tatum, were
breech-loading rifles and ammunition. Another chief laid out the Kiowas' modus operandi: go on the warpath, kill some people and steal a
good many horses, get the soldiers to chase them for a while, and then
wait for the government to bribe them with annuity goods to quit raiding. The Kiowas, Tatum concluded, "seemed very sanguine that they
could not be restrained."[10]

But Tatum would try. He found a kindred spirit in Colonel Benjamin H. Grierson, the commanding officer at Fort Sill. Grierson
pledged to help Tatum in the spirit "contemplated by the philanthropic

and good people of the land," assuring the agent that there would be no killing Indians for the pleasure of "genocidal" Texans so long as he was in command. Which might not be much longer. Grierson's reformist sympathies rendered him odious to Sheridan. The only thing standing between the humane colonel and dismissal was Grierson's friendship with Sherman and Grant, both of whom esteemed him for his superb Civil War record.

Sheridan's doubts about Grierson's suitability had merit. The Comanches and the Kiowas construed Grierson's restraint as weakness, and they accordingly grew more audacious. Reservation Comanches opened the 1870 raiding season by stealing twenty agency horses and scalping a man within view of Tatum's office. Not to be outdone, a Kiowa war party stole a mule herd and killed three soldiers. The young war leader Big Tree tried to seize the horses of the Tenth Cavalry. He would have succeeded had a warrior not fired a premature shot that alerted the Buffalo Soldiers. Even Kicking Bird went on the warpath. Satanta had taunted him as weak and cowardly for choosing the white man's road. To restore his honor, Kicking Bird did something Satanta would never have dared. He led a Kiowa war party against a cavalry detachment in open battle, killing three soldiers and wounding twelve without losing a man; he even ran a soldier through with his lance. It would be his final fight, however. By this audacious act, Kicking Bird had shown his people that he wanted peace out of conviction, not from fear of grappling with white soldiers. Sherman apparently understood Kicking Bird's strategy; in any event, he did not punish him.

What Sherman could not abide, however, were Texans who accused Tatum and Grierson of supplying war parties with arms and ammunition earmarked for peaceable Indians—a blurred distinction, to be sure. Sherman thought it part of a Texas scheme to divert the army from its Reconstruction duties in the state by exaggerating the Indian threat, and he set out to learn the truth, traveling with an armed escort from San Antonio to Fort Richardson. Encountering no hostile Indians, Sherman concluded that Texans should look to their own defense—at least until he arrived at Fort Richardson on May 18, 1871. A dying teamster had just staggered into the post with a harrowing story: a large war party had waylaid the wagon train of one Henry Warren outside nearby Jacksboro and butchered seven of his companions. Sherman was stunned. Only a few hours earlier, he had crossed the same ground. After ordering the commanding officer at Fort Richardson, Colonel

Ranald S. Mackenzie, to track down the culprits, Sherman hastened to Fort Sill to learn from Tatum and Grierson whether the warriors were reservation Indians.[11]

∗

Ranald S. Mackenzie was a curious character. Born into wealth, he entered West Point at age eighteen in 1858, a year behind George Armstrong Custer. The similarities between the two were as striking as the differences. Like Custer, Mackenzie was gregarious and fun loving. Unlike Custer, he was modest, gentlemanly, and a far better student. Custer graduated last in the class of 1861; Mackenzie graduated first a year later. Both were daring and gifted young field commanders, but Custer enjoyed better luck. He emerged from the Civil War unscathed. Mackenzie, on the other hand, suffered six wounds, including the loss of the first two fingers of his right hand. Soldiers of the Fourth Cavalry labeled him Three Finger Jack. The Indians called him Bad Hand. When agitated, Mackenzie snapped the finger stumps vigorously. Caustic and critical of his subordinates, with a well-deserved reputation as a martinet, Mackenzie was oddly diffident around women. Custer had his beautiful and tempestuous Libbie to anchor him; Mackenzie was a confirmed bachelor.

Mackenzie and Custer both rose to division command during the Civil War. The dashing Custer might have been the public's darling, a boy general who graced the cover of *Harper's Weekly*, but Mackenzie enjoyed higher regard within the service. At war's end, General Grant thought him "the most promising young officer in the army." After three years of Reconstruction duty as the colonel of a black regiment, Mackenzie became commander of the Fourth Cavalry in 1870. The regiment held no great affection for their commander, but they bowed to his will, eventually becoming a crack unit superior to Custer's Seventh Cavalry in discipline and combat effectiveness.[12]

∗

The adjutant of the Fourth Cavalry was with the patrol that found the remnants of the Warren wagon train. The spectacle burned itself in his memory, and he reported every gruesome detail. Scattered about were nude, scalped, and beheaded bodies bristling with arrows. Brains had been scooped out, and penises severed and shoved in the victims' mouths. The evidence of torture was unmistakable. Bowels had been opened while the victims were still alive and live coals placed upon them, and a scorched corpse, chained between two wagons, slumped over a smoldering fire.

That Sherman had not suffered a similar fate was the consequence of a Kiowa's dream. The night before the Warren wagon-train raid, a long-dead ancestor had told the war party's leader, Maman-ti, that he must refrain from attacking the first party that passed his planned ambush site. Maman-ti's medicine was strong, and no one presumed to challenge him or his vision. Few whites knew of Maman-ti, who worked in the shadows, instigating nearly every major Kiowa raid in the early 1870s.[13]

Satanta, who participated in the raid as a subordinate, spared Sherman the trouble of investigating the affair. When the Kiowa chiefs— less Maman-ti, who kept clear of whites unless to kill them—came to the agency on May 28 to draw their weekly rations, Satanta boasted to Tatum that *he* had led the raid. He also implicated his cousin Big Tree and the aged chief Satank in the affair. Then, for good measure, he demanded arms and ammunition to kill more Texans. That was too much even for a Quaker to bear. Tatum rid himself of Satanta with a suggestion that he talk instead to the great soldier-chief then visiting Fort Sill. After Satanta left the agent's office quite satisfied with himself, Tatum hurriedly wrote to Grierson, asking the colonel to summon the Kiowa chiefs on the pretense of an interview with General Sherman and then arrest Satanta, Satank, and Big Tree.

Satanta arrived to find Sherman pacing Grierson's front porch. Gradually, the other chiefs assembled. Curious Kiowas crowded around them. Puffed up by the presence of an audience, Satanta repeated his version of the raid. Fine, Sherman answered; Satanta, Satank, and Big Tree were now under arrest and would be sent to Jacksboro to stand trial for murder. Satanta hesitated a moment in wonder; no white man had ever threatened him. And then, pushing aside his blanket, Satanta reached for his revolver, shouting that he would die before he would face a Texas court. Sherman gave a prearranged signal, window shutters banged opened, and Satanta found himself staring into the rifle barrels of a squad of Tenth Cavalry Buffalo Soldiers. The great Kiowa braggart wilted. Meekly, he told Sherman that he had been only a reluctant member of the war party.

The tension eased. Soon another detachment of the Tenth Cavalry appeared leading a disheveled Big Tree, who had tried to sneak off. With Big Tree's inglorious appearance, tempers flared. As Kicking Bird talked with Sherman, another chief aimed an arrow at the general. A levelheaded Kiowa warrior struck him on the arm, and the arrow missed its mark. Then Chief Lone Wolf, who had joined the gathering at Kicking Bird's insistence, raised his rifle. Lunging toward Lone Wolf, Grierson inadvertently upended Kicking Bird, and the three men crashed to the porch. Sherman's nerve held. He ordered the soldiers to withhold their fire. The colonel and the chiefs untangled themselves, and the Kiowas quieted down. Sherman had escaped his second brush with death in Texas. During the commotion, Satank sat calmly smoking his pipe. "If you want to crawl out of this affair by telling pitiful stories," he told Satanta, "that is your affair. I am sitting here saying nothing."[14]

Satank had been a member of Maman-ti's war party, but he had signed on solely to avenge the death of his favorite son, killed while on a raid the previous summer. The old chief was nearly mad with grief. Since finding his son's buzzard-stripped remains on the Texas prairie, a suicidal Satank had wandered sorrowfully through Kiowa villages leading a horse carrying his son's bones.

Sherman ordered Satanta, Satank, and Big Tree manacled and tossed into the guardhouse. On June 8, soldiers loaded them into wagons for the trip to Jacksboro. It was a journey Satank did not intend to complete. He belonged to a society that comprised the ten bravest Kiowas, committed to death before dishonor. As the wagons creaked onto the prairie, Satank covered himself with a blanket and intoned the society's death song. While he sang, Satank struggled free from the handcuffs, tearing his flesh as he tugged. Drawing a knife concealed in his breechcloth, he threw off his blanket and then stabbed one guard and grabbed the carbine of the other. Before Satank could use it, a corporal in the next wagon fired two bullets into his chest. Colonel Mackenzie dumped his body beside the trail.[15]

For Satanta and Big Tree, cowboy justice in Jacksboro was swift and predictable. They were found guilty of murder and sentenced to hang. But the presiding judge and Lawrie Tatum, both convinced that permanent confinement would be a harsher punishment than a quick gallows death, prevailed upon the governor of Texas to commute the sentences to life imprisonment in the Texas state penitentiary. The governor's decision outraged not only Texans but also General Sherman, who told Grierson that if he ever heard those Indians again brag of murders, "I won't bother the courts but will have the graves dug at once."[16]

But first he had to find the Kiowas, who had fled the agency the instant the chiefs were arrested. Grierson and Tatum presumed they were somewhere between Fort Sill and the Staked Plain; their temper, however, was anyone's guess. Mackenzie stepped forward with a solution: find, dismount, disarm, and then force the Comanches and the Kiowas to become farmers.

Sherman bade Mackenzie try. For five weeks, the Fourth Cavalry combed the sunbaked Texas prairie in search of roving Comanche and Kiowa bands. It was Mackenzie's introduction to campaigning in the Kiowa-Comanche country, and the experience was excruciating. Water was scarce, hot, and stank of gypsum. Buffalo excrement floated on its urine-streaked surface. Men and animals sickened. There was neither grass nor—due largely to Satanta's fear of the hangman's noose—Kiowas on the loose. Before leaving Fort Sill, Satanta had told his people to behave. Most heeded his counsel and returned to the reservation.

Although the arrest of the three Kiowa chiefs shifted the tribal balance of power to Lone Wolf and the war faction, Kicking Bird nonetheless labored on for peace. He rounded up forty-one stolen mules and gave them to Tatum to indemnify Henry Warren in accordance with Sherman's peace terms. The commanding general kept his part of the bargain and recalled Mackenzie, who displayed a disappointment that his adjutant said "seemed to possess his soul and disturb his peace of mind."[17]

Fortunately for the morbidly driven young colonel, there remained another enemy for him to fight—the mystic and terrible Quahadi Comanches.

*

The Peace Policy barred Mackenzie from the Comanche-Kiowa Reservation but left him a free hand in Texas, and he meant to make the most of it. On October 3, 1871, Mackenzie set out with six hundred officers and men and twenty-four Tonkawa scouts on an expedition against the Quahadi Comanches, the undisputed lords of the Staked Plain. Fiercely independent and inveterately hostile, the Quahadis had never tasted defeat. Theirs was a high-plains country larger than New

England, a semiarid vastness that actually teemed with animal life and good water, if one knew where to find it. There was, however, no mistaking its formidability. Seen from the east, the Staked Plain resembled an impregnable fortress. In the central panhandle, the higher Staked Plain yielded to the Texas low plains in a precipitous drop of stunning magnitude called the Caprock Escarpment, a toothlike succession of buttes, ridges, ravines, and fissured crevices interrupted by Palo Duro Canyon, the second-largest canyon in North America and a favorite campsite of the Quahadis. The Quahadis also frequented the broad but gentle Blanco Canyon and the headwaters of McClellan Creek, one of many Texas tributaries originating at the Caprock.

Fellow Comanches agreed that the Quahadis were the most skillful—and vicious—warriors in the tribe. Some Comanches even feared them. All Southern Plains Indians envied their wealth, as measured in horses. They were said to have a herd of fifteen thousand (the Quahadis numbered no more than twelve hundred people). The Quahadis' only contact with whites was to kill, kidnap, or rob them. They bartered their immense stock of stolen Texas cattle, together with captive women and children, to renegade New Mexico traders called Comancheros in exchange for guns, ammunition, and whiskey.

Mackenzie's route led toward the village of the brilliant young Comanche war chief Quanah. Just twenty-three years old, Quanah was the son of a prominent Comanche war chief and Cynthia Parker, daughter of an early Texas settler. Taken captive at age nine, she grew up Comanche. Quanah lost his parents at age twelve to the Texas Rangers, who killed his father and "freed" his mother, much against her will. Needless to say, Quanah harbored a burning hatred of the whites. Among his own people, Quanah was a gregarious optimist, a darkly handsome, large, and long-limbed man whose Anglo blood showed itself in his aquiline nose and gray eyes. Prowess in war won Quanah the allegiance of nearly half the Quahadis.[18]

Mackenzie reached the foot of the Staked Plain at a point less than a dozen miles from Quanah's village, catching the young war leader in a rare moment of unpreparedness. Fortunately for Quanah, Mackenzie had no idea he was so near the enemy, and on the night of October 9 he camped near the mouth of Blanco Canyon, taking only rudimentary precautions against attack.

Quanah struck at midnight. Yelling, jingling bells, and waving buffalo blankets, the Quahadis galloped over Mackenzie's perimeter guards and rode down the horse herd, terrifying the soldiers. Blinding muzzle flashes lit the night. Snorting horses plunged and kicked, the iron picket pins that held them in place whistling through the air like shell fragments. Soldiers who grabbed at lariats were dragged along the ground or had their hands burned and lacerated when the ropes slipped from their grasp. The Quahadis made off with sixty-three horses, including Mackenzie's.

Quanah had hoped to send the soldiers home on foot. But Mackenzie kept coming, forcing Quanah to fight a rear-guard action on October 10 to cover the escape of the tribe's women and children. Quanah shot a terrified trooper in the head at point-blank range, the only soldier lost in what the army called the Battle of Blanco Canyon. Afterward, he tried multiple ploys to elude Mackenzie's Tonkawa Indian trackers (the Tonkawas were mortal enemies of the Comanches). He broke up the village, climbed and descended the Caprock repeatedly, crisscrossed his trails, and doubled back on the pursuers. These time-honored tricks failed him, however, and on October 12 the Tonkawas tracked the reunited Quahadi village onto the Staked Plain. Behind the scouts, Mackenzie and his troopers climbed the Caprock Escarpment under darkening skies. On the Staked Plain, the temperature plummeted. A frigid wind whipped through their ranks. Comanche warriors stung Mackenzie's flanks "like angry bees," trying to lure the soldiers away from the women and children. When the village at last came into view a mile away, the sky opened with sleet and snow. The troopers waited expectantly for the order to charge, most believing the village as good as captured. But Mackenzie called a halt, and the Indians melted into the storm.

Mackenzie never explained his reasons for not attacking, but it was a prudent decision. His horses were gaunt and wobbly, the men running on pure adrenaline. Supplies were far too low for Mackenzie to assume the burden of women and children captives, particularly because Quanah's warriors could be counted upon to contest every inch of the march. The campaign, however, had not been for naught. Mackenzie had learned valuable lessons in Indian fighting. More important, he had proven the Quahadis could be hunted down in their homeland.[19]

*

And what of the Kiowas? They had kept quiet for ten months out of concern for their captive chiefs, but in April 1872 boredom got the better of the young warriors of the tribe, and war parties swept through

Texas. In June, Lawrie Tatum authorized the army to strike hostile Kiowas wherever encountered—the reservation included. That was welcome news to the army, but Tatum was badly out of step with his Quaker superior, the superintendent for Kansas and Indian Territory, who scolded him and discounted his reports of Indian atrocities. Convinced that moral suasion would succeed because God would will it so, the superintendent called a general council of Indian Territory tribes, which served only as a venue for the Kiowas to boast of their recent depredations and, for good measure, demand the removal of Fort Sill.

The secretary of the interior tried his hand next. He brought a delegation of Kiowa and Comanche chiefs to Washington for the usual purpose of intimidating Indians with the white man's might. He succeeded in overawing the chiefs, who went home dispirited and robbed of much of their fighting spirit. Tribesmen, however, scoffed at their talk of huge stone tipis large enough to hold all the Kiowas and masses of white men more plentiful than buffalo as illusions conjured by the white man's medicine. The chiefs did return with a bit of welcome news: the commissioner of Indian affairs had promised to release Satanta and Big Tree if the Kiowas behaved.

The commissioner had overstepped his bounds badly. The prisoners belonged to Texas, and only the governor could pardon them. Tatum's Quaker superiors celebrated the commissioner's toothless pledge. Tatum did not. Tired of working at cross-purposes with his idealistic co-religionists, he tendered his resignation. If someone else thought he could tame the Kiowas with kindness, Tatum concluded, "he ought to have the opportunity."[20]

✳

The year 1872 treated Ranald Mackenzie better than it had Tatum. Bold new superior officers took charge. Christopher C. Augur, who had cleaned the Dog Soldiers out of western Kansas, assumed command of the Department of Texas. General Sherman, now painfully aware of realities on the Texas frontier, engineered the transfer of the Department of Texas to Sheridan's Military Division of the Missouri, shifting the army's mission in the Lone Star State from reforming ex-Confederates to suppressing hostile Indians.

In addition to gaining aggressive bosses, Mackenzie scored an intelligence coup when a cavalry patrol captured a Comanchero willing to exchange the secret of navigating the Staked Plain for his life. There was, he said, a good wagon road with abundant sources of water on the Staked Plain over which the Comancheros ran bartered cattle to New Mexico Territory, as well as an equally good return route farther north. Dragging along the informant, Mackenzie ranged the Staked Plain for most of the summer under orders from Augur to break up the Comanchero trade. Although both the Comancheros and the Comanches eluded him, he had learned how to operate—and survive—on their ground.[21]

Mackenzie refitted and returned to the Staked Plain in September. Eight days out, his Tonkawa scouts found a fresh trail that led to the camp of the Kotsoteka Comanche chief Mow-way, a notorious marauder and close ally of Quanah's who had once told government negotiators that "when Indians in here [the reservation] are treated better than we are outside, it will be time enough to come in." Perhaps Mow-way sensed that time was near, because he had absented himself from the village in order to speak with white "peace people" just before Mackenzie struck.

The Fourth Cavalry obliterated Mow-way's village, slaying fifty-two Indians and capturing a hundred and thirty, mostly women and children, together with the entire Kotsoteka pony herd. The Tonkawas, who had found the village, proved better trackers than herd guards. That night, Kotsoteka warriors not only recovered their own ponies but also divested the Tonkawas of theirs. The next morning, the scouts walked "woefully sheepish and dejected" into camp, leading a small burro bearing their saddles. Mackenzie was furious. "After that," said a sergeant, "no effort was ever made to hold a herd of wild captured Indian ponies. *They were all shot.*"[22]

Despite the loss of the captured ponies, the Battle of the North Fork of the Red River was a singular victory for the army. Never before had the Comanches lost so many warriors killed or people captured, nor had they been so powerless to avenge a defeat. Hundreds of shocked and contrite non-reservation Comanches streamed into the agency. Even some Quahadis came in, surrendering white hostages and pledging to send their children to school and take up farming. It was all just a ruse, however, to induce the government to return the Kotsoteka women and children, and it worked. The hopelessly naive Quaker superintendent (Tatum's former boss) released the captives in June 1873. Within days, Comanche warriors were back on the warpath in Texas.

Mackenzie was no longer there to stop them. Sheridan had ordered him to the Rio Grande to put an end to Kickapoo Indian raids from Mexico. Plans for the final crushing of Comanche resistance would have to await his return.[23]

*

Bloodied and battered on the southern plains, the Peace Policy none-theless continued to cast a long and generally benevolent shadow. In October 1873, it shaded the Kiowas, who, having sworn off the war-path that year, were rewarded with the return of Satanta and Big Tree, paroled by the governor of Texas on the condition the Kiowas keep the peace. Only Kicking Bird's faction complied, however. No sooner had the captive chiefs been released than Kiowa raiders were slashing their way south all the way to Mexico. General Sherman excoriated the gov-ernor for releasing the chiefs. "With a small escort I ran the risk of my life, and . . . I now say to you, that I will never again voluntarily assume that risk in the interest of your frontier, that I believe Satanta and Big Tree will have their revenge . . . and that if they are to have scalps, that yours is the first that should be taken."[24]

Sherman was wrong about Satanta. The chief understood the terms of his parole. For perhaps the first and only time, Kiowa raiders did not ride forth with the devious chief's blessing. During negotiations for his release, Satanta had promised to "take my Texas father to my breast and hold him there," and he meant it. Lone Wolf, on the other hand, seethed with murderous rage. His son had been one of the first to return to the warpath, and soldiers had gunned him down near the Rio Grande. When the war party brought home the young man's body, Lone Wolf cut off his own hair, killed his horses, burned his lodges, and vowed revenge.

In the unending hatred between peoples, Kicking Bird foresaw an apocalyptic end for all. "I fear blood must flow, and my heart is sad," he told a Quaker friend. "The white man is strong, but he cannot destroy us all in one year. It will take him two or three, maybe four years. And then the world will turn to water or burn up. It is our mother and can-not live when the Indians are all dead."[25]

The circle around the Southern Plains tribes grew tighter. The Southern Cheyennes and Arapahos had been reservation Indians since 1869. The Comanches were crippled. Only the Quahadi band remained entirely free. Comanche and Kiowa raiders were finding their forays into Texas increasingly costly, as Lone Wolf could attest. Such was the state of affairs within the limits of Kicking Bird's world. Beyond his horizon, the Lakotas and the Northern Cheyennes continued to hold sway on the northern plains. Whites had not yet threatened the Unceded Indian Territory, but pressure on the eastern boundary of the Lakota domain was growing, and since Red Cloud's War there had been sporadic small clashes between the Lakotas and the army. Yet more than half of the Lakotas and Northern Cheyennes, and nearly all of the Arapahos, had made their way to agencies on the Great Sioux Reservation voluntarily. Few resided on the reservation year-round, however. They clung to the life of the hunt, following the buffalo in fair weather and repairing to their agencies only during the harsh plains winters. Although the process of making Christian farmers of the Indians was far from being realized, it could at least be said that—with the exception of Texas—the plains were relatively tranquil. In that sense, at least, the Peace Policy seemed to be succeeding.

And then, on the far-off Oregon-California border, a tiny tribe rose up to resist the reservation process in a sudden, violent revolt that shocked the nation, embarrassed the army, and shook the foundations of the Peace Policy nearly to collapse.

PART TWO

CHAPTER 8

TRAGEDY IN THE LAVA BEDS

O N T H E N I G H T O F April 10, 1873, Captain Jack and his band of fifty-six Modoc warriors weighed the merits of murder. Huddled in the caves of Northern California's Lava Beds, they and their families, numbering perhaps 150 in all, were nearly surrounded by five hundred U.S. soldiers, amassed to intimidate the warriors into returning peaceably to their reservation. In a last-ditch effort to reach a pacific solution, the Modoc head chief was to meet with Brigadier General Edward R. S. Canby and a small peace commission the next morning. Should Captain Jack parley with the commissioners in good faith, the warriors debated, or would it be better to ambush and kill them and send a warning to the government to put a stop to the plundering of the tribe's lands and way of life?

By the flames of a sagebrush fire, Jack listened to the hard words of his rivals within the tribe. Emotions were raw. The band's shaman, Curly-Headed Doctor, argued to kill the commissioners. Eliminate them, he predicted, and the soldiers that threatened the band's stronghold would leave. Recent events had enhanced Curly-Headed Doctor's standing. Four months earlier, when the troubles had started, he had uttered incantations that had apparently protected the Modocs. The warriors had not yet lost a single man, and in skirmishes with the white troops they had shot nearly their number in soldiers. Most of the tribe was willing to accept the shaman's latest guarantee.

Chief Schonchin John echoed Curly-Headed Doctor's call to kill. There had been enough talk. Every day brought more soldiers. When Chief Hooker Jim and his band killed fourteen settlers four months earlier in retaliation for an unprovoked attack on the tribe, he argued, they had all but guaranteed U.S. government retaliation, probably through hanging. Peace was now impossible.

Captain Jack finally rose to speak. He said that he would try to persuade the peace commissioner Canby to pardon Hooker Jim's men and allow the Modocs to live in their homeland. The men responded with heckles and curses. One of them shouted, "Jack, you will never save your people. You can't do it." The army had artillery and was near enough to use it, he said. The commissioners intended to make peace by blowing off Captain Jack's head.

"You are like an old squaw; you have never done any fighting yet. You are not fit to be a chief," agreed Hooker Jim. "You kill Canby or we will kill you."

Killing Canby would be a "coward's act," Captain Jack said. With that, the warriors grabbed him, threw a shawl and a woman's hat over his head, and pushed Captain Jack to the ground. They called him a white-faced squaw whose heart the white men had stolen.

Stung, Captain Jack rolled out of the clothes and yielded to the majority. "I am a Modoc. I am your chief. I will do it. I know it is a coward's work, but I will do it. I will kill Canby, although I know it will cost me my life and all the lives of my people."[1]

※

Captain Jack's people belonged to a small but fiercely independent tribe. For three hundred years, the Modocs had occupied a five-thousand-square-mile tract along the present-day California-Oregon border. They had a reputation among other Indians as merciless raiders, trading humans for horses and dealing to strong tribes the female captives they had seized from weaker tribes. When in the 1840s the Modocs first made contact with Americans, the tribe numbered just eight hundred. Settlers called them "Digger Indians," a pejorative applied to root eaters (the Modoc dietary staple was water-lily roots), whom the whites considered a particularly low form of Indian. The Modocs returned the compliment with violence.

The trouble began in 1846 when a pair of settlers, Lindsay and Jesse Applegate, followed a shortcut to the Willamette valley through Modoc country between Klamath and Goose Lakes. For two years, immigrant trains rumbled over the Applegate Trail safely. But the settlers left the scourge of smallpox in their wake, and the disease ravaged Modoc villages. Only four hundred Modocs survived. In retaliation, the warriors hit the Applegate Trail hard until the autumn of 1852, when a posse from Yreka, California, attacked a Modoc village, killing and scalping forty-one of the forty-six Modoc men present. The slaughter stunned the Modocs into making peace, from which they profited, in a manner of speaking. Modoc men took odd jobs in Yreka or on the large ranches, and boys found work as house servants. They cut their hair short, wore white men's clothes, and accepted the sometimes unflattering names Californians gave them. Many learned English. Modoc men disinclined to work prostituted their women to gold miners. Particularly adept as a pander was Kintpuash, born in 1837 to the late chief of the Lost River Modocs. Kintpuash was five feet six inches tall, the average height of a Modoc man. He was slender but strongly built, with a square jaw and a handsome face. He parted his jet-black hair in the middle and wore it just below the ears.

Kintpuash spoke little English but claimed to "know the white man's heart," which he found in the main to be good. His closest white friend was the Yreka lawyer Elijah Steele, who purportedly gave Kintpuash the name Captain Jack because of his resemblance to an Yreka miner and his penchant for military ornaments. Captain Jack's sister shared her brother's good looks and used them to her advantage, making a small fortune for Jack and herself as the mistress of five miners, each of whom she cleaned out.[2]

*

Not all relationships between miners and Modoc females were casual or cash based. In the California gold country—as in other parts of the West where eligible white women were scarce—some liaisons bloomed into real love matches. Overcoming barriers of language, culture, and racial prejudice, these mixed unions helped ease suspicion between Indians and frontiersmen.

One such enduring relationship was that of Frank and Toby Riddle. Born in 1832 in Kentucky, eighteen-year-old Frank Riddle had joined the ragged procession of restless young men making their way west to the California goldfields. Although he earned a reputation among his fellow miners as a kind and temperate companion, Riddle was unsuccessful as a miner. But he was a good hunter, and no one challenged his claim to have slain 132 bears.

Toby Riddle was Captain Jack's cousin. Her people were said to have called her Nan-ook-to-wa, the "strange child," because she was something of a loner and also uncommonly curious about the white man's culture. In 1862, her father brought Nan-ook-to-wa, attractive and apparently well developed for her twelve years, to the cabin of Frank Riddle, then thirty, and asked him in sign language if he "wanted to buy a squaw." Because she was an Indian, the difference in age would have bothered no one, but Riddle declined. Father and daughter visited Frank Riddle a second time. This time Nan-ook-to-wa made known in sign language that she wanted to be his "property." Again he demurred. Ten days later, she came back alone with her belongings and moved into the cabin. Riddle relented. He gave her father two horses, and the deal was sealed. Within a year, the couple had a son.[3]

Nan-ook-to-wa took the name Toby and adapted easily to the white people's ways. The Riddles won the affection and trust of both whites and Modocs. Each had a genuine concern for the well-being of the other's people. They accepted work as government interpreters with the Oregon superintendent of Indian affairs, Alfred B. Meacham, a man prominent in state politics who genuinely sympathized with the Indians. But times were challenging for Superintendent Meacham. Sporadic Modoc raids on wagon trains had continued until 1860, when immigration tapered off. Then the Civil War brought a rush of families availing themselves of the Homestead Act or simply distancing themselves from the conflict. To prevent bloodshed between settlers and Indians, the government negotiated a treaty with the Modocs and their Klamath neighbors by which both tribes ceded everything but a 768,000-acre tract north of Lost River valley that would become the Klamath Indian Reservation.

It was good land and should have been more than enough to meet the needs of the Klamaths and the Modocs, who spoke the same language and had once been close allies. But the reservation was in Klamath country, so the Klamaths felt entitled to tribute from the Modocs. By April 1870, Jack and his followers had had enough. They left the reservation to return to Lost River but were met there with increasing numbers of settlers. Angry at this encroachment on what they felt was their land, the warriors began harassing the settlers, entering their homes uninvited and leaving only after having been fed, frightening (but never harming) women and children, and generally making

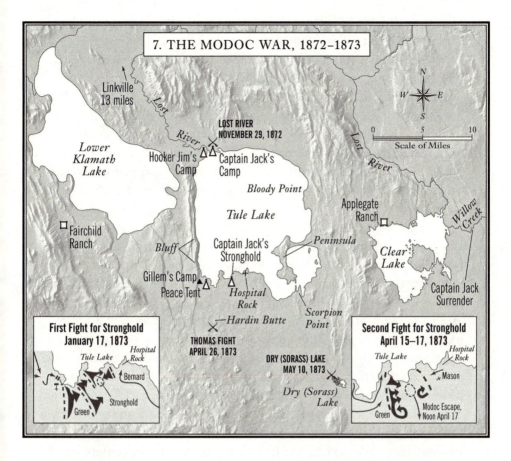

a nuisance of themselves. Although the Indians' offenses were minor, nervous settlers demonized them as "desperados, a squalid band of miserable savages" who placed the country on the "verge of a desolating Indian war."[4]

Tensions in the Lost River country mounted. In early February 1872, frustrated settlers appealed to General Canby to force Captain Jack's Modocs back onto the Klamath Reservation. Sorting through the evidence from his headquarters in Portland, Canby recommended that no action be taken until the Interior Department settled the question of a permanent home for them.

Canby had more experience with Indians than most of his fellow generals. Before the Civil War, he had fought Seminoles in Florida and Navajos in the New Mexico Territory and negotiated the unconditional surrender of twenty-four hostile Navajo chiefs. During his thirty-three-year army career, Canby had compiled a solid if not spectacular record. "Prudent" was how most fellow officers described him. Of limited ambition and conciliatory by nature, Canby was the only general officer in the regular army with no known enemies. He did what he was told and went where he was told.

Until 1870, that is. Four years of field service in the Civil War, followed by five years of Reconstruction duty in a hostile South, had taken its toll on the fifty-two-year-old general. In one of the few selfish acts of his career, he asked for command of the Department of the Columbia in order to get some rest. General Sherman obliged him, seeing General Canby and his wife off for Oregon with "best wishes for a pleasant trip."[5]

Canby's hope for a peaceful tour faded fast as agitation against the Modocs increased. In early April 1872, the Interior Department replaced Meacham with Thomas B. Odeneal, an Oregon county judge of little patience and even less understanding of Indians, and instructed him to relocate the Modocs "if practicable."

The summer of 1872 passed quietly enough. Captain Jack promised to control his people, asking in return that settlers be kept away from the mouth of Lost River, where the Modocs wintered. Odeneal, however, was disinclined to negotiate. Instead, he issued the Modocs an ultimatum: move or be moved. Predictably, Captain Jack ignored the order. Once the weather soured, Odeneal acted swiftly and recklessly. On November 26, he sent the agency interpreter Ivan Applegate (of the trailblazing family) to Captain Jack to summon him to a conference in Linkville. Jack refused. He was "tired of being talked to and done with talking." As was Odeneal. Bypassing both Canby and the district commander, Colonel Frank Wheaton, Odeneal dispatched Applegate to the commanding officer at Fort Klamath, Major John Green, with orders for the major to remove the Modocs.[6]

At dawn on November 28, Applegate delivered his instructions to Lieutenant Frazier A. Boutelle, the officer of the day at Fort Klamath. Learning from Applegate of Odeneal's extra-official machinations and doubting the ability of the understrength Fort Klamath garrison to round up the Modocs, Boutelle was consequently "amazed" to receive orders from his company commander, Captain James Jackson, to saddle up thirty-five troopers at noon and ride to Lost River.

Jackson's tiny command struggled over muddy trails and through heavy sagebrush beneath a cold, battering sleet. At daylight on November 29, they halted a mile west of Captain Jack's camp. Reeling with fatigue, the men dismounted and, following Boutelle's example, strapped their frozen coats over their saddles. "If I was going into a fight," Boutelle told Jackson, "I wanted my deck cleared for action."

The soldiers galloped into Captain Jack's camp on the west side of Lost River and then dismounted and deployed into line. Not all the Modocs were with Captain Jack; Hooker Jim was camped with fourteen warriors and their families on the east bank. Just as the soldiers arrived, Scarfaced Charley, the most respected warrior in the Lost River band and normally a peaceable man, returned from a night of gambling in Hooker Jim's camp. Perhaps drunk, he slipped on the riverbank, and his rifle went off. No one panicked, but the Modocs were nervous. Women and children vanished, and men in war paint emerged from the lodges. Scarfaced Charley distributed rifles to the men and shouted at the soldiers to leave.

The sleet fell harder. "Mr. Boutelle, what do you think of the situation?" asked Jackson. "There is going to be a fight," the lieutenant warned, "and the sooner you open it the better." Jackson told Boutelle to arrest Scarfaced Charley. Boutelle leveled his pistol and barked, "You son of a bitch." Charley answered, "Me no dog. Me no 'fraid of you." The two fired at each other and missed. Then everyone began shooting. Eight soldiers fell, and the rest ran. The Modoc warriors—less one killed—scattered into canoes and paddled away. Among them was Captain Jack, who had been in his lodge pulling on his clothes when the shooting started.

Hooker Jim and his band had a brief fight of their own. Getting wind of Jackson's plans, a dozen settlers crept into Hooker Jim's camp at dawn to demand his surrender. Hooker Jim's warriors drove them off with a single volley, but not before an Oregonian fired a load of buckshot that mangled a baby and wounded the dead infant's mother.[7]

That afternoon, Captain Jack's band and the women and children of Hooker Jim's band paddled across Tule Lake to the Lava Beds. Abutting the lake on the southern edge of Modoc country and sprawling six miles from east to west and ten miles north to south, the Lava Beds contained seven hundred caves, thirty lava flows, and countless cinder and spatter cones. Three hundred yards short of the lakeshore sat a mass of boulder formations and caves, joined by labyrinthine paths. The Modocs called it their "stone house," a place to retreat in times of trouble. The army would come to call the fortress Captain Jack's Stronghold.

Safe in his stronghold, Jack wanted no further trouble with the whites. But Hooker Jim was full of fight and fury. On a two-day ride to the Lava Beds, he, Curly-Headed Doctor, and twelve other men had made a shambles of the white settlements along Tule Lake. Because settlers had attacked them unprovoked, they felt justified in killing any they came across. Odeneal had failed to warn the settlers of the planned arrest of the Modocs, and fourteen unsuspecting men died. Hooker Jim's band spared the women and children. "We are Modocs; we do not kill women or children," Hooker Jim reassured a new widow.

The Hot Creek band of Shacknasty Jim wanted to keep out of the fray, and Jim went for advice to the rancher John Fairchild, a level-headed man and friend to the Modocs. Fairchild persuaded him and his forty-five followers to go to the Klamath Reservation and agreed to act as their escort. Word of their approach leaked, and some loudmouthed drunks formed a posse to "hang a few Modocs." Fairchild persuaded the would-be lynch mob, which the crisp December air had sobered up, to turn back. But their brush with the noose panicked the Modocs, and they slipped away to the Lava Beds to join Captain Jack, who welcomed their arrival. But Captain Jack was horrified when Hooker Jim's men rode in boasting of their butchery. Captain Jack knew their presence would make it impossible for Shacknasty Jim or him to surrender, but having too few supporters to oust Hooker Jim, he instead withdrew with his family to the largest cave, and the three Modoc bands settled uneasily into the stronghold to await the coming of the soldiers.[8]

The Modocs had a long wait. Command confusion and winter storms inhibited army operations. The first inkling Canby had of the Lost River clash came on December 2 when he received an appeal from the governor of Oregon for troops to protect the settlements. Determined to prevent a second disaster, Canby methodically assembled troops from throughout his department. Colonel Wheaton, who superseded Major Green as field commander on December 21, was also cautious. While his idle troops slept in the snow on the windswept plateau and survived on crackers and bacon, Wheaton waited two weeks for mountain howitzers from Fort Vancouver. Not until January 15 was he ready to attack. He had 214 regular soldiers (three troops of cavalry and two companies of infantry); 60 Oregonians commanded by Brigadier General John E. Ross of the state militia; 24 Californians under a reluctant John Fairchild; 30 Klamath scouts of doubtful loyalty; and 15 Snake scouts, for a total force of 343. Opposing them, Wheaton wrongly imagined, were at least 150 Modoc warriors.[9]

Wheaton's plan was simple. At dawn on January 17, two cavalry troops under Captain Reuben F. Bernard would attack from a lakeshore elevation two miles east of Captain Jack's Stronghold. At the same hour, the main body under Green, which included the Oregon volunteers, would advance from an elevation two miles west of the stronghold later called Gillem Bluff. The ground on either side of the stronghold was a flat plain, so thoroughly covered with bunchgrass and sagebrush as to render the lava rocks underfoot nearly invisible. All the troops would fight dismounted. Wheaton intended for Green's right flank to join Bernard's left to prevent the Modocs from escaping into the lava flow south of Captain Jack's Stronghold. Artillery fire would cover the advance from the west. Wheaton thought serious resistance unlikely but swore that if the Modocs tried to "make good their boast to whip a thousand soldiers, all will be satisfied." The soldiers were more crassly colorful. One said he planned to "eat Modoc steak" after the fight; another was going to snatch a Modoc woman to "wash his dishes."

In the stronghold, the Modocs struggled with doubt. Captain Jack advocated surrender. Curly-Headed Doctor, who wanted to fight, swore that his medicine would protect the Modocs. The Modoc men put the matter to a vote. Fourteen were for surrender, but the rest agreed to give Curly-Headed Doctor's medicine a chance, and Captain Jack submitted to the dictates of the majority.

The shaman went to work. Around the perimeter of the stronghold, he ran a rope of tule fiber several hundred feet long, through which, he said, no soldier would pass. That night, he erected a dog-skin medicine pole and enjoined his people to dance around the council fire. As they danced, the Modocs threw sacrifices of meat and roots on the fire. Curly-Headed Doctor inhaled the smoke and collapsed, jerking and twitching. It was a good omen.[10]

*

January 17, 1873, dawned damp and foggy over the Lava Beds. At 6:30 a.m., Wheaton's howitzers fired three signal shots, and Major Green's troops dispersed into a skirmish line. Before they started forward, muzzle flashes stung the fog, and down went an Oregonian. Tearing their boots on the razor-sharp lava, stumbling, and cursing, the soldiers inched ahead. No one could see a thing. Bullets ricocheted off rocks and occasionally struck flesh. No sooner did soldiers approach a protruding finger of lava rocks than its Modoc defenders, camouflaged with sagebrush, dropped back unseen. Fighting a phantom foe who taunted them in English infuriated the soldiers. When a captain was hit in the elbow, the Modocs derided his cry of "Oh, I'm shot." Came a woman's voice from the fog, "You come here to fight Indians and you make noise like that; you no man, you squaw."[11]

It took Green four hours to cover two miles, which was farther than Bernard went. After losing a lieutenant and four men, Bernard huddled with his command among the icy rocks east of the stronghold. The Klamath scouts kept moving—not to fight the Modocs, but to pass them ammunition. With no chance of linking flanks south of the stronghold, Green slipped most of his command around the northern edge and joined up with Bernard's right. The battle was over. Eight soldiers had been killed and eighteen wounded. The volunteers suffered four dead and eight wounded. That night, Green and Bernard limped back to a ranch thirteen miles east of the stronghold. The next day, Wheaton withdrew to Lost River Ford, also well clear of the Modocs.

Victory strengthened the hold that the hard-liner Schonchin John and the fanatical Curly-Headed Doctor enjoyed over the Modocs. The battle had turned out as the shaman had foretold; the Modocs had not lost a single man, and no soldiers had penetrated Curly-Headed Doctor's magic ring of tule rope. Captain Jack's supporters dwindled to a dozen.[12]

Unaware of Captain Jack's weakened position, the government sought to negotiate with him. Meacham persuaded the secretary of the interior that a peace commission might talk Captain Jack out of the stronghold more easily than the army could blast him out. With the Modoc revolt threatening to undermine the Peace Policy, President Grant readily approved and named Meacham lead commissioner. Canby was ordered to suspend offensive military operations and cooperate with Meacham. At the Lava Beds, the conciliatory general found morale abysmal under the new commander, Colonel Alvan Gillem. Wheaton had earned a star during the Civil War for repeated gallantry under fire; Gillem, a blustering incompetent, had seen little action and owed his star to the patronage of the former president Andrew Johnson.

Peace would not come easy, Modoc women visiting the army camp told the commissioners; Captain Jack wanted to reach terms, they said, but was hopelessly outnumbered by militants who preferred to fight than hang for murder. Not even Captain Jack's old friend Elijah Steele, who prided himself on his disinterestedness and the fact that he was one of the few men in Yreka never to have slept with a prostituted Modoc woman, could make any headway. Barely escaping a visit to the stronghold with his life, Steele warned Canby that the Modocs had no interest in talking. Canby forged ahead with negotiations anyway, working in concert with Meacham and the other two commissioners: the Klamath agent Leroy S. Dyar and the Reverend Eleazer Thomas, who had been appointed to appease eastern humanitarians.

In the meantime, six more regular companies arrived, and Canby now had just over five hundred men, evenly divided between Gillem and Major E. C. Mason, who had assumed command of Captain Bernard's units. Canby hoped that the mere sight of the massing soldiers might intimidate the Modocs into making peace. On April 1, he moved his headquarters and Gillem's troops to the east side of Gillem Bluff, three miles west of the stronghold. Six days later, Major Mason advanced from the east to within two miles of the stronghold. In clear violation of the truce, a cavalry company scooped up thirty-four Modoc ponies.[13]

It was while inspecting the stronghold from atop Gillem Bluff that Canby first met Captain Jack, who was also out reconnoitering. In the hastily arranged council that followed, Canby, who called Jack "the most prosy of all Indians," largely listened, saying only that he had moved the army closer to make communications easier. Captain Jack, with Curly-Headed Doctor hovering ominously by his side, demanded the Modoc ponies back and said he wanted the soldiers to leave. Captain Jack, Canby wrote to his wife, acted the part of a man under duress, "sullen and reticent."

Undaunted, Canby and the other commissioners held a four-hour talk on April 2 with Captain Jack, and on April 7 Canby sent Toby Riddle into the stronghold to tell the Modoc chief that the army would protect anyone who surrendered. Each session ended with Hooker Jim's and Shacknasty Jim's men not only refusing to leave the stronghold but also threatening to kill any Modoc who tried to give up.

Although Meacham and Dyar saw nothing to be gained by another council, Canby decided on one last try. He accepted Captain Jack's request to meet him and five unarmed Modocs on April 11 at the council tent halfway between the lines. In the meantime, Captain Jack had exacted a concession from his more murderous tribesmen. He would kill Canby, he told them, but only if the general refused to give the Modocs a home in their country. "I will ask him many times," Captain

Jack said. "If he comes to my terms, I will not kill him." The lives of General Canby, the peace commissioners, and ultimately every Modoc Indian depended on Captain Jack's powers of persuasion.[14]

*

Good Friday, April 11, 1873, opened clear and cool. Each commissioner prepared himself for the conference in his own way. The Reverend Eleazer Thomas took his "pet" Modocs, Bogus Charley and Boston Charley, to the sutler's store and bought them new suits of clothes. The two had passed the night in the army camp. Although both carried rifles, neither looked particularly harmful (Boston Charley was only five feet tall), and Thomas seemed inclined to accept their word that all would go well. Meacham, on the other hand, was resigned to the worst. Dyar was also opposed to the council, but like Meacham he agreed to attend out of a sense of honor. Before setting out, he ran to his tent and pocketed his derringer.

Dressed in his finest uniform and carrying a box of cigars, General Canby stopped by Gillem's tent long enough to hear Frank Riddle tell Gillem that he would take no blame for any trouble. A cousin of Toby's had warned her that the Modoc war faction had gained the upper hand and was pressuring Captain Jack to murder the commissioners at the next meeting. Toby had never lied to him, said Frank, and he had no cause to doubt her now. As Canby stepped outside the tent, Toby caught the general by the arm and begged him one last time not to go, but Thomas intervened, assuring her, "Sister Toby, the Modocs will not hurt us. God will not allow it."

Rebuffed by Canby and Thomas, Toby grabbed the bridle of Meacham's horse and fell to the ground in tears. Meacham gently urged her away and then started off to follow Canby and Boston Charley, who led the way on foot. Toby trailed on horseback. Frank walked beside her. Bringing up their rear were Bogus Charley, Dyar, and Thomas. At the council tent, the commissioners found six Modocs, not five as promised. All carried revolvers. Bogus Charley and Boston Charley loitered on the periphery, rifles in hand. Dressed in a slouch hat and filthy gray coat, Captain Jack sat beside a small campfire, looking downcast and nervous. Canby sat down opposite Jack. He calmly offered the Modocs cigars and spoke of his friendly feelings toward the Indians. Meacham could not tell whether Canby suspected trouble. As

Canby spoke, Hooker Jim swaggered over to Meacham's horse. Taking Meacham's overcoat from the bridle, Hooker Jim announced, "Me Old Man Meacham now. Bogus, you think me look like Old Man Meacham." Meacham tried to treat the implied threat as a jest. "Hooker Jim, you'd better take my hat, also." "I will, bye and bye," retorted Hooker Jim. "Don't hurry, Old Man."

Dyar and Frank Riddle blanched, and Meacham felt seized with the chill of death. Now it was Jack's turn to talk. Leaning close to Canby, he pleaded with the general to take away the soldiers and let the Modocs alone. Only after the soldiers departed would the Modocs talk about leaving the stronghold. Meacham glanced hopefully at Canby. "All seemed to feel that if he assented to the withdrawal of the army the trouble would be passed over." Canby, however, could not lie to save his life. The army would stay, he said, and the Modocs must surrender unconditionally. Captain Jack walked a few steps off, saying he had to relieve himself. Schonchin John began to harangue the commissioners. A moment later, two young Modocs jumped up from behind a low line of lava rocks thirty feet away and ran toward the council, carrying armloads of rifles. Canby and Meacham stood up abruptly. "Captain Jack, what does this mean?" demanded Meacham. Captain Jack spun around, drew his revolver, and yelled, "All ready." The time was 12:12 p.m.

Captain Jack snapped his revolver in Canby's face, but the cap popped harmlessly. As Canby stood frozen, Captain Jack cocked the hammer again and shot him through the left eye. To everyone's amazement, the mortally wounded general rose to his feet and ran forty or fifty yards until Captain Jack and the warrior Ellen's Man caught up with him. Ellen's Man shoved his rifle against Canby's head and fired, and Captain Jack stabbed Canby in the throat for good measure. Together they stripped off his uniform and ran with it back to the stronghold.

At the first shot, Dyar and Frank Riddle broke for camp. Neither Frank nor Toby was in any real danger. Scarfaced Charley had threatened to kill any Modoc who harmed them, and he now lay behind some rocks a few dozen yards off, ready if necessary to ambush the ambushers. Boston Charley fired the second shot and dropped the Reverend Thomas with a bullet through the heart. Schonchin John and Shacknasty Jim took aim at Meacham. Toby tried to stop them, but a bullet from each knocked Meacham unconscious. Slapping Toby to the ground, Boston Charley drew his knife and cut into Meacham's forehead, trying to lift the bald man's scalp until Toby cleverly screamed,

"The soldiers are coming." None were, but Boston Charley did not wait around to find out. When soldiers at last swept down off Gillem Bluff, they were too late to catch any of the culprits. Instead, they found only the naked corpses of Canby and Thomas, and Toby clinging to Meacham's body. Remarkably, Meacham recovered.[15]

*

The murder of Canby horrified the nation. The press called it a severe blow to Grant's Peace Policy, and the saying made it so. Calls for retribution were virtually universal; even newspapers strongly supportive of the Peace Policy demanded that the guilty Modocs hang for "a crime so unhuman, so deliberate, so utterly wanton and base."[16]

Not since the Fetterman disaster six years earlier had the War Department enjoyed such popular support in the struggle for the nation's conscience over the plight of the Indian. General Sherman inferred public revulsion to mean he had carte blanche to sustain "any measure of severity against the savages." He replaced Canby with a man well fitted for the job, Colonel Jefferson C. Davis (no relation to the former Confederate president). Unyielding and brutal, in the Civil War Davis had murdered a fellow general who insulted him—and had gotten away with it.

Davis would need at least two weeks to reach the Lava Beds. In the meantime, the war belonged to Gillem. On April 15, he ordered Green and Mason to attack the stronghold, but even under a clear spring sky the soldiers came no closer to the stronghold than they had in the January fog. They did kill one Modoc warrior, however, and held their ground, building stone breastworks behind which they passed the night safely. The Modocs had not expected the soldiers to stay; neither were they prepared for the small mortars that lobbed shells into their sanctuary, killing another Modoc. The following morning, Gillem renewed the attack. Unable to join flanks on the south, Green and Mason linked up north of the stronghold and inched into its outer defenses before dark. Again the troops dug in for the night.

That day marked a turning point for the Modocs. Soldiers had crossed Curly-Headed Doctor's magic tule-rope line, and two Modocs had died. The shaman's medicine had failed, and the dispirited Modocs turned to Captain Jack for leadership.

Captain Jack took the only sane course of action. Leaving behind

those too old and ill to move, he led the remaining Modocs along a concealed path out of the stronghold. By daybreak on April 17, they were
deep into the southern reaches of the Lava Beds. Instead of pursuing
the Modocs, Gillem had his men fortify the stronghold against counterattack, as if there were any prospect of fifty-five warriors assaulting
five hundred soldiers. For the moment, the Modocs were safe. "Apathy
had settled on Colonel Gillem," said one officer, "and like a nightmare
seemed to follow him about." He resisted pressure from Majors Green
and Mason to attack, relenting only insofar as to send out a sixty-four-
man patrol on April 26 under Captain Evan Thomas, who failed to take
even the most rudimentary precautions.

The Modocs slaughtered the detachment without losing a man.
Scarfaced Charley broke off the battle after two hours, yelling, "All
you fellows that ain't dead had better go home. We don't want to kill
you all in one day." Pelted by blowing snow during the day and paralyzed by fear at night, a relief party needed thirty-six hours to retrieve
the wounded. Army officers blamed the disaster not on Thomas but on
Gillem for having ordered the patrol.[17]

Colonel Davis arrived a week later. What he found disgusted him.
"A great many of the enlisted men here," he wrote to headquarters, "are
utterly unfit for Indian fighting of this kind, being only cowardly beef-
eaters." The high command sent him more "beef-eaters," lifting his
dubious force to nearly one thousand men. Making the best of what he
had, Davis, according to an admiring lieutenant, "infused new life into
a command demoralized by mismanagement."

Of particular value to Davis were seventy Warm Springs Indians who reported to him as scouts the first week of May. Unlike the
Klamaths, these Indians had no compunction about killing Modocs.
From them, Davis learned that the Modocs were moving toward the
southeast. Immediately, he sent the Warm Springs Indians and three
mounted companies under Captain Henry C. Hasbrouck to find them.
Hasbrouck made camp on the night of May 9 alongside a morass of
muddy sludge that the troops dubbed Sorass Lake. Within range of a
bluff four hundred yards away, the soldiers bedded down wherever they
pleased. The stage seemed set for another Thomas disaster.

At dawn on May 10, Scarfaced Charley and thirty-two warriors
opened fire from the bluff. Eight soldiers fell, and the horses stampeded. But Hasbrouck kept his head. He sent the scouts galloping
around either flank of the Modocs. A cavalry sergeant yelled, "God

damn it, let's charge," and sprinted toward the Modocs with a handful of soldiers. Taken from in front and both flanks, the Modocs fled into the lava flows. The defeat unnerved the Modocs, and after a heated argument they split up. The subchief Black Jim, Curly-Headed Doctor, Hooker Jim, Shacknasty Jim, and thirteen warriors and their families headed west. Captain Jack and Schonchin John, suddenly allied, headed east.[18]

Cavalry patrols combed the country, giving the Modocs no rest. Near Fairchild's ranch, Hasbrouck caught up with Black Jim's group, killing five. On May 22, Fairchild went up the mountain near his ranch and brought in sixty-three hungry Modocs clothed in tatters, riding gaunt ponies that "seem scarcely able to bear the women and children who were literally piled upon them." With the prospect of the noose dangling before him, Hooker Jim offered to help catch Captain Jack. Colonel Davis sized up Hooker Jim as "an unmitigated cutthroat with well-earned claims to the halter." Nevertheless, calculating that the betrayal of one Modoc leader by another would have a salutary effect on other tribes that might contemplate war, he accepted Hooker Jim's offer. Bogus Charley and Shacknasty Jim also turned traitor.

On May 28, Hooker Jim and the other Modoc bloodhounds cornered Captain Jack on Willow Creek, east of Clear Lake. Captain Jack dismissed Hooker Jim contemptuously. The next day, the cavalry and Warm Springs scouts surprised Jack's camp, scattering the occupants. For four days, the cavalry pursued Captain Jack in what Davis called "more of a chase after wild beasts than war." Finally, on June 1, Hooker Jim and his compatriots helped a cavalry patrol surround a cave in which Jack and his family were hiding. Captain Jack emerged unarmed, approached the officer in command, and shook his hand, saying that he had quit running because his "legs had given out."[19]

Colonel Davis wanted the murderers of Canby and Thomas dead as quickly as he could erect scaffolds. An immediate "chastisement" of the guilty Modocs, he told a newspaperman, "would quiet restless tribes emboldened by the prestige the Modocs have gained." Official Washington intervened to stop the lynching, however. The attorney general ruled that the Modoc resistance "constituted war in a technical sense that crimes afterwards committed against the laws of war are triable and punishable by military commissions."

On July 1, a panel of officers took evidence. Captain Jack, Schonchin John, Boston Charley, the warrior Black Jim (who had only fired a few halfhearted shots at Frank Riddle), and the two boys who had brought rifles to them were charged with "murder in violation of the laws of war" and "assault with intent to kill, in violation of the laws of war." They had no legal counsel.

The Modocs might not have understood military law, but they did recognize injustice. Reflecting on the killing of the Modoc woman and her child by the Oregonians at Lost River, Jack said,

> If the white men that killed our women and children had been tried and punished, I would not have thought so much of myself and companions. Do we Indians stand any show for justice with you white people, with your own laws? I say no. I know it. You people can shoot any Indians any time you want whether we are in war or in peace. I charge the white people with wholesale murder.[20]

Some whites agreed. The son of the Reverend Eleazer Thomas declared it was the "wickedness of white men that caused my father's death." A California congressman demanded a full investigation of the war, saying, "There was never a time since the organization of our government that there was so much corruption and swindling as is today practiced on Indian Reservations on this Coast." But the only investigation that followed was into what the war had cost the Treasury.

The price had been considerable, over half a million dollars. The value of the two thousand acres on Lost River the Modocs had asked for was less than ten thousand dollars.

No one gained from the Modoc War. The human cost had been high—for the army and its Warm Springs Indian allies, sixty-eight killed and seventy-five wounded, which represented nearly a quarter of those who actually saw action during the conflict. No heroes emerged. On the contrary, in the public eye, the army came off as inept, thanks in no small measure to the ham-handed performance of Gillem.

In the five-month war, the Modocs lost five dead and three wounded. The Interior Department ordered the 155 survivors exiled to a two-and-a-half-square-mile tract of land in Indian Territory, where disease killed dozens in the first years.

After he recovered, Meacham formed a lecture company and for nearly two years toured from Sacramento to New York City with a small troupe that included Frank and Toby Riddle, Scarfaced Charley, and Shacknasty Jim. As the months passed, attendance at Meacham's programs dwindled. Few cared any longer to hear about the happenings in the Lava Beds. After four months, a homesick and depressed Toby turned suicidal, and Frank hustled her back to Oregon as soon as he could scrape together the money. When the tour finally broke up, Scarfaced Charley returned to Indian Territory to assume the role of chief of the agency Modocs.

At 9:45 a.m. on October 3, 1873, Captain Jack, Boston Charley, and Black Jim mounted the gallows. As the nooses were fitted, an Oregon settler yelled, "Jack, what would you give me to take your place?" "Five hundred ponies and both my wives," replied Jack. With that macabre joke, Captain Jack's life ended.

The army was not content merely to kill Captain Jack. After he was lowered from the gallows, Captain Jack was decapitated. His head was mailed to the Army Medical Museum, where it was added to its collection of Indian craniums.[21]

The Peace Policy weathered the Modoc crisis, barely. The perfidy of Captain Jack, however, ensured that the government would be considerably less inclined to indulge recalcitrant Indians with talk. The next unrest, provoked or otherwise, was likely to be met first with force. And as the white noose tightened on the Indians, some "poor devils," to use General Sherman's expression, were certain to "wriggle against their doom" with all the might they could muster.

CHAPTER 9

THE BUFFALO WAR

JOSIAH WRIGHT MOOAR came to the southern plains in 1870 with no thought of killing Indians; certainly the nineteen-year-old New Englander never dreamed that he would threaten their way of life. Mooar was drawn by the same vague dreams of "grandeur and danger" that lured tens of thousands of restless young men west after the Civil War, and like most of them he found only disappointment. Flat broke, Mooar took work at Fort Hays, Kansas, chopping and hauling wood for the army. He soon learned that there was better money to be had easier; those earning it were the buffalo hunters who supplied the Fort Hays commissary with meat.

Mooar wanted in. He had an idea for making big money from buffalo. Hunters took only the choicest cuts and discarded the rest of the carcass. Mooar saw the potential for turning the hides into commercial leather. A British company with a similar interest had contracted a Fort Hays hunter named Charlie Rath for five hundred hides to test the market, and Rath asked his close friend Mooar to help fill the order. It was a good choice. Mooar was an excellent shot, and he and Rath exceeded their quota. Mooar shipped his share of the surplus hides east to his brother John, who offered them to New York tanneries. John Mooar found a buyer and joined Josiah in Kansas with a contract for two thousand hides at fifty cents each. Other firms capitalized on the Mooar brothers' success, and the hide market boomed. With hunters in high demand, practically anyone capable of handling the deadly accurate .50-caliber buffalo rifle and mounted telescope was hired, and in the Mooar brothers' wake came scores of misfits, miscreants, outlaws, and fugitives, drawn to the vast Kansas herds like flies to putrefying buffalo carcasses.

Fort Dodge, in southwestern Kansas, became the center of the trade. In just three years, railroad cars hauled a staggering 4,373,730 hides to eastern markets. The Southern Plains tribes abhorred the wanton slaughter, but so long as the hunters remained north of the Arkansas River, the Indians had no recourse, short of war. South of the river matters were different, because the Medicine Lodge Treaty had granted the Indians exclusive hunting rights from the Arkansas River to the southern border of Indian Territory.

Treaties, however, meant nothing to the hide hunters. In 1872, after decimating the Kansas herds, hunters crossed the Arkansas River "deadline" and continued the slaughter on Cheyenne and Arapaho land. By the end of 1873, the country between the Arkansas and the Cimarron Rivers had become a vast abattoir. The tribes reeled before the juggernaut, struggling to find a foothold, while the hunters laid plans to cross the Canadian River into the Kiowa and Comanche hunting grounds in 1874.

The Indians implored the government to eject the hunters from their country. The Kiowa peace chief Kicking Bird tried to explain what the buffalo meant to the Indian in terms white men could comprehend. "The buffalo is our money," he explained. "It is our only resource with which to buy what we do not receive from the government. Just as it makes a white man feel to have his money carried away, so it makes us feel to see others killing and stealing our buffalo." Kicking Bird understated Indian fears, which amounted to apocalyptic dread. For the Plains Indian, extermination of the buffalo meant death—both physical and spiritual.

Few besides the Indians cared. The secretary of the interior told Congress he "would not seriously regret the total disappearance of the buffalo as a means of hastening their sense of dependence on the products of the soil." Phil Sheridan reveled in the slaughter. Hide hunters, he told Texas legislators contemplating a buffalo-conservation bill, "had done more to settle the Indian problem in two years than the army had done in thirty. For the sake of lasting peace, let them kill and skin until the buffalo are exterminated."

Sheridan's sentiments rippled down through the ranks. In the winter of 1873, Kansas buffalo hunters made tentative plans to cross the Canadian River come summer. A delegation of hunters visited Lieutenant

Colonel Richard I. Dodge, who was responsible for keeping hunters off Indian land, to ascertain the probable legal consequences. "Colonel," inquired Josiah Wright Mooar, "if we cross into Texas, what will be the government's attitude toward us?"

"Boys," Dodge answered, "if I were a buffalo hunter, I would hunt buffalo where the buffalo were."

That settled the question. In the spring of 1874, a now-prosperous Charlie Rath and his chief competitor, A. C. "Charlie" Myers, moved their hide businesses from Dodge City to the south bank of the Canadian River. A saloon keeper and a blacksmith followed them. The frontier entrepreneurs erected four timber-reinforced sod shacks near the ruins of an abandoned trading post called Adobe Walls and settled in to await the profits of the summer hunt. That their penetration deeper into Indian land might finally provoke a war with the southern tribes was a risk the hunters and hide merchants were willing to run.[1]

*

Phil Sheridan's bludgeoning of the Southern Cheyennes in the 1868–1869 campaign had silenced the tribe for four years. But the rosy promises of the Peace Policy had not bloomed on the Cheyenne-Arapaho Reservation. Instead, peace had brought a slow death dreadful for tribal elders to contemplate. Moral degradation and the hopeless tedium of reservation life in Indian Territory corroded Cheyenne culture. As for the Arapahos, their accommodating nature only accelerated their decline.

Liquor was the agent of ruin. The Cheyennes and the Arapahos fell easy prey to Kansas bootleggers, who divested them of a fortune in buffalo robes and ponies in exchange for rotgut whiskey. Horse thieves cleaned up what the whiskey peddlers missed, stealing thousands of ponies from the reservation Indians. Even the faithful peace chief Little Robe lost his pony herd. The Arapahos had become too dependent on the white man's goods and too pacific to reverse course. The Cheyennes, however, retained enough fighting spirit to remain dangerous, something their pragmatic Quaker agent well understood.

Farther south, on the Fort Sill Reservation, tensions ran high. The Kiowas and the Comanches were less prone to alcoholism, but white horse thieves preyed on their herds no less than they did on those of the Cheyennes and the Arapahos. The presence of government surveyors

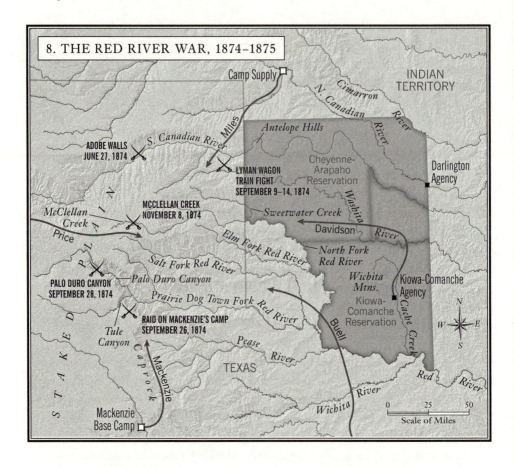

also troubled the Kiowas. "This country was given by Washington to his red children," Kicking Bird told a white friend. "It was a country of peace. Now see white men in it making lines, setting up stones and sticks with marks on them. We do not know what it means, but are afraid it is not for our good."[2]

As difficult as they were to bear, these accumulated wrongs had not provoked an outbreak. It was the specter of starvation during the long, hard winter of 1873–1874 that finally pushed the Indians over the edge. Blizzards blocked the delivery of government rations to the reservations. The Indians had relied on their agents' promises to feed them. When no food came and their meager supply of buffalo meat ran out, the men butchered their ponies for food. The snow melted in late April, but still no rations came. Freight haulers bickered with the government over technicalities and refused to deliver food until they were paid. The Cheyenne-Arapaho agent, meanwhile, importuned the Indian Bureau to act: "It is *very important* NOW that these people be *fed*." No reply came.

War awaited only a unifying leader.[3]

*

He arose in early 1874 in the person of Isa-tai, a young Quahadi medicine man and close friend of Quanah's. He had an unfortunate name; Isa-tai translates as coyote vagina or wolf vulva. But Isa-tai had strong medicine. He claimed to have resurrected the dead and boasted his imperviousness to the white man's bullet, and he had credulous "witnesses" to his feats. Men said they had seen him spit up a wagonload of cartridges and then swallow it again. Others swore they had watched him ascend into the clouds to the great beyond, where, Isa-tai said, the Great Spirit had given him the power to wipe out the white man and restore the Comanche nation to its old glory. Two of Isa-tai's prophecies had apparently come to pass already. In 1873, Isa-tai had divined the day on which a brilliant comet would vanish from the summer sky. He had also predicted the winter of anguish that followed. With each arctic blast, his medicine grew stronger and scoffers fewer.

In May 1874, Isa-tai convoked the first Sun Dance in Comanche history. It was a clarion call to war under the protective cloak of his medicine. Nearly all the Comanches came, but only half agreed to follow him—which was the closest thing to unified action in Comanche history. With Quanah at his side, Isa-tai also proselytized outside the tribe, promising to share his divine power with all believers. Their evangelical results were mixed. The Kiowa council of chiefs refused to consider war until after their own Sun Dance in July. Only six Kiowas agreed then and there to fight; those six, however, included Satanta and Big Tree. Fewer than two dozen Arapaho warriors answered Isa-tai's call, and they only came to observe. The Cheyennes, however, enlisted en masse. Even without Kiowa and Arapaho participation, Isa-tai and Quanah had assembled the largest war party ever seen on the southern plains.

On June 25, 1874, the war of redemption began. The hardened war leader Quanah, the mystic firebrand Isa-tai, the parole-breaking Satanta and Big Tree, and five hundred warriors weaved their snorting ponies through the putrefying remains of tens of thousands of skinned buffalo toward the despised buffalo hunters' gathering place at Adobe

Walls, where only twenty-nine whites were congregated. The war-riors rode stripped to their breechcloths, their bodies splashed with the sacred golden ocher Isa-tai said would protect them from bullets. Confidence ran high. "Isa-Tai make big talk at that time," recalled Quanah. "He says, 'God tell me we going to kill lots white men—I stop bullets in guns. We kill them all, just like old women.'" But Isa-tai had not reckoned with the mighty Sharps .50-caliber buffalo rifle, a weapon so powerful it could knock down an animal at a thousand yards. In the hands of experienced hunters using telescopic sights, the rifles were uncannily accurate.[4]

In the flint gray dawn of June 27, 1874, the war party marshaled on a steep red ridge a half mile east of Adobe Walls. A deserter from the Buffalo Soldiers waited to signal the attack with bugle blasts. But impetuous young warriors spilled down the ridge before Quanah gave the order. The "young men go too fast. Pretty soon [I] yelled, 'All right go ahead,' and we charged down on [the] houses in wild charge, throwing up the dust high."

The doors of the four sod shacks slammed shut, and the Indians began circling in the classic maneuver of Plains warfare. Clinging to the far sides of their ponies at full gallop and firing from beneath the animals' throats, the warriors drew nearer with each pass. Quanah broke from the circle and charged a shack to "kill some white men and make my heart good." He drove his lance through a trembling boy who had lingered too long outdoors and then whirled his pony and slammed the animal against the shack door. It held. Inside, the racket from rifles and Indian yells deafened the defenders. Billowing gun smoke blinded them. Fear narrowed the hunters' focus, and they fought with adrenaline-fed rage. Repeatedly, the warriors withdrew, regrouped, and then came on again. Nothing, however, went as Isa-tai had promised. The white hunters' bullets found victims at ranges incomprehensible to the warriors. "Sometimes we would be standing 'way off, resting and hardly thinking of the fight," a stunned Comanche marveled, "and they would kill our horses."[5]

A Sharps bullet struck Quanah's pony, and the war leader fell hard. As he crawled behind a buffalo carcass to catch his breath, a ricocheted bullet grazed his neck and temporarily paralyzed his left arm. With Quanah down, the leaderless war party disintegrated. On a bluff half a mile distant, Isa-tai and a cluster of war leaders watched the fight go terribly wrong. Isa-tai was stark naked, his body coated solid with war paint. Any lingering faith the chiefs had in Isa-tai's medicine vanished when a bullet split open the forehead of his pony. An enraged Cheyenne bent over and slapped him with his quirt. "Your medicine no good. Yours pole-cat medicine." Isa-tai had a ready alibi: someone had killed a skunk, and that had broken his power.[6]

For the next three days, the Indians taunted the whites from a safe distance. On the night of June 30, a hunter slipped through the Indian lines and rode to Fort Dodge, Kansas, for help. No one at Fort Dodge had the authority to dispatch troops, so the governor interceded with the senior military officer of the region, Brigadier General John Pope, the commander of the Department of the Missouri.

The governor had gone to the wrong man. Pope saw the situation for what it was. "Indians, like white men," he said, "are not reconciled to starve peacefully." Pope refused the governor's appeal. "The buffalo hunters have justly earned all that may befall them. If [I] were to send troops to the locality of these unlawful establishments, it would be to break them up and not to protect them."

As it turned out, the hunters had no need of army help. They had killed or wounded nearly a hundred Indians and lost only two men. After Adobe Walls, the war party splintered. Enraged warriors fanned out from Texas to eastern Colorado, killing at least a hundred whites in a final, frenzied fight for their way of life. The Kiowas did not join them, however. Adobe Walls had strengthened Kicking Bird's hand, and after the Sun Dance three-quarters of the tribe returned with him to the reservation. Satanta surrendered his chieftaincy in despair, and Big Tree grew morose. Only Lone Wolf and Maman-ti remained defiant. In mid-July, they cut deep into Texas, killing seven, including a hated Texas Ranger. Lone Wolf chopped the ranger's head to pieces and scooped out his bowels. Then he prayed aloud. "Thank you, Oh thank you for what has been done today. My poor son has been paid back. His spirit is satisfied."[7]

*

Adobe Walls ended the Peace Policy on the southern plains. When General Sherman demanded permission to launch an all-out offensive unfettered by reservation boundaries, no one objected. Even the Quakers were fed up. Most important, President Grant believed that he had given the Indians ample opportunity to beat scalping knives into plowshares. So long as care was taken not to strike "innocent and friendly" Indians, Sherman could make war on his own terms. On July 20, Sherman unleashed Sheridan.

It would be the total war of 1868–1869 revisited. This time, however, there would be no waiting for winter. Sheridan issued orders for multiple columns from the Departments of the Missouri and Texas to converge on the Texas Panhandle haunts of the hostile bands as quickly as they could be assembled. He erased department boundaries to facilitate pursuit. The Indians were to be kept on the run with no respite to hunt. It would be reservation life on government terms or death by bullets or by starvation. Sheridan intended this to be the last campaign on the southern plains.[8]

Sheridan left the details to Generals Augur and Pope, who adopted similar plans independently of each other. Augur organized three expeditions: the first, under Colonel John W. Davidson, would march west from Fort Sill with six companies of the Tenth Cavalry and three infantry companies. Colonel George P. Buell would push up from the south with a comparable force. Colonel Mackenzie, from whom Augur expected the most, would sweep northeast from Fort Concho with the Fourth Cavalry and five infantry companies. General Pope organized two expeditions. He instructed Major William R. Price to strike east with the Eighth Cavalry from Fort Bascom in the New Mexico Territory as far as the eastern fringe of the Staked Plain and ordered Colonel Nelson A. Miles, commander of the Fifth Infantry, to proceed to Fort Dodge and assume command of eight companies of cavalry and four of infantry. Enjoining quartermaster and subsistence departments to "promptly comply with all requisitions for supplies" that Miles might make, Pope cloaked the colonel with wide discretionary authority to conduct operations as he judged best.

Miles would have tolerated nothing less. In fact, he expected Pope to give him command of Price's force as well. It was absurd, he told his wife, for Pope to think he could direct movements of forces that were ten days from the nearest telegraph lines and five hundred miles from headquarters. Miles's objection made good military sense, but that wasn't why he complained. He wanted out from under Pope. In fact, he wanted to be clear of anyone who he thought might impede his rapid rise through the ranks. Miles's vaulting ambition made him the most unpopular senior officer on the frontier, but none could deny his competence.

Miles had come up the hard way. Born into a farm family too poor to send him to secondary school, Miles migrated to Boston at age six-teen. He clerked in a crockery store, took night classes, and, with a passionate interest in all things martial, studied military drill and tactics under an old French veteran. He learned his lessons well, rising from lieutenant to brevet major general of volunteers during the Civil War. Unlike Custer, who had reverted to the rank of captain in the regular army, Miles emerged from the war with a regular army colonelcy and a huge chip on his shoulder. Despite his rank, he was convinced that the best jobs went to West Pointers. Detractors accused him of marrying General Sherman's niece in 1868 solely to further his career, but they were wrong. Miles loved his wife. And it was good he did, because her uncle loathed favoritism. So long as Sherman commanded the army, battlefield success was the sole road to field promotions.[9]

For Miles, that meant finding and defeating the Indians before Mackenzie. In mid-August, Miles marched out of Fort Dodge into blast-furnace heat and a prolonged drought that the Cheyennes called the Great Dry Time. Temperatures soared above 110 degrees. Streams evaporated, rivers withered, and springs dried up. Miles drove his soldiers twenty-five miles a day, accelerating the pace on August 27 after his scouts discovered the trail of the main Cheyenne village at the base of the Caprock. Three days later, Miles caught up with the Cheyennes, chasing five hundred warriors for twelve miles over what the colonel called "the roughest ground that I had until that time ever seen men fight upon." On the sand-covered bed of the Prairie Dog Town Fork of the Red River near Tule Canyon, Miles ended the pursuit. One captain added a touch of grim humor to the inconsequential running fight, exhorting his exhausted men from bluff to bluff with the promise "If any man is killed I will make him a corporal."[10]

There was, however, a far greater chance of men dying from dehydration than Indian fire. Canteens were empty, and the Prairie Dog Town Fork was a watercourse in name only. Delirious soldiers slit their arms and moistened their lips with their own blood. Still, Miles drove them on. The morning after the Prairie Dog Town Fork frolic, his command climbed out of Tule Canyon onto the Staked Plain. Tactically, it was a wasted effort, because the Cheyennes were well on their way to Palo Duro Canyon. But the soldiers did find a stream. With rations low and the odds of encountering another water source nil, Miles made camp while his wagon train returned to Camp Supply for food and forage.[11]

The field was open to Mackenzie.

*

In his haste to outpace Mackenzie, Miles had inadvertently allowed a Cheyenne war party under Chief Medicine Water to slip behind him and wreak havoc in western Kansas. The marauders' first victims were a party of government surveyors, the second a family of poor home-steaders traveling from rural Georgia to Colorado.

They were John German, his wife, and their seven children, and they were just one day short of Fort Wallace when Medicine Water's war party descended on them and exacted revenge for Adobe Walls. The warriors shot John German and his son, and Medicine Water's wife split open the skull of German's pregnant wife. The eldest daughter, Rebecca, was wounded defending herself with an ax and then gang-raped, wrapped in blankets, and tossed into a fire. The Cheyennes rode off with Rebecca's five sisters: petite, blue-eyed Catherine German, aged seventeen; fifteen-year-old Joanna, a long-haired blonde; Sophia, a pretty brunette who looked older than her twelve years; Julia, aged seven; and Adelaide, aged five. After a nine-mile ride, they halted to appraise the girls.

Joanna's long hair doomed her. She was raped, killed, and scalped, her hair fashioned into five trophy scalps, each signifying a dead member of the German family. When the war party returned home, Medicine Water handed the German girls to the women of the village. They stripped Catherine and tied her to a horse that was set loose on the prairie for the men to chase; she became the property of the warrior who caught her.

Several days later, a patrol from Fort Wallace chanced upon the German massacre site. In the dirt beside the charred wagon lay four corpses; among the scattered effects was the family Bible with nine names written on the flyleaf. Finding the five missing girls became a cause célèbre without parallel in the annals of the Indian-fighting army.[12]

*

Meanwhile, back on the reservations in Indian Territory, the work of separating friendly from potentially hostile Indians was proving difficult. At the Darlington Agency, the task was straightforward: most of the Arapahos submitted to enrollment; nearly all of the Cheyennes were absent on the warpath. But at Fort Sill, the lines blurred. Kicking

Bird's band went peaceably to a confinement camp near the fort, but the rest of the Kiowas and some Comanches clashed with the army before escaping onto the Staked Plain. By the close of August, eighteen hundred Cheyennes, two thousand Comanches, and one thousand Kiowas were on the loose, including Lone Wolf, Maman-ti, Satanta, and Big Tree, all carrying incriminating enrollment papers.

On September 9, the renegades attacked Colonel Miles's fully laden supply train on its return trip from Camp Supply. Lone Wolf and Maman-ti orchestrated the assault, which proved an abject failure. The train commander, Captain Wyllys Lyman, corralled the wagons on a low rise two miles north of the Washita River. His detachment of fifty-six soldiers and teamsters repelled several charges. At nightfall, both sides dug rifle pits. For the next five days, the soldiers and the Indians fired harmlessly at each other.[13]

As always, there were irrepressible young warriors in search of war honors. A seventeen-year-old Kiowa mixed blood, Botalye, made quite a name for himself on the last day of the battle. It was Botalye's first encounter with soldiers, and he had a compelling reason to prove himself. During a boyhood wrestling match with two of Satanta's sons, Botalye had accidentally kicked hot coals against the side of the chief's sacred red lodge, setting it ablaze. Satanta promised to thrash him if he ever showed cowardice in combat. With Satanta's threat looming large in his mind, Botalye told a medicine man he intended to ride through the corralled wagons to a buffalo wallow, the soldiers' only source of water, to see how much was left. Try once, and only once, the medicine man said. Off went Botalye. "I dashed between the trenches and the wagons. The soldiers couldn't shoot at me for fearing of hitting their own men. I raced on through and up the ridge on the far side . . . and tried to holler. I wanted to make it sound like the cry of a wild goose, but only a frightened squawk came out." Botalye repeated his feat twice before Maman-ti ordered him to stop. "But I was feeling great. I said that I would make a fourth run." And he did. When Botalye returned, Satanta laughingly told him, "If you hadn't done it, I was going to whip you," and then he embraced the boy. "I wasn't really going to whip anyone as brave as you. I couldn't have made a fourth run myself. No one ever comes back the fourth time."

"Everyone listen!" a chief exclaimed. "I'm going to give Botalye a new name . . . I name him *Eadle-tau-hain*—He Wouldn't Listen!"[14]

Satanta had enjoyed perhaps the last good laugh of his life. Quite abruptly, Major Price's column appeared nearby, and the warriors withdrew. Early in the afternoon, black clouds gathered over the horizon. A cold wind swept down from the north. Thunder rolled across the prairie, and rain fell in blinding sheets. The warriors wrapped themselves in their blankets and turned west. The Great Dry Time of heat and drought was over, and the Kiowa leadership was in disarray. Colonel Davidson's pursuing army column had prevented warriors from hunting buffalo, leaving the women and children cold, wet, and hungry. Lone Wolf and Maman-ti led most of the Kiowas on a desperate and miserable march through rain, sleet, and ice to Palo Duro Canyon. Gambling on the mercy of the government, Satanta, Big Tree, and their followers surrendered at the Darlington Agency. Satanta said he was finished with war—insisting he had not fired a shot in anger since leaving Fort Sill—and wanted only to farm. No one believed him, and he was hustled back to the Texas penitentiary. Satanta never stood a chance with Sherman, but Sheridan believed Big Tree had redeeming qualities. He held him at Fort Sill under light guard, intending to release him as soon as the Kiowas surrendered.

The Indian agent Lawrie Tatum had been right when he predicted that the loss of freedom would prove a fate more terrible than death for Satanta. On October 9, 1878, after the State of Texas rejected yet another of his ceaseless requests for a pardon, a despairing Satanta jumped headfirst from a second-story window in the penitentiary hospital, smashing his body on a brick wall. He died two days later. Big Tree, on the other hand, elected to assimilate. As General Sheridan had hoped, the Kiowa chief became an advocate of the white man's road. Ordained a deacon in the Baptist church in 1897, Big Tree died peacefully at his home in Anadarko in 1929.

*

Satanta's suicide was still four years in the future. While the once imperious chief threw himself on the mercy of the government, in early autumn 1874 Lone Wolf and Maman-ti slogged through drenching rains toward Palo Duro Canyon. The weather was their sole enemy. Miles and Price were at Camp Supply refitting their commands. After an unproductive scout of the Caprock, Davidson had returned to Fort Sill. Colonel Buell, who did not even get started until late September, stopped after just five days to build a base camp. But Mackenzie was on the move, and that meant that Miles's worst fears were about to become reality.[15]

*

Colonel Mackenzie left little to chance. While Miles fretted at Tule Canyon over his tardy wagon train, Mackenzie stockpiled provisions in Blanco Canyon, carefully crafting his campaign in close consultation with General Augur. A week after Miles withdrew, Mackenzie moved onto the Staked Plain under a cold hard rain, occupying the very ground Miles had abandoned. Three years earlier, fierce storms and low supplies had forced Mackenzie off the Staked Plain, but he had learned well the lessons of his abortive campaign against Quanah. Mackenzie patiently rode out the storms, comfortable in the knowledge that the Fourth Cavalry carried sufficient rations, with resupply just a day's march away. When the skies cleared, Mackenzie sent scouting parties onto the Staked Plain to find the hostile villages.

The Indians tried Quanah's tactics to thwart Mackenzie. On the night of September 26, a large Comanche war party fell upon the Fourth Cavalry's camp to run off their horses, but Mackenzie was ready for them. Every animal was hobbled, clusters of troops surrounded the herd, and a soldier stood guard every fifteen feet around the camp. The Indians recoiled from a withering fire. While they considered their options, Mackenzie counterattacked at dawn.

The warriors gave way, regrouped out of range, and then turned leisurely east, a ruse that was obvious to Mackenzie. Concluding that the warriors' eastward course meant their villages lay to the north, Mackenzie prepared a deception of his own. He followed the war party until sunset and then made camp in plain sight. At nightfall, he abruptly saddled up his command and pounded north to the rim of Palo Duro Canyon, arriving there early on the morning of September 28. Mackenzie's gambit succeeded. Stretching for two miles along the canyon floor were nearly four hundred lodges containing three thousand Indians, about equally divided between the Kiowa villages of Lone Wolf and Maman-ti and two large Cheyenne and Comanche camps.

The receding predawn twilight revealed to the soldiers an eerily spectacular sight. Wide swaths of red ocher bled down the walls into a dense growth of cedar trees five hundred yards below the rim. The Indian lodges looked like tiny coins, and the grazing ponies resembled a gaggle of geese. There were no sentinels. Maman-ti, whose medicine the assembled bands trusted implicitly, had assured them they were safe—a reasonable assumption, considering that the jagged canyon walls appeared impassable to man or beast. But Mackenzie had found a trail to his liking—"narrow, dizzy, [and] winding, such as a goat could hardly travel," an officer called it. Down the men went leading their horses, stumbling and sliding single file. For an instant, it appeared the troopers might forfeit the element of surprise. An early-rising Kiowa subchief whose camp stood near the trail's end spotted the troops. Instead of warning the village, however, he nervously squeezed off two shots and then ducked into his lodge to put on his war paint. Indians awakened by the shots assumed a hunting party had fired them and then went back to sleep. Once safely on the canyon floor, Mackenzie deployed his troops in a long skirmish line and then charged.

The villages fell without resistance. Lodges and winter stockpiles of food went up in flames. Some women and children clawed their way out of the canyon, yanking their possessions up behind them with ropes. Others milled about senselessly. A Kiowa warrior noticed his addled sister running toward instead of away from the soldiers. "She had a little baby boy on her back. I told her to give me the baby. She said no, let's throw it away. I said that I would rather leave her than the baby." The warrior hoisted them onto his pony and galloped off.

Meanwhile, a returning war party gathered on the rim athwart Mackenzie's back trail. Warriors from the villages regrouped behind rocks and trees along the canyon slopes and began sniping at the soldiers. With the outcome suddenly in doubt, a frightened cavalryman asked Mackenzie how he planned to extricate them. "I brought you in," retorted the colonel, "I will take you out," and he did, not only withdrawing his command through the mouth of the canyon with just one man wounded, but also bringing with him the entire Indian pony herd. Five warriors died in the Battle of Palo Duro Canyon, as did the subchief who had neglected to sound the alarm. The human casualties, however, were of small account when measured against the loss of the ponies. This time the Indians would have no chance to reclaim them. After the Tonkawa scouts took the best animals for themselves, Mackenzie had the remaining 1,046 ponies shot.[16]

*

Palo Duro Canyon broke the back of Indian resistance. Without their ponies, the Indians could neither wage war nor hunt buffalo, and the crippled tribes dispersed on the Staked Plain to their separate fates. Miles and Price closed in from the north. East of the Staked Plain, Colonel Buell burned 550 lodges in two abandoned villages. The Indians called the ensuing weeks of rain and constant flight the Wrinkled Hand Chase.[17]

Palo Duro Canyon also put Mackenzie one step closer to a general's star, but a stroke of good fortune kept Miles in the race. On November 8, while leading home an empty wagon train near the mouth of McClellan Creek, Miles's most trusted subordinate, the aggressive lieutenant Frank D. Baldwin, chanced upon the village of the Cheyenne war chief Gray Beard. Baldwin had only one infantry company, two cavalry companies, and a single howitzer—perhaps eighty men in all. They were too few to launch a conventional attack against an enemy he correctly calculated at two hundred warriors, so the lieutenant improvised. Forming his twenty-three wagons in two columns, Baldwin placed an infantryman or two in each wagon and a cavalry company on either flank. He fired six artillery rounds into the unsuspecting village and then waved the wagons forward along a low narrow mesa. The warriors offered little resistance; most had no ammunition. Baldwin seized their pony herd and burned the lodges. In the abandoned village, Baldwin found a prize far more precious than ponies. The Cheyennes had left behind young Adelaide and Julia German, emaciated and nearly naked. From their starved state, Baldwin assumed, probably incorrectly, that the Indians had mistreated them. In fact, the Cheyennes themselves were no better off than the girls.

Colonel Miles sent the orphans to his wife at Fort Leavenworth. The fate of the older sisters weighed heavily on his mind, and he promised her that he would continue the search so long as he was able. But headquarters stripped him of all but three companies, leaving Miles with scarcely enough men for a limited reconnaissance.

There was nothing personal in Sheridan's decision to recall the troops. Supplies were failing, and the weather was too tempestuous to contemplate a repeat of the 1868 winter campaign. Ice storms raged for days on end. Temperatures sank well below zero. During one storm, ninety of Colonel Davidson's horses froze to death, and twenty-six men were incapacitated with frostbite.

With conditions on the open plains unbearable, destitute Indians streamed into the agencies to surrender. In February 1875, Kicking Bird induced Lone Wolf and Maman-ti to lay down their arms. On March 6, the peace chief Stone Calf brought in most of the remaining Cheyennes. With him were the elder German sisters. Stone Calf had purchased the girls from their captors, but the impoverished chief had been able to offer them little more than kindness.[18]

Rather than capitulate, some Southern Cheyennes fled north. Stone Forehead, keeper of the Sacred Medicine Arrows, reached the Northern Cheyennes with the holy objects and a handful of warriors. Chief Little Bull's band of seventy Southern Cheyennes, on the other hand, was butchered in flight. On the snowy morning of April 23, 1875, Lieutenant Austin Henely attacked their camp on Sappa Creek in northwest Kansas. Half the Indians escaped on horseback; the remainder sought cover behind the riverbank or in holes dug the night before as defensive positions. The protection was illusory. Henely surrounded the spot with forty soldiers and opened fire on the Indians huddled below, killing nineteen warriors and seven women and children. The lieutenant took no prisoners. A sergeant later accused Henely of ordering the cold-blooded murder of a Cheyenne woman and child, whose bodies he said were tossed into a burning lodge to destroy the evidence.[19]

Sappa Creek was the last clash of what the army called the Red River War. More misery awaited the subjugated tribes, however. General Sheridan wanted to try the "ringleaders" before a drumhead military commission. The Indian Bureau protested to the attorney general, who ruled that the army lacked the authority to sit in judgment of government wards, hostile or otherwise. President Grant intervened, directing that instigators and "criminals" be taken from their families and imprisoned without trial at Fort Marion, Florida. Based on information gleaned from Indian informants, the government set a quota of seventy-five ringleaders.

The execution of Grant's directive was a cruel farce. At the Darlington Agency, the Cheyenne warriors were lined up to enable Catherine and Sophia German to identify the rapists and murderers. When the girls proved able to point out only three with certainty, the post commander stepped in. Too drunk to distinguish one warrior from the other, he chose thirty-three others at random to fill the Cheyenne quota.

Kicking Bird protested that the Kiowa quota of twenty-seven was grossly unjust, pointing out that the Comanches, who had started the war, were required to offer up only seven warriors. Sherman's long-standing grudge against the Kiowas was probably behind the discrepancy. To Kicking Bird's mortification, the army coerced him into selecting the Kiowas to be incarcerated. He chose Lone Wolf, Maman-ti, three lesser chiefs, and then—in order to ease the burden on the tribe—filled out the rolls with Mexican captives and tribal delinquents.

Kicking Bird's reluctant complicity cost him friends and hardened his enemies. As Kicking Bird saw the prisoners off with words of affection and a promise their imprisonment would be brief, Maman-ti hexed him. "You think you have done well. You think you are free, a big man with the whites. But you will not live long; I will see to that." The next day, Kicking Bird died after drinking a cup of coffee. The post surgeon said he had been poisoned with strychnine. "I have taken the white man's road, and am not sorry," the dying Kicking Bird whispered to the surgeon. "Tell my people to take the good path."[20]

By early 1875, Quanah was also advocating the white man's road. In a vision that winter, a wolf had approached him out of a mystic mist, howled, and then turned toward Fort Sill. From then on, Quanah counseled surrender as the only alternative to perpetual flight. An ultimatum from Mackenzie, now the commanding officer at Fort Sill with authority over Indian Territory and the agencies, strengthened his conviction. Bad Hand promised no harm would come to the Quahadis if they came in voluntarily, but if he had to track them down, his troops would do to them what they had done to Maman-ti at Palo Duro Canyon. The Quahadis knew that Mackenzie was capable of making good on his threat. On June 6, Quanah and Isa-tai led the last free Comanches into Fort Sill.

Mackenzie was as good as his word, telling Sheridan, "I think better of this band than of any other on the reserve. I shall let them down as easily as I can." He saw to it that no warriors were imprisoned or exiled and defended their pony herds against white horse thieves, ordering his troops to shoot any white man who tried to steal Indian stock. And he formed a friendship with Quanah based on mutual respect. They spent long hours in Mackenzie's quarters, where the young colonel patiently taught the young chief how to navigate the white man's world.

The aftermath of the Red River War might have brought out the best in Mackenzie, but it triggered the worst in Miles, who schemed to deprive Mackenzie of half of the Fourth Cavalry and command of Indian Territory. Mackenzie took Miles's machinations in stride. "I have no word to say against Colonel Miles," Mackenzie told Sherman. "On the contrary I regard him as a very fine officer. But I am not in the slightest degree jealous of him. I regard him not as my superior in any way and in some particulars I am sure he is not my equal." Mackenzie prevailed. For the moment at least, Miles had met his match.[21]

*

The outcome of the Red River War exceeded even Phil Sheridan's high expectations. His victory could not be measured in the number of Indians killed, which apart from the Sappa Creek affair was trifling. The Red River War was decisive because it deprived the Indians of the means to make war. The government confiscated their weapons and sold their war ponies at public auction. One chief insisted his captors accept his son's toy bow and arrows; the boy, he said, would have no need for them on the white man's road. Great cattle ranches sprawled over land once home to formidable Comanche villages. Country formerly blanketed with buffalo was fenced in tight. From the Rio Grande to eastern Colorado, settlers slept tranquilly in the knowledge their scalps were safe.

The circle had closed. A way of life had ended. The wild tribes of the southern plains had been conquered, and they knew it. Before starting for Florida, the Cheyenne chiefs Gray Beard and Minimic asked the officer commanding the army escort to write a letter for them to their Indian agent. It contained this message to their people:

Your Gray Beard and Minimic want me to write you to tell their people to settle down at their agency and do all that the government requires of them. They say, tell them to plant corn and send their children to school, and be careful not to get in any trouble; that we want them to travel in the white man's road. The white men are as many as the leaves on the trees, and we are only a few people.[22]

*

So much had changed in ten years. In 1865, the Little Arkansas Treaty had promised perpetual peace between the government and the Indians of the southern plains and had presumed to set in motion the reservation process. The peace commissioners and the chiefs had signed the treaty as equals, if not in fact, then at least for legal purposes. By 1875, the tribes were thoroughly subjugated wards of the government with little voice in their future.

During that decade of decision on the southern plains, the desert Southwest had seen its share of upheaval. There had been hard fighting and brutal conquests. The Peace Policy had been tried there also, with results that were as yet uncertain. As the southern plains were gradually tamed, and the northern plains simmered, the public mind was increasingly drawn to the alien reaches of Apacheria.

CHAPTER 10

NO REST, NO PEACE

IN APRIL 1871, Aravaipa Creek was an oasis of peace in the blood-soaked desert of the southern Arizona Territory. Along its cottonwood-fringed banks, 500 Apaches camped, grateful to live under the protection of Lieutenant Royal E. Whitman, commander of nearby Camp Grant. Chief Eskiminzin and his 150 half-starved followers, who lived in constant dread of attack by the army and local volunteers, had been the first Apaches to come in. To Eskiminzin's plea that his people be permitted to make peace and "raise cattle and corn and live like your people," Whitman could offer only rations and temporary sanctuary until he received instructions from department headquarters. Satisfied with the terms, the Aravaipas turned over their weapons. Whitman hired the Indians to cut hay and chop wood for the post, and neighboring ranchers engaged them to bring in their barley harvest. As word of Whitman's kindness spread, 350 other Apaches found their way to his informal reservation.[1]

Seventy miles southwest of Camp Grant, the residents of Tucson seethed. Since Whitman had undertaken his experiment in peace, Apache raids in the area had claimed six lives. There was no evidence that Whitman's Indians were to blame, but they made handy targets for Arizonans, who demanded to know if the army would continue to coddle his "murderous wards." A deputation from Tucson's self-appointed Committee of Public Safety took the people's case to the department commander, Colonel George Stoneman. The colonel told them to take care of the problem themselves.

They did. Abandoned by the army, a group of Mexican-Americans, whites, and Papago Indians banded together to mete out frontier justice to the "fiends" at Camp Grant. At dawn on April 30, the vigilantes quietly surrounded Eskiminzin's camp. By prearranged signal, the Papagos clubbed, hacked, and stoned the sleeping villagers, while the whites and the Mexicans poured rifle volleys into those who escaped the Papago war clubs and knives. Upward of 144 Apaches died, nearly all women and children. Eskiminzin survived but lost four wives and five children. Not a single attacker fell, principally because there was no resistance.

The slaughter at Camp Grant delighted most Arizonans, the territorial press labeling it "righteous retribution worthy of emulation at every opportunity." Eastern humanitarians denounced the massacre, and President Grant threatened to place the territory under martial law if the culprits were not arraigned.

Eskiminzin held out little hope for justice; no Arizona court, he told Whitman, would punish a white man for killing Apaches. He was right. Tucsonans burned the prosecuting attorney in effigy, and the jury acquitted the killers on the grounds of self-defense.[2]

*

No Indians elicited less sympathy from frontier citizenry than did the Apaches. Their incessant raiding kept Arizonans in a perpetual state of turmoil. The agony they inflicted on their captives, torturing them with exquisite cruelty, nauseated people of the territory and instilled in them a burning thirst for revenge on any and all Apaches, as the Camp Grant Massacre demonstrated. Until the army proved capable of arresting Apache atrocities, Arizonans' antipathy to the Apaches would continue to glow white-hot.

Subduing the warlike elements among the Apaches and the Yavapais—the latter, a central Arizona indigenous people who were often mistaken for Apaches—would be difficult. As guerrilla fighters, the Apaches were matchless, the Yavapais only slightly less so. The Apaches had no use for the individual bravado that often animated Plains Indian warriors. The Apache, said a captain who fought them, "would prefer to skulk like the coyote for hours, and then kill his enemy rather than, by injudicious exposure, receive a wound, fatal or otherwise. The precautions taken for his safety prove that he is an exceptionally skillful soldier."

By the early 1870s, the Apaches were far better armed than any other Indians in the West. Nearly every warrior owned a repeating rifle. Bows and arrows were used principally for hunting, if at all. The Apaches believed that supernatural power was critical to success on raids or in war, and they adhered to its requirements and taboos as closely as did the Plains Indians. Apache warriors were mediocre horsemen, a short-coming they more than compensated for with remarkable endurance on foot. Unlike the Plains Indians, who took pride in their elaborate tipis, the Apaches lived in simple, dome-shaped circular shelters called wickiups, made of boughs and saplings bent together and covered with canvas or blankets or thatched with brush. The ease with which wicki-ups were made gave the Chiricahuas—and to a lesser degree the Western Apaches—far greater mobility year-round than the Plains Indians enjoyed.[3]

*

Colonel Stoneman's cavalier attitude toward Apache and Yavapai raid-ing epitomized the sorry state of military affairs in the Arizona Terri-tory, where two thousand troops were scattered among a dozen posts. Morale was low, desertion common. More troops would have deserted had there been somewhere to go, but settlements were sparse and widely separated, their occupants often "miserable vagabonds and fugi-tives from justice" more likely to rob and kill a deserter than help him.

Living conditions for the army in Arizona were execrable—so bad that one young army doctor feared he would blow his brains out before his tour was up. At Fort McDowell, the Potemkin village of Arizona posts, the gravel parade ground blazed a blinding white during the day, absorbing enough heat to keep the night air nearly as hot as the day-time temperature, which an officer said often exceeded 115 degrees in the shade "or would have done so if any shade could have been found." Officers and men lived in crude adobe structures that swarmed with venomous red ants and stank when the horse manure used to pack roof beams dampened. There were no vegetables or fruits, and dysentery was rampant. Hostile Indians prowled the perimeter at night, picking bullets out of targets and scrounging for glass bottles and tin cans, from which they fashioned arrowheads, which together with the recy-cled bullets they used against the soldiers.

For a multitude of reasons, garrisons frequently lacked the means to strike back. Transportation was limited and unreliable. Army wagons fell to pieces in the intense desert heat, and the want of horses often crippled the cavalry. Ammunition stocks were always low. The general reorganization of the army in July 1866 resulted in an intolerable breakdown in command cohesion in Apacheria: the New Mexico Territory became a district in the Department of the Missouri; the Arizona Territory was carved into four separate districts of the Department of California. With no stage line operating in Arizona, it took weeks for messages to reach department headquarters at San Francisco. Army doctrine, with its emphasis on conventional combat, was useless to officers waging counterguerrilla warfare in the desert. Despite these disadvantages, between 1866 and 1870 the army somehow managed to kill more Indians in Arizona than it lost in soldiers. Raids continued nonetheless. Territorial residents weighed the army's performance on the scale of raids and found it lacking. The Indians knew better: their losses in warriors were becoming unsustainable.

No Apache leader understood the grim logic of attrition better than Cochise, whose war against the Americans entered its tenth year in 1870. From his stronghold in the Dragoon Mountains of southeastern Arizona, Cochise continued to direct the struggle, until in August he did the unexpected: he proposed peace talks to the commanding officer at Camp Apache, Major John Green. "He was tired and wanted to sleep," reported Green. "The troops had killed almost all his band and worried him nearly to death." Calculating that "we were about even," Cochise called for a truce, but Green lacked the authority to treat with him. Persevering, Cochise went next to the Cañada Alamosa (Canyon of the Cottonwoods) Reservation, home to the Chihenne band of Chiricahuas. There he met a former Indian trader named Thomas Jeffords, with whom he developed a close friendship. At Cañada Alamosa, Cochise also spoke with an Indian Bureau special agent, to whom he reiterated his desire for peace and asked for permission to settle among the Chihennes. Returning to his mountain haunts to await a government decision, Cochise tried to control his warriors, but collisions with civilian posses and army patrols were inevitable. Cochise could find, as he put it, "no rest, no peace."

Cochise needed peace not only for his people, already reduced by war to fewer than four hundred, but also to prolong his own life. The warrior chief who had bested the U.S. Army for a decade was losing a slow battle with stomach cancer.[4]

*

Cochise's peace overtures coincided with a shake-up in the military administration of the Arizona Territory. In early 1870, Governor Anson P. K. Safford had persuaded the War Department to consolidate the territory's feckless military districts as the Department of Arizona. Unfortunately for Arizonans, Colonel Stoneman had received the command. Apathetic and out of touch, Stoneman refused to move his headquarters from San Francisco to the "hot, sickly town of Tucson," and he showed little concern for the endless Apache and Yavapai raids that paralyzed travel and forced ranchers and farmers to remain indoors during daylight hours. In December 1870, Stoneman tried to mollify Arizonans with a general order promising to prosecute "a relentless winter campaign," a pledge intended as a public-relations sop to the citizenry. Stoneman's heart was simply not in his work; he told General Sherman he expected peace commissioners to solve the Apache/Yavapai problem for him by an "exercise of moral and religious influence." So oblivious was Stoneman to the deteriorating conditions in his department that just two weeks before the Camp Grant Massacre he recommended that five posts be closed and the troops sent to other departments. An incredulous Safford demanded Stoneman's dismissal.[5]

The governor knew just the man to replace Stoneman: Lieutenant Colonel George Crook, then in San Francisco on a "Benzine Board" convened to weed out subpar officers. Crook, however, wanted nothing to do with the Arizona Territory. The command had been offered to him a year earlier; he had declined it on the grounds that "Indian fighting entailed hard work without any corresponding benefits." Besides, he had said, Arizona's blistering heat would ruin his health. Over Crook's objections, the governor pressed Washington to give him the command. Although the secretary of war and General Sherman both counseled against the appointment on the grounds that as a lieutenant colonel Crook was too junior for the job, President Grant acceded to Safford's entreaties. On May 17, 1871, Crook was assigned to command of the Department of Arizona until a suitable general could be found. Crook despaired. He not only found the notion of a "temporary command" distasteful, particularly in Arizona, but also worried his elevation over senior colonels would arouse the ire of the officer corps, which it did.[6]

No one could object to Crook's assignment on the basis of his

Indian-fighting record. Before coming to Arizona, he had seen longer and more arduous post–Civil War service against Indians than any other field-grade officer in the regular army. In December 1866, Crook had taken command of the District of Boise—the worst army command in the West. For two years, the Northern Paiutes had been waging a vicious guerrilla war with eastern Oregon and Idaho settlers. The army had proven worse than useless, with drunkenness and apathy rife among the officers. Crook had changed everything. Shortly after he arrived, Paiute war parties struck settlements near his headquarters. Crook took a cavalry company, a toothbrush, and a change of underwear and set off after them. He had intended to be gone only a week. "But," Crook recalled, "I got interested after the Indians and did not return there again for over two years." Crook pacified the country and then treated the defeated Indians wisely. He enlisted the toughest warriors as scouts and to the formerly hostile bands "made few promises, and none that he could not keep," said an aide, "and the peace then concluded lasted for a period of ten years. When broken . . . I am not so sure that it was not the fault of the white man."[7]

Although they praised the change in department commanders, Arizonans found the forty-year-old Crook something of a cipher. Independent-minded, stubborn, and sometimes hermetic, Crook seemed to delight in sparring with senior officers. He loved backwoods life, being, a staff officer said, "more of an Indian than the Indian himself." There was certainly little military in his appearance. He sported enormous blond muttonchops joined by a scraggly chin beard. On campaign, Crook braided his whiskers and tucked them into his blouse. In the field, he seldom wore a uniform.

At West Point, Crook had shown little promise, graduating near the bottom of his class, but he came into his own during the Civil War, rising from captain to major general of volunteers. During the 1864 Shenandoah Campaign, he commanded a corps under his friend and West Point roommate Phil Sheridan, who—placing ambition before friendship—took credit rightly due Crook for one particularly stunning Union victory. Crook never forgave Sheridan.[8]

Arriving in Arizona in June 1871, Crook established his headquarters at Whipple Barracks in Prescott and selected Lieutenant John G. Bourke of the Third Cavalry as aide-de-camp. From the standpoint of his image, Crook could not have chosen better. Capable, courageous, highly articulate, and intellectually curious, the young lieutenant became his commander's informal public-relations man. For the next fifteen years, their fortunes would be inextricably linked.[9]

Crook made his first target Cochise, whom he chalked up as an "uncompromising enemy to all civilization" despite his peace overtures, which the general dismissed as insincere. In July, Crook set out for Cochise's Dragoon Mountain stronghold with five cavalry companies. His chances of surprising Cochise, who had lookouts everywhere, were minimal at best, and they vanished altogether after an inept captain led his company across a valley in plain sight of every Apache within miles. Understandably furious, Crook canceled the operations. The outcome, however, was for the best: anything short of Cochise's destruction would likely have driven the ailing chief from his tentative path to peace back to full-scale war. Also, Crook's foray against the Apaches had given him firsthand knowledge of the theater of operations and had persuaded White Mountain Apaches—who had no love for the Chiricahuas—to sign on as scouts, an achievement Crook rightly judged "the entering wedge into solving the Apache problem."[10]

The wedge, however, would not immediately be widened by force. While planning a second campaign against Cochise, Crook unexpectedly received orders to stand down. A special commissioner was on his way from Washington to, as Crook put it, "make peace with the Apaches by the grace of God."

Although Crook bristled at the meddling, he was partly to blame for it. On assuming command, he had vowed to throttle the Apaches into submission, much as he had the Northern Paiutes. The well-intentioned philanthropists of the Board of Indian Commissioners cried foul, claiming that Crook's bellicosity ran contrary to the tenets of the newly inaugurated Peace Policy, which contemplated whenever possible the peaceable shepherding of the Indians onto reservations, where they were to be "civilized." The trouble was, Cochise's intentions were as yet uncertain, and there were in any event no reservations in Arizona to which Cochise's people might repair. It was the task of the special commissioner, the Indian Board's secretary, Vincent Colyer, to both negotiate peace and select suitable reservations. Convinced Colyer was a cat's-paw of Arizona's chapter of the consortium of swindlers and crooked officials known nationally as the Indian Ring, a disgusted Crook assailed both his motives and his competence. Bourke outdid his boss in contumely, calling Colyer a "spawn of hell." Territorial newspapers fitted rhetorical nooses around the commissioner's neck.[11]

While traveling through the Arizona Territory, Colyer created the vast White Mountain Indian Reservation to accommodate the thousands of Indians he assumed would yield to his supplications.[12] Otherwise, he accomplished nothing. Indian raids resumed as soon as Colyer departed. On November 5, 1871, a Yavapai war party ambushed a stagecoach near Wickenburg, killing seven of eight passengers. The so-called Wickenburg Massacre outraged the nation and discredited Colyer. Delighted to learn that "Vincent the Good" had been "decapitated," Crook readied his troops to take the field before other soft-headed peace emissaries appeared. In December, Crook announced that he would treat as hostile any Indian not on a reservation. He assured his superior officer, Major General John M. Schofield, that he would conquer a peace by spring; all he required "were a few more horses and to be let alone."[13]

Again the eastern peace element upset his calculations. Less than a week before Crook's offensive was to begin, Schofield ordered him to postpone operations to give another special commissioner a chance to carry on Colyer's work and, most important, to find and make peace with Cochise. The new commissioner was Brigadier General Oliver O. Howard.

There was no irony in Grant's selecting a soldier to forge peace without bloodshed. Called the Christian General, sometimes derisively, by his fellow officers, the forty-one-year-old New Englander was a deeply caring and humane man of genuine faith. Howard had lost an arm in battle, and after the Civil War was one of the privileged few to obtain a brigadier general's billet in the regular army. In May 1865, President Andrew Johnson appointed Howard commissioner of the newly created Bureau of Refugees, Freedmen, and Abandoned Lands to help emancipated slaves find their way in a free society. Although the Freedmen's Bureau fell afoul of partisan politics and stank of corruption, a guiltless Howard emerged untainted.

Howard and Crook had never met, and neither came away from Howard's courtesy call at department headquarters impressed with the other. Howard found Crook "peculiar and difficult to gauge," with eyes that "were really not open and transparent windows to his soul." Crook considered Howard delusional. "He told me that he thought the Creator had placed him on earth to be the Moses to the Negro. Having accomplished this mission, he felt satisfied his next mission was with the Indian. I was at a loss to make out whether it was his vanity or his cheek that enabled him to hold up his head in this lofty manner."[14]

Howard's religious fervor nearly sabotaged his mission. On April 30, 1872—exactly one year after the Camp Grant Massacre—he invited chiefs of the Western Apaches and their hereditary enemies the Pimas and the Papagos to a peace conference at Camp Grant. As he approached the Indian assemblage, Howard abruptly dropped to his knees and began to pray aloud, whereupon the chiefs scattered like quail. They returned only after Lieutenant Whitman assured them that the one-armed general's strange behavior had not been an act of bad medicine. After much speech making, they all agreed to a permanent peace, a promise they would keep. Much to Crook's relief—Howard's work at Camp Grant had failed to impress him—Howard left soon thereafter, having been unable to make contact with Cochise.

Crook, however, had not heard the last of Howard. Four months later, the Christian General returned to Apacheria determined to see Cochise, even at the cost of his own life. He made straight for Fort Tularosa, home to a new Chihenne Apache reservation. Members of Cochise's Chokonen band were known to frequent the place. Cochise's close friend Tom Jeffords was also there, building a trading post. Howard asked Jeffords to find Cochise and bring him in for a talk. Jeffords had no idea what to make of Howard, but he certainly had neither the time nor the inclination to act as his messenger, particularly when he believed Howard might well prove incapable of dealing with the fiery Chokonens "on account of his well-known humanitarian ideas, and to my mind, posing as a Christian soldier."

Jeffords thought he had an easy way out. "General Howard," he said, "Cochise won't come in. The man that wants to talk to Cochise must go where he is . . . I'll tell you what I'll do. I will take you to Cochise. Will you go there with me without soldiers?" To Jeffords's surprise, the general not only agreed but also appointed Jeffords agent for the "Cochise Reservation," which he intended to establish at Cañada Ala-mosa, assuming the chief agreed to his terms.

Howard had snared Jeffords. On September 19, 1872, they set out on the three-hundred-mile ride to Cochise's stronghold in the Dra-goon Mountains, accompanied by Howard's aide-de-camp and two of Cochise's relatives. The unlikely party rode between thirty and forty miles a day beneath a scorching desert sun, a merciless test of endur-ance for a man lacking a limb. On October 1, Howard and Cochise met. Their discussions were frank. Howard, who said he had come at the Great Father's behest to make peace, proposed uniting the Cho-

konens and the Chihennes at Cañada Alamosa. Cochise was pleased—
"nobody wants peace more than I do," he told Howard—but feared
the move would break up his band. He suggested instead a reservation
in the Chokonen homeland, a proposition his subchiefs agreed would
"cancel all old scores." In the interest of peace, Howard acquiesced. No
one committed the agreement to paper, but Howard reported the terms
as follows: The Chokonens would be granted a fifty-mile-wide reservation between the Dragoon and the Chiricahua Mountains from which
the army would be barred; Thomas Jeffords would be their agent; and
the government would supply the Chokonens with food and clothing.
In return, Cochise agreed to cease warring on Arizonans.

Jeffords confessed that his first impression of Howard had been
wrong. "I doubt if there is any other person that could have been sent
here [and] performed the mission as well," he said. "Certainly none
could have performed it better." Governor Safford, who visited Cochise a month later and came away admiring the former scourge of the
territory, warmly thanked General Howard for "having done his duty
nobly." Crook, on the other hand, abstained from the chorus of accolades, claiming only to know that Howard had reached some sort of
agreement with the Apaches "by the grace of God and prayer."[15]

Crook's pettiness did him no credit. He should have thanked Howard. Despite his insistence on diplomacy with Cochise, Howard agreed
that only force would bring the hostile Yavapais and Western Apaches
to terms. Official Washington concurred. Cochise was off-limits, but
Crook at last was free to launch an offensive against the other troublesome tribes.

*

Crook's force would be unorthodox, to say the least. Availing himself of
the innate Apache love of fighting, he offered full army pay to warriors
willing to turn against their own people (he had plenty of takers). In
violation of army regulations, Crook hired experienced civilian mule
packers to create a pack-train service capable of negotiating the most
rugged Arizona terrain. He showed his faith in the ornery beasts of
burden by riding a mule in the field himself.

His operational plan was simple. He would send preliminary columns against the Yavapais west of the Verde River, battling bands that
stood their ground and driving the rest over the Mazatzal Mountains

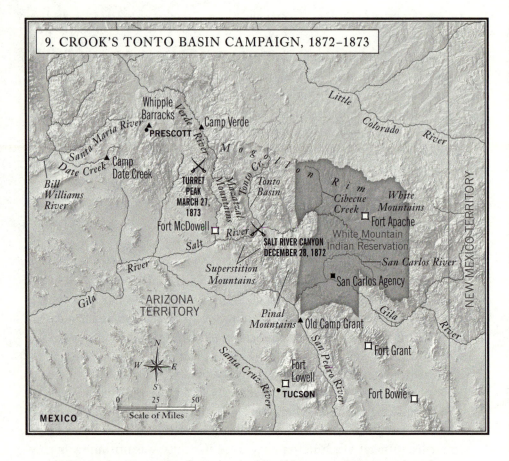

9. CROOK'S TONTO BASIN CAMPAIGN, 1872–1873

and into the Tonto Basin, a semiarid wilderness of chaparral and ponderosa pine that was home not only to the Yavapais but also to several hostile Western Apache bands. Crook would then close the ring with converging columns of Indian scouts and soldiers—starving, freezing, or fighting the Indians into surrender. Column commanders were to make every effort to spare women and children, to treat prisoners of both sexes humanely, and to encourage male prisoners to enlist as scouts. No excuse would be tolerated for quitting the field; if the horses played out, the soldiers were to continue on foot. Crook expected the campaign to be "short, sharp, and decisive."[16]

The columns took the field on November 15, 1872. Crook's new aide-de-camp, Lieutenant Bourke, decided to accompany Major William H. Brown's 220-man force of two dismounted cavalry companies and detachment of Pima and Apache scouts, which proved to be a good choice for a junior officer in search of action. After five weeks in the field, Brown's scouts found a fresh trail in the rugged Mazatzal

Mountains that led to a narrow mesa terminating in a Yavapai strong-hold. The difficulty rested in getting there, because the trail was narrow and rocky, with a steep cactus-studded slope falling away on one side to the swift-flowing Salt River far below. A sharp wind swirled through the mountains, seemingly calculated to trip up the unwary. Brown rested his men for a day and then, on the cold and cloudy afternoon of December 28, set out to find the stronghold. To muffle their approach, the soldiers marched in moccasins. The night came on cold and moonless, but the pitch dark was no obstacle to finding the Yavapais. A roaring bonfire beckoned Brown to their stronghold—a small, elliptical cave carved into a rocky palisade and screened by a ten-foot-high sandstone rampart. On the near side, warriors danced in celebration of recent raids while children looked on and women cooked. The Yavapais had posted no sentinels. No outsiders had ever penetrated their mountain fastness, and they had no reason to believe this night would be different.

Brown's men crept to within thirty-five yards of the Yavapais and then opened fire with a crashing volley that reverberated in the dark mountains. Terrified women and children stumbled into the cave. Startled warriors ducked behind the rampart and fired blindly through the bonfire. Major Brown called on them to surrender; the Yavapais responded with hoots of derision—that is, until rocks rained down on them, hurled by soldiers who had clawed up the palisade to the bluff overlooking the cave. From inside came the baleful and monotonous intoning of death songs. Determined to finish the business rapidly, Major Brown ordered his men to ricochet bullets off the roof of the cave into the unseen mass of Indians. In three minutes, the cave fell silent. Lieutenant Bourke stepped inside. "A horrible spectacle was disclosed to view. In one corner eleven dead bodies were huddled, in another four; and in different crevices they were piled to the extent of the little cave." Fifty-seven warriors and nineteen women and children perished in the Battle of Salt River Canyon (also known as the Battle of Skull Cave or Skeleton Cave). Brown had obliterated the Yavapai band of a chief whom Vincent Colyer had showered with gifts the year before and who had boasted to Colyer that "no troops had found his retreat and none ever would."[17]

Crook's columns clashed with the Yavapais and the Western Apaches nineteen times in the Tonto Basin during the winter of 1872–1873, killing an estimated 150 Indians. But the survivors slipped through the army cordon and defiantly raided isolated homesteads and ambushed unwary travelers. Crook retaliated with more punitive expeditions. On the evening of March 27, 1873, one of his columns struck a Yavapai *ranchería* atop Turret Peak on the west bank of the Verde River. The slaughter exceeded Crook's expectations, and he reported, "So secure did [the Indians] feel in this almost impregnable position that they lost all presence of mind. Some jumped off the precipice and were mashed into a shapeless mass. All of the men were killed; most of the women and children were taken prisoner."

Turret Peak broke the back of Yavapai resistance. Indians drifted into the army camps, emaciated and clothed in rags. "We surrender to you not because we love you but because you have directed some of our [people] against us," the principal Yavapai chief told Crook when surrendering his twenty-three hundred followers. "You have divided our tribe in two . . . So I want to make peace and will do exactly what you tell me to do." Crook the warrior had triumphed. Now Crook the humanitarian stepped forward. He told the chief that "if he would promise to live in peace and stop killing people, he would be the best friend he ever had." Crook kept his promise, helping the Yavapais establish farms on the Camp Verde Reservation. He admonished his officers not to judge Indians harshly for small crimes against the white man's laws, being careful to treat them as "children in ignorance, not in innocence."[18]

The Grant administration amply rewarded Crook for his success, jumping him from lieutenant colonel to brigadier general and making his assignment as department commander permanent. As Crook had feared, his promotion infuriated the army's officer corps. None harbored greater bitterness than Colonel Nelson Miles. From that day forward, he loathed Crook. The defeated Yavapais, on the other hand, harbored no ill will against their conqueror. They respected a white man whose actions matched his words, even if those actions came at their expense. And Crook's ability to penetrate their most remote sanctuaries overawed them. Certain that a sacred predator must have favored him with the power of stealth, they named him Nantan Lupan, the "Gray Wolf Chief."

Nantan Lupan was not above giving himself and his men a hearty pat on the back. Proclaiming the Tonto Basin Campaign "second to none in the annals of Indian warfare," Crook imprudently boasted that he had "closed an Indian war that has been waged since the days of Cortez."

Six weeks later, the reservations erupted in violence.

*

The trouble began on the White Mountain Reservation, where the scoundrel of an Indian agent encouraged discord among the Western Apaches, employing a turbulent faction to browbeat honest agency employees who questioned his crooked contracts. The agent's combustible mix of intimidation and pampering ignited on ration day in May 1873, when the agent's Indian thugs murdered a young lieutenant during a scuffle. Having thus signed their own death warrants, they set out to despoil settlements. A furious Crook gave notice that no surrender would be accepted until the leaders were brought in, dead or alive, preferably the latter. No sooner had the White Mountain Reservation boiled over than the Yavapai chief Delshay, who had tearfully begged mercy on surrendering a month earlier, quit the Camp Verde Reservation and went on the warpath.[19]

Before unleashing his troops and Apache scouts, Crook offered the renegades a way out: bring in the heads of the wanted leaders and their sins would be forgiven. When no heads materialized, Crook commenced operations, battering the hostile bands mercilessly. Dozens of warriors perished, but the leaders always managed to slip away. Crook's terms began to look more appealing to their dwindling followers, who now vied with Apache scouts for the chance to decapitate the chiefs. Within a year, the heads of all but Delshay were brought in and neatly displayed on the Camp Apache parade ground. When Delshay's head finally rolled, it drew rival claimants. Three Tonto Apaches from Camp Verde swore they had killed him and brought in a scalp and an ear to prove it. A warrior from the White Mountain Reservation claimed the honor, offering as evidence a severed head. The gruesome competition amused Crook. "Being satisfied that both parties were earnest in their beliefs, and the bringing in of an extra head was not amiss, I paid both parties."[20]

*

There was one Apache head, metaphorically speaking, that remained beyond Crook's grasp—that of Cochise. Contemptuous of Howard's work, Crook cast about for a pretext to make war. When Cochise's warriors resumed their time-honored raids in Mexico just weeks after Howard had departed, Crook thought he had a legitimate reason to attack. Given the power of the peace element in Washington, however, he needed to be certain, and so in late January 1873 he sent Major Brown, fresh from his victory at Salt River Canyon, to ask Cochise what he and Howard had agreed upon respecting Mexico. "The Mexicans are on one side in this matter and the Americans on another," Cochise told Brown. "There are many young people whose parents and relatives have been killed by the Mexicans, and now these young people are liable to go down from time to time and do a little damage to the Mexicans. I don't want to lie about this thing; they go, but I don't send them." That was not what Crook had wanted to hear. It was evident, however, Cochise considered himself in compliance with Howard's treaty. Reluctantly, Crook scrapped plans to fight the Chokonens.[21]

It really didn't matter. Cochise would not trouble Crook much longer. He was dying of stomach cancer. To relieve the incessant pain, Cochise drank heavily. He grew feeble and thin. Nightmares plagued his sleep. He was certain the spirits of the white men he had killed had returned to torment him. He watched for omens in the dancing flames of campfires. He told his warriors that a visiting Chihenne female had bewitched him. They nearly burned the woman to death before cooler heads prevailed. Despite his agony, Cochise remained lucid enough to remember his pledge to General Howard. His last instructions to his people were "to forever live at peace" with the whites and to do as their agent Tom Jeffords instructed them. Cochise named his elder son, Taza, by nature a peaceable young man, to succeed him as chief.

On the evening of June 7, 1874, Jeffords and Cochise talked for the last time. Cochise asked Jeffords if he thought they would see each other in the hereafter. Jeffords had no answer. "I have been thinking a good deal about it while I have been sick here, and I believe we will," said Cochise, pointing to the sky. "Good friends will meet again—up there." Cochise died the next morning in the fastness of his Dragoon Mountain stronghold. Nine months later, General Crook departed to assume command of the distant Department of the Platte. His replacement was Colonel August V. "Dutch" Kautz, a mediocre officer whose Indian-fighting credentials were nil. At a farewell reception, Crook assured Arizonans, perhaps disingenuously, that they could reckon on Kautz to be "a man of action and deeds."[22]

He would have to be. Out of the general peace prevailing in the Arizona Territory, the Indian Bureau had fashioned a ticking time bomb. In late 1874, Washington bureaucrats had decided Arizona was ready for the concentration policy, whereby Indians already settled on small reservations would be moved—forcibly if necessary—to large reservations, there to be freed, theoretically at least, from the baleful influence of frontier ruffians. No one seemed to reckon on the chance that the ruffians who preyed upon the smaller reservations would simply relocate to the larger and more lucrative targets. In any case, the Yavapais, Western Apaches, and Chiricahuas would be brought together on the 2.5-million-acre White Mountain Indian Reservation in eastern Arizona, which Colyer had created and General Howard expanded during their peace missions. The San Carlos Agency, at the confluence of the Gila and San Carlos Rivers in the desert wasteland that constituted the southern extremity of the reservation, would administer the sprawling concern. The army post Camp Apache served as an informal agency for those Indians living in the picturesque, game-rich mountain country of the northern half of the reservation.

In endorsing the concentration policy, the Board of Indian Commissioners had urged the government to keep hereditary enemies apart. In the Arizona Territory, the Indian Bureau ignored its own counsel. As mutually hostile tribes and bands were thrown together at White Mountain, the timer began ticking toward trouble.

The first Indian agent at the White Mountain Reservation was John P. Clum. An arrogant and ambitious twenty-two-year-old, "hardly out of baby grass," as one scornful Apache put it, Clum accelerated the countdown. Contentious by nature, he went out of his way to antagonize the army. He particularly resented the influence that the military leadership at Camp Apache exercised over the northern bands. The only way Clum could fight back was to congregate as many Indians as possible in the idle desert of the San Carlos Agency. And so he did.

First Clum drove the high-country Yavapais from the farms and fields they had carefully cultivated at the Camp Verde Reservation under Crook's benevolent administration. Then he burned the Camp Apache Agency of the White Mountain Reservation and carted off its supplies to San Carlos to compel the White Mountain Apaches to move. Seven hundred northerners followed him, but eleven hundred refused to relocate, including the Indian scouts at Camp Apache and their families. Clum knew better than to press the matter.

The Chiricahuas' turn came in June 1876. By then the easygoing administration of Tom Jeffords had attracted nearly as many Apaches from other bands as there were Chokonens on the Chiricahua Reservation. Cochise's son Taza, meanwhile, was proving a weak leader. He commanded the loyalty of only a third of the Indians, perhaps 325 in all. Honoring his late father's stricture on violence against whites, Taza and his followers went quietly to San Carlos.

"San Carlos! That was the worst place in all the great territory stolen from Apaches," remembered a Chiricahua warrior. "The heat was terrible. The insects were terrible. The water was terrible. At times it was so hot that I am sure the thermometer registered well above 120 degrees." All in all, said another warrior, "it was considered a good place for the Apaches—a good place for them to die." Fast on the heels of the departed Chiricahuas, settlers and ranchers poured onto their former reservation, and the Chokonen homeland abruptly vanished.

Not all the Chiricahuas accepted the exodus, however. Nearly four hundred who rejected Taza's authority fled to Sonora, where they melted into old haunts in the Sierra Madre and pursued their favorite pastime of plundering Mexicans. Among their leaders was a mercurial medicine man named Geronimo.[23]

CHAPTER 11

SITTING BULL AND CRAZY HORSE

"I SEE. I KNOW. I began to see when I was not yet born; when I was not in my mother's arms, but inside of my mother's belly. It was there that I began to study about my people," Chief Sitting Bull once told a reporter. "God gave me the power to see out of the womb. I studied there, in the womb, about many things. I studied about the small-pox that was killing my people—the great sickness that was killing the women and children. I was so interested that I turned over on my side."[1]

Sitting Bull never ceased to study about his people, the Hunkpapa Lakotas. Their welfare was his obsession. No threats, no bribes, no offers of annuities or gifts, no peace overtures, could sway him from a fixed determination to fight for his people, their land, and the traditional way of life. He spoke, and people listened.

Sitting Bull was born in 1831 below the mouth of the Yellowstone River. His mother named him Jumping Badger. At age fourteen, Jumping Badger counted his first coup, after which, as was customary, his father, Buffalo Bull Sits Down, bestowed his name on his son, a name whites incorrectly translated as Sitting Bull. Over the next decade, young Sitting Bull counted at least two dozen more coups and was wounded three times in fights with the Crows and the Pawnees, including a bullet wound in the foot that gave him a permanent limp. Sitting Bull became an officer in four men's societies, which was a remarkable achievement, because most warriors were fortunate merely to gain membership in one society. By the mid-1860s, only Sitting Bull's uncle Four Horns stood higher than he in the Hunkpapa war hierarchy. Sitting Bull also enjoyed a growing reputation as a *Wichasha Wakan*, a holy man with the gift of prophecy obtained from dreams, visions, and direct communication with *Wakan Tanka*, the Great Mystery, source of all seen and unseen.

Sitting Bull the war leader and holy man personified the four Lakota cardinal virtues of bravery, fortitude, generosity, and wisdom. But he remained humble, even timid by some accounts. Sitting Bull dressed simply, abjuring the warbonnet in favor of a single white eagle feather (signifying his first coup) or occasionally a second eagle feather painted red (signifying his first wound). He was a good listener and did not interrupt others. He made no claims to superiority and took no offense when people rejected his counsel or discounted his visions. He had a keen sense of humor and excelled at pantomime and mimicry. He also suffered from deep spells of depression. The two constants in his character were his distrust of white men and his belief, which he forced upon no one, that God had chosen him "to be the judge of all other Indians." Soon Sitting Bull's fame extended throughout the Lakota tribes. "Yet he seems to have taken it in a dull sort of way," said a missionary. "It took an occasion—a crisis—to arouse him out of his introverted, contemplative satisfaction to extrovert action."[2]

*

The crisis that first stirred Sitting Bull to leadership against the whites was the construction in 1866 of Fort Buford at the confluence of the Yellowstone and Missouri Rivers. Just as Forts C. F. Smith and Phil Kearny—also built in 1866—had threatened the hunting grounds of Red Cloud's Oglalas, so too did Fort Buford presage an intolerable white intrusion into the Hunkpapa country. Sitting Bull could not match Red Cloud's exploits, however. In two and a half years of intermittent warfare, he was unable to overwhelm a garrison that often mustered no more than fifty men. But Fort Buford's resilience did not diminish Sitting Bull's determination to resist. To an abject group of reservation Assiniboins, Sitting Bull articulated his creed. Better to go deep into the buffalo country and fend for oneself than depend on the white man's gifts to survive. "Look at me," he challenged his listeners. "See if I am poor, or my people either. The whites may get me at last, as you say, but I will have good times till then. You are fools to make yourselves slaves to a piece of bacon, some hardtack, and a little sugar and coffee."[3]

By Sitting Bull's reckoning, most of the Lakotas had become fools when Red Cloud and his chiefs signed the Fort Laramie Treaty in 1868. Within four years, the "fools" made up nearly 90 percent of an estimated Lakota population of 15,000. Only half of the 2,000 Hunkpapas stood by Sitting Bull. Fewer than one in four of the 4,000 Oglalas rejected the treaty; the remainder, together with some 1,500 Cheyennes and 1,000 Northern Arapahos, gravitated to the Red Cloud Agency. Nearly all of the estimated Brulé population of 4,050 lived on the Spotted Tail Agency. Sitting Bull and the others who spurned the 1868 Fort Laramie Treaty became known as the non-treaty bands—or as hostiles when it suited the government's purpose.[4]

Categorizing Lakotas as reservation or non-treaty was problematic at best. Non-treaty Lakotas frequently visited their kinsmen on the reservations and even attached themselves to agencies to draw rations, particularly during the winter months. Conversely, the Unceded Indian Territory offered a refuge for reservation Indians disgruntled with government regulations or who merely wanted an occasional taste of the old freedom. Each spring, Lakotas left the reservations to join their free-roaming relatives, returning to the agencies after the autumn buffalo hunt. The Lakota tide in the Unceded Indian Territory thus rose in the summer and ebbed in the winter.

Sitting Bull rode no tide save his own constant adherence to the old life. Red Cloud and the Oglalas might do as they wish. As for himself, he would sell no part of his people's country. Neither would he repudiate the time-honored Lakota practice of expanding its domain by forcibly displacing other tribes. For nearly two decades, the Lakotas had struggled to wrest the buffalo-rich Powder River country from the Crows, an objective they obtained in the early 1860's. Within a decade, however, the largest herds had migrated deeper into what remained of the Crow country. For the next six years, Sitting Bull would dedicate his efforts to driving the Crows entirely from the plains and into the mountains. The whites, who as yet only rubbed against the eastern fringe of his world, he deemed a lesser threat.[5]

Sitting Bull's actions carried far greater weight now. No longer was he merely a Hunkpapa war chief. At a grand council of non-treaty Lakotas in the summer of 1869, his uncle Four Horns had engineered his nephew's promotion to supreme chief of the Lakotas—or rather, of those Lakotas who rejected reservation life. It had been a bold move, and many had refused to accept Sitting Bull's ascension to a position alien to the Lakotas' political culture. But hundreds of Hunkpapas, Blackfeet, Sans Arcs, Oglalas, Miniconjous, and even Northern Cheyennes, to whom Sitting Bull was an unknown quantity, had supported Four Horns's proposal. At the conclusion of the ceremony, Four Horns had turned to his nephew and said, "For your bravery on the battlefields and as the greatest warrior of our bands, we have elected you as our war chief, leader of the entire Sioux nation. When you tell us to fight, we shall fight, when you tell us to make peace, we shall make peace."[6]

Sitting Bull was not the only prominent Lakota to espouse the old ways. There was a strange young Oglala war leader, not yet known to him, who was just as passionately committed to the same cause. His name was Crazy Horse.

*

People thought Crazy Horse peculiar, a loner fit only for war. He often wandered the prairies alone—seeking visions, hunting, or stealing horses from enemy tribes. When in camp, he seldom spoke, appearing distracted, distant, as if human contact were more than he could bear. He shunned councils and peace talks—anything that smacked of politics, scheming, or intrigue, not merely with whites, but also with fellow Lakotas. He had no interest in the annual Sun Dance, which was the greatest of all Lakota religious ceremonies, nor did he trouble himself with sacred rituals. He never posed for a photograph, for fear the camera would rob him of his soul. He dressed plainly, lived in poverty, and gave his best horses and the fruits of the hunt to the poor. Crazy Horse never owned a warbonnet, and he rode into combat naked except for a breechcloth. His physiognomy mystified both Indians and whites. According to a warrior who knew him as well as anyone could, he was "not very tall and not very short, neither broad nor thin. His hair was very light [and he] had a light complexion, much lighter than other Indians. His face was not broad, and he had a high, sharp nose." Although given to sidelong glances, Crazy Horse "didn't miss much that was going on, all the same." His perpetually youthful appearance, pale skin, and fine hip-length hair imparted to him an androgynous quality. An Indian agent described the man at age thirty-six as a "bashful girlish looking boy."

Upon one point all agreed: Crazy Horse was an outstanding warrior, perhaps the ablest of his generation on the northern plains. The

Oglalas understood and accepted him for what he was. "Crazy Horse was not accounted good for anything among the Indians but to make war," asserted his personal medicine man. War honors and trophies, however, were unimportant to Crazy Horse. He never took scalps and often permitted aspiring warriors to count coups that were rightfully his. Crazy Horse closely followed the military adage of inflicting maximum casualties at minimal expense. A friend admired his reluctance to do battle "unless he had it all planned out in his head and knew he was going to win. He always used [good] judgment and played [it] safe."

Except when it came to romance. Still single at thirty, he wanted a woman who was another man's wife. Not only was she married, but Black Buffalo Woman was also the niece of Red Cloud. On top of that, her husband was Crazy Horse's rival as war leader. Crazy Horse's lust for Black Buffalo Woman, however, got the better of him, and he made off with her while her husband was away fighting the Crows. When he returned, the cuckold tracked the couple down and shot Crazy Horse in the head with a revolver at point-blank range. Remarkably, after a long convalescence, Crazy Horse recovered, but the incident traumatized the entire Oglala tribe. Crazy Horse had committed adultery while a "shirt wearer." There were four shirt wearers in each Lakota tribe, elected by the tribal council of elders to enforce council edicts and set standards of moral rectitude. Needless to say, Crazy Horse had failed miserably on the latter score, and he was stripped of his office. No one replaced him, and soon afterward the position of shirt wearer lost its meaning. Despite his transgression, Crazy Horse's martial talents and his sway over the young men were too great to cast him aside. His personal life might have been in tatters, but Crazy Horse's best days as a war leader lay ahead of him.[7]

*

After Sitting Bull's investiture as head chief of the non-treaty Lakotas, his uncle Four Horns advised him to "be a little against fighting. But when anyone shoots be ready to fight him."

Four Horns's counsel, however, applied only to whites; Crows continued to be fair game. Sitting Bull and Crazy Horse led the push to dispossess the Crows of their remaining hunting grounds in the early 1870s, but many from the treaty bands fought with them, as did the Northern Cheyennes and, to a lesser degree, their Northern Arapaho allies. The architects of the Fort Laramie Treaty of 1868 had included Crow land within the Unceded Indian Territory, which made Lakota aggression perfectly legal. But it threatened the citizens of southwestern Montana, who had counted on the Crows as a buffer between themselves and Lakotas, and the governor appealed for federal intervention. Generals Sherman and Sheridan made it a matter of unofficial policy to supply the Crows with arms. Each side benefited: settlers felt safer, and the army winked at Crow retaliatory raids against the Lakotas.[8]

The Crows had it hard, but none suffered more for their fidelity to the Great Father than did the Pawnees. Agency Oglala and Brulé warriors raided Pawnee villages in central Nebraska with the implicit support of Red Cloud and Spotted Tail, who saw nothing amiss in young warriors sating their hunger for war honors at the expense of tribal enemies. Certainly it was preferable to unwinnable wars with the whites. In August 1873, at least eight hundred Lakota warriors, perhaps led by Spotted Tail himself, fell upon a Pawnee hunting party in southwestern Nebraska, killing a hundred, of whom nearly half were women and children. Only the timely appearance of a cavalry detachment prevented a greater slaughter.

The massacre broke the spirit of the Pawnees. Nebraskans who recalled the protection that the Pawnees had afforded Union Pacific work crews in their state were outraged and demanded the government give the Pawnees the best available arms in order to meet the Lakotas on an equal footing. Instead, the Indian Bureau banished the Pawnees to Indian Territory. In their single-minded ambition to remake the *hostile* tribes into white men, the eastern humanitarians did not lift a finger to forestall this unpardonable act of bad faith.[9]

*

While the non-treaty Northern Cheyennes and Lakotas drove the Crows westward, a threat developed in the rear of the allied tribes, courtesy of the financier Jay Cooke. God had put Cooke on this earth to do his work—at least that's what Jay Cooke believed. During the Civil War, Cooke had become a multimillionaire selling Treasury notes for the government. In 1869, he found a new undertaking worthy of the Lord's instrument: financing the moribund Northern Pacific Railway. Four years earlier, Congress had enacted legislation providing land grants to aid in the construction of a railroad line from Lake

Superior to Puget Sound. Perhaps because a northerly route through untamed, unsettled, and unknown country offered little prospect of near-term economic gain, Congress offered no mileage loans to finance the work, such as had been granted the Union Pacific and Central Pacific Railroads.

In 1869, few questioned the importance of transcontinental railroads in settling the "Indian question." Secretary of the Interior Jacob D. Cox stood in awe of the newly completed Union Pacific. It had "totally changed the conditions under which the civilized populations of the country come in contact with the wild tribes. Instead of slowly advancing the tide of immigration, making its gradual inroads upon the circumference of the great interior wilderness, the very center of the desert has been pierced."[10]

Seemingly every railroad station, be it small and ramshackle or large and grandly built, had become, where the land permitted, the nucleus of an agricultural settlement and a base for mineral explorers. A leapfrogging population also eliminated the need for a huge cordon of troops to protect a slow-moving white frontier. To the poorly funded and understrength postwar regular army, the benefit was incalculable. General Sherman had made protection of the Union Pacific construction crews the army's top priority on the frontier in the first years after the Civil War. Now he was prepared to offer the same shield to the Northern Pacific. Sherman reckoned the effort a fair gamble if it helped to close the circle on the recalcitrant Northern Plains bands.

Until Jay Cooke & Company, the nation's largest banking firm, stepped in to finance the operation, the Northern Pacific had existed largely in blueprints and the imaginations of a corrupt board of directors. Surveys had been completed from Duluth, Minnesota, west to the Missouri River, and from Tacoma, Washington, east to Bozeman in the Montana Territory. The prospect of losing their scalps to nontreaty Lakotas, however, had kept surveyors out of the intervening Yellowstone River valley.

Bankrolled by Cooke, the Northern Pacific sent two survey parties with strong military escorts into the uncharted region in autumn 1871. The Lakotas did not interfere. Adhering to Four Horns's counsel that he maintain a strictly defensive posture against the whites, Sitting Bull dispatched emissaries to inquire whether they meant to run the iron horse through the Yellowstone country.

Crazy Horse also favored a defensive posture. He and Sitting Bull had only just met that summer during the annual midyear mingling of non-treaty Lakotas in the Powder River country, and they had a natural affinity for each other. Thenceforward, the roving Oglalas and Hunkpapas would be bound by a common destiny.[11]

Sitting Bull's emissaries returned without having gotten a clear answer. The government's intentions, however, became obvious the following spring when a second pair of survey teams with an even heavier military presence squeezed the Lakota country from two directions. Their objective was to complete the final 225 miles of the Northern Pacific survey, through the Yellowstone valley from Glendive Creek to present-day Billings. The expedition commanders were Major Eugene M. Baker, the perpetrator of the Piegan Massacre, and Colonel David S. Stanley. Baker would march east from Bozeman, Stanley west from Fort Rice, near the future site of Bismarck, North Dakota. Neither commander was such as to inspire confidence. Baker was still a hopeless drunk. Colonel Stanley had compiled an estimable record during the Civil War, but the postwar years had been hard on the forty-three-year-old Ohioan, and he too turned to the bottle until, by the date of the expedition, he teetered on the brink of alcoholism. Prolonged stress in particular caused him to binge drink. Assuming these commanding officers remained sober and all proceeded according to plan, the expeditions would meet at the confluence of the Yellowstone and Powder Rivers.[12]

Stanley got a foretaste of what he might be up against when the Sans Arc war chief Spotted Eagle called on him at Fort Sully in April 1872 to warn that "he would fight the railroad people as long as he lived, would tear up the road, and kill its builders." To Stanley's objection that such action would not only be futile but also doom his people, Spotted Eagle said that the railroads drove away the buffalo, which meant certain death in any event.

Before Stanley started, the assistant secretary of the interior traveled to Fort Peck, Montana Territory, to hold a council with the non-treaty chiefs. Attending in his place, Sitting Bull's brother-in-law said the chief wanted no trouble with the whites. He intended to fight the Crows and would come in and talk peace "when the snow flies."

But Baker's expedition upended his plans. Sitting Bull and Crazy Horse were traveling west with one thousand warriors to kill Crows when wolves brought word that Baker's camp lay within easy striking distance. The chiefs were outraged; hadn't Spotted Eagle made clear their objections to survey parties on the Yellowstone? On the evening of August 13, the war party halted undetected on the south bank of the Powder opposite Baker's camp, which was nestled in a cottonwood stand on the north bank near the junction of the Powder River and a narrow, meandering stream called Arrow, or Pryor, Creek.

The chiefs gathered to debate a course of action. During the night, their young warriors grew weary of waiting. First a trickle and then a flood of young men—including Sitting Bull's nephew White Bull, who had bluffed his way past a cordon of *akicitas* (village police) with the excuse that he needed to "pass water"—crossed the Yellowstone and inched toward the sleeping soldiers. Most of the army camp was in bed, including Baker, who lay dead drunk in his tent. The action opened when an overeager warrior startled a sleeping civilian, and a blind exchange of gunfire ensued. A senior captain darted into Baker's tent for orders, but the major was too "stupefied with drink" to recognize the danger. The captain took charge and repulsed the warriors.[13]

When Sitting Bull came on the scene at daybreak, he found the warriors arrayed on a long, low bluff north of Baker's camp. Heavy Indian fire kept the soldiers pinned down in the timber. Neither side seemed inclined to break the stalemate; that is, until four soldiers tossed the body of a Hunkpapa killed in the opening fray onto a campfire. That stirred a cocky and ambitious warrior named Long Holy into a reckless display of braggadocio. He had had a vision, the typical my-power-will-render-you-bulletproof dream. Long Holy persuaded White Bull and six other men to follow him down the bluff. Within minutes, four of his seven followers were wounded. Sitting Bull galloped onto the plain to halt the pointless display; White Bull was happy to stand down, but not Long Holy. He sulked about the bluff, blaming the setback on a follower who wore a color that broke his medicine and complaining about Sitting Bull's interference. "The great warrior Tatanka Ioytake [Sitting Bull] perhaps has forgotten what it takes to be brave," challenged Long Holy. "It is said with age, blood upsets a man's stomach!" The young upstart had, in effect, accused the supreme chief of cowardice.

Sitting Bull took his pipe bag and tobacco and limped down the bluff. After reaching a spot midway between the lines, he sat down and calmly began the pipe-smoking ceremony. Glancing back, Sitting Bull shouted, "Any Indians who wish to smoke with me, come on!" Long Holy skulked away. But White Bull and three other warriors—two of them Cheyennes—accepted the challenge. Leaving their horses behind, they joined Sitting Bull and then squatted opposite him. After a leisurely smoke, Sitting Bull handed the pipe to the warriors. "We wasted no time," said White Bull. "Our hearts beat rapidly, and we smoked as fast as we could. All around us the bullets were kicking up the dust. But Sitting Bull was not afraid. He just sat there quietly, looking around as if he were at home in his tent, and smoked peacefully." White Bull, on the other hand, closed his eyes, lowered his head to his knees, and prepared to die. The pipe empty, Sitting Bull cleaned the bowl, gathered up the paraphernalia, and hobbled back to the bluff. White Bull and the others sprinted past him, one warrior so shaken up that he left his bow and arrows behind. Sitting Bull's exhibition of courage silenced his critics. When he said, "That's enough, we must quit," everyone obeyed.

The Indians drew off. Their first challenge to the Northern Pacific had fallen short of Spotted Eagle's threat to kill all the builders, but the fight at Pryor Creek unnerved Major Baker, who declined to escort the surveyors farther. Understandably, they were unwilling to go on alone, and so on August 20, well short of the planned rendezvous with Stanley, the expedition turned back.

Stanley had also failed the field-sobriety test. On at least three occasions, he had gone on a bender, remaining sober just often enough to shepherd the survey team safely to its objective, where, instead of finding Baker as planned, Stanley encountered the Hunkpapa chief Gall, a close friend and able ally of Sitting Bull's who threatened to "bring all the bands and give us a big fight."

Nothing came of Gall's threat. Nevertheless, Lakota defiance had raised serious doubts about the viability of building the Northern Pacific Railway through the Yellowstone River country. The army's Crow allies judged the soldiers beaten. "You say the railroad is coming," a Crow chief said, "that it is like the whirlwind and cannot be turned back. I don't think it will come. The Sioux are in the way, and you are afraid of them; they will turn the whirlwind back."[14]

Generals Sherman and Sheridan were not so easily deterred. "That Northern Pacific Railroad is going to give you a great deal of trouble," Sherman wrote to Sheridan confidentially in late 1872. "Yet I think our interest is to favor the undertaking of the road, as it will help to bring the Indian problem to a final solution." Reminding a parsimonious Congress that "the railroad was a national enterprise demanding army protection," he and Sheridan pleaded for more cavalry to guard the survey teams and work crews. And the right man for the job was not only available but also eager to return to frontier duty. That man was George Armstrong Custer.[15]

*

Custer's triumphant return from his early 1869 campaign against the Southern Cheyennes had marked the start of a tumultuous four years of personal anguish and exaltation, elusive fortune and shining celebrity, boredom and excitement. Whether a consequence of his probable dalliance with the Cheyenne girl Monahsetah or a rumored wandering eye, Custer's storybook marriage had briefly foundered. No sooner had his personal life mended than the Seventh Cavalry was reassigned to Reconstruction duty. Custer paused to consider his future. In the shrinking regular army, the prospects for advancement appeared dim. Obtaining a seven-month leave of absence, he went to New York City to explore business opportunities, and Libbie returned to Monroe. Custer the human whirlwind promoted a Colorado mining scheme to wealthy financiers, cultivated conservative Democrats and newspaper editors hostile to the Grant administration, partied with high society, attended horse races at Saratoga, and frequented casinos. He made no headway toward a civilian career, however. For the foreseeable future at least, he remained wedded to the army.

In February 1873, Custer, then thirty-three, returned to the plains. General Sheridan had reassigned the Seventh Cavalry to a military post under construction named Fort Abraham Lincoln, on the west bank of the Missouri opposite Bismarck, Dakota Territory. That summer, the Northern Pacific Railway reached Bismarck.

Fort Abraham Lincoln became home to as dysfunctional a cadre of regimental officers as could be found in the regular army. Smoldering anger over Custer's perceived abandonment of Major Elliott at the Washita and his tendency to surround himself with a fiercely loyal clique—his "royal family," as those outside the Custer circle termed them—rekindled old dissension and deepened factionalism. In the weeks ahead, however, the Seventh Cavalry officer corps would be preoccupied with matters more pressing than nursing grudges and scheming. General Sheridan had charged the new commander of the Department of Dakota, Brigadier General Alfred H. Terry, with assembling a military force formidable enough to deter Lakota aggression against the Northern Pacific's third surveying team, which would set out from Fort Rice for the Yellowstone River in June 1873. The result was the largest military presence on the Great Plains since General Hancock's bungled 1867 campaign. Colonel Stanley commanded the fifteen-hundred-man expedition, which included ten companies of the Seventh Cavalry. Terry advised Stanley to keep a tight leash on Custer, whose tendency to freelance was well established.

The expedition began inauspiciously. A week of pounding rain and hail liquefied the prairie. Men and horses grew fatigued, and tempers frayed. Stanley and Custer soon fell to bickering; Stanley was drinking too much, and Custer resented supervision by an inebriate. Their relationship hit rock bottom when Stanley, while deep in his cups, arrested Custer for using a nonregulation cooking stove and ordered him to the rear of the column. When he sobered up, a contrite Stanley restored Custer to his command. Thereafter, Stanley permitted Custer to do largely as he wished.[16]

And what of Sitting Bull? Simply put, the discordant team of Stanley and Custer were about to catch him with his guard down. No one in his village of four hundred Hunkpapa and Miniconjou lodges on the Yellowstone River had the vaguest idea that soldiers were in the vicinity. Sitting Bull's wolves had failed him, and he only learned of the danger from a passing Oglala hunting party. Ordering camp struck, Sitting Bull dispatched several dozen men under the war leaders Gall and Rain-in-the-Face to harass the soldiers while the village escaped.[17]

*

August 4, 1873, was a brutally hot day in the Yellowstone country. At 2:00 p.m., the thermometer touched 110 degrees, and Stanley called a halt. Infantrymen crawled under wagons. Cavalrymen rested in the shade of their listless horses. Even Custer had reached the limit of his endurance. That morning, Stanley had sent him on ahead with two companies to reconnoiter a good bivouac site, which he found in a cottonwood grove on the near bank of the Yellowstone. He sent a courier back to Stanley, and his duty done, Armstrong and his brother Tom led the men to the woods, ordered horses unsaddled to graze, posted half a dozen guards, and then fell fast asleep in the tall grass, unaware that a war party lurked in another cottonwood grove two miles farther downriver. As the camp grew quiet, Gall and Rain-in-the-Face made

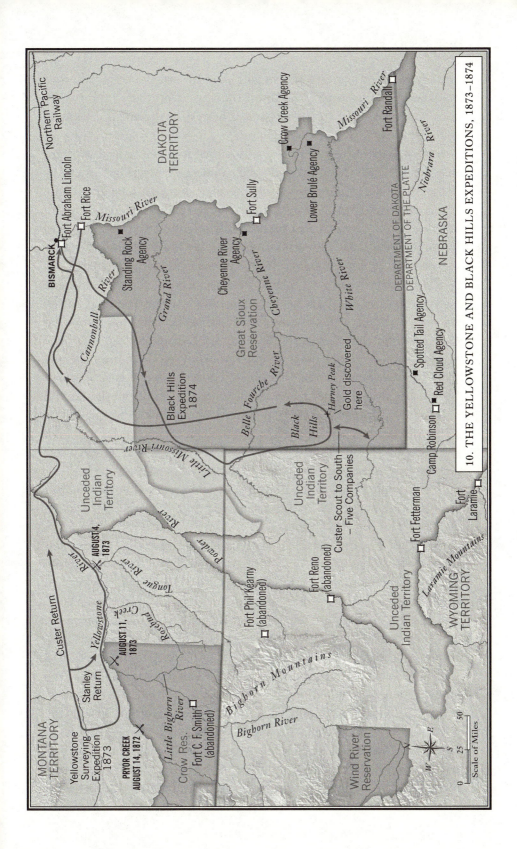

10. THE YELLOWSTONE AND BLACK HILLS EXPEDITIONS, 1873–1874

their move, sending six warriors galloping toward the cavalry horses. Awakened by the pickets' carbines, the Custer brothers took twenty men and gave chase to the Indians. The rest of the small command followed in support.

The Indians retreated just rapidly enough to maintain a constant distance between themselves and the troopers. Armstrong Custer saw through the decoy ploy but decided to play along. Accompanied only by his orderly, he trotted forward until abreast of a second cottonwood stand. There he paused. He released his orderly with orders for Tom Custer to form a dismounted skirmish line and then, keeping a weather eye on the tree line, rode in a circle, signifying he wanted to parley.

The Indians waiting to spring the trap included several Cheyenne survivors of the Washita, who recognized Custer as the long-haired soldier chief who had destroyed their village. Their rage propelled them from the timber, spoiling the ambush. Gall and Rain-in-the-Face waved forward the war party, swelled to nearly 250 by reinforcements from the village. Wheeling his horse, Custer galloped back through his brother's skirmish line. The twenty troopers rose from the ground and delivered two quick volleys that shocked the Indians to a halt. The remaining seventy troopers arrived, and the Indians fell back a short distance. In the open and outnumbered at least three to one, Custer seemed in danger of sharing Captain Fetterman's fate. But he kept his cool and, edging back to the first cottonwood grove, deployed his men in a 250-yard semicircle with his flanks anchored on the Yellowstone River.[18]

The Indians fanned out. Muzzle flashes winked from the timber. Three Cheyennes tumbled from their ponies. For three hours, the Indians attacked in the blistering heat with a persistence Custer had never witnessed. At one point, fifty warriors broke from the main body and vanished. A few minutes later, they turned up behind Custer's line, crawling single file along the riverbank toward the horses, but something spooked the Indians, and they sprinted away. After that tactic had failed, the Indians attempted to set grass fires on the open plain, but the stalks were too green to burn.

At 3:00 p.m., Custer noticed "an unusual commotion" among the attackers. "Looking far to the right," he recalled, "we could see an immense column of dust rapidly approaching." It was eight companies of the Seventh Cavalry, ordered forward by Stanley. Never one to wait for help, Custer followed the Indians with his exhausted troopers until the warriors outdistanced him. "The only satisfaction we had," Custer said, "was to drive at full speed for several miles." Custer had flirted with disaster, but once again "Custer's Luck" had rescued him from his own rashness.

With Stanley's permission, he pressed on, straining to overtake Sitting Bull's village. Six days of relentless pursuit brought him to the north bank of the turbulent Yellowstone River, near its junction with the Bighorn River, no closer to Sitting Bull than he had been when he first gave chase. Two days earlier, the Lakotas had negotiated the Yellowstone handily, something they did every hunting season when following the buffalo. But for Custer, the effort proved a near catastrophe. He fashioned makeshift rafts, which foundered. The troopers drove their mounts into the river, but the rapid current nearly dragged them down, and it was a minor miracle that no men or horses drowned. That night, Custer camped on a long sandbar beside the north bank, intent on trying again in the morning before the Lakotas were too far away to catch.

Unbeknownst to Custer, Sitting Bull was finished running. Having summoned warriors from every Lakota and Cheyenne village within a day's ride, Sitting Bull returned to the river in the early hours of August 11 with at least five hundred men. As the warriors entered into timber opposite Custer's bivouac, Sitting Bull and the Indian families climbed a long granite bluff overlooking the Yellowstone to watch the action unfold.

The warriors did a poor job of concealing their approach. Lieutenant Charles Braden, in command of the night guards, was certain he heard horses galloping in the dark. Braden assumed some cavalry mounts had stampeded, but a Crow scout told him the sounds were made by Indian ponies and that an attack would come at dawn. Braden warned Custer, who dismissed him archly. "His manner indicated that he was annoyed at being awakened. I also was annoyed at the manner of my early reception and went back to the guard," Braden recalled.

Daybreak vindicated Braden. "As the mist on the river became dissipated by the rising sun, a hot fire was opened upon us. The cooks, preparing coffee, were the only ones astir, and for all but the scout and myself, it was a complete surprise." Custer reacted well, however, sending two companies downriver and two upriver to prevent Indians from crossing beyond his flanks. Meanwhile, Braden ascended a bluff with twenty men to watch for Indians. Down on the sandbar, a newspaper reporter recorded a string of insults flung by the Lakotas from across the river, which the Crow scouts translated for him into English. "We're coming over to give you hell. You'll see more Indians than you ever saw before in your life," went a typical Lakota taunt, to which a Crow responded, "Shoot, you son of a bitch."

The Lakotas indeed came over, swimming their ponies across the Yellowstone to take Custer in both flanks. Braden, meanwhile, was in trouble the instant he crested the bluff, because before him was what appeared to the stunned lieutenant to be the entire Lakota warrior population bearing down on his platoon. His troopers swung their carbines into action moments before the warriors overran their line. The Indians gave way, only to be replaced by another wave of warriors. A bullet fired at point-blank range bore through Braden's left leg, shattering the bone and leaving him a cripple for life. Custer dispatched a squadron to scatter the Indians, who broke for the river.

On the sandbar, the Seventh Cavalry beat back an attack from the south just as the booming of cannon echoed up the valley to announce Stanley's approach. Ordering the regimental band to strike up "Garryowen," Custer galloped toward the war party. A chance shot toppled Gall's pony, and the Indians pulled back. The Seventh Cavalry chased them for eight miles, over open prairie, through gullies, and around coulees until, as Custer reported, the Indians "were completely dispersed." Stanley's cannon, meanwhile, drove Sitting Bull and the gathered families from the bluff on the far bank of the Yellowstone.

Custer had emerged victorious. At a cost of four killed and three wounded, he had repelled two Indian charges and inflicted forty casualties. A civilian observer wondered at Custer's daring—and his legendary luck. "Custer came riding toward us with his band and a flag bearer with the American flag flying. He was on a white horse and wore a red shirt, a clear target, but the Indians have not yet succeeded in getting him, even though he always rides in front leading his soldiers."[19]

Afterward, a small war party returned to fire a few harmless shots at a gaggle of cavalrymen bathing in the Yellowstone. Apart from sending the troopers scampering naked out of the water, no harm was done. That was the last anyone saw of the hostile Indians. Having demonstrated their objection to Stanley's incursion—without risking the lives needed to drive them from the Yellowstone country—the Lakotas and the Cheyennes returned to their principal pursuit: making war on the Crows.

The remainder of the Yellowstone Expedition proved routine. Surveyors reached their objective, completing the work Major Baker had abandoned. The official verdict on the expedition was mixed. Convinced that the majority of Indian combatants were temporary defectors from the agencies, the commissioner of Indian affairs feared the army's inability to score a victory would embolden them. Sherman also lamented the absence of a decisive blow, but for the time being nothing more could be done. There were too few troops in the Department of Dakota to even consider a winter war. "I suppose," he told Sheridan, "we had better let things take their natural course until the mass of Indians commit some act that will warrant a final war."[20] Custer returned to Fort Abraham Lincoln on September 22, 1873. Abundant press coverage of his two clashes on the Yellowstone paraded him before the American people more favorably than at any time since the Washita. Unlike the Washita with its tally of dead women and children, Custer's skirmishes on the Yellowstone River were clean, unambiguous fights between soldiers and warriors. Custer, one newspaper said, was once again the nation's "Glorious Boy." Colonel Stanley, on the other hand, exited into obscurity. He penned a brief report in which he praised Custer and extolled the "handsome" conduct of his troopers and then returned to Fort Sully and the bottle.[21]

*

Ironically, the Yellowstone Expedition not only accomplished nothing of lasting importance but also hastened the demise of the Northern Pacific Railway enterprise and with it Jay Cooke's millions. Simply put, Lakota resistance spooked investors into shedding Northern Pacific bonds. Echoing their fears, *The New York Times* editorialized, "If several thousand of our best soldiers . . . can only hold the ground on their narrow line of march for 150 or 200 miles west of the Upper Missouri, what will peaceful bodies of railroad workmen be able to do, or what can emigrants accomplish in such a dangerous region?"[22]

For the moment, it seemed, nothing. A bankrupt Jay Cooke & Company closed its doors, precipitating the panic of 1873 and the onset of a six-year-long depression. For the foreseeable future at least, the Northern Pacific Railway would go no farther west than the Missouri River. Sitting Bull and his people knew nothing of economics. They knew only that the white tide had receded.

CHAPTER 12

THE THIEVES' ROAD

JUST AS THE Yellowstone Expedition had restored the luster to Custer's public image, so too did it enhance Sitting Bull's standing among the non-treaty Lakotas and their Cheyenne allies. His uncompromising ways also impressed reservation Oglalas, and that spelled trouble for Red Cloud. The latter's 1870 visit to Washington, D.C., might have reinforced the government's perception of his authority, but it caused many of his people to wonder if he had sold out to the white man. Red Cloud's behavior grew erratic. Recognizing he would forfeit the respect of his warriors if he capitulated to all of the Great Father's demands, he reneged on an agreement to relocate the agency to the White River, a place farther removed from white traders. Only after most reservation Oglalas warmed to the idea did he agree to the move. Red Cloud's personal commitment to peace was genuine, however, and nothing could induce him to return to the warpath. Non-treaty Lakotas took that as a sign that the once-great war leader had gone soft. Defying him, in late 1873 hundreds of warriors from the Unceded Indian Territory descended on the Red Cloud Agency to demand rations. Some shuttled between the Red Cloud and the Spotted Tail Agencies, drawing rations at both places. They so roiled the normally tractable Brulés that Spotted Tail's people seized the agency's beef herd to keep it out of their hands.[1]

General Sherman's patience with the roaming Lakotas had worn thin. "Sooner or later," he told Phil Sheridan, "these Sioux will have to be wiped out or made to stay just where they are put." Neither general would have objected to an immediate showdown, but the Lakotas had yet to furnish sufficient provocation to convince the Grant administration that the time for war had come. Indeed, as Sheridan was forced to confess in his annual report, with the exception of the troubles at the agencies, conditions were "remarkably quiet."

If he could not kill Lakotas, Sheridan could at least try to make them stay put. To check the reservation Indians, he established Camp Robinson within hailing distance of the Red Cloud Agency and Camp Sheridan near the Spotted Tail Agency. Protecting Nebraskans from non-treaty bands was more problematic. For that, he would need to build a fort somewhere in the Unceded Indian Territory. The spot that Sheridan recommended, and that the War and Interior Departments approved, was the Black Hills, a natural fortress of splintered precipices and dark defiles that sprawled over the western portion of the Great Sioux Reservation. Although rumors of gold abounded, few white men had dared enter the hills.

That was because the Paha Sapa, the "Hills That Are Black," belonged to the Lakotas by both treaty and right of conquest, and they had no intention of parting with them. Neither, however, would they live in the Paha Sapa, except on occasion, and then only briefly. Severe thunderstorms with huge dancing bolts of lightning, of which all Plains Indians stood in dreadful awe, regularly rocked the region. A vague spiritual power also hung over the hills. Lakotas spoke of a "spirit hole" somewhere in its inner recesses—a cave in which dwelled an old man with a flowing white beard, "without beginning of days or end of years"—yet the Lakotas most esteemed the Paha Sapa for its material bounty, not, as some have assumed, for its mystic aura. The hills were their "meat pack," to use Sitting Bull's words, a game reserve to be tapped in times of hunger. Their sheltered meadows made for comfortable campsites, and the blanketing pine trees were ideal for fashioning lodge poles. Every spring, Lakotas ventured into the Paha Sapa to replenish their supply.[2]

Sheridan originally intended to outfit a Black Hills expedition from Fort Laramie. But because the route from Fort Laramie to the Black Hills led past the Red Cloud Agency, the unsettled state of affairs there and the bad temper of the agency Indians led him to think better of it. An approach from the north, while it ran the risk of colliding with the non-treaty bands, seemed to Sheridan the lesser of two evils. And so he turned to Custer and the Seventh Cavalry at Fort Abraham Lincoln. Although Custer did not expect the Indians to "strew flowers on our pathway," he was not overly concerned; with the Seventh Cavalry, he boasted to a newspaperman, he could "whip all the Indians in the Northwest." Nonetheless, Custer ordered his troops not to provoke them. Private Theodore Ewert, a perspicacious former captain of Union volunteers, interpreted that as mere subterfuge to disguise a great wrong. "The United States Government," opined Ewert, "forgot its honor, forgot the sacred treaty, forgot its integrity, and ordered an expedition for the invasion of the Black Hills."

If the Lakotas chose to fight, the expedition appeared large enough to take care of itself. By the time the engineering detachments and civilian scientists arrived, Custer had assembled a command of 951 soldiers and teamsters, augmented by 61 Arikara scouts—blood enemies of the Lakotas; 2 "practical miners" purportedly fitted out at Custer's own expense; and 3 newspapermen. Custer also invited President Grant's son Fred, recently graduated from West Point, to come along.

Eastern humanitarians contemplated Custer's mission and cried foul. The expedition, they said, violated the 1868 Fort Laramie Treaty provision that prohibited whites from entering the Great Sioux Reservation without Lakota permission. Not so, responded Generals Sherman and Terry, who argued that military personnel in the discharge of their duties were exempt from the prohibition. Had the expedition been staged solely to reconnoiter possible sites for a new fort, their interpretation of the treaty would have been legitimate. But its unspoken ancillary purpose—to search for gold—clearly violated treaty terms.[3]

On July 2, 1874, Custer's expedition departed Fort Abraham Lincoln for the agonizing aridness of the Dakota Badlands. Burning billows of white alkaline powder blinded the men, and blood from the cactus-torn fetlocks of cavalry mounts stained the trail, which provided the only sanguinary incidents in the journey. Occasional clusters of reservation warriors watched the plodding whites from a respectful distance; none, however, tried to impede Custer's advance. The lodge-pole-cutting season was over, which meant the Black Hills were vacant, or nearly so. The reservation Indians wanted to believe the soldiers' presence on the Great Sioux Reservation benign, and Red Cloud was too busy bickering with his Indian agent over short rations and sundry other matters to give the matter much thought.

Nothing was seen of the non-treaty Lakotas. Sitting Bull and his followers ranged well north of Custer's route, hunting buffalo or battling Crows, and Crazy Horse's band was far to the west in the Unceded

Indian Territory engaged in similar pursuits. Crazy Horse himself was lost in mourning. His passion for Black Buffalo Woman having finally subsided, shortly after recovering from his grievous face wound, he had married a young woman with whom he had a daughter. The child succumbed to cholera just as Custer was setting out on his invasion of the Black Hills. While Custer plodded toward the Paha Sapa, Crazy Horse lay sobbing beneath his daughter's burial scaffold. Friends said he was never again the same man.[4]

As the dusty and begrimed bluecoats entered the Black Hills, the weather cooled, the air cleared, and the expedition took on the aspect of an armed picnic. The march led through achingly beautiful meadows. Custer, who had never seen such a profuse display of flowers, found it strange to "glance back at the advancing columns of cavalry and behold men with beautiful bouquets in their hand, while the head gear of their horses was decorated with wreaths of flowers fit to crown a queen of May."

On July 27, Custer's two miners went to work. Five days later, they hit pay dirt. It wasn't much, they told Custer, enough perhaps to yield fifty to seventy dollars a day in gold to organized mines—hardly worth the efforts of individual prospectors. The gold fever gripped the camp nevertheless. A perplexed Indian scout watched soldiers laugh, weep, shout, toss hats in the air, and run about in circles. Perhaps, he told Private Ewert, the mountain spirits had made them all crazy. No, answered Ewert, nothing sacred had struck the soldiers, only visions of earthly wealth. For two days, the troopers panned for gold before Custer put a stop to the activity. A few glittering grains, no more than two or three cents' worth of gold per pan, were the richest take.[5]

All the while, the American people waited hopefully for news from the Black Hills. Mired in the depression brought on by the panic of 1873, the country longed for a gold bonanza. On August 7, one of Custer's white scouts carried a field report to General Sheridan in which Custer lauded the logging and stock-raising potential of the Black Hills. Regarding gold, Custer was circumspect, but the scout delivered more than just Custer's guarded assessment of the hills' gold wealth, because newspapermen had prevailed upon the scout to file their dispatches for them. Most were measured in their reporting. But the fanciful, frenetic scribbling of a Chicago correspondent, trumpeting "ten dollar diggins'" and "pay dirt from the grass roots down," created a frenzy. Prospecting expeditions soon fitted out all along the frontier. Enterprising writers with more imagination than experience churned out guidebooks to the "New Eldorado," and opportunistic frontier merchants stocked up on prospecting gear.

Custer returned to Fort Abraham Lincoln on August 31, having marched 1,025 miles. Before leaving the Black Hills, he conducted a perfunctory search for a place to build Sheridan's fort but came up empty. No one cared.

The Lakotas had a name for the trail Custer blazed through the Black Hills. They called it the Thieves' Road. And they had a name for Custer. They called him Pehin Hanska, "Long Hair." His Crow scouts called him Son of the Morning Star.[6]

*

Once back at Fort Abraham Lincoln, Custer came down with gold fever. He now proclaimed not only that accounts of a bonanza in the Black Hills were true but that the prospects were "even better than represented." While Custer fanned the fevered dreams of jobless men, General Sheridan tried to calm the hysteria. "The color of gold can be found almost anywhere in any of the now existing western territories," he reminded a heedless nation, "but often its quantity is confined to a few particles which make the color." Sheridan remained fixated on building a fort in or near the Black Hills, and the sooner the better.

Not everyone bought Custer's new story. The expedition geologist, an eminent professor, had seen no gold. He speculated publicly that Custer's handpicked miners had planted it. A college professor could be written off as addlepated and his opinion therefore suspect. But not so the president's son Fred Grant, who wholeheartedly concurred with the professor. Eastern newspapers had a field day, ridiculing the gold mania as a hoax gotten up by speculators to resuscitate the Northern Pacific Railway. The debate was academic, however, because hopeful miners were already pouring into the Black Hills. General Sheridan made a good-faith effort to expel them, but he lacked the authority to keep them out. No sooner had cavalry patrols escorted miners out of the hills than they snuck back in.

By the spring of 1875, the army was fed up with the assignment. "It's the same old story," mused General Sherman, "the story of Adam and Eve and the forbidden fruit." But did the fruit really exist? The government needed an authoritative answer, not merely to settle the debate, but also, if the Black Hills indeed bore a bonanza, to begin the process of "extinguishing Indian title" to the Paha Sapa—in other words, to wrest from the Lakotas part of the reservation that had been promised them in perpetuity. And so the geologist Walter P. Jenney entered the Black Hills to investigate, infuriating Sheridan. The entire endeavor undercut his efforts to keep out miners.

Sheridan worried needlessly. The Black Hills were already teeming with miners—nearly a thousand by Jenney's reckoning. Hundreds more had attached themselves to his expedition, rendering "great assistance in prospecting the country." The farce of governmental collusion with white trespassers to decide the fate of the Lakota country lasted five months. On November 8, 1875, Jenney submitted his findings to the secretary of Indian affairs. He basically reiterated what Custer's miners had said the year before: there was insufficient gold for prospectors panning creek beds, but a good return could be had with sluices and a moderate amount of shared capital. Even had Jenney condemned the hills as sterile, it would have changed nothing. Five days before receiving Jenney's report, the Grant administration secretly decided the fate of the Paha Sapa.[7]

In point of fact, the government had taken the first steps toward dispossessing the Lakotas of the Black Hills even before Professor Jenney set foot in them. For several months, Red Cloud had been agitating for a meeting with the Great Father to demand a new agent, alleging that the incumbent shortchanged the Oglalas on rations and annuity goods. In May 1875, the Indian Bureau granted Red Cloud's request, but not for the purpose the Oglala chief intended. That all was not as it seemed became apparent when the Lakota delegation traveling to Washington crossed paths with Jenney's party en route to the Black Hills.

Nothing in Washington went Red Cloud's way. The Great Father had no ear to lend Lakota grievances. Instead, President Grant bluntly advised the chiefs to ponder a few unpleasant truths. First, the government's treaty obligation to issue rations had run out and could be unilaterally revoked; rations continued only because of Washington's kind feelings toward the Lakotas. Second, he, the Great Father, was powerless to prevent miners from overrunning the Black Hills; the Lakotas must either cede them or risk losing their rations. Grant even suggested they vacate their reservation and move to Indian Territory.

Red Cloud and the other Lakota chiefs left the White House "all at sea." For three weeks, they alternated between discordant encounters with hectoring bureaucrats and bleak hotel caucuses among themselves. At last, the chiefs concluded to break off the talks, and they returned to the reservation "disgusted and not conciliated."[8]

In the interim, General Sheridan had not been idle. He had rethought the matter of a fort in the Black Hills and decided it would be insufficient in the event of war. He wanted the forts closer to water traffic, and so he dispatched his military aide by steamboat far up the Yellowstone River to reconnoiter suitable sites.

All summer long, miners poured into the Black Hills. The thankless task of expelling the interlopers fell to General Crook, recently arrived from Arizona to command the Department of the Platte. Crook knew precious little about the Lakotas and the Cheyennes or their grievances. Neither was he eager to learn, because his sympathies clearly rested with the miners. In July, he issued an edict evicting them, but before they pulled up stakes, Crook suggested the trespassers record their claims in order to secure them before the country opened up. Amid general guffawing, the miners did as Crook suggested and then scattered to await the voiding of the Lakota title.

Not that the Lakotas had given the government any cause to strong-arm them. "How do the bands that sometimes roam off from the agencies on the plains behave now?" a reporter asked Crook in early August.

"Well," he confessed, "they are quiet."

"Do you perceive any immediate danger of an Indian war?" the reporter persisted.

"Not just now," answered Crook. "There is undoubtedly to be a great fight yet. The government has to whip the Sioux. The sooner it is done the better."[9]

*

Sitting Bull was determined not to contest the whites alone. While Sheridan's aide poked around the Yellowstone country, Professor Jenney chiseled in the Black Hills, and General Crook issued his pseudo ultimatum to the miners, the Hunkpapa chief worked to forge a united front. At his behest, Lakota and Northern Cheyenne bands assembled in June for an unprecedented intertribal Sun Dance, the sanguinary culmination of a twelve-day religious ceremony central to the Lakota faith and to that of most other Plains Indians. Five tribal circles took form on Rosebud Creek. There were Sitting Bull's own Hunkpapas;

Crazy Horse's Oglalas; Sans Arcs under the fire-eater Spotted Eagle, who had threatened Stanley with annihilation two years earlier; a loosely led band of Miniconjous; and Northern Cheyennes under the moderately accommodationist chief Little Wolf, who well represented the mood of most of the tribe.

The Northern Cheyennes had been at peace with the whites since the end of Red Cloud's War seven years earlier. Many had settled at the Red Cloud Agency; others had made their home in the Powder River country. They were still fearsome warriors, as the Crows and the Pawnees could attest. But thus far they had accepted the white man's presence, limited as it was, and their agreeable disposition freed up army resources to deal with their beleaguered southern kinsmen. All that, however, was about to change. The Paha Sapa represented more to the Northern Cheyennes than simply the hunting reserve (or "meat pack," to use Sitting Bull's definition) that it was to the Lakotas. For all Cheyennes, the Paha Sapa truly was holy ground, the home of Noahvose, the "Sacred Mountain." Cheyenne tradition held that in the distant past, in a cave deep within Noahvose, the Creator himself had given the Cheyenne people the revered Sacred Medicine Arrows. That the Cheyennes had refrained from responding to the white invasion of the Black Hills was the consequence of a loss in the tribe's spiritual direction. Two years earlier, a half-mad Cheyenne woman had ripped a horn off the Sacred Buffalo Hat, second only to the Sacred Medicine Arrows in its holy power. The tragedy had enervated the council chiefs and cast a pall over the Northern Cheyenne people. It took the harsh winter of 1874–1875, when starving agency Cheyennes were reduced to eating their ponies, to reawaken the tribe. The Indian Bureau's remedy was to pressure the Northern Cheyennes to move to Indian Territory. It was a bad idea that only bred anger. Young men flocked to the camps of the non-treaty bands, and Cheyenne chiefs became receptive to a stronger alliance with these freedom-loving Lakotas.

Not so the Northern Arapahos. At heart a compliant people, they had entirely lost the will to resist. (In fact, the Northern Arapahos soon would permit the government to resettle them on the distant Wind River Reservation, home of their traditional enemies the Shoshones.) Their absence was a serious blow to Sitting Bull's nascent alliance and the death knell of the Cheyenne-Arapaho confederation.

With the Arapahos neutralized, the importance of holding the Cheyennes close was not lost on Sitting Bull, who presided over the unifying Sun Dance. His performance was calculated to win over the wavering, not only among Cheyennes, but also within the non-treaty Lakota bands. Clad only in a breechcloth, his body painted yellow, and wearing a warbonnet (something he rarely did), Sitting Bull entered the Sun Dance lodge on a fine black war pony, a gift from a Cheyenne holy man. First he danced with the animal beside him. Then he stopped to ask the Cheyenne and Hunkpapa chiefs to fill their pipes and smoke as one people. As they did, he resumed dancing—forward and back, making signs that signified an approaching enemy. Three times he pantomimed an ambush, saying, "I have nearly got them." The fourth time he brought his arms together and declared, "We have them. The Great Spirit has given our enemy into our power." The lodge erupted in a song of triumph. Sitting Bull silenced the gathering and cautioned against hasty assumptions, reminding them that war with the Crows was not yet over and that conflict with the whites had scarcely begun. "The Great Spirit has given our enemies to us," Sitting Bull said. "We are to destroy them. We do not know who they are. They may be soldiers."[10]

Or they may be agents of the Great Father. After Red Cloud left the capital, President Grant directed the Interior Department to appoint a commission to hold a "grand council" with the chiefs at a place of the Lakotas' choosing on the Great Sioux Reservation. The purpose: to buy mining rights to the Black Hills, as well as "such other rights as could be secured and as might be thought desirable for the Government." The commissioners were to attempt conciliation, but they were also instructed to remind the chiefs that the government was no longer obliged to feed their people, the implication being that the rations would cease if the Lakotas refused to come to terms.

It was a rather sorry assemblage the government sent to negotiate so sensitive a matter. Senator William B. Allison of Iowa chaired the nine-member commission. His sole qualification was loyalty to the Grant administration. Seven of the remaining eight commissioners were equally ignorant of Indian affairs. Only General Terry knew the Lakotas, and he had no stomach for coercing them into ceding the Black Hills. Why not, he suggested, encourage them to farm and raise livestock in the hills?

Terry was an unlikely soldier. Soft-spoken, kind, urbane, gracious, and affable, the forty-seven-year-old, baggy-eyed bachelor lived with his mother and sister in St. Paul, Minnesota, headquarters of the Department of Dakota. Born into affluence, Terry obtained a law degree from Yale University. Grant had taken a liking to him during the Civil War, and Terry's performance had been such that he received a coveted brigadier general's commission in the regular army. That decided him on a military career. He had no desire to fight Indians, however. Pushing papers in the comfort of his urban headquarters was more to his liking than field duty on the frontier. In the event of hostilities, Terry could be expected to delegate operational command to his principal subordinate, Custer. Although they had little in common, Terry and Custer got along well.

✳

The Allison commission arrived at the Red Cloud Agency on September 4, 1875, to find the reservation chiefs no more pliable than they had been in Washington. Allison sent runners to invite non-treaty Lakotas to the grand council, a gesture as impolitic (reservation chiefs and their roaming counterparts had little use for each other) as it was naive. Crazy Horse answered that he would rather fight than make a treaty. Sitting Bull, picking up a pinch of dirt, responded, "I do not want to sell or lease any land to the government—not even as much as this." Subchiefs and warriors from Sitting Bull's and Crazy Horse's villages attended the council—not to negotiate, but rather to threaten with death any agency chief who yielded.[11]

Not that there seemed much chance of the chiefs agreeing to anything. Red Cloud and Spotted Tail wrangled for nearly two weeks over the council site; each wanted the meeting held at or near his own agency. In the end, the commissioners chose a location that pleased no one. Meanwhile, gate-crashing whites—some well-meaning and others of questionable intent—advised the chiefs that the Black Hills were worth tens of millions of dollars, a sum astronomically higher than the commission was prepared to offer.

The council opened amid much bickering and belligerence. Five thousand agency Lakotas attended as observers. Well-armed young warriors from the non-treaty bands weaved menacingly through the crowd, evidently ready to make good on their threats. Chairman Allison botched the negotiations from the beginning. Pleading the impossibility of keeping whites out of the Black Hills, Allison said the government only wanted the Lakotas to permit mining until gold and precious metal stocks were exhausted, after which the country would revert to the Indians. (The senator neglected to explain how the government would evict the whites.) Apparently forgetting the blood that the Lakotas had shed to close down the Bozeman Trail forts, Allison, in a supremely stupid move, also asked the Lakotas to sell the Bighorn Mountain country.

The chiefs responded with rare unanimity. The Bighorn country, they said, was not for sale or lease. As for the Black Hills, they would sell on the condition that the government pay enough to sustain their people for seven generations to come; Spotted Tail thought sixty million dollars a fair price (the commission had been authorized to offer less than a tenth that amount). The talks sputtered and died, and the commissioners departed, incensed that an offer they considered "ample and liberal" had met with "derisive laughter from the Indians as inadequate." Only one option remained. The Indians, opined Allison, could not be brought to terms "except by the mild exercise, at least, of force in the beginning." Congress should fix a price for the Black Hills and insist the Indians accept it. If they refused, the senator concluded, then the Indians should be starved into submission.

President Grant had a still more radical solution in mind—war. There was no reasonable excuse for it. For all their threats and bluster in council, the Indians had displayed remarkable restraint toward the Black Hills' miners. The army reported no hostile encounters on the northern plains during 1875. The western press contained no salacious stories of Indian depredations. And white travelers to the Black Hills found the Lakotas surprisingly docile. But Grant was confronted with an insoluble dilemma. On the one hand, clamor for annexing the Black Hills was growing, and not merely in the western states. A nation mired in the throes of economic depression demanded that the hills be opened. Preparations to storm the Black Hills had reached a fever pitch, and hundreds of hopeful miners were already braving winter snows to make the journey. On the other hand, treaty obligations and sheer morality compelled the administration to defend Lakota rights. In effect, Grant was forced to choose between the electorate and the Indians. Although a lame-duck president, for the sake of his party and national prosperity, he yielded to the former.

On November 3, Grant held a secret meeting in the White House with a select few like-minded generals and civilian officials to map out a war plan. On that day, the Peace Policy breathed its last. Generals Sheridan and Crook were present; General Sherman was not. He had fallen out with Secretary of War William W. Belknap and moved his headquarters from Washington to St. Louis. It is doubtful that anyone regretted Sherman's absence; more scrupulous than Sheridan, he might have objected to a plan that he considered illegal or unethical. Also absent was the peace proponent General Terry, in whose department the non-treaty bands wintered. The hawkish and morally bankrupt secretary Belknap attended. So too did the anti-Indian secretary of the interior, Zachariah Chandler. It is a sad reflection of the moral cesspool into which the Grant administration had sunk that the first instance of real cooperation between the War Department and the Bureau of Indian Affairs involved the most egregious treachery ever contemplated by the government against the Plains Indians.

The conferees agreed on a two-phase plan. The president's edict reaffirming Lakota ownership of the Black Hills would stand, but the army would no longer enforce it. If the Lakotas retaliated against white trespassers, so much the better. Hostilities would help legitimize the secret second phase of the operation. To wit, the non-treaty Lakotas were to be given an impossibly short deadline to report to their agencies; the Indian Bureau was to fabricate complaints against them; and General Sheridan would begin preparations for his favorite form of warfare: a winter campaign against unsuspecting Indian villages.

The conspirators believed that intimidation by the non-treaty bands had dissuaded the agency chiefs from reaching an agreement with the Allison commission. Crush the non-treaty bands, their reasoning went, and the agency chiefs would yield. Six days after the conference, Sheridan sent Terry confidential orders to quietly mobilize. Crook returned to the Department of the Platte and began preparations of his own.[12]

To prime the public for war, the government leaked an inflammatory report of a routine tour of the Dakota and Montana Indian agencies by an Indian Bureau inspector dated nine days *after* the secret White House conference. The report was a put-up job to suit the administration's secret purpose. The "wild and hostile bands of Sioux Indians," roared the inspector, "richly merit punishment for their incessant warfare, and their numerous murders of settlers and their families, or white men wherever found unarmed." The true policy, the bureau cat's-paw concluded, was to whip them into subjection, the sooner the better.

On December 3, Secretary Chandler set the first phase of the scheme in motion. He directed the Indian Bureau to inform Sitting Bull and the other "hostile" chiefs that they had until January 31, 1876, to report to the agencies; otherwise, the army would march against them. Sheridan was delighted. "The matter will in all probability be regarded as a good joke by the Indians," he wrote to Sherman.

All appeared neatly in order to commence a war of naked aggression.[13]

CHAPTER 13

GUARD US AGAINST
ALL MISFORTUNE

C OLONEL JOHN GIBBON, the commander of the District of Montana, had little to occupy his time in December 1875. Like his commanding officer, General Terry, the colonel was not privy to the White House decision to blame the non-treaty Lakotas for the hostilities that President Grant hoped to provoke. Availing himself of the semi-hibernation of winter garrison life, Gibbon penned a long and distinctly unmilitary missive to the editors of the *Army and Navy Journal*. He wanted the army, the public, and official Washington to know precisely where he stood on the subject of Indian wars. A West Point graduate and Civil War hero whose division had blunted Pickett's Charge at Gettysburg, Gibbon was hardly soft or sentimental. But he was an honest man with a strong sense of justice. And so he asked his readers to consider the Indians' point of view:

> Put yourself in his place and let the white man ask himself this question: What would I do if threatened as the Indian has been and is? Suppose a race superior to mine were to land upon the shores of this great continent, trade or cheat us out of our land foot by foot, gradually encroach upon our domain until we were finally driven, a degraded, demoralized band into a small corner of the continent, where to live at all it was necessary to steal, perhaps to do worse? Suppose that in a spirit of justice, this superior race should recognize the fact that it was in duty bound to place food in our mouths and blankets on our backs, what would we do in the premises? I have seen one who hates an Indian as he does a snake, and thinks there is no

good Indian but a dead one, on having the proposition put to him in this way, grind his teeth in rage and exclaim, "I would cut the heart out of everyone I could lay my hand on," and so he would; and so we all would.[1]

Three hundred miles southeast of Fort Shaw, the non-treaty Lakotas wintered in villages scattered along the Powder and Yellowstone Rivers. Neither degraded nor demoralized, as Gibbon would have them, nor thieves (except of Crow and Shoshone horses), these hard-core traditionalists were sometimes called "winter roamers," to differentiate them from the so-called summer roamers—reservation Indians who swelled their ranks during the warmer months to hunt with them, renew family ties and friendships, and breathe if only briefly the heady air of freedom. As the New Year opened, the attitude of the non-treaty Lakotas remained unchanged; that is to say, they had no quarrel with the whites so long as the whites stayed out of the Unceded Indian Territory, which their chiefs had made abundantly clear they had no intention of surrendering. Consequently, the government demand that they report to the Indian agencies no later than January 31, 1876, bewildered them. Their response was unthreatening and, from an Indian perspective, quite practical: They appreciated the invitation to come in and talk but were settled in for the winter. When spring came and their ponies grew strong, then would be the proper time for a council to discuss their future. In the meantime, they intended no one any harm.

The commissioner of Indian affairs pigeonholed the Lakota reply and stuck to the official line scripted in November. The Lakotas, he declared, were "defiant and hostile," so much so that he saw no point in waiting until the January 31, 1876, deadline to permit the army to take military action against them. Secretary Chandler duly endorsed the fiction. "Sitting Bull still refuses to comply with the directions of the commissioners," he told the secretary of war, to whose authority he released the non-treaty Lakotas, together with the Cheyennes who were wintering in the Unceded Indian Territory, for whatever action the army deemed appropriate.

Sheridan had the green light. On February 8, he ordered Terry to march west from Fort Abraham Lincoln with Custer and the Seventh Cavalry toward the Powder River country and Crook to march north from Fort Fetterman in Wyoming Territory. If they were able to coordinate their movements, so much the better. Terry's expedition, however, never got started. Heavy snow shut down the Northern Pacific Railway, preventing supplies from reaching Fort Abraham Lincoln. Hopeful that Gibbon might contribute something in Custer's stead, Terry told the colonel to move east from Fort Ellis along the Yellowstone River to cut off any Indians that Crook might drive northward. But Gibbon was also snowbound and would need the entire month of March to assemble his troops.[2]

Matters appeared more promising in Crook's department. Despite the foul weather, he succeeded in gathering sufficient supplies and on March 1, 1876, started from Fort Fetterman with 692 officers and men, a sizable pack-mule train to carry food and ammunition, and a large and cumbersome horse-drawn wagon train. Officially, Colonel Joseph J. Reynolds, the fifty-four-year-old commander of the Third Cavalry, led the expedition, with Crook playing the part of observer. Although a relatively competent corps commander during the Civil War, Reynolds had proved inept on the frontier. The Powder River Expedition was Crook's way of giving Reynolds a chance to redeem himself.

Crook's expectations, however, were low. "I am here on an expedition against the famous 'Sitting Bull of the North,'" he confided to his close friend and confidant the future president Rutherford B. Hayes. "I don't feel very sanguine of success, as they have so much advantage over us." And they would have more. No sooner had Crook left Fort Fetterman than winter threw all its weight against the expedition. Whipping snows blinded the hunters and masked the hunted. On the first night of the expedition, a small raiding party made off with the beef herd, over which Reynolds had neglected to post guards. Four nights later, a second band of raiders nearly stampeded the cavalry horses. Warriors tracked the column and hung on its flanks with no attempt to conceal themselves. An exasperated Crook shunted aside Reynolds and took charge. Ostentatiously sending his infantry and wagon train back toward Fort Fetterman to mislead the Indians, on the bitterly cold and cloudless night of March 7 he cut loose with the cavalry toward the presumed site of Crazy Horse's village on Powder River and into the teeth of one of the worst winter storms in plains history. It snowed relentlessly. The temperature plunged to forty below zero. Crook's war was now with nature. "Men could only use their bacon by slowly splintering off pieces with axes; the few loaves of soft bread were frozen solid as rocks," a shivering journalist scribbled in his diary. "Weapons and knives adhered to fingers as though each had been freshly coated with adhesive plaster, and ice on [the Tongue] river was from eighteen inches to three feet thick."[3]

Opportunely for Crook, on March 16 two Indian hunters nearly stumbled into his camp before disappearing into the squall. Crook sent Reynolds with three battalions—15 officers and 359 men—guided by the able scout Frank Grouard on a night march to find Crazy Horse, from whose camp Crook assumed the hunters had come. The newspaperman Robert Strahorn and the aide-de-camp Lieutenant John G. Bourke tagged along.

Crook remained in camp with the mule train. "His orders were very strict," recalled Grouard. "We should jump the village and capture the horses, take all the dried meat we could get, burn the village and hold [it] until we could get a courier back to him. We were to capture the Indians if possible. That was the purport of General Crook's verbal orders to Reynolds."

Reynolds's column set out after dark. It was the coldest night Grouard had ever known. An icy wind lashed at the soldiers. Snow fell fitfully, and heavy clouds shrouded the moon. Jet-black gulches and glassy ravines crisscrossed the dim trail. Strahorn marveled at Grouard, "now down on his hands and knees in the deep snow, scrutinizing the faint hoof prints, then losing the trail for an instant, darting to and fro until it was found." Toward morning the clouds parted. The snow stopped, and the temperature fell further—down to sixty below, some thought. They were near the Powder River now, and at 2:30 a.m. the cavalry huddled in a deep ravine while Grouard went on alone. Hungry, exhausted, and benumbed, several troopers toppled from the saddle and would surely have frozen to death had the officers not kicked and shook them awake. Mercifully, Grouard returned at daybreak; he had found Crazy Horse's village. Or so the veteran scout thought. In reality, the encampment consisted of sixty-five Cheyenne lodges under two peace chiefs who intended to report to the Red Cloud Agency in the spring.[4]

The Washita had demonstrated that dawn was the ideal winter hour for a sneak attack. It was well after sunrise, however, before Reynolds and his officers reached a high, broken ridge overlooking the Cheyenne encampment, which lay nestled in a cottonwood grove on the west bank of the Powder River two miles distant. Between the base of the ridge and the river, the surface was level and free from snow—good ground for a cavalry charge. In this natural pasturage south of the village, a thousand ponies grazed in small clusters on both sides of the frozen Powder River. When they saw young warriors walking among the tipis, Reynolds and his shivering subordinates feared they had lost the element of surprise.

Actually, they never entirely possessed it. The Cheyennes knew there were soldiers in the area, but being peaceably inclined, they assumed Crook would leave them alone. As Reynolds began his night march, the chiefs held a council. No one suggested moving the village. Prudence, however, dictated watchfulness, and so the chiefs sent ten wolves into the storm to find and watch the soldiers. An outer line of sentinels stood a frigid guard on the scattered hills northwest of the village. As chance would have it, there were none on the ridge where Reynolds had assembled his command for the assault. As for the Cheyenne wolves, they had become lost in the snowstorm; by the time they found the cavalry's trail, their ponies were too exhausted to reach camp ahead of the soldiers.

Reynolds's plan was simple. He would send Captain Henry E. Noyes's battalion down the ridge and into the village, while that of Captain Alexander Moore provided covering fire from the crest. What should have been a straightforward assault instead unfolded as a tactical foul-up of the first order. The icy ravines lacing the ridge disoriented Noyes, and his battalion struck the valley floor a mile south of the camp, the horses near collapse. Captain James Egan's company, armed with revolvers, took the lead. By the time they had weaved their way through the Cheyenne pony herd, Egan and his forty-seven troopers could only muster a slow trot for their charge. A dense undergrowth of wild-plum bushes slowed them further. Nevertheless, the assault had the desired effect. "Women screamed, [and] children cried for their mothers," recalled a Cheyenne warrior. "Old people tottered away to get out of reach of the bullets singing among the lodges."

The turmoil in the village was brief. Harangued by their chiefs to "fight like men," the warriors rallied north of the camp and delivered a withering return fire. Six cavalry horses fell, and four troopers toppled dead or wounded from their saddles. As Indian resistance stiffened, Egan dismounted his men among the tipis and waited for fire support from the bluff.

None came. Moore had been unaccountably slow getting his men into line. When his battalion finally opened fire, their shots fell mostly in the midst of Egan's men. Captain Noyes, meanwhile, was well to the rear with the second company, leading off the Cheyenne pony herd.

Reynolds, for his part, was of no use to anyone. He had neglected even to give a mission to his third battalion commander, Anson Mills, so the captain took it upon himself to reinforce Egan. He drove the warriors several hundred yards beyond the village and then applied the torch to the tipis, which were heavily stocked with ammunition. Exploding cartridge boxes hurled torn tipi canvas and splintered lodge poles high in the air. Pony saddles popped apart with a puff. Buffalo robes, finely embroidered elk-hide trunks, elegant eagle-feather warbonnets, blankets, bells, silk ribbons, silverware, pots, and kettles—all succumbed to the flames. Reynolds ordered everything burned, including a thousand pounds of fresh buffalo meat and venison. The wanton destruction of much-needed meat shocked Lieutenant Bourke, who judged Reynolds "incapable of learning the first principles of Indian warfare," which included retrieving one's casualties. Retreating with untoward haste, he abandoned two dead troopers and a wounded man unable to walk. Reynolds did come away with seven hundred Indian ponies but then neglected to post guards over them. That night, a raiding party of ten warriors recaptured nearly all of the ponies.

On March 27, 1876, General Crook's dispirited column trudged into Fort Fetterman. The winter campaign had served only to put the nontreaty tribes on notice that they were in mortal danger. Quick to deflect blame for the debacle, Crook filed court-martial charges against Reynolds for what Bourke labeled the colonel's "imbecility and incapacity."

Two warriors had died in the five-hour engagement, which the army called the Battle of Powder River. To Egan and Mills's credit, no women or children had been shot. A head count of the Indians revealed only one person missing, an old blind woman too feeble to flee. Returning to the smoldering ruins of their camp, several Cheyenne warriors found the woman's tipi still standing and she unharmed. "We talked about this matter," said one, "all agreeing that the act showed the soldiers had good hearts."[5]

Perhaps, but they had crippled the Cheyennes notwithstanding. Half-starved and frostbitten, the homeless Indians tramped through the subzero cold and deep snows for three days until at last they reached Crazy Horse. The Oglalas did what they could to help the refugees, but Crazy Horse's village contained fewer than four hundred people, too few to attend to all the Cheyennes' needs. Recognizing that he was also vulnerable to attack, Crazy Horse broke camp. Together the Cheyennes and the Oglalas journeyed sixty miles to Sitting Bull's large

Hunkpapa and Miniconjou village at the junction of the Powder and Little Missouri Rivers, where they were greeted with an outpouring of goodwill and an abundance of food, blankets, and tipis. While the Cheyenne people availed themselves of the Hunkpapas' generosity, the chiefs of both tribes held a great council at which all agreed to stay together.

"We supposed that the combined camps would frighten off the soldiers," the Cheyenne warrior Wooden Leg said. "We hoped thus to be freed from their annoyance. Then we could resume our quiet wandering and hunting." The gathered tribes looked to Sitting Bull for leadership. "He had come now into admiration by all Indians as a man whose medicine was good—that is, as a man having a kind heart and good judgment as to the best course of conduct," explained Wooden Leg. In keeping with Sitting Bull and Crazy Horse's policy of defensive war, the council agreed that the Indians would fight only if threatened. But they were angry. Before soldiers had trespassed to guard railroad builders or explore. Now they came to kill.[6]

*

Sheridan's winter war had failed miserably. The army had not gained an inch of ground in the Unceded Indian Territory, nor was the Grant administration one step closer to realizing its secret designs. The non-treaty Indians had been untouched. Instead of dealing a hard blow to Crazy Horse, Crook had attacked a peaceable Cheyenne village. All this served only to alert a foe who would become fully mobile with the advent of spring. Worse yet, the army's stumbling performance had hardly impressed Red Cloud and the treaty chiefs with the need to cede the Black Hills. On the contrary, the reservation Indians who now began their annual migration to the Unceded Indian Territory to hunt buffalo came prepared to join their non-treaty brethren in fighting for what little liberty remained to them all.

Sheridan had no choice but to mount a summer campaign. He had little enthusiasm for the enterprise, however, leaving its conduct entirely to his department commanders, whose plans were not particularly imaginative. Crook intended to again march northward from Fort Fetterman in search of Crazy Horse. Terry reissued orders to Gibbon to move east along the Yellowstone River while he built a supply base on the river from which the Seventh Cavalry could operate.

As his subordinates readied their expeditions, Sheridan learned that Indians were streaming from the reservation in record numbers. Although it was disquieting news, he was more concerned that the enemy would scatter before his generals could bring them to battle. "As hostile Indians, in any great numbers, cannot keep the field as a body for a week or at most ten days," he told General Sherman, "I therefore consider—and so do Terry and Crook—that each column will be able to take care of itself, and of chastising the Indians should it have the opportunity."

Withal, Sheridan had no expectation of delivering a knockout blow. Although hopeful his generals would at least drive the hostiles onto the reservation temporarily, he knew that as soon as the troops quit the field, the non-treaty Indians would decamp, and the whole process would have to be repeated. Sheridan believed that a lasting peace could only be obtained if the Indian agencies were placed under army authority and the two posts he wanted on the Yellowstone River were built. For the moment at least, these were mere flights of fancy. Public opinion east of the Mississippi ruled out military control of the agencies; congressional parsimony precluded the building of new posts; and General Sherman had other worries beyond corralling obstreperous Indians, including rising violence in the Reconstruction South. "Now as to yourself," he told Sheridan, "of course we all recognize the fact that you are the man to deal with Indians, but the South may become again the theater of trouble, and here you are equally necessary." Better, he concluded, to leave it to Crook and Terry "to finish this Sioux business which is about the last of the Indians."[7]

Sherman and Sheridan also had one other troublesome matter demanding their attention: what to do with Custer.

*

Custer knew no more of the politics that were about to trigger an Indian war than what he read in the newspapers. While Sheridan and Crook had been mapping out the winter campaign, Armstrong and Libbie enjoyed an extended holiday in New York City, where high society fawned over the celebrated Indian fighter and his lovely wife.

Had Custer contented himself with an active social calendar, all would have gone well for him. But the outspoken Democrat could not resist playing politics, a game for which he had little aptitude. He met frequently with his good friend James Gordon Bennett, publisher of the vociferously anti-Republican *New York Herald*. Mired in multiple scandals, the Grant administration was an easy target for Bennett. In February 1876, the *Herald* published a searing indictment of malfeasance in the War Department in which it accused Secretary of War Belknap of selling frontier post traderships for personal gain. Using the *Herald* story as a club with which to bludgeon the president, a Democrat-controlled House special committee gathered evidence of kickbacks paid to Belknap by the post trader at Fort Sill. Under pressure from Grant, Belknap resigned to avoid impeachment.

Custer had suspected similar malfeasance at posts on the upper Missouri River, Fort Abraham Lincoln included. In the summer of 1875, with Custer's connivance, Bennett had sent a correspondent to Bismarck to ferret out fraud. The reporter discovered a cesspool of corruption involving licenses for both Indian agency and post traderships that implicated not only Belknap but also President Grant's brother Orvil.

Nine months later, the house committee summoned Custer to testify on the charges. Sensing trouble, Terry suggested that he respond by telegram. Custer, however, either from a sense of duty or perhaps hoping to twist the knife in Belknap's political cadaver, answered the summons.

It was a terrible miscalculation. Custer's open admiration for the committee chairman—they strolled about the capital and dined together—won him no friends in the administration. Custer's actual testimony consisted of secondhand information supplemented by his own suspicions—hardly enough to convict in a court of law, but sufficient to infuriate President Grant, who ordered Custer banished from the forthcoming campaign.

Custer was crushed. "With tears in his eyes," General Terry later confided to friends, "[Custer] begged my aid. How could I resist it?" Terry dictated a telegram for Custer to send to the president, appealing to him as a fellow soldier to spare Custer the "humiliation of seeing my regiment march to meet the enemy, and I not to share its dangers." Terry had ulterior motives for helping Custer: he feared taking the field without him; in fact, he did not want to take the field at all. Grant relented, to a degree. He gave permission for Custer to lead the Seventh Cavalry but not the expedition; Terry would have to hit the trail after all. Custer blurted out the news to Terry's chief engineer, adding

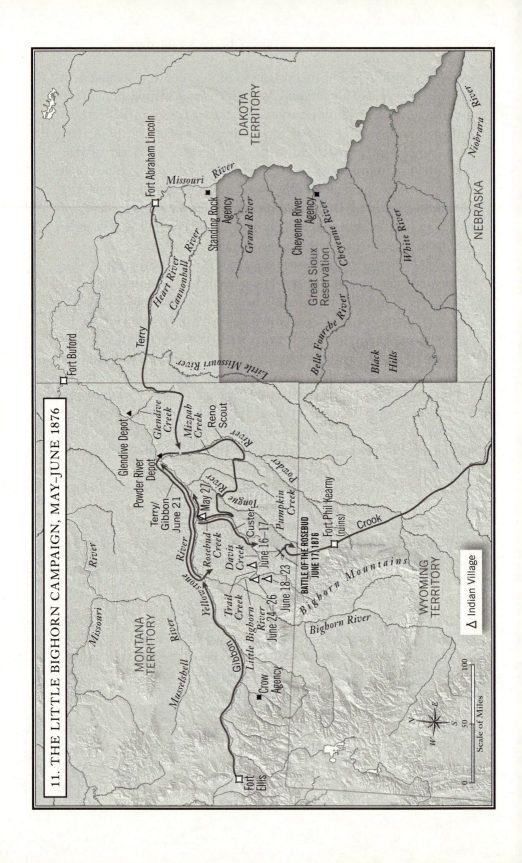

11. THE LITTLE BIGHORN CAMPAIGN, MAY–JUNE 1876

DAKOTA
TERRITORY

NEBRASKA

Fort Abraham Lincoln

Missouri River

Standing Rock
Agency

Grand River

Cheyenne River
Agency

Cheyenne River

White River

Niobrara River

Heart River

Cannonball River

Great Sioux
Reservation

Belle Fourche River

Black
Hills

Terry

Fort Buford

Little Missouri River

Glendive Depot

Glendive Creek

Powder River
Depot

Mizpah Creek

Reno
Scout

Powder River

Fort Phil Kearny
(ruins)

Crook

Terry/
Gibbon
June 21

May 27

Tongue River

Custer
June 16–17

Pumpkin Creek

BATTLE OF THE ROSEBUD
JUNE 17, 1876

Rosebud Creek

Davis
Creek

June 18–23

Bighorn Mountains

MONTANA
TERRITORY

Missouri River

Yellowstone River

Musselshell River

Gibbon

Trail Creek

Little Bighorn River

June 24–26

Bighorn River

WYOMING
TERRITORY

Crow
Agency

Fort
Ellis

△ Indian Village

N
W   E
S

Scale of Miles
0   50   100

indiscreetly that he would "cut loose" from Terry at the first opportunity; he had "got away with Stanley and would be able to swing clear of Terry." Custer's gratitude to his department commander would apparently take a backseat to his ambition.[8]

✳

General Crook was no less ambitious than Custer. He was also not one to repeat a mistake. There would be no more delegating operations to subordinates, certainly not to anyone needing to restore a tarnished reputation. Instead, Crook would lead the Wyoming Column himself. On May 29, 1876, he started north from Fort Fetterman with a 1,051-man command, a force seemingly sufficient to overawe any Indians it might encounter. Not only was Crook's new expedition larger than the Powder River Expedition had been, but it was also better officered. The dependable lieutenant colonel William B. Royall commanded the four cavalry battalions, all of which were led by solid officers. Major Alexander Chambers, a West Point classmate of Crook's, commanded the infantry.

Crook's immediate destination was the ruins of old Fort Reno, eighty miles north of Fort Fetterman, where at least two hundred Crow and Shoshone allies were expected to rendezvous with his command. From there the expedition would continue into the Montana Territory along either the Tongue River or Rosebud Creek, depending on where hostile trails led, and deliver a hard blow with overwhelming numbers. At least, that was Crook's plan.[9]

Crook had not the slightest idea what he was up against. The reports Sheridan had received were true. Lakotas from the reservations were flocking to Sitting Bull. On April 1, his village had numbered 250 lodges. By early June, it had climbed to 461 lodges. That represented a population of three thousand, of whom eight hundred were warriors. A third of the lodges were Hunkpapa, but every Lakota tribe was represented. Thanks to Crook's misdirected Powder River attack, 100 Cheyenne lodges had also placed themselves under Sitting Bull's protection. During the late spring, the village followed the buffalo herds west through the upper Powder River country. The amount of available grass and firewood dictated how long a village remained in one place; once these resources were exhausted—usually within three days—the village picked up and moved in the direction indicated by scouts on the lookout for buffalo herds. Other wolves scoured the countryside for signs of soldiers.

The council chiefs endorsed Sitting Bull and Crazy Horse's defensive policy, reminding their warriors that their energy was better spent hunting buffalo than grappling with soldiers. But the admonitions of the elderly fell on deaf ears. As always, aspiring warriors, ever in search of honors and prestige, marched to a different drum—the war drum. Reining them in was a constant challenge for the chiefs.[10]

In late May, the roving Indian village camped near the mouth of Rosebud Creek. For a *Wichasha Wakan* of Sitting Bull's sensibility, it was a place of staggering spiritual power. An unseen, irresistible force beckoned the Hunkpapa holy man to ascend a nearby butte and commune with *Wakan Tanka*. Atop the butte, he prayed, meditated, and then drifted off to sleep. Dreamed winds of gale force blew into his face. Looking east, Sitting Bull saw a huge dust cloud on the horizon swirl toward him. At the same time, a white cloud in the shape of an Indian village resting beneath snowcapped mountains sailed gently against the gale from the opposite direction. As the gale bore down on the village, Sitting Bull glimpsed countless soldiers with glittering guns riding behind the dust cloud. The two air masses collided. There was a terrific crash, such as Sitting Bull had never heard, and the sky erupted with thunder and lightning. A downpour obliterated the dust cloud. As the storm abated, the white cloud drifted serenely eastward. Sitting Bull awoke profoundly moved. He recounted his dream to the council chiefs. The gale and the dust cloud, he said, represented the army coming to wipe out the Lakotas; the white cloud was the Lakota and Cheyenne village. The meaning was clear. The Indians would annihilate the soldiers in a great battle.

A few days after his vision, Sitting Bull summoned his nephew White Bull and three other men to accompany him to a hilltop to hear him pray for the Lakota people. Sitting Bull dressed humbly, his face unpainted and his waist-length hair loose. After a lengthy pipe ceremony, Sitting Bull rose, faced the setting sun, and implored *Wakan Tanka* to give his people ample food and to maintain unity among the Lakota tribes. In exchange, Sitting Bull promised to undergo the Sun Dance ritual for two days and two nights and later to make *Wakan Tanka* an offering of a buffalo.

Sitting Bull organized the Sun Dance in the shadows of the Deer Medicine Rocks, a place sacred to both the Lakotas and the Cheyennes.

LEFT Chief Quanah of the Quahadi Comanches, son of a war chief and Cynthia Parker, the daughter of an early Texas settler. His Anglo blood showed itself in his aquiline nose and gray eyes.

BELOW, LEFT Kicking Bird, peace chief of the Kiowas. Before he died, he told an army surgeon, "I have taken the white man's road, and am not sorry. Tell my people to take the good path."

BELOW, RIGHT Chief Lone Wolf. A fierce Kiowa war leader, he chopped a Texas Ranger to pieces to avenge the death of his son, killed on a horse-stealing raid in Texas.

LEFT Nelson A. Miles's vaulting ambition and ruthless quest for advancement made him unpopular with fellow officers, but he was just and humane in his dealings with defeated Indians.

MIDDLE The Red River War. A soldier in the foreground is moistening his lips with his own blood to ease his thirst, an extremity to which many were driven.

BOTTOM Palo Duro Canyon, scene of the decisive battle of the Red River War. On the morning of September 28, 1874, Mackenzie's Fourth Cavalry descended the canyon wall to attack a combined Comanche, Kiowa, and Cheyenne village on the canyon floor.

RIGHT Captain Jack, reluctant leader of the Modoc resistance. He claimed to "know the white man's heart," which he found in the main to be good.

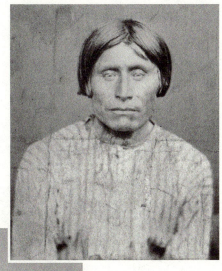

LEFT Edward R. S. Canby, an "honorable and simple-hearted" soul whose limited ambition made him the only general officer in the regular army with no known enemies.

LEFT Toby Riddle, the selfless Modoc wife of a gold miner. She acted as intermediary between Captain Jack and General Canby.

RIGHT George Crook near the end of his career. A staff officer said Crook was "more of an Indian than the Indian himself."

Sitting Bull, Hunkpapa Lakota chief and holy man. He once said, "The white man never lived who loved an Indian, and no true Indian ever lived that did not hate the white man."

Custer's expedition into the Black Hills. Custer appears in the left foreground wearing light clothing. Behind him are the expedition's 110 Studebaker covered wagons.

The septuagenarian Eastern Shoshone Chief Washakie (standing right center, holding hat and wearing the presidential peace medal) and his subchiefs and headmen. Washakie and eighty-six Shoshones fought with General Crook at the Battle of the Rosebud.

Alfred H. Terry, urbane and independently wealthy, preferred the comforts of his St. Paul, Minnesota, headquarters to the rigors of the campaign.

John Gibbon empathized with the non-reservation Lakotas. Gibbon said that if he were an Indian whose way of life was threatened he "would cut the heart out of everyone I could lay my hands on."

The Custer Fight, by famed Western artist Charles Marion Russell. The destruction of Custer and the remnant of his battalion on Last Stand Hill from the Indian perspective.

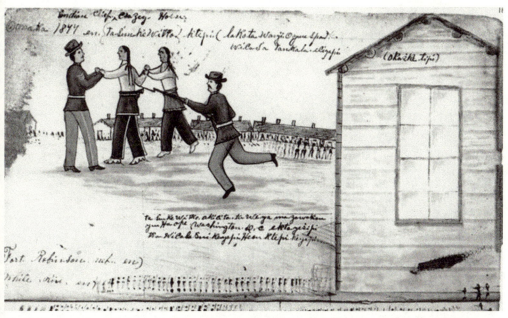

The killing of the Oglala war leader Crazy Horse, as depicted by Amos Bad Heart Bull, a famous Lakota artist who painted in the Ledger Art tradition. There is no known photograph of Crazy Horse.

LEFT Little Wolf (standing) and Dull Knife (seated), Northern Cheyenne chiefs

BELOW Soldiers overwhelm the starving and exhausted remnant of Dull Knife's Cheyenne band on January 22, 1879.

All the non-treaty Indians attended. On June 6, Sitting Bull fulfilled the first of his vows. First he purified himself in a sweat lodge. Next, in the dance lodge, Sitting Bull performed a pipe ceremony. Then he sat against the dance pole, arms and legs akimbo. Fifty match-head-sized bits of flesh were gouged from each of Sitting Bull's arms with an awl. As the blood flowed, Sitting Bull supplicated *Wakan Tanka*. He danced around the pole, all the while staring into the sun. After a time, he stopped and fainted without falling. Onlookers gently placed him on the ground and dabbed his face with water. Awakening, Sitting Bull spoke of a vision. Just below the sun, he had seen many soldiers and horses plunging upside down from the sky like so many grasshoppers into an Indian village; there were some Indians falling headfirst also. "These soldiers do not possess ears," a voice told Sitting Bull. "They are to die, but you are not supposed to take their spoils." Afterward, Sitting Bull fulfilled his remaining pledge, offering a buffalo carcass to *Wakan Tanka*.

Sitting Bull's second vision electrified the village. The meaning was clear: The Lakotas and the Cheyennes would soon win a spectacular victory. But to reap its benefits, Sitting Bull reiterated, they must not plunder the dead soldiers.[11]

*

Two hundred miles to the southwest, Crook was having a hard time of it. When he arrived at the ruins of Fort Reno on June 2, there was no sign of the Crows or the Shoshones who were to have met him there. Crook dispatched his only scouts, led by the indispensable Frank Grouard, to go to their agencies beyond the Bighorn Mountains and find them. Three days later, Crook's column labored blindly past the remnants of Fort Phil Kearny, hardly an uplifting experience. A cavalry lieutenant moonlighting as a newspaper reporter used the ill-starred fort as a metaphor for public indifference to the frontier soldier. "The bodies of [Captain William Judd] Fetterman and his band lie buried in a trench in the graveyard, but one more sad commentary on the gratitude—or absolute want of it—of this our model republic," he wrote. "I saw within the ruins of the old enclosure, which once surrounded the burial place, human bones lying unburied and bleaching in the sun, having been doubtless exhumed by the coyote."

Leaving the sad sight behind, Crook crossed the Montana border and promptly lost his way. On the night of June 7, a small war party skirmished with Crook's pickets. No damage was done, but with the element of surprise obviously lost, Crook withdrew toward the Bighorn Mountains. And then, Lieutenant Bourke jotted in his journal, the command "settled down in the somnolent apathy of permanent camp life looking for our friends." Crook himself only pretended apathy. Deeply troubled, he masked his emotions with endless games of whist and hunting trips into the hills.

A week later, Grouard returned with 176 Crow warriors. Later in the day, eighty-six well-armed and brightly adorned Shoshones trotted into camp in perfect military order, two American flags flapping crisply at the head of their column. Leading the colorful procession was the seventy-eight-year-old chief Washakie, a frontier legend. He spoke both French and English and encouraged missionaries to proselytize his people. In appreciation of the chief's goodwill, the army named the military post near his reservation Fort Washakie, the only fort ever named for an Indian. For all their loyalty, the Crows sided with the army principally to settle scores with the Lakotas; the Shoshones, however, served with the soldiers out of genuine affection for them.[12]

Grouard had brought not only the Indian allies but also flawed intelligence; he calculated the Lakota and Cheyenne strength at twenty-five hundred warriors (the correct number was closer to a thousand) from a village located on the Rosebud, forty-five miles distant (the village actually rested on a divide between the Rosebud and the Little Bighorn River). The supposed numerical superiority of the hostiles did not trouble Crook, who doubted that the Indians were either capable of concentrating their forces or willing to risk open battle.

At daybreak on June 16, Crook's cavalcade started confidently for the headwaters of Rosebud Creek. After a thirty-five-mile march, Crook bivouacked, taking care to assemble his horses and mules inside a hollow square to protect them from raiding parties. Few doubted that the enemy was near. During the march, scattered buffalo had crossed the column's path; the Crows said they were running from Lakota hunters. Late in the day, Crow scouts found a cooking fire with buffalo meat still on it. That night the Crows and the Shoshones readied themselves for battle, singing and dancing until dawn. "We are now right in among the hostiles and may strike or be struck at any hour," a sleepless Bourke wrote in his diary. He would not have long to wait.[13]

The Crow scouts had interrupted the hasty meal of a Cheyenne raiding party out for stray army horses. The raiders were long gone, having galloped the forty miles back to the village to report their discovery of Crook's massive column. Criers sounded the alarm. Women hurriedly packed family belongings and dismantled tipis. Young men painted themselves for war. The chiefs urged restraint, but Sitting Bull's vision of victory undercut their words of caution; buoyed by a feeling of invincibility, their warriors took matters into their own hands. "As darkness came on we slipped away," said the Cheyenne warrior Wooden Leg. "Warriors came from every camp circle. We had our weapons, war clothing, paints, and medicines. I had my six-shooter. We traveled all night." Unable to stop them, the chiefs joined the procession. As the sun rose over the big bend of the Rosebud on June 17, 1876, Sitting Bull, his swollen arms rendered all but useless by the flesh-giving ritual, Crazy Horse, Gall, and a host of lesser war chiefs rode toward an unsuspecting foe at the head of nearly a thousand supremely confident Lakota and Cheyenne warriors.[14]

Crook knew nothing of their approach. Since encountering the Cheyenne raiding party, the Crows and the Shoshones had grown painfully diffident. They clung to the soldiers, venturing no farther than necessary to shoot a few buffalo. Only Frank Grouard had demonstrated any pluck. From insults traded with Lakota wolves, he deduced that the hostile village lay twenty miles up the valley of Rosebud Creek. Armed only with Grouard's uncertain surmise, at dawn on June 17 Crook edged a tentative three miles downriver and then halted, intending to stage a surprise attack that night. The bivouac site was pleasant enough but difficult to defend should the need arise. A steep bluff bordered it on the south, and interminable ridges rolled off to the north. Several of the Crow scouts, having regained their nerve, edged over the ridges.

The morning was hot and still, the big Montana skies crystal blue. A heavy languor settled over the camp. Crook passed the time playing whist, while the soldiers dozed in the shade of their saddle blankets. Scribbling a few lines of column, a newspaperman observed that there was "nothing to suggest an enemy might be near."

Nothing, that is, until the Crows suddenly spilled over the nearest ridge and made straight for Crook's card table. The Lakotas, they announced, were coming. Unaccountably, Crook paid them no heed. Giving up on the general, the Crows and the Shoshones painted themselves for battle and started for the front of their own accord. Minutes later, they were back, hallooing that the Lakotas were charging down on them. Bullets kicked up dust in their wake, angrily punctuating the plain truth: Crook had been caught napping.

Only the near exhaustion of the enemy saved Crook. "We found the soldiers about 8:00 a.m.," said Wooden Leg. "We had slept only a little, our horses were very tired, so we did not hurry our attack. But always in such cases there are eager or foolish ones who begin too soon." A stunned cavalry lieutenant watched several young hotheads gallop straight into the midst of his disorganized ranks and slap soldiers with quirts until they were shot from their ponies.

The overeager warriors included eighteen-year-old Jack Red Cloud, son of the great Oglala chief. He had slipped off the reservation with his father's warbonnet and intricately decorated repeating rifle, neither of which proved of much use to him. After a soldier's bullet felled Jack Red Cloud's war pony, Wooden Leg observed the young Oglala do the unpardonable. "According to the Indian way," Wooden Leg later explained, "a warrior was supposed to stop and take off the bridle from the killed horse to show how cool he could conduct himself." Not the son of Red Cloud. No sooner had his pony hit the ground than he scampered off with three mounted Crows close behind. Weeping hysterically, Jack Red Cloud begged for mercy. The Crows, who were merely out for fun, lashed him with their pony whips and jerked off his warbonnet. Wooden Leg enjoyed the playful display. "They did not try to kill him. They only teased him, telling him he was a boy and ought not to be wearing a warbonnet."[15]

In marked contrast to Jack Red Cloud's cowardice stood the heroism of a Cheyenne girl whose brother had also lost his pony near Crook's camp. His comrades held back, but she darted from the Cheyenne lines. Pulling rein beside her brother, she helped him mount and then galloped off with him to safety. In her honor, the Cheyennes named the ensuing clash the Where the Young Girl Saved Her Brother Fight.[16]

For three hours, over a three-mile-long front, the battle rolled and roiled without result. Plains Indian tactics were unfamiliar to many of the officers, Crook included, and his response—a series of unco-ordinated counterattacks—was ineffectual. As the soldiers advanced, the Indians simply retired from one ridge to another until, finding good defensive ground, they dismounted and drove off the attackers while their well-trained war ponies grazed quietly behind them. Captain Anson Mills found the Indian tactics frustrating beyond measure. When the Indians chose to attack, they "came not in line like soldiers but in flocks, hanging on with one arm around the neck and one leg over the horse, firing and lancing from underneath the horses' necks, so that there was no part of the Indian at which to aim." And then there was their "hideous" appearance—Mills used the word "hideous" three times in one paragraph—which terrified the army horses. Mills might have been repulsed by their feathers, horns, and the multitude of colors splashed in undecipherable designs on man and pony, but he had to admit that "the Indians proved then and there that they were the best cavalry soldiers on earth."

Crook tried to appear master of a situation too fluid and confused to comprehend. Nothing in his years of tracking small bands of Snakes, Paiutes, and Apaches, all of whom preferred quick ambushes and hasty retreats to stand-up battle, had prepared him for this moment. Never had he seen so many hostile Indians, nor faced an Indian foe who refused to run. Indeed, Crook would have liked to run himself. During a lull, a captain dared ask, "General, many say that they get so hardened to this sort of thing that they don't mind it, and I often wonder whether you feel like I do in a position of this kind?"

"How do you feel?" asked Crook.

"Why, just as though, if you were not in sight, I'd be running like hell."

"Well, I feel exactly that way myself."[17]

At 11:00 a.m., Crook made a decision that nearly cost him the battle. Hoping to regain the initiative, he ordered Captain Mills to extricate himself, ride northward down the canyon of Rosebud valley with two battalions, and strike the hostile village. Mills's departure left Crook to defend a long ridge with only Chambers's infantry, the Indian scouts, and a platoon of mule packers.

On a parallel ridge three-quarters of a mile to the west, with a broad valley and wisp of a watercourse called Kollmar Creek intervening, Colonel Royall and 225 troopers bore the brunt of an assault by at least twice as many Indians. Crook had never wanted Royall so far from the main body, but in the muddled opening moments of the battle Royall had acted on his own initiative. Now it cost him dearly. His men fought standing or kneeling in a ragged skirmish line against an enemy sheltered behind sagebrush, rocks, ravines, and bumps in the ground. Despite the unpromising odds, Royall's men were holding their own when a staff officer from Crook galloped up with orders for the colonel to withdraw. Royall duly pulled Guy Henry's battalion from the line. It was then that the slaughter started. A large .44-caliber bullet bore through Henry's face, obliterating his left eye and shattering his sinuses before emerging beneath his right eye. The captain swayed from the saddle, choking on his own blood. Crow and Shoshone scouts rushed forward and saved him before Lakota warriors closed in. As the skirmish line disintegrated, half a dozen troopers were surrounded and shot dead. Only an aggressive counterattack by the Crow and Shoshone scouts and several well-aimed volleys from Chambers's infantry enabled Royall to extricate himself without heavier losses.[18]

As his lines wavered, Crook ordered Mills's recall. The timing was excellent, if unintentional. Mills had pounded four miles down the narrow Rosebud valley without finding the village. Now he climbed from the canyon and struck the Indians' left flank just as they were gathering for another assault. The Indians dispersed, quitting the battlefield in clusters around their war leaders. Welcome though it was to Crook's beleaguered troops, Captain Mills's timely reappearance was not the primary cause of the Indian withdrawal. The warriors had ridden all night and fought for six hours. They were hungry and exhausted. Scores of ponies either had been shot or were too worn to go on. The Indians, moreover, had come not to annihilate the soldiers but to frighten them off. Convinced they had succeeded, the Lakota and Cheyenne chiefs were well pleased with the battle's outcome. Excepting one mortally wounded Cheyenne and twenty dead Lakotas—thirteen of whom lost their scalps to Crows or Shoshones—and perhaps another sixty wounded, it had also been a good day for individual warriors, especially Sitting Bull's nephew White Bull, who counted five coups. A Cheyenne war chief thought the clash "a great fight, [with] much smoke and dust."[19]

Too much, without a doubt, for Crook's taste. Captain Mills encountered the general an hour after the Indians had gone, looking "more dejected" than any man he had ever seen. Mills asked Crook why he had recalled him. "Well," replied Crook, "I found it a more serious engagement than I thought. We have lost about fifty killed and wounded, and the doctors refused to remain with the wounded unless I left the infantry and one of the squadrons with them. I knew I could not keep my promise to support you with the remainder of the force."

Crook had lost fewer men than he supposed. Only nine soldiers, one Crow, and one Shoshone were killed and one officer, nineteen soldiers, four Crows, and two Shoshones wounded—the low casualties a consequence of both poor Indian marksmanship and their aversion to close-quarters combat. Crook, however, had forfeited something more precious to his campaign than lives: He had lost the confidence of his Crow and Shoshone allies. They now called him Squaw Chief, the epitome of cowardice. Captain Mills was only slightly less damning of his commander, dismissing the entire expedition as a tragicomic debacle. "I do not think General Crook knew where the [hostiles] were," he wrote later, "and I do not think our friendly Indians knew where they were, and no one conceived we would find them in the great force we did."[20]

Crook indeed had a great deal to learn about Plains Indian warfare. He was in no hurry to enlighten himself, however. Deprived of the Crows and the Shoshones, who left for their agencies with a lukewarm pledge to return in time for the next campaign, Crook hustled his command back to the base of the Bighorn Mountains. Beneath Cloud Peak, the highest elevation in the range, he set up camp.

Crook's first order of business was to write to Sheridan of his misfortune. Employing the dubious maxim that whoever holds the field last is the victor, he excused his ultimate withdrawal on the grounds that the men were low on food and his wounded needed proper care. Replenishing supplies was the work of a day, but Crook made clear that he intended a prolonged stay. "I expect to find those Indians in rough places all the time," he informed Sheridan on June 19, "and so have ordered up five companies of infantry, and shall not probably make any extended movement until they arrive." What Crook hoped to accomplish with a few score additional infantrymen against swift-riding Indians, he failed to say.

While Crook made excuses to headquarters, his command enjoyed what amounted to a vacation amid breathtakingly beautiful surroundings. Everyone from the general to the lowest private went hunting or fished. Crook also found time for bird collecting and, of course, endless games of whist. On the Fourth of July, he received Sheridan's reply to his abbreviated report of the Battle of the Rosebud. He was to hit the hostiles again and hit them hard.

Crook ignored Sheridan. The only thing he intended to hit hard was the sportsman's trail. Crumpling up the order, Crook wandered off to make good his vow to bag a hundred trout in one day. Lieutenant Bourke, meanwhile, devoted endless hours to his diary, which included a delusional July 6 entry that cast the Rosebud imbroglio as a victory for the commander he revered. "The absence of hostile demonstrations since our fight of June 17 speaks very plainly of the severe handling the Sioux received that day," wrote Bourke. "Were they victorious or had the day been even undecided, our camp would long since have been beleaguered by their sharpshooters." Evidently, it did not occur to Bourke that the Indians might have fought only to protect their village.[21]

Removing himself from the campaign was bad enough. But Crook had not only lost his stomach for a fight but also neglected to inform Terry of the battle on the Rosebud, the immensity of the Indian force, or his present whereabouts. His incomprehensible negligence left Terry to operate in the dark, with consequences that were to prove more tragic than anyone could have imagined.

That there would be more fighting, and closer to home, Sitting Bull had no doubt. His vision had not been fulfilled. Thus far, no soldiers had fallen upside down into the Lakota camp.

*

Much had transpired in Terry's command since Crook opened his ill-fated campaign on June 2. Seemingly no worse for his brush with official oblivion, Custer had returned to Fort Abraham Lincoln. "Dressed in a dashing suit of buckskin," gushed an admiring newspaperman, "he is prominent everywhere, flitting to and fro in his quick eager way . . . full of perfect readiness for a fray with the hostile red devils, and woe to the body of scalp-lifters that comes within reach of himself and brave companions in arms." With Custer back, the Dakota Column certainly appeared, as General Sheridan put it, "to be fully equal to all the Sioux which can be brought against it." For the first time, all twelve companies of the Seventh Cavalry would campaign together. How much Terry himself would contribute to the campaign was an open question, but with three infantry companies, a Gatling gun platoon, and 40 Arikara scouts in addition to Custer's command, he had a total of 925 men with which to operate.

It was an impressive force; on paper, that is. The "Fighting Seventh" had not fired a shot in anger in three years. The regiment's only real brush with Indians since the Battle of the Washita eight years earlier had been the skirmishes on the Yellowstone in 1873, which had principally served to restore Custer to the public eye and raise Sitting Bull higher in the estimation of the non-treaty bands. Few Washita veterans remained in the ranks of the Seventh. Nearly a quarter of the seven hundred enlisted men were raw recruits. Only twenty-eight of the regiment's authorized forty-three officers were present, and of these just half had Indian-fighting experience. The chain of command was fractious, to put it mildly. Custer's relations with his two wing commanders—Captain Frederick Benteen and Major Marcus A. Reno—were arguably the worst between a regimental commander and his chief subordinates anywhere in the frontier army. Captain Benteen detested Custer. Five years older than his colonel, the gallant, capable, but irascible captain not only blamed Custer for Major Elliott's death at the Washita but also believed himself far better qualified than Custer to command a regiment.

Major Reno seemed to hate not only Custer but also life itself. Sullen by nature and socially inept, Reno had seen his world crumble since the death of his vivacious and politically well-connected wife two years earlier. Now only the army remained to him, and he was sabotaging his career with heavy drinking. The officers in the Seventh Cavalry, Custer included, respected Benteen and trusted his judgment in battle. Few officers, however, liked or trusted Reno. Although Custer knew that Benteen and Reno hated him, an impartial subordinate swore that he "was considerate of them and always ready to do the [men] favors."[22]

Custer's admirable willingness to shrive troublesome subordinates was about to be tested in the unforgiving classroom of active campaigning. In the predawn hours of May 17, 1876, the staccato bugle notes of "Boots and Saddles" pierced the black stillness at Fort Abraham Lincoln. The field exam had begun. The regiment mounted, the band struck up "Garryowen," and in the receding darkness the Seventh Cavalry passed in review. General Terry permitted married officers and men a brief pause for a farewell embrace with their families. The band changed tunes to "The Girl I Left Behind Me," and the long column snaked west onto the prairie. A furtive light knifed through the fog to reveal a singular mirage: the marching cavalry appeared suspended between earth and sky. Libbie Custer shivered with a presentiment of tragedy. "The future of the heroic band seemed revealed, and already there seemed a premonition in the supernatural translation as their forms were reflected from the opaque mist of the early dawn."[23]

Terry's campaign to humble the Lakotas unfolded haltingly and for the moment was in little danger. The Dakota Column reached the lower

Powder River on June 9 without having seen a single Indian or, for that matter, heard a word from Crook, who had left Fort Fetterman nine days earlier. Gibbon, who was making his way slowly down the Yellowstone toward a junction with Terry, had sent him only a vague dispatch dated May 27, in which he hinted at an Indian sighting somewhere near the river. That clearly would not do. Having expected more energy and clearer reporting from Gibbon, Terry summoned him aboard the steamboat *Far West*, which the general had chartered to carry supplies down the Yellowstone. Leaving his command behind, Gibbon at least made good time to the steamboat.

Gibbon's oral report was a sad saga of lassitude and missed opportunities. He had departed Fort Ellis on April 1 with 424 men, keeping north of the Yellowstone River as Terry had instructed. The Indians, it turned out, had known Gibbon's location every step of the way. Thanks to his vigorous chief of scouts, Lieutenant James H. Bradley, Gibbon briefly knew theirs. On May 16, the far-ranging Bradley had glimpsed the Lakota village in the lower Tongue River valley. Gibbon had intended to attack but was unable to negotiate a crossing of the Yellowstone. Inexplicably, he had neglected to report to Terry either Bradley's discovery of what was undoubtedly the principal village of the winter roamers or his own abortive attempt at attacking it. Similarly baffling was his subsequent failure to keep the village under constant observation.

On May 26, Bradley again located Sitting Bull's village, this time in the valley of the Rosebud, just eighteen miles from Gibbon's camp. The Indians were clearly traveling away from Terry, either up the Rosebud or toward the Bighorn country. It was critical intelligence, but to Bradley's astonishment Gibbon merely pocketed the lieutenant's report and leisurely resumed his march down the Yellowstone, leaving the Indians behind him. "Everybody wondered why we were not ordered over to attack the village," puzzled Bradley. "It was pretty big odds, but I imagine the majority of our officers would not have hesitated to give them a trial."[24]

Terry could forgive Gibbon's reluctance to attack a foe that likely outnumbered him two to one, particularly when neither he nor Gibbon knew of Crook's whereabouts. But Gibbon's silence regarding Bradley's rediscovery of the Indian village defied comprehension. It is not known what words passed between Terry and Gibbon during their June 9 meeting on the *Far West*. The upshot, however, was that Terry told

Gibbon to return posthaste to his former position opposite the Rose-bud and prepare to take the offensive jointly with the Dakota Column, then camped at the mouth of the Powder River. With luck, they might catch the Indians in a pincer.

Before Terry could march farther west, however, he had to ensure there were no stray Indians east of Rosebud Creek. To that end, he ordered Major Reno to reconnoiter the country with six companies of the Seventh. Custer was dead set against the Reno reconnaissance, and in an anonymous letter to the *New York Herald* he made sure the nation knew it. Although improperly registered, Custer's reservations were sound. Reno's scout would consume at least a week and, Custer observed, "require the entire remaining portion of the expedition to lie in idleness within two marches of the locality where it was generally believed the hostile village would be discovered on the Rosebud, the danger being that the Indians, ever on the alert, would discover the presence of the troops and take advantage of the opportunity to make their escape."[25]

Reno was out nine days. When he returned on June 20, he told Terry that he had exceeded his orders and scouted the Rosebud itself, where he had found four successive Indian campsites, each more recently abandoned than the last, and broad lodge-pole trails heading southwest—presumably toward the Little Bighorn River. The capable scout Mitch Boyer, who knew the country intimately, estimated that the hostile village numbered four hundred lodges containing eight hundred warriors.

Reno's freelancing infuriated Terry, and he vented his anger in a persnickety but private letter to his sisters; Custer, on the other hand, again took up his anonymous pen to fustigate the major publicly. "Reno has so misconducted his force as to embarrass, if not seriously and permanently mar, all hopes of future success," readers of the *New York Herald* learned. "A court-martial is strongly hinted at, and if one is not ordered it will not be because it is not richly deserved."[26]

Custer's hyperbolic accusation is indefensible. Terry, at least, recognized that Reno's insubordination had spared him the embarrassment of attacking a vacated campsite, and he formed his plans accordingly. They were necessarily more hopeful than precise. On the morning of June 21, Terry wired Sheridan his intentions, to wit: Gibbon's Montana Column (accompanied by Terry) would leave later in the day and retrace its steps along the north side of the Yellowstone, cross the river at the mouth of the Bighorn River, and then march to the mouth of the

Little Bighorn. Custer, meanwhile, would proceed up the Rosebud on the morning of June 22 with the entire Seventh Cavalry. Assuming he found no Indians on the Rosebud, Custer was to continue southwest to the headwaters of the Little Bighorn and then north down the river. Terry told Sheridan that he "could only hope that one of the two columns will find the Indians."[27]

That afternoon (June 21), Terry called Gibbon and Custer aboard the *Far West* to review the plan and to work out as many details as the nebulous intelligence on Sitting Bull's whereabouts permitted. The day before, Gibbon's scouts had reported large fires toward the Little Bighorn. That seemingly confirmed Sitting Bull's presence either on the headwaters of the Rosebud or fifteen miles farther west on the upper Little Bighorn, as Reno's reconnaissance had suggested. Terry and Gibbon accepted Mitch Boyer's estimate of eight hundred warriors. Only Custer seemed to consider the possibility that summer roamers might have swelled that number to as many as fifteen hundred. Not that it mattered. No one believed the Indians would stand and fight. Neither did the absence of news from Crook concern the conferees. Preventing the Indians' escape, Gibbon recollected, "was the idea pervading the minds of all of us." And that could only be done with a swift attack.

All agreed it best to unleash Custer and hope he would not only find the Indians but also strike them in such a way as to drive their village into Gibbon's "blocking force." That said, the conferees also concurred that all movements "must be controlled by circumstances as they arise." Terry's written orders to Custer were framed as suggestions, which Terry expected the colonel to heed unless Custer saw "sufficient reason for departing from them." Concerned that the Indians might slip the noose and escape southward, he *asked* Custer to "feel constantly" to his left.

Custer exuded confidence. He declined a proffered Gatling gun platoon as apt to slow his march and four extra cavalry companies as superfluous, boasting that the Seventh "can whip anything it meets." Being unfamiliar with the country, however, Custer readily accepted the services of Mitch Boyer and Bradley's best Crow scouts. As the conference broke up, Gibbon asked Custer to give the Montana Column a chance to participate in the fight. Custer merely laughed.[28]

Not that Gibbon had expected a favorable response. "Though it is General Terry's expectation that we will arrive in the neighborhood of the Sioux village about the same time and assist each other in the attack, it is understood that if Custer arrives first he is at liberty to attack at once if he deems prudent," Lieutenant Bradley wrote in his diary that night. "We have little hope of being in at the death, as Custer will undoubtedly exert himself to the utmost to get there first and win all the laurels for himself and his regiment."[29]

And why not? Terry clearly expected no less. Knowing that she delighted in expressions of confidence in her "dear Bo," before setting out on June 22 Custer sent Libbie a last letter with this telling extract from Terry's official order to him: "It is of course impossible to give you any definite instructions in regard to this movement, and, were it not impossible to do so, the Department Commander places too much confidence in your zeal, energy, and ability to impose on you precise orders which might hamper your action when nearly in contact with the enemy." Custer, in short, had Terry's blessing to do as he thought best.

Back at Fort Abraham Lincoln, Libbie was haunted by the mystifying mirage of a month earlier. Did it portend disaster? "Oh Autie," she wrote her husband, also on June 22. "How I feel about your going away so long without our hearing . . . Your safety is ever in my mind. My thoughts, my dreams, my prayers, are all for you. God bless and keep my darling. Ever your own Libbie." Perhaps she also thought of the other family members in harm's way. Besides Armstrong and Captain Tom Custer, their younger brother, Boston, accompanied the expedition. Also along for the adventure was their half sister's only son, eighteen-year-old Harry Armstrong "Autie" Reed.

At noon, Custer bade Terry and Gibbon farewell. As Custer turned to leave, Gibbon jokingly called out, "Now Custer, don't be greedy, but wait for us." With a wave of the hand and a hearty laugh, Custer replied, "No, I will not."[30]

*

Custer departed with 31 officers, 578 enlisted men, 45 scouts and guides, and several civilians, for a total of about 660 men. He wore a fringed buckskin jacket and pants, a dark blue wide-collared shirt, a light gray broad-brimmed hat, and a red scarf. He carried a Remington sporting rifle, a hunting knife, and two British-made revolvers. While at Fort Abraham Lincoln, Custer had cropped his reddish blond hair. Many officers had done the same; several others were also clothed in buckskin. The enlisted men were a nondescript lot. Most wore badly stained blue-flannel blouses and sky-blue pants reinforced in the legs and seat with whitish canvas. They sported a wide variety of headgear, from the regulation black-wool campaign hats to light straw hats. Beards and shaggy hair predominated. They were armed with single-shot breech-loading 1873 Springfield carbines—a weapon that boasted excellent stopping power but was prone to jam—and Colt .45 revolvers.[31]

Custer halted at 4:00 p.m. on June 22 after a twelve-mile march. His mood had inexplicably darkened, and his officers had trouble ascertaining his intentions. Lieutenant Edward S. Godfrey found officers' call that evening a dismal assemblage. "Everyone seemed to be in a serious mood, and the little conversation carried on before all had arrived was in undertones." Custer spoke in a rambling, almost diffident fashion. Absent was his customary brusqueness. He took pains to impress upon his officers that he trusted their judgment, discretion, and loyalty. They might face up to fifteen hundred warriors, Custer said, but he had rejected Terry's offer of four additional companies. If the Indians could whip the Seventh Cavalry, he told them, they would be able to defeat a much larger force; the implication being that reinforcements could not save the Seventh from defeat. Custer asked his officers to make, "then or at any time, any suggestions they thought fit."

Godfrey left the gathering perplexed. The opinions of subordinates had never mattered to Custer. Was he depressed? Did he sense that "Custer's Luck" was about to run out? Lieutenant George Wallace offered an answer: "Godfrey, I believe General Custer is going to be killed."

"Why, Wallace," replied Godfrey, "what makes you think so?"

"Because I have never heard Custer talk in that way before."[32]

*

The Lakotas and the Cheyennes had no interest in killing more soldiers. With Crook's retreat, they considered the war over. The young Cheyenne warrior Wooden Leg had "no thought of any fighting being done in the future." He was more interested in courting girls. Another Cheyenne spoke of the general sense of relief when the village entered Little Bighorn valley after the Battle of the Rosebud. "Everybody thought, 'Now we are out of the white man's country. He can live there, we will live here.' "

The burgeoning size of the village was a great cause of comfort. It now stood at 960 lodges. Seven thousand Indians camped together, of whom eighteen hundred were warriors. The pony herd probably exceeded twenty-five thousand. Although few people from the Red Cloud and Spotted Tail Agencies were present, every Lakota tribe was represented in the village. It was the largest Indian gathering on the northern plains since the 1851 Fort Laramie council.

On the afternoon of June 24, the Indians raised their tipis on bottomland along the west bank of the winding Greasy Grass River, the Lakota name for the Little Bighorn. It was a delightful spot. The waters of the Greasy Grass were cold and pure, fed by melting snows from the Bighorn Mountains. Cottonwood and willow fringed the riverbanks. A chain of ragged bluffs rose from the east bank. Beyond the bluffs lay soapweed-mottled prairie, scorched brown by the summer sun. Ravines wrinkled the land, which receded into a horizon of overwhelming vastness. Immediately west of the village was a gentle bench with plenty of scraggly but nutritious grama grass for the pony herd. The Bighorn Mountains rose blue on the horizon ten miles to the southwest.

The village was a mile long and divided into tribal circles. The Cheyenne circle rested at the lower (northern) end of the village. At the upper (southern) end, two sweeping river bends cradled the large Hunkpapa circle. Sitting Bull's lodge stood on the southern margin and housed thirteen people, including the chief's two wives. Crazy Horse's Oglalas camped midway between the Cheyenne and the Hunkpapa circles.

For six days after the Rosebud, the Lakotas and the Cheyennes had held victory dances, feasted, and recited martial deeds nonstop. On June 24, the celebration took a lighter turn. There were social dances for the young men and women and games for the children. It seemed to an ebullient Wooden Leg that "peace and happiness was prevailing all over the world; that nowhere was any man planning to lift his hand against his fellow man."

Sitting Bull knew better. Sensing his Sun Dance vision was about to be fulfilled, he climbed a knoll on the east side of the Greasy Grass. There at sunset on June 24, he performed a sacred ceremony of offering. On the hilltop, he placed a buffalo robe, a ceremonial pipe, and some tobacco wrapped in buckskin tied to a carved cherry stick—gifts for the Great Mystery *Wakan Tanka*. Then he prayed,

Wakantanka, pity me. In the name of the tribe I offer you this peace-pipe. Wherever the sun, the moon, the earth, the four points of the wind, there you are always. Father, save the tribe, I beg you. Pity me. We want to live. Guard us against all misfortunes or calamities. Pity me.[33]

CHAPTER 14

LAST STAND

W HILE SITTING BULL performed his ceremony of supplication, twenty-five miles to the east, in a bend of Rosebud Creek, the Seventh Cavalry went into bivouac. June 24 had been a difficult day for Custer. The Seventh had marched twenty-eight fitful miles while the scouts examined deserted campsites—all large, and each fresher than the last. The heat had been intense, the trail dry and dusty. The tracks of thousands of lodge poles, dragged behind Indian ponies, scarred the Rosebud valley. Wider, heavily beaten trails told of immense pony herds. And there had been ill omens. A white man's scalp found dangling from the frame of an abandoned Sun Dance lodge suggested to the Arikara scouts the presence of strong Lakota medicine. As Custer and his officers gathered to inspect the area, a stiff breeze came up and blew down the headquarters flag with the tip of the staff pointing rearward. Lieutenant Godfrey picked up the flag and shoved the staff in the ground. Again the flag fell rearward. Finally, he dug a hole. Braced by sagebrush, the staff at last held. Godfrey gave the matter no further thought. But a fellow officer told him he'd divined the hidden significance behind the falling standard: the Seventh Cavalry would be defeated.

Custer's scouts, meanwhile, had divined defeat in the lodge-pole trails, which were not diverging, as Custer assumed, but converging, made by summer roamers flocking from the agencies to Sitting Bull's village. That evening the half-Arikara, half-Lakota chief scout Bloody Knife, who was Custer's favorite, warned his fellow Indians that they were headed for a big fight. "I know what is going to happen to me," he confided. "I shall not see the sun."

The trooper William O. Taylor rested near the single "A" tent that constituted regimental headquarters. Inside, Custer sat alone, apparently lost in thought. "I was lying on my side, facing him, and it was my fancy, or the gathering twilight that made his face take on an expression of sadness that was new to me. Was it because his thoughts were back to Fort Lincoln where he had left a most beloved wife," Taylor wondered, "and was his heart filled with premonition of what was to happen on the morrow?" Custer's reverie was interrupted by a group of young lieutenants singing the doxology. Taylor thought it rather strange for officers on campaign to sing hymns.[1]

At 9:00 p.m., Crow scouts galloped into camp with momentous news: they had located the principal Lakota trail, leading west from the Rosebud valley. They also told Custer of a spruce-mottled prominence (later called the Crow's Nest) on the divide between the Rosebud and the Little Bighorn valleys that offered an unimpeded view all the way to the Little Bighorn, thirteen miles distant. If the Lakotas were in the valley of the Little Bighorn, the Crows said, their campfire smoke would be visible at dawn.

Custer faced a dilemma. General Terry had "suggested" that he reconnoiter the head of Rosebud Creek before turning west toward the Little Bighorn. Continuing down the Rosebud might trap the Indians between himself and Gibbon—assuming Gibbon had reached his assigned position—and also prevent the Indians from retreating south into the Bighorn Mountains. On the other hand, it also entailed the risk of discovery by Lakota wolves or of condemning Gibbon to fight alone. Finding an Indian village of any size was difficult enough; to pass it up once discovered violated a fundamental rule of frontier warfare. And Terry had accorded Custer the discretion to do as he deemed best should the situation warrant a departure from orders.

Custer needed less than twenty minutes to decide on a course of action: he would attack the Indian village. At 9:20 p.m., Custer sent the chief of scouts, Lieutenant Charles Varnum, with the Crows to the prominence. At dawn, the Crows saw what they had expected—campfire smoke and the dim outline of a distant pony herd. So too did Mitch Boyer. But not Varnum, whose eyes were inflamed by the trail dust. Taking the scouts at their word, he reported their findings to Custer, who was already on the trail to the divide. There he intended to conceal the regiment on June 25 to allow ample time for rest and final preparations and then attack at dawn the next day.

Few would forget the midnight march. It had a weird, almost surreal quality. The moon had set, and the night was dark as pitch. Heavy dust clouds enveloped the column. The last rank of each company banged mess cups to help trailing companies keep to the path. Here and there, men and horses lost their way and tumbled into ravines.

Atop the Crow's Nest at 9:00 a.m. on Sunday, June 25, with the regiment an hour behind him, Custer stared toward the valley. "I've got about as good eyes as anybody," he began, "and I can't see any village, Indians, or anything else." "Well, General," interjected Mitch Boyer, "if you don't find more Indians in that valley than you ever saw together you can hang me." Springing to his feet, Custer retorted, "It would do a damned sight of good to hang you, now wouldn't it?" and then started down the hill with Varnum. "I recall his remark," Varnum wrote later, "particularly because of the word damn, as it was the nearest to swearing I ever heard him come."

The Crows begged Custer to attack. A party of Lakota warriors had ridden in plain sight toward the Little Bighorn, and the Crows assumed that the Lakotas had spotted them. Custer not only declined their advice but also doubted that a large village lay directly ahead. In short, he did not credit what he could not see. Then Tom Custer rode up with troubling news: there were Indians on the back trail. A pack mule had dropped its load, and when a detail went back to retrieve it, they had found a group of young Cheyenne warriors huddled around a box of hardtack. A few shots had dispersed the Indians.

That cinched it. Convinced now that the all-important element of surprise had been lost, Custer decided to attack at once. (Unbeknownst to Custer, the Cheyennes had decided to follow the soldiers rather than warn the village.) The potential size of the Indian village, assuming the Crows were correct about its location, did not trouble Custer; his overriding concern was that it would scatter before he reached it. Mitch Boyer again tried to dissuade Custer. He had been on the northern plains for thirty years and never heard of a larger village. If they entered Little Bighorn valley that afternoon, Boyer predicted, they would wake up in hell the next morning. Custer ignored him.[2]

At 11:45 a.m., the Seventh Cavalry started down the divide. After a half mile, Custer called forward Reno and Benteen. Apparently concluding he might find it advisable to assault the hostile village from multiple directions, such as he had done at the Washita, Custer now divided the regiment into four parts. He assigned a three-company battalion and the Arikara scouts to Major Reno (175 men) and three companies to Captain Benteen (115 men) and augmented Captain Thomas M. McDougall's company (136 men) to protect the pack train. Custer retained five companies (221 men) led by his favorites—his brother Tom, Captains George Yates and Myles Keogh, his brother-in-law Lieutenant James Calhoun, and Lieutenant Algernon Smith. Custer told Benteen to reconnoiter a chain of bluffs a mile to the southwest; if they were vacant, he was to rejoin the main body immediately. Custer and Reno would follow a narrow stream (later named Reno Creek) to the Little Bighorn. McDougall and the cumbersome pack train were to follow the main body.

Before Benteen departed, a Crow scout approached Custer. "Do not divide your men," he said. "There are too many of the enemy for us, even if we all stay together. If you must fight, keep us all together."

Custer had heard enough dismal talk. "You do the scouting, and I will attend to the fighting," he replied. The Crow stripped and began to paint his face. "Why are you doing this?" asked Custer.

"Because," he answered, "you and I are going home today, and by a trail that is strange to us both."[3]

Custer was then fifteen miles from the knoll on which Sitting Bull had prayed for divine intercession the evening before.

*

Custer and Reno moved at a brisk walk under clear skies and a blazing midday sun. Dust clouds billowed from the trail. Men shed their blouses and discarded excess gear. After five miles, the columns came upon an elaborately decorated tipi. Inside was the corpse of a warrior killed at the Rosebud. (Of course Custer knew nothing of Crook's battle, so the discovery held no particular significance for him.) From a bluff beside the tipi, Mitch Boyer and the Crow Indians spotted fifty warriors on the horizon. To Custer, it could only mean one thing: the village was indeed near, and the warriors encountered earlier on the back trail were now on the way to spread the alarm.

It was nearly 2:30 p.m. Benteen had not come up, and time was at a premium. Custer waved the Arikara scouts forward, but they refused to move without the soldiers. The regimental adjutant, Lieutenant William W. Cooke, delivered orders to Reno: "The Indians are about two and a half miles ahead—they are on the jump. Go forward as fast as you think proper and charge them wherever you find them and he will support you." When the major rode by, Custer reiterated his pledge of support and told Reno to take the scouts with him. That was the extent of Custer's battle plan. The situation was fluid and unfolding fast; there was little more to offer Reno. As for Benteen, he knew nothing of Custer's intentions because Custer had no idea where either the nettlesome captain or the pack train, which was far behind everyone, might be. The command structure of the Seventh Cavalry was unraveling, and the only shots fired in anger had been at the Cheyenne biscuit thieves.

Mitch Boyer advised Custer a final time to hold up. "But Son of the Morning Star," recalled a Crow, "was like a feather borne by the wind and had to go."[4]

✳

Major Reno needed a bracer. As his men paused to water their horses in a shallow ford at the confluence of Trail Creek and the Little Bighorn at 3:00 p.m., he took a long draft from his whiskey flask. At that instant, a lieutenant splashed past him. "What are you trying to do?" snapped Reno. "Drown me before I am killed?"

A few minutes later, Reno's battalion and the Arikara scouts started down the valley on the west side of the Little Bighorn toward a dust cloud two miles distant, presumably raised by the Indians "on the jump" that Custer had instructed Reno to overtake. Bringing all three companies on line and accelerating the advance from a fast trot to a gallop, Reno yelled, "Charge!" To Private William Taylor, the order sounded slurred. Glancing back, he saw Reno take a healthy swig from a quart flask. Taylor had no idea what to expect next: "Over sage and bullberry bushes, over prickly pears and through a prairie dog village without a thought we rode. To most of us it was our first real battle at close range. Many, of whom I was one, had never fired a shot from a horse's back."

Nor would Taylor have an opportunity now. Through rifts in the dust cloud, Reno glimpsed tipis—hundreds of them—still standing. The major was caught up in an alcohol-blurred conundrum. Custer had ordered him to chase the rear guard of a small fleeing village; instead, he found himself confronting a defiant foe screening a large, stationary Indian camp. The Arikaras, who had veered to the left to drive off the

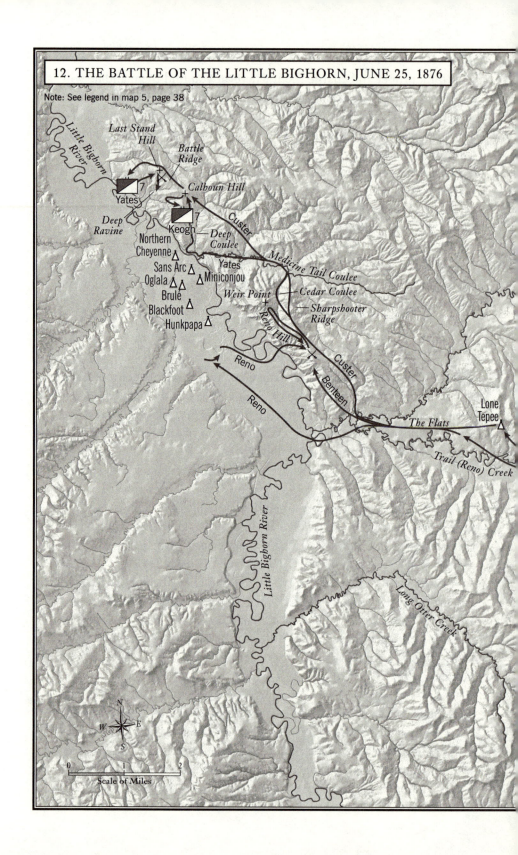

12. THE BATTLE OF THE LITTLE BIGHORN, JUNE 25, 1876

Note: See legend in map 5, page 38

Little Bighorn River

Last Stand Hill

Battle Ridge

Yates 7

Calhoun Hill

Deep Ravine

Keogh 7

Deep Coulee

Northern Cheyenne

Sans Arc

Oglala

Brule

Blackfoot

Hunkpapa

Yates

Miniconjou

Custer

Medicine Tail Coulee

Weir Point

Cedar Coulee

Sharpshooter Ridge

Reno Hill

Reno

Reno

Custer

Benteen

The Flats

Lone Tepee

Trail (Reno) Creek

Little Bighorn River

Long Otter Creek

N
W E
S

0   1   2

Scale of Miles

Lakota pony herd, as was their duty, had also run up against unexpected opposition. It was Major Reno's first taste of Indian fighting, and there was no sign of Custer. Knowing nothing of Custer's intentions beyond his vague promise of support, Reno dismounted six hundred yards short of the Hunkpapa circle. The "horse-holders," numbering one man in every four, led the mounts into a stand of timber along the riverbank. With ninety-five troopers, Reno formed an attenuated skirmish line across the bottomland. The men were in remarkably good spirits—or perhaps just giddy from adrenaline—talking and laughing as they fired. Officers exchanged banter and boasted of their marksmanship. No one, except perhaps Reno, seemed to apprehend defeat by a foe who seemed content simply to stir up dust at a distance.[5]

*

Before Reno appeared, the Lakota and Cheyenne village had been drowsing in the hot mid-afternoon sun. There were rumors of cavalry far to the east, but no one expected trouble that day. The adolescent Oglala Black Elk was greasing his body for a swim when he heard a Hunkpapa village crier yell out, "They are charging, the chargers are coming. Where the [lone] tipi is they say the chargers are coming." A woman who stepped from her lodge in the Hunkpapa circle just as Reno formed his skirmish line heard a terrific volley of carbines. "The bullets shattered the tipi poles. Women and children were running away from the gunfire. In the tumult I heard old men and women singing death songs for their warriors who were now ready to attack the soldiers."

The Hunkpapa war chief Gall said he lost two wives and three children in the first volley. That made his heart "bad," and he resolved to fight the soldiers "with the hatchet"—in other words, to mutilate indiscriminately. Nearby, carrying a Winchester rifle and a six-shooter, his old friend Sitting Bull rode a black horse amid the lodges, exhorting the warriors to "brave up." Resistance was spontaneous, leadership minimal. Warriors who had kept their war ponies beside their lodges entered the fray first, pausing just long enough to apply a modicum of war paint.[6]

There was no need for bold tactics to unsettle Major Reno; sheer numbers alone sufficed. As a swarm of warriors drove the Arikaras from the pony herd and threatened to envelop his left flank, Reno retracted his skirmish line and withdrew into the timber, reuniting soldiers and their mounts. The move mystified some of the men. Reno's casualties had been negligible; only one trooper was wounded during the twenty minutes the skirmish line held. The major had glimpsed Custer watching the action from a bluff on the east bank, a mile distant. Before wheeling his horse out of sight, Custer had waved his hat. Reno took the gesture as approval of his decision to form a skirmish line.

The Indians had kept a healthy distance from the cavalry carbines. But as the warriors' ranks swelled, so too did their audacity. The Hunkpapa war chief Iron Hawk gathered a party along the riverbank behind Reno's right, ready to infiltrate his lines. Individual warriors crept forward to set fire to the underbrush at the timber's edge. "Arrows were showered into the timber . . . while we extended our curved line farther and farther around the big grove of trees," recalled a Cheyenne warrior. "It seemed to me the [soldiers] would not live many hours longer."

Major Reno reached the same conclusion. Five minutes after entering the timber, he shouted at the men to mount up and make ready to gallop for the ford two miles upriver whence they had entered the valley. Once on the east bank of the Little Bighorn, Reno reasoned, he could join forces with Custer or with Benteen, wherever they may be. The possibility that Custer might stage a flank attack against the village to relieve pressure on Reno might have entered the major's mind. But in his view, there was no time to wait around to find out. Although Reno's decision meant a long ride over open ground with Indians in pursuit, at least one trooper found the order to leave a relief. "We could not see the Indians, but they were signaling all the time to each other with their bone whistles, and they seemed to be on all sides."[7]

Sound though Reno's plan might have been, its execution was faulty. The major had no trumpeter, which meant that the order to mount passed orally down the ranks. Few beyond earshot even knew of Reno's command. And Reno neglected to cover his withdrawal; everyone who got the order mounted more or less simultaneously. When the soldiers ceased fire, Iron Hawk's war party broke through the timber and delivered a point-blank volley. A bullet found the scout Bloody Knife, spattering blood, brains, and bone chips in Reno's face and down his blouse. Shock and liquor conspired to render Reno incoherent. First he told the men to dismount. Then he ordered them to mount. And then he simply yelled, "Any of you men who wish to make your escape, follow me," and bolted.

The major's panic infected the ranks. Someone screamed, "Every man for himself," and all who were able galloped after Reno. The Indians nearest the treeline gave way, but what the Cheyenne warrior Wooden Leg called a "great throng of Sioux" blocked the cavalry's path up the valley, forcing them to the left along a narrow trail that spilled into the Little Bighorn a mile downstream from the mouth of Trail Creek. One Lakota war chief likened the ensuing pursuit to a grand buffalo chase.

In the vanguard, Wooden Leg watched the soldiers' jaded horses tremble and lurch. The Indians' ponies, by contrast, were "lively," and the warriors rapidly gained on the troopers. The fighting now became hand-to-hand. Wooden Leg squeezed off four shots wildly with his revolver and then watched a Lakota with steadier nerves drive an arrow into the back of a soldier's head. Lance thrusts and blows from stone war clubs toppled troopers left and right. The Indians interspersed their war cries with derisive jeers. "You are only boys. You ought not to be fighting. You should have brought more Crows or Shoshones with you to do your fighting."[8]

The driving force behind Wooden Leg's "great throng of Sioux" was Crazy Horse, who had arrived on the field moments before Reno's troopers spilled out of the timber. The Indians already in action took his appearance for granted. His closest friends, however, had wondered if he would ever reach the fight. Crazy Horse had been bathing in the Little Bighorn when the shooting started upriver. Rather than ride directly to the sound of the guns, he first consulted with a medicine man. Together they invoked the spirits needed to fortify Crazy Horse's personal medicine. Outside the lodge, his warriors grew impatient. Finally, Crazy Horse emerged. His war dress was even simpler than usual. He wore no feathers, his hair hung loose, and he had painted only a few spots on his face. Leaping onto his pinto pony, Crazy Horse led the Oglalas up the valley. Other Lakotas, and even a few Cheyennes, fell in behind him. When he arrived at the riverbank, Crazy Horse flung his warriors against the flank of the retreating soldiers, herding them into the killing zone. "Indians covered the flat," remembered a Cheyenne. "They began to drive the soldiers all mixed up—Sioux, then soldiers, then more Sioux, all shooting. The air was full of smoke and dust. I saw the soldiers fall back and drop into the riverbed like buffalo fleeing."

Together with several other youths, Black Elk rode behind the warriors. Near the river a writhing soldier caught his attention. "Boy, get off and scalp him," ordered a warrior. Black Elk dismounted and with his hunting knife sliced off the trooper's closely cropped hair, and the skin with it. "Probably it hurt because he began to grind his teeth. After I did this I took my pistol out and shot him in the forehead."[9]

Private Taylor took precautions against meeting a similar fate, firing off all but one round of his revolver, intending to save the last bullet for himself. But in the rush from the timber, he accidentally dropped the weapon. Hastening along to the riverbank, Taylor saw "a struggling mass of men and horses from whom little streams of blood was coloring the water near them."

Where Taylor struck the riverbank, the Little Bighorn varied in width from twenty-five to fifty feet, the icy water belly-deep to a horse. The east bank was eight feet high, a difficult jump for tired mounts and terrified riders. Those who made it across faced a hard climb up a steep and slippery bluff interspersed with narrow ravines. The clay surface offered little traction for the horses, many of which had grown uncontrollable. But upward the men struggled, riding or leading their horses. Losing his hat during the climb, Reno was one of the first to reach the top of the hill that was to bear his name. With a red bandanna wrapped around his head and a wild look in his eyes, the major darted about the crest. Around him, men dropped from fatigue. Some wept; others cursed. Most felt they had been badly licked. Dr. Henry Porter, an army surgeon who had been in several Indian scrapes, remarked to Reno, "Major, the men were pretty well demoralized, weren't they?"

"That was a charge, sir!" was Reno's bizarre explanation of his panicked retreat.

Reno's charge to the rear had cost him dearly. The corpses of thirty-two troopers, three officers, and three civilians littered the bottomland or floated in the river. Survivors on the summit watched helplessly as warriors stripped, scalped, and mutilated the fallen. Two Arikara scouts were dead; most of the rest escaped up the valley leading Lakota ponies. Twenty soldiers were missing. Left behind in the timber, most of them would eventually find their way up Reno Hill. Thirteen wounded troopers also made it to the summit. Had it not been for the dust raised by hundreds of pounding hooves, which cut visibility to fifty feet, many more men might have been lost.

Once on the hillcrest, Reno's men were safe, at least for the moment. No warriors pursued them; on the contrary, the Indians were rapidly quitting the field, galloping northward for a purpose Reno and his men could not then divine.[10]

✳

Sitting Bull stayed behind. He had not taken part in the action. Now he rode over the valley floor viewing the carnage. Soldiers had fallen into camp, just as the voice in his vision had promised. But Sitting Bull's people had forgotten the mystic speaker's command that they not desecrate the dead. Women and children were finishing off the wounded and then butchering and plundering the corpses. Bleeding profusely from a chest wound but still alive was Isaiah Dorman, a black man married to a Lakota woman. He had signed on with Custer as an interpreter. As a knot of warriors gathered around him, he begged, "My friends, you have already killed me; don't count coups on me." Dorman had once done Sitting Bull a good turn. Now the chief intervened on his behalf.

"Don't kill that man, he is a friend of mine," Sitting Bull said as he dismounted and poured Dorman a drink of water. The warriors obeyed, but the women paid him no heed. After Sitting Bull left, a Hunkpapa woman shot Dorman dead. To ensure his agony continued into the afterlife, she and her companions slashed him with butcher knives, shot arrows into his corpse, drove an iron picket pin through his testicles, and then cut off his penis and stuffed it in his mouth.

Sitting Bull joined the cavalcade of warriors galloping north to challenge a new band of soldiers threatening the lower end of the village. As befitted a senior chief, he went not to fight but to safeguard the noncombatants. "There was so much doubt about the issue of the battle," Sitting Bull later explained, "that I started down there to tell the squaws to pack up the lodges and get ready to move away."[11]

✳

Only Custer knew what he had meant when he told Reno that he would support him. He might have intended to follow the major, as Reno expected. Unforeseen developments, however, dictated another course of action. Varnum had appeared while Custer's men were watering their horses to confirm that the Indian village lay just down the valley. Then word came that Indians were standing their ground against Reno. The best tactic, Custer apparently decided, was a flank attack to trap the Indians between his battalion and Reno's. He would rather have waited for Benteen, but time was pressing. Victory seemed assured, and

Custer's enthusiasm was contagious. As Lieutenant Varnum rode off to rejoin his scouts, Custer swung his hat in the air and sang out, "Thirty days' furlough to the man who gets the first scalp."

At 3:00 p.m., Custer led his command in a column of twos, all five companies abreast, across the Little Bighorn and onto the high ground above the east bank in search of a suitable fording site. And then he caught his first glimpse of the largest Indian village any white man had ever laid eyes on. Not that he or his men found the spectacle at all discouraging. Some troops cheered; others had trouble reining in their mounts. "Hold your horses in, boys," hollered Custer. "There are plenty of them down there for us all."

As promising as the prospect of a second Washita might have appeared to Custer, the sheer enormity of the Indian village gave new urgency to the situation. Waving over Sergeant Daniel Kanipe, Tom Custer, on his brother's behalf, told the seasoned noncommissioned officer, "Go to Captain McDougall. Tell him to bring the pack train straight across the country. If any packs come loose, cut them and come on quick—a big Indian camp. If you see Captain Benteen, tell him to come quick—a big Indian camp."

Moving at a gallop now, Custer's column hit the southern edge of a cedar-lined coulee. While the troopers tightened cinches and caught their breath, the Custer brothers climbed a hill. The scene before them was sobering but, in their judgment, still favorable. There were few warriors in the village; those with ponies at hand had left to fight Reno, while others had run to the pony herd to grab theirs. Reno's skirmish line appeared to be holding firm (his withdrawal into the trees would come twenty minutes later; the mad dash for safety across the river ten minutes after that). Returning to his waiting troops, Custer announced, "We will go down and make a crossing and capture the village." He told Mitch Boyer that the Crow scouts were free to leave; they had done their duty. But where was Benteen? To the trumpeter Giovanni Martini (an Italian immigrant who had changed his name to John Martin at enlistment), Custer barked an order: "I want you to take a message to [Captain] Benteen. Ride as fast as you can and tell him to hurry. Tell him it's a big village and I want him to be quick, and to bring ammunition packs." Distrusting Martin's uncertain command of English, Adjutant William Cooke scribbled a message for the trumpeter to carry: "Benteen. Come on. Big Village. Be quick. Bring Pack. W. W. Cooke. P. bring pacs [*sic*]." Spurring his horse up the back trail,

Martin glanced behind him long enough to see the command gallop down Cedar Coulee. It was approximately 3:30 p.m.[12]

*

There ends the army-eyewitness version of Custer's last battle. Three Crow Indians who lingered on a ridge above the village to watch a while longer later gave garbled accounts of minimal value. Custer's movements after the trumpeter Martin left are thus necessarily conjectural, the subject of ever-changing theories drawn from markers denoting where officers and men supposedly fell, the lay of the land, the pattern of bullets recovered in an archaeological dig, an ongoing assumption of Custer's innate aggressiveness, and the words of Indian combatants. The scenario that follows is drawn from Indian testimony and the most thoughtful modern studies of the battle.[13]

*

Custer's battalion continued north down Cedar Coulee until it terminated at a broad ravine called Medicine Tail Coulee, which led to the river. Custer now faced two apparent options: descend Medicine Tail Coulee and hope to find a suitable ford, or hold his command on high ground overlooking the coulee until Benteen and the pack train arrived.

The information available to Custer would have given cause for both hope and alarm. Leaving his place of safety with the pack train, young Boston Custer had galloped up from the south to join in the action. Boston would have been able to tell his older brother that the back trail was clear and that Benteen had taken up Custer's route. Mitch Boyer, on the other hand, brought troubling news. He and a Crow scout had remained on the bluff overlooking the Little Bighorn. There they witnessed Reno's recall of his skirmish line and withdrawal into the trees.

In the hope of drawing warriors away from Reno, Custer compromised, leading two companies under Captain Yates down Medicine Tail Coulee to feint against the village. He assigned the remaining three companies to Captain Keogh, posting them on a hill overlooking the twin coulees, both to protect his rear and to act as a beacon for Benteen. The maneuver almost worked. There were fewer than fifty warriors crouched amid the cottonwood trees at Medicine Tail ford when Custer and Yates approached. But they were enough to turn back the attackers. Several troopers pitched into the river dead or wounded; the remaining eighty or so swung north up a drainage called Deep Coulee. Hundreds of warriors returning from the Reno fight coalesced around the ford. Burning for vengeance, the bad-hearted chief Gall, who had lost five family members to Reno's opening volley, led the warriors across the Little Bighorn. Dismounted skirmishers fired ragged volleys at the Indians to little effect. Sitting Bull attributed the soldiers' poor showing to exhaustion. "When they got off from their horses they could not stand firmly on their feet. They swayed to and fro—so my young men have told me—like the limbs of cypresses in a great wind."

In the meantime, Captain Keogh had fallen back to a gentle rise later known as Calhoun Hill, a mile north of the lower limit of the Indian village. Calhoun Hill represented the southern end of a wavy, barren "backbone" today called Battle Ridge. A tumble of grassy ravines marked the course from the ridge to the river. Trending northwest for about a mile, Battle Ridge terminated in the small knoll with a panoramic view where Sitting Bull had prayed the evening before.

Shortly before 5:00 p.m., Custer and Yates reunited with Keogh on Calhoun Hill. While Custer considered his next move, Keogh deployed half his men in a skirmish line to hold off warriors edging up Deep Coulee and tucked the remaining troopers behind the crest in reserve. Custer had to act fast. Hundreds of warriors were now on his side of the Little Bighorn. The Indians, however, were in no hurry. This was a day for deliberate killing, not reckless mounted dashes to prove one's courage. They crawled through the sagebrush, jumping up to fire and then jerking themselves down just as quickly. A few warriors were hit nonetheless. Wooden Leg glimpsed a wounded Lakota stagger off. "As he passed near to where I was I saw that his whole lower jaw was shot away. The sight of him made me sick. I had to vomit."[14]

Unlike their assailants, Calhoun's men were easy targets. They knelt or stood, silhouetted along the barren hilltop. Arrows rained down on them. Bullets kicked up dust or entered flesh with a sickening thud. Terrified horses grappled with their holders. Carbines jammed. And still no sign of Benteen. Before Calhoun's line buckled, Custer led Yates's two companies in a charge along the ridge, hoping to ford the Little Bighorn two miles north of the village and then capture women and children who had fled the village. It was a desperate, almost ludicrous gambit. Custer had no more than seventy men, yet somehow he hoped to force his way into a throng of nearly five thousand Indian noncombatants and take enough prisoners to compel the warriors to break off the battle.

Not a man made it to the ford. Clustered in brush beside the river, Cheyenne warriors sent a hail of arrows and bullets into Custer's front ranks. Another contingent of warriors swept north around the women and children and charged his flank. Wheeling their horses, the troopers retreated toward the northern knoll. The initiative now rested entirely with the Indians. "Custer's Luck" was rapidly running out.

Keogh was doomed the instant Crazy Horse entered the fray. Skirting the captain's defenses, the Oglala war chief met up with Sitting Bull's nephew White Bull in a ravine east of Battle Ridge. White Bull, who was pumping rounds from his Winchester as fast as he could pull the lever, was not particularly pleased to see Crazy Horse, who had almost cost him his life in a bravery run against Custer on the Yellowstone River three years earlier. Now Crazy Horse challenged him to repeat the feat. Reluctantly, White Bull accepted. Crying, "Only heaven and earth last long," he galloped with Crazy Horse through a gap in the soldiers' ranks. Returning unscathed, they made a second run. Others followed their example. As the soldiers paused to reload, warriors on the southern slope surged forward on foot. Army horses dashed toward the river in the confusion. The Indians said that the stranded troopers "became foolish" and that a few shot themselves or threw aside their carbines and raised their hands. Others were said to have fallen on their knees and pleaded.[15]

But this was no day to show mercy. "My heart was bad. I was like one that has no mind," said the Lakota war chief Rain-in-the-Face. Rushing up the ridge, he grabbed a cavalry guidon just as his pony was shot dead. He untied the thong that bound him to the animal, brained the flag bearer with his war club, and then darted downhill. "The Long Sword's blood and brains splashed in my face. It felt hot, and blood ran in my mouth. I could taste it. I was mad. I got a fresh pony and rushed back, shooting, cutting, and slashing." An elementary moral calculus drove the Indian combatants. The Lakota warrior Iron Hawk later explained why he had pounded a trooper's head into jelly. "These white men wanted it, they called for it, and I let them have it."[16]

As Keogh's position crumbled—twenty men perished while gathered around the captain—Custer gathered the remnants of Yates's battalion and the survivors of Keogh's command on the knoll at the northern edge of Battle Ridge, where he ordered the horses shot to form breastworks. Perhaps ninety men in all were now clustered on the hill.[17] Their fear was beyond reckoning. They could see all the men behind them dead, and at least fifteen hundred Indians surrounding them: How could they not think this was their last stand? Soldiers behaved so erratically that the Indians thought them inebriated. "They shot like drunken men," said Iron Hawk, "firing into the ground, into the air, wildly in every way."

No one can say with certainty, because the Indians were unaware that they were fighting "Yellow Hair," but Custer was apparently one of the last to die. A bullet slammed into his chest; a second shot crashed into his right temple. He collapsed across the corpses of two or three troopers in such a manner that his back scarcely touched the earth. Tom Custer crumpled to the ground twenty feet from his brother.[18]

In the final struggle, forty men broke through a narrow gap in the Indian cordon and ran toward the river, most scrambling down a ravine that deepened as it wound toward the Little Bighorn. Their attempted flight was pathetic to behold. A young Lakota bystander watched them "making their arms go as though they were running, but they were only walking. We could see some Indians right on top of them whirling around all over the place. It seems as though the Indians could have just trampled them down even if we had not had weapons." But weapons they had aplenty, and the warriors on the slopes of the ravine methodically shot most of the soldiers in the back. Boston Custer and Autie Reed were both killed in the abortive breakout.

By 5:30 p.m., it was over. The dust settled, and the gun smoke dissipated. Women poured forth from the village with clubs, rocks, butcher knives, hatchets, and sewing awls. They bludgeoned the wounded and plundered, stripped, and mutilated the dead. The warriors did not linger for long. On a high point three miles to the southeast, a knot of troopers had gathered. Leaving the women to their bloody work, the warriors departed to do battle for a third time that day. Wooden Leg was not with them. On the knoll later christened Last Stand Hill, he had found an intriguing corpse—a buckskin-clad soldier with long, bushy sideburns. "Here is a new kind of scalp," he told a friend. Wooden Leg sliced off one side of the face and half the chin, tying the strange scalp to an arrow shaft. Deaf to Sitting Bull's injunction against despoiling the dead, he returned to the village quite pleased with himself. "I had on a soldier's coat and breeches, two metal bottles of whiskey, and the beard scalp." It had been a good day.[19]

*

While Custer's men fought, wept, and wondered at their solitude, Captain Benteen's battalion shuffled toward the Little Bighorn at a slow walk. Brooding all the way, Benteen was convinced that Custer had sent him "valley hunting ad infinitum" solely to exclude him from the moment of victory. Near the lone tipi, the captain encountered Sergeant Kanipe. His report did nothing to improve Benteen's humor. Custer had found a large Indian village and wanted the captain to hurry—to pick over the dregs of Custer's triumph perhaps? Certainly Kanipe gave the impression the battle had been all but won, yelling as he continued on to find the pack train, "We've got 'em boys! They're licking the stuffing out of them." Benteen resumed the march at a fast walk.[20]

At the river, Benteen encountered John Martin. The trumpeter handed him Lieutenant Cooke's scrawled order for Benteen to be quick and bring packs but then added in his broken English that the Indians were "skedaddling." Here, Benteen imagined, was further evidence that Custer alone would wear the laurels. The captain grumbled, increased his pace to a trot, and ascended the bluffs along the trail Custer had blazed an hour earlier. Fifteen minutes later, he found himself face-to-face with Reno. Troopers were still toiling up the hill or dying in the attempt.

"For God's sake, Benteen, halt your command and help me! I've lost half my men," Reno stammered.

"Where's Custer?" Benteen asked.

"I don't know," replied Reno. "He went off downstream and I haven't seen or heard anything of him since."[21]

When the Indians unexpectedly broke contact, Benteen—now alert to the very real possibility that Custer was in trouble—showed Reno the "Come quick" note and suggested the major join him in "making a junction" with Custer. Reno, however, refused to budge until the pack train arrived with ammunition. Benteen neither pressed the point nor pressed ahead with his own battalion. He "supposed General Custer was able to take care of himself."

Reno, it was clear, was of no use to anyone. According to many officers and men, after Benteen arrived, the intoxicated major returned to his principal worry—whiskey. "Look here," he allegedly boasted to the commanding officer of the pack train when it reached Reno Hill at 5:20 p.m. (about the time Custer died), "I have got half a bottle yet."

While Reno imbibed and Benteen hesitated, the troopers on Reno Hill listened as a continual crash of rifle fire rolled toward them from far downstream and wondered why no one ordered an advance. "The three troops that had been engaged in the valley were, it is true, somewhat demoralized," Private Taylor later wrote. "But that was no excuse for the whole command to remain inactive." Captain Thomas B. Weir agreed, and after an hour of speculating on the source of the gunfire, he led his company out onto an elevation a mile northwest of Reno Hill. Other company commanders followed. From the prominence, which became known as Weir Point, the Indian village was clearly visible a mile to the west. Three miles to the north, a dark dust cloud hung over the horizon. By the time Benteen and Reno joined Weir and the others at 6:00 p.m., the shooting had subsided. With binoculars, some officers thought they made out Indians milling about and firing arrows at objects on the ground. They puzzled at the strange sight and speculated on Custer's whereabouts. That his battalion might have been obliterated never crossed their minds.[22]

The contemplative officers were far from safe themselves, as the dust cloud roiling their way suggested. Within minutes, the entire Indian force swarmed toward Weir Point. Neither Reno nor Benteen issued any orders. Companies withdrew to Reno Hill when their commanders saw fit. Returning to the hill, Reno hunkered down with his bottle. Disorder threatened until Benteen took charge and established a defensive perimeter in a saucer-shaped depression. Dr. Porter created a makeshift hospital in the center of the hollow. Pack mules provided a flesh-and-blood barrier to Indian fire.

The troopers defending Reno Hill were still in grave danger. There was scarcely a scrap of natural cover and only three spades in the entire command. Men pieced together breastworks with whatever they could find—boxes, saddles, forage bags, dead animals. It was scant protection against the warriors who surrounded the hill. The Indians fought in shifts, coming and going from the village, until the shooting sputtered out at nightfall.[23]

*

June 26 dawned to the promise of another blistering day. At sunrise, the Indians reopened the battle with long-range sniping. Although seldom sustained, the fire was effective. Of the 367 defenders of Reno Hill,

7 were killed and 41 wounded that day. As the morning progressed and the heat climbed, water became a greater concern than Indian bullets. The wounded were dangerously dehydrated, and one soldier went insane from thirst. Men chewed sunburned grass, sucked on pebbles, or gnawed lead bullets to work up a little saliva. Benteen was at his best. He staged a counterattack that swept away the nearest warriors, some of whom had crept close enough to chuck dirt clods into the soldiers' faces, and then called for volunteers to draw water from the river. More stepped forward than were needed, and the captain detailed a dozen to descend a craggy ravine laden with camp kettles and canteens. All returned alive.

Prospects for the besieged at last brightened. Indians began abandoning their positions, and by 3:00 p.m. the firing had ceased. Four hours later, concealed behind a cloak of brush fires, Sitting Bull's village moved south toward the Bighorn Mountains. The consensus among Seventh Cavalry officers was either that the Indians had run low on ammunition or that Custer was coming with reinforcements. They were wrong on both counts. The Indians departed because wolves (scouts) had brought word that a large body of soldiers was moving up Little Bighorn valley. Wooden Leg said that the young men were unanimous in wanting to give battle but that the council of chiefs prevailed. "They decided we should continue our same course—not to fight any soldiers if we could get away without doing so."

The next morning, a tearful general Terry rode into Reno's lines at the head of Colonel Gibbon's column. The defenders gave three cheers. Terry acknowledged the gesture by removing his hat. Benteen posed the question on every man's mind: Where was Custer? "To the best of my knowledge and belief," Terry replied, "he lies on this ridge about four miles below here with all his command killed." The captain's hatred of Custer got the better of him. "I can hardly believe it. I think he is somewhere down the Bighorn grazing his horses. At the Battle of the Washita he went off and left part of his command, and I think he would do it again." Terry cut him off. "I think you are mistaken, and you will take your company and go down where the dead are lying and investigate for yourself." Benteen did so and returned pale. "We found them," he stammered upon returning, "but I did not expect we would."

Most of the survivors mourned dead comrades or damned the Indians—and in some cases Custer—to perdition; Private Taylor, on the other hand, ruminated over a Lakota corpse:

In a little depression there lay outstretched a stalwart Sioux warrior, stark naked with the exception of a breech clout and moccasins. I could not help feeling a sorrow as I stood gazing upon him. He was within a few hundred yards of his home and family, which we had attempted to destroy and he had tried to defend. The home of the slayer was perhaps a thousand miles away. In a few days the wolves and buzzards would have his remains torn asunder and scattered, for the soldiers had no disposition to bury a dead Indian.[24]

The disparity in casualties at the two-day Battle of the Little Bighorn was enormous. Thirty-one warriors, 6 women, and 4 children are known to have been killed; an indeterminate number of Indians, probably not exceeding a hundred, were wounded. The Seventh Cavalry lost 258 killed and 60 wounded, along with 3 civilians and 3 Indian scouts dead, the asymmetry in losses largely a consequence both of Custer's splitting his outnumbered command in the face of a much larger force and of the Indians' having refrained from exposing themselves unnecessarily.[25]

"I feel sorry that too many were killed on each side," Sitting Bull later said. "But when Indians must fight, they must."[26]

The Lakota-Cheyenne alliance had achieved a great victory in a battle they had not sought. But it bore every prospect of becoming a triumph more devastating for the Indians than defeat would likely have been. After a decade of temporizing and unrealized threats, the U.S. government—the president, the cabinet, the War Department, the Interior Department, the army, and the Indian agents—was united in a single objective: to crush Sitting Bull and Crazy Horse and lock up the Lakotas and the Cheyennes on reservations once and for all.

CHAPTER 15

THE GREAT FATHER'S FURY

G ENERAL TERRY shuffled about the steamer *Far West*, his normally full face drawn and haggard. There was no masking his
anguish. Calling the ship's captain to his cabin, Terry implored the
man to make the trip a safe one. "You have on board the most precious
cargo a boat ever carried," Terry said. "Every soldier here who is suffering with wounds is the victim of a terrible blunder; a sad and terrible
blunder."

But whose blunder? Terry knew that the nation would demand an
answer. By the time the *Far West* nosed into the Bismarck landing near
midnight on July 5, 1876, Terry had regained his composure. Concern
for his career trumped contrition, and instead of accepting responsibility for the Little Bighorn, he prevaricated. Before Custer started on
his fateful expedition, Terry had told Sheridan the best hope was that
either Custer or Gibbon might find and engage the hostiles. Now he
claimed to have ordered Custer to attack only in conjunction with Gibbon and not before June 26. In a word, it was all Custer's fault. For the
good of the service, Sheridan accepted Terry's lie. Publicly, he attributed the Little Bighorn debacle to "a misapprehension and [Custer's]
superabundance of courage." Still smarting over Custer's congressional testimony, President Grant had no difficulty excoriating the dead
colonel for the "wholly unnecessary" sacrifice of lives "brought on by
Custer himself." The official blame game had begun.[1]

All this might have been of great matter to the public, but Congress was less concerned with Custer's possible culpability in his own
defeat than it was with the need for the war in the first place. Two

weeks after the Little Bighorn, the Senate had called on the president to explain the war's origins and the government's objectives. Well practiced in the art of deception where the Lakotas were concerned, the Grant administration obfuscated shamelessly. Military operations were targeted not against the Sioux nation, Secretary of War J. Donald Cameron testified, but rather against "certain hostile parts" that defied the government—in other words, the element that lived in the Unceded Indian Territory as the 1868 treaty seemingly permitted. And the Black Hills were a red herring. "The accidental discovery of gold on the western border of the Sioux reservation and the intrusion of our people thereon, have not caused this war," Cameron swore, "and have only complicated it by the uncertainty of numbers to be encountered." If Cameron were to be believed, the innate war lust of young warriors had caused the war, plain and simple.[2]

Certainly many congressmen recognized Cameron's chicanery for what it was. But with the nation clamoring for swift and harsh retribution, they dared not dispute the administration's line nor deny the army whatever it asked for. And General Sheridan wanted three things, all of which were unimaginable before the Little Bighorn: a larger army, two permanent forts on the Yellowstone River in the heart of the Unceded Indian Territory (a request Sheridan had made repeatedly), and military control of the Indian agencies.

Congress moved swiftly to oblige the army, and Sheridan got all that he wanted and more. On July 8, Congress appropriated $200,000 for the Yellowstone forts. Two weeks later, the Interior Department handed over the Red Cloud and Spotted Tail Agencies to military control and authorized Sheridan to treat any Indians off the reservation as hostile. In early August, Congress increased the strength of cavalry companies on the frontier to a hundred men, which would bring twenty-five hundred new volunteers, dubbed the Custer Avengers, into the field. Congress also raised the authorized number of enlisted Indian auxiliaries from three hundred to a thousand. Sheridan now had near-absolute authority to deal with the Lakotas and the Cheyennes—friendly or hostile—however he saw fit, irrespective of treaty or law.[3]

What Sheridan lacked were commanders who were willing to fight. Neither Terry nor Crook appeared eager or psychologically able to face the Indians. Without Custer, Terry was adrift; the remnants of the Dakota Column remained glued to their base camp, with morale shattered and sickness rampant. Sheridan had ordered the one man always

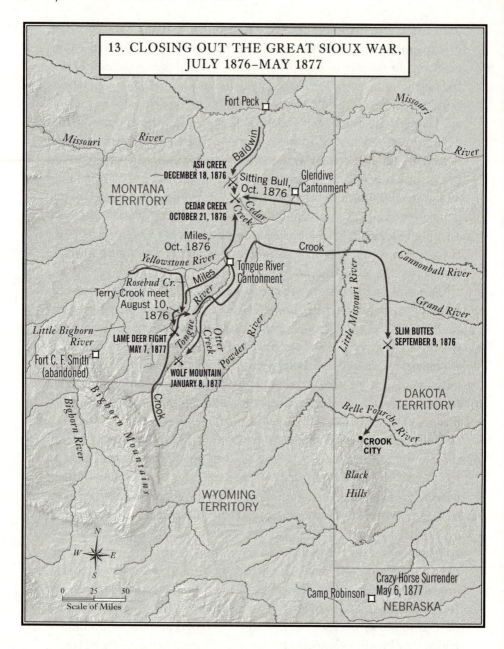

13. CLOSING OUT THE GREAT SIOUX WAR, JULY 1876–MAY 1877

eager to fight, Nelson Miles, then on duty on the southern plains, to report to Terry with the Fifth Infantry. But Miles would need at least a month to relocate his regiment.

At Camp Cloud Peak, eighty miles south of Terry's column, Crook's force had recuperated and was in good condition for renewed campaigning. The same, however, could not be said of its commander, who literally walked away from his responsibilities after the Rosebud. On the Fourth of July, Crook had received an order from Sheridan to "hit [the Lakotas] again and hit them hard." Instead, he had gone fishing. When couriers arrived six days later with the news of the Little Bighorn and repeated instructions from Sheridan that he "hit the Indians the hardest blow possible," Crook was not in camp to receive them, having walked off alone to hunt in the Bighorn Mountains. Bourke was beside himself. "The general has set an example of recklessness that cannot be too strongly condemned; this rashness must be foregone in the future. Else someday his mutilated corpse will be found and this whole scheme of Sioux pacification fall to the ground."

Crook returned that afternoon. A few hours later, 213 Shoshone warriors under Chief Washakie rode into camp. The old chief warned Crook that the Lakotas outnumbered the soldiers three to one. The actual odds were about even, but to Crook's addled mind Washakie's calculations seemed entirely reasonable. Sheridan steadied Crook somewhat with a promise to send him Colonel Wesley Merritt's Fifth Cavalry. As the days passed with no word from Merritt, Crook relapsed into a "nervous unhappiness." On July 23, he all but conceded defeat. "Immeasurably embarrassed" by Merritt's nonappearance, Crook confessed to Sheridan his constant dread of an attack, adding, "I am at a loss what to do."

Crook's timidity exhausted Sheridan's patience. "Merritt will reach you on August 1 or 2," he responded on July 28. "If you do not feel strong enough to attack and defeat the Indians, it is best for you to form a conjunction with General Terry at once. I have sent to you and General Terry every available man that can be spared in the Division, and if it has not made the columns strong enough, Terry and you should unite your forces."[4]

Crook's fears were baseless. The last thing the Lakota and Cheyenne chiefs wanted was another battle. They could not know that in beating back Crook on the Rosebud and rubbing out Long Hair on the Greasy Grass, they had decreed their own downfall. That the soldiers would return, however, they were certain. Two considerations drove Indian actions: keep as far from the army as possible and, once clear of danger, begin the belated summer buffalo hunt. After a lengthy victory celebration in the Bighorn Mountains, the Indians turned eastward, burning the prairie behind them to discourage pursuit.

It was an arduous trek. Game was scarce. The people grew hungry, and ponies weakened. Not until they had put 150 miles between themselves and Crook did the Indians feel safe enough to camp in one place for more than one night. At a grand council, the chiefs decided that the tribes should separate to improve their chances of finding sufficient game. The Cheyennes elected to remain in the Powder River country. The Lakotas continued on to the Little Missouri River, where they split up. Sitting Bull took the Hunkpapas and most of the Miniconjous and Sans Arcs northeast into the Montana Territory, while Crazy Horse led the Oglalas south toward the Black Hills. Not surprisingly, Indian traffic to and from the agencies grew confused. Some non-treaty Lakotas lost heart and drifted in at the same time that many agency Lakotas and Cheyennes, wary of the increased military presence on the reservations, left for the Unceded Indian Territory. By early August, the great Lakota and Cheyenne alliance that had made possible victory on the Little Bighorn was in tatters.[5]

*

The arrival of Wesley Merritt, a businesslike, "soldierly but cordial" Sheridan protégé, at Camp Cloud Peak at last roused Crook to action. On August 5, he set out, hoping to trap the Indians between himself and Terry. Crook called his command the Bighorn and Yellowstone Expedition. He had 1,500 cavalry under Merritt, 450 infantry, 250 Indian auxiliaries, and a handful of white scouts. The troops marched in light order over the burned prairie. A stripped-down mule pack train carried rations and extra ammunition.

The movement was a minor fiasco. Two days of blast-furnace heat and thick dust were followed by three days of cold driving rains that obliterated the Indian trail. Lacking ponchos or tents, the men suffered intensely. On August 10, the sun broke through and the heat returned. The troops were filthy and hungry, and the horses gaunt from lack of grass or forage. That afternoon, Terry and Crook linked up on Rosebud Creek after almost mistaking each other's command for hostile Indians. When he identified the approaching column, a befuddled Terry is said to have uttered to a staff member, "Why, Colonel, that is Crook. Where in the world are the Indians?" The caustic colonel Miles, who had reported for duty with Terry four days earlier, asked himself the same question. Always critical of superiors who kept too tight a rein on him, he also denounced Terry to Sheridan's staff. The general, he said, had lost heart. As for Terry's troops, Miles had never seen a "command so completely stampeded—either in the volunteer or regular service." With genuine emotion, he wrote to his wife, "The more I see of movements here the more admiration I have for Custer, and I am satisfied his like will not be found very soon again."[6]

Grown suddenly arrogant and cocksure, General Crook also told Merritt that his and Terry's combined five-thousand-man force was too large to be effective, an odd opinion from a man who two weeks earlier had feared for his own survival. But Crook's comment proved prescient. In a week of miserable marching, he and Terry encountered only relentless thunderstorms that drowned morale and persuaded the Shoshones and the Crows to head for home. Crook too had had enough. After drawing a fifteen-day supply of field rations, he "skipped out with his men one fine morning [August 26] in the mud without any pretense of a courteous leave-taking," said a Terry subordinate.[7]

Crook left Terry because the two had reached an impasse. Terry believed that Sitting Bull's band, which he called the "heart and soul of the Indian mutiny," had crossed the Yellowstone River and started north. Although he conceded that Crazy Horse might have gone south, as Crook contended, he nonetheless thought the two commands should stick together to "destroy the nucleus" of the hostiles. Crook, on the other hand, considered the danger to the Black Hills settlements and mining camps too great to leave them unprotected. As commander of the Department of the Platte, it was his responsibility to protect them. Terry conceded the point and released Crook, taking his own column north. Crook continued east in search of Crazy Horse's trail. Perhaps he could yet salvage something from the campaign and with it his tarnished reputation.[8]

Crook was correct regarding Crazy Horse's movements but wrong as to his intentions. The Oglala war leader had halted fifty miles north of the Black Hills. Small war parties staged scattered strikes in the Black Hills, which would continue until late August, but Crazy Horse and the council chiefs had no interest in launching a concerted attack on the whites. They wanted only to be left in peace in the country they called home.[9]

There now began what was perhaps the most dismal march in the history of the frontier army. Cold penetrating rains punctuated by hailstones the size of hen's eggs battered Crook's expedition. Horses sank in mud up to their knee joints. Chronic diarrhea, neuralgia, rheumatism, and malaria stalked the men. In ten days, Crook's "drowned-rat brigade" managed only one hundred miles. On September 5, the general faced a crucial decision. He had found Indian trails leading south toward the Black Hills. The hills, however, were two hundred miles away, and rations were nearly exhausted. Fort Abraham Lincoln lay fifty miles closer to the east, but there was no sign of Indians moving in that direction. Regardless of which way Crook went, food would run out before he reached his objective. He elected to make for the Black Hills. To a friendly war correspondent, he confided that only two and a half days of rations remained. "We must make them last for seven at least," whispered Crook. "The miners must be protected, and we must punish the Sioux on our way south, or leave this campaign entirely unfinished. If necessary, we can eat our horses."

Which they did. Heavy rains fell, and the singed prairie became, in Bourke's words, "as wet as a sponge but without elasticity." Cavalry mounts played out by the score. The troops fared little better. Contrary to Crook's expectations of stretching the meager rations of rain-soaked hardtack and rancid meat, hunger drove some soldiers to consume theirs in a single sitting, after which horse meat became a staple. "You can gather no realization of the suffering of the men," one of Crook's officers wrote home. "I have seen men become so exhausted that they were actually insane. I saw men who were very plucky, sit down and cry like children because they could not hold out." Walking alongside his horseless troopers, Merritt heard their talk turn ugly. Jests about "Rosebud George" and his "Horse Meat March" were acceptable soldierly griping; suggestions that Crook suffered from "aberrations of the mind" and "ought to be hung" were another matter. Merritt had a frank discussion with the general.

Crook had known he needed help even before Merritt told him of the mutinous temper of the men. He had ordered part of the pack train, escorted by the reliable captain Anson Mills with 150 troopers, to make for Deadwood in the Black Hills, then one hundred miles distant. The pack-train commander said that Crook admonished Mills to avoid contact with the Indians; Mills, however, would later claim that Crook had given him verbal orders to attack any village he might encounter. In either case, Crook intended to rest his men all day on September 8 (which happened to be his forty-sixth birthday), a clear indication Mills could not expect timely support if he ran into Indians.

Mills nonetheless elected to gamble. Thirty miles south of Crook's camp, he spotted a small pony herd. Obviously an Indian village lay nearby; how large was anyone's guess. Rather than risk discovery by conducting a close reconnaissance, Mills concealed his force in a ravine under a hard rain, intending to attack at dawn.

The object of Mills's assault were forty-eight lodges under the Miniconjou chiefs American Horse and Red Horse containing perhaps 250 people who were en route to their agency to surrender. The peaceable village lay in a broad depression beneath a chain of chalk-white bluffs called Slim Buttes.

Mills's troopers galloped into the village through a thick mist, pistols cracking. Slashing open the sides of their tipis, the Indians fled, many of them naked. "We caught up what arms we could in the dark, the women taking the children and hiding in the rocks," said Red Horse. "We gathered up a few horses and put our families on them and went to the main [Crazy Horse's] camp, where we told what had happened."

Not all the Indians ran. A handful, including American Horse, gathered in a gully. Others taunted the troopers from the bluffs, a sure sign they expected reinforcements. Fortunately for Mills, Crook arrived at noon, having decided to make a birthday march. Although he upbraided the captain for attacking, he could hardly object to the five thousand pounds of dried meat the village yielded. With so much booty at hand, Crook lost all control over the troops. An officer unable to rally his men had never seen such a sight. "Two thousand men were scattered through it in orderless confusion, picking up buffalo robes and other articles, and burning the lodges." Twenty troopers volunteered to clear out American Horse. They went at it with a will, cursing and yelling. The shrieks of terrified women answered their imprecations. Crook hurriedly ordered a cease-fire. It came too late for some, including a cluster of women and children that Bourke saw "covered with dirt and blood and screaming in perfect agony of terror [and] weltering in their own gore." American Horse emerged from the ravine clutching his stomach to contain his bullet-ripped intestines. He died the next morning.

At 4:00 p.m., Crazy Horse appeared on the bluffs with four hundred warriors. The two sides exchanged fire until dusk, when a cavalry charge through a blinding fog drove the Indians off. Crook claimed victory at Slim Buttes, but it was at best a brittle palm. He had disrupted the Lakota buffalo hunt at the cost of enraging several hundred

Indians who had intended to return to the agencies. Instead, they cast their fate with Crazy Horse or Sitting Bull.

On September 14, Crook's ordeal ended. Filthy, ragged, and half-starved, his troops were greeted by wagons laden with supplies from the "grateful" citizens of the Black Hills, who purveyed goods at exorbitant prices. Full stomachs, however, did not dull the soldiers' anger over what Crook had subjected them to. The "Horse Meat March" represented "maladministration in its worst form," averred a cavalry lieutenant. "It is a lamentable thing when a want of foresight, a jealous disposition, or selfish ambition sits at the helm." A perceptive private agreed: "The expedition has been nothing but disaster, and a depletion of the public purse. Custer and his brave soldiers still remain unavenged, and the Indian Question is further from solution than ever."[10]

*

In fact, Congress had taken an enormous step toward solving the Sioux problem. On August 15, 1876, President Grant signed into law a rider to the annual Sioux Appropriation Bill that if faithfully administrated and backed by the threat of force would inevitably destroy the Lakota culture. The bill itself included an increase of one million dollars for food rations in recognition of what most Lakotas already knew: that they could no longer rely on the hunt to sustain them year-round. Of course no food would be given to hostile bands, at least not knowingly. And there was a menacing proviso: No future appropriations for rations for any of the Lakotas would be entertained until they relinquished all claim to the Unceded Indian Territory and to that portion of the Great Sioux Reservation lying west of the 103rd meridian, including the Black Hills. They also must grant right-of-way for three roads across the reservation into the hills, consent to receive supplies at new agencies on the Missouri River "in order to reduce freight charges," and agree to till the soil and send their children to school. The Lakotas, in effect, were to be given the choice of ceding or starving.[11]

Grant appointed a commission of Christian reformers to present the reservation Lakotas with the administration's ultimatum. At the Red Cloud Agency, the chiefs gave long speeches that betrayed confusion over what exactly was being demanded of them. After enduring the usual government palaver to silence them, the chiefs signed. Caught between the army, which had beefed up its presence near the agencies, and their non-treaty kinsmen, whose defeat the agency chiefs knew was inevitable, they really had little alternative.

There was no cheer in the proceedings. One chief blindfolded himself before signing. Red Cloud, looking "grimly meditative and sullen," told the commissioners, "You have come here with the words of the Great Father; therefore, because I am his friend I have said yes to what he has said to me, and I suppose that makes you happy." A bit of the old fire remained in Red Cloud, however. After the council, he and the Brulé chief Red Leaf demanded that rations be brought to their villages.

From the Red Cloud Agency, the commissioners traveled on to the Spotted Tail Agency. Spotted Tail recognized extortion when he saw it. Threats of ration cuts, starvation, rough handling by the army, and forced relocation were more than even the friendliest and most "progressive" Lakota leader could bear in silence.

> My friend, your words are like a man knocking me in the head with a club. By your speech you have put great fear upon us. Whatever the white people ask of us, wherever we go, we always say *Yes—yes—yes!* Whenever we don't agree to what is asked of us in council, you always reply: *You won't get anything to eat! You won't get anything to eat!*[12]

Having spoken his heart, Spotted Tail reluctantly "touched the pen." After that, the dominoes fell easily. In rapid order, the commission secured signatures at the Standing Rock, Cheyenne River, Crow Creek, Lower Brulé, and Santee Agencies. Reported the chairman sententiously, "We finished our labors with our hearts full of gratitude to God, who had guarded and protected us, and directed our labors to a successful issue."[13]

The deed was done, pending only Senate ratification, which in this instance came rapidly. The agency chiefs had relinquished the Unceded Indian Territory. The Black Hills were gone, and the Great Sioux Reservation was reduced by a third. There remained one further indignity for the agency Indians to endure, and Phil Sheridan was about to administer it.

*

On September 22, while the commission wrapped up its work at the Red Cloud Agency, General Sheridan summoned Crook and Ranald

Mackenzie, whose reassignment with the Fourth Cavalry to Crook's department Sheridan had engineered, to Fort Laramie. The purpose: to decide when and how to disarm and dismount the reservation Indians. It might have been a strained meeting. Mackenzie had become subject to violent mood swings and was certain his fellow officers all were his secret enemies. Crook too had imagined foes. Having been twice humiliated by the Lakotas, he ached to wreak vicarious vengeance on the agency chiefs, who were guilty of nothing beyond a measured sympathy for Sitting Bull.

Sheridan assigned Crook overall responsibility for the operation. Colonel Mackenzie would move against the nearby Red Cloud Agency. Wesley Merritt would support him as needed. It is evident from Crook's instructions to Merritt, then scouting the Black Hills country, that he expected violence. "Do all in your power to avoid a conflict," Crook told Merritt, "but should that alternative be forced upon us, we must do them all the damage we can consistent with civilized warfare."[14]

Merritt was spared the worry. False rumors circulated by dubious informants, warning that Red Cloud and Red Leaf intended to join the hostiles, persuaded Crook to act before Merritt arrived. Mackenzie completed the mission without bloodshed, but it did him no credit. Expecting to find hidden arsenals in the villages, he uncovered just a handful of old rifles. And he turned a blind eye as troops ransacked tipis and the Pawnees made off with Lakota ponies. The vandalism aside, Crook was delighted with the outcome. "I feel," he told Sheridan, "that this is the first gleam of daylight we have had in this business." Then Crook deposed Red Cloud and appointed Spotted Tail—whom he found "decidedly the most intelligent and loyal"—as head chief of the Lakotas. Crook had intended to curb Red Cloud's influence; instead, the chief's divestiture enhanced his standing with reservation Oglalas.

Crook's next move was shrewd. Disobeying Sheridan's order to cripple the agency Indians, he permitted all but the immediate followers of Red Cloud and Red Leaf to retain their arms and ponies. To have moved against the "loyal" bands, he told Sheridan, "would simply have arrayed the white man against the Indian and placed the loyal and disloyal on the same footing." Crook thought this tangible act of good faith did more to win the allegiance of the agency Indians than all past assurances of the Great Father's friendship combined, and he was right. Nearly five hundred reservation Lakotas signed on as scouts. Pitting Lakotas against Lakotas "will have a decided effect in inducing the hostiles [to] surrender [and] is the entering wedge by which the tribal organization is broken up, making way for civilizing and Christianizing influences," explained Crook. Unimpressed with his willful subordinate's rationale, Sheridan officially disapproved his actions. But Crook had presented him with a fait accompli. All Sheridan could do from Chicago was seethe, when he should have cheered.[15]

The frontier army had taken a huge leap forward. The Lakota people had been rent irreparably when Red Cloud had made his separate peace eight years earlier. But relations between the non-treaty bands and the reservation Lakotas (if not their chiefs) generally had been close and amicable. Indeed, without the presence of large numbers of reservation warriors at the Little Bighorn, Custer would likely have triumphed. Now, just two months afterward, these very same warriors were signing up to help the government subjugate their defiant kinsmen. As had been the case on the southern plains, disunity among the northern tribes would greatly facilitate their physical conquest and ultimately the demise of their way of life. It is ironic that the absolute freedom to decide one's destiny so cherished by the Indians would prove to be a deciding factor in their inability to preserve it. None of this, however, was yet apparent to Sitting Bull and Crazy Horse, who clung to the old ways with fierce tenacity.

*

Watching the summer campaign sputter to its inglorious end, Colonel Miles told his wife, "Terry means well enough, but he has little experience and is too much under the influence of those slow inefficient men like Gibbon to reap good results. This business to be successful should be conducted on sound military principles first, and then with great energy and persistency." In Miles's view, Terry had done neither. After only a week of following cold trails north of the Yellowstone River, in late September 1876 Terry disbanded the Montana and Dakota Columns. "As the Sioux have failed to find us," joked a Seventh Cavalry captain, "we are going home."[16]

Terry's troops were quitting the Lakota country, but that did not mean that Phil Sheridan intended to leave the field open to the Indians. Instead, he ordered Terry to direct Miles and his Fifth Infantry to erect a cantonment at the mouth of the Tongue River, solidly in the heart of the Lakota winter homeland. Beyond keeping Miles's garrison alive with supply trains, Sheridan had no plans to challenge the subarctic northern plains winter. He failed to reckon with Miles's aggressive temperament and restless ambition, however, and Miles immediately requested permission to take the offensive, promising to sweep the region clean of Indians before the snows melted. Terry denied his appeal on the grounds that a winter campaign was impossible.

Sitting Bull unwittingly gave Miles the chance to prove Terry wrong. The Hunkpapas needed to lay in large stores of buffalo meat before the snows fell, and the region north of the Yellowstone teemed with bison. What Sitting Bull did not know was that the Yellowstone country was now home to an army officer with a tenacity rivaling his own.

On October 10, as Sitting Bull's village crossed the Yellowstone, Lakota wolves reported an army supply train nearby. Sitting Bull counseled against attack, but the young men ignored him; fully laden wagons were too great a prize for them to forgo. The next day, a large war party struck. The small infantry escort drove the warriors away, but not before they ran off enough mules to cripple the train and stampede the civilian teamsters. Four days later, a reconstituted and heavily escorted supply train rumbled into range. Sitting Bull and the elder chiefs again urged restraint. Again the young warriors disregarded their counsel.

That included Sitting Bull's nephew White Bull. Slinging his buffalo-tail war charm over his right shoulder, he grabbed his Winchester rifle and made for the wagons to count coups. When measured against his pipe-smoking episode with Sitting Bull four years earlier on the Yellowstone, or his bravery run with Crazy Horse at the Little Bighorn, a galloping pass at a wagon train did not seem particularly risky. White Bull's medicine, however, had run out. A .45-caliber rifle slug slammed into his upper left arm, shattering the bone. The shock knocked him unconscious. Two friends grabbed the pony's bridle and led White Bull to safety. The soldiers proved too much for the war party, which rejoined Sitting Bull's village on its northward trek into the buffalo country. Respectful Lakota warriors dubbed the infantrymen "walk-a-heaps."

Unbeknownst to the Lakotas, Colonel Miles, fearing trouble when the wagon train did not arrive at the cantonment on schedule, had set out to find it and was now hard on the Indians' trail with the Fifth Infantry. On the morning of October 20, he overtook them near the headwaters of Cedar Creek in southern Montana Territory, deploying his five hundred soldiers along a ridge a mile west of the Lakota camp. Three hundred warriors hurriedly assembled on a parallel ridge to shield the village. Caught unawares with their families vulnerable to attack, Sitting Bull and the chiefs consented to a council between the lines.

The day was clear but bitterly cold. Sitting Bull dressed in buckskin leggings and wrapped himself in a thick buffalo robe. Miles wore a fur cap and long overcoat trimmed with bear fur and covered with an army cape, which earned him the Lakota moniker Man with the Bear Coat, or Bear Coat for short.

Scrutinizing the famed vanquisher of Custer, Miles found him "courteous, but evidently void of any genuine respect for the white race." Despite his thinly disguised animosity, Sitting Bull followed council proprieties, spreading a buffalo robe on the ground and inviting Miles to sit. The colonel refused, which immediately chilled the proceedings, and the two men stood and sparred verbally with the robe between them. Miles said he meant to bring the Lakotas to the reservation—peacefully if possible, forcibly if necessary. Bristling at the threat, Sitting Bull demanded Miles leave so that the Lakotas could conduct the fall buffalo hunt.

Expounding on larger themes of war and peace, Sitting Bull soon struck at the heart of the matter. He told Miles that there could be no reconciliation between the races, because "the white man never lived who loved an Indian, and that no true Indian ever lived that did not hate the white man." Boldly, he declared that "God Almighty made him an Indian and did not make him an agency Indian either, and he did not intend to be one."

Miles, who had spies in the Lakota village, faced Sitting Bull down by laying out the Lakota plans with an accuracy that "excited the wild, savage ferocity of [Sitting Bull's] nature." Grudgingly, Sitting Bull consented to meet again the next morning, having suffered a psychological defeat in his first verbal encounter with Bear Coat Miles.

Miles pressed his advantage at the second parley. This time he brought the buffalo robe and invited Sitting Bull to sit. When he predictably declined, Miles invited the other chiefs to sit in Sitting Bull's place, and they accepted. Badly shaken by their breaking ranks, Sitting Bull presented his pipe to the Great Spirit and implored him to have mercy on the Lakotas. Otherwise, he spoke little. "We talk," a Hunkpapa orator said by way of excuse for Sitting Bull's visible melancholy, "but he is our fighting chief." Miles was not buying it. "I think he feels that his strength is somewhat exhausted, and he appeared much depressed, suffering from nervous excitement and loss of power," the colonel wrote to his wife that evening after the council ended in a deadlock.[17]

The two sides now squared off to fight. Miles opened the action, ordering his infantry forward in line of battle. The Lakotas set fire to the prairie grass and slowly gave ground to cover the escape of the village. Not all were for retreating. As the troops drew near the dismantled camp, White Bull, his arm in a sling, yelled, "Come on, let's go and rub them out!" No sooner had he started than Sitting Bull caught his bridle rein and sent his wounded nephew to the rear.

White Bull did not miss much. Only one Indian was killed and two soldiers wounded in the clash at Cedar Creek, but the walk-a-heaps kept on the heels of the fleeing Lakotas, scooping up precious winter supplies and fracturing Sitting Bull's coalition. Sitting Bull and Gall continued north toward the Missouri River with four hundred people, mostly Hunkpapas. With the prospect of a winter of hunger before them, the Sans Arcs and the Miniconjous surrendered to Miles. The delighted colonel, who believed that lasting peace rested on magnanimous treatment of surrendering Indians, gave them a generous stock of rations and freedom to report to the Cheyenne River Agency unguarded. Many reneged and found their way to Crazy Horse's camp but not White Bull. Judging his nephew too badly wounded to make what might prove a fighting trek to the Missouri River, Sitting Bull told White Bull to report to the agency. His warrior days were over.[18]

The clash with Miles not only wrecked Sitting Bull's alliance but also stunned all the winter roamers. Before, soldiers had come, provoked a fight, occasionally talked, and then left. But Miles meant to stay. The Cheyenne warrior Wooden Leg, traveling with Crazy Horse's village, voiced the growing despair of the winter roamers:

Wherever we went, the soldiers came to kill us, and it was all our own country. It was ours already when the Wasichus [whites] made the treaty with Red Cloud that said it would be ours as long as grass should grow and water flow. That was only eight winters before, and they were chasing us now because we remembered and they forgot. We were not happy anymore, because so many of our people had untied their horses' tails [left the warpath] and gone over to the

Wasichus. We went back deep into our country. The bison had gone away, and a hard winter came early.[19]

*

George Crook itched for action. In less than one month, Nelson Miles had inflicted more damage on the non-treaty Lakotas than Crook had in eight. Sitting Bull was beyond his reach, but Crazy Horse's camp presumably lay within striking distance (although Crook had no idea exactly where). Having twice failed to find him—first the ignominious Powder River Campaign in March 1876, and then the quixotic march in September—Crook was determined to settle scores before year's end. And so, amid great fanfare, in November he launched his third campaign against the elusive Lakota war chief. He called it the Powder River Expedition. Once again Crook mustered a huge force. On this occasion, fifteen hundred regulars, including Mackenzie's Fourth Cavalry; three hundred civilian teamsters; and nearly four hundred Indian auxiliaries marched out of Fort Fetterman.

Regardless of what the campaign might bring, Crook had already scored a diplomatic victory more significant in its long-term implications for the non-treaty bands than any battlefield triumph he could expect to win. In the process of recruiting Indians for the expedition, something of the old, cunning Crook had reemerged. Warriors from eight tribes, some of them with long histories of mutual hostility, rode under Crook. Pawnees and Shoshones predominated, but there were also reservation Lakotas, Cheyennes, Arapahos, Utes, Bannocks, and Nez Perces. The logic of Crook's recruiting pitch was not lost on the chiefs. The buffalo were vanishing, Crook reminded them, while the white settlements were growing. The Indians, he declared, must "come together as friends" or perish. A Pawnee chief who agreed with Crook voiced a sentiment previously unthinkable. "Brothers," he said, "we are all of the same color, and we are all Indians." And, he might have added, they were all on the Great Father's side. Crook had done what the mightiest war chiefs had been unable to do: he had kindled a sense of "Indianness" and common interests among the tribes of the northern plains and the Pacific Northwest. It so happened that it was channeled against their own freedom.[20]

Lieutenant Colonel Richard I. Dodge, the astute observer of Indian life and veteran of three decades on the frontier, commanded Crook's infantry. The Powder River Expedition was the largest and best equipped he had ever seen. Formidable though it appeared, without their Indian allies Crook's column might have searched for months without encountering a single "hostile." Providentially for the general, his Lakota and Arapaho scouts tricked a young Cheyenne warrior into revealing the whereabouts of both Crazy Horse's village on Rosebud Creek and that of the Northern Cheyennes at the southwestern base of the Bighorn Mountains. Crook prepared to strike Crazy Horse, who was nearer to him. No sooner had Crook readied his command, however, than he learned that the camp of the voluble Cheyenne prisoner had taken flight toward Crazy Horse's village. The Lakotas were now certain to be alerted to Crook's presence. Unwilling to concede defeat, he sent Mackenzie with the cavalry and Indian auxiliaries to the Bighorn Mountains to launch an unprovoked attack on the Cheyenne village. Although many of the Cheyennes had been present at the Little Bighorn, the majority of the villagers had only just arrived from the Red Cloud Agency, "not bothering any white people nor wanting to see any of them," as one warrior put it. But any Indians roaming free were fair game for the army. If Crook could not have Crazy Horse, he would settle for the Northern Cheyennes.

Crook had given Mackenzie a difficult mission. The Cheyenne village—consisting of 173 lodges with approximately twelve hundred occupants, including three hundred warriors—lay nestled at the far end of a deep, half-mile-wide, and nearly inaccessible canyon of the Red Fork of the Powder River. It pulsated with spiritual energy. The tribe's two most revered "Old-Man chiefs," Dull Knife, aged sixty-six, and Little Wolf, ten years his junior, were there. Compassionate and selfless, a gallant warrior and superior tactician, Little Wolf was the Sweet Medicine Chief, the human embodiment of the Cheyenne faith. The village was also home to the holiest of Cheyenne objects—the Sacred Medicine Arrows and the Sacred Buffalo Hat—and their guardians. It was the first time the objects had been in the same village in over a decade. Unfortunately, the village also included the thuggish Last Bull and his imperious Kit Fox warrior society.

There had been ominous auguries. On November 20, wolves dispatched by the council chiefs discovered Crook's cantonment. Four days later, Box Elder, a venerated, blind octogenarian holy man, was visited with a sunrise vision of soldiers and enemy Indians charging toward the village. That alone convinced most Cheyennes the time had

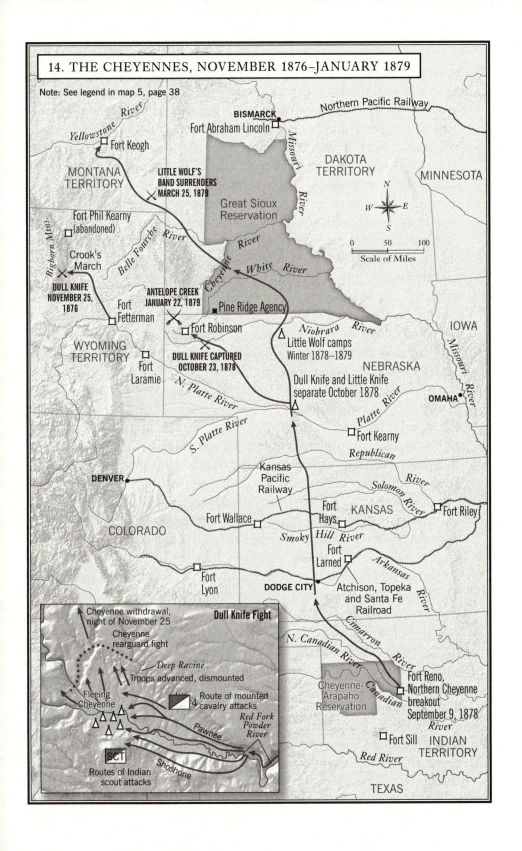

14. THE CHEYENNES, NOVEMBER 1876–JANUARY 1879

Note: See legend in map 5, page 38

BISMARCK
Fort Abraham Lincoln

Northern Pacific Railway

Yellowstone River
Fort Keogh

MONTANA
TERRITORY

LITTLE WOLF'S
BAND SURRENDERS
MARCH 25, 1879

Missouri River

DAKOTA
TERRITORY

MINNESOTA

Great Sioux
Reservation

N
W   E
S

0   50   100
Scale of Miles

Fort Phil Kearny
(abandoned)

Belle Fourche River

Cheyenne River

White River

Crook's
March

Bighorn Mtns

DULL KNIFE
NOVEMBER 25,
1876

Fort
Fetterman

ANTELOPE CREEK
JANUARY 22, 1879

Pine Ridge Agency

WYOMING
TERRITORY

Fort Robinson

DULL KNIFE CAPTURED
OCTOBER 23, 1878

Niobrara River

Little Wolf camps
Winter 1878–1879

IOWA

Missouri River

Fort
Laramie

N. Platte River

Dull Knife and Little Knife
separate October 1878

NEBRASKA

OMAHA

S. Platte River

Platte River

DENVER

Fort Kearny

Republican

Kansas
Pacific
Railway

Solomon River

River

KANSAS

Fort Riley

Fort Wallace

Fort
Hays

Smoky Hill River

COLORADO

Fort
Larned

Arkansas River

Fort
Lyon

DODGE CITY

Atchison, Topeka
and Santa Fe
Railroad

N. Canadian River

Cimarron River

Canadian River

Fort Reno,
Northern Cheyenne
breakout
September 9, 1878

Cheyenne-
Arapaho
Reservation

River

Fort Sill

INDIAN
TERRITORY

Red River

TEXAS

Cheyenne withdrawal,
night of November 25

Cheyenne
rearguard fight

Dull Knife Fight

Deep Ravine
Troops advanced, dismounted

Fleeing
Cheyenne

Route of mounted
cavalry attacks

Red Fork
Powder
River

Pawnee

SCT

Shoshone

Routes of Indian
scout attacks

come to move. But Last Bull's warriors were on duty as *akicitas* (village police). In an unprecedented usurpation of council authority, Last Bull told his men to whip anyone who tried to leave and to slaughter their ponies. The Kit Fox warrior society had killed twenty Shoshones in a recent raid, and Last Bull insisted everyone participate in their victory dance. All night long, a celebratory fire taller than a tipi lit up the village. Drumbeats echoed from the beetled canyon walls. Snow carpeted the camp. The moon set early on the night of November 24; in its place, a heavy mist settled over the canyon floor.[21]

While Last Bull's reluctant celebrants sang and danced, Mackenzie groped through a slight gap in the canyon's sharp, white-sandstone northern wall. As the gray light of an uncertain daybreak overspread the canyon, he arrayed his force a mile east of the nearest tipi. A dense growth of willow thickets lined the Red Fork, and thick brush obscured the village. Only the pony herd was visible, grazing on a grassy bench, but there was no time for a reconnaissance. Like Custer five months earlier, Mackenzie would go in blindly. He had, however, three important advantages that Custer had lacked: a large force of friendly Indians thirsty for Cheyenne blood, the protective cloak of a dull winter dawn, and superior numbers. A "last stand" hardly seemed in the cards.

The attackers broke from a walk into a gallop, Indian auxiliaries along the south bank and the cavalry on the north bank of the Red Fork. While the cavalry charged the pony herd, howling Pawnees surged into the village, shooting fast and indiscriminately. From atop the canyon's red-sandstone southern wall, the Shoshones fired down on the village. One Cheyenne warrior likened the sound of bullets striking the lodges to hailstones; another Cheyenne, who had been shot through the body, said that "it seemed as if I was walking on bullets." The Kit Fox–imposed festivities had ended just before the assault came. Cheyenne girls, laced together to prevent young men from slipping off with them during the dance, now fell in panicked heaps until warriors cut the ropes. Once freed, they hastened toward a chain of bluffs west of the camp.

Cheyennes who had quit the dance early tumbled from their lodges naked or wrapped only in a blanket or robe. Men whose weapons were in their lodges grabbed them and formed a ragged line to cover the people's escape. They endured a heavy fire. Chief Little Wolf was hit six times. The blood coagulated quickly in the cold, and he kept on fighting. To the left of Little Wolf's line, nine warriors in a deep gully died making a stand that temporarily blunted the cavalry charge. Behind them, Cheyenne women built stone breastworks above the canyon's deep western recesses. Throughout the struggle, the blind holy man Box Elder sat on a knoll singing his death song. He survived the ordeal, as did the Sacred Medicine Arrows and the Sacred Buffalo Hat.

Little else of the Northern Cheyennes' material culture escaped destruction. The village fell in less than fifteen minutes, and Mackenzie put it to the torch. Strikingly decorated lodges, sacred scalp shirts and warbonnets, richly painted buffalo hides, holy clothing, and heirloom war shields were lost forever. Soldiers tossed into the fire the sacred ears of corn that Cheyennes believed were gifts of the Creator. Tons of dried buffalo meat and pemmican meant to sustain the Cheyennes until spring crackled in the flames.

The troopers relished their destructive work. They had uncovered enough evidence to convince them they had wrought just retribution on the Cheyennes. A bag containing the severed right hands of twelve Shoshone babies, beaded necklaces decorated with dried fingers, a white girl's scalp, a Seventh Cavalry guidon, and a bloodstained buckskin coat thought to have belonged to Tom Custer all were found in the village.[22]

The battle soon settled into a long-range exchange of gunfire. Mackenzie saw no need for another charge. The village and the pony herd were in his hands, and the Cheyennes were clearly beaten, their leaders divided. Under a truce flag, Dull Knife told an army interpreter that he had lost two sons and wanted to surrender but that the other chiefs had held him back. The sight of Lakotas and Cheyennes serving with the soldiers infuriated him. "Go home, you have no business here," Dull Knife yelled. "We can whip the white soldiers alone, but can't fight you too." Little Wolf seemed resigned to the worst. "You have killed and hurt a heap of our people," he told the interpreter. "You may as well stay now and kill the rest of us."

Mackenzie decided to let hunger and the elements finish the work. On the morning of November 26, he left the canyon to rejoin Crook. Mackenzie had lost one officer and five enlisted men killed, and twenty-one enlisted men and one Shoshone scout were wounded in what became known as the Dull Knife Fight. Cheyenne losses approximated forty dead, 120 wounded, and their entire heritage.[23]

In one sense, Mackenzie may be counted among the army casualties. For no rational reason, after dark his mind began to unravel. His orderly eavesdropped on his colonel's anguish. "We were right near the hospital and could hear the wounded groaning all night. Every time I awoke I could see the general walking up and down. I don't believe he slept a bit that night. He must have been troubled about something. I don't know what, for he is the bravest I ever saw." A week later, in the presence of Colonel Dodge, Mackenzie suffered a nervous collapse. He ranted about having botched the battle with the Cheyennes, called himself a coward on a downward spiral, and swore that if he could muster the courage he would blow his brains out. "He talked more like a crazy man than the sane commander of a splendid body of cavalry," attested Dodge, who "bullied and encouraged him" with a reminder that everyone considered the Dull Knife Fight to have been a "grand success." That quieted Mackenzie, at least for the moment, and Dodge hastened to inform Crook of the colonel's breakdown. At a loss what to do, Crook distracted Mackenzie with games of whist until the colonel's mood lifted.[24]

Besides a suicidal subordinate, Crook had problems of his own making. After the Dull Knife Fight, he led his column in an abject search for Crazy Horse. For three weeks, he wandered amid battering blizzards and fifty-below-zero cold before calling off the campaign in late December. Crook publicly blamed his failure on inadequate transportation and the "meager appropriation" Sheridan had allotted for purchasing forage. When he learned of Crook's accusation, Sheridan's confidence in his refractory subordinate, already fragile after the Rosebud and Horse Meat March debacles, dropped even further.[25]

*

The Northern Cheyennes were lost in incomprehensible suffering of their own. On the night of November 25, the temperature, which had risen high enough during the day for the soldiers to have fought in their shirtsleeves, dropped to minus thirty. Eleven Cheyenne babies died in the mountains that night; three others perished the next evening. At least a dozen adults also froze to death. The Cheyennes' only chance for survival lay in reaching Crazy Horse's camp, and the odds against them appeared immense. It snowed relentlessly. The first day out, warriors ran off a party of Pawnee scouts and recovered seventy-five horses, without which the band would have perished. The Cheyennes butchered the horses, stuffed unconscious and half-frozen small children into the animals' steaming stomachs to resuscitate them, and then subsisted on the meat of the slaughtered animals. Lacking moccasins, they wrapped their feet in strips of horse hide or bits of cloth. Many wore only a single buffalo robe.

Eleven days after the battle, the Cheyennes reached Crazy Horse's village, only to find the Oglalas were also destitute. Although some Cheyennes thought the Oglalas stingy, Crazy Horse's people fitted them out with tipis and supplies as best they were able, and the two peoples remained together. They alternately battled and eluded Bear Coat Miles's walk-a-heaps until February 1877, when the Cheyennes made a break for the Little Bighorn country, hopeful the soldiers would leave them in peace.[26]

But Miles dogged their trail. He had captured four Northern Cheyenne women a month earlier. Now he released the eldest to deliver an ultimatum to the tribe: Surrender yourselves, your weapons, and your ponies, and I will see that no harm comes to you. Reject my terms, and I will destroy you. The council of chiefs yielded.

Then Crook got involved. Loath to see Miles get credit for capturing Indians he had hounded for months, he dispatched agency Cheyennes from Nebraska with a better offer. He would permit any Cheyennes who surrendered to him at Camp Robinson not only to keep their weapons and ponies but also to return to the White River Agency in the Cheyenne country. This new wrinkle fractured the consensus among the chiefs, and the tribe splintered just as the Lakotas had. About three hundred Northern Cheyennes under minor chiefs surrendered to Miles, who treated them kindly and enlisted half the warriors as scouts. Nearly a thousand Cheyennes under Little Wolf and Dull Knife surrendered to Crook, who promptly reneged on his promises. He fed them well enough—one starved warrior died of surfeit—but as a quid pro quo demanded they surrender their arms and mounts. And they would not be going home to White River. Crook told the Cheyennes that they must choose between relocating to agencies on the Missouri River, an option the chiefs instantly rejected, and joining the Southern Cheyennes in Indian Territory. Such was the will of the Great Father. Crook had known this all along, even if publicly he bragged of never making a promise to an Indian he couldn't keep.

The Cheyenne chiefs acceded to relocate only because General Crook and Colonel Mackenzie had assured them the tribe could return north if they found conditions in Indian Territory unsatisfactory. Both

Crook and Mackenzie later denied this. In any case, being unarmed, dismounted, and dependent on government rations, the Northern Cheyennes had little choice but to comply. And so, on May 28, 1877, Little Wolf and Dull Knife led 972 Northern Cheyennes under army escort on a journey along trails they had used to visit their southern relatives, over a country now foreign to them. Where once had roamed enormous buffalo herds, there were now cattle ranches and farms. Countless settlements lay just east of the route, and three railroads crossed plains formerly the domain of the Cheyennes. Whatever he might or might not have guaranteed the Northern Cheyennes, Colonel Mackenzie honestly believed resettlement in Indian Territory would be best for their "ultimate prosperity." He told the chiefs that "as a people, they must under pressure of circumstances change their mode of life." But, he was careful to add, "such a change, wherever they were, would be accompanied by much suffering."[27]

On August 5, the Northern Cheyennes arrived at the Darlington Agency in Indian Territory. Suffering stalked them from the start. The Southern Cheyennes tormented the northerners; the last thing they wanted were more mouths at the agency to consume the already insufficient government rations. And they were no longer one people. In the thirteen years since the last tribal Sun Dance, the Northern and Southern Cheyennes had diverged in their customs, in their dress, and even in their vocabulary. Scornful of the frequent intermarriage between Northern Cheyennes and Lakotas, a southern chief asked his northern kinsmen, "What are you Sioux doing here?"

The answer was obvious. They were dying. The weekly beef issue scarcely sufficed for two days. Malaria cut through them like a scythe. During the winter of 1877–1878, a measles epidemic killed fifty Northern Cheyenne children already weakened by hunger. Mosquitoes, heat, and homesickness enervated those whom disease spared. Of the Northern Cheyennes' first year on the reservation, the Indian agent John D. Miles reported, "They have lived and that is about all."[28]

When Colonel Mackenzie returned to Indian Territory in 1878 as district commander, the condition of the Northern Cheyennes at the Darlington Agency appalled him. "I am expected to see that Indians behave properly whom the government is starving," he complained to Sheridan, "and not only that, but starving in flagrant violation of agreement." Mackenzie also told the commanding officer at Fort Reno to turn a blind eye if the Cheyennes wandered off the reservation to hunt;

otherwise, he said, "the troops will be placed in the position of assisting in a great wrong." The difficulty was, there were no buffalo left to hunt.

General Sheridan shared Mackenzie's outrage. With the scales at last dropping from his eyes, he deprecated the appalling conditions not only at the Darlington Agency but also at all Plains Indian agencies. In his 1878 annual report, Sheridan declared,

> There has been an insufficiency of food, and as the game is gone, hunger has made the Indians in some cases desperate, and almost any race of man will fight rather than starve. The question of justice and right to the Indian is past and cannot be recalled. We have occupied his country, taken away his lordly domain, destroyed his herds of game, penned him up on reservations, and reduced him to poverty. For humanity's sake, let's give him enough to eat and integrity in the agent over him.[29]

Most of the Northern Cheyennes attempted to mend ties with the Southern Cheyennes and make the best of a bad situation. Not so Little Wolf. Determined to go home rather than acquiesce in a life of misery, he implored the Indian agent either to allow him and his followers to leave or to permit the chief to petition the Indian Bureau directly. The agent denied both requests. Shocked and angry, Little Wolf and his subchiefs were convinced the refusal contravened what they understood to have been Crook and Mackenzie's promise. "If we could have been allowed to go back to our old reservation," Chief Wild Hog later said, "we would have been willing to go to farming, or to have done anything the government required of us in that country."[30]

But not on the pestilential southern plains. On September 9, Little Wolf addressed the Indian agent and the commanding officer of Fort Reno with a polite but firm finality:

> My friends, I am now going to my camp. I do not wish the ground about this agency to be made bloody, but now listen to what I say to you. I am going to leave here; I am going north to my own country. I do not want to see blood spilt about this agency. If you are going to send your soldiers after me, I wish that you would first let me get a little distance away from this agency. Then if you want to fight, I will fight you, and we can make the ground bloody at that place.[31]

That night, Chiefs Little Wolf, Dull Knife, Wild Hog, and 353 people left the agency with their lodges standing and cooking fires burning. Most were women, children, and old men. Only sixty were seasoned warriors. Ominously, the keeper of the Sacred Buffalo Hat, which had always resided with the Northern Cheyennes, opted out, meaning that Little Wolf's people would travel without the protection of a sacred relic. Wooden Leg and his father also remained behind. "We sympathized fully with our deceived and suffering people," he explained, "and both of us had a high admiration for Little Wolf. But we settled our minds to stay here and keep out of trouble."[32]

As Little Wolf had expected, trouble pursued him with unwavering persistence. First, a cavalry battalion from Fort Reno overtook the Cheyennes just below the Kansas border. Little Wolf tried to avoid bloodshed. As he parleyed with the commander, shots were fired. The Cheyennes easily bested the troopers, and the next morning resumed their flight.

Little Wolf's reluctance to spill white blood was genuine but unrealistic. The Northern Cheyennes needed fresh horses and cattle for the long journey. Kansas cattlemen, however, were not accustomed to surrendering their livestock without a fight. By the time the Cheyennes crossed the Arkansas River midway through Kansas, their foraging parties had killed ten ranchers.

The army dragnet was now fully in place. General Sheridan had formed two lines to intercept the Cheyennes—the first along the Kansas Pacific Railway, and a second line farther north on the Union Pacific. Soldiers and cattlemen pursued them across Kansas. In one clash, the Cheyennes lost sixty ponies, together with most of their dried meat and other supplies. It was then that the exodus turned truly ugly. War parties composed of what Chief Wild Hog called the "wilder young men" of the band ravaged farms and ranches in northwest Kansas, running off livestock and raping and killing indiscriminately. Little Wolf tried vainly to prevent the carnage. Forty civilians, mostly foreign immigrants who had never laid eyes on an Indian, perished before the Cheyennes crossed into sparsely populated western Nebraska. Public opinion, initially favorable to the Cheyennes, now swung decisively against them, and soldiers steeled themselves for a brutal campaign.[33]

The Northern Cheyennes eluded the army, only to fall victim to internal discord. Little Wolf wanted to press on to the game-rich Powder River country. Dull Knife, however, was determined to go to the Red Cloud Agency, where he assumed the Cheyennes would be permitted to live. "Now we have again reached our own ground," proclaimed the old chief, "and from this time forth we will fight no more or harm any white people." Unbeknownst to Dull Knife, the government had resettled Red Cloud's Oglalas on the Pine Ridge Agency in the Dakota Territory.

In the Sandhills country of northcentral Nebraska, Little Wolf and Dull Knife parted company. Little Wolf's people hunkered down for the winter in the Sandhills, while Dull Knife led 149 Northern Cheyennes toward the defunct Red Cloud Agency. Instead of finding sanctuary, they stumbled upon soldiers from Fort (previously Camp) Robinson. Heavily outnumbered, Dull Knife capitulated. He had traveled eight hundred miles since leaving the Indian Territory.[34]

At first, life at Fort Robinson was good. The army installed the Cheyennes in a barracks as prisoners of war, with the full freedom of the post grounds. But powerful forces were at work to return them to Indian Territory or worse. Sheridan argued that although the Cheyennes' condition was pitiable, failure to send them back would jeopardize the stability of the reservation system. The governor of Kansas wanted to prosecute and hang alleged perpetrators of atrocities in his state. Neither the War Department nor the Interior Department contested the request, and in mid-December orders went out to General Sheridan to send the Cheyennes to Fort Leavenworth, where the wanted men would be turned over to Kansas courts and the remainder returned to Indian Territory.

Red Cloud urged Dull Knife to go peacefully. "Our hearts are sorry for you," he told the Cheyenne chiefs in a parley at Fort Robinson. "But what can we do? The Great Father is all powerful. His people fill the whole earth . . . So listen to your old friend and do without complaint what the Great Father tells you." Dull Knife was immovable. The Northern Cheyennes had bowed once to the Great Father's will, and it had brought them only sickness and hunger. They would not yield a second time. Dull Knife asked the post commander, Captain Henry W. Wessells, to "tell the Great Father if he lets us stay here [my] people will hurt no one. Tell him if he tried to send us back we will butcher each other with our own knives."

The Nebraska winter hardened. On New Year's Day 1879, Captain Wessells called another council. "If you will allow us to remain we will do anything the Great Father may require of us," pleaded Wild Hog. "We will live like white people, work and wear their clothes. We will never make trouble." Dull Knife had fallen dangerously ill, but his will to resist a return to Indian Territory remained strong. "The only way you can get us there," he said, "is to come in here with clubs, knock us on the head, drag us out and take us down there dead." Little did he know that their supposed friend George Crook was willing to employ harsh measures to break them.[35]

Confronted with what he called Cheyenne "intransigence," Crook concluded to "starve or freeze" them out. Accordingly, on January 3, 1879, Captain Wessells withheld food and firewood, rationalizing that it was more humane "than to knock the building down with field pieces." The Cheyennes held firm. Five days later, Wessells cut off water to the barracks. He urged the Indians to release their children to his care. Inside the barracks, the young warriors had wrested control from Dull Knife. "They would eat their children," a warrior was said to have yelled from a window, "and when they were consumed [they] would eat their women and it was no use to try to persuade them—they would all die before they would go back south." Wessells ordered the barracks door boarded up and chained. The next day, he took Wild Hog hostage. It was a gross miscalculation. Rather than break their will to resist, the arrest of Wild Hog convinced the Cheyennes that their only hope lay in escape.[36]

At sunset on January 9, the Northern Cheyennes made their melancholy preparations to break out of the barracks. They covered the windows with blankets and tore up a floorboard beneath the stove where they had secreted a dozen rifles and five revolvers, reassembled from parts the women and children had worn as jewelry or hidden beneath their clothing. They had only a few rounds of ammunition. Warriors painted their faces and donned the bits of war clothing left to them. There were 125 Cheyennes in the barracks, 44 of whom were men of fighting age. None held out much hope of seeing the next sunrise. "It is true that we must die," they told one another, "but we will not die shut up here like dogs; we will die on the prairie; we will die fighting."

Outside, the mercury hovered near zero. Six inches of snow covered the ground, and the moon shone full in a cloudless sky. At 10:00 p.m., the Cheyennes smashed the barracks windows and shot the nearest sentries. Half-starved and wild with thirst, their clothing frozen hard to their bodies, the Indians lurched toward a bridge over the nearby White River. Several paused to drink and were gunned down on the riverbank. Once over the bridge, the remaining Cheyennes staggered toward a chain of sandstone bluffs a mile distant. Five warriors formed a rear guard against a company of hastily awakened troopers clad only in their winter underwear. All the warriors were killed. A Cheyenne woman likened the slaughter to shooting cattle, her people "dropping dead one after another as we ran." From beneath the bluffs, officers called on the survivors to surrender. When they refused, the soldiers riddled them with bullets, killing twenty-six Cheyennes and wounding thirty more.

It took twelve days for six well-mounted cavalry companies to ride down the last of the enfeebled "fugitives." Too weak to go on, the thirty-two remaining Cheyennes halted in a shallow pit northwest of Fort Robinson. There they erected breastworks and prepared to die. On January 22, Captain Wessells and 151 cavalrymen surrounded the Indians. Only eighteen were warriors. A bitter struggle ensued at near-point-blank range. During a lull, a young girl raised a carbine above the breastworks in a gesture of surrender. Her mother yanked her daughter to the ground, slit her throat, and then stabbed herself to death. The shooting resumed. Three warriors leaped from the pit and were shot to pieces. Then the pit fell silent. Twenty-three bodies were removed from the washout; three wounded Cheyennes died the next day. Only six Cheyennes emerged unscathed.

Dull Knife and his family had vanished. Wessells presumed them dead of exposure somewhere on the prairie. But they were alive—barely. For ten days, they hid in a cave before daring to show themselves. A friendly white rancher took them in. His Lakota wife fed them until they were strong enough to reach the Pine Ridge Agency, where the Oglalas spirited them to a well-provisioned lodge far from inquisitive officials. Only later did Dull Knife learn how his people had fled, fought, and died without their chief.[37]

Fate was kinder to Little Wolf's people. After wintering undetected in the Sandhills country, Little Wolf resumed his journey toward the Powder River. Rather than apply force, the department commander, General Terry, hoped to talk the band into surrender. In late February, he dispatched Lieutenant William Philo Clark to find and confer with Little Wolf, who along with many of his warriors had served under Clark as scouts before their banishment.

Terry's diplomatic gambit succeeded. On March 25, 1879, Little Wolf and his 114 followers surrendered to Clark, ending their eight-month, twelve-hundred-mile odyssey. The bloodless denouement pleased Little Wolf. "You are the only one who has offered to talk before fighting," he told Clark. "It looks as though the wind, which has made our hearts flutter for so long, would now go down. I am very glad we did not fight and that none of my people or yours have been killed . . . There are only a few of us left, and we only wanted a little ground, where we could live."[38]

They would have it. At the recommendation of Lieutenant Clark and General Terry, the government permitted the band to remain at Fort Keogh (the former Tongue River Cantonment). Grateful for Clark's support, Little Wolf enlisted as a sergeant in his scout company.

Little Wolf had profited from public revulsion over the army's treatment of Dull Knife's band. President Rutherford B. Hayes, disturbed by the "unnecessary cruelty" at Fort Robinson, had ordered an investigation. "In every respect it would have been better to treat the prisoners well than to treat them harshly," said Secretary of the Interior Carl Schurz. "Freezing and starving them was not the way to reconcile them to their fate." The government allowed the fifty-eight survivors of Dull Knife's decimated band to join their chief at Pine Ridge, and a Kansas jury acquitted Wild Hog and his co-defendants on all charges.

Captain Wessells did not suffer for his actions, nor did Crook for ordering them. Wessells served with distinction during the Spanish-American War and retired a brigadier general. Five years before his death, he recapitulated the Fort Robinson tragedy in a letter to a friend. "All right," he conceded, "was on the side of those Indians."

Before January 9, 1879, no one in the government or the army believed Dull Knife's Northern Cheyennes would fight to the finish for their birthright. A month later, an astonished investigative board concluded that the Northern Cheyennes, on that bright and frigid winter's night at Fort Robinson, had literally "gone out to die."[39]

The smashing of the Northern Cheyennes by Ranald Mackenzie in November 1876 left only the non-treaty bands of Sitting Bull and Crazy Horse to challenge government control of the northern plains. With the end of the centennial year, the white circle around the Plains Indians had all but closed. Only the buffalo-rich Hunkpapa country between the Yellowstone and the Missouri Rivers in northern Montana remained purely Indian. To the roaming Lakotas, it represented the final refuge, the last hope for preserving the old ways. Their bastion, however, was about to be breached.

CHAPTER 16

A WARRIOR I HAVE BEEN

Nelson miles never made idle threats. At their abortive October 1876 parleys, the colonel had warned Sitting Bull he would hound him all winter. He did, and the high command was delighted. General Sherman relished the prospect of Miles "crowning his success by capturing or killing Sitting Bull and his remnant of outlaws," and he assured the press that the army "will dog them till they succumb." He and Sheridan hoped the Indian Bureau would agree to place the defeated Indians—stripped of their guns and ponies—on reservations along the Missouri River, where they might be more easily controlled.

But first Miles had to find the hostiles, and that presented a monumental challenge. The heart of the Hunkpapa country was terra incognita to the whites. On army maps, the region appeared as a large blank space. All Miles knew was that Sitting Bull habitually wintered near the Fort Peck trading post on the Missouri River, 150 miles north of Tongue River Cantonment. With only a compass to guide his course, on November 5, 1876, Miles marched out of the cantonment and into the teeth of a raging Montana blizzard. Visibility was nil, but at least the troops were warm. The Fifth Infantry had prepared itself for the arctic blasts of a northern plains winter as well as ingenuity and individual effort permitted. That which army quartermaster stocks lacked the soldiers made up for with mittens, underwear, and masks fashioned from their own woolen blankets. Nearly all the men wore long, heavy buffalo coats that warded off the cold but made walking in snow a tribulation.[1]

Miles and his heavily bundled walk-a-heaps reached Fort Peck two weeks later. Sitting Bull was gone, no one seemed to know where. Miles combed the country for another two weeks and then headed home to Tongue River Cantonment to rest and refit. His favorite subordinate, Captain Frank Baldwin, kept at it with a small detachment. On December 7, Baldwin chanced upon the elusive Hunkpapa chief, who had returned to Fort Peck to trade for ammunition. It was not for himself but for Crazy Horse that Sitting Bull had risked detection. Encumbered with Dull Knife's destitute Cheyennes, low on ammunition, and fearing attack, Crazy Horse had urged Sitting Bull to join him—and to bring bullets. Having gotten what he came for, Sitting Bull withdrew from Fort Peck after a brief skirmish with Baldwin and journeyed south along the Redwater River. It was too cold and the snow too deep to make the long march to the Powder River without rest, and so Sitting Bull paused to camp under a sheltering range of bluffs along the timber-lined Ash Creek, a tributary of the Redwater.

Captain Baldwin was close behind but struggling. The temperatures had dropped so low that even the soldiers' buffalo coats and thick mittens were insufficient to protect them, and frostbite or fatigue had relegated nearly a third of the men to riding in the wagons. After toppling benumbed from his horse, the captain wisely ordered the heartiest men to fix bayonets and prod the unresponsive—himself included. On the afternoon of December 18, the sight of a low cloud of campfire smoke on the horizon revived everyone. Sick and frostbitten soldiers climbed from the wagons to fight with their companies, and the command lumbered toward the Hunkpapa village. They came on slowly enough for the few warriors on hand—most were out hunting—to cover the retreat of the women and children and save the ammunition train. But the 122 lodges and all their contents, as well as part of the pony herd, were lost. Well satisfied with the outcome, Baldwin shot the ponies and started for Tongue River Cantonment. The encounter cost Sitting Bull his last vestige of influence over the non-Hunkpapas, most of whom went their own way. With his own band now as destitute as the Cheyennes, Sitting Bull traveled on to share in Crazy Horse's meager resources.

Ten years earlier, almost to the day, the Lakotas, Cheyennes, and Arapahos had annihilated Captain William Judd Fetterman and eighty officers and men in the shadows of the Bighorn Mountains. To the horror-struck garrison of Fort Phil Kearny, the northern tribes had seemed unconquerable. Now their situation appeared hopeless. Winter was no longer an ally. The Hunkpapa homeland—the last Lakota sanctuary—had been breached. For a moment, it had looked as if peace might obtain without further bloodshed. Two days before Baldwin humbled Sitting Bull, a delegation of five influential Miniconjou chiefs from Crazy Horse's coalition had approached Tongue River Cantonment under a flag of truce to learn what terms Bear Coat might offer. Regrettably, they never reached Miles; his Crow scouts murdered them. Miles disarmed and dismounted the Crows and sent their ponies to the Miniconjous to apologize for the "cruel and cowardly murders." But the damage had been done. The peace element had lost face, and the war faction refused to negotiate. The combat would continue.[2]

Which actually suited Miles's purposes. With Crook no longer in the field, the way was open for him to score the victory over Crazy Horse that had eluded his rival and by so doing put himself one step closer to a brigadier general's star. Intending, as he told General Sherman, to "have a good fight with Crazy Horse," Miles left Tongue River Cantonment on December 29 with the thermometer tottering at thirty below zero and his troops not yet recovered from the exertions of the Fort Peck Expedition. "Miles is working his men to death," observed a major who remained behind. "[They] are tired and worn and all men and officers seem dissatisfied . . . I am afraid if he met with a large body of Indians his men would not be able physically to compete with them."[3]

*

Crazy Horse wanted to fight as badly as did Miles. Employing loyal *akicitas* to silence dissenters, he coerced the coalition chiefs into taking the offensive. They would crush Bear Coat, he promised, and recover the lost Lakota hunting grounds. Armed with that assurance, fifty decoys set out for Tongue River Cantonment to lure Miles up the narrow and winding Tongue River valley. It was ideal country for an ambush. Before Crazy Horse could spring his trap, however, army scouts captured several Cheyenne women and children who had become disoriented in the rugged wilds. Enraged warriors dashed toward Miles's bivouac to rescue them. A snow squall supervened, and they drew off empty-handed.[4]

Miles bivouacked in scattered cottonwood groves behind a barren ridge, the icy Tongue River twisting along his front and flanks. At daybreak on January 8, 1877, a long column of mounted warriors appeared opposite his camp. The soldiers "would eat no more fat," they declared, meaning this was their last breakfast. The army interpreters told them to stop yelling like women and start fighting like men.

Crazy Horse commanded the war party. Fewer than 400 of the 600 fighting men in the village were with him. Most of the Miniconjous and Sans Arcs hung well back, preferring to let the soldiers come to them rather than to risk an attack—a sure sign Crazy Horse's sway over the non-Oglalas had waned. His tactics also left much to be desired. Crazy Horse went first for the heart of Miles's line and was handily repulsed. Between charges, the lightly clothed Indians huddled by fires, while the fur-clad troops stamped their feet in the ranks to keep warm. A blowing snow came up, adding an urgency to the battle. Breaking off the futile lunges at Miles's center, Crazy Horse led 250 warriors upstream to a butte beyond Miles's left. There he halted.

The snow fell faster. A Cheyenne medicine man who thought himself impervious to bullets walked back and forth along the ridge, challenging the soldiers to shoot at him. No one mimicked his heroics, Wooden Leg, who fought beside Crazy Horse, confessing, "All of us kept behind the rocks, only peeking around at times to shoot. Bullets glanced off the shielding rocks, but none hit us." Finally, a bullet found the medicine man. He writhed and moaned until Wooden Leg and three others risked their lives to drag him to safety. The medicine man's fall was the cue for Miles to advance. The warriors, nearly out of ammunition, scurried off the butte. Crazy Horse formed a small but unnecessary rear guard. A full-blown blizzard had set in, stopping the soldiers in their tracks.

The Battle of Wolf Mountain ended at noon. Casualties in the five-hour engagement were minimal. The Cheyenne medicine man and two Lakotas were known to have been killed, and perhaps two dozen warriors were wounded. Miles suffered five dead and another eight wounded. The strategic consequences, however, were enormous. Amid the swirling snows at Wolf Mountain, Lakota offensive power was forever broken, and Crazy Horse's reputation for military genius had been dealt a shattering blow.

Diminishing supplies compelled Miles to return to Tongue River Cantonment. The Indians withdrew far upriver to find a precarious refuge in the Bighorn Mountain country. But no place was truly safe from the walk-a-heaps. As Miles adduced, "The engagement demonstrated that we could move in any part of the country in the midst of winter and hunt the enemy down in their camps wherever they might take refuge." It was the beginning of the end for the battered bands of Lakota holdouts.[5]

✳

Sitting Bull reached Crazy Horse's village on January 15, 1877. It was a dismal place. The Miniconjous and the Sans Arcs were ready to quit. "I am tired of being always on the watch for troops," said a Miniconjou subchief, whose sole desire was to get his family "where they can sleep without being continually in the expectation of attack." The Oglalas wanted to keep up the struggle. The Northern Cheyennes wanted to go their own way.

After Mackenzie's destruction of Dull Knife's village, Crazy Horse had used muscle to hold the winter roamers together. When the Miniconjous tried to leave, Oglala *akicitas* had torn apart their lodges and killed their ponies. Crazy Horse, however, dared not threaten such measures against the mighty Sitting Bull. And at the end of January, Sitting Bull stunned Crazy Horse by deciding to go north—far north. Many Hunkpapas had obtained asylum in the "Grandmother's Land," Canada. "They told us this line was considered holy," remembered a boy in Sitting Bull's village. "They called that a holy trail. They believe things are different when you cross from one side to another. You are altogether different. On one side you are perfectly free to do as you please. On the other you are in danger."[6]

Sitting Bull told Crazy Horse that he would camp near Fort Peck and wait to hear how his kinsmen fared in Canada before making a final decision. In reality, his people were deciding for him. Most had already taken the *chanku wakan*, or sacred road, across the border. Sitting Bull, who eight months earlier had presided over thousands, was left with just ten lodges. Crazy Horse also saw his world slipping away. Emboldened by Sitting Bull's departure, the Miniconjous and the Sans Arcs quit his camp in early February. Some followed the Hunkpapas north; most drifted uncertainly toward the agencies, hoping to negotiate favorable surrender terms. Sitting Bull's defection had dealt the unity of the non-treaty Lakotas, always tenuous at best after the Little Bighorn, a fatal blow. The end could not be far off.

As Crazy Horse's martial law crumbled, Oglala waverers reasserted themselves. The *akicitas* shifted their loyalty to chiefs who favored peace talks. Confused and angry, Crazy Horse reverted to his customary diffidence in council. He seldom spoke and spent little time in camp. Finally, on March 5, he and his wife packed their tipi and walked off into the wilderness.

Crazy Horse had embarked on a vision quest. Perhaps the spirits would tell him how he might yet save his people and their country. For days on end, he fasted and prayed, braved blizzards, and waited for divine guidance. None came, and Crazy Horse returned to the village a pariah. In his absence, the chiefs had agreed to surrender to Crook at Fort Robinson; the time, they said, had come to walk the white man's road. "You see all the people here in rags," Chief Iron Hawk told Crazy Horse. "They all need clothing; we might as well go in." Broken in spirit, Crazy Horse posed no objection.

Chief Spotted Tail had engineered the capitulation. He had agreed to undertake a peace mission on the strength of Crook's word that prisoners would be treated liberally, no leaders would be punished, and the planned relocation of the Red Cloud and Spotted Tail Agencies to the Missouri River would be scrapped. Spotted Tail's message to the non-treaty chiefs was direct and terse: surrender or be hunted down like dogs. The Lakota youth Black Elk found the chief repellent, grown fat with the white man's food, while they were thin with famine. His father told him that Spotted Tail had come to induce Crazy Horse to give up "because our own people had turned against us, and in the spring, when the grass was high enough for the horses, many soldiers would come and fight us, and many Shoshones and Crows and even Lakotas would come against us with the Wasichus." They were hard words but true.[7]

After fifty days with the winter roamers, Spotted Tail returned to Fort Robinson. Although he had not seen his nephew, Spotted Tail was certain Crazy Horse would surrender. General Crook, however, wanted Crazy Horse sooner rather than later. And so he turned to Red Cloud, whom he had deposed as head chief of agency Lakotas in favor of Spotted Tail the previous fall. Appealing to the chief's vanity, he tacitly promised to restore him to office if Red Cloud expedited his son-in-law Crazy Horse's capitulation. Crook authorized Red Cloud to modify the surrender terms in two respects: Crazy Horse would be permitted to organize a buffalo hunt once all the "hostiles" had come in and also to visit the Great Father, should he wish. Red Cloud set out in mid-April.

Red Cloud's mission proved superfluous, because Crazy Horse fully intended to submit. He had "untied his pony's tail," a Lakota metaphor for peace. On May 6, Crazy Horse rode into Fort Robinson with 889 followers and nearly two thousand ponies. Lieutenant Philo Clark, who had facilitated the capitulation of the Cheyenne chief Little Wolf, was on hand to greet him. Crazy Horse offered the lieutenant his left hand, a Lakota gesture expressing the wish for lasting peace. Lieutenant John Bourke watched him ride in with Clark. "Crazy Horse behaved with stolidity, like a man who saw he had to give in to fate, but would do so as doggedly as possible."[8]

The day after Crazy Horse shook Lieutenant Clark's hand, Sitting Bull crossed the mystic line into the Grandmother's Land. There remained one mopping-up action—which Miles effected in May—against a small Miniconjou band that had rejected Spotted Tail's peace overtures. But it was the capitulation of Crazy Horse that effectively brought down the curtain on the Great Sioux War.[9]

*

With the bloodless denouement at Fort Robinson, Crook had wrested the headlines from Miles. The army high command, however, knew that Miles deserved the credit for defeating the non-treaty Lakotas. It was his relentless winter campaigning that so wore them down that surrender or sanctuary in Canada had become their only alternatives. Crook's diplomacy had simply accelerated the inevitable. The best that can be said of Crook and Terry is that they had had the good sense to give Miles and Mackenzie free rein. "The fact of the case is, the operations of Generals Terry and Crook will not bear criticism," General Sheridan reminded Sherman as the war wound down, "and my only thought has been to let them sleep. I approved what was done, for the sake of the troops, but in doing so, I was not approving much, as you well know."[10]

Crazy Horse had two requests when he turned himself in: that his people be accorded an agency of their own west of the Black Hills, and that Crook make good on his promise of a buffalo hunt. There was a pathos to Crazy Horse's sincere entreaties. He could not grasp that every aspect of the old life was irrevocably gone or that Crook had lied to him. The Lakotas were on the government dole. They were expected to take up farming, not wander off on land that was no longer theirs. Crook disingenuously agreed to present Crazy Horse's request for an agency to the Great Father, knowing full well a decision to remove all of the Lakotas to the Missouri River had already been made. As the weeks passed, Crazy Horse grew restive. The army encouraged him to join a Lakota delegation on a visit to the Great Father, but he declined, saying that there was no "Great Father between him and the Great Spirit." He refused to sign for rations, as chiefs were required to do before they were issued, and spoke of taking his people beyond the Black Hills—acts of defiance that enhanced the war chief's standing with Oglala warriors whose support Red Cloud needed to maintain his authority. And Red Cloud was not one to indulge potential rivals.

Jealousy and mistrust generated a whirlwind of rumors and accusations at the Red Cloud Agency. Friends of Crazy Horse warned him that the proffered Washington trip had been a "decoy" to lure him to a distant place, where he would be imprisoned or killed. Friends of Red Cloud whispered falsely to the old chief that General Crook intended to replace him with Crazy Horse as chief of the agency Oglalas, which only deepened Red Cloud's hostility toward his son-in-law. Spotted Tail, who also saw Crazy Horse as a threat to the established order, closed ranks with Red Cloud. The army, however, gave Crazy Horse the benefit of the doubt. "Crazy Horse [is] all right," a captain at Camp Sheridan reassured officers there. "If they would let him alone and not 'buzz' him so much he would come out all right." Lieutenant Clark agreed. Crazy Horse, he told General Crook, "wanted to do right."[11]

Crook and Crazy Horse, however, had vastly different understandings of the meaning of "doing right." Crook expected him to help the government defeat its few remaining Indian enemies. Crazy Horse, having committed himself to peace, found the notion repellent, as Lieutenant Clark learned on August 1 when he asked Crazy Horse to recruit warriors to join the army in quelling an outbreak of the Nez Perce Indians. Although he initially refused, Crazy Horse changed his mind the next day. Reminding Clark that he had forsworn war, Crazy Horse expressed surprise that "the same men who had desired to have this pledge from him were urging him to go killing men again." Nevertheless, he "would take his warriors north" and "camp beside the soldiers and fight with them until all the Nez Perces were killed."

There then occurred a tragic error. The interpreter Frank Grouard mistranslated Crazy Horse's words as "We will go north and fight until not a *white man* [italics added] is left." It might have been a case of willful misrepresentation on the part of the normally reliable Grouard; he had double-crossed Crazy Horse several years earlier and likely wanted him out of the way. Or he might have misunderstood Crazy Horse. Deliberate or otherwise, Grouard's faulty rendering had the desired effect. Clark exploded. As the lieutenant upbraided Crazy Horse, Grouard slipped out of the room. Flabbergasted, the other interpreter present tried to convey Crazy Horse's reply correctly. But Clark was in no mood to listen. Unaware of the mistranslation, Crazy Horse enumerated his conditions for participating in the Nez Perce War. Confused and affronted by Clark's anger, Crazy Horse lost his temper and stormed out of the council. The situation spiraled out of control. Clark telegraphed Crook that Crazy Horse meant to break out. The post commander, Lieutenant Colonel Luther P. Bradley, warned Crook that "Crazy Horse is behaving badly. Every influence that kindness could suggest has been exhausted on him." Then Bradley asked for reinforcements that would swell the troop strength at Fort Robinson to seven hundred soldiers and three hundred Indian auxiliaries. Bradley also telegraphed General Sheridan of the emergency. Sheridan told Crook to take charge of the matter personally.[12]

Crook arrived at Fort Robinson on September 2. Hoping to defuse the crisis, he had Clark call a meeting with Crazy Horse for the next morning, but it never came off. As Crook made his way to the council grounds, a nephew of Red Cloud's intercepted him, possibly at the chief's behest. Crazy Horse, the warrior warned, intended to kill the general. Crook canceled the council.

That night, Crook met with Red Cloud and his chiefs to decide how best to neutralize Crazy Horse. Red Cloud wanted to kill him outright. Crook thought that a bit drastic. He told Red Cloud to have his men arrest Crazy Horse secretly the next night. The war leader was not to be harmed—unless he resisted. His unseemly business concluded, Crook departed Fort Robinson.

Matters did not unfold as Crook expected. When he learned of the planned operation, Colonel Bradley took it upon himself to halt what he condemned as vigilante justice. A man of Crazy Horse's prestige, he wired Crook, should be arrested in broad daylight, adding, "The life of Crazy Horse is just as dear to him as my life is to me." To intimidate Crazy Horse and his people, Bradley ordered eight cavalry companies to accompany Red Cloud's men.[13]

On the morning of September 4, nearly a thousand soldiers and Oglala warriors left Fort Robinson to apprehend one man. Forewarned of their approach, Crazy Horse now found himself a fugitive. As his followers scattered, he rode first to the village of a Miniconjou friend at the Spotted Tail Agency. Wanting no trouble with the army, the friend persuaded Crazy Horse to go to Camp Sheridan, where Spotted Tail and the commanding officer, Major John Burke, awaited him. Crazy Horse pleaded with his uncle Spotted Tail to give him a home at his agency, but the chief was unwelcoming. In the presence of hundreds of Indian onlookers, he rebuked his nephew. "We never have trouble here! I am chief here! We Brulés keep the peace! Every Indian who comes here must obey me! You say you want to come to this agency to live peaceably. If you stay here, you must listen to me! That is all!"

Crazy Horse wilted. Major Burke and Lieutenant Jesse Lee, the officer in charge at the Spotted Tail Agency, coaxed him into Burke's quarters for a talk. Lee pitied Crazy Horse, who "seemed like a frightened, trembling wild animal brought to bay, hoping for confidence one moment and fearing treachery the next."

"I want no trouble," Crazy Horse told the officers. "I came here because it is peace here. I want to get away from the trouble at Red Cloud. They have misunderstood and misinterpreted me there ... I would like to be transferred to this agency. They gave me no rest at Red Cloud. I was talked to night and day and my brain is in a whirl. I want to do what is right."[14]

Burke and Lee could only suggest that Crazy Horse return to Camp Robinson and plead his case to Bradley. If the colonel approved, they would grant him a home among the Brulés. Crazy Horse agreed, and the next morning, September 5, 1877, he traveled to Fort Robinson with Lee and several agency chiefs. Lee did not like the look of things when they arrived. The parade ground overflowed with Red Cloud's warriors—many in war paint—and mounted cavalrymen, rifles in hand. Crazy Horse's followers mingled on the periphery. Bradley's adjutant told Lee to turn Crazy Horse over to the officer of the day, Captain James Kennington, who informed Lee that there was to be no interview with the colonel. Lee was mortified. Without telling Crazy Horse what Kennington had said, he asked Crazy Horse to wait in the adjutant's office and then went to see Bradley. The colonel was no less disturbed than Lee. But he could do nothing. "T'was no use. It was too late to talk," Bradley told Lee. General Sheridan had ordered the immediate arrest of Crazy Horse. Bradley was to transport him under guard to division headquarters in Chicago. From there, Crazy Horse would be shipped to a prison cell on the Dry Tortugas off the Florida coast to rot.

In the faint hope that Bradley might reconsider his role in the impending treachery, Lee dissembled to Crazy Horse. "I told [him] that the night was coming on and the soldier chief said it was too late for a talk; that he said for him to go with the officer of the day and he would be taken care of and not harmed." Unaware he was headed for the guardhouse, Crazy Horse smiled hopefully and shook Kennington's hand. Crazy Horse's friend Little Big Man and the captain each took hold of one of Crazy Horse's wrists and led him outside. Two soldiers followed. The party veered toward the guardhouse. The cell with its small grated window came into view. Inside, there were men shackled to black iron balls. Crazy Horse recoiled. "I won't go in there. It is the place where prisoners are kept!"[15]

It was over in an instant. Breaking free from Little Big Man and Captain Kennington, Crazy Horse knocked the two guards against the wall. Little Big Man grabbed his wrist. Crazy Horse drew out a hidden knife and slashed his friend's arm. As Crazy Horse lurched into the open, Kennington barked, "Stab the son-of-a-bitch! Stab the son-of-a-bitch." A private of the guard thrust his bayonet into Crazy Horse's back, piercing a kidney and a lung. Crazy Horse screamed, and the soldier impaled him again. The great Oglala war leader collapsed. Shoving his way through the throng, the post surgeon Valentine T. McGillycuddy examined him. Crazy Horse, he later reported, "was frothing at the mouth, pulse weak and intermittent, [and] blood trickling from the upper edge of his [right] hip." As McGillycuddy set to work to save his life, carbines and rifles emerged from beneath the blankets of Crazy Horse's men. Red Cloud's warriors raised their weapons in answer, but no one really wanted to shoot. Tempers cooled, rifles were lowered, and the crowd dispersed. Soldiers carried Crazy Horse on a blanket into the adjutant's office and, at his own wish, placed him on the floor. Crazy Horse lingered in agony for hours. Occasionally, he spoke. "I don't know why they stabbed me," he told the interpreter Louis Bordeaux. "No white man is to blame for this . . . I blame the Indians." Crazy Horse's father was more specific. He alleged that the jealousy of Red Cloud and Spotted Tail had killed his son.

Crazy Horse died at 11:40 p.m. Moments before slipping into unconsciousness, he murmured, "All I wanted was to be left alone." Dr. McGillycuddy cut to the core of the tragedy when he said, "A combination of treachery, jealousy, and unreliable reports simply resulted in a frame up, and he was railroaded to his death."

"It is good," an old Miniconjou ally said when Crazy Horse expired. "He has looked for death, and it has come." Drawing the blanket over Crazy Horse's face, he pointed to the corpse and uttered, "There lies his lodge," then, gesturing upward, said, "The chief has gone above."[16]

*

Sitting Bull wanted very much to live. "I am looking to the north for my life," he said of his decision to seek sanctuary in the Grandmother's Land. And for a time, life there was good. No menacing columns of soldiers roamed the country, only a few dozen North-West Mounted Police, good and honest men who promised to protect the Lakotas so long as they kept north of the international border and abided by the Grandmother Queen Victoria's laws. Anyone who returned to the United States to steal or kill, however, would forfeit his or her Canadian asylum. Sitting Bull embraced these unambiguous terms and the Mounties who enforced them. Here, he thought, were white men worthy of trust.

In October 1877, the U.S. government sent a delegation under General Terry to Sitting Bull's village in a halfhearted attempt to talk the Lakotas back across the border. "Don't you say two more words," Sitting Bull barked at Terry during the brief council. "Go back home where you came from." Terry cheerfully obliged him. In truth, the United States did not want Sitting Bull and his people. Neither did the British, who hoped the Lakotas would leave of their own accord before a cross-border raid precipitated a diplomatic crisis. But the Lakota population in Canada only grew. By the spring of 1878, the village in exile had swelled to nearly five thousand.

The flush times were short-lived. Within a year, the Canadian buffalo herds were gone. Hunting parties drifted south into Montana Territory, and despite Sitting Bull's best efforts to stop them, war parties raided frontier settlements. In July 1879, Colonel Miles clashed with a Lakota hunting camp in northern Montana that included Sitting Bull himself. After that, Canadian policy hardened. The U.S. government, also concerned about border incidents that might strain bilateral relations, reversed course and sent emissaries to lure the Lakota refugees onto reservations. Homesick and hungry, thousands were ready to accept reservation life. Sitting Bull tried to stem defections with *akici-*

tas, but even his most loyal chiefs abandoned him. By early 1881, only the weak and the elderly stood by Sitting Bull, subsisting on fish, small game, and handouts from friendly traders. Clothing rotted and fell from their bodies. War parties of Canadian Indians circled their tattered village like vultures. On July 20, Sitting Bull surrendered at Fort Buford, Dakota Territory. "Nothing but nakedness and starvation has driven this man to submission," concluded a sympathetic army officer, "and that not on his own account but for the sake of his children, of whom he is very fond."

On the eve of the Little Bighorn five years earlier, twins had been born to Sitting Bull. Now Sitting Bull handed one of them his Winchester rifle and told him to give it to the commanding officer, saying, "I surrender this rifle to you through my young son, whom I now desire to teach in this manner that he become a friend of the Americans. I wish him to learn the habits of the whites and to be educated as their sons are educated. This boy has given it to you, and he now wants to know how he is going to make a living."

By farming, the major said. Sitting Bull and his people would be taken down the Missouri River to the Standing Rock Agency, where they would be treated no differently than reservation Indians.

Sitting Bull composed this simple song to mourn the moment when he forswore his freedom:

> A warrior
> I have been
> Now
> It is all over
> A hard time
> I have.

It would become harder yet. A steamboat transported Sitting Bull and his people down the Missouri River, past Standing Rock, and on to Fort Randall, where they were incarcerated on War Department orders as prisoners of war. The white man had lied again.[17]

✳

The military conquest of the Great Plains was complete. The nation cheered and made ready to exploit the Lakotas' lost land, and the army settled into garrison life and police duty. And then, as the specter of future Indian wars subsided, conflict erupted in the Pacific Northwest, which had been tranquil since the Modoc defeat. The source of the strife was familiar. Whites had turned a covetous eye on the homeland of a peaceable Indian people who had not yet tasted agency life. Negotiations to move them foundered. The white circle tightened, the Indians grew fearful, and a racial tinder touched off war. In this instance, the victims were some of the truest Indian friends that the whites had ever had in the West.

PART THREE

———◆———

CHAPTER 17

I WILL FIGHT NO MORE FOREVER

THE NEZ PERCES were a handsome, dignified people who called themselves the Ni-mii-puu (the Real People). They were exceptional warriors but not intrinsically warlike, and they were open-minded and accommodating toward the whites. Indeed, Nez Perce charity had saved Meriwether Lewis and William Clark when their Corps of Discovery was near starvation, moving Clark to report glowingly of their "immortal honor" and "great acts of hospitality," which included a bedmate by whom Clark might have had a mixed-blood son.

The Nez Perce country was beautiful and bountiful, embracing twenty-five thousand square miles of natural magnificence in what is today southeastern Washington, northeastern Oregon, and north-central Idaho. The Bitterroot Mountains marked the eastern boundary, and the Blue and Wallowa ranges traced much of the western limit of Nez Perce country. The principal rivers in the Nez Perce homeland were the Snake, which runs north, and the Clearwater and Salmon, which enter the Snake from the east. All three teemed with salmon, the staple of the Nez Perce diet.

Although they called themselves the Real People, in truth the Nez Perces were a tribe physically and culturally divided. The northern bands, which lived along the Clearwater River, were adventuresome and excelled as horsemen. Annual buffalo hunts took their warriors to the Great Plains and an alliance with the Crows. The northerners fashioned themselves the *k'usaynu-ti-to-gan*, "the sophisticates." The southern bands lived along the Snake and Salmon Rivers. Because these traditionalists seldom ventured beyond the Nez Perce country, their northern cousins dubbed them the *eneynu*, "the provincials." The government simply called northerners and southerners the Upper and Lower Nez Perces.

The Nez Perces had no supreme chief. The council of chiefs might appoint a man to represent the tribe in dealings with outsiders, but he had no role beyond that of an intermediary. Unlike the Plains tribes, the Nez Perces had occupied their country for several centuries. Spiritual ties to the land ran deep. In the interest of amity, however, in 1855 they relinquished the perimeter. The consequent treaty defined their country as a reservation. Because the land conceded was minimal and the government made no effort to alter the Nez Perce way of life, the chiefs gave the matter little further thought.[1]

Gold, the great despoiler of Indian lands and beacon to avaricious whites, changed everything. In the fall of 1860, white prospectors found a few glittering flecks in the Clearwater River. Within two years, almost fifteen thousand miners—five times the total Nez Perce population—swarmed into the Upper Nez Perce country. In their wake came farmers and stockmen. The army built a fort, and the Indian Bureau established an agency. The Nez Perces entreated the Great Father to remove the white intruders; instead, Washington proposed a new treaty reducing the Nez Perce Reservation by 90 percent. The remaining 10 percent—a coffin-shaped twelve-thousand-square-mile tract along the Clearwater River—would be known as the Lapwai Reservation.

The Upper Nez Perces signed. Because the proposed reservation embraced the entirety of their homeland, they stood to lose nothing. Also, they had grown sedentary. Many farmed or raised cattle. Fewer young men hunted buffalo. Christianity had taken firm root. All this had transpired without coercion or bloodshed. The Upper Nez Perces, who constituted nearly three-quarters of the tribe, became the government's model Indians. Not so the Lower Nez Perce bands of Chiefs Toohoolhoolzote, White Bird, and Old Joseph, whose lands lay outside the reduced reservation. They refused to sign what they called the "thief treaty." Although his village lay within reservation limits, Chief Looking Glass also declined to sign as a matter of principle.

The 1863 treaty completed the rupture between the Upper and the Lower Nez Perces. Their world shaken, many Lower Nez Perces turned to the teachings of Smohalla, the chief and medicine man of a small Columbia basin tribe. Smohalla claimed that the Creator had taught him how to resurrect the dead and repopulate the land with game—in short, to create a golden age in which the white presence "would fade away into a dim but horrible dream peopled by ghastly souls." To achieve this transformation, he needed a vanguard of adherents willing to reject the white man's road, leave the earth untouched, and perform a ritualistic dance. The "Dreamer" religion was pacifistic, but the government—fearful of what it did not understand—regarded faith as an incitement to violence. Apart from adopting the distinctive pompadour hairstyle of the Dreamers, few Lower Nez Perces paid Smohalla's doctrine more than hopeful lip service. They went on farming and ranching, more interested in material gain than a visionary new creed. But in Washington's view, any Indian even remotely associated with the "Prophet" Smohalla's teachings was suspect.

For a time, the government tolerated noncompliance with the 1863 treaty. Nonetheless, the future looked bleak to Old Joseph, who died in 1871 just as the first homesteaders entered the Wallowa valley. His eldest son and successor to the Wallowa band chieftainship, thirty-one-year-old Young Joseph, vowed never to relinquish the country, his credo being "A man who would not love his father's grave is worse than a wild animal."

The Wallowa valley became the litmus test for federal indulgence of the non-treaty Nez Perces. Unable to stop the settlers, the government tried to broker a compromise. In June 1873, President Grant signed an executive order giving Joseph's band exclusive rights to half the Wallowa valley, only to revoke it two years later under political pressure from territorial representatives. The Wallowa valley became public domain, and whites overran the land, killing Nez Perce men without cause and raping their women. To retaliate invited destruction. "We were like deer. They were like grizzly bears," Young Joseph later said. "We had a small country. Their country was large. We were contented to let things remain as the Great Spirit Chief made them. They were not, and would change the rivers and mountains if it did not suit them."[2]

✳

The Wallowa band forswore vengeance until June 1876, when two farmers killed a warrior wrongly accused of horse stealing. When the Nez Perce agent's promise to bring the guilty whites to justice did not materialize, infuriated warriors laid siege to Wallowa ranches. Civilian

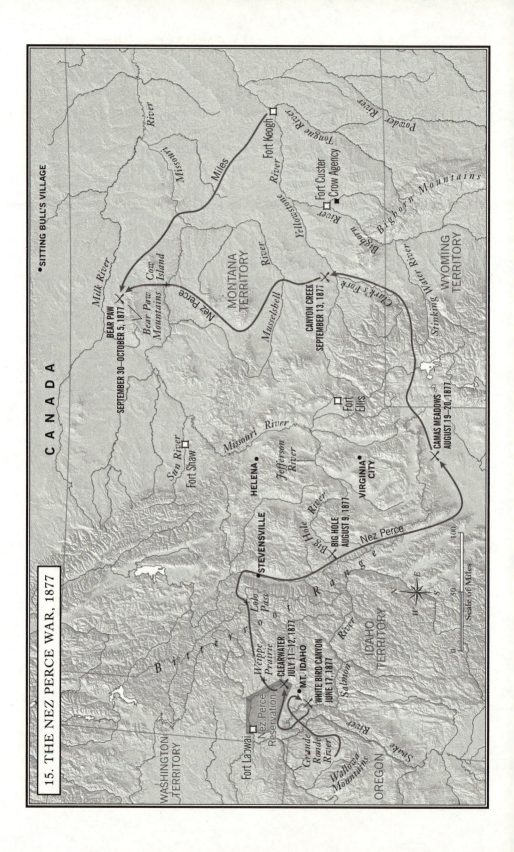

15. THE NEZ PERCE WAR, 1877

CANADA

• SITTING BULL'S VILLAGE

WASHINGTON TERRITORY

OREGON

IDAHO TERRITORY

MONTANA TERRITORY

WYOMING TERRITORY

Fort Lapwai

Nez Perce Reservation

Weippe Prairie

Lolo Pass

CLEARWATER
JULY 11–12, 1877

MT. IDAHO

WHITE BIRD CANYON
JUNE 17, 1877

Grande Ronde River

Wallowa Mountains

Snake River

Salmon River

Bitterroot

STEVENSVILLE

Big Hole River

BIG HOLE
AUGUST 9, 1877

Nez Perce

Range

HELENA

Jefferson River

VIRGINIA CITY

Fort Ellis

CAMAS MEADOWS
AUGUST 19–20, 1877

Sun River
Fort Shaw

Missouri River

Musselshell River

Yellowstone River

Stinking Water River

CANYON CREEK
SEPTEMBER 13, 1877

Clark's Fork

Bighorn River

Bighorn Mountains

BEAR PAW
SEPTEMBER 30–OCTOBER 5, 1877

Bear Paw Mountains

Cow Island

Nez Perce

Milk River

Missouri River

Miles

River

River

Fort Keogh

Tongue River

Fort Custer
Crow Agency

Powder River

N
W   E
S

Scale of Miles
0   50   100

volunteers assembled to repel them. Only the intervention of Young Joseph and his younger brother Ollokot averted a war.

The sons of Old Joseph complemented each other. A born diplomat who abhorred killing, Young Joseph, now thirty-six years old and known as Chief Joseph, led the band in civil affairs. Ollokot, two or three years younger, was the fighter in the family. He excelled in intertribal warfare and enjoyed the allegiance of the Wallowa band's young men, who also appreciated his amiable and open ways. Neither brother wanted war with the whites.

But Washington viewed violence as inevitable so long as whites and the non-reservation Nez Perces lived in proximity to each other. Consequently, in November 1876, the Interior Department created a commission, of which Major General Oliver O. Howard, commander of the Department of the Columbia and the only member with Indian experience, became de facto head. Although the commission was ostensibly appointed to hear Nez Perce grievances, its real purpose was to get the non-treaty bands onto the Lapwai Reservation.

Howard had mixed feelings about the assignment. In negotiating peace with Cochise four years earlier, he had had a free hand; now the Christian General was under "positive military orders" to enforce Indian Bureau policy. Not that he opposed that policy. Although sympathetic to the Lower Nez Perces, Howard and his fellow commissioners shared the bureau's conviction that stern measures were necessary to break Dreamer "fanaticism." They recommended that the military occupy the Wallowa valley and—unless the Wallowa band moved voluntarily within "a reasonable time"—that Chief Joseph's people be coerced onto Lapwai. The Interior Department was well pleased, but the War Department cautioned Howard to go slow. On May 3, the commission met with the non-treaty chiefs in an effort to avert a crisis.

The Lapwai council became a primer in cross-cultural misunderstanding. The chiefs elected Toohoolhoolzote, a devout Dreamer, to defend for them oratorically what they could never relinquish—their homeland. Still virile at seventy, the old Dreamer spoke with an arrogance that Howard misinterpreted as a "strong and settled hatred of all Caucasians." Toohoolhoolzote held forth for four days before Howard ran out of patience. "Twenty times over I hear that the earth is your mother," the general told the Dreamer. "I want to hear it no more, but come to business at once." Would Toohoolhoolzote submit?

"The Indians may do as they like," replied Toohoolhoolzote, "but

I have a prick, that which belongs to a man, and will not go on the reservation!"[3]

Those were Toohoolhoolzote's final words in council. Howard arrested him and then dragged Chiefs Joseph and White Bird around Lapwai to select homes for their peoples. Again the general and the chiefs spoke past one another. Howard thought he and the chiefs had found mutually agreeable village sites; Joseph, on the other hand, remembered riding all day without encountering any unoccupied land of good quality. Regardless of what transpired, there was no misconstruing Howard's ultimatum: the chiefs had thirty days to move; otherwise, soldiers would force them onto the reservation.[4]

Disturbed and bewildered, the chiefs held council on Camas Prairie, eight miles south of Lapwai. They had six hundred adherents. Only twenty-four hours remained before Howard's deadline expired. Chief Joseph had already decided to submit. Looking Glass also counseled compliance. All the chiefs recognized the magnitude of the moment. None were given to rashness. Their seventy-year peace pact with the white man was at stake. The elderly White Bird, a powerful shaman and a great warrior in his day, had no love for the gold hunters who had overrun his country, but he was nonconfrontational. Even Toohoolhoolzote, for all his fiery rhetoric, preferred oratory to combat.

While the chiefs talked, a hotheaded warrior named Wahlitits and two inebriated companions settled the matter by murdering four whites notorious for their abuse of the Nez Perces. The next day, a Nez Perce war party swept through the Camas Prairie settlements, burning ranches, stealing livestock, killing eighteen men, and raping at least one woman in two days.

Chief Joseph abhorred the violence, but he understood what drove the warriors.

> I know that the young men did a great wrong, but I ask who was first to blame. They had been insulted a thousand times; their fathers and brothers had been killed; their mothers and wives had been disgraced; they had been driven to madness by the whiskey sold to them by the white men . . . and added to all this, they were homeless and desperate.[5]

Assuming all Lower Nez Perces would suffer alike, Joseph and Ollokot cast their fortunes with the guilty bands. Looking Glass, on the other hand, wanted no part in the affair; his hands, he told Joseph and Ollokot, "were clean of white men's blood and they shall so remain."

The fugitives moved to White Bird Canyon, high above the Salmon River. Concerned but not yet alarmed, Howard wired higher headquarters that "we shall make short work of it." His prediction would prove perhaps the most egregious underestimation of the war-making abilities of Indians that any frontier-army general ever made.

At White Bird Canyon, the Lower Nez Perce chiefs tried to parley with the commander of two cavalry companies Howard had sent to bring in the Indians, but a local reprobate riding with the soldiers fired on Nez Perces bearing a white flag. A return shot killed an army bugler, and the battle was on. In what was to become an all-too-familiar pattern, the Nez Perces made fools of the army, chasing the terrified troopers and their citizen auxiliaries until the chiefs commanded, "Let the soldiers go! We have done them enough!" The Nez Perces, in fact, had done them more than enough. Although outnumbered two to one, they had slain thirty-four soldiers and wounded two others at a cost of two warriors wounded. An army sergeant said the warriors afterward boasted that the fight had been great fun, no more dangerous than hunting buffalo.[6]

The Battle of White Bird Canyon stunned the military establishment. Nez Perce combat ability far exceeded that of the Lakotas and the Cheyennes at the Little Bighorn. Like Terry after that disaster, Howard now prevaricated, reporting the Nez Perces had heavily outnumbered the cavalry. It was the cleanest way to disguise command bungling and poor soldiering, as well as to prepare the nation for what might well prove a long and costly contest.

Certainly it would not be the "short work" Howard had presumed. As reinforcements sped to him from every corner, Howard unthinkingly strengthened his foe. Accepting baseless rumors that Looking Glass intended to join the belligerents, Howard dispatched two fresh cavalry companies to "surprise and capture this chief and all that belonged to him."

There was nothing remotely hostile about Looking Glass's village. His vegetable-growing and cattle-raising band had never troubled anyone. The chief was at breakfast when told that soldiers were approaching. Both he and the cavalry commander were inclined to talk. But another trigger-happy civilian volunteer precipitated a clash, gunning down an elderly Nez Perce before a word was said, whereupon the hillside erupted in gunfire. Bullets perforated tipis and riddled cattle. A terrified woman flung herself and her baby into the Clearwater, where both drowned. There was no return fire; the Nez Perces were intent only on escape. Unable to catch them, the soldiers instead razed their deserted village and drove off their cattle. "Of course," Howard wrote when he learned of the debacle, "we thus stirred up a new hornet's nest."[7]

After White Bird Canyon, the other Nez Perce bands had crossed the Salmon River. It was a cunning move. If Howard followed them, the chiefs could double back at a place of their choosing, slip behind Howard, and head for the Clearwater River, all the while leading the soldiers on a merry chase.

Howard took the bait. Handily eluding him, the Nez Perces dubbed him Day After Tomorrow Howard. Not only had Howard forfeited the respect of his foe, but he was also losing the battle for public opinion. Newspapers nationwide had called the Camas Prairie murders "wanton and preconcerted," part of a Dreamer conspiracy to upend the Pacific Northwest, but after White Bird Canyon the press reconsidered. Unlike other Indians "on the warpath," the Nez Perces had neither scalped nor mutilated slain soldiers. And they treated settlers kindly, even paying old debts at local stores. In a word, the Nez Perces were adhering to the white man's code of war, leading a local newspaper critical of Howard to declare, "Chief Joseph's magnanimity may save us, and that is all."[8]

On July 2, the Nez Perces recrossed the Salmon River. Five days later, they joined Chief Looking Glass on the South Fork of the Clearwater River. The "hostiles" now numbered 750, including 200 warriors. No one exercised overall command, and with Howard far behind, the Nez Perces relaxed their vigilance. The location of the Nez Perce camp—dominated by steep, boulder-strewn bluffs on the opposite bank, with only a narrow canyon behind the village as a means of egress—reflected their disinclination to give battle. They were on the run, plain and simple. Unfortunately for them, they tarried on the Clearwater too long.

Howard stumbled on them on July 11 with 400 regulars and 150 scouts and volunteers, including several Upper Nez Perces. It was a sultry afternoon, the temperature teetering near a hundred degrees. The Indians suspected nothing. Young men and boys raced horses. Ollokot's second wife waded in the bracing waters of the Clearwater. The warrior Yellow Wolf sat lost in thought until the boom of a cannon from the east bank interrupted his reverie. Men hurriedly stripped for battle and slung cartridge belts around their shoulders. Yellow Wolf joined a group of two dozen warriors called together by Toohoolhoolzote and splashed across the river and up a wooded ravine. At the top, the Indians dismounted behind a clump of thornbushes, piled up stones for shelter, and then opened fire on the soldiers, who approached hesitantly.

Toohoolhoolzote's furious stand confused Howard, who deployed his men haphazardly. Subordinates had no idea what he expected of them, and soldiers squeezed off rounds randomly, firing as often on friends as on foes. The Nez Perces, on the other hand, shot with deadly accuracy, dropping ten soldiers for every warrior hit. A single Nez Perce sharpshooter picked off several men before an artillery round blew him to pieces.

Gradually, Howard established an elliptical line of battle. There being few trees, he assembled the pack train and horses on open ground behind the firing line. Behind them, he set up headquarters and a crude field hospital.

Toohoolhoolzote quit the battle after three hours. In his wake came two assault parties. One group under Ollokot struck Howard's right flank and, according to Nez Perce accounts, nearly captured the general. A second party charged up a ravine toward Howard's artillery, dissolving into small clusters before the guns could be trained on them. Warriors slid from the saddle, took deliberate aim, and then remounted their placidly grazing ponies. Toward sunset, Howard launched two limited counterattacks. The Nez Perces fell back and then fortified behind small outcrops. The crack and flash of Indian rifles kept officers and men on edge all night.[9]

Unquestionably, the day's combat had unnerved Howard. He thought himself outnumbered, when in fact fewer than a hundred warriors had nearly bested five times their number. "In spite of our successful charges," Howard later reported, "matters were not very bright at dark." Neither did they seem much more promising at dawn on July 12. But the Nez Perce warriors began to drift off, until at noon fewer than fifty remained. Most saw little point in risking their lives when the soldiers had made no attempt at the village.

Around noon, their calculus abruptly changed. An officer fed up with the stalemate decided to end the battle himself—or lose his command trying. Sent to escort some approaching wagons to safety, he instead wheeled his men and made for the few warriors still on the field.

The Nez Perces fired a few volleys and then bolted. "Everybody was running," a warrior later confessed, "some leading, [and] some falling behind. All were skipping for their lives for the camp."[10]

It was worse in the village. Cannon boomed and Gatling guns rattled, hurling shot after shot after the fleeing families. Yellow Wolf and a companion were the last men to leave the bluffs. Riding into camp, Yellow Wolf glimpsed Chief Joseph's wife grapple with a bucking pony as shells burst dangerously close. Her newborn daughter lay on the ground wrapped in a cradleboard. Yellow Wolf scooped up the infant and passed it to her. Together they galloped toward the narrow canyon and safety. Joseph stayed behind until the last noncombatants were clear of danger.[11]

The barrage wounded only one Nez Perce, but the precipitate retreat cost them most of their possessions. Howard's cavalry belatedly splashed across the river into the deserted camp. The commander was about to give chase when Howard, who had somehow concluded that the Indians were returning, ordered him to ferry the foot soldiers across the river. While the Nez Perce village burned—at whose order Howard never said—the general committed a second grievous blunder. Four hours of daylight remained, plenty of time to disperse and defeat the shattered bands, but Howard let the Nez Perces go, confident he could catch them the next day.[12]

He was wrong. Brushing off the cavalry, the Nez Perces made for Weippe Prairie, where, seventy-two years earlier, the tribe had welcomed Lewis and Clark. Now the chiefs assembled to debate a future unimaginable, forced on them by a people to whom the Nez Perces had pledged eternal peace. Joseph wanted to turn back and make a last stand on native soil. Looking Glass offered a more hopeful alternative. Having long fought with the Crows against the Lakotas, he was certain they would grant the Nez Perces sanctuary on their reservation. Looking Glass presented a compelling case. True, the going would be hard. The way to the Crow country led along the tortuous Lolo Trail, over the backbone of the Bitterroot Mountains and then southward into Montana's Bitterroot valley. But Looking Glass said the whites who lived in the Bitterroot country had always been friendly. So long as the Nez Perces behaved themselves, the Montanans would surely let them pass in peace. The war, after all, had been an Idaho affair. Once the troubles in Idaho were forgotten, Looking Glass promised, the government would permit the Nez Perces to return home. The council not only assented to his proposal (Joseph and Ollokot reluctantly) but also placed Looking Glass in command of the march, a decision that left a depressed Joseph resigned to drift "as the tribe desired."

Events unfolded as Chief Looking Glass had predicted—at least at first. On the Lolo Trail, the Nez Perces easily outdistanced Howard, bypassed a small blocking force, and then debouched into the Bitterroot valley without losses. Looking Glass kept a close rein on the Nez Perces during their sojourn through the Bitterroot valley, compelling warriors to pay for supplies they could have stolen with impunity.[13]

The Montanans were friendly, and Looking Glass became complacent and imperious. His own people, on the other hand, grew impatient. Wahlitits, who had started the war, galloped about one morning speaking of dream visions of impending disaster. Chief White Bird urged Looking Glass to pick up the pace, to no avail. Once again, Looking Glass offered compelling arguments in favor of his course of action: Day After Tomorrow Howard had undoubtedly fallen far behind them, the Montanans were unthreatening, and the Continental Divide was within sight. On the far side of the divide beckoned the broad and tranquil Big Hole valley, an old haunt of Nez Perce buffalo hunters. The Crow country lay just three hundred winding but largely hospitable miles farther east. Again the council bowed to Looking Glass.

On August 8, Looking Glass ordered a halt on the east bank of the North Fork of the Big Hole River in the shadow of a long, tall, sharply rising hill, partially blanketed with pine trees. The pony herd was pastured partway up the slope without guards. Looking Glass refused to allow scouting parties to comb the back trail, saying, "No more fighting! War is quit!"

But menacing dreams persisted. A respected medicine man thought haste essential. "While I slept," he told Looking Glass, "my medicine told me to move on, that death is approaching us. If you take my advice, we can avoid death, and that advice is to speed through this country. If not, there will be tears in our eyes in a short time." Looking Glass ignored him. Most of the Nez Perces gradually relaxed. Families raised their tipis in a V-shaped village of eighty-nine lodges. Children played along the riverbank. Warriors sang or gambled until well after midnight. The warrior Yellow Wolf shared in the revelry. "Everybody was with good feeling. We were going to the buffalo country!"[14]

On the hillside near the Nez Perce pony herd, huddled beneath blankets, unseen soldiers waited for dawn.

✳

The army high command had been busy. With Sitting Bull in Canada and the non-treaty Lakotas and their Cheyenne allies only recently pacified, the last thing General Sherman needed was a volatile new ingredient cast into the delicate mix of diplomacy and coercion that he had crafted. He had no sympathy for the Nez Perces. Possessing a hopelessly warped view of the origins of the conflict, he wanted the Nez Perces "made to answer for the murders they committed and punished as a tribe for going to war without any just cause or provocation." Subordinates were expected to hunt down the Nez Perces heedless of department boundaries. When the Nez Perces entered the Bitterroot valley, they had traded General Howard's Department of the Columbia for Colonel John Gibbon's District of Montana, a part of General Terry's Department of Dakota. Gibbon had only a handful of badly scattered, understrength companies, which placed the burden on Howard. But the one-armed general lagged far behind the Nez Perces, slowed by pounding rainstorms and his decision to await reinforcements to protect the Idaho settlements, in the event the Nez Perces doubled back on him.[15]

So the battle, if there were to be one, would be fought by Gibbon. His performance in the Little Bighorn Campaign hardly inspired confidence. But the fifty-year-old colonel had found renewed vigor. On July 28, he left Fort Shaw with 17 officers and 146 enlisted men from his Seventh Infantry. Gibbon's skeleton force moved so rapidly through the Bitterroot valley that by August 7 they were just a day's march behind the Nez Perces. Gibbon had gained men along the way—34 settlers unmoved by Nez Perce benevolence. Gibbon assigned the Montanans to Lieutenant James H. Bradley. Miscalculating the distance to the Nez Perce village, on the night of August 8, Gibbon nearly lost the reliable subaltern, the dubious Montanans, and a company of mounted infantry, sending the tiny contingent ahead to find and disperse the Nez Perce pony herd with the assurance he would soon be up. Fortunately for Bradley, his instincts told him to wait. It was midnight before Gibbon reached Bradley, whereupon the colonel fell asleep beneath a pine tree. Two hours later, his reunited command was on the move.

The moon was down; the night black—welcome conditions for a stealth march. But the deep darkness also made for surprises. Near the base of the hill, Gibbon stumbled onto the Nez Perce pony herd. The startled animals whinnied and pawed the earth. Camp dogs took up the alarm, and for an instant Gibbon feared discovery. But the barking subsided, the ponies wandered uphill away from the soldiers, and the camp, now dimly visible a few hundred yards distant, showed no signs of stirring. Gibbon wanted his guide to take a detail and run off the herd, but the man, who had spent his life among the Indians, convinced the colonel that the Nez Perces would never allow their war ponies to roam unguarded. That was not the case; Looking Glass had neglected even the most rudimentary precautions against attack.[16]

With nothing better to occupy his time until dawn, Gibbon meditated on the morality of what he was about to do. As he later told the bishop of Montana,

> Knowing our peaceful disposition as you do can you fancy us seated for two hours in the darkness of night within plain hearing of a parcel of crying babies and the talk of their fathers and mothers, waiting for light enough to commence a slaughter which we knew from the nature of the case must necessarily be promiscuous. We had ample time for reflection, and I for one could not help thinking that this inhuman task was forced upon us by a system of fraud and injustice which had compelled these poor wretches to assume a hostile attitude towards the whites.[17]

Dawn approached. Emerging from their tipis, the Indian women kindled breakfast fires. Gibbon formed his soldiers in an attenuated skirmish line. At 4:00 a.m., he waved them forward. Wading through waist-high sloughs and gingerly pushing aside brushwood, the soldiers and the civilian volunteers edged across the boggy stream between them and the village. From the hillside, Gibbon squinted at the advancing shadows "with every sense on the strain for the first sign of alarm." Suddenly a rifle shot on the far left shattered the stillness. A soldier had shot dead a half-blind old Nez Perce man who had wandered too close to the pony herd.

Thereafter, events eluded Gibbon's grasp. "As if answering the shot as a signal, the whole line opened, and the men, rushing forward with a shout, plunged into the stream and climbed up the opposite bank, shooting down the startled Indians as they rushed from their [tipis] pell-mell, men, women, and children, together." A chance shot struck Bradley. With his death, the lieutenant's detail bunched up on the main body, leaving the northern end of the Nez Perce camp untouched when the soldiers struck the village.[18]

The Nez Perces had no idea what hit them. A cacophony of "cheers, savage yells, shrieks, curses, and groans" rent the morning air as the villagers stumbled about "dazed and in shock." One of the first to die was Wahlitits, the angry young man whose act of vengeance had begun the war. Running from his tipi with his pregnant wife, he threw himself on the ground behind a log near the riverbank and killed the first soldier to emerge from the brush. The next man shot Wahlitits through the chin. As Wahlitits tumbled backward, his wife grabbed his rifle and killed her husband's slayer. Then a bullet slammed into her throat, and she collapsed on Wahlitits's corpse.

The panic and horror of the opening moments of the battle were forever seared in the memory of ten-year-old Young White Bird. His father had stepped outside the family lodge when the shooting erupted. The boy cringed at the impact of "bullets like hail on the tipis, ripping the walls." Young White Bird's mother took his hand, and they ran toward a bend in the creek. A bullet sliced off two of her fingers and Young White Bird's right thumb. Without breaking stride, she dragged him along. Splashing neck-deep into the frigid water, they hid behind a fringe of brush. Nearby, a woman scooping out a hole in the sand pitched into the creek, shot through the left breast. Moments later, a soldier spotted Young White Bird and his mother. He motioned to other troops, who swung their rifles up and took aim at the pair. "Mother ducked my head under the water. When I raised out, I saw her hand up. She called out, 'Women, only women!'" An officer apparently ordered the soldiers to desist because they lowered their weapons. Some left; others waded into the water and shook hands with the women to reassure them.

Most of the women and children had fled away from the river onto an open plain east of camp, where dozens of unarmed warriors milled. Yellow Wolf, who had been sleeping off the night's revelry in Chief Joseph's lodge, at least had his war club. Spying a soldier "crawling like a drunken man," Yellow Wolf caved in his brains and took the dead man's rifle and ammunition belt. Chief Joseph had darted from the lodge barefoot, clad only in a shirt and blanket. Mounting their favorite war ponies, which had been tied to their lodges, he and another man galloped up the slope past the soldiers and led the pony herd out of danger.

Down on the plain, Chief White Bird strove to instill a bit of Joseph's clearheadedness into the stunned fighting men. "Why are we retreating?" he yelled. "Since the world was made, brave men fight for their women and children. Are we going to run to the mountains and let the whites kill our women and children before our eyes? These soldiers cannot fight harder than the ones we defeated in White Bird Canyon. Fight! Shoot them down!" The men rallied and followed White Bird back to the camp. Yellow Wolf and his companions found themselves "mixed with those soldiers badly. We could hit each other with our guns. They acted as if drinking. We thought some got killed by being drunk."[19]

Perhaps so. But most of the soldiers who fell in the Nez Perce counterattack died because Gibbon made a snap decision to burn the village rather than press his advantage. The rancher John B. Caitlin, "captain" of the Montana volunteers, thought it silly to lose valuable time burning lodges too heavy with frost to ignite. "If we whipped the Indians, the lodges could be burned when we had more time for that kind of work."

Gibbon's orders indeed proved a thundering error. The soldiers' preoccupation with wrecking the village gave White Bird time to launch a counterattack that overwhelmed Gibbon's small force. Not only did warriors grapple with the troops in the village, but several Nez Perces also slipped behind them onto higher ground on the far side of the stream. What had been a neat army skirmish line deteriorated into a ragged circle. After a bullet mangled his leg, Gibbon ordered a retreat. His objective was a stand of small pine trees near the base of the hill half a mile west of the lower end of the village. Again Caitlin saw cause to find fault with Gibbon. "I had long since learned to never back up, but always go ahead, or an Indian will think you are whipped and thus renew his courage."

Which is what happened. Nez Perce marksmen dropped at least two dozen of Gibbon's men scrambling uphill. Had all the warriors possessed guns, hardly a white man would have reached the pine stand alive. As it was, several dozen warriors swarmed up the slope above Gibbon's chosen defensive site. Those with rifles rained a heavy fire down on the frightened soldiers and civilians, who frantically dug rifle pits with bayonets or their bare hands. Stumbling into the defensive perimeter, now nearly surrounded by Nez Perces, Caitlin demanded to know, "Who in hell called a halt here?" Colonel Gibbon had, replied someone. "I don't give a damn," Caitlin snarled. "It's a hell of a place to camp!"[20]

Gibbon had hoped for help from his howitzer, which rolled into view shortly after the troops congregated in the pines. But a war party pounced on the gun, killing one man and wounding two others before dismantling the howitzer. Simultaneously, the warriors on the slope set fire to dry brush, trying to smoke out the soldiers. As the flames rolled toward them, Gibbon shouted, "If the fire reaches us, we will charge through it to the river, taking our wounded with us, and then from the cover of the banks send the redskins to a hotter place than they have prepared for us." The colonel's histrionics fooled no one; every man knew the flames would drive them into the deadly accurate rifle fire of the Nez Perces. But the wind shifted, and the flames receded.

The shooting stopped at dusk. That evening, all of the warriors drifted off the hill except twelve under Ollokot, whose wife lay in their lodge mortally wounded. What remained of the village sickened Yellow Wolf. "It was not good to see women and children lying dead and wounded. A few soldiers and warriors lay as they had fallen—some almost together. Wounded children screamed with pain. Women and men cried, wailing for their scattered dead. The air was heavy with sorrow. I would not want to hear, I would not want to see [that] again."

Throughout the bitter night, curses and shrieks of pain emanated from Gibbon's blood-soaked bivouac. Casualties had been horrific. Seventy-four of the 182 men who had entered the battle were either dead or wounded. The only food was a dead horse, which its owner sliced up and distributed in small bits. And a Nez Perce assault at dawn appeared inevitable.

The Nez Perce chiefs, however, wanted only to reach the Crows. Between sixty and ninety Nez Perces died at the Big Hole, most of them women and children. "The Nez Perces never make war on women and children," Chief Joseph later said truthfully. "We could have killed a great many women and children while the war lasted, but we would feel ashamed to do so cowardly an act." Had they wished, the Nez Perces could also have annihilated Gibbon's decimated command. But they were in a hurry now; the lives of their wives and children meant everything to the warriors; killing for the sake of killing—or for revenge—had no place in their plans.[21]

Burdened with their wounded, the Nez Perces resumed their flight. A disgraced Looking Glass led only his own band; control of the march had passed to Poker Joe, a mixed-blood resident of the Bitterroot valley with an inordinate love of cards. Poker Joe had not meant to get involved with the Idaho Nez Perces. He and his small, peaceable Nez Perce band had lived in the Montana Territory for several years. They had assumed themselves part of the community until white neighbors accused them of having fought in Idaho, whereupon an incensed Poker Joe cast his lot with the fugitives as they passed through the Bitterroot country.

Poker Joe's presence proved a godsend. A natural leader, he knew every trail in western Montana. With Poker Joe in charge, leisurely marches were over. He set an exacting pace of nearly fifty miles a day, and it was good he did. Day After Tomorrow Howard was catching up. On August 11, he relieved Gibbon, who gratefully returned to Fort Shaw with his shattered command. A week later, Howard's cavalry closed to within fifteen miles of the Nez Perces. Howard was unaware the Indians were so near, however, and on the evening of August 19 he erected an undefended camp in Camas Meadows, forty miles west of Yellowstone National Park. Seeing a chance to redeem himself, Looking Glass prevailed upon the other war chiefs to join him in a nocturnal horse-stealing raid. They caught the cavalry completely unawares. The Nez Perces went home in high spirits, leading what they thought were army mounts. Then dawn broke, revealing their prize for what it was—a handful of obstreperous pack mules.[22]

The Camas Meadows raid did not help Looking Glass, but it did hobble the army pack train. More important, it shattered the fragile morale in Howard's weakening command. Having marched five hundred miles in twenty-six days, the infantrymen were near collapse. Summer uniforms were in tatters, shoes worn through. Some soldiers were barefoot, and a few had only a single blanket with which to ward off the high-mountain cold. Howard's chief medical officer demanded that he halt, and the Christian General made camp a day's march from Yellowstone National Park and the Wyoming border, the eastern limit of the Military Division of the Pacific.

In truth, General Howard had grown as weary of the chase as had his soldiers, and he telegraphed General Sherman for permission to hand off the Nez Perces to commanders in General Sheridan's Military Division of the Missouri. Not unreasonably, Howard thought he had done more than his share. Although the Nez Perces had slipped away, it had not been for want of effort on Howard's part. But Sherman rebuked him nonetheless. Reminding the dispirited general that his were the only troops immediately available, he told Howard to "pursue the Nez

Perces to the death, lead where they may." Then he struck a nerve: "If you are tired, give the command to some energetic officer and let him follow them, go where they may." A riled Howard responded that he never flagged; it was his men who were worn out "by a most extraordinary march." Resupplied and somewhat rested, Howard resumed the pursuit at the end of August.[23]

Sherman's pique owed less to Howard's performance than to a contrary tide of public opinion. The Nez Perce flight had become a national drama, a sort of David and Goliath encounter in which nearly everyone outside the military and the government pulled for the Indian underdogs. Satirists mocked the army and magnified its defeats. The Nez Perces even won over the exterminationist western press, which conceded that their war making "has been almost universally marked by the highest characteristics recognized by civilized nations." Attention centered on Joseph. Because he had represented the Nez Perces in prewar talks with Howard, he was assumed to be their war leader as well. A flattering if fanciful engraved portrait of the chief even graced the pages of *Harper's Weekly*.

None of this sat well with Sherman. He wanted the Nez Perces captured and their leaders executed by sentence of civil courts. "What are left should be treated like the Modocs, sent to some other country," he told Sheridan. "There should be extreme severity, else other tribes alike situated may imitate their example."[24]

Sheridan found himself hard-pressed to satisfy his petulant superior. The department commanders Terry and Crook were on temporary duty in the East quelling railroad labor riots. Colonel Miles at Fort Keogh (formerly Tongue River Cantonment) was three hundred miles from the probable Nez Perce line of march. All Sheridan could do was instruct Miles to send Colonel Samuel D. Sturgis—who after seven years of detached duty had reluctantly resumed his place as commander of the Seventh Cavalry—to try to bottle up the Nez Perce in the tangled Absaroka Range, the last natural obstacle between the Indians and the northern plains. The effort failed, however, and the Nez Perces slid past him and entered the Crow country on September 10.

*

What should have been a cause for celebration among the Nez Perces became instead a nightmare of betrayal. The Crows had welcomed Nez

Perce help in their battles with the Lakotas and the Cheyennes so long as it entailed no obligations on their part. Certainly they had never expected to find nearly a quarter of the tribe on their doorstep. To grant the Nez Perces sanctuary would put the Crows on a collision course with their great benefactor, the U.S. government. And so they not only sent them packing but, to reaffirm their fidelity to the Great Father, also contributed their best warriors to Sturgis's command.

It was now clear to even his staunchest followers that Looking Glass had taken the Nez Perces on a twelve-hundred-mile fool's errand. Their only remaining chance for freedom was to reach Canada ahead of the army—a course of action Poker Joe had always advocated—and hope that their mortal enemies, Sitting Bull's Hunkpapa Lakotas, would accept them as fellow victims of white aggression. With this slim hope, they pressed north over the barrens of eastern Montana.

General Howard linked up with Sturgis the day after the Nez Perces slipped past the Seventh Cavalry. Although doubting Sturgis could overtake them, Howard granted him permission to try. Sturgis did manage to catch up with the Nez Perces at Canyon Creek, just north of the Yellowstone River, where poor tactics on Sturgis's part and a strong Nez Perce rear guard earned him a stinging reverse. The Nez Perces escaped with just three men wounded but at a heavy cost in animals.[25]

Eager for plunder, Crow warriors nipped at the Nez Perces' flanks and rear. As hope receded and Poker Joe's pace accelerated, the elderly and the infirm began to drop out, many falling victim to Crow scalping knives. By the time the Nez Perces reached the Musselshell River, two hundred miles from the Canadian border, their leadership was in disarray. Advocates of slowing the march—Looking Glass foremost among them—reasserted themselves. Women, children, and the elderly were near exhaustion, they argued, and horses on the verge of collapse. Day After Tomorrow Howard and the Seventh Cavalry were now far behind; surely there was nothing more to fear from the army.[26]

*

Colonel Miles had yet to make a move. Unaware of Sturgis's setback or of the Nez Perces' whereabouts, he knew only that if Sitting Bull were to descend from Canada to help the Nez Perces, then his twelve months of hard campaigning against the Lakotas would have been for naught and his prospects for promotion diminished accordingly.

Ruminating over that unpleasant scenario as he stood beside the Yellowstone River on the evening of September 17, 1877, Miles descried a lone rider on the western horizon. It was a courier from the Seventh Cavalry. "Have you had a fight?" inquired Miles as the trooper pulled rein. "No," the man replied, handing the colonel an envelope. "But we have had a good chance." The envelope contained two notes. One was a confession from Sturgis that the Indians had left him "hopelessly in their rear." The second note came from Howard, who begged Miles to intercept the Nez Perces or "at least to hold them in check until I can overtake them."[27]

Miles needed no further urging. He started from Fort Keogh with a 520-man strike force consisting of three Seventh Cavalry companies that Sturgis had left behind, three Second Cavalry companies, and three Fifth Infantry companies mounted on captured Lakota ponies. Miles was 150 miles east of the last known Nez Perce position, and Howard's appeal was five days old. With only stale intelligence to guide him, he headed for the junction of the Musselshell and Missouri Rivers. But the Nez Perces, still under the fortunate sway of Poker Joe, crossed the Missouri River ahead of him. The chiefs held a council. Canada beckoned, its border just eighty miles distant—at most a three days' journey at Poker Joe's pace.

Poker Joe, however, had been impeached. At this supremely critical juncture, Chief Looking Glass prevailed upon the council to slow the pace and to reinstate him as commander of the march. "All right, Looking Glass, you can lead," Poker Joe is said to have remarked. "I am trying to save the people, doing my best to cross into Canada before the soldiers find us. You can take command, but I think we will be caught and killed."

For four days, the Nez Perces inched across the drab and sterile prairie. On September 29, they entered a rippled landscape between the Bear Paw Mountains and the Little Rockies. Early that afternoon, they made camp near the northeastern edge of the Bear Paw. The Canadian border now lay a mere forty miles distant. The subchief Yellow Bull shared in the prevailing desire to press on. "But Looking Glass again had his own way, and so we stopped and began to dry buffalo skins and meat."[28]

The Nez Perce camp rested in a six-acre, kidney-shaped depression on the east bank of Snake Creek. Winding north, the watercourse emptied into the Milk River, the last natural obstacle between the Nez

Perces and Canada. A few Nez Perces raised threadbare tipis; most made do with canvas-topped brush shelters. The Nez Perces grazed their ponies on an open plateau on the west bank. Near sunset the skies turned leaden. A stinging rain fell, changing to snow during the night.

The village stirred slowly on the morning of September 30. A chill mist hung in the hollow. Children played, and women tended breakfast fires. Only a few of the Nez Perces had retrieved their ponies and begun to pack. Suddenly two scouts galloped from the south shouting, "Stampeding buffaloes. Soldiers! Soldiers!" Looking Glass scoffed at their warning. Howard was at least two suns behind them. "Do not hurry!" he commanded. "Go slow! Plenty, plenty time. Let children eat all wanted!"

"Because of Looking Glass," Yellow Wolf later declared, "we were caught."[29]

*

Miles had bivouacked ten miles southeast of the Nez Perces. At daybreak on September 30, his Cheyenne scouts discovered their day-old tracks. Elated, Miles ordered his mounted force into a trot and then a gallop. His surgeon delighted in the moment: "To be astride a good horse on the open prairie, rifle in hand, has an exhilarating effect on most of the men. To be one of four hundred horsemen, galloping on a hot trail, sends a thrill through the body which is but seldom experienced." Miles agreed heartily. "This gallop forward, preceding the charge, was one of the most brilliant and inspiring sights I ever witnessed on any field. It was the crowning glory of our twelve days' forced marching."[30]

Two miles south of the Nez Perce camp, Miles divided his command. The Cheyenne scouts were already well out in front and making straight for the Nez Perce herd. Their precipitous charge forced Miles literally to make his plans on the gallop. Diverting the three companies of the Second Cavalry to support the scouts, he ordered the three Seventh Cavalry companies to charge the village head-on from the south.

An hour after Looking Glass's ill-considered admonition to take it slow, a Nez Perce scout appeared atop a steep ridge above the east side of the village. Circling his horse, he frantically waved his blanket to signal the enemy was nearly upon them. "A wild stir hit the people," said Yellow Bull, who grabbed his rifle and took position with a group of warriors along a lower ridge south of camp. From beyond came a rumble one warrior likened to running buffalo. A contingent under Poker Joe and Ollokot formed on the eastern ridge. Before he left the village, Yellow Wolf glimpsed his uncle Chief Joseph leap from their lodge shouting, "Horses! Horses! Save the horses!" Moments before the Cheyennes and the Second Cavalry reached the animals, Joseph led seventy men across the creek on foot. The shock of the Cheyenne charge scattered the warriors, and the herd was lost. Helpless to prevent the calamity, Joseph turned back toward camp. "With a prayer to the Great Spirit Chief who rules above, I dashed unarmed through the line of soldiers. It seemed to me that there were guns on every side, before and behind me. My clothes were cut to pieces and my horse wounded, but I was not hurt. As I reached the door of my lodge, my wife handed me my rifle, saying, 'Here's your gun. Fight!' "[31]

And fight the Nez Perces did. A withering fire at thirty yards decimated the Seventh Cavalry. Many of the troopers—the so-called Custer Avengers—froze with fear or milled about aimlessly. As the cavalry crumbled, Miles ordered a mounted infantry detachment forward. It suffered the same fate. So too did another infantry column that charged along the east bank of Snake Creek. The Seventh Cavalry made one more go of it in the afternoon. Dismounted troopers edged forward along the eastern ridge until heavy volleys again sent them reeling. All told, the Seventh Cavalry lost 55 of 116 men engaged, a blow reminiscent of the Reno disaster at the Little Bighorn. The rout shocked Miles. A blood-soaked young lieutenant approached him, shouting, with understandable hyperbole, "I'm the only damned man of the 7th Cavalry wearing shoulder straps who's alive." All the while, the Nez Perces verbally abused the colonel. During a lull, Miles yelled to a unit, "Charge them to hell!" To which a warrior retorted in English, "Charge? Hell, you God damn sons of bitches! You ain't fighting Sioux!" With 20 percent of his strike force dead or wounded, Miles gave up on charges. He encircled the Nez Perces and then settled in for a siege.

The Nez Perces had also been hurt badly. Chief Joseph said eighteen warriors and three women were killed that day. Toohoolhoolzote was dead. Poker Joe was dead, mistakenly shot by a Nez Perce warrior. And Joseph's brother Ollokot, the guiding spirit of the young warriors, was dead.[32]

Two thoughts troubled Miles in about equal measure: that Sitting

Bull would rescue the Nez Perces, and that General Howard would arrive and relieve him of command. Sitting Bull also loomed large in the imaginings of the Nez Perces. After dark, six warriors crept through the lines and started for Canada to find the Lakota chief, their last hope.

In the Nez Perce camp, the grim business of survival went on. Women dug shelters with hooks and butcher knives. Warriors improvised rifle pits with captured army bayonets. Overnight it grew colder. The wind blew harder. Five inches of snow fell. Corpses stiffened. Children whimpered, and death wails rode on the blackness. Yellow Wolf sensed the coming end. "All for which we had suffered lost! Thoughts came of my country when only Indians were there. I felt as if I were dreaming."[33]

The darkness melted into a gray dawn. The gale increased in strength, whipping fallen snow into the faces of the combatants. An occasional rifle crack rent the grieving wind. At noon, the storm subsided, and as the skies partially cleared, everyone looked north. On the horizon, two long lines of black objects advanced "with all the regularity and precision of soldiers." Miles assumed them to be Lakota warriors come to raise the siege. The "formidable [Indian] reinforcements" he feared turned out to be buffalo, but the momentary scare prompted the colonel to parley with the Nez Perces.[34]

Looking Glass and White Bird refused to negotiate. Chief Joseph, however, came to Miles's tent under a white flag to hear his terms. What passed between them is uncertain, but the talks apparently stalled when Miles insisted that the Nez Perces surrender their arms. When Joseph attempted to leave, the colonel detained him overnight "as his guest." Miles might have intended to hold the chief hostage. Whatever his thought, he was forced to release him the next morning because the Nez Perces had seized a lieutenant who had wandered into their rifle pits, perhaps under instructions from Miles to reconnoiter their defenses. Even now, reduced to the extremes of desperation, the Nez Perces maintained their sense of honor and decency. They permitted the lieutenant to retain his sidearm, and White Bird gave him two blankets. The Nez Perces occasionally bantered and jested with the officer, but mostly they spoke of their hope that Sitting Bull would come and save them.

On the blustery afternoon of October 2, Miles reluctantly exchanged Joseph for the lieutenant. The agonizing routine of the siege resumed.

It snowed again. Sporadic rifle fire kept everyone on edge. Huddled in the pits, the Nez Perce women and children slept fitfully. The next day, Miles's wagon train arrived with a cannon. A chance shot collapsed a dugout, burying four women and two children alive.[35]

When General Howard showed up on October 4 with a small escort, one of Miles's two great fears seemed realized. But the general waived his right to command. "You shall receive the surrender," Howard assured him. "Not until after that will I assume command."

A Nez Perce surrender, however, remained far from certain. Howard had brought with him two elderly Upper Nez Perces to negotiate on his behalf. Both men had daughters in the hostile camp. On October 5, they told the chiefs Howard and Miles's terms: the Nez Perces would be treated honorably as prisoners of war; none would be punished for the Idaho killings; and when spring came, the army would escort them to the Lapwai Reservation. The chiefs held a final council. Looking Glass upbraided a wavering Chief Joseph with a dire warning: "I am older than you. I have my experiences with a man of two faces and two tongues. If you surrender you will be sorry; and in your sorrow you will feel rather to be dead, than suffer that deception." He and White Bird would instead make a break for Canada with their bands.

Looking Glass never got the chance. While he was smoking with his warriors in an exposed rifle pit, his attention was called to a mounted Indian approaching from the north—surely the man was a Lakota. Looking Glass sprang up to see for himself. A rifle volley rippled from the army ranks, and a bullet crashed into his forehead, hurling him down the hill, dead. The rider turned out to be a Cheyenne scout.

Joseph had had enough. The Wallowa band, at least, was finished fighting and running: "I could not bear to see my wounded men and women suffer any longer; we had lost enough already. Colonel Miles had promised that we might return to our country with what stock we had left. I thought we could start again. I believed Colonel Miles, *or I never would have surrendered.*"[36]

One of the Upper Nez Perce chiefs conveyed Joseph's words of surrender to Miles and Howard, whose adjutant transcribed the message as follows:

Tell General Howard I know his heart. What he told me before I have in my heart. I am tired of fighting. Our chiefs are killed; Looking Glass is dead; Toohoolhoolzote is dead. The old men are all dead.

It is the young men who say yes or no. He who led the young men is dead. It is cold, and we have no blankets; the little children are freezing to death. My people, some of them, have run away to the hills and have no blankets, no food. No one knows where they are—perhaps freezing to death. I want to have time to look for my children and see how many of them I can find. Maybe I shall find them among the dead. Hear me, my chiefs! I am tired; my heart is sick and sad. From where the sun now stands, I will fight no more forever.[37]

Chief Joseph rode slowly from the Nez Perce entrenchments toward Howard and Miles, hands crossed on the pommel of his saddle. His Winchester rifle rested across his knees, and his shoulders drooped. Bullet holes in his shirt and leggings showed how lucky he was to be alive. Dismounting, Joseph offered his Winchester to Howard, who motioned to him to hand it to Miles. Smiling sadly, Joseph did so. Then he shook hands with both officers.

The Nez Perce hegira was over. Four hundred and forty-eight Nez Perces surrendered. All but eighty-seven were women and children. The Nez Perces had traveled seventeen hundred miles. They had slain 180 whites and wounded another 150 at a loss of 120 killed and perhaps as many wounded. Man for man, they had proven far superior to the soldiers sent out to stop them. White Bird escaped to Canada. Yellow Wolf also snuck off. Approximately 233 Nez Perces, nearly half of them warriors, reached Sitting Bull's village, where they received a warm welcome. For capturing the Nez Perces—or two-thirds of them at any rate—Miles won the glory he craved. But he also came away from Bear Paw Mountain with an enduring admiration for his former enemy. Recognizing that "fraud and injustice" had precipitated the conflict, he thought the Nez Perces could "be made loyal friends in six months with anything like honesty and justice on the part of the government."[38]

Miles was the lone voice of reason within the military establishment. Perversely obsessed, General Sherman insisted on punishing the Nez Perces. He rammed orders through the War and Interior Departments banishing them to Fort Leavenworth, Kansas, where dozens succumbed to disease. From Kansas, they were shunted off to Indian Territory. Nearly every baby born there died.

The Nez Perces' plight brought out the best in Miles.[39] He championed their cause at considerable risk to his own career, appealing unsuccessfully to President Rutherford B. Hayes to permit Joseph and his people to settle in Idaho. On several occasions, Joseph himself visited Washington, D.C., to plead his case, becoming a national celebrity. Support for Chief Joseph came from every corner except Idaho, where the Wallowa band remained under indictment for the revenge murders that had precipitated the war and of which they were innocent. In 1885, the Interior Department resettled White Bird's and Looking Glass's peoples at Lapwai. Joseph and his band were shunted to the Colville Reservation in eastern Washington. For two decades, with Miles's assistance, Joseph continued his petitions to return to Idaho. Finally, in 1900, he was permitted to visit his father's grave. He tried to buy a tract of land in the Wallowa valley, but the white residents refused to sell to him.

Chief Joseph passed away on September 21, 1904. The Colville Agency physician said he died of a broken heart.[40]

CHAPTER 18

THE UTES MUST GO!

O N AUGUST 1, 1876, President Ulysses S. Grant proclaimed Colorado the thirty-eighth state. The road to statehood had been dark and bloody, stained by the slaughter of innocent Indians at Sand Creek and scores of miners and settlers killed in retaliation. The Cheyennes and the Arapahos were gone forever. Only one tribe remained in the state, the Utes of the Rocky Mountains.

The federal government had guaranteed the Utes a reservation in perpetuity: twelve million acres in the western part of the state, representing nearly a third of the arable land in Colorado. Politicians denounced this "obstacle to the advancement" of business. Governor Frederick W. Pitkin and the state legislature vowed to expel the Utes within a decade. Denver newspapers wanted the job done at once. But no one outside Colorado listened. So long as the Utes remained peaceable, federal authorities had no intention of moving them.[1]

*

The Utes were a small tribe, with no more than four thousand members divided into seven autonomous bands. There was no supreme Ute chief, nor was there a tribal council. The Utes wintered in tipis tucked away in secluded river valleys below seven thousand feet, where snow fell lightly and winter grass grew thick. In the spring, hunting parties ranged upward into deep forests and alpine tundra abounding in deer, bear, elk, and antelope or out onto the high, aspen-fringed basins of central Colorado known as the North, Middle, and South Parks to hunt buffalo. The Utes were hereditary enemies of the Lakotas and the

Cheyennes, whose war parties seldom left the Utes' Rocky Mountain stronghold alive.

Until settlers and miners poured into the Rocky Mountains after the Civil War, the Utes roamed the eastern half of present-day Utah, the northern half of New Mexico, and most of Colorado. They clashed sporadically with the intruders but for the most part chose accommodation. In 1863, the Ute Indian agent sent a delegation of Uncompahgres (the largest Ute band) to Washington to sign a treaty on behalf of the entire tribe conceding the eastern slope of the Rocky Mountains and the San Luis Valley. Much of the land the Uncompahgres surrendered belonged to other Ute bands, but the distinction was lost on the Bureau of Indian Affairs. As a mark of gratitude, the government named the Uncompahgre leader Ouray (Arrow) head chief of the Utes.

Although few Utes besides the Uncompahgres recognized Ouray's authority, he had the uncommon advantage of having personally bridged the cultural divide between Indians and whites. Educated by Catholic friars in Taos, he spoke fluent Spanish and passable English. Ouray rose to the Uncompahgre chieftainship by virtue of his prowess in battles against the Plains tribes, but he saw no future in war with the whites. Acculturation and farming became matters of faith with him. Although Ouray genuinely cared about all Utes, he was a despot within his band. In one year alone, his henchmen murdered four of his rivals, which caused a white friend to comment that Ouray's "summary methods of disposing of his enemies is probably without a parallel in the annals of the American Indians."

In 1868, Ouray returned to Washington, D.C., with chiefs from the seven bands to conclude a new treaty establishing the boundaries of the Ute territory. Ouray negotiated shrewdly and played to pro-Indian sentiments in the East. When the Indian Bureau tried to coerce the Utes, he appealed to the press. "The agreement an Indian makes to a United States treaty is like the agreement a buffalo makes with his hunters when pierced with arrows," he told reporters. "All he can do is lie down and give in." The bullying ceased.[2]

The Ute Treaty of 1868 accorded the Utes sixteen million acres, from the western slopes of the Rockies to the Utah border, and granted them hunting rights in North and Middle Parks, which lay outside the reservation. Two permanent Ute agencies were created: one at Los Pinos for the southern bands, the other on White River in the remote northern reaches of the reservation for the united Yampa and Grande

River bands, known to whites as the White River Utes. The Uintah band, already prospering as farmers in eastern Utah, had their own agency. In terms of acreage, the Ute Treaty was the most generous Indian land grant ever made. But the promises of 1868 proved fleeting. Trespassing prospectors found gold in the San Juan Mountains of southwestern Colorado, and the federal government was powerless to expel them. The Utes again chose accommodation over war, signing away the southern quarter of the reservation in 1873 in exchange for a government pledge to contain the miners. Ouray, who had resigned himself to submission, knew it was an empty gesture on the government's part. Untouched by the treaty, the northern bands clung to the traditional life. They did so peaceably, but the risk of an inadvertent clash was real. "One day," Ouray told a white friend, "some of these troublesome Utes may do something that may bring the troops down on us, and we will be destroyed."[3]

*

One hundred and fifty miles east of the White River Agency, an aging, mentally unbalanced social reformer named Nathan C. Meeker was struggling to preserve a floundering agricultural cooperative and stave off financial ruin.

Meeker had devoted much of his life to the search for the perfect society. As a young man, he embraced agrarian socialism. In the 1840s, he joined an Ohio farming commune that collapsed after two years. Afterward, Meeker made a modest living penning agricultural essays. He also wrote a novel, *Life and Adventures of Capt. Jacob D. Armstrong*, about a shipwrecked seafarer—his fantasy alter ego—who molded South Pacific savages into modern utopists. Meeker mailed the manuscript to Horace Greeley, the crusading editor of the *New-York Tribune*, who liked it. The book was a commercial flop, but it did begin Meeker's association with America's most influential journalist, who hired him on as an agricultural editor.

While on assignment in eastern Colorado in 1869, Meeker fell under the spell of land hucksters. They rekindled his utopian dreams with glittering talk of railroads to be built and limitless fertile land waiting to be farmed. Meeker persuaded Greeley, something of a utopian himself, to sponsor the Union Colony in the promised mecca outside Denver, with Meeker as president in residence and editor of the town newspaper, *The Greeley Tribune*. Exhibiting astonishing incapacity, he bought farm lots sight unseen at inflated rates, with predictable consequences. The land was arid, and as the colony sank deeply into debt, Meeker grew morose and dictatorial. Facing bankruptcy, in the fall of 1877, at the age of sixty, Meeker asked the Colorado senator Henry M. Teller, whom he had supported for reelection, to advocate his appointment as agent to the White River Utes, hopeful the salary would allow him to settle his debts.

Teller was glad to return the favor. He persuaded the commissioner of Indian affairs to recommend Meeker to Secretary of the Interior Carl Schurz, a dedicated reformer who advocated farming and individual ownership of land as the cornerstones of a new Indian policy. From what Schurz was told, Meeker seemed the right man to ease the Utes into farming. Had Schurz seen an editorial Meeker had penned for the Massachusetts *Springfield Republican*, he might not have supported this fateful choice. In it, Meeker ridiculed the notion that Indians—who possessed "small brains organized upon an animal standard"—could become farmers. Nonetheless, Meeker was determined to try. Success against these odds would not only restore his utopian credentials but also save the Utes. "I doubt whether they understand [that] their fate is to be overthrown by prospectors and others," Meeker wrote to Senator Teller just before setting off for the White River wilds. "It seems to me . . . that this agency . . . should be placed on a self-sustaining position as soon as possible, preparing for the evil day."

Of course no one bothered to ask the White River Utes, who were quite satisfied with the status quo. Life in their mountain fastness had never been better, and danger seemed remote. The nearest soldiers were at Fort Steele, in Wyoming Territory, a hundred miles and a three days' journey north of the White River Agency, and they had never set foot on the reservation. The Utes ranged over the North Park basin, maintaining friendly relations with the scattered settlers and hunting off the reservation as the 1868 treaty permitted. Their agents posed no objections, and in return the Utes planted a few potato and vegetable gardens—just enough to enable the agents to send glowing reports to Washington about the Utes' fine progress on the path to civilization. Both parties profited from the deception. Agents hauled Ute hides in Indian Bureau wagons to the railroad for auction in the East. With their share of the earnings, the Utes increased their vast pony herds and also bought new-model rifles, revolvers, and ammunition.[4]

With his wife, Arvilla, and daughter Josephine, Nathan C. Meeker swept into the White River Agency in May 1878. "Father" Meeker, as he insisted the Utes call him, immediately ordered the agency relocated twelve miles downriver to a large open valley at a lower altitude called Powell Park, where it seldom snowed and the soil was fertile. Powell Park also happened to be choice grazing land and the site of pony races, the Utes' favorite pastime. Ute protests at the move were to no avail; Meeker would make farmers of them or die in the effort.

His greatest ally in his plan to cultivate Powell Park was the perennial instability of Indian leadership. There were two claimants to the White River chieftainship: Douglass, a pliant old man whom the government recognized as head chief; and Nicagaat, a charismatic young war leader whom the whites called Ute Jack, or sometimes simply Jack. Meeker exploited the rivalry between Douglass and Jack, paying Douglass's men fifteen dollars a day and giving them extra rations to plow land and dig an irrigation ditch in Powell Park. Jack's followers heckled the laborers as women but inwardly seethed at their preferential treatment. Jack, however, bore no ill will toward whites. He had led a detachment of Ute auxiliaries during the Great Sioux War and had enjoyed the company of soldiers; they in turn had found the Ute scout's familiarity with the taciturn George Crook amusing, as did Crook. "Hello, Clook," Jack would say. "How you getting' on. Where you tink dem Crazy Hoss 'n Sittin' Bull is now, Clook." Jack's fighting ability won him the allegiance of two hundred warriors, while only forty men, most well past their prime, stood behind Douglass. Rather than resist Meeker and jeopardize their friendship with the whites, Jack and his men abandoned the agency and melted into the mountains. Meeker hated him for it.

At first, Meeker was careful not to overplay his hand. Both Jack's and Douglass's factions respected the band's burly medicine man Canavish (Johnson to the whites), who ran the pony races. Meeker left Johnson's racecourse alone and, after Johnson planted a potato patch to show his gratitude, gave the medicine man a farm and livestock. With Douglass and his paltry following and Johnson on his side, Meeker believed he had the Utes "well on the road to civilization." But, he told the Indian Bureau, he must be allowed to complete his "experiment" without interference, particularly from the army. He could handle any Utes who refused to till the soil. "I propose to cut every Indian to bare starvation if he will not work," Meeker told Senator Teller. He would realize his dream of an agrarian utopia, even if it were only with Indians.[5]

*

Winter passed. The high-country snows receded, and in Powell Park barbed-wire fences glittered beneath an unrelenting sun. Douglass and Johnson tilled the agency acreage. Elderly Utes whispered that the efforts were wasted: the auguries foretold a summer without rain. In North Park, Jack and his men prepared for the annual spring hunt. They had no idea that Meeker had become obsessed with getting them back on the reservation, the agent going so far as to advise the commanding officer at Fort Steele, Major Thomas T. "Tip" Thornburgh, that Jack intended to carry arms and ammunition to hostile Indians four hundred miles away. Meeker insisted Thornburgh arrest Jack and drag his men to the agency. Generals Sheridan and Sherman dismissed Meeker's report as absurd, which it was, and the War Department refused to dispatch troops. No one in authority, however, thought to question Meeker's sanity.[6]

Drought came as the Ute elders had foretold. It rained only once between April and July. Meeker's infant crops withered. Wildfires caused by lightning or careless railroad workers devastated northwestern Colorado. Ever eager for a pretense to drive the Utes from Colorado, Governor Pitkin told Washington the fires represented "an organized effort on the part of the Indians to destroy the timber of Colorado." Meeker endorsed the lie. Not only had Jack's warriors set North Park ablaze, he assured the Indian Bureau, but they also threatened local whites. "Whether the commandant at Fort Steele will pay any attention to my request to drive them out of the park is doubtful," Meeker snarled, "as hitherto he has paid no regard to my requests." The War Department shrugged its bureaucratic shoulders and told Major Thornburgh to investigate the allegations. Though he had no combat experience, having won his rank through politics, he was a fair-minded man, not the sort to stir up trouble. Thornburgh duly interviewed the whites in North Park, and finding they had no complaints against the Utes, he accordingly stood down.[7]

Meeker, meanwhile, was becoming increasingly enraged by the Utes' refusal to knuckle under and plow fast enough to suit him. He disparaged the Utes to the Indian Bureau, complaining that they were a

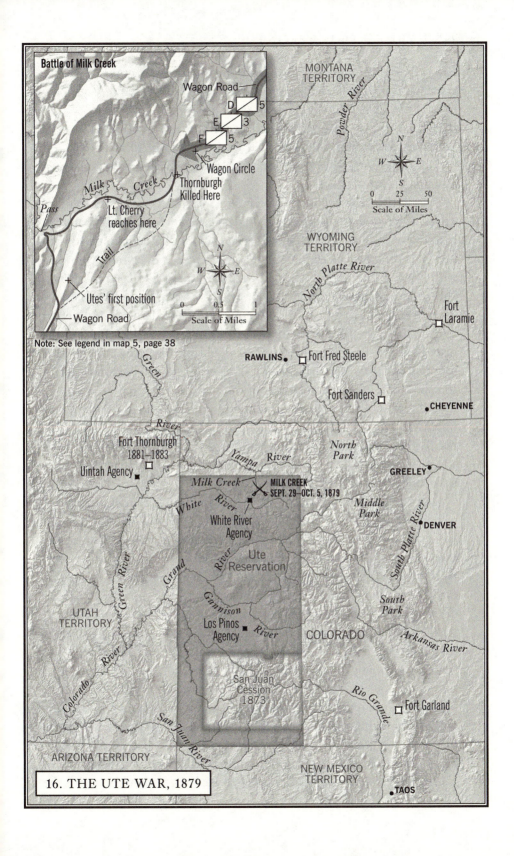

Battle of Milk Creek

Wagon Road

D 5

E 3

F 5

Wagon Circle

Thornburgh
Killed Here

Milk Creek

Pass

Lt. Cherry
reaches here

Trail

Utes' first position

Wagon Road

Scale of Miles
0   0.5   1

Note: See legend in map 5, page 38

MONTANA
TERRITORY

Powder River

North Platte River

Fort
Laramie

RAWLINS

Fort Fred Steele

Fort Sanders

CHEYENNE

WYOMING
TERRITORY

Scale of Miles
0   25   50

Green

River

Fort Thornburgh
1881–1883

Uintah Agency

Yampa River

North
Park

GREELEY

Milk Creek

MILK CREEK
SEPT. 29–OCT. 5, 1879

White River
Agency

White

River

Middle
Park

DENVER

South Platte River

Grand

River

Ute
Reservation

UTAH
TERRITORY

Green River

Gunnison

Los Pinos
Agency

River

COLORADO

South
Park

Arkansas River

Colorado

River

San Juan
Cession
1873

Rio Grande

Fort Garland

San Juan River

ARIZONA TERRITORY

NEW MEXICO
TERRITORY

TAOS

16. THE UTE WAR, 1879

cowardly and contemptible race, constantly running off to steal horses, trade hides for guns, and conspire with white "ruffians and renegades" to steal the agency cattle. None of these accusations were true.

By mid-August, Meeker had succeeded merely in alienating seven hundred reservation Utes who, fed up with his lunatic demands, left to join Jack. Only Douglass, Johnson, and twenty or thirty old men remained loyal to the agent.

Finally, Meeker snapped. He ordered Johnson's racetrack plowed under. Agency employees and Douglass begged Meeker to spare the racecourse; even Jack returned to the agency long enough to plead with him, but the now clearly paranoid agent rebuffed everyone. "Plowing will proceed," he advised the Indian Bureau in early September 1879, "but whether unmolested I cannot say. This is a bad lot of Indians. They had had free rations so long and have been flattered and petted so much that they think themselves lords of all." When Johnson protested, Meeker laughed him off. "The trouble is this, Johnson. You have too many ponies. You had better kill some of them." An angry Johnson shoved Meeker out the door of the agent's office and up against a hitching post. Amid a peal of laughter from Utes who had gathered to watch the exchange, Meeker tumbled over the rail, injuring his shoulder. Before departing, Johnson suggested that Meeker pack his bags and make way for "another agent to come, who was a good man and was not talking such things."[8]

Jack urged Meeker to let the insult pass, calling it a small matter, not worth making a fuss over. But Meeker had no intention of being bullied by Johnson or counseled by Jack. On September 10, he telegraphed the commissioner of Indian Affairs an exaggerated account of the incident. "I have been assaulted by a leading chief, Johnson, forced out of my own house, and injured badly but was rescued by employees . . . Life of self, family, and employees not safe. Want protection immediately."

Meeker's urgent demand forced the military's hand. On September 16, 1879, Thornburgh received orders to arrest malefactors, "enforce obedience to the requirements of Agent Meeker," and "afford him such protection as the exigency of the case requires."[9]

Thornburgh quickly assembled three cavalry companies, one infantry company, and perhaps two dozen civilian wagoners, for a total force of about two hundred men. On September 19, Thornburgh loaded troops, animals, and supply wagons onto freight cars for the short train ride to Rawlins, Wyoming. Because Meeker's correspondence with the

Bureau of Indian Affairs was short on details, the major's orders were necessarily vague. Superiors offered reinforcements, but Thornburgh elected to march with the force at hand. Ranchers and prospectors drifted into camp bearing rumors of agency buildings burned and Utes armed for battle. Five days passed with no word from Meeker. On September 25, midway between Rawlins and White River, Thornburgh sent a guide ahead with a letter to the agent, assuming he was still alive, asking for information. Thornburgh left his infantry behind in order to make better time, and the next morning (September 26) wrote to department headquarters hopefully, "I don't believe they will fight."[10]

Major Thornburgh was right, up to a point. No act of Meeker's had so infuriated the White River Utes as his summons of soldiers. Word spread among the Indians that the troops came at the agent's behest to put them in chains and drag them to Indian Territory. The Douglass and Jack factions united against the common threat, haranguing Meeker and demanding he recant. The Utes stopped short of violence, however. They had broken no treaty provisions and would fight only if the soldiers entered the reservation.

The only way onto the White River Reservation was the 170-mile-long, rocky wagon road from Rawlins, over which Thornburgh and his 150 cavalrymen plodded blindly through sand-streaked gorges and over rocky hills, their wagon train heaving and lurching in the whirl of dust.

Major Thornburgh took the measure of Ute anger when he met Jack fifty miles northeast of the agency on the afternoon of September 26. Jack said he had come to avert war, but Thornburgh's officers thought he was there to size up their strength. The truth is that Jack had come for both purposes. Thornburgh permitted Jack to count his command and said he had come in peace to find out if Meeker was safe. Jack cursed Meeker "in the most vituperative terms," according to one officer, but assured Thornburgh that no harm had come to him and suggested that the major and a small escort accompany him to the agency so that they could see for themselves whether the Indians had mistreated their agent. Thornburgh declined, and Jack departed. The next day, Thornburgh advanced to within twenty miles of the agency. That night, a second Ute delegation brought a letter from a frightened Meeker, who clearly regretted his appeal for troops. He seconded Jack's suggestion that Thornburgh leave his command behind and come to the agency so that "a talk and better understanding can be had," adding that the Utes "consider the advance of your troops as a declaration of real war. In this," Meeker said, "I am laboring to undeceive them."

The Utes, however, were in no mood to listen to Meeker. So that there would be no misunderstanding their position, Colorow also visited Thornburgh's camp, evidently on behalf of Jack. Once a great war leader, Colorow had grown soft on whiskey and biscuits begged from cattlemen and prospectors. Jack had been cordial to all and gregarious with officers he knew from shared duty under Crook. Colorow, on the other hand, was sullen and suspicious. He presented Thornburgh with an unambiguous ultimatum: leave his troops on the far side of Milk Creek (the northeastern boundary of the reservation) and come himself to the agency to talk as Jack and Meeker requested, or cross onto Ute land prepared for battle, adding significantly, "You have too many soldiers for peace but not enough for war."

The Ute position could not have been clearer. Unfortunately, Thornburgh succumbed to a harebrained, deceitful scheme by his second-in-command, Captain J. Scott Payne. Believing false rumors from unreliable locals that the Utes had gone on the warpath and intended to ambush Thornburgh's small party before they reached the agency, reports that rendered the major indecisive, Payne proposed that Thornburgh camp on the far side of Milk Creek the next morning and then march the entire command after dark to the agency, where the troops would be in position either to rescue Meeker or, should the worst have occurred, to punish his murderers.

At the White River Agency, Meeker listened warily to the war drums that beat late into the night on September 28. The young warriors were stirring.[11]

*

Captain Payne swung into the saddle on September 29 in high spirits. The morning was clear and balmy, the sunbathed chain of bluffs and hills on either side of the narrow Milk Creek valley seemingly tranquil. At 9:30 a.m., the cavalry entered the valley on foot. Save for the soldiers, not a living creature was in sight.[12]

Perhaps not in sight, but three miles to the west, lurking behind the hills south of Milk Creek, were at least two hundred Ute warriors. From a vantage point above them, Jack watched the soldiers approach. Thornburgh had broken his word to leave them behind and come himself to the agency for a talk, but Jack still hoped the troops would turn back of their own accord.

Shortly before 10:30 a.m., Thornburgh reached Milk Creek. The Utes had burned the grass on the west bank, and the creek ran dry. With no place in the immediate vicinity to camp, Thornburgh faced a critical decision. He could proceed to the agency with a small guard as he had promised the Utes and order his troops back to their well-watered camp of the night before or cross Milk Creek with his entire command in search of water and grass. Thornburgh chose the latter course. He left the wagons and a cavalry company on the far bank and sent Lieutenant Samuel Cherry across the creek with twenty men to reconnoiter. Then Thornburgh ordered his two remaining companies to dismount and inch their way forward in two ragged V-shaped formations of about fifty men each.

The young Ute warriors in the hills painted their faces for war. They clutched new-model repeating rifles bought from white traders and laughed or sang songs to steady their nerves. Jack awaited the clash that now appeared inevitable. "I was with General Crook the year before fighting the Sioux, and I knew in a minute that as soon as this officer deployed his men out in that way it meant a fight; so I told my men to deploy too." There was a brief moment of goodwill. Cherry spotted the Utes and waved his hat in a friendly gesture. Several Utes waved their rifles casually in return. Jack started down the slope to talk with Cherry. Then someone—Cherry said an Indian; Jack did not know who—fired a shot, and the battle was on. Jack sent a courier back to the agency to warn Douglass the soldiers were coming. He picked up his rifle, took a last look at the valley that roiled and churned beneath a curtain of blue gun smoke, fustigated the warriors for their foolishness in bringing on a fight, and then rode off. Jack had tried to keep the peace; now he was going home.

Colorow took command. He sized up the situation and concluded the best course lay in separating the soldiers from their supplies. Calling on the warriors nearest him, Colorow led a mounted charge on the wagon train. As the Indians spilled down the hills, Thornburgh ordered Payne to withdraw the cavalry and then galloped toward the train to organize a defense. At the creek bed, a bullet from a Ute sharpshooter slammed into Thornburgh's chest, and he careened from the saddle. His corpse became the object of Ute fury. Passing warriors fired bullets through Thornburgh's eye sockets and slit deep gashes in his forehead, arms, and legs. They scalped him, stripped him, and stuffed the photograph of a scowling Ute warrior in his mouth.[13]

Meanwhile, the retreating cavalrymen fought off Colorow's dash on the circled wagons. Once inside the corral, the soldiers barricaded themselves behind bedrolls and corn sacks. They wrapped the dead in blankets and added them to the defenses. Ute sharpshooters killed three-quarters of the 339 horses and mules crowded into the corral, and the troops dragged the carcasses outside and made breastworks of them. As always, there were cowards and shirkers. First Sergeant John Dolan, a thirty-seven-year veteran already on the retired list, upbraided them gruffly. "If you don't get out and help, I will kill you myself." As he finished the sentence, a Ute bullet felled him.

During the afternoon, the Utes employed the old Indian tactic of setting grass fires and advancing behind the flames. Six soldiers were killed, and Captain Payne suffered a second wound before the blaze was extinguished and the warriors drew back. At sunset, the shooting subsided. Payne ordered the men to dig rifle pits while he counted his losses. They were considerable. Thirteen had died, and forty-three had been wounded. "I believe that we can hold out until reinforcements reach us if they are hurried through," Payne wrote in a measured appeal. At midnight, four volunteers slipped through the Indian lines with Payne's note for the long trek back to Fort Steele.[14]

*

Nathan C. Meeker passed the last hours of his life ignorant of the happenings on Milk Creek. Douglass had called on the agent that morning to insist he keep the soldiers off the reservation, but Meeker casually dismissed him. Later a Ute from Milk Creek brought news of the clash to Douglass. The matter was clear. The soldiers had spilled Ute blood; Meeker had lied yet again. Douglass assembled twenty armed Utes and marched on Meeker's home.

At noon, the Meekers dined. At 1:00 p.m., Meeker wrote to Thornburgh that he expected to leave with Douglass momentarily to meet with the major, adding that all was peaceful and Douglass was flying the Stars and Stripes over his cabin. An hour later, the male employees of the agency were dead and the agency buildings ablaze. Douglass and his people melted into the mountains, the warriors carrying off Arvilla and Josephine and the wife of an agency employee as hostages and sexual plunder. Nathan C. Meeker lay faceup outside his home, naked from the waist down, a bullet hole in his head, and a logging chain wrapped around his neck. The Utes had clubbed his skull and pounded a metal stake down his throat. He would tell no more lies.[15]

∗

The outcome of the day's combat at Milk Creek pleased Colorow. "This will not be so bad," he assured his warriors after they shot down the last army horse. "This bad smell will bring big, fat, blue flies. Those flies will get even fatter on those dead horses, and when the soldiers run out of food, they can roast them." During the night, icy winds swirled through the valley, and sleet pelted the ground. Most of the warriors lost interest in the battle and drifted off. After three days, only Colorow and sixty men remained on the field. The fight had gone out of the Utes; if the soldiers showed a disposition to leave, they would pose no obstacle.

Instead, more soldiers came. On October 2, Company D, Ninth Cavalry, which had been patrolling Middle Park, trotted into Milk Creek valley. More curious about their skin color than any threat they might pose, the Utes held their fire while the Buffalo Soldiers entered Payne's barricade. To Payne's grateful survivors, reinforcements of any hue were welcome, and they set aside their bigotry. "Why, we took those darkies in right along with us in the pits," said one soldier. "We let 'em sleep with us, and they took their knives and cut off slips of bacon from the same sides as we did."[16]

Untainted adulation greeted Colonel Wesley Merritt when he arrived at daybreak on October 5 at the head of four companies of the Fifth Cavalry, having covered the 170 miles from Rawlins in forty-eight hours with animals that arrived almost as fresh as when they had started. The colonel attributed his success to strict discipline and careful attention to the welfare of horses and men—in that order.[17]

Few Utes witnessed Merritt's arrival; fewer still shot at the soldiers. Most were huddled under the hills with Jack, who had returned to the front to ponder a letter from Ouray imploring them to cease hostilities immediately. The Uncompahgre chief had no authority over the White River Utes. Nonetheless, Ouray's letter gave Jack the clout necessary to end the fighting, and on October 5 he proposed a cease-fire, to which Merritt agreed on the condition that the Utes not oppose his continuing on to the agency. Unaware of the bloody events that had transpired there or the abduction of Meeker's wife and daughter, Merritt made no attempt to impede the Utes' departure from the battlefield, a bit of magnanimity he would later regret. Jack and his warriors rode south into the mountains to join Douglass, Johnson, and the white captives and await their fate.[18]

*

If the Colorado exterminationists and the army had their way, destruction would be the Utes' destiny. "Either the [Utes] go or we go, and we are not going," proclaimed a Denver daily. "The Western Empire is an inexorable fact. He who gets in the way will be crushed." Governor Pitkin falsely accused the entire Ute tribe of complicity in what the press labeled the Meeker Massacre and threatened to call out twenty-five thousand volunteers to replicate Sand Creek on a grand scale. Neither Sheridan nor Sherman, however, believed the unrest extended beyond the White River Reservation, and they had little sympathy for Meeker, who they now realized had brought on the war by his "mismanagement and ignorance of Indian character." But the generals were bent on avenging Thornburgh's death, which Sherman attributed to "base and murderous" treachery. The White River Utes could either surrender unconditionally or face destruction. "There will be no halfway measures this time," Sherman promised Sheridan. "If necessary I will send every man from the Atlantic coast to go after the Utes." On October 11, Colonel Merritt marched from the White River Agency to flush out the White River Utes, while nearly three thousand troops converged on the Ute country from as far away as Minnesota.

Fortunately, cooler heads prevailed. Chief Ouray assured the Indian Bureau that his Uncompahgres and the southern bands wanted no trouble and that the White River Utes would fight only if provoked. He suggested that a peace commission be formed "to investigate facts and let blame rest where it may." Carl Schurz also favored diplomacy over force. Fearful that a large-scale offensive would drag all the Utes into war and doom the women captives, Schurz persuaded Sherman to hold the army in check while he negotiated for their release. The former Ute agent Charles Adams, a just and prudent man, agreed to act as Schurz's emissary.[19]

General Sheridan fumed over the recall order. "We went to the agency at the solicitation of the Indian Bureau whose agent was murdered, and our men killed and wounded, and now we are left in the heart of the mountains with our hands tied and the danger of being snowed in staring us in the face," he griped to Sherman. "I am not easily discouraged, but it looks as though we had been pretty badly sold out in the business."[20]

In the end, it was the Utes who were sold out. Douglass surrendered the women hostages to Adams in the naive hope it would smooth things over. But he asked for too much. He had raped Arvilla Meeker and then taken her as a second wife, a young warrior had raped and then "wed" Josephine Meeker, and Johnson had taken the third woman. Learning of these outrages, Coloradans demanded a Ute genocide. If only for the sake of their survival, Secretary Schurz concluded that the White River Utes had to be gotten out of Colorado and resettled on Utah's small Uintah Ute Reservation. He appointed a peace commission composed of Adams, Ouray, and Colonel Edward Hatch to arrange it.

The proceedings, however, did not go entirely as Schurz had expected. The commissioners exonerated Jack, Colorow, and the Milk Creek warriors on the grounds they had not intended to fight Thornburgh. But the agency killings were another matter. The Meeker women identified twelve Utes as perpetrators, including Douglass and Johnson. Colonel Hatch wanted the "cowardly dogs" brought to justice and expected Chief Ouray to deliver the accused to the commission. Rightly objecting that no Ute could expect a fair hearing in Colorado, Ouray refused to cooperate unless the men were guaranteed a trial in Washington, D.C., and he and the chiefs were permitted to speak with Schurz.[21]

Schurz's back was against the wall. The Colorado state legislature narrowly defeated a bill titled "An Act for the Destruction of Indians and Skunks," which offered a bounty of twenty-five dollars to anyone presenting authorities with either a dead skunk or a Ute scalp. Representing the mining interests, a Colorado senator gave the secretary an ultimatum: either buy the Ute land, or step away so that others might take "more extreme measures."

Time had run out. On January 7, 1880, Schurz dissolved the peace commission and put the Ute question before the cabinet. President Rutherford B. Hayes approved a nonnegotiable treaty, which Schurz drafted, expelling the White River Utes from Colorado and resettling the peaceable bands in the southwest corner of the state. On March 16,

1880, Ouray and a delegation of chiefs conceded to the terms, surrendering twelve million acres for fifty thousand dollars and past-due annuities. The suspects in the agency killings never materialized, and the government did not press the issue.[22]

While in Washington to sign the treaty, Ouray had his meeting with Schurz. The secretary came away pleased. Calling Ouray "the brightest Indian" he had ever met, Schurz said the chief understood the "utter hopelessness of the Indians against the progress of civilization [and] that nothing was left to them but to accommodate themselves to civilized ways or perish."

The secretary could hardly have failed to notice that Ouray was dying. For nearly a year, he had been wasting away from acute nephritis. Sudden attacks of excruciating back pain and severe vomiting frequently interrupted his service on the peace commission. His face grew puffy, and breathing came hard. As the end drew near, Ouray discarded the white man's clothing he had been accustomed to wearing in favor of Ute buckskin and told his followers that he regretted having so often cooperated with the government. Ouray died on August 24, 1880, at his farmhouse at Los Pinos. A week later, a New York newspaper announced to the world, "The greatest Indian that ever lived is dead."[23]

Death spared Ouray the agony of witnessing a gross injustice dealt his own band when the Colorado legislature voted to displace the Uncompahgres from their promised new homes in southwestern Colorado. Baited with annuities, most White River Utes acquiesced to life on the Uintah Reservation. The blameless Uncompahgres, on the other hand, relented only after the army intervened.

In the blink of an eye, the Ute culture had vanished. An army captain marveled at the sudden transformation of the Ute country. "As we pushed the Indians onward, we permitted the whites to follow, and in three days the rich lands of the Uncompahgres were all occupied, towns were being laid out, and lots being sold at high prices. In short order the Uncompahgre Valley—previously a desert—became the garden spot of Colorado, covered with bountiful farmland and orchards."[24]

*

Jack never adjusted to reservation life. He despised the pacifistic Uintah farmers, who in turn had little use for the White River band. In November 1881, Jack slipped off the Uintah Reservation. The Indian

Bureau ordered the army to return him. A spy tracked Jack to his lodge on the Shoshone reservation near Fort Washakie, and on April 28, 1882, a cavalry company rode out to arrest him. Jack refused to surrender and shot a sergeant who came too close. The detachment commander rolled a howitzer up to the tipi and fired. When the smoke cleared, the troops picked up Jack's scattered remains and deposited them in a salt bag. Like the Modoc chief whose name he shared, Jack had died a violent death in the poisoned aftermath of a war that he had tried to prevent.[25]

———•———

CHAPTER 19

RETURN TO APACHERIA

WITH THE END OF THE Ute War, the white subjugation of the Indians of the Rocky Mountains was complete. The decade of the 1870s, which had opened hopefully with President Grant's conciliatory Peace Policy, closed with ironfisted intolerance of tribes that did not unconditionally indulge the United States' limitless appetite for land and confine themselves to the limits of their reservations.

In Apacheria, events during the latter years of the 1870s unfolded independent of the happenings elsewhere in the West, though ultimately with the same painful trajectory for the Indians involved. In Arizona Territory in 1876, the Indian agent John Clum's draconian application of the concentration policy had brought the Yavapais, the Western Apaches, and all the Chiricahua Apaches except the Chihennes together on the White Mountain Reservation and its hellish vortex, the San Carlos Agency.

Since the murder of Mangas Coloradas in 1863, the Chihennes had lived apart from other Chiricahuas on a "permanent" reservation in the heart of their homeland at Cañada Alamosa in southwestern New Mexico Territory, just west of the Rio Grande. The Chihennes felt a profound oneness with their country that other Chiricahuas lacked. And with good reason. At Cañada Alamosa, they wanted for nothing. Game was plentiful. The land was semiarid, but the climate temperate. When the Chihennes took ill, which was seldom, they traveled up the canyon to Ojo Caliente (Warm Springs) to seek relief in the mystical healing power of its mineral water. It was at Ojo Caliente in times immemorial that the Chihennes believed their deities had imparted the rituals and beliefs that defined the band.

There was an unsavory aspect to the Ojo Caliente Reservation, however. Life in a nearly idyllic homeland could not cure the Chihennes of the deep-seated Apache raiding impulse, and they regularly slashed their way across northern Mexico. Needing a safe place at which to barter their plunder, the Chihennes encouraged shady Mexican and American traders to build a village in Cañada Alamosa. The arrangement was mutually beneficial—that is, until Vincent Colyer stepped in. The Ojo Caliente Reservation was one of the stops on his 1871 peacemaking circuit. The dogmatic Indian Board secretary gave the Chihennes' love of country short shrift. In common with his fellow eastern humanitarians, he believed that "wild" Indians needed to learn to farm and to live in isolation until they had been "civilized." In his estimation, Cañada Alamosa lacked arable land and swarmed with frontier ruffians (the dealers in Chihenne plunder), and so he decreed that the reservation be closed and the Chihennes moved to the Tularosa valley, a hundred miles northwest of Cañada Alamosa. Somehow he deluded himself into thinking it the perfect home for the Chihennes, "remote from white settlements, surrounded by mountains and not easily crossed, [with] sufficient arable land, good water, and plenty of wood." The Chihennes were appalled. Colyer's paradise was a Chihenne hell, a land blighted by sterile mountains and fetid marshes, the legendary home of evil spirits who dealt death to the Chihennes. The army also deplored Colyer's decision as both unjust and dangerous, viewing Tularosa's innumerable gorges and canyons as excellent hiding places for hostile Indians.

Chiefs Victorio and Loco, who wanted good relations with the Americans, represented the Chihennes in their dealings with Colyer. They were cousins, born between 1820 and 1825, whose Mexican enemies knew them as daring warriors and skillful war leaders and named them accordingly. Victorio literally meant "the victorious one." Loco was not "crazy," as his moniker suggested, but was so named by the Mexicans because of his uncontrollable fury as a young warrior, which included battling grizzly bears. During one such scuffle, he lost an eye. The ferocious warrior and bear wrestler mellowed with age, however. By the time he met Colyer, Loco had become the acknowledged peacemaker of the band. For his part, Victorio had always been a reasonable man, and he was more predictable in his behavior than his cousin Loco. As far as is known, Victorio never indulged in the well-refined Apache practice of torturing prisoners, and unlike most Apache chiefs he was both monogamous and abstemious. In dealings with government representatives, Victorio was forthright, honest, and accommodating. An

Indian Bureau official who came to admire him described Victorio as "short and stout, with a heavy, firm-set jaw and an eye not unlike a facile politician." Victorio and Loco protested vigorously Colyer's demand that they leave Cañada Alamosa, but in the interest of peace they eventually yielded.[1]

The chiefs almost instantly regretted their decision. Tularosa was all they feared and worse. Winter winds swirled down from the mountains and cut through the brushwood frames and ragged-mat coverings of their fragile wickiups. Early frosts withered crops. The water was impure. Women weakened, and children died. During a council at Fort Tularosa in September 1872, Victorio and Loco implored General Howard, who had succeeded Colyer as special Indian commissioner, to intercede with the Great Father for their return to Ojo Caliente. Turbulent young Chihenne warriors—whom an increasingly morose Victorio could not control—were quitting the reservation in droves and, the chiefs warned Howard, might provoke war with the whites of the New Mexico Territory. "I will speak the truth, let the fault be where it may," said Victorio. "We do not feel contented here, and want to go to Cañada Alamosa where the sun shines upon us and we feel well and where the ground is our own." Victorio's appeal moved Howard, who promised to do what he could for the Chihennes. It took two years for the government to undo the mess Colyer had created, but finally, in July 1874, the Chihennes were allowed to return to a reopened Ojo Caliente.[2]

Back on their homeland, the Chihennes prospered until tumult at Arizona's San Carlos Agency spilled over onto Ojo Caliente. The disruptive element was a small but violent faction of their Chokonen kinsmen that had rebelled against the agent John Clum's closure of Tom Jeffords's Chiricahua Reservation in mid-1876 with a string of bloody raids, seeking Ojo Caliente as a sanctuary between forays. Loco wanted to expel them, but Victorio, in deference to the strong ties between the bands, allowed them to stay. Although Victorio refused to join in their depredations, whites equated tolerance with complicity. A clamor arose for again closing down Ojo Caliente and not only removing the Chokonen renegades but also relocating Victorio's people to San Carlos. Once again the army protested; uprooting the Chihennes, the generals felt, would be a gross breach of good faith, but their objections fell on deaf ears, and the Indian Bureau ordered the San Carlos agent, John Clum, to round up everyone.[3]

Oliver Otis Howard, called the Christian General, at the close of his career. He saw more hard service in the West than any other general, excepting George Crook.

Chief Joseph of the Wallowa band of the Nez Perce Indians. He never forgot his dying father's admonition to "stop your ears whenever you are asked to sign a treaty selling your home." Joseph later said, "A man who would not love his father's grave is worse than a wild animal."

Ollokot, brother of Chief Joseph. War leader of the Wallowa band, he also was the guiding spirit of the young warriors in the Nez Perce War. Like his brother, Ollokot wears the pompadour hairstyle of adherents of the Dreamer religion.

Chief Looking Glass led the Nez Perce flight.

Nathan C. Meeker, the mentally unstable Indian agent whose obsession with converting the peaceable Ute Indians into agrarian utopists precipitated the Ute War

Ute Jack, charismatic war leader of the Utes, scouted for General Crook during the Great Sioux War. A victim of Meeker's irrational wrath, he did not want to fight the whites.

ABOVE Besieged troopers at the Battle of Milk Creek, September 29–October 5, 1879

LEFT Chief Victorio of the Chihenne (Eastern Chiricahua) Apaches, the greatest Apache guerrilla fighter of them all

LEFT Geronimo, the Bedonkohe shaman. His fellow Chiricahuas believed he possessed great mystic powers uniquely valuable in warfare and raiding. Many Apaches feared him, but few liked him.

RIGHT Chihenne Chief Loco, a man of peace whose band sat out Victorio's War

Geronimo (*squatting third from left*) and General Crook (*seated second from right*) in council at Cañon de los Embudos (Canyon of the Funnels) in Sonora, Mexico, on March 27, 1886. "What is the matter that you don't speak to me?" Geronimo asked Crook. "Your mouth talks too many ways," the general replied.

Chiricahua prisoners of war en route to Fort Marion, Florida. This trackside photograph was taken on September 10, 1886, near the Nueces River in Texas. Geronimo and Naiche, son of Cochise, are in the front row, third and fourth from the right.

Sitting Bull's cabin. A local photographer staged a reenactment of his arrest for the camera. The cabin was dismantled and shipped to Chicago for display at the 1892 Columbian Exposition.

The Opening of the Fight at Wounded Knee. Frederic Remington made this sketch after interviewing Seventh Cavalry participants. It may be considered an accurate depiction of the first volleys.

Chief Big Foot of the Miniconjou Lakotas, lying frozen where he died at Wounded Knee on December 29, 1890. The photograph was taken on January 3, 1891, when the burial detail arrived.

In April 1877, Victorio and Loco reluctantly led 343 Chihennes to San Carlos. Victorio hedged his bets, counseling his warriors to cache their arms in case San Carlos proved unbearable, which it soon did: The Chihenne tract was a gravelly flat near the San Carlos Agency, its monotony broken only by dejected rows of cottonwoods. In summer, the heat was relentless. Flies and mosquitoes blanketed the river bottom. Dust storms provided the only relief from the infestation. Rations were chronically insufficient, but Clum, who never warmed to the Chihennes, forbade them to hunt. White Mountain Apaches frequently provoked fights with the Chihennes, which at least offered an interlude to the endless tedium.

Under these circumstances, Victorio and Loco's authority slipped rapidly. As the social fabric of the Chihennes unraveled, some of their warriors fell under the sway of a psychotic Chokonen raider on the run from the army. Faced with a choice between leadership and irrelevance, on September 1, 1877, Victorio and Loco led 310 Chihennes in a break for Cañada Alamosa. Before leaving, they stole a herd of White Mountain Apache horses, more out of necessity than spite.

The Chihennes never came close to their homeland. The army sealed off Ojo Caliente, and cavalry detachments and Indian police from the San Carlos Agency (mostly White Mountain Apaches) chased the Chihennes across the New Mexico Territory. As their animals gave out, the desperate Chihennes stole horses and cattle, killing ranchers who resisted. With nowhere to run, Victorio and Loco surrendered on October 11.[4]

The Chihennes were now prisoners of war under army control, which proved providential for them. Brigadier General John Pope, commander of the Department of the Missouri, permitted the Chihennes to return to Ojo Caliente, and the district commander, Colonel Edward Hatch, pledged to Victorio that he would strive to make their stay permanent if they would "prove themselves to be good Indians and plant crops." Even Phil Sheridan spoke up on Victorio's behalf. When the Indian Bureau toyed with the idea of banishing the Chihennes to the Fort Sill Reservation in Indian Territory (a particularly perverse interpretation of the concentration policy), the secretary of war persuaded President Grant to squelch the plan. The army wanted peace no less than did the Chihennes.

Victorio dutifully tilled the soil and kept his warriors in check. Hatch reciprocated with supplementary rations and generous gifts of surplus army clothing. He also withdrew troops from the reservation, effectively leaving Victorio's people as prisoners under their own recognizance. Victorio and Loco told an army inspector that they were the most content they had ever been. Even the Apache-loathing *Arizona Star* conceded that the behavior of Victorio's band was exemplary.

Good intentions notwithstanding, the army could not maintain the Chihennes indefinitely. In June 1878, Sheridan and Sherman demanded the Indian Bureau resume responsibility for them. That broke the bureaucratic inertia, but the outcome mortified the generals. Ignorant of the true nature of affairs in the Southwest, Secretary of the Interior Carl Schurz, who would later risk his job to do right by the Utes, now asked the War Department to send the Chihennes to San Carlos.

Loco consented to go, but Victorio refused. He had reached the limit of his tolerance of government duplicity. On October 25, 1878, Loco started for San Carlos with 172 Chihennes, only 22 of whom were warriors, while Victorio took to the mountains with 90 followers, including 44 warriors. Frontiersmen excoriated the Indian Bureau for its foolhardy decision. "The whole community on the Rio Grande felt secure," said the *Tucson Weekly Star*. "No outrages had been committed and the sudden removal to San Carlos was as much a surprise to the people as it was wrong and unjust to Victorio."[5]

Nothing went right for Victorio that winter. Savage snowstorms battered his high-country sanctuary. Game was scarce. A slow but steady trickle of defections began. Rather than watch his band dissolve, in February 1879 Victorio agreed to surrender on the condition his people not be returned to San Carlos. The Indian Bureau consented to relocate them on the Mescalero Apache Reservation, eighty miles east of Ojo Caliente. The Mescaleros were friends, and their reservation was a far more agreeable place than San Carlos. Everyone but the vengeful residents of Silver City was satisfied. Victorio had raided near the southwestern New Mexico mining town during his flight from San Carlos, and in July a local grand jury indicted him for murder and horse thieving. An uneasy Victorio kept his promise to remain on the Mescalero Reservation, but when the Silver City judge and prosecuting attorney passed through the reservation on a hunting trip later that summer, the Chihennes panicked. Confronting the Mescalero agent, Victorio angrily jerked his beard, whistled in the Chihenne pony horse herd, ordered the women to break camp, and made for the mountain country around Ojo Caliente. On September 4, Victorio and sixty warriors ran off the horse herd of the Ninth Cavalry company stationed at their former agency and killed eight Buffalo Soldiers. Rampaging southward, they butchered seventeen men, women, and children.

Victorio had declared war on the whites.[6]

＊

The army found Victorio as formidable a foe in war as he had been a staunch friend when treated fairly in times of peace. Indeed, he showed himself more skilled at guerrilla warfare than Cochise. Two weeks after stealing the horses at Ojo Caliente, Victorio lured two pursuing Ninth Cavalry companies into a textbook ambush in Las Animas Canyon, forty miles south of the reservation. Only the appearance of two companies drawn by the echoing gunfire and Victorio's tactic of shooting horses before men saved the Buffalo Soldiers. As it was, nine troopers died. Victorio retired into the rugged Mimbres Mountains without the loss of a man. Reflecting on the action, one of Victorio's men boasted, "I think we may have invented trench warfare, and we infinitely preferred a mountain at our backs. When closely pursued we killed our horses and scaled cliffs no enemy could climb." All of which, to the army's chagrin, would repeatedly prove true.[7]

Victorio's success dumbfounded Colonel Hatch. "The Indians are thoroughly armed, and as evidence [that] they are abundantly supplied with ammunition their fire in action is incessant," he reported to General Pope. "It is impossible to describe the exceeding roughness of such mountains as the Black Range and San Mateo. The well-known Modoc Lava Beds are a lawn compared to them." He needed help, and Pope sent him the best he had—Lieutenant Charles B. Gatewood's White Mountain Apache Company. Hatch assigned them to the Ninth Cavalry squadron of Major Albert P. Morrow, whom he tasked with defeating Victorio.

The White Mountain Apaches welcomed the opportunity to kill Chihennes. On September 28, in a combined operation with Morrow's Buffalo Soldiers, they discovered Victorio's camp and dealt the Chihennes their first casualties in a drawn fight near Cuchillo Negro Creek in the heart of the Black Range. Bested on his own ground, Victorio angrily retaliated with lightning raids up and down the Rio Grande valley. Morrow gave chase, but Victorio was not to be taken unawares a second time. He knew the sunbaked country and its scattered water holes intimately, replenished his stock regularly with stolen horses, and fought only on his own terms. By the end of October, hard marching had reduced Morrow's command to less than half its original strength. Obsessed with cornering Victorio, Morrow followed him into Mexico—a blatantly illegal act that, if discovered, could lead to war. It was also a stupid move on its own merits. Once in Mexico, Morrow's force withered under the desert sun. Horses gave out and were shot. Men offered a month's pay for a swallow of water. After riding seventy miles without finding a single water hole, the major's ragged command at last chanced upon a tank of cool and clear water, only to discover the Chihennes had tossed a disemboweled coyote into it and "otherwise disgustingly poisoned the water." Victorio was practicing the desert variant of a scorched-earth policy.

After a month of sparring with the Chihennes south of the border, Morrow called it quits. He had pushed his men 1,125 miles in forty-nine days. "I am heartily sick of this business," the captain told a friend after hobbling home to Fort Bayard. "I have had eight engagements with the Victorio Indians, and in each have driven them, but there is no appreciable advantage."[8]

Morrow hadn't driven Victorio anywhere. The Chihenne chief had entered Mexico not to bait the major but rather to rest his people in the remote, well-watered Candelaria Mountains, a favorite refuge. Victorio also needed fresh horses, which he stole from the closest village, Carrizal. The mayor found fifteen men foolish enough to follow the Chihenne raiders, and Victorio killed them all. Having gotten what he came for, Victorio left his mountain sanctuary in January 1880 and headed north, his ranks swelled by fifty or sixty Mescalero warriors who had grown bored with reservation life. New Mexicans braced for a return of the Apache "hell hounds."

To their immense relief, Victorio had returned not to raid but to make peace. Eleven months on the run had brought him no closer to finding a permanent home than the day he broke out of San Carlos. Eluding Major Morrow, who was back in the field, Victorio cautiously approached Ojo Caliente and asked a trusted agency employee to inquire of the Indian Bureau on what terms it would accept Victorio's surrender. The man telegraphed Secretary Schurz directly, with a reminder that "the Indians have not been treated fair." Victorio repaired to the San Mateo Mountains to await a reply. Morrow caught up with him the next day, and the adversaries talked. Victorio told Morrow he would go to Ojo Caliente and surrender if the government repatriated the Chihennes still at San Carlos. Here was a chance to end the bloodshed. All Morrow had to do was promise to relay Victorio's request and then back off. Instead, he insisted that Victorio's warriors first give up their horses and weapons, terms no sane Apache chief would entertain. The parley ended, and the shooting began. Morrow lost three men; Victorio escaped without casualties. To his credit, Morrow recognized his error and passed along Victorio's proposal to Colonel Hatch, who strongly endorsed it, as did Generals Pope and Sherman. But the Indian Bureau was obdurate: Victorio had to either accept reservation life at San Carlos or be killed by the army. In late February, Victorio again offered his hand in friendship, this time to the Mescalero agent, who declined to negotiate without Indian Bureau approval. Victorio had suffered his last rebuff. In the future, he would talk to white men only through the muzzle of his rifle.[9]

Victorio would have plenty of opportunities. Heartily tired of five months of fruitless chases by his subordinates and near ambushes, Colonel Hatch assumed field command himself, assembling every available man in his district. General Pope ordered Colonel Benjamin H. Grierson, commander of the District of the Pecos, and his Tenth Cavalry Buffalo Soldiers from Fort Concho, Texas, to cooperate with Hatch in denying Victorio access to the Mescalero Apache Reservation, a ready source of supplies and recruits for the Chihennes. But Hatch deviated from Pope's orders. His scouts had reported Victorio holed up in Hembrillo Canyon, a yawning defile in the San Andres Mountains midway between the Rio Grande and the Mescalero Reservation. To strike Victorio in the San Andres required only a seventy-five-mile detour. Hatch decided to attack "for the effect it would have upon the Mescalero Indians . . . and the possibility of throwing enough troops around [Victorio's] position to capture or destroy it."

It was a reasonable risk, and Hatch planned carefully. He divided the Ninth Cavalry and his Apache scout company into three converging expeditions. Grierson waited on the Texas border to intercept any hostiles who escaped Hatch's net. Hatch's plan might well have worked had the environment and simple luck not intervened on Victorio's behalf. The first of the colonel's columns was struck with acute diarrhea when the men and horses drank from a gypsum-laced spring. Mad with thirst, the troopers staggered on to the next known source of water, which happened to be in Hembrillo Canyon, under the guns of Victorio. Six

Buffalo Soldiers and their commanding officer were wounded in a mad dash for the spring. The timely appearance of the second column saved them from almost certain annihilation. As usual, the Chihennes disappeared into rough country where pursuit was useless.[10]

Despite these successes, Victorio was in a perilous position. Low on ammunition and burdened with women and children, he had to break free from the barren San Andres Mountains. Deploying his warriors as a rear guard, Victorio started south along a narrow trail that debouched onto a torrid desert skillet called Jornada del Muerto (Journey of the Dead Man). Unbeknownst to the chief, Hatch had started north that morning with his third column over the same trail. In Victorio's present state—his women and children between the warriors and the soldiers—the Chihennes were easy prey for Hatch's fresh command.

Victorio had entrusted the women and children to Nana, a septuagenarian war leader whose skills remained undiminished with age. What should have been a tiring but otherwise uneventful run for safety instead turned into a brush with slaughter. "The trail was very rocky and there was little dust to warn us of the coming of an enemy until they were almost upon us," remembered Nana's grandson. "As the cavalry rounded a point of rocks pretty well lined with mesquite, Grandfather sent the people east, following a rocky ledge, to the shelter of an arroyo." Nana told a few boys to backtrack slowly, sweeping the footprints and hoofprints off the trail until they reached the arroyo a quarter mile away, where they were to secrete themselves. Now the fate of the party rested on Chihenne grit—and luck. "Taking advantage of every clump of vegetation, every rock, our people stood with hands ready to press the nostrils of our horses so that they would not betray our position," continued Nana's grandson. "Mother took off [the baby's] cradle and handed it to Grandmother, freeing her to use her rifle. If the baby had opened her mouth to make a sound it would have been necessary to smother her."

The old woman was spared the horror of infanticide. Hatch's Apache scouts rode right past them without even a glance in their direction. Next Hatch and the cavalry rode by, equally oblivious to the Chihenne presence. As the last troopers turned a bend, Nana rushed his people down the trail toward the Jornada del Muerto. Hatch had no second chance at the Chihennes. Victorio had seen Hatch coming and had passed an anxious fifteen minutes before the soldiers turned off the mountain. By changing his course, Hatch had lost an opportunity to end the war.[11]

After leaving the San Andres, the combatants went their separate ways. Victorio and Nana made for the Black Range, less most of the Mescalero warriors, who headed home, their appetite for war sated. Colonel Hatch continued on to the Mescalero Reservation and joined Grierson in arresting every Mescalero male they could lay their hands on. A few warriors returned to Victorio, but the army quarantine of the Mescalero Reservation cost the chief his safe haven.

Victorio's reason for returning to the Black Range, which teemed with soldiers, is obscure. Perhaps he reasoned that it was better to die fighting for their homeland than be hunted down and slaughtered like animals in a strange and forlorn country. Or perhaps seven months of running dulled his tactical instinct. Whatever the case, Victorio's decision proved disastrous for the Chihennes because he made the same mistake his opponents had repeatedly committed: he allowed himself to be trapped. On May 23, "Captain" Henry K. Parker, a tough Indian fighter from Texas whom Hatch had hired as chief of scouts, ferreted out Victorio's camp in the canyon headwaters of the Palomas River at the base of the Black Range. After dark, his seventy Indian scouts quietly surrounded the sleeping Chihennes, some creeping to within fifty yards of Victorio's camp undetected.

At daybreak, Parker opened fire, catching the Chihennes completely by surprise. In their haste to find cover, some warriors left their rifles in their wickiups. Others used their women as human shields while they heaped together rock breastworks. Victorio fell early in the action with a leg wound. Parker's scouts shouted to the Chihenne men to surrender their women and children, promising no harm would come to them. The women responded with vile imprecations. One screamed that if Victorio died, "they would eat him, so that no white man should see his body."

Parker held the Indians in check for two days before a lack of water and ammunition forced his withdrawal. Thirty Chihenne men, women, and children died in the encounter, while Parker suffered no losses. Victorio's wound was minor, but Parker had dealt his aura of invincibility a mortal blow. Chihenne morale suffered accordingly; nearly half the band deserted him and disappeared among reservation Indians. Victorio headed for Mexico with the faithful, killing and pillaging as they went, each mile taking them farther from their beloved Cañada Alamosa.[12]

*

The Chihennes' bloody peregrinations brought them perilously near the West Texas military district of Colonel Benjamin Grierson, whom Phil Sheridan had relieved of command at Fort Sill eight years earlier because he had been too lenient with the Indians to suit Sheridan's taste. The colonel was eager to settle the score. "Thank God," Grierson wrote to his wife, "my back is not broken, and mark what I tell you, sooner or later, I will get even with this man."[13] A brilliant victory would certainly help, but the chance of achieving one in a region largely devoid of both Indians and whites appeared remote. That is, until Victorio appeared on the scene. When the Chihenne chief retreated to Mexico after his thrashing by Parker, General Pope initially ordered Grierson and his Tenth Cavalry to reinforce Hatch in New Mexico. Grierson suggested a change in tactics. Rather than wear down his command in long and fruitless pursuits as Morrow had done, he proposed guarding the water holes and mountain passes along the Rio Grande in order to "intercept and punish the marauders in case they attempted to cross into Texas." Pope concurred.[14]

Victorio, meanwhile, was finding Mexico no longer an easy touch. His slaughter of the citizen-volunteers from Carrizal had galvanized the Mexican government into action. Five hundred Mexican regulars kept on his trail until, with nowhere else left to turn, he made for West Texas. On the morning of July 30, 1880, Victorio splashed across the Rio Grande near Quitman Canyon, seventy miles southeast of El Paso, with a hundred warriors. His immediate destination was a water hole called Tinaja de las Palmas. To reach it, he would have to get past Colonel Grierson himself, on patrol near the water hole with six soldiers and his nineteen-year-old son, Robert, just out of school and eager for adventure, which, the colonel later joked, "he suddenly found."[15]

When a courier brought word of Victorio's approach, Colonel Grierson built a rock barricade on high ground near Tinaja de las Palmas. A lieutenant reported in from a nearby outpost with fifteen troopers, slightly improving the chances Grierson and his son would come out alive. Robert slept well that night, seemingly oblivious to the danger. And he reveled in what the morning brought. Robert had just finished breakfast when the vedettes hollered, "Here come the Indians." Robert grabbed his rifle. "We let fly from our fortifications at the Indians about three hundred yards off and golly, you ought to've seen 'em turn tail and strike for the hills." Colonel Grierson held Victorio at bay for another hour before two companies of Buffalo Soldiers appeared and drove the Apaches back across the Rio Grande. It had been a close call for the Griersons.[16]

Four days later, Victorio returned. He was desperate now. Slipping through Grierson's cavalry screen, he made for the distant Mescalero Reservation. Surely he knew his chance of reaching it was slim. West Texas was terra incognita to the Chihennes, and for once Victorio had to go slowly. Grierson, on the other hand, was on familiar ground, and on August 6, 1880, he savaged Victorio's parched and straggling war party near a precious water hole with the uninviting name of Rattlesnake Springs. Beaten and dispirited, soldiers nipping at his heels, Victorio reversed course for Mexico. He had lost thirty warriors killed or wounded, along with his cattle herd and most of his supplies.

Grierson's victory won him nothing but empty accolades. His military district was abolished as superfluous, and Grierson and the Tenth Cavalry returned to purgatory at Fort Concho. Yet Grierson could take satisfaction in knowing he had brought a "feeling of security, heretofore unknown," to West Texas. Settlements sprang up, and within a year two transcontinental rail lines traversed the region.[17]

In his annual report published in September 1880, General Pope excoriated the policies that had driven Victorio to war. "I do not know the reasons of the Interior Department for insisting upon their removal to San Carlos, but certainly they should be cogent to justify the great trouble and severe losses occasioned by the attempts to coerce the removal." With Victorio resolved to fight to the finish rather than waste away at San Carlos, there could be no turning back the clock. Military operations must proceed until his band was killed or captured. "The capture is not very probable," concluded Pope, "but the killing—cruel as it will be—can, I suppose, be done in time."[18]

*

Time ran out for Victorio sooner than Pope had expected. Down to a handful of cartridges and hungry, with no end in sight but violent death, Victorio's few remaining Mescalero allies tried to defect. To keep them in line, Victorio killed their chief, a desperate act that accomplished nothing. On October 14, a combined force of three hundred Mexican soldiers and Indian scouts under Colonel Joaquin Terrazas, as resourceful and resolute an Indian fighter as Mexico ever produced, found Victorio holed up in a place called Tres Castillos, which translates as Three Castles, a rather lofty appellation for three barren hummocks that rose just one hundred feet above the desert floor. The battle that followed was the culmination of an exodus to nowhere, a year of fighting and feeling for peace that took Victorio's band from a land of broken promises to a land devoid of hope. With the Mexicans hovering just out of rifle range and ammunition running out, Victorio's band settled in behind rock walls and waited.

At first light, the Mexicans scaled the slopes on foot and horseback. Victorio's men squeezed off their last rounds and then grappled with their assailants, "the combatants wrestling with each other and getting hold of each other's heads." At least that was Terrazas's version of events. Because the colonel lost just three men, it is more likely the Mexicans murdered the Chihennes after the warriors ran out of ammunition. However he accomplished the bloody work, Terrazas slew seventy-eight Chihennes and Mescaleros, including sixty-two warriors, his men scalping the dead for bounty money. The colonel's share of the spoils was sixty-eight women and children prisoners, whom he sold into slavery. Only seventeen members of Victorio's band escaped from Tres Castillos. Old Nana, who had been down on the Castillos plains with a dozen warriors when the battle occurred, headed for the Sierra Madre with the survivors.

No one knows how Victorio died or who slew him, but the State of Chihuahua awarded the honor of killing Victorio—along with a fancy nickeled rifle and a hefty reward—to the captain of the Tarahumara Indian scouts. An elderly Chihenne woman who had been near Victorio and some of his men when they fell said no Mexicans killed them. "They were out of ammunition and Victorio did not want to be taken prisoner, so they used their knives on themselves."[19]

To citizens of the American Southwest, the manner of Victorio's passing was inconsequential; that he was dead was cause enough for celebration. "Glory Hallelujah! Victorio killed! War Ended! Peace!" proclaimed the headlines of a New Mexico daily. Two weeks after Victorio's death, President Hayes traveled through the New Mexico Territory on the recently completed Santa Fe Railroad. At a small-town whistle-stop, he spoke of the territory's bright future. "The advantages of health and climate, to say nothing of your great mineral interest, bespeak for you wonders," the president told the delighted crowd. "Those who come among you feel the fact that they are not only in a land of promise, but that the flag of our common country floats over them, guaranteeing liberty and independence and awakening a feeling of love and patriotism known only to America."[20]

*

The stars had at last aligned for the citizens of the Southwest. Hadn't the president said as much? Large ranches were laid out. Silver and coal mines flourished. Between 1880 and 1882, the white population of the territory doubled from forty thousand to eighty thousand. Few of the newcomers ever saw an Indian, much less a hostile one. The Yumas, the Pimas, and the Papagos lived quietly on their reservations, and as for the "human tigers," as General Crook had called the Apaches and the Yavapais, those not exterminated had been gathered in the number of five thousand on the White Mountain Indian Reservation. Apacheria had seemingly been tamed.

The tranquillity was tenuous, however. The reservation had become a powder keg with multiple fuses. Nowhere in the West was the government's failure to match good intentions with enlightened administration more acute than on the White Mountain Reservation, where crooked contractors conspired with the pliable and greedy agents to cheat the Indians out of rations and annuity goods and secretly sow disaffection among the Indians in the hope of provoking war, which had always proven a reliable source of lucrative government contracts. The corruption was not merely local; the reformist secretary of the interior, Carl Schurz, summarily dismissed his commissioner of Indian affairs for collusion in the illegal business. Truly, lamented the president of the independent Board of Indian Commissioners, "our Indian administration is made a stench in the nostrils of honest men by the shameful practices and personal conduct of our officials [at] San Carlos."[21]

Well aware of the fortunes being made at their expense, in 1879 the chiefs of the Yavapai and Apache tribes put aside personal enmities and held councils to consider quitting the reservation. They chose as their leader Cochise's younger son, Naiche. Elders advised against a breakout, and Naiche refused to defy his late father's admonition to keep the peace, but the discontent was palpable. "Everywhere the naked, hungry, dirty, frightened little Indian children, darting behind bush or into wickiup at the sight of you," said a young lieutenant after inspecting San Carlos. "Everywhere the sullen, stolid, hopeless, suspicious faces of the older Indians challenging you. You felt the challenge in your very marrow—that unspoken challenge to prove yourself anything else than one more liar and thief."[22]

The Indians felt the white noose tighten around the White Mountain Reservation, and it frightened them. Mining operations on the western boundary eventually spilled over onto reservation land. East of the reservation, farmers diverted water from the Gila River, withering the crops of Apache farmers farther upriver. Northwest of Fort Apache, Mormons settled along the edge of the White Mountain Apache homeland. The discovery of coal south of the reservation brought miners to within fourteen miles of the San Carlos Agency before the army ousted them. And pecking at the boundaries like starved vultures were the inevitable whiskey peddlers and gun merchants.

Honest and efficient administration came to San Carlos for a year with the temporary assignment of Captain Adna R. Chaffee as agent in July 1879. He went to work with a dogged single-mindedness, ferreting out corruption and doing what he could to improve the lot of the Apaches. Chaffee issued hundreds of renewable passes to ease overcrowding around the agency and enable Apaches so inclined to plant crops in the healthful northern part of the reservation. Chaffee also released the White Mountain Apaches whom John Clum had dragged to San Carlos. Returning home to Fort Apache, they soon became self-sufficient. With fewer mouths to feed and honest accounting, Chaffee was able to issue full rations to the Indians still living near the agency.

Chaffee's successor, Joseph C. Tiffany, continued the captain's regime. In May 1881, Nock-ay-det-klinne, a thirty-six-year-old Cibecue Apache chief and medicine man, applied for a pass to take his people north. Tiffany saw no reason to deny his request. Army officers and agency employees liked "Bobby-ti-klen-ni," as the whites called him. His reputation as a mystic and healer offered no cause for alarm; one officer described him as "a kindly herb doctor." With a complexion paler than many whites, he hardly looked Apache at all. A mere wisp of a man, Nock-ay-det-klinne stood five feet six inches tall and weighed just 125 pounds. But he had the aura of a mystic and eyes that hypnotized.[23]

With his pass in hand, Nock-ay-det-klinne took his people to a remote site along Cibecue Creek, forty-five miles northwest of Camp Apache. There they planted corn and barley, hunted, herded, and held dances. But as Agent Tiffany would soon learn, Nock-ay-det-klinne's dances were unlike any other in Apache history.

*

The Cibecue and White Mountain bands were home, but for how long? Passes were revocable, and agents were capricious. The Apaches felt themselves doomed to do the white man's bidding forever. Then Nock-ay-det-klinne offered a way out. Something about him had changed since coming to Cibecue Creek. Perhaps he had had a powerful vision; perhaps he had merely become greedy. In any event, in June he professed the power to resurrect Apache dead and to restore the old way of life—provided believers first gave him gifts of ponies, cattle, blankets, and food and performed a peculiar new dance that he would teach them.

A paroxysm of fervent devotion gripped the White Mountain and Cibecue people. Nock-ay-det-klinne grew wealthy from their offerings. The dances went on through the month of July. Hundreds of Apaches participated in frenzied expectancy. But the dead remained dead. Some devotees began to smell a rat and demanded their property back. Others threatened to kill Nock-ay-det-klinne if he failed to deliver on his augury. Confronted with likely defectors and potential assassins, Nock-ay-det-klinne modified his prophecy. He said the dead would not materialize until the whites vanished, which would occur during the corn harvest in late August. The cornered shaman did not advocate violence against the whites, but a truculent minority of his followers interpreted his words as an injunction to kill. The ambiguity in his message made even the most faithful Apache friends of the whites uneasy, and the normally cheerful and voluble White Mountain scouts became sullen and uncommunicative. Doubting their fidelity, Lieutenant Thomas Cruse, Gatewood's successor as commanding officer of the Indian scout company at Camp Apache, recommended his men be discharged and replaced with friendly Yuma Indians. Colonel Eugene Carr, the commanding officer at Camp Apache, agreed. While awaiting permission from department headquarters to dismiss Cruse's scouts, Carr seized their rifles and ammunition, an act of bad faith that probably contributed to the very disloyalty that Cruse and Carr feared. One scout wondered if there was something "wrong with his head" to make Carr act as he had.[24]

Meanwhile, Apache informers had warned Agent Tiffany that Nock-ay-det-klinne was fomenting unrest on Cibecue Creek, and he summoned the shaman to San Carlos to explain himself. When Nock-ay-det-klinne declined to come in, Tiffany grew furious, demanding that Carr "arrest or kill him or both"—the sooner the better. Taken aback by Tiffany's extreme solution, in early August Carr telegraphed the commander of the Department of Arizona, Colonel Orlando B. Willcox, for instructions. Instead, Willcox left the matter to Carr's discretion. No sooner had Carr received Willcox's reply than torrential rainstorms severed the only telegraph line between Fort Apache and the outside world.

Carr fretted and temporized. He invited Nock-ay-det-klinne to Fort Apache for a talk, but the medicine man demurred. Most of Carr's officers expected hostilities. A friendly White Mountain chief, however, assured him that Nock-ay-det-klinne was about to face his come-uppance from followers who felt he had swindled them. The colonel didn't know whom or what to believe.[25]

Two weeks passed. The corn harvest, which the Apaches celebrated with prolonged drunks and frequent gunplay, drew near. Tiffany's orders to kill or arrest the shaman stood, and with the telegraph line still down Carr saw no alternative but to bring in Nock-ay-det-klinne. On August 29, 1881, he started for the shaman's village with two cavalry companies and Cruse's twenty-three Apache scouts, who remained a sullen lot. The colonel's decision to bring them along was unpopular with at least one officer. "Are you for us or are you going to help the Indians at the Cibecue?" he chided them on the march. The scouts kept silent.[26]

On the hot, bright afternoon of August 30, Carr's column entered the broad Cibecue Creek valley, Cruse and the scouts in the lead. As they neared Nock-ay-det-klinne's wickiup, the medicine man emerged, adorned in eagle feathers and body paint of many hues. He greeted Cruse gravely.[27]

Carr cantered up with the cavalry. He and the interpreter dismounted and approached the shaman. Seventy-nine troopers deployed in a mounted line of battle facing his wickiup. Armed warriors, women, children, and White Mountain scouts mingled within earshot of Carr. What they heard could hardly have reassured the Indians. Carr told Nock-ay-det-klinne to come back to the fort with him for a talk. If all went well, Nock-ay-det-klinne would be free to return to his *ranchería*. No harm would come to him unless he tried to escape—in which case, Carr said, he would kill him. The shaman smiled and replied that he was perfectly willing to go. The colonel seemed unable to quit while he was ahead. He told Nock-ay-det-klinne that any rescue attempt would also end in his death. The shaman smiled again. Carr ordered First Sergeant Cut-Mouth Moses of the scout company and Sergeant John F. McDonald to take charge of the prisoner and then started off with Captain Edmund C. Hentig and his cavalry company to make camp two miles downstream. Carr and Hentig congratulated each other on a job well done. Carr confessed that he "was rather ashamed to come out with all this force to arrest one poor little Indian." Hentig, for his part, considered the matter "a case of great cry and little wool."[28]

Lieutenant Cruse wasn't so sure. Had Carr spared a moment to look behind him, he might have noticed that half his command was unaccounted for. Nock-ay-det-klinne had not been quite ready to go. After Carr's abbreviated column vanished around a bend in the stream, he had asked for, and Sergeant McDonald had granted him, time to eat a hasty meal, gather his family, and have his pony brought in. While the scouts and the rest of the cavalry waited, the mood of the village turned ugly. One hundred armed warriors gathered on an adjacent mesa. The pony was slow in coming, and as the minutes passed, the tension grew. Cruse felt "as if I was standing on a can of dynamite with a quick fuse attached." At last, the pony appeared, and Nock-ay-det-klinne departed quietly in custody, but behind him the crowd of watching Indians buzzed like an angry rattlesnake.[29]

Carr pitched camp on a low mesa beside Cibecue Creek. Cruse reported in with the prisoner a short time later. Close behind came the armed Apache throng. "Those Indians mustn't come into camp!" snapped an obviously surprised Carr. "Direct troop commanders to keep them out!" Captain Hentig started toward the Indians, yelling, "U-ka-she! U-ka-she! Get away! Get away!" The Indians halted, all but one, whom Hentig caught by the arm. "U-ka-she!" Hentig repeated. The man told Hentig he was a scout, and the agitated captain shoved him toward the camp. A minute later, Lieutenant Cruse recalled, "all hell broke loose." Who fired first will never be known. One thing is certain, however, and that is the identity of the first casualty—Captain Hentig. According to a cavalry farrier standing fifteen feet away, after the opening volley the scout that Hentig had shoved spun around, knelt, and shot the captain in the back at point-blank range. He was likely dead before he hit the ground.

"Kill the medicine man!" shouted Carr. Cut-Mouth Moses was sitting beside Nock-ay-det-klinne on a packsaddle when Carr gave the order. Sergeant McDonald fired once and missed. He shot again, and Nock-ay-det-klinne, with a bullet in his skull, slumped over silently. Moses jumped behind the saddle. "That's all I saw. I could hear the doctor breathing." Observing his chest rise and fall, a young trumpeter placed his pistol muzzle against the medicine man's neck and pulled the trigger.[30]

The shooting of Nock-ay-det-klinne infuriated the Apache scouts, and without warning or premeditation they mutinied, firing two ragged volleys at the soldiers and then joining Cibecue warriors in the underbrush along the creek bottom. Other scouts, startled by the turn of events, fled from the scene when the soldiers returned the fire.[31]

Lieutenant Cruse could make no sense of the melee. "Practically all that happened occurred explosively, almost simultaneously." There was no mistaking Colonel Carr's actions, however. He moved among his supine soldiers calmly on horseback. "For God's sake, General, get under cover or you'll be killed sure," the first sergeant cried. "Oh, God damn these whelps, they can't hit me," replied Carr coolly. "God damn 'em."[32]

Finding his command "unanimous in the wish to get out of there," Carr withdrew after dusk. The colonel had lost one officer (Captain Hentig) and six enlisted men killed and two troopers wounded. All of the scouts except Cut-Mouth Moses were gone. Carr estimated that fewer than sixty Indians, including the mutinous scouts, had grappled with his command at the onset of the affair and that no more than two hundred had fought him at any time.

The only known Indian casualty was Nock-ay-det-klinne, and he proved a hard man to kill. Before quitting the field, Carr told his adjutant, Lieutenant William H. Carter, to examine the medicine man's body. Carter found him saturated with blood from head to chest. Part of his skull was caved in. But Nock-ay-det-klinne clung to life. There remained only one option—finish him off quietly. Setting aside his rifle, Carr's civilian guide split Nock-ay-det-klinne's skull in twain with an ax. "The recovery of this Indian, if left in the hands of his friends," a subordinate later wrote by way of legitimizing the murder, "would have given him a commanding influence over these superstitious people, which would have resulted in endless war."[33]

*

Nock-ay-det-klinne achieved no martyrdom in death. On the contrary, the medicine man's failure to resurrect even himself disillusioned his adherents. Those who had come to Cibecue Creek strictly to dance and pay homage to him hurried home to San Carlos. Left without the symbolic, unifying presence of Nock-ay-det-klinne, his warriors broke into loose bands. They killed three Mormon travelers and a detail of three soldiers and then reunited just long enough to strike Fort Apache on September 1, setting several outbuildings ablaze and running off a herd of cattle before Carr's exhausted troopers and the infantry garrison repelled them. The brief attack had the distinction of being the only purposeful assault on an army post during the Indian Wars. The scouts, meanwhile, being officially classified as deserters, had scattered to the wind. A few holed up as far west as Salt River Canyon.[34]

With the telegraph line to Fort Apache still down, wild rumors circulated about the fate of Carr and his men. Newspapers cast Cibecue Creek as another Custer massacre, with not a man left alive to tell the tale. The army high command panicked. General Willcox wired his superior, the Division of the Pacific commander, Major General Irvin McDowell, that the Navajos had left their reservation in northern New Mexico to hold war dances near San Carlos. General McDowell took the madness a step further. He telegraphed General Sherman that the entire Arizona Territory was ablaze and that Apache war parties were even waylaying railroad trains. On September 8, the telegraph operator at Fort Apache tapped out the first message from the post in nearly a month. The telegram should have reassured the army leadership. There had been no grand outbreak. Carr and most of his troops were alive, and the partly charred Fort Apache still flew the Stars and Stripes. Although the Indians' whereabouts were uncertain, General Pope speculated that they were in hiding, "as much stampeded about what they have done as the people of Arizona are."

Pope was correct. General Willcox had four strong columns sweeping the reservation for the hostiles, who themselves were hurrying to the San Carlos Agency to give up before the army caught them. All they wanted was a fair trial and good legal counsel. Even some of the ex-scouts turned themselves in. Willcox continued military operations nevertheless but moved too slowly to suit Sherman, who still thought he had a major Indian war on his hands. "I want this annual Apache stampede to end right now," he wired General McDowell on September 16, "and to effect that result will send every available man in the whole army if necessary." By the time the first reinforcements arrived, the last of the Cibecue warriors had surrendered, thus ending the imagined Apache war.[35]

Three months later, under calmer conditions, General McDowell made a careful study of the official reports of events leading up to the Cibecue imbroglio and concluded that Nock-ay-det-klinne's arrest had been unjust. "It was not for any overt act," McDowell wrote, "but for what he said—or it was said he had said—not for anything done but for something feared" that he had been killed. McDowell also believed that the medicine man's warriors were blameless of any wrongdoing beyond trying "to rescue an influential man of their tribe who, whatever he may have been to them—as demagogue, quack, pretender, fortune teller, swindler, or simply fanatic, had committed no act of hostility on the whites." General Willcox had incarcerated sixty-eight warriors and wanted them exiled from Arizona. McDowell dissented and appealed to the secretary of war to return to the reservation all but those few who had committed murders subsequent to the Cibecue affair, for which they merited trial by civil courts. The secretary agreed and ordered their immediate release.

The mutinous scouts, however, were another matter. For them, McDowell felt no compassion. He approved the court-martial of five— all of whom had surrendered voluntarily—on charges of mutiny, desertion, and murder. Two were dishonorably discharged and sentenced to long terms at Alcatraz. Three scouts—including Sergeant Dead Shot, who stood accused of inciting the scouts to fire on the soldiers—were hanged. Later that day, Dead Shot's wife hanged herself. Lieutenant Cruse believed the sentence unjust. "I have always regretted the fate of Dead Shot. [He] was the sage of the company. I doubted at the time if he had [an] intentional part in the firing upon us. It seemed to me that he was swept into the fight by excitement and the force of evil circumstances."[36]

Cruse's judgment was a fitting epitaph for all who died at Cibecue Creek. If the demise of Nock-ay-det-klinne had brought a lasting peace to Apacheria, then it might have been said that something good had emerged from the tragedy—that perhaps a lesson in restraint and mutual understanding had at last been learned. But the confused shots fired on Cibecue Creek in August 1881 would prove merely the opening volley of six long years of renewed violence in Apacheria. Before it was over, Apache raiders would cut a bloody swath across southeastern Arizona, the U.S. Army would plunge into the Sierra Madre of Mexico and undergo assassinations and betrayal, one Chiricahua band would be all but obliterated, and the entire tribe would be exiled to a distant land. For much of the tumult, one man would bear the blame. His name was Geronimo.

CHAPTER 20

LIKE SO MANY VULTURES,
GREEDY FOR BLOOD

M ANY YEARS after the Apache Wars were over, Chatto, who was a rising Chokonen leader in the early 1880s, would declare, "I have known Geronimo all my life up to his death and have never known anything good about him." The daughter of the Chokonen chief Naiche agreed. "Geronimo was not a great man at all. I never heard any good of him. People never say he [did] good." A reliable interpreter and licensed trader who lived on good terms with the Chiricahuas for two decades said they distrusted and feared Geronimo, especially when he was inebriated. Once while hopelessly drunk, he berated a nephew, "for no reason at all," so severely that the young man committed suicide. After sobering up, a shamed Geronimo packed up his family and bolted from the reservation for several months.[1]

Army officers otherwise sympathetic to the Apaches detested Geronimo. Lieutenant Bourke found him "a depraved rascal whose neck I should like to stretch." He was a "thoroughly vicious, intractable, and treacherous man," agreed Lieutenant Britton Davis, who would come to know him all too well. "His only redeeming traits were courage and determination."[2]

And "power," Davis might have added, had he understood the concept. What the whites dismissed as superstition was quite real to the Chiricahuas. That Geronimo possessed mystic attributes uniquely valuable in raids and war, few Apaches doubted. Rifles were said to jam or misfire when aimed at him. Some warriors thought the mere act of riding with Geronimo would render them impervious to bullets, a belief this consummate troublemaker heartily encouraged. Many Chiricahuas also attributed to him the gift of divination. Others thought him able to make it rain or to prevent the sun from rising. Geronimo also enjoyed a reputation as a master herbalist and surgeon. Despite his supposed powers, he was too strongly disliked to ever become a chief. His baleful countenance, locked in a perpetual scowl, probably didn't help. All told, Geronimo's personal following never exceeded thirty warriors.[3]

The minatory shaman of the Bedonkohe band was born Goyahkla, meaning "He Who Yawns," in 1829. Because he was saddled with such a singularly uninspiring name, it is little wonder he assumed the name Geronimo, which the Mexicans had bestowed on him. The Spanish equivalent of Jerome, it lacked the verve of Victorio but certainly was a better name than Goyahkla. Unlike Victorio, Geronimo felt no compelling ties to the place of his birth. He fought not to defend a homeland but to avenge the murder of his mother, first wife, and children by Mexican soldiers and because he enjoyed taking lives. "I have killed many Mexicans; I do not know how many. Some of them were not worth counting," he said shortly before his death. If he were young again, Geronimo added, "and followed the warpath, it would lead into Old Mexico."

Geronimo's forays into Mexico often led him to the Sierra Madre, home to the Nednhi Chiricahua band of Chief Juh, one of his few real friends. Although a better war leader than Geronimo, Juh lacked the shaman's gift for oratory. When excited, particularly in battle, Juh stuttered so badly that he had to use hand signals to communicate or rely on Geronimo to make his intentions known. Both men were wary of Americans. Juh had had little contact with them; he was naturally suspicious of everyone. Geronimo's distrust derived from personal experience—first the murderous betrayal of Mangas Coloradas in 1863, and then his own humiliating arrest at Ojo Caliente and lockup at San Carlos by Agent John Clum in 1877.[4]

*

In January 1880, Juh and Geronimo settled at the Chiricahua subagency, surprising everyone. Their halfhearted decision did not derive from any sudden fondness for Americans. Rather, they had suffered a series of heavy blows from an increasingly competent Mexican army. (Victorio was also abandoning his Mexican haunts.)

San Carlos had become a byword for discord and despair. No uniting figure had emerged after Cochise's death, and in less than a decade warfare and disease had reduced the Chiricahua population from 1,244 to just over 800. The Chihennes were split between Loco's following at San Carlos and Victorio's soon-to-be-decimated people. The Bedonko- hes no longer existed as a separate band. The extended family group to which Geronimo belonged merged with the Nednhis, but most of the Bedonkohes cast their lot with the Chokonens. Geronimo shuttled between both troubled Bedonkohe groups. The Chokonens too had more than their share of problems. While on a visit to Washington, D.C., Cochise's elder son, the peaceable Taza, had died of pneumonia. Cochise's younger son, twenty-three-year-old Naiche, succeeded Taza as Chokonen chief.[5]

Naiche was no Cochise, and he knew it. Standing six feet two, strong, slender, and strikingly handsome, he bore an uncanny resem- blance to his father. But there the similarity ended. Naiche was an able warrior. Affable and fair-minded, he also made a reasonably competent chief in times of peace. He lacked, however, both the temperament of a war leader and mystical power, the latter a critical shortcoming that Geronimo happily exploited, formulating strategy and making the hard decisions for Naiche, whose distinguished lineage in turn lent Geron- imo a modicum of respectability. Theirs might have been a symbiotic relationship, but it was also a tense one. Naiche sometimes resented Geronimo, and they were never friends.[6]

Not all the Chiricahuas bowed to Geronimo. Chatto and Chihua- hua, two important Chokonen leaders, were utterly immune to him. In contrast to his low opinion of Geronimo, Lieutenant Davis came to regard Chatto as one of the finest men he had ever known. Chatto would cooperate with Geronimo only when it suited his purposes. Chi- huahua was a year older than Geronimo. A subchief of great courage and ability, dignified and polite, Chihuahua was also his own man. In 1879, while Juh and Geronimo were busy despoiling Mexican villages, Chihuahua served as an army scout in the operations against Victorio.

Such was the fragile and fragmented state of Chiricahua society. It took an army blunder, a chief's lies, and an underlying paranoia to unite the discordant Chiricahua leaders.[7]

*

September 30, 1881, was ration day at the San Carlos subagency. By regulation, the chiefs drew rations for their bands and distributed them.

Among the chiefs receiving rations at the subagency were the White Mountain Apaches Bonito and George, whose *rancherías* lay near those of the Chiricahuas. Bonito and George also happened to be suspects in the attack on Fort Apache that had followed the Cibecue Creek affair. The two had agreed to turn themselves in that afternoon to an army major who was waiting at the subagency with three troops of cavalry. Bonito was about to surrender when George reneged on his promise. The vexed major sent his scouts to George's *ranchería* to arrest him, but they botched the assignment, seizing nearly everyone in the village except George, who fled to the Chiricahua camps with an absurd story calculated to arouse them. The soldiers, he announced, were coming to kill their women and children, arrest and shackle the chiefs, and then deport them to some distant place. George offered no reason why the army wanted the Chiricahuas, but his lie had the desired effect. That evening, the chiefs held a council to decide on a course of action. Geronimo and Juh announced their intention to break out rather than risk Mangas Coloradas's fate. Chatto put in with them. Geronimo's persuasive powers got the better of Naiche, and he too agreed to go. Chihuahua hesitated; he bolted only after he mistakenly thought he saw troops heading toward his *ranchería*.

On the night of September 30, 1881, 375 Chiricahuas, including 74 warriors, slipped silently away from San Carlos. Chief George was not among them. He had double-crossed the Chiricahuas and returned to his *ranchería*. Bonito, on the other hand, joined the exodus.

The Chiricahuas struck out for Juh's stronghold in the Sierra Madre. En route, they killed anyone who came between them and their destination. General Willcox was powerless to stop the Chiricahuas, because most of his troops were tracking down fugitives from the Cibecue. After a four-day, unimpeded flight, they crossed the international border and linked up with Nana's band of Tres Castillos survivors, bringing the number of Chiricahuas in Mexico to 450. Once ensconced in the Sierra Madre, they established a routine of alternately negotiating with Mexican authorities and killing Mexican civilians.[8]

When not occupied with the Mexicans, the Chiricahua chiefs gave considerable thought to "freeing" Chiricahuas still at San Carlos. Two small bands under the inconsequential chiefs Zele and Chiva could easily be induced to leave. Chief Loco's Chihennes, however, presented a problem. By all accounts, Loco's people were content. The agents at San Carlos might have been corrupt, but all except John Clum showed a genuine interest in the Chihennes, granting them off-reservation privileges to hunt or to work for wages on white-owned ranches. Other Chihennes found jobs with the agency police force. Most raised livestock, and a few had taken up farming.

The prosperity of the Chihennes galled Geronimo. Loco had always aroused his antipathy, the more so now that it appeared his peaceable ways had paid off. Dragging Loco's people into Mexico was a potent attraction to Chiricahua warriors with time on their hands. And so Geronimo proposed an expedition to San Carlos to liberate the unwilling and to steal their livestock, only to find all the leaders wanting in enthusiasm except the pliable Naiche, and with good cause: there were more than two thousand American soldiers deployed in southern Arizona. Only after the hot-tempered, pistol-toting wife of a subchief declared her intention to join Geronimo did the wavering leaders feel sufficiently shamed to join the enterprise.

If Geronimo's dislike of Loco merely reflected his general contempt for peaceable and prosperous souls, Loco, on the other hand, had profound cause to despise Geronimo. It was the Bedonkohe shaman who had led the troublemaking squatters on the Ojo Caliente Reservation in 1877, which provoked the government into deporting the Chihennes to San Carlos. That began the downward spiral for the band that ended at Tres Castillos. In a very real sense, Geronimo was the agent of Victorio's ultimate destruction.

Geronimo made no attempt to disguise his intentions. He sent three separate messengers to Loco, threatening the chief with forced removal and giving the date for his abduction as early April 1882. Loco apprised Tiffany of Geronimo's intentions, and the agent relocated the band's *ranchería* to within a mile of the San Carlos Agency, while the army laid a heavy dragnet across Geronimo's probable path. Loco also offered a foolproof solution to the renegade Chiricahuas' threat to the peaceable Chihennes: Why not move his people to the Navajo Reservation in faraway northern New Mexico?

There was nothing far-fetched about Loco's proposal. He had already discussed the possibility with a Navajo chief to whom he was related by marriage. Both the Navajos and the Chihennes unanimously endorsed the move. Almost everyone in both the civilian and the army chains of command in Arizona liked the idea, but the military division commander vetoed the idea, sealing Loco's fate.

On April 19, Geronimo struck. A half century later, the Chihenne

Jason Betzinez, who was then a teenager—he could hardly be called a warrior, because neither he nor the thirty-two men of Loco's band owned weapons—recalled the fateful moment, when at sunrise "we heard shouts along the river. Running out of our [wickiup] we saw a line of Apache warriors coming our way with guns in their hands. Geronimo repeatedly shouted, 'Take them all! Shoot down anyone who refuses to go with us!' "

Loco tried to reason with Geronimo until Chatto stuck a gun in the Chihenne chief's face; after that, "We did everything they told us to do," said Betzinez, who with the other 179 Chihennes was driven from his village on foot "with nothing but a handful of clothing and other belongings."[9]

That afternoon, Loco's captors chanced upon three freight wagons laden with nine hundred gallons of liquor. While they drank, Loco slipped his eldest wife and twenty-five other relatives out of camp and told them to head for the Navajo Reservation. After Geronimo and the raiders sobered up, they herded Loco and the remaining Chihennes toward the Mexican border. Along the way, Geronimo fought an inconclusive skirmish with the army, pillaged ranches, swept up livestock, and killed randomly, torturing men in every imaginable way, roasting women alive, and tossing children into nests of needle-crowned cacti.

Geronimo had staged the greatest raid in Apache history, but his leadership on the return trip to the Sierra Madre left much to be desired. On April 28, two troops of U.S. cavalry that had crossed illegally into Mexico attacked Geronimo while he held a two-day bacchanalia at a desert oasis forty miles short of the Sierra Madre stronghold. Twelve men and several women, most of them innocent Chihennes, were killed and dozens more wounded. After that, Geronimo restored a modicum of order to the march, establishing a strong rear guard under his command two miles behind Loco's people and assigning Naiche and Chatto to scout ahead of the Chihennes.

At daylight on April 29, the Sierra Madre grew visible, five miles distant. The way to the mountains followed the bone-dry Alisos Creek through a small arroyo. As the Chihennes plodded along beside the creek, Naiche, Chatto, and their warriors galloped on to sheltering foothills a mile and a half away, where they paused to smoke and contemplate the two hundred Mexican soldiers hidden in a shallow ravine astride the Chihennes' path. Inexplicably, they neither warned the Chihennes nor lifted a finger to prevent the ambush that followed. The

Mexicans might have been unaware that the Chihennes traveled as captives. Not that the knowledge would have changed what followed; to the Mexicans, all Apaches were alike and equally deserving of death.

The Chihennes, none of them armed, filed into the streambed, and Alisos Creek exploded with gunfire. Jason Betzinez scarcely trusted his senses. "Whole families were slaughtered on the spot, unable to defend themselves. These were people who had never been off the reservation, had never given any trouble, and were from the most peace-loving band of Apaches." Geronimo and his warriors repelled several Mexican attacks and then left the Chihennes to fend for themselves. Before Geronimo pulled out, some of the Chihennes claimed that he told the women to strangle their babies and small children to prevent them from crying and revealing his movements. The story may be apocryphal slander. What is certain, however, is that Geronimo abandoned the Chihennes at the first opportunity and that Naiche and Chatto, for reasons known only to themselves, remained mere observers of the slaughter.

The Alisos Creek massacre was the crowning catastrophe for the Chihennes. Seventy-eight Chiricahuas died, nearly all of them Chihennes. Thirty-three Chihenne women and girls were captured and sold into slavery, including Loco's beautiful fifteen-year-old daughter. Of the 180 Chihennes who had been abducted from San Carlos, perhaps 40 survived. These Geronimo gathered up and took to Juh's stronghold. Hardly pleased to see the Nednhis—Betzinez called Juh's people "outlaw Indians who when they couldn't find anyone else to mistreat fought among themselves"—the Chihennes settled in for what they knew would be a long stay. In the eyes of the U.S. government, they too were now outlaws.[10]

✻

With trouble aplenty closer to home, General Willcox had little interest in the Chiricahuas in Mexico. After Cibecue Creek, fifty-three recalcitrant warriors and seven fugitive scouts had coalesced under the leadership of the Cibecue subchief Na-ti-o-tish. For nearly a year, they hid in the deepest recesses of the White Mountain Reservation, where, Willcox told the War Department, they presented "a standing menace . . . and a nucleus for renegades." He requested permission to post a liberal reward for their capture, dead or alive, which the War Department denied while also reminding the general that troops were forbidden to operate on the reservation. Willcox's hands were tied.

Na-ti-o-tish inadvertently untied them. On July 6, 1882, he ambushed the San Carlos Agency Indian police and then headed for the Tonto Basin, one step ahead of pursuing soldiers, stealing cattle and killing settlers. On July 17, Na-ti-o-tish challenged the army to a stand-up fight atop Mogollon Rim. Believing he faced only one troop of cavalry, Na-ti-o-tish deployed his warriors along the edge of a deep, narrow canyon called Big Dry Wash in ambush. In fact, there were five cavalry troops—over 150 men—converging on his position. In the ensuing clash, Na-ti-o-tish and twenty-seven Apaches were killed. The rest melted back onto the reservation. Willcox had achieved a decisive victory, but it came too late. Cibecue Creek and Geronimo's San Carlos raid had cost him the confidence of General Sherman and infuriated Arizonans; Apache unrest was bad for business, frightening off big mining interests and wealthy cattlemen, and the territorial press helped orchestrate his removal. In August, Willcox left for New York, where he marked time until his retirement four years later.

Sherman turned to the one man he knew capable of restoring order in Arizona: George Crook.[11]

*

General Crook assumed command of the Department of Arizona on September 4, 1882, with mixed feelings. The "constant wear and tear" of thirty-one years of field service had taken a heavy toll on him. The general was bone tired and wanted a desk job. But the assignment fed his ego. Events had born out his oft-repeated, and just as frequently ignored, prediction that the Howard-Cochise accord had only postponed the day of reckoning with the Chiricahuas. That the government considered him the only man capable of subduing Geronimo pleased Crook immensely.[12]

For the moment, however, Geronimo would have to wait. Affairs in Arizona demanded Crook's full attention. A week after his arrival, Crook saddled up his mule Apache, donned his familiar canvas suit and pith helmet, and rode out from department headquarters to hear the reservation Apaches' grievances. Warriors and ex-scouts hidden in the mountains since the Cibecue now flocked to him, and Apaches who had remained loyal told Crook they had been punished without cause; one chief was even thrown in the guardhouse for six months because he had offered to help track down the renegades.[13]

Finding the Apaches' complaints uniformly credible, Crook was grateful for their "remarkable forbearance in remaining at peace," and he worked fast to make certain they stayed that way. Admonishing his officers to redress all Indian grievances and to employ force only as a last resort, Crook also absolved the Apaches of guilt in the Cibecue Creek affair, mutinous scouts excepted. Speaking of Nock-ay-det-klinne's followers, he observed, "If these Indians had been in earnest, not one of our soldiers could have gotten away from there alive."[14]

Crook assembled the Apache and Yavapai chiefs and headmen at San Carlos to explain the new order. To maintain discipline, every male of fighting age (of which there were some fifteen hundred on the reservation) would be issued a numbered tag. Those found off the reservation or without tags would be treated as hostile. On the reservation, the Indians would be permitted to settle wherever they pleased; their chiefs would be held accountable for their conduct. In exchange for the privilege of selecting their homes, they must cultivate crops and raise stock. With that concession, Crook won over the Cibecue and White Mountain Apaches, who could finally put San Carlos behind them for good. Crook said he would enlist as scouts only men of the highest character and standing. When the scouts were not on campaign, he expected them to guide their people toward self-government. Army officers would implement Crook's policies: Captain Emmet Crawford as military commander of the White Mountain Reservation; Lieutenant Charles B. Gatewood as commander of the Apache scouts, with headquarters at Fort Apache; and Lieutenant Britton Davis as chief of the Indian police at the San Carlos Agency. They would prove to be the wisest personnel assignments Crook made during his long career, and all three would play crucial roles in the events to come.[15]

The thirty-eight-year-old Crawford epitomized the ideal officer. Superiors and subordinates alike esteemed him, and the Indians respected him for his fairness and devotion to their best interests. "Gallant," "noble," "gentlemanly," "chivalrous," and "kindhearted" were the words his army contemporaries most frequently used to describe Crawford. His long and narrow head, Vandyke beard, and piercing gray eyes gave the six-foot-one Crawford the appearance of a middle-aged Don Quixote. In common with the legendary knight errant, his greatest wish was that "he might die in the act of saving others." The Apaches called him Tall Chief.

A veteran of the Victorio Campaign, Charles B. Gatewood shared Captain Crawford's remarkable courage and high principles. Unlike Crawford, however, he never truly warmed to the Apaches, who called him Beak Chief.

Fresh out of the military academy, twenty-two-year-old Britton Davis carried himself with poise unusual in one so young. Quick thinking and sharp-witted, Davis dealt squarely with the Apaches and came to relish their company. They called him Stout Chief.

None of Crook's program would have been possible without the cooperation of the Indian agent Philip P. Wilcox, who endorsed Crook's concept of shared military-civilian control over the reservation, in part because he wanted to spend as little time in Arizona—which he called "a hole not fit for a dog"—as necessary to keep his job. To excuse his absence, Wilcox proclaimed, "The days for general [Apache] outbreaks are over; there will be no more of them; the last wrinkle has been taken out of their war blankets, and they are as gentle and docile as lambs." Crook shared the truant agent's optimism, telling the secretary of the interior that he had so perfected the military administration at San Carlos that "scarcely a pin can drop" among the Indians without his officers knowing of it at once.[16]

Restoring order to the White Mountain Reservation had been no small achievement. Achieving a lasting peace in the Arizona Territory, however, would be impossible so long as Chiricahuas in large numbers lurked in the Sierra Madre. A cross-border raid by the renegades was inevitable, but running them down once they slipped into Arizona would be like chasing the wind. Crook insisted that the only way to beat the hostile Chiricahuas was to surprise them in their Sierra Madre sanctuary. Crook was right, but a foray into Mexico hinged on four factors: first, he must have just cause to cross the border; second, he needed a reliable guide to lead him to the Chiricahuas; third, he needed the cooperation of, or at least no interference from, Mexican authorities; and fourth, he needed permission from his own superiors.[17]

The expected raid came on March 21, 1883, when a party led by Chatto swept into Arizona. Things didn't go quite as intended. The raiders ran off plenty of horses and killed whites who stood in their way, but when they approached the San Carlos Agency to recruit and to pilfer agency supplies, not only did the reservation Apaches shun them, but some also volunteered to repel the raiders. Chatto's chagrined warriors fled empty-handed, less one man killed and one defector. The turncoat was a Cibecue Apache named Pah-na-yo-tishn, whom the sol-

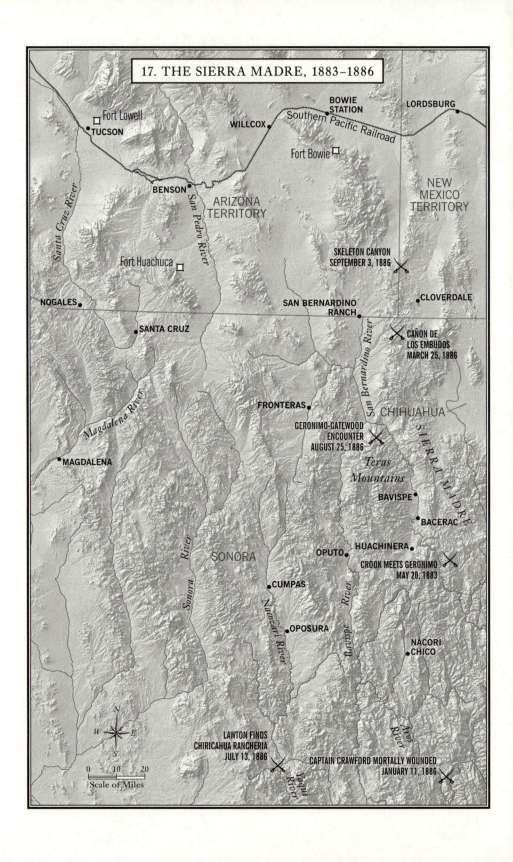

17. THE SIERRA MADRE, 1883–1886

LORDSBURG

BOWIE
STATION

WILLCOX

Southern Pacific Railroad

☐ Fort Lowell
TUCSON

Fort Bowie ☐

NEW
MEXICO
TERRITORY

BENSON

ARIZONA
TERRITORY

Santa Cruz River

San Pedro River

Fort Huachuca ☐

SKELETON CANYON
SEPTEMBER 3, 1886 ✕

CLOVERDALE

NOGALES

SAN BERNARDINO
RANCH

SANTA CRUZ

CAÑON DE
LOS EMBUDOS
MARCH 25, 1886 ✕

San Bernardino River

Magdalena River

FRONTERAS

CHIHUAHUA

GERONIMO-GATEWOOD
ENCOUNTER
AUGUST 25, 1886 ✕

S I E R R A   M A D R E

MAGDALENA

*Teras
Mountains*

BAVISPE

BACERAC

Sonora River

SONORA

OPUTO

HUACHINERA

CROOK MEETS GERONIMO
MAY 20, 1883 ✕

CUMPAS

Bavispe River

Nacozari River

OPOSURA

NACORI
CHICO

N
W   E
S

Aros River

LAWTON FINDS
CHIRICAHUA RANCHERIA
JULY 13, 1886 ✕

CAPTAIN CRAWFORD MORTALLY WOUNDED
JANUARY 11, 1886 ✕

Yaqui River

0   10   20
Scale of Miles

diers nicknamed Peaches because of his light complexion and smooth skin. Peaches offered to lead Crook to the Chiricahua stronghold, and Crook heartily accepted.[18]

Chatto's raid was a godsend to Crook, giving him both a persuasive reason to enter Mexico and a guide. He hastened to meet with Mexican authorities in Chihuahua and Sonora who promised to interpose no objections to his proposed campaign. But Crook still faced a dilemma, because the existing convention between the United States and Mexico permitted American troops to enter Mexico only in "hot pursuit" of Indian marauders, and the campaign a hundred miles beyond the border that Crook contemplated hardly qualified as "hot pursuit." The secretary of war reminded him that "*no* military movements must be made into or within Mexico not authorized [by treaty]," an order Crook acknowledged, then set about to circumvent. Crook was walking himself onto a fragile limb. Should his expedition fail or the Mexicans create difficulties for him, Crook could count his career finished. It was a hazard he was willing to accept.

✳

On May 1, 1883, General Crook crossed the border with the most militarily unorthodox Indian-fighting force ever seen on the western frontier, consisting of 193 Western Apache auxiliaries under Lieutenant Gatewood; 2 civilian scouts; 3 interpreters; an immense train of pack mules tended by 79 packers; Crook's factotum John Bourke, now a captain; and 45 cavalrymen. Crook told higher headquarters to expect him back in two months. That was the last anyone would hear from him for more than a month.[19]

The cavalry company was largely ornamental; success depended on the fidelity and tracking abilities of Peaches and the Apache auxiliaries. It was a great risk, but one that Crook had to run. "In warfare with the Indians it has been my policy—and the only effective one—to use them against each other," he told a reporter before leaving on the expedition. "Nothing breaks them up like turning their own people against them." Although their willingness to actually shoot fellow Apaches might be in doubt, there was no question that Crook's Indians wanted to find them and put a stop to the outbreaks that left San Carlos in a state of near-constant turmoil. As Crook was about to discover to his immense satisfaction, of all the Indians the army was to make war with in the

American West, the Apaches would prove the most disunited and the most willing to turn on one another.

For three days, Crook's column traveled due south without seeing a single human being. Decades of Apache raids had blighted the landscape. Where once there had been prosperous haciendas, there were now only lonely ruins. In the villages, hollow-eyed Mexicans gawked at the soldiers and cast terrified glances at the Apache scouts. Food was scarce. Only mescal liquor was to be had in abundance. Bourke, who spoke fluent Spanish, said that the people lived "in a condition of squalor and poverty beyond description . . . in a worse position than that now occupied by the Chiricahuas. Even the scouts felt sorry for them."[20]

On May 8, Crook ascended the Sierra Madre until at forty-six hundred feet above sea level the main trail unraveled in a perplexing web of paths strewn with the detritus of Apache despolation. Bourke found the going unendurable. "We led our horses and mules up and down, up and down, the animals sweating, and we bathed in perspiration," the captain wrote in his diary. "To look at this country is grand; to travel in it is Hell. And yet, up and down these ridges our Apache scouts, when the idea seized them, ran like deer."

The next day, Peaches warned Crook that the hostile *rancherías* were near; it was time to unleash the Apache auxiliaries. On the afternoon of May 10, Crook held a final conference and found the Apaches unanimous in the opinion that Geronimo and Juh should be summarily shot if found. Admonishing them to spare women and children, Crook saw off Crawford and his Apaches the next morning. Four days later, they fell upon the *rancherías*. All the leaders except Chihuahua and most of the men were out plundering Mexicans. Stunned to find their sanctuary invaded, the few warriors who remained offered only token resistance.[21]

Geronimo was 120 miles away when his devotees claimed the distant attack awakened his mystic power. The impressionable Jason Betzinez, now a devotee of the shaman, marveled at his supposed gift of divination. "We were sitting there eating, Geronimo with a knife in one hand and a chunk of beef in the other. All at once he dropped the knife, saying, 'Men, our people whom we left at our base camp are now in the hands of U.S. troops! What shall we do?'" Everyone agreed to return at once. Of Geronimo's clairvoyance, Betzinez could offer no explanation beyond "I was there and saw it."[22]

Meanwhile, the demoralized renegades gradually drifted into

Crook's camp. Chihuahua confessed to him that the Chiricahuas had assumed the Sierra Madre to be impenetrable. But now that American soldiers and their Western Apache allies had breached their sanctuary, Chihuahua said the time had come to surrender. On the morning of May 20, Geronimo and his men appeared on the bluffs above Crook's camp. They looked, Bourke said, "like so many vultures, greedy for blood." But Geronimo was a broken man. Clearly Crook possessed stronger power than he, for in no other way could an American have found the Chiricahuas' remote *rancherías*.

Crook took full advantage of Geronimo's frayed nerves. When Geronimo attempted to parley, Crook told him to go to hell; he was tired of broken Chiricahua promises. If they wanted a fight, he would accommodate them. Otherwise, the Mexican troops were closing in fast, Crook said, and "it was only a matter of days until the last of [the Chiricahuas] should be under the ground." Geronimo departed visibly shaken. Having humbled him, Crook softened his stance over breakfast the next morning, telling Geronimo, Naiche, and Chatto that he had come not to make war but to take them back to San Carlos as friends. Then he made a shrewd concession. Because he did not fear the Chiricahuas, he would not deprive them of their arms. But they must decide: Was it to be war or the reservation? Geronimo acquiesced. "We give up. Do with us as you please." He, Naiche, and the subchiefs, however, were not yet ready to leave Mexico. First they had to round up their people. With rations running dangerously low and several hundred new mouths to feed, Crook could not tarry. Taking Geronimo at his word, he started home.[23]

One Chiricahua leader had been notable by his absence from the councils—Juh. In January 1883, the Mexicans had done the unimaginable; they had surprised the Nednhi chief in his winter camp, killing fourteen and seizing three dozen, including Juh's wife, Chatto's wife and two children, and two of Geronimo's wives. The remaining Nednhis abandoned him. Irremediably disgraced, Juh wandered off deep into the Sierra Madre, losing himself in liquor and despair. That autumn, he rode his horse off a cliff.[24]

*

On June 10, 1883, Crook reentered the United States amid general applause with 325 Chiricahuas, including an appreciative Chief Loco. General Sherman predicted that the Sierra Madre campaign presaged a permanent resolution of the Apache problem. Basking in the accolades, Crook waited for Geronimo and the Chiricahua chiefs to make good their promise—and waited. Months passed with no sign of them. As reports of renewed Apache atrocities in Mexico filtered northward, adulation of Crook turned to acrimony. Arizona newspapers that had eulogized him as a "conquering hero" now called upon Arizonans to censure him. Congress discussed baseless allegations that it had been Geronimo who had captured Crook.

The most significant change in the army high command in two decades compounded Crook's woes. In the autumn of 1883, General Sherman retired, and Phil Sheridan became the commanding general of the U.S. Army. A shake-up of division commands followed. Major General John M. Schofield moved to Chicago as the new commander of the Military Division of the Missouri, and John Pope was appointed major general to succeed Schofield as commander of the Military Division of the Pacific. Like Schofield, General Pope supported Crook's policies and his military operations. General Sheridan, however, favored a harder line, and the nonappearance of the Chiricahuas lessened his confidence in Crook, which had been brittle at best since Crook's generally sorry performance in the Great Sioux War.[25]

The Chiricahua chiefs meant to keep their word, but they needed to replenish their horse herds, and that meant a final round of raids. The Chiricahuas also hoped to grab hostages to exchange for kinsmen that the Mexicans had captured. Negotiations, however, went nowhere. Mexican authorities were bent on eradicating the Chiricahuas, not talking about prisoner swaps, and the chiefs began to filter northward. In November 1883, Naiche arrived at San Carlos. Chatto and Chihuahua followed three months later. Geronimo appeared last, having sent his son secretly to San Carlos to make sure there were no "bad people" waiting there to arrest him. Geronimo's capitulation vindicated Crook's unorthodox tactics. He had won the Sierra Madre campaign not by killing Chiricahuas but because he had shown he could mobilize Apaches against Apaches and penetrate the inner recesses of the renegades' supposedly impregnable Sierra Madre bastion.[26]

But Crook's troubles were not over. The agency Apaches wanted nothing to do with the Chiricahuas, vowing to slaughter the returned renegades if they caused the slightest disturbance. To prevent a massacre, Crook permitted them to choose their own home on the reservation. All but Geronimo opted for Turkey Creek, a location near Fort

Apache that Britton Davis called "a beauty spot and a game paradise." Crook appointed Davis to oversee the five hundred Chiricahuas at Turkey Creek, which included a reluctant Geronimo.

Their future appeared bright, especially when the now-prosperous White Mountain Apaches agreed to forgive past Chiricahua offenses. Chatto hoped the army would also pardon earlier transgressions. He had "been on a crooked trail," Chatto told Captain Crawford, but now he wanted the treaty to "last as long as the sun." Accepting Lieutenant Davis's offer of first sergeant's job in a new scout company recruited entirely from formerly hostile Chiricahua warriors, Chatto gave the army his unswerving loyalty. Naiche seemed resigned to reservation life, and nearly all the Chiricahuas wanted to keep the peace. But for all his fine talk, Geronimo was an unreconstructed nuisance. He told Captain Crawford he had come in with the express understanding that his every wish would be granted, a notion of which Crawford quickly disabused him. Sullen and suspicious, Geronimo remained aloof. Chihuahua and Mangas, the peace-loving but easily manipulated son of Mangas Coloradas, also kept their distance. Their followers mimicked them, which worried Lieutenant Davis. "None of the Indians were making anything more than a bluff at farming. Most of them contented themselves with loafing and gambling, or trading ponies for things they wanted from the White Mountains." The men were bored, and boredom in warriors spelled trouble.

At this delicate juncture, General Crook made an egregious error in judgment. He banned three traditional Apache practices: wife beating, the mutilating of adulterous women's noses, and the brewing and consumption of corn liquor (*tiswin*). Crook not unreasonably considered the bans necessary steps in "civilizing" the Chiricahuas. He underestimated the backlash, however. The chiefs reminded Crook that renunciation of nose butchering and spousal abuse had not been part of the bargain. The *tiswin* ban annoyed nearly everyone, but it especially incensed Chihuahua, who, Davis observed laconically, "liked his toddy." It also threatened the livelihood of Mangas's wife, who ran a lucrative *tiswin*-brewing business, and she browbeat her husband into opposing the prohibition. Weary of reservation life and believing as always that "bad people"—in this instance, Davis, Chatto, and Crook—were conspiring to harm him, Geronimo encouraged the discontent.

A showdown was inevitable. On the morning of May 15, 1885, Chihuahua, Mangas, Loco, Nana, Naiche, and Geronimo all staggered into Davis's tent. They had been on an all-night *tiswin* drunk. Chihuahua was still inebriated, and the others nursed hangovers. They demanded to know if the lieutenant intended to punish them. Davis took the safest possible course: he stalled for time. Telling them that only Nantan Lupan could adjudicate so weighty an issue, Davis promised to telegraph the general at once. Somewhat mollified, the Indians agreed to wait.[27]

Fittingly, alcohol subverted Davis's plan. Regulations required that the lieutenant send his message through his immediate superior. Captain Crawford would have understood the gravity of the problem, but he had left the reservation two months earlier. His successor, who had been at San Carlos only two months, took Davis's telegram to the chief of scouts, Al Sieber, normally the most reliable of men and a favorite of Crook's, for his opinion. Inopportunely, Sieber had been on a bender of his own that night. Shaking him awake, the captain handed the glassy-eyed scout the message. Sieber waved him off. "Oh, it's just another tiswin drunk, Davis can handle it." The officer thereupon pigeonholed the message.[28]

Two days came and went without a reply. Lieutenant Davis passed the time playing poker and umpiring baseball games. Geronimo counted the hours and planned mayhem. Certain that Crook intended to arrest him, Geronimo decided to bolt. Mangas's entrepreneurial wife coerced her husband into joining him. Geronimo and Mangas could muster only fifteen warriors between them, however; they needed Chihuahua and Naiche. But the sobered and repentant chiefs demurred. The phantoms of Geronimo's febrile mind whispered a way to force their hand: assassinate Chatto and Davis. Geronimo brought Mangas into the irrational plot and hired two of his own cousins to do the job. He then told Chihuahua and Naiche that Chatto and Davis were dead, the scouts had deserted, and all the Chiricahuas were about to quit the reservation. The credulous chiefs fell in with Geronimo and Mangas, as did Nana, the incorrigible old Chihenne lieutenant of Victorio. All told, thirty-four men, eight adolescent boys, and ninety-two women and children fled Turkey Creek at dusk on May 17. Nearly four hundred Chiricahuas—representing three-quarters of the tribe and most of the fighting men—stayed on the reservation. Put another way, less than 3 percent of the five thousand Indians at San Carlos participated in the outbreak. Fewer still felt any sympathy for the renegades.

Unbeknownst to Geronimo, Davis and Chatto were very much

alive, the would-be assassins having lost their nerve. Davis reported the breakout, assembled the agency police, and galloped after the fugitives. When Chihuahua learned of Geronimo's deceit, he went to the slippery shaman's wickiup after nightfall to kill him, only to discover that he and Mangas had struck out for Mexico. Chihuahua intended to return to the reservation after the excitement died down, but Davis found his *ranchería* first, and a skirmish ensued. Wrongly branded a hostile, Chihuahua became one. He staged one rage-filled raid after another against Arizona and New Mexico ranches and mines, killing at least twenty-seven unsuspecting civilians over the course of a month before making for the Sierra Madre.[29]

*

Crook prepared for another long and arduous campaign. This time, however, he would remain behind. Most southwestern newspapers branded him as partially culpable for the bloodletting, charging that his relative leniency in 1883 had emboldened rather than pacified the Chiricahuas. The political landscape had also changed. Both the new president, Grover Cleveland, and the new secretary of war doubted Crook's war-making methods, particularly his reliance on Apache scouts. They credited every hyperbolic rant from the territorial newspapers, including bogus stories of huge Apache war parties running amok in Arizona (Chihuahua had already entered Mexico). Sheridan still supported Crook but with far less enthusiasm than had Sherman.

Crook's strategy was straightforward. Two mobile columns, each consisting of one cavalry troop and two Apache-scout companies, would penetrate the Sierra Madre to flush out the hostiles. Captain Crawford would lead one column, and Captain Wirt Davis, an outstanding cavalry officer, would command the other. To prevent the renegades from raiding north, Crook blanketed the border with troops.

Davis and Crawford combed the Sierra Madre for three months, enduring heat, dust, thirst, fatigue, and swarms of insects. Wirt Davis's scouts found Geronimo and Mangas's *ranchería*, but the braying of a startled mule alerted the fugitives. At the first fire, Geronimo grabbed his young son and fled. Fifteen women and children fell captive, however, including Mangas's *tiswin*-brewing wife and three of Geronimo's five wives. The clash bankrupted the creditability of Geronimo's power, and Mangas deserted him. Now free from his domineering spouse,

Mangas hid in the mountains and caused no further trouble, only waiting for the opportune moment to surrender. In October, Crawford and
Wirt Davis put in at Fort Bowie, Arizona, to rest, refit, and prepare
for another assault on the Sierra Madre. Britton Davis would not be
joining them. Disillusioned and exhausted, the young lieutenant had
resigned from the army.[30]

No sooner had Crawford and Davis departed than the renegades
counterattacked. Chihuahua's younger brother Ulzana and eleven warriors slipped through Crook's cordon and headed for Fort Apache in
a daredevil attempt to "liberate" family left behind at Turkey Creek
and to assassinate Chatto. In just under eight weeks, Ulzana's raiders
traveled twelve hundred miles, killing thirty-eight whites, butchering
twenty-one White Mountain Apaches on the reservation, and stealing
250 horses. Cavalry and Indian scouts scoured the mountains north
of the border, but they turned up only cold trails. For all the mayhem
they had wrought, Ulzana's men had been unable to find their families
or kill Chatto. Ulzana's exploits had also won him no converts. Not a
single reservation Apache so much as lifted a finger to help him.[31]

Not that it mattered to the territorial press. Editors formerly his
friends now branded Crook a "liar, coward, and murderer." Calls went
out for vigilante posses to "KKK" the reservation Apaches. The locals
were all talk, but not Phil Sheridan. With the new commanding general, the constancy of the reservation Chiricahuas counted for nothing when measured against the terror wrought by Ulzana's raid. He
saw San Carlos as nothing short of an incubator for future hostiles.
Sheridan's solution? Remove every last Chiricahua from the Southwest permanently. The secretary of war supported Sheridan's plan, and
with President Grover Cleveland's blessing it became official policy. In
November, Sheridan traveled to Fort Bowie, not to consult with Crook,
but to present a fait accompli. Both Crook and Captain Crawford, who
had just enlisted two new companies of Chiricahua scouts, objected
strenuously. How, Crawford asked the commanding general, could the
army expect the scouts to serve faithfully when it intended to betray
them? Sheridan took the point and backed off for the moment.

What the army asked of the Chiricahua scouts was difficult enough
without Sheridan complicating matters. None of the scouts relished the
idea of tracking down their own people, much less shooting at them.
That is, with one exception. Nearly every scout wanted the honor of
killing Geronimo. The Chihennes ached to even the score for Alisos

Creek; others resented the suspicion that his activities had cast on the reservation Indians.

Captain Crawford, meanwhile, was lost in a private nightmare. The captain spoke privately of a premonition that would do Geronimo credit. He appreciated Crook's confidence in him to lead the proposed expedition, but he dreaded the assignment. "When I go down into Mexico," Crawford told a friend, "I will not return."[32]

———◆———

CHAPTER 21

ONCE I MOVED LIKE THE WIND

C APTAIN CRAWFORD entered Mexico on December 11, 1885, with four officers and a hundred Apache scouts, nearly half of them Chiricahuas. The dependable lieutenant Marion P. Maus, who had been Miles's chief of scouts in the Nez Perce War, and Lieutenant William E. Shipp, just two years out of West Point and on his first campaign, commanded two Apache scout companies each. The only other white men on the expedition were the scouts Tom Horn and William H. Harrison and the chief mule packer Henry W. Daly and his twenty assistants.

After a few days on the trail, Daly got the distinct impression that the White Mountain Apaches, perhaps out of fear, were withholding knowledge of the hostiles' whereabouts. He shared his impression with Crawford, who in turn harangued the scouts with uncharacteristic vehemence. None denied the accusation, and the White Mountain medicine man stepped forward to steady them with a sacred *hoddentin* (cattail rush pollen) ceremony, taking around a small buckskin bag for each scout to kiss. "Each repeated after him some form of vow or obligation," recalled Henry Daly. "I then became convinced of their sincerity and that they would find the hostiles."[1]

At dusk on January 9, 1886, Crawford's lead scouts located Geronimo and Naiche's winter *ranchería* in the remote Espinazo del Diablo (Devil's Spine), an unearthly patchwork of sawtooth mountains and deep canyons about two hundred miles south of the border. The news placed Crawford in a difficult predicament. The command had marched all day without food. Even the Chiricahuas were near exhaustion, and the pack train was far in the rear. Judging the risk of discovery too great to rest, Crawford pushed on. The night was moonless, and the going slow and treacherous. For twelve hours, the scouts inched forward in blackness. In poor health and utterly exhausted, Captain Crawford hobbled along with his rifle as a walking stick. Lieutenant Maus was convinced that Crawford survived the ordeal by "sheer force of will."

Crawford reached the *ranchería* before daybreak. Not a soul stirred, and no sentinels stood watch. Crawford whispered orders: Lieutenants Maus and Shipp and the scout Tom Horn were to take one detachment each and work their way into position in the hills above the hostiles. A giddy lieutenant Shipp thought the campaign was all but over. After all, the scouts need only complete the encirclement of the *ranchería*, wait until dawn, and then with a single rush capture the renegades. But Shipp had not accounted for the roughness of the terrain. In the darkness, some of the scouts tripped. Loosened stones trickled downhill, alerting the renegades' mules and burros—the "watchdogs of an Indian camp." Three warriors emerged from their wickiups to investigate the braying.

As so often happened, overeager Indian scouts spoiled what would otherwise have been near-certain surprise. In this case, the culprits were White Mountain Apaches who had lost relatives in Ulzana's raid. Understandably vengeful, they ignored orders and opened fire the instant their target came into view. With their positions now compromised, Maus and Shipp urged their Chiricahua scouts to charge. They too ignored orders, seeking cover among the rocks and firing a few halfhearted, poorly aimed volleys. Shipp understood the reluctance of the Chiricahua scouts to push their advantage. All had friends or family members in the *ranchería*. "They wanted peace, but not at the expense of much bloodshed." The White Mountain Apaches, for their part, were too fearful of the renegades to chance close combat.

The scouts' diffidence cost Crawford little. The hostiles scattered, leaving behind their food stock and animals. That afternoon, an old woman appeared bearing a message from Naiche. The renegades were ready to surrender and return to the reservation. Terms might have been negotiated then and there, but Crawford's Apache interpreter had been too tired to make the night march. With nothing to fear from the hostiles, Crawford's command bedded down for the night beside roaring campfires in the high-country cold.[2]

✳

A chill fog rolled over the hills before dawn on January 11. The scouts tended breakfast fires. Shipp and Maus lounged under their blankets and chatted. Then the unthinkable happened. Through the mist, a straggling line of shabbily clad but heavily armed men appeared on a ridge above Crawford's camp and opened fire. The scouts ducked behind rocks and held their fire.

Their assailants drew nearer. The fog lifted, and daybreak revealed their identity—two hundred Mexican Tarahumara Indians out for plunder and Apache scalps. Lieutenant Maus and Captain Crawford dashed forward. In plain sight, Crawford climbed a large rock between the opposing lines and waved a white handkerchief. Tom Horn, standing nearby, yelled his lungs out in fluent Spanish, telling the Tarahumaras that they were firing on American soldiers. The shooting stopped, and the Mexican commander came forward with his officers. Crawford told Lieutenant Maus to go back and make sure the scouts kept quiet while he parleyed.

No sooner had Maus turned his back than a single shot rang out. He whirled around to find Crawford crumpled in the mud, his brains seeping from a gaping hole in his forehead. Enraged Apaches riddled the Mexican officers. "No power could stop the firing," said Maus. The Tarahumaras and the Chiricahuas, bitter adversaries, taunted each other between volleys, the Tarahumaras boasting that they had collected two thousand dollars for the scalp of Victorio. The skirmish ended only after the Tarahumaras realized they had come up against more Apaches than they had bargained for.[3]

From bluffs across the river, Geronimo and Naiche had watched the firefight. Cautiously, they entered Lieutenant Maus's camp with a message for Crook: they wanted to meet with Nantan Lupan in one month near the border, swearing to cease raiding until then, a promise they had no intention of keeping. But Maus, who was short of food and ammunition, felt compelled to trust them, and he set out the next day with the unconscious captain Crawford, who, borne on a crude litter, lingered for seven days before dying.[4]

While Maus struggled back to the border, Geronimo and Naiche slashed through remote northern Sonora, plundering to make good their losses. But they kept the rendezvous. On March 25–27, 1886, General Crook met them at Cañon de los Embudos (Canyon of the Funnels) just over the Arizona border in Mexico. The circumstances were hardly conducive to sober discussion. The hostile Chiricahuas had fortified themselves on a lava-strewn hill half a mile from Crook's camp. From a shanty set up near their stronghold, a cattle rustler named Charles Tribolet and his brother dispensed copious quantities of whiskey and mescal. The Chiricahuas had been on a raucous drunk, and Geronimo nursed a hangover. General Crook entered the council ground with the strange sensation of reliving General Canby's last moments with the Modocs.[5]

Crook disguised his unease well. Geronimo, shaking as he spoke, did most of the talking. He rambled on about how he had been wronged by false rumors and blamed the breakout on Britton Davis and Chatto, who he alleged had been out to hang him. While the delusional shaman rattled off one lie after another, Crook stared hard at the ground. Nantan Lupan's silence disconcerted Geronimo, who perspired profusely, less from the heat than from the aftereffects of his nocturnal binge. "What is the matter that you don't speak to me? It would be better if you would speak to me and look with a pleasant face," Geronimo pleaded. "I want you to look and smile at me."

Crook made no reply. Denying any knowledge of a plot to kill Chatto and Davis, Geronimo resumed his monologue until the disgusted general called him a liar. Geronimo's warriors fidgeted with their rifles and grumbled, but Naiche silenced them with a wave of his hand. Crook closed the conference with an ultimatum: either they surrender unconditionally or they fight, the choice was theirs. If they fought, Crook promised to kill them all "if it took fifty years."[6]

The war of nerves continued into the night. Crook sent two Chiricahua scouts into the hostiles' *ranchería* to foment discord by preaching the merits of capitulation. His gambit had mixed results. Chihuahua, who had mended fences with Geronimo, and Naiche decided to give up, but not Geronimo, who stormed about, ranting and threatening to shoot the scouts. By morning, he had calmed down enough to accompany Chihuahua and Naiche for a private talk with Crook, who denied their request to return to the reservation without telling them that the Great Father had decreed their permanent deportation. Geronimo and Naiche changed tack. They would accept a two-year exile on the condition their families accompany them; otherwise, they would return to the Sierra Madre. Knowing he had to act quickly or face war "with all its attendant horrors," Crook accepted terms he knew he could not honor. The site of their "temporary" banishment, he told Geronimo and Naiche, would be the military prison at Fort Marion, Florida—a name and a place with no meaning to the Apaches.

On March 27, the Chiricahuas formally submitted. To Geronimo's annoyance, Chihuahua did most of the talking. He expressed his confidence in Crook's honesty and offered a lengthy apology for his past transgressions. Naiche also apologized. "What Chihuahua says, I say. I think now it is best for us to surrender and not remain out in the mountains like fools as we have been doing." All eyes turned to Geronimo. After a pregnant pause, he muttered, "Two or three words are enough. I surrender. Once I moved about like the wind. Now I surrender to you, and that is all."

But it was not all. Chihuahua, who had a good idea of what to expect, gathered up his followers and camped with Crook that night, begging the general to keep Geronimo as far from his band as possible. Geronimo and Naiche returned to their stronghold and guzzled five gallons of Tribolet's rotgut whiskey. Naiche shot his wife in the knee when she flirted with a man; he then passed out, while drunken warriors fired a few harmless shots at the mule packers' camp. Despite these contretemps, Crook set out with Captain Bourke for Fort Bowie the next morning, leaving the hostiles in Lieutenant Maus's care. A few miles north of Cañon de los Embudos, he ran into Geronimo and three warriors, swaying on two mules, "drunk as lords." Embracing Bourke, Geronimo reassured the captain of his commitment to peace. Recoiling from the alcohol fumes, Bourke advised Crook to "have Tribolet killed as a foe to human society. If you don't," he warned, "it will be the biggest mistake of your life."[7]

Crook declined Bourke's counsel and went on to Fort Bowie. Geronimo and Naiche kept drinking, and as they drank, they pondered their fate. Crook's brusqueness and casual departure puzzled and frightened them. In their liquored imaginings, they glimpsed two nooses with their names on them at Fort Bowie, with a grinning Chatto as the high chief and executioner. Fear of what exile might bring, assuming they weren't hanged first, also tugged at them. It was all more than they could bear. On March 30, Geronimo and Naiche broke for the Sierra Madre, taking with them eighteen warriors and twenty-two women and children. Chihuahua and Ulzana, on the other hand, kept their word. On April 7, they and seventy-seven other Chiricahuas, including two of Geronimo's wives, three of his children, and Naiche's family, boarded railcars at Bowie Station, Arizona, bound for Florida. Crook never told Chihuahua that he would never see his homeland again.

Four days later, Crook himself boarded a train bound for Omaha, Nebraska. Like the Chiricahuas, he had been banished from Arizona.[8]

*

Crook's promise of a two-year deportation in contravention of government policy had angered Sheridan, and Geronimo and Naiche's flight snapped their tenuous thread of friendship. Sheridan had never cared for Crook's reliance on Apache scouts, and to his way of thinking Geronimo's escape could only have been the result of collaboration between the scouts and the hostiles, a suggestion a prickly Crook sharply dismissed. When Sheridan demanded that he renege on his pledge to permit Chihuahua's band to return to Arizona after a short exile, Crook replied that it would "result in their scattering to the mountains." As for the hostiles, Crook thought the chances of rounding them up slim.

Sheridan threw up his hands. "I do not see what you can do now except to concentrate your troops at the best points and give protection to the people." Reminding Crook that he had at his disposal forty-six companies of infantry and forty companies of cavalry in the Arizona and New Mexico Territories, Sheridan said that he expected them to be put to good use in a defensive posture—a scarcely subtle repudiation of Crook's reliance on Indian scouts and on aggressive strikes into Mexico.

Crook had had enough. On April 1, he offered his resignation. To the delight of both President Cleveland and the secretary of war, Sheridan immediately accepted it. He kicked Crook upstairs to command of the Military Division of the Missouri, turning the coveted billet into a retirement post and appointed Crook's nemesis Nelson A. Miles, now a brigadier general, to command in the Southwest. Sheridan made certain there would be no misunderstanding on Miles's part: he was to subdue Geronimo with "vigorous operations" conducted by the regular army. Apache scouts—none of them Chiricahuas, whom Sheridan deemed unreliable—were to be employed sparingly and only to find the enemy. The soldiers would do the fighting. President Cleveland forbade any attempt at diplomacy: unconditional surrender or extirpation were the only terms Miles was authorized to offer. That sat poorly with

Miles, who honestly said later that he "never had any desire to engage in a campaign of that character."

With few exceptions, Arizona newspapers welcomed Crook's departure. "Everyone in Tucson is wondering whether General Miles can do any better than General Crook," commented the *Tombstone Epitaph*. "[We] in Tombstone are wondering whether he can do any worse." A New Mexico correspondent on assignment at department headquarters told General Crook that he was sorry to see him leave. "Well, I'm not," snapped Crook. "I have had to worry along with these [Apaches] for eight years, and have got enough of them. Now let some of the others try their hand."[9]

Crook's Indian-fighting days were over. For more than thirty years, he had given his heart, his soul, and his very health to helping win the West for the whites. He might have reneged on promises to the Indians or obfuscated on uncomfortable truths, but their welfare was always of deep concern to him. Henceforth, he would dedicate what remained of his career to championing Indian rights.

*

Nelson Miles arrived at Fort Bowie, Arizona, on April 11. A week on the ground convinced him that Crook's methods had been sound. Miles had a conscience, and, Cleveland's instructions notwithstanding, he hoped to talk before shooting. Miles asked Sheridan to release the Chiricahua raider Ulzana from Fort Marion as a peace emissary, a request Sheridan tersely rejected. The commanding general wanted no parleys. He reminded Miles that he expected him to protect the people of the Southwest and to pry the hostiles from their Sierra Madre strongholds with the regular army—a strategy, mused the former lieutenant Britton Davis, akin to using "Londoners against the Alpine Swiss."[10]

Miles dutifully set about implementing Sheridan's fanciful plans. He carved southern Arizona and New Mexico Territories up into twenty-seven "districts of observation," deploying infantry to seal off strategic mountain passes and cavalry to run down Chiricahua raiding parties. In one of American military history's greatest examples of overkill, Miles eventually marshaled nearly five thousand troops along the international border to prevent possible incursions by the eighteen warriors left to Geronimo and Naiche. On the highest peaks in each district,

Miles placed observers equipped with state-of-the-art telescopes and field glasses to spot Apache movements and with heliographs (tripod-mounted glass mirrors that reflected sunlight) to flash messages. The heliograph stations might have been useful had the hostiles shown themselves during the day. But they traveled by night, when the heliograph was useless. Once his defenses were in place, Miles readied an elite strike force of regular army troops to enter Mexico. It would be the third army foray beyond the border in as many years.[11]

Geronimo and Naiche, however, operated according to their own timetable. While Miles tinkered with his plans, they struck. Entering Arizona near Nogales on April 27, a small war party rampaged down the Santa Cruz valley on a blitz cut short by pursuing cavalry. The hunters and the hunted spilled into northern Sonora. On May 3, a troop of Tenth Cavalry Buffalo Soldiers skirmished with the Chiricahuas twenty miles south of the border. Two weeks later, the raiders lost their stock to the cavalry. They recovered the animals, but Geronimo and Naiche were demoralized; they had never encountered cavalry so skillful and persistent. But Naiche would not abandon hope. Longing to see his family and perhaps to put out peace feelers to Crook (who unbeknownst to him was gone), Naiche struck out for Fort Apache with most of the warriors, while Geronimo, restrained by the specter of the noose, stayed behind. Along the way, Naiche killed whoever stood in his path. Four years later, Crook asked Naiche why he had murdered civilians when his intentions had been pacific. "Because we were afraid. It was war. Anybody who saw us would kill us, and we did the same thing. We had to if we wanted to live."

Naiche's risky gambit brought him nothing but heartache. Under the cover of darkness, he slipped into his mother's lodge in the Chiricahua camp at Turkey Creek, only to learn that General Crook had shipped off his family with Chihuahua's people. Naiche rejoined Geronimo in early June, and their reunited bands withdrew deep into Sonora.[12]

The way was now open for Miles. To command his strike force, he chose Captain Henry Lawton of the Fourth Cavalry. A lion of a man, Lawton stood six feet five and weighed a muscular 230 pounds. He fought hard and drank harder. Joining Lawton was Captain Leonard Wood, a twenty-five-year-old Harvard graduate and army assistant surgeon. The fair-haired, blue-eyed Wood had a gentler mien than Lawton but was equally robust. With Lawton and Wood went the thirty-five troopers of Lawton's Fourth Cavalry troop, twenty handpicked infantrymen, twenty White Mountain and San Carlos Apache scouts—Miles had recognized that it took Apaches to find Apaches—and thirty mule packers with a hundred pack mules.[13]

Lawton entered Mexico in a foul mood. "This is a godforsaken country and godforsaken people live in it," he wrote to his wife. "I really do not feel any sympathy when I hear that the Indians have killed a half a dozen or more of the people. I think the Indians [are] better than the Mexicans." Lawton had accepted the assignment solely to curry Miles's favor. Now the ambitious captain wondered if he had erred. Five days after plunging into the Sierra Madre, he wrote to his mother, "The whole country is a mass of gigantic mountains through which we are laboriously working on the trail of the ever fleeing and never fighting Indian." Temperatures soared to 120 degrees, and rifle barrels became too hot to touch. Officers and men shed their uniforms and marched in their underwear and in moccasins. Frequent, violent rainstorms transformed dry canyons into raging torrents. Captain Lawton got ptomaine poisoning from a can of rancid Armour corned beef. For a few hours, his life hung in the balance. A tarantula bite almost killed Wood. Nearly everyone suffered from acute diarrhea.

On July 13, Lawton's scouts discovered Geronimo and Naiche's *ranchería*. Lawton hurried forward the infantry, now led by Captain Wood (the original commander had been evacuated desperately ill). It was a moment fraught with grand possibilities: for Lawton, the chance to end a monthlong ordeal with one blow and emerge a hero; for Wood, the opportunity to prove himself as a combat leader.

Lawton split his command. He sent the scouts on a flanking march to the far bluff, while he and Wood ascended the near bluff with the troops. The scouts were to attack first—hardly a Sheridan-esque approach.

Wood gazed upon the tranquil *ranchería* far below. "Fires were burning, Indian ponies picketed out, and a good many Indians moving about in all directions . . . There seemed to be no outlet, but we knew there must be a good one or the Indians would not be there." Indeed there was. A warrior out hunting chanced upon a red headband lost by a scout. He alerted the camp, and the Chiricahuas escaped before the scouts were able to seal the exit. Lawton captured everything in the *ranchería* except the Indians. "I was so disappointed as to be almost sick, for here was the opportunity we had been looking for for so long and it slipped from me." For three weeks thereafter, he stumbled about the

Aros River country, while Geronimo and Naiche headed for the border. Naiche was ill and unstrung, and the sudden appearance of American soldiers so deep in the Sierra Madre made him feel like "giving up." Had he known what was about to transpire at far-off Fort Apache, Naiche might well have surrendered then and there.[14]

*

Shortly after assuming command in Arizona, General Miles became seized with an idea that would forever change the Chiricahua world. The Chiricahua villages at Fort Apache, he believed, were "the arsenal, the breeding place, the recruiting depot, the hospital, [and] the asylum of the hostiles." Nothing could have been further from the truth. Chatto and several other former Chokonen war leaders had become farmers and sheep ranchers, with no sympathy whatsoever for the renegades. Three-quarters of the eighty-one Chokonen warriors on the reservation had served as scouts, and all had remained at peace since surrendering to General Crook three years earlier. Even General Sheridan now believed the Chiricahuas should be "controlled where they are."

Unfortunately, when Miles visited Fort Apache to investigate conditions there, the Chiricahuas were in the midst of a prolonged *tiswin* drunk. Miles thought "it was dangerous to go near them. The young men were insolent, violent, and restless . . . and I received reliable information that another outbreak was then being arranged by them." The so-called reliable informants were the White Mountain Apaches, who had grown weary of the Chiricahuas in their midst. Once again, the divided Apaches proved their own worst enemies.

Miles pleaded his case for removal to Sheridan: "The 440 men, women, and children now living [at] Fort Apache are nominally prisoners of war, yet they have never been disarmed . . . and are in better condition than ever before . . . The boys of today will become the Geronimos of a few years hence." Among those named in Miles's preposterous assertion were Chief Loco and the long-suffering Chihennes. Miles suggested relocating all the Chiricahuas near the Wichita Mountains in Indian Territory, where the "clear water of the mountains, the climate, and the fertile soil would be congenial and beneficial to them."[15]

In the meantime, Miles again tried to orchestrate the surrender of Naiche and Geronimo, being careful to hide this olive branch from

Sheridan. Miles wanted "men who had been out with Geronimo" to carry terms to the hostile camp, so he sent the warriors Martine and Kayitah, who had relatives with Geronimo. Miles offered each of them seventy-five thousand dollars and a fine farm at Fort Apache if they succeeded, though they undertook the mission less for profit than to save their families from further harm. Neither knew what the general had in store for the Chiricahuas.[16]

To lead the peace delegation, Miles needed an officer Geronimo trusted. Captain Crawford was dead, and Britton Davis had resigned, leaving only Lieutenant Gatewood, then on duty in New Mexico. "Beak Chief" was in poor health and wanted no part of what he considered a "fool's errand," and only after Miles offered him a future staff job did he accept the assignment.

On July 18, Gatewood, Martine, and Kayitah departed. Two weeks and three hundred miles later, they found Lawton on the Aros River. Neither Lawton nor Gatewood himself had any faith in Miles's scheme. Suffering from dysentery and an inflamed bladder that made riding sheer torture, Gatewood wanted to go home, and he asked Wood to certify him unfit for duty and send him back to Fort Bowie, a request the worn-out doctor refused. Lawton, for his part, wanted to shoot first and talk later. Martine and Kayitah expressed their opinion of Miles's plan by getting roaring drunk.

With no idea of Geronimo's whereabouts, Lawton meandered northward. Rations spoiled in the tropical heat, and the men grew dangerously thin (Lawton himself dropped forty pounds during the expedition). As his command withered, Lawton grew more amenable to Gatewood's peace mission. Learning from a passing Mexican burro train that Geronimo had been to Fronteras, just fifty miles shy of the border, Lawton ordered Gatewood to hurry ahead and open communications with him. When Lawton arrived four days later and found Gatewood tarrying about Fronteras, he drank himself into an angered stupor, while a sober captain Wood peremptorily ordered Gatewood to find Geronimo and open negotiations.

*

In the *ranchería* overlooking the Bavispe River, sentiment for surrender ran high. The Chiricahuas were exhausted. The brutal and increasingly competent Mexican army haunted their sleep. Geronimo and Naiche longed to see their families. When Kayitah and Martine met them on August 24, the renegades were recovering from a mescal drunk. Watching their approach through a field glass, a brain-fogged Geronimo told his men to shoot them when they came into range. Three sober warriors stood up to Geronimo, an act unthinkable in the shaman's heyday. They threatened to kill the first man who followed his order, and the emissaries delivered their message unmolested.

The next morning, Geronimo and Gatewood met in a canebrake beside the river. Naiche stood on the sidelines. Armed warriors squatted close by. After cigarettes and a meal, Gatewood delivered Miles's terms: "Surrender and you will be sent to join the rest of your people in Florida, there to await the decision of the President of the United States. Accept these terms, or fight it out to the bitter end." The Chiricahuas greeted the message with icy stares, and Gatewood prepared for the worst. "Geronimo sat on the log beside me, as close as he could get. I could feel his six-shooter against my hip."

Geronimo made a move—not for his pistol, but to extend his trembling hands and beg Gatewood for a drink. Geronimo gulped down a draft and then, the tension eased, offered counter-terms: they would submit, but only if they were returned to the reservation and exempted from punishment. That was how it had always been, and Geronimo saw no reason why things should be different now. (Why on earth he expected the army to trust him this time only Geronimo knew.) Gatewood held firm. An exasperated Geronimo said it was asking too much of the Chiricahuas to give up all their land "to a race of intruders." They were willing to cede all of it but the reservation. "Take us to the reservation or fight" was Geronimo's ultimatum. Uncertain what to do next, Gatewood dissembled. "I informed [them] that the rest of their people—the mother and daughter of Naiche among them—had been removed to Florida to join Chihuahua's band."

Geronimo was crestfallen. He peppered Gatewood with questions about General Miles. What kind of man was he? Does he look you in the eyes when he talks? Was he cruel or kindhearted? Would he keep his promises? Did he have a large heart or a small one? After Gatewood painted a favorable picture of Miles, Geronimo interjected, "He must be a good man, since the Great Father sent him from Washington, and he sent you all this distance to us." There was just one more thing. "We want your advice. Consider yourself one of us and not a white man. Remember all that has been said today, and as an Apache, what would you advise us to do under the circumstances? Should [we] surrender, or should [we] fight it out?"

"I would trust General Miles and take him at his word," replied Gatewood. With that, the council concluded for the day.

When the parties reassembled the next morning, Geronimo offered to meet Miles across the border at Skeleton Canyon, sixty miles south-east of Fort Bowie, and discuss terms—provided Gatewood remain with his band and Lawton accompany them at a respectful distance to ward off roving Mexican army units. Gatewood and Lawton agreed, and on August 28 the two cavalcades set out for the proposed rendez-vous point.[17]

In the waning days of August, Miles had concerns more pressing than a peace council with Geronimo. President Cleveland had accepted Miles's proposal to exile the Chiricahuas but rejected his proposed destination. Seven years earlier, Congress had passed legislation pro-hibiting the resettlement of Apaches in Indian Territory, and Cleve-land was adamant that no Apaches be located anywhere west of the Missouri River. Sheridan suggested sending the adult males to join Chihuahua's band at Fort Marion, Florida, a proposal that Cleveland enlarged to include the entire Chiricahua people. To his credit, Miles protested the deportation to Florida. He implored Sheridan to prevail upon the administration to find "some safe place away from Arizona that would be agreeable to them." But the president was obdurate. All Chiricahuas—including former scouts and their families—were to be sent without further delay to Fort Marion as prisoners of war.[18]

*

Sunday, August 29, 1886, was ration day at Fort Apache. The White Mountain Apaches had had a *tiswin* drunk the night before and killed one of their own; unbeknownst to the Chiricahuas, their antagonistic neighbors had laid blame for the murder on them. But the day began no differently than any other ration day. The Chiricahuas lined up at noon to receive their weekly ration tickets. Five Chiricahua scouts maintained order. An infantry company stationed at Fort Apache formed ranks. There was nothing out of the ordinary about that. A group of White Mountain scouts looked on, which was odd but not troubling. What happened next baffled the Chiricahuas. A former Chiricahua scout watched a cavalry detachment materialize "as if they were going somewhere. But it turned and joined with the infantry and [White Mountain] scouts and surrounded us." The troopers disarmed the five Chiricahua scouts. Then one by one the rest of the Chiricahua men had their rifles taken from them. No one resisted. The post commander superintended the disarmament. He told the Chiricahuas that they were going to a good country where they would have more and better cattle.

Miles now turned his attention to Geronimo. On September 3, the antagonists met at the mouth of Skeleton Canyon. Gatewood and Lawton sat close behind them. Naiche was in the hills a few miles away, mourning for his brother, who had gone back into Mexico to retrieve his favorite pony and was now presumed dead. General Miles repeated to Geronimo what Gatewood had promised: that they would be sent to Florida, there to await the final action of the president of the United States. Turning to Gatewood, Geronimo smiled and said in Apache, "Good, you told the truth." And for once in his lifetime of lies, Geronimo was sincere. "He shook hands with the general and said he himself was going with him, no matter what the others might do," recalled Gatewood. "He followed our commander wherever he went, as if fearing he might go away and leave his captives behind."

On the contrary, Miles wanted to remove Geronimo and Naiche from his department quickly. Early on the morning of September 6, Miles, Geronimo, and Naiche left for Fort Bowie in the general's ambulance, covering the sixty miles in a single day. Two days later, General Sheridan informed Miles that President Cleveland had directed that Geronimo and Naiche be detained at Fort Bowie until they could be turned over to territorial authorities, presumably to be tried and then hanged. Miles pigeonholed the telegram. He had made an agreement with Geronimo and Naiche, who had surrendered as "brave men to brave men."[19]

On the morning of September 8, Lawton's command rode into Fort Bowie with the remaining renegades. Soldiers lined them up on the parade ground and took their weapons from them—and from Martine and Kayitah. Miles might have promised the two scouts fine farms and handsome bounties, but the Cleveland administration, which saw all Chiricahuas as equally dangerous, rewarded their loyalty with exile. The friendly Chiricahuas, together with Geronimo, Naiche, and their followers, were loaded onto wagons for the short trip to Bowie Station, where a special train waited to carry them east. As the wagons rolled onto the desert, the Fort Bowie band struck up "Auld Lang Syne." At 2:55 p.m., the train pulled out of the station. The Chiricahuas would never again see their native land. The struggle for Apacheria, which had begun in 1861 just four hundred yards from Fort Bowie when a foolish young lieutenant betrayed Cochise, was over. In the quarter century of conflict that followed, more than half of the Chiricahuas perished.[20]

White participants with a sense of proportion found the denouement shameful. "The final surrender of Geronimo and his small band was brought about only through Chiricahuas who had remained friendly to the government. For their allegiance they have all been rewarded alike—by captivity in a strange land," said Crook. "There is no more disgraceful page in the history of our relations with the American Indians," averred Captain Bourke, "than that which conceals the treachery visited upon the Chiricahuas who remained faithful in their allegiance to our people."[21]

*

Geronimo lived for twenty-three years after his surrender. In 1893, the government resettled Geronimo and the Chiricahuas—still prisoners of war—at Fort Sill, Oklahoma, home to the Kiowa-Comanche Reservation. They received plots of land to farm, and the men were taught the techniques of the range cattle industry. Geronimo went through something of a metamorphosis, becoming a model farmer and impressing his growing circle of white friends as a "kind old man." He said he had learned much of the whites during his long years of captivity, finding them to be "a very kind and peaceful people." In his later years, Geronimo also enjoyed celebrity. He appeared regularly at fairs and festivals, including the 1904 Louisiana Purchase Exposition in St. Louis, where at age seventy-five he joined in calf-roping contests and sold signed photographs of himself. In 1905, Geronimo rode in President Theodore Roosevelt's inaugural parade and dictated his autobiography, which, over the army's objection, was published with Roosevelt's permission.

Although he never lost faith in his personal power, Geronimo embraced Christianity, more to supplement than to supplant traditional Apache beliefs. "Since my life as a prisoner has begun I have heard the teachings of the white man's religion, and in many respects believe it to be better than the religion of my fathers. However, I have always prayed, and I believe that the Almighty has always protected me."

Geronimo's divine protection ran out on a cold day in February 1909, when he rode into Lawton, Oklahoma, alone to sell some bows and arrows. With the proceeds, the old shaman bought whiskey, for which he had never lost his fondness, and began the return ride after dark deeply intoxicated. He was almost home when he fell off his horse beside a creek. A neighbor found him the next morning, lying partially submerged in the freezing water. Four days later, at age seventy-nine, the man whom no bullet could ever kill died in bed of pneumonia.[22]

PART FOUR

CHAPTER 22

A CLASH OF VISIONS

CHIEF SITTING BULL'S two-year incarceration at Fort Randall, Dakota Territory, ended in April 1883, three years before the Chiricahua Apache exile. The government never told Sitting Bull why he had been made a prisoner of war. He was never tried nor convicted of any crime. The War Department had simply tucked him away to languish under army surveillance until, for reasons equally unclear, it returned him to Interior Department control. On May 10, 1883, Sitting Bull disembarked from a Missouri River steamboat at the Standing Rock Agency. He was now the very person he had so long despised—an agency Indian.

There was no other choice available to him. The free and open Lakota country he had left behind when he took the holy trail into the Grandmother's Land had passed out of existence, its end hastened by the iron horse. Sitting Bull had battled survey expeditions along the Yellowstone River, successfully he thought, but it had been the depression brought on by the panic of 1873 and not Lakota resistance that had checked the railroad's progress. When, after six years, the nation emerged from the depression and capital once again flowed freely, the Northern Pacific Railway resumed construction in the Dakota Territory. With the Lakotas either in Canada or under the government's thumb on the Great Sioux Reservation, track laying proceeded unimpeded, westward through Montana Territory and into the Rocky Mountains. Moving apace with railroad construction crews were professional buffalo hunters, eager to feed eastern markets still hungry for hides. The slaughter was as rapid and prodigious on the northern plains as it had been on the southern plains. In 1876, more than two million buffalo had blanketed the river valleys of Wyoming and Montana. Six years later, a rancher traveling across the northern plains said he was "never out of sight of a dead buffalo and never in sight of a live one." In the bison's place came cattle by the hundreds of thousands. By the mid-1880s, at the peak of the beef bonanza, there were more open-range cattle in the Lakota country than there had ever been buffalo.

Few were better pleased with the transformation of the Lakota country than William T. Sherman. He had devoted half his military career to pacifying the plains. In February 1884, he retired from the army with a sense of mission accomplished. The Indians, he declared in his last report as commanding general, had been "substantially eliminated from the problems of the Army."[1]

Sherman's strategy of supporting the railroad builders with all available army resources had succeeded. There was no place left for Indians but the reservations. Stockmen ruled the former Unceded Indian Territory. Long-horned cattle grazed the Staked Plain, once the impenetrable stronghold of the Comanches. Mining towns chained off the Rocky Mountains ranges once home to the Utes and the Nez Perces. Even Mexico's long-impenetrable Sierra Madre had ceased to be a reliable safe haven for the Apaches.

What to do with the vanquished Indians now became the paramount question. In the latter half of the 1860s and in the 1870s, the government's objective had been to consolidate the tribes on reservations well removed from the overland travel routes and white settlements; if the Indian could be "civilized" in the bargain, so much the better. In those years, the efforts of eastern humanitarian reformers had been sporadic and poorly coordinated. But with the opening of the 1880s, a host of high-minded reformist groups sprang up dedicated to lift the Indians "from the night of barbarism into the fair dawn of Christian civilization." As such, the reformers doubled as cultural exterminators. Few of them saw anything in the traditional Indian way of life worth preserving. In its place, they would impose individual ownership of the land and a white man's education. The Earth Mother was the rightful property of the men who exploited her, and the sooner the Indians learned that, reasoned the reformers, the better their chance of survival. The reformers also held one critical interest in common with westerners: they wanted reservations cut to the bare minimum and surplus Indian land thrown open to homesteaders. The Indian reform movement of the 1880s, then, held something for everyone—be they humanitarians, philanthropists, investors, pioneers, politicians, or land-grabbers—everyone, that is, except those Indians who wanted to remain true to their traditions.[2]

There of course was nothing new in what the reformers proposed. The same high-minded—in the eyes of the whites at least—proposals had been advanced since the birth of the Republic. What had changed was the Indians' ability to deflect the Christianizing impulses. They could no longer resist, nor find anywhere free from whites to which they might retreat.

Now that the Indian Wars were presumably over, most reformers would have no truck with the army, which they saw as a corrupting influence on the Indians. This was base snobbery. In point of fact, senior army officers not only shared the reformers' ideals but also had a far more realistic understanding of the impediments to realizing them. The weightiest trammel, as the officers saw it, was the government's inability to meet the basic needs of reservation Indians. "No races of men," General Pope reminded the reformers, "are in a condition to profit much by the lessons of kindness and charity taught by well-fed apostles whilst they themselves are suffering from want and hunger."

Many thoughtful generals considered the reformers' plan to remake Indian warriors into farmers to be the greatest obstacle to their acculturation. "You might as well take an Indian from the plains into the Elgin watch factory and expect to make a good workman of him," said General Terry. "The first step toward the solution of the Indian question is to give the Indians cattle and let them lead a pastoral life, which is closely allied to their own natural life." Pope, Miles, and Mackenzie agreed with him.[3]

Whatever might be the best path to integrating the Indians into white society, their actual plight disturbed senior officers. Colonel Henry B. Carrington, so ignominiously routed by Red Cloud on the Bozeman Trail, had found his thoughts wandering to the Indian plight when loading onto wagons the frozen and mangled dead from the Fetterman Fight. "In [that] extreme hour, when all I held dear was in danger of self-immolation, or slow death at the hands of the red man, I knew that if I had been a red man, I should have fought as bitterly, if not brutally, as the Indian fought." Their suffering sickened Carrington no less than had the sight of the cordwood dead of his command. "I have seen all ages, and both sexes, half naked and yet reckless of exposure, fording the Platte [River] while ice ran fast and mercury was below the zero mark, for the single purpose of gathering from a post slaughterhouse the last scrap, all offal, however nauseous, that they might use it in lieu of the precious game which our occupation was driving from its haunts." The words of an old Lakota chief whom he had fought to open the Bozeman Trail to white gold seekers forever haunted Carrington: "White man wants all. He will have it all, but the red man will die where his father died."[4]

The Cheyenne and Arapaho cultures had been upended after the 1868–1869 campaign. Now, in the 1880s, reservation life struck the Lakotas with sudden and devastating impact. Without the buffalo, the traditional Lakota economy collapsed. No longer able to trade hides for guns and ammunition, much less to feed themselves, the Lakotas became utterly dependent on the government dole. Withholding rations became a potent weapon in the agent's arsenal.

∗

When Sitting Bull reached the Great Sioux Reservation in May 1883, it had already sunk into six seas of misery, each swirling around a separate agency island. Five years earlier, the government had closed down the Red Cloud and Spotted Tail Agencies because they lay outside the reservation boundaries. Red Cloud's seventy-three hundred Oglalas now resided on the Pine Ridge Agency, fifty miles southeast of the Black Hills in the Dakota Territory. Spotted Tail's four thousand Upper Brulés belonged to the Rosebud Agency, ninety-five miles east of Pine Ridge. About a thousand Lower Brulés lived at their agency on the west bank of the Missouri. Some three thousand Miniconjous, Blackfeet, Sans Arcs, and Two Kettles congregated around the Cheyenne River Agency. North of them, seventeen hundred Hunkpapas, Blackfeet, and Upper Yanktonais were enrolled at the Standing Rock Agency. The total Lakota reservation population approached seventeen thousand, nearly half of whom had been branded hostiles between 1876 and 1881.

Without war and raiding, Lakota men lost their paths to prestige and status. Warrior societies declined in membership and meaning. The Indian Bureau filled the void with the Indian police. Uniformed and salaried, fiercely loyal to the government, and often Christianized, Indian policemen became the agent's *akicitas*. Even had the Lakotas possessed the means, there was nowhere for them to go. By mid-decade, the white population of the Dakota Territory had climbed to 500,000.

Well-armed cowboys quite capable of defending themselves covered the country more thoroughly than could cavalry patrols. The Great Sioux Reservation, in short, had become a sealed laboratory for social engineering.

Anticipating the reformers, in 1881 the commissioner of Indian affairs had set the official course for the decade when he told Congress that "to domesticate wild Indians is a noble work, [the] crown of glory to any nation. But to allow them to drag along in their old superstitions, laziness, and filth, when we have the power to elevate them in the scale of humanity, would be a lasting disgrace to our government." The chief duty of an Indian agent was now to "induce his Indian to labor in civilized pursuits." Agents were instructed to stamp out "demoralizing and barbarous customs," which included plural marriages, pagan "medicine-making," and traditional ceremonies—particularly the Sun Dance. Removing the Sun Dance from Plains Indian religion was analogous to banishing Christ from Christian churches. With its proscription—the last Sun Dance was held in 1883—the social and religious fabric of Lakota society unraveled.[5]

Government policies, however, were only as effective as the agents charged with executing them. And in the 1880s, the Lakotas were visited with two of the strongest agents in Indian Bureau history, James McLaughlin at Standing Rock and Valentine McGillycuddy at Pine Ridge. McLaughlin, a former blacksmith with a mixed-blood wife, was every bit the equal of Sitting Bull in strength of character, integrity, and firmness of vision. Adroit at "managing" Indians—that is to say, playing one faction against another—he had won over two of Sitting Bull's most influential former lieutenants, the war chiefs Gall and Crow King. Both were now "progressives," the title that agents accorded chiefs who cooperated with government programs. As for Sitting Bull, McLaughlin cast him as a reactionary, or "non-progressive," chief who must be broken.

McLaughlin did the Lakota holy man a rank injustice. Sitting Bull resented McLaughlin's lack of respect, and he stood up for his people, but he was not categorically opposed to change. Mostly, after his release from army custody, Sitting Bull wanted to go it alone in these bewildering times. At Pine Ridge, on the other hand, Chief Red Cloud sparred aggressively with Agent McGillycuddy, the former army surgeon who had attended to a dying Crazy Horse. Highly competent but mercurial, McGillycuddy respected Red Cloud as "one of the greatest, if not the greatest war chiefs of his people, [who] never forgot his love of his people." But "the old man was a reactionary in a high degree, and it was one eternal war between us for seven years." Wounded pride played a part, because Red Cloud resented the Great Father's imposition of a mere "boy" as his agent. (McGillycuddy was just thirty when he came to Pine Ridge.)

Chief Spotted Tail found it all quite amusing. He visited McGillycuddy in the fall of 1879, shortly after the agent's appointment, in good humor. "We were old acquaintances," recalled McGillycuddy, "and he had heard of the innovations at Pine Ridge, of my organizing the police force to offset Red Cloud and the soldier bands. On leaving he remarked, 'Brother Red Cloud, you'd better look out, that boy the Great Father has sent you will break you before he gets through.'"

Red Cloud weathered McGillycuddy's tenure, but Spotted Tail died at an assassin's hand two years after warning the old chief to watch out. His murderer was Crow Dog, a member of a Brulé cabal intent on setting up one of their own as head chief. The self-styled heirs to the head chieftainship squabbled and intrigued, but none possessed the character or influence to succeed the slain Spotted Tail. Many Lakotas had written off Spotted Tail as the white man's cat's-paw, which he decidedly was not. Spotted Tail had been a pragmatist, dedicating thirty years of his life to preserving what he could of Lakota culture while easing his people into inevitable white domination on the most favorable terms possible. With his death, the Brulés disintegrated as a tribe.[6]

✳

The Brulés, and in fact all the Lakotas, were to sink even further. On February 8, 1887, eastern reformers and western land promoters celebrated a watershed victory. On that day, President Grover Cleveland signed into law the General Allotment Act—also known as the Dawes Act—opening huge swaths of Indian reservations to homesteaders. The act was the brainchild of Senator Henry L. Dawes, who shared the reformers' vision of Indian assimilation. The legislation authorized the president to survey the reservations and to allot reservation land suitable for farming or grazing to the Indians in severalty, after which the government could negotiate with the Indians for the purchase of surplus acreage. In plain language, the Dawes Act provided the legal framework for dismantling treaties.

Dakota Territory promoters hustled through Congress a bill applying the Dawes Act to the Great Sioux Reservation—with one important qualification. The Sioux Bill of 1888 permitted negotiations for surplus lands *before* surveys were run and land allotted to the Indians. Prospective Dakota boomers stood to gain nine million acres, or roughly half of the Great Sioux Reservation. Captain Richard Pratt, the founder of the Carlisle Indian Industrial School in Pennsylvania, took a delegation west to negotiate the purchase. Pratt was a terrible choice. His boarding school was the ultimate expression of the reformers' goal of Americanizing young Indians. Corporal punishment was unknown in Indian families, but Pratt was not above beating Native behavior out of his students, nor did he shrink from strong-arming Plains Indian families into surrendering their children to his faraway school. The Lakotas understandably despised him, and the chiefs sent him back to Washington empty-handed.[7]

That clearly would not do. Rickety "claims-shacks" had mushroomed on the margins of the reservation, and some had already trickled onto Lakota land. In March 1889, President Benjamin Harrison appointed a new commission to hurry the acquisition of the excess acreage. A few sweeteners were added, such as an increase in the purchase price from fifty cents to $1.25 an acre. Also, Congress conceded that any agreement must be ratified by three-quarters of adult males, as called for under the 1868 Fort Laramie Treaty. The blueprint was simple: existing agencies were to become autonomous reservations, in some cases separated physically by land ceded to the government. Thus, the Pine Ridge Agency of the Great Sioux Reservation would become the Pine Ridge Reservation, the Rosebud Agency would become the Rosebud Reservation, and so forth.

General Crook dominated the three-man commission, but he faced staunch opposition from the chiefs. Deploring the commissioners' "talk of sugar," Red Cloud opposed the cession loudly and openly. Sitting Bull, for his part, worked quietly through intermediaries to defeat the sale on the grounds that the government would renege on its obligations. Crook, however, was not interested in Lakota objections. He bluntly educated the Lakotas in the dismal truth, which was that they would never get better terms than they were now being offered. "It strikes me," he told the chiefs, "that you are in the position of a person who had his effects in the bed of a dry stream when there was a flood coming down, and instead of finding fault with the Creator for sending it down, you should try to save what you can. And that when you can't get what you like best you had better take what is the best for you."[8]

Crook wished to save the Lakotas from themselves, but he used questionable methods. After three months of cajolery, bribery, and exploiting factional rivalries, Crook obtained the three-quarters majority needed for Lakota ratification. Before signing the land cession agreement in June 1889, the Lakota progressives had exacted from Crook a promise that rations would not be cut anytime soon; the government's intention of making the Indians self-supporting and eventually abolishing rations was an open secret on the reservation. No sooner had the commission concluded its business, however, than orders came slashing beef rations at the Rosebud Agency by two million pounds and at other agencies in proportional quantities. The rations cut was a consequence of ill-timed congressional economizing, and Crook was powerless to right the wrong.

The need for full rations had never been greater. After the three-month negotiations ended, the Lakotas returned home to find their neglected crops withered or trampled under. White rustlers and horse thieves had run off much of their livestock and pony herds. Then drought came, drying up creeks and destroying what few crops remained. Rather than close ranks after the government betrayal, the Lakotas sank deeper into discord. Traditionalists derided those who signed the agreement as "dupes and fools"; children took their parents' dispute into agency schools, and brawls became commonplace.[9]

*

The winter of 1889–1890 came on hard. Families struggled to keep their kettles full. Epidemics of measles, whooping cough, and influenza swept the reservations, cutting down malnourished children, the infirm, and the elderly. Idleness and brooding made abject alcoholics out of once-proud warriors. The young medicine man Black Elk gazed upon the bleak landscape of squat gray cabins and desolate fields and grieved. "The people seemed heavy to me, heavy and dark; so heavy it seemed they could not be lifted; so dark that they could not be made to see anymore. Hunger was among us now. There were many lies, but we could not eat them."[10]

Then came the ultimate act of bad faith and from the Great Father himself. In February 1890, on the flimsy pretext that the Sioux Land Commission agreement had been nonbinding, President Harrison threw open the ceded reservation lands to settlement. No surveys had been conducted to mark the boundaries, nor had the many Lakotas living in the ceded land been given allotments on the reduced reservations. In fact, no Lakota knew what land was his and what was not. "The very earth," said a missionary, "seemed sliding from beneath their feet." And then, on March 21, the Lakotas lost a powerful advocate when George Crook died of a massive coronary at age fifty-nine. He had been engaged in his morning weight-lifting routine at his headquarters in Chicago when his three decades of hard frontier service at last caught up with him. The Lakotas heard the news and wept. Said Red Cloud to the Catholic missionary at Pine Ridge, "Then General Crook came . . . He promised to see that his promises would be kept. He, at least, had never lied to us. They signed. They hoped. He died. Their hope died with him. Despair came again."[11]

But something mysterious was afoot. Early in 1889, vague rumors had reached the Lakotas of a messiah come to earth beyond the Rocky Mountains to liberate all Indians from the white man's yoke. After the ration cuts came, the Oglala chiefs dispatched a delegation to the Pacific Northwest for an audience with the messiah. "There was no hope on earth," lamented Red Cloud, "and God seemed to have forgotten us." Perhaps something had induced the Great Spirit to remember.

In March 1890, the Lakota delegation returned with startling news. They had seen the messiah descend from the sky. He was the son of the Great Spirit, sent to earth to deliver the Indians from their sins and to bring unto them an earthly paradise free from whites, whom he would wipe from the face of the earth. It would all happen in the spring of 1891.

For the great millennial event to occur, vouchsafed Lakota disciples, believers must perform a sacred ritual taught by the messiah. It was called the Ghost Dance. The strong of faith would "die" while dancing and gain a glimpse of the coming world. So long as they wore sacred clothing called Ghost Shirts, worshippers need fear nothing. "If the high priests would make for the dancers [ghost] shirts and pray over them, no harm would come to the wearer," a disciple assured them, adding that "the bullets of any whites that desired to stop the dance would fall to the ground without doing anyone harm, and the person firing such shots would drop dead."

It was a heady creed. A dance into immortality in an earthly paradise, a violent death to any whites who dared interfere and to all whites at the appointed hour. There was just one problem. Unbeknownst to reservation Lakotas, the messiah taught no such thing.[12]

*

The messiah's earthly name was Wovoka, or Jack Wilson to his white friends, of whom he had many. Gentle and mild-tempered, Wovoka was a thirty-five-year-old Paiute medicine man. He wore white man's clothing and worked for a western Nevada rancher, from whom he learned both English and a confused version of Christian theology. During a solar eclipse in early 1889, a vision had come to Wovoka. He had been violently ill, and in his fevered state he had felt himself ascend into heaven. There God had given him the Good News. Jesus, whom the whites had killed, had returned to earth to inaugurate the Indian millennium. The whites would evanesce, but not by violence. Come the spring of 1891, the Great Spirit would simply send them back from whence they had come. Until then, Wovoka had told his disciples, they must perform the Ghost Dance faithfully and also keep on good terms with the whites. Arapahos and Shoshones had been the first to bear Wovoka's words beyond the Paiute country. Within a matter of months, perhaps weeks, Wovoka's message had spread to every tribe in the American West. Ghost Dances, peaceable as Wovoka intended, swept the reservations. For the Lakota emissaries, however, anger over the land cessions and reduced rations was too raw for them to accept a wholly pacific doctrine. So they added their own militant touches, creating a potentially explosive heresy.[13]

It was the heresy of a millennial fantasy that even in its pacific manifestation could do the Indians no good: a false hope that, like a narcotic, temporarily deadened the soul-wrenching pain of cultural disintegration. To peoples so afflicted, the promises of a prophet are a compelling summons. Throughout history, temporal conditions grown unendurable have called forth spiritual solutions. Remarkably, in view of their circumstances, at the outset few Lakotas embraced the Ghost Dance religion—or the "Messiah Craze," as the government called the theosophical phenomenon. Progressives dismissed the new faith as so much nonsense. Traditionalists were receptive but skeptical. Red Cloud was evasive. If the new faith were real, he told the Pine Ridge agent, "it would spread all over the world." If it were false, "it would melt like the snow under the hot sun."[14]

Then summer came. Hot winds scorched the prairie. Crops died. Even range grass wilted. Hundreds of white settlers living near the reservation abandoned their homesteads and headed east. But the Lakotas had nowhere to go. And so they suffered. The baked soil became fertile ground for the new faith, and hunger nourished its growth. Valentine McGillycuddy, who had left Pine Ridge three years earlier, sympathized with the Lakotas: "The dance and its ceremonies was like the voice of a feast to a starving man. Had these people been well fed the Ghost Dance would never have been heard of . . . The prayer in the dance was for food for themselves; for their women and their children; they cried for help from above, all other help having failed."

Or as the Oglala progressive chief Big Road put it, "White men pray because they want to go to Heaven. Indians want to go to Heaven too, so they prayed, and they also prayed for food enough to keep them out of Heaven until it was time to go."[15]

On the Cheyenne River Reservation, rations were irregular and always short. Hungry Brulés at the Rosebud Agency begged "for the refuse from the slaughter pen and from the company kitchens." Progressive chiefs implored their agents to "give us just [as] you have promised," saying that if they did, the Ghost Dance movement would collapse. Neighboring whites agreed. The Ghost Dance, said a Nebraska editor, was the consequence of "bad faith on the part of the government, bad rations, and not enough of them." But Congress dithered. Without renewed funding, Indian Bureau authority to feed the Indians would expire on October 1, 1890. Nonetheless, it was late August before Congress passed the Indian Appropriations Act for 1891, too late for supplemental rations and most annuity goods to reach the Indians before winter.

By autumn, the Ghost Dance was in full flower. Its spiritual center was the Pine Ridge Reservation. Northern Cheyennes at Pine Ridge rejected the faith, but nearly 40 percent of the Oglalas converted. At the Rosebud Reservation, one in three Brulés were dedicated dancers; at Cheyenne River, one in five Lakotas were practitioners. The principal Lakota apostles of the Ghost Dance religion were the Oglala warrior Kicking Bear (a cousin of Crazy Horse's) and the Brulé medicine man Short Bull. Both were about forty-five years old and had been delegates to Wovoka. It was they who had distorted the messiah's teachings.

All Lakotas had ample cause to embrace the faith, but most of its practitioners were traditionalists—the so-called non-progressives of Crazy Horse's and Sitting Bull's bands who had been among the last to surrender. Under the steadying hand of the Oglala chiefs American Horse and Young Man Afraid of His Horses at Pine Ridge and the

Hunkpapa war chief Gall at Standing Rock, the progressives largely shunned the Ghost Dance. That which Wovoka had intended as a unifying pan-Indian religion served instead to deepen the schism within the Lakota people.[16]

As the chill of autumn set in, the Ghost Dance continued to burn white-hot. Day upon day, devotees of all ages and both sexes danced and sang fervently, hoping to induce the trance that would transport their spirits temporarily to the other side, where they would meet deceased friends and relatives, and perhaps the messiah himself, and taste of the prosperity to come.

To the uninitiated, the Ghost Dance was a fearful spectacle to behold. Large dance circles undulated with unrestrained frenzy. Here and there, dancers collapsed in the dust in ersatz rigor mortis; others foamed at the mouth or screamed in seeming insanity. All were bathed in perspiration. Among the whites, sympathy for the Lakotas' suffering was replaced with dread of a bloody Indian breakout. An exodus from ranches and farms bordering the reservations began, the refugees sped along by newspaper speculation that "buck Indians are holding their savage dance of death, with Winchesters on their backs and [bad] blood in their hearts." Lakota men, it was rumored, were buying up all the ammunition to be had in area hardware stores. Clearheaded editors tried to restore calm, pointing out that the dancers had not harmed anyone and, apart from stealing an occasional sheep or head of cattle, had kept to themselves. But young male Lakota dancers in fact were growing restive. When the agent at Rosebud tried to stop them from slaughtering reservation breeding stock, the men told him that they would rather die fighting than from starvation; besides, they had nothing to fear: they would be resurrected when the millennium came.[17]

And it would come sooner than expected, if Short Bull were to be believed. To forestall white meddling, he assured the Ghost Dancers that he would personally advance the millennium to an unspecified date, perhaps as soon as the next moon. And the dancers need not worry should soldiers appear. "Pay no attention to them," he enjoined a gathering near Pine Ridge on October 30. "Continue to dance. If the soldiers surround you four deep, three of you upon whom I have put [Ghost] shirts will sing songs which I have taught you and some of them will drop dead, then the rest will start to run but their horses will sink into the earth." An army officer reported—and local newspapers published—Short Bull's speech. Some read Short Bull's words as a call to war, which they were not. But their antagonistic tone deepened the apprehension of Dakotans.[18]

*

The tragedy of Nathan C. Meeker and the Utes should have demonstrated beyond any doubt the grave damage that unqualified Indian agents could inflict upon both the Indians and the army. But nothing had changed. Thirteen years after the Milk River fiasco, the patronage system continued to dictate agency appointments. A South Dakota senator claimed Pine Ridge, and he engineered the appointment as agent of thirty-six-year-old Daniel F. Royer—a physician, newspaperman, banker, two-term territorial delegate, druggist, and quite possibly narcotics addict. Not only did Royer lack relevant experience, but the mere sight of Indians also made him uneasy. Quick to take his measure, the Oglalas called him Young Man Afraid of Indians. On October 12, just four days after assuming his duties, Royer told the Indian Bureau that troops might be needed to keep order.

The new commander of the Military Division of the Missouri was having nothing to do with Royer's alarmism. General Crook's death had bestowed on Nelson A. Miles a second star and the top job in the West. In late October, a visit to Pine Ridge left Miles convinced the messiah craze would run its course naturally. Nevertheless, he warned the Oglalas that should they cause trouble, he would "whale the hell out of them." The Ghost Dancers scoffed at Miles's threat. Had not Short Bull promised that the messiah would soon come and rub out Bear Coat and all his soldiers? They took Royer even less seriously. When the timorous agent later demanded the Ghost Dance leaders halt the dances, "they simply laughed and said that they would keep it up as long as they pleased."[19]

On ration day, November 10, the last vestige of Royer's authority crumbled when he ordered a Ghost Dancer arrested for killing a steer contrary to agency policy. As the agency police moved in to arrest the man, Ghost Dancers surrounded them. Calls to kill the police came from the crowd. Upbraiding the mob for threatening "their own race," Chief American Horse prevented bloodshed. A terrified Royer withdrew to his office and began a drumbeat of telegrams to the Indian Bureau demanding soldiers be sent to protect agency employees from "these crazy dancers." As for himself, Royer wanted out. The delicacy of the situation, he told the Indian Bureau, demanded that he brief Washington officials personally; the acting commissioner told him to remain at his post and do his duty.

Unbeknownst to the Indian Bureau, Royer had taken his case public, telling the local press that the Ghost Dancers were loading up on ammunition, which they were not, and planned to use it. "Bloodshed," he insisted, "is all that will stop them now." Royer's alarmism was unwarranted. True, the situation at both Pine Ridge and Rosebud was tense and unstable, and some of the Ghost Dancers had indeed grown insubordinate, but there was no credible evidence that any of the leaders contemplated violence. If Royer hoped to instill enough fear in official circles to induce Washington to act, he succeeded. On November 13, President Harrison ordered the secretary of war "to assume responsibility for the suppression of any threatened outbreak, and to take such steps as may be necessary to that end."

Two days later, Royer issued a final, frenetic appeal; the Indians, he said, were "dancing in the snow and are wild and crazy." That forced General Miles's hand. He dispatched twelve hundred soldiers to Pine Ridge and another three hundred to the Rosebud Agency. The commanding officer of the Department of the Platte, Brigadier General John R. Brooke, a punctilious officer long on good intentions but short on Indian experience, assumed operational command, setting up headquarters in Royer's vacant office; the agent had abandoned his post and taken his family to the nearest town.

General Miles intended to exercise caution. So too did the commanding general of the army, Major General John M. Schofield. In Schofield's judgment, "the ghost dancers should not be disturbed for the present, nor anything be done to precipitate a crisis." But should Miles find it necessary to "whale the hell" out of the Ghost Dancers, as he had threatened to do, there was one regiment at Pine Ridge well acquainted with the Lakota manner of war making: the Seventh Cavalry.[20]

*

The army's appearance on the Pine Ridge Reservation forced Red Cloud to take a stand, and he came down on the side of the government. "Those Indians are fools," he said of the Ghost Dancers. "The winter weather will stop it, I think. Anyway, it will be all over by spring. I don't

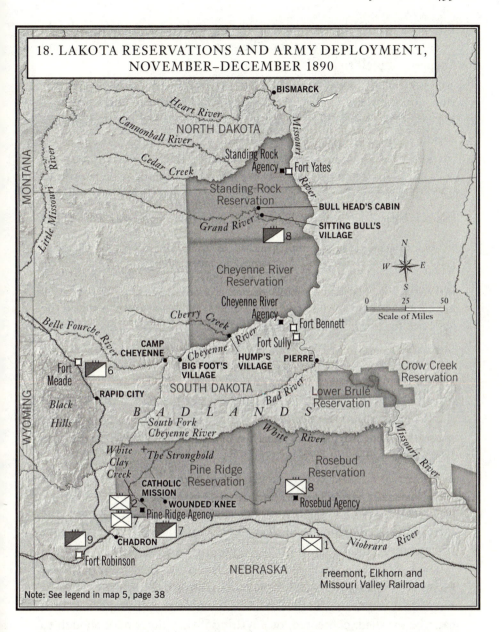

18. LAKOTA RESERVATIONS AND ARMY DEPLOYMENT, NOVEMBER–DECEMBER 1890

Note: See legend in map 5, page 38

think there will be any trouble." He hadn't seen the dance for himself; his vision had grown too weak, and his eyes were too sore. "When they get well, I will go to see it [and] try to stop it," he assured visiting newspapermen. That Red Cloud would succeed was highly doubtful. He persuaded his son Jack Red Cloud to quit the dance, but the sixty-eight-year-old chief himself had grown too feeble even to challenge the military presence. "When we made our treaty it was promised there should be no troops on the reservation," he said. "They are here, though, and I suppose it is all right."[21]

It was not all right. No soldiers had ever set foot on a Lakota reservation, and their coming touched off a panic. The Brulé Ghost Dancers, led by Short Bull and Kicking Bear, abandoned the Rosebud Reservation in order to worship unmolested. Nonbelievers also fled. Two Strike's and Crow Dog's traditionalist bands joined the Ghost Dancers to avoid being caught in an army roundup. All told, close to two thousand Brulés left the reservation. With only a few hundred "progressives" remaining behind, the army occupiers found the agency tranquil and duty dull.

The Brulés on the run had hoped to obtain refuge at Pine Ridge. But when they learned the army was there as well, they turned north toward the Badlands. Along the way, they wrecked the vacant homes and stole abandoned property of progressive Lakotas, who were streaming to the agencies for protection. Once in the Badlands, the Brulés erected their village on a nearly inaccessible corner of a broad, grassy plateau. The army dubbed the forbidding spot the Stronghold. In late November, several hundred Oglala Ghost Dancers and two thousand Lakota progressives, fearful the army would disarm and dismount them, joined the Brulés. By December 1, nearly four thousand Lakotas crowded the mesa. It was the largest off-reservation gathering of Northern Plains Indians since the Little Bighorn.[22]

Neither General Brooke at Pine Ridge nor General Miles in Chicago wanted to provoke a confrontation. While Brooke sent peace emissaries to talk the Lakotas out of the Badlands, Miles began to assemble the forces necessary to surround the reservations and awe the recalcitrant Indians into submission. Both Miles and Brooke empathized with the Lakotas. "My eyes have been opened very wide since coming here," General Brooke scolded Agent Royer. "Too little, too little, entirely too little. I don't care whether they are Indians or what they are. People can't be satisfied, contented, or anything if they don't have enough to eat, and the government should be finding it out pretty soon."[23]

It did. On November 28, General Miles went to Washington, D.C., to lay before the Harrison administration and Congress the unvarnished truth: the Indians needed food at once; otherwise, war was inevitable. He bludgeoned the secretary of war into buying additional rations out of army appropriations and the secretary of the interior into using discretionary funds to bring rations temporarily to the 1889 treaty level. He also came with a personal shopping list. Taking a page from Sheridan's Great Sioux War playbook, Miles demanded army control over the "police and management" of the Lakota agencies, permission to summon troops from across the country as needed, and authority to arrest and remove the "principal leaders and organizers" of the Ghost Dance. Miles got everything he asked for and within two weeks had cordoned off the reservations with eight regiments totaling almost five thousand men, or one-quarter of the fighting strength of the United States, some rushed in by railroad from as far away as San Francisco.

Miles's detractors found his operation oddly reminiscent of the Geronimo Campaign, when he had assembled a similarly huge force to hunt down a handful of Apaches. Brigadier General Wesley Merritt accused Miles of exaggerating the danger in order to further his career. There might have been an element of truth to Merritt's accusation, but Miles's strategy was sound. By mid-December, diplomacy, adequate rations, and the implicit threat of force had induced runaway progressive Oglalas and the bands of Two Strike and Crow Dog to return to the agencies. Hostilities now appeared unlikely. Only a few hundred hard-core Brulé and Oglala Ghost Dancers clung to the Stronghold, and they were caught up in dancing and prayers, threatening no one. Given time, Miles believed they could be talked into surrendering. Of the three thousand Lakotas on the Cheyenne River Reservation, only the bands of Chiefs Big Foot and Hump—at most six hundred Miniconjous—were Ghost Dancers. And at Standing Rock, no more than four hundred Hunkpapas, representing less than a quarter of the agency Indians, practiced the faith. The three remaining Lakota reservations had few if any converts. The messiah craze had, in a large part, fizzled. Miles, however, knew better than to declare victory. He understood that only Congress could effect a lasting solution by fulfilling the "treaty obligations in which the Indians were entreated and coerced into signing."[24]

Having isolated the Ghost Dancers, Miles turned to phase two of his plan: the arrest and deportation of their leaders. Sitting Bull's prestige made him the greatest threat, and so Miles moved against him first with the eager cooperation of Agent McLaughlin, who in the course of five years of wrangling with the chief had worked himself into an irrational lather. Sitting Bull was a "mindless obstructionist" and should be taken from Standing Rock to a military prison, McLaughlin told the Indian Bureau in October 1890. Not only did Sitting Bull bear the standard of reaction, McLaughlin insisted, but he was also a coward, "a polygamist libertine, and habitual liar; a man of low cunning, devoid of a single manly principle in his nature, or an honorable trait of character, capable of inciting others to any amount of mischief."

For a time, it had looked as if McLaughlin and Sitting Bull might make peace. Hopeful an understanding of the white man's power would make Sitting Bull more tractable, McLaughlin had permitted him to join Buffalo Bill Cody's Wild West show for the 1885 season. McLaughlin's plan backfired, however. Sitting Bill returned from the East with an enlarged worldview that not only made him more independent of the agent but also deepened his contempt of the white way of life. First, Sitting Bull set his people straight on the Great Father. The agents had lied: white men did not hold the Great Father sacred. On the contrary, Sitting Bull told them, "half the people in the hotels were always making fun of him and trying to get him out of his place and some other man into his place." As for members of Congress, "they loved their whores more than their wives." And like most white men, they drank too much. Indeed, Sitting Bull told friends, "the soul of a white man is so odored with whiskey that it will have to hang around here on earth for hundreds of years before the winds and storms will so purify it that the people in the other life can endure the smell of it there, and let them in." Once he was back home at Standing Rock, Sitting Bull occasionally took up women's work. When asked why, he would say, "I am trying to learn to be as we will all have to be when the white man gets us."

Sitting Bull was spreading it on a bit thick. He genuinely enjoyed farming. Together with most of the Hunkpapas, he settled on Grand River, thirty miles southwest of the agency and forty miles from Fort Yates. Living in a cluster of cabins with his large family, Sitting Bull cultivated vegetables, harvested oats, bred cattle, kept a large flock of chickens, and dug a root cellar. The "non-progressive" promised to make his living from the soil, and he did it better than most Indians under McLaughlin's tutelage.[25]

Apart from speaking out against the 1889 land cession, Sitting Bull had kept a low profile. Stories of the new religion intrigued him, however. In October 1890, he invited Kicking Bear to Grand River to teach the Hunkpapas the Ghost Dance. McLaughlin's police ejected Kicking Bear from the reservation but not before he had instructed Sitting Bull in the rudiments of the faith. Well pleased, Sitting Bull summoned the Hunkpapas to his settlement to initiate a Ghost Dance. Fewer than five hundred responded, but they made up with fervor what they lacked in numbers. Sitting Bull presided over the dances and interpreted the revelations of dancers who visited the spirit world. He never said whether he believed in the new faith or not. Probably he saw in it a chance to reassert his authority, much of which he had lost to Gall, the war chief and Little Bighorn hero (to the Lakotas at least) now turned progressive. Sitting Bull was just fifty-nine years old; unlike the failing Red Cloud, he was still vigorous enough to stage a comeback.[26]

McLaughlin's solution, with which the commanding officer at Fort Yates concurred, was to use agency police *ceska maza* (or "metal breasts," a reference to their badges) to arrest Sitting Bull at his home on ration day, December 20, when most of the Hunkpapas would be at the agency, and then hand him off to a waiting cavalry squadron from Fort Yates. It would be a tough operation to pull off, because Sitting Bull and McLaughlin had spies in each other's camps. Lieutenant Henry Bull Head, a Christianized Lakota who had once fought under Sitting Bull, was McLaughlin's man at Grand River. The agent quietly reinforced him with small detachments that Bull Head placed above and below Sitting Bull's settlement. With police keeping watch and cavalry on call at Fort Yates, there was nothing more for McLaughlin to do but wait for ration day.

Sitting Bull unwittingly altered their timetable. He had received an invitation from Short Bull and Kicking Bear to visit the Stronghold, and he intended to go. Eavesdropping on Sitting Bull's council, two of Lieutenant Bull Head's informers reported that the chief would leave on the morning of December 15 and would shoot any metal breasts who got in his way. McLaughlin concurred with Bull Head's recommendation that the chief be grabbed at once. On the evening of December 14, Bull Head ordered the police to assemble at his cabin. He had received a formal order from McLaughlin to effect the arrest peaceably. But it contained a caveat: Bull Head was not to allow Sitting Bull to escape under any circumstances.[27]

*

The Hunkpapa *ceska maza* John Lone Man was a committed pilgrim on the white man's road. Transformed from a skilled warrior who had fought Custer into a devout Catholic farmer, he exemplified the "pro-gressive" spirit that McLaughlin hoped to instill in all his charges; that is to say, the "whiteman-izing" that Sitting Bull condemned. Lone Man was at home mending his police saddle when his fellow *ceska maza* Charles Afraid of Hawk brought word that Lieutenant Bull Head wanted the police to meet at his cabin three miles northwest of Sitting Bull's village. For Lone Man, it meant a thirty-mile trip on his day off. He and Afraid of Hawk speculated that the purpose of their summons was to arrest Sitting Bull, a prospect that saddened them. As they rode to the rendezvous, other policemen fell in with the apprehensive pair. "Of course we had quite a lot to say on the way among ourselves, know-ing full well that we were called to take a final action to suppress this Ghost Dance, which was becoming a menace to the tribe."[28]

Lone Man and his companions reached Bull Head's cramped cabin at 7:00 p.m. Four volunteers also showed up. One of them was Sitting Bull's brother-in-law; another was a nephew of Sitting Bull's who had formed a cattle-raising partnership with the chief's stepson and then turned informer for McLaughlin. Past loyalties were yielding to the changed realities of the Lakota world that Sitting Bull had so dreaded.[29]

After dinner, Lieutenant Bull Head confirmed the reason for the summons: they were to arrest Sitting Bull on the agent's order. Bull Head assigned two men to grab and saddle Sitting Bull's favorite horse, a gift from Buffalo Bill Cody, while he and the sergeants entered the chief's cabin. The rest of the men would form a perimeter outside. Lone Man, whose place would be beside the door, sensed "big trouble ahead."

The policemen passed the long winter night halfheartedly telling war stories. Before dawn, Bull Head led them in Christian prayer. At 4:00 a.m., December 15, 1890, under an icy drizzle, the metal breasts mounted in a column of twos. "Hopo," the lieutenant commanded, and they trotted into the darkness. The ride was eerie. Lone Man's imagi-nation got the better of him. "As we went through the Grand River bottoms it seemed as if the owls were hooting at us and the coyotes were howling . . . a warning [to] beware."[30]

A mile from their destination, the police broke into a gallop. At a quarter mile's distance, they charged. Dogs barked, and the camp awakened. The policemen dismounted at Sitting Bull's cabin. Bull Head and his first sergeant pushed open the door and lit matches. On a mattress in the flickering light with one of his wives and his small chil-dren sat Sitting Bull, stark naked. His fourteen-year-old son squatted in a corner. Sitting Bull arose, and the officers shoved him toward the door. "This is a great way to do things," he protested, "not to give me a chance to put on my clothes in wintertime." They relented long enough for Sitting Bull's wife to fetch his clothes from an adjacent cabin. The chief dressed, and the three men walked to the door.

Outside, the policemen confronted a growing throng of Ghost Dancers. The atmosphere was tense and uncertain. Catch the Bear, a companion of the chief's since youth, stepped forward. "Now here are the *ceska maza*," he spat, "just as we had expected all the time. You think you are going to take him. You shall not do it." To the crowd he yelled, "Come on now, let us protect our Chief." The police line wavered. Inside the cabin, Sitting Bull's son taunted his father. "Well, you always called yourself a brave chief. Now you are allowing yourself to be taken by the *ceska maza*." Sitting Bull hesitated. "Then I shall not go," he said, gripping the doorway. "Come, now, do not listen to any-one," begged Bull Head. "Uncle, nobody is going to harm you," Lone Man interjected. "The agent wants to see you and then you are com-ing back, so please don't make any trouble." But Sitting Bull refused to budge. Bull Head grabbed his right arm, and another policeman took hold of his left, while a third shoved the chief into the yard from behind. The people shook their fists and cursed. "The police tried to keep order," Lone Man said, but "[it] was useless—like trying to extin-guish a treacherous prairie fire."

Without warning, Catch the Bear threw off his blanket, raised his Winchester rifle, and shot Bull Head in the side. Still clutching Sit-ting Bull's arm, Bull Head squeezed off a round from his revolver that struck Sitting Bull in the sternum, tearing apart his chest. A hand-to-hand struggle ensued between the police and the crowd. Three more bullets plowed into Bull Head, mortally wounding him. Catch the Bear took aim at Lone Man, but his rifle misfired. Yanking it away, Lone Man clubbed him across the forehead, cleared the chamber, and then shot the instigator dead.

The Ghost Dancers withdrew into a belt of timber, firing as they fell back, and the police returned the fire from behind sheds and corrals. After the shooting subsided, Lone Man noticed a stirring behind a cur-tain in Sitting Bull's cabin. Pulling it aside, he stood face-to-face with Sitting Bull's son. "My uncles, do not kill me. I do not wish to die," the boy begged. Lone Man glanced at Bull Head. "Do what you like with him," groaned the mortally wounded lieutenant. "He is one of them that has caused this trouble." Lone Man and another man pumped bullets into the boy and then flung his corpse out the door.[31]

From a ridge across the Grand River, a cannon boomed, dispersing Sitting Bull's followers. Although day had dawned, a gray mist covered the settlement. Aiming blindly, the cannon shifted fire toward Sitting Bull's cabins. Between explosions, Lone Man darted about waving a white flag until the cannon fell silent and a cavalry squadron charged down from the heights. To the accompanying wails of Sitting Bull's widows, the squadron commander dismounted and picked up a branch. Counting coup on Sitting Bull, he said, "Sitting Bull—big chief, you brought this disaster upon yourself and your people." Relatives of the dead policemen released their rage on the chief's remains. Several emptied their revolvers into the body. One man sliced open the holy man's face with an ax; another cut it with a knife. A third man seized an ox yoke or club—accounts differ—and beat Sitting Bull's head into a shapeless mass. "What the hell did you do that for?" a soldier asked. "The man is dead. Leave him alone." To keep Sitting Bull's body from freezing to the large pool of blood on the cabin floor, an army sergeant dragged it outside.

The police placed their wounded in a cavalry ambulance and their dead in an old farm wagon. When a police sergeant told them to toss Sitting Bull's body into the wagon as well, the men objected; to put him in the same wagon, they said, would dishonor their fallen comrades. The sergeant insisted. The men obeyed, in a manner of speaking; they flipped Sitting Bull's mangled corpse facedown on the wagon bed beneath their dead.

Grieving and terrified, Sitting Bull's Hunkpapas journeyed south toward the Cheyenne River Reservation in the hope of finding sanctuary with the Miniconjous. They would come to call the tragedy that they had just witnessed the Battle in the Dark.[32]

Two days after the killing of Sitting Bull, Lone Man took his family to the agency to attend the funeral for the dead policemen. A combined Catholic and Protestant service was held in the Congregational mission, and the *ceska maza* were buried in the church cemetery with full military honors. A company of soldiers fired three volleys over the graves, and an army bugler blew taps. After the burial, James McLaughlin attended another interment, this one at Fort Yates. Together with three army officers, he watched a rough wooden coffin with Sitting Bull's remains lowered into the equivalent of a pauper's grave at the far corner of the post cemetery. Four guardhouse prisoners shoveled dirt into the hole. No service was held. No words were read over the grave.

Later in the day, John Lone Man paid a call on McLaughlin. Laying his hands on Lone Man's shoulders, the agent told him how proud he was of his conduct in the struggle with the Ghost Dancers. "I was not very brave right at that moment," Lone Man later confessed. "His comment nearly set me a crying."[33]

CHAPTER 23

THE PLACE
OF THE BIG KILLINGS

F EW BESIDES Lone Man and Sitting Bull's small band of followers wept over the great chief's passing. Westerners, of course,
applauded his demise, while reformers grieved only over the manner of
his death. The eastern press sneered that the "murderous old wretch"
had met a "richly deserved fate." On the Lakota reservations, Sitting
Bull's death occasioned scarcely a murmur of protest. At Standing Rock,
the progressives expressed what McLaughlin called "satisfaction at the
result of the fight." At Pine Ridge, General Brooke said the friendly
chiefs, which presumably included Red Cloud, "recognized the justice
of Sitting Bull's death and said it was a good thing that he had met
his fate." In the Stronghold, the reaction was also muted. Small raiding parties went on stealing cattle, mostly within the confines of the
Pine Ridge Reservation. But no whites were molested; in fact, the only
killing came when Short Bull's men grappled with several progressive
Lakotas who wanted to go home. Giving the rather ironic reason that
he couldn't bear to watch Lakotas kill one another, Crow Dog, the
assassin of Spotted Tail, packed up and headed for the reservation with
his band and half of the village in tow, leaving fewer than two hundred
warriors and their families in the Stronghold. Time was on General
Miles's side.[1]

The death of Sitting Bull left the Miniconjous Hump and Big Foot
of the Cheyenne River Reservation as the only two Lakota chiefs outside the Stronghold still practicing the Ghost Dance. Neither had any
thought of stirring up trouble. Hump had led the Miniconjou contingent
at the Little Bighorn, but his resolve to resist the whites had never been

strong. During the Great Sioux War, he had surrendered to General Miles at the first opportunity. When the Ghost Dance began, Hump, momentarily overcome with religious zeal, took his village upriver to worship, but he regretted the decision almost immediately. Soon after, his friend Chief Big Foot's band, who had thrown themselves into the Ghost Dance with a genuine fervor, joined Hump's camp. No sooner had they done so than Hump returned to the reservation and enlisted as an army scout under his old friend Bear Coat Miles.

Big Foot was crestfallen. At heart a peaceable man, the sixty-five-year-old Miniconjou chief was revered by the Lakotas as an intra-tribal mediator. Although a traditionalist, he promoted schooling for Lakota children, always seeking to strike a balance between the old ways and the new. After Hump defected, Big Foot took his band back to their village and shunned the Ghost Dance. His young men, however, kept their Ghost Shirts and clung to the faith. Lieutenant Colonel Edwin V. Sumner Jr., whose task it was to keep an eye on Big Foot from a "camp of observation" near the chief's village, found him friendly and "anxious to obey" orders, but the colonel was also worried. He believed Big Foot meant well, but he also saw how tenuous the chief's hold over his warriors had grown.

As Sumner feared, nothing went as Big Foot had intended. Setting out for home on December 17, the great Miniconjou mediator received an appeal from Red Cloud to come to Pine Ridge to help restore order, with a promise of a hundred ponies for his trouble. Big Foot was inclined to ignore the request; that is, until he learned that troops were marching on his village from Fort Bennett, the army post nearest the Cheyenne River Agency. The next day came more disturbing news. Two young Hunkpapas staggered into the Miniconjou camp with news of Sitting Bull's death and the flight of their people. In keeping with the Lakota tradition of charity, Big Foot dispatched ten men to offer the Stand Rocking refugees the hospitality of his camp.[2]

Big Foot's emissaries found the Hunkpapas in an abject state. Hump was there too, rounding up the Hunkpapas for the army and threatening to kill Big Foot's emissaries if they interfered. With a small group of Hunkpapas who had escaped Hump's clutches, Big Foot set out for home. Two days after his brush with Hump, he ran into Colonel Sumner, only to find that pressure from higher headquarters had caused the colonel to turn against him. Because Big Foot had been among the first to embrace the Ghost Dance religion, General Miles considered him second only to Sitting Bull in his baleful influence on the Lakotas. Miles, who had come from his Chicago headquarters to Rapid City, South Dakota, to oversee operations, had wired Sumner that "it was desirable that Big Foot be arrested." Although not a direct order to detain Big Foot, the telegram signaled that Sumner had been out of step with his superiors.[3]

The suddenly frosty Sumner demanded to know why Big Foot harbored the Hunkpapas. Because they were brother Lakotas, "almost naked, hungry, footsore, and weary," the chief replied, "and no one with any heart could do any less." Sumner softened. "The Standing Rock Indians answered his description perfectly," he later reported, "and were, in fact, so pitiable a sight that I at once dropped all thought of their being hostile or even worthy of capture. Still, my instructions were to take them, and I intended to do so."

That would not be easy. Big Foot's subchiefs refused to countenance a betrayal of the Hunkpapas. Big Foot persuaded Sumner not to force the matter; he would instruct his people to deliver up the Hunkpapas the next day, December 23. Unfortunately, Big Foot was no longer able to deliver on his promises, having contracted pneumonia; he collapsed after his parley with Sumner. With their chief prostrated, the Miniconjous passed December 23 quietly in their cabins with their Hunkpapa friends. That evening, Sumner started back to Big Foot's village. Before bedding down for the night, he asked a local rancher whom the Miniconjous trusted to ride ahead and try to persuade Big Foot to at least go to Fort Bennett.

Sumner had sent the wrong man. Galloping to Big Foot's cabin, the breathless rancher gave the chief a horribly garbled—or intentionally embellished—version of Sumner's message and urged the Miniconjous instead to go at once to the Pine Ridge Reservation "if you want to save your lives." Easing their grievously ill chief into a wagon, the Miniconjous and the Hunkpapas made for Pine Ridge, fifty wintry miles to the south.[4]

Colonel Sumner spent a dismal Christmas Eve in the empty Miniconjou village. A courier had delivered a telegram from Miles informing him that Big Foot was clearly "both defiant and hostile." Sumner was to arrest and disarm his band at once. The colonel could only shrug in wonderment. Clearly Miles was out of touch with reality. "If Big Foot had been hostile or defiant in attitude," Sumner later wrote, "I was not aware of it until receiving the orders making him so."[5]

Big Foot's escape—for that is what Miles called the Miniconjou detour to Pine Ridge—infuriated the general. Everything had pointed to a peaceful resolution of the Ghost Dance crisis. In the Stronghold, howling winter winds and an influenza outbreak were dampening the enthusiasm of the holdouts. Friendly Brulé and Oglala chiefs and headmen had held talks with Short Bull and Kicking Bear, who appeared ready to capitulate. But now Big Foot was on the loose. Should the "recalcitrant" chief reach the Stronghold, reasoned Miles, he might rouse the Ghost Dancers to war. New orders went out to all units in the field: find the fugitive Miniconjous before, as Miles phrased it, they were able to "turn all the scale against the efforts that have been made to avoid an Indian War." He would tolerate no half measures. "I hope you will round up the whole body of them, disarm them, and keep them all under close guard," he telegraphed General Brooke at Pine Ridge. "Big Foot is cunning and his Indians are very bad."[6]

✳

Miles could not have been more off the mark. Nothing about Big Foot suggested malice. He was dressed for the frigid trip to Pine Ridge in a heavy overcoat, trousers, a jacket, and wool underwear, looking more like an impoverished farmhand than a Lakota chief. Around his head, Big Foot wore a large scarf, which lent him a gaunt and grandmotherly aspect. And even if he were so inclined, Big Foot was too sick to foment unrest. Jostled about on the bed of a cold, springless farmer's wagon, he was declining fast.

As for Big Foot's "bad Indians," far from making for the Stronghold as Miles supposed, his people had no idea it even existed nor that there had been an outbreak from Pine Ridge. The empty Lakota cabins on the road to Pine Ridge baffled them until their scouts met an Oglala who told them what had transpired at the agency and of the coming of the soldiers. The Oglala added that all would be well, because the chiefs at Pine Ridge had gone to the Stronghold to negotiate a surrender. (Unbeknownst to the Oglala traveler, Short Bull and Kicking Bear were, in fact, already on their way in.) Big Foot was pleased. In a hoarse whisper, spitting up blood as he spoke, he told the Oglala he came in peace and would follow the main road to the agency.

If he lived. Their chief's precarious health was the first concern of the Miniconjous. After crossing the icy White River on Christmas Day, they camped for two days. The final forty miles to the agency would not be easy. Five creeks lay between White River and Pine Ridge, and the weather had turned miserable. Strong prairie winds churned dust into blinding clouds. Leaden skies hinted at snow. Better, they reckoned, to let Big Foot rest and then take it slow.[7]

Meanwhile, the army's search for the Miniconjous was on. There were no secrets at Pine Ridge. Indian informers kept General Brooke apprised of Big Foot's whereabouts. On the afternoon of December 26, Brooke directed Major Samuel M. Whitside to take the First Squadron of the Seventh Cavalry, two hundred strong, to intercept, dismount, and disarm the Miniconjous. A sensible man, Brooke would have preferred to undertake the errand himself, and alone, so as not to frighten the Miniconjous, but orders were orders. To discourage resistance, he gave Whitside two Hotchkiss guns. Looking more like a mounted popgun than an army fieldpiece, the small-caliber Hotchkiss could sustain an accurate and astoundingly rapid rate of fire that more than compensated for its diminutive size.[8]

Big Foot's band was neither hiding nor looking for a fight. As the Miniconjous broke camp on December 28, runners from Short Bull warned them of cavalry patrolling Wounded Knee Creek and suggested they detour around the soldiers. Big Foot waved them away, telling his people they must go directly to the soldiers' camp and show that they were peaceable.

Early that afternoon, the Seventh Cavalry and the Miniconjous met. As the two parties edged near each other, Whitside drew up a battle line with the Hotchkiss guns in the center, loaded for action. Big Foot's men drew back, but the chief told them to approach the soldiers "calmly and confidently showing no fear." The twenty-eight-year-old warrior Dewey Beard was one of those who obeyed. Expecting to die for his fidelity but determined to exit the world with a flourish, Dewey Beard dismounted beside a Hotchkiss gun and shoved his arm into the barrel.[9]

The creak of Big Foot's approaching wagon interrupted Dewey Beard's improvised death ritual. The chief's condition stunned Whitside. Instead of the inveterate hostile he had been told to expect, he saw before him a pain-racked old man. Whitside stared a moment and then pulled back the blanket to get a better look at the chief's drawn and bloody face. "Can you talk; are you able to talk," Whitside asked.

"How."

"How, Cola [Hello, friend]," the major replied as Big Foot weakly shook his hand. "I heard you were coming hostile; but now I see you here today, and I'm very glad to see you. I want you to come to the camp with me."

"All right," said Big Foot. "I am going there."

Whitside spoke through the interpreter John Shangrau. "John, I want the horses and guns."

"Look here, Major, if you do that there is liable to be a fight here; and if there is you will kill all these women and children and the men will get away from you."

"But I have an order to do that wherever I catch them."

"Well, that may be," said Shangrau, "but we better take them to camp and then take their horses away from them and their guns."

"All right; you tell Big Foot to move down to camp at Wounded Knee."

Big Foot agreed. Whitside offered the chief an army ambulance for greater comfort, a gesture the Indians appreciated.

The Miniconjou warrior Joseph Horn Cloud, who spoke English, eavesdropped on the conversation. He recalled that Whitside asked Big Foot to relinquish twenty-five rifles as an act of good faith, a request the chief politely declined, saying he feared some harm might come to his people, promising to turn all their guns over once they reached the agency.[10]

While their leaders parleyed, the soldiers and the warriors mingled amicably. The Miniconjous found the Hotchkiss guns of particular interest. "Heap good, heap big guns," they said, tapping the barrels.[11]

*

The Seventh Cavalry and the Lakotas halted at sunset on a bleak, six-hundred-yard-wide plain on the west bank of Wounded Knee Creek, home to a small community of agency Oglalas, frightened off during the Ghost Dance scare. Abandoned log cabins dotted the landscape, and barbed-wire fences enclosed a scattering of fallow fields.

It was a dismal bivouac site for both parties. Major Whitside directed the Indians to a two-acre tract with their backs up against a broad, sharply sloped, twenty-five-foot-deep ravine. Densely thicketed in places, the ravine snaked eastward across the treeless expanse and emptied into Wounded Knee Creek. The cavalry encamped three hundred yards northeast of the Indians. A small field separated the cavalry camp and the Indian village. Whitside had a Sibley conical tent, warmed by a stove, erected for the chief and his wife on the southern edge of the cavalry bivouac. Soldiers raised five more Sibley tents in the Indian village to shelter those without tipis. The major issued rations of coffee, sugar, and bacon to the Indians and permitted them to graze their ponies.[12]

Whitside's kindness was balanced with tactical preparedness. He posted the Hotchkiss guns on a knob west of the cavalry camp, their barrels trained on the ragged rows of tipis, and ringed the Miniconjou village with twenty picket stations, permitting only women drawing water from the creek to pass through the lines. Convinced "that otherwise trouble might ensue," Whitside asked for help to disarm Big Foot's warriors. General Brooke wired Miles the day's news. Miles's reply was perfunctory: "All right. Use force enough. Congratulations." Brooke ordered out the Second Squadron of the Seventh Cavalry, augmented by two more Hotchkiss guns and a company of Cheyenne and Oglala scouts, to reinforce Whitside. He also asked Father Francis M. Craft, a Jesuit missionary fluent in Lakota for whom the Indians had real affection, to accompany the column and assist the regimental commander, Colonel James W. Forsyth, in winning the Indians' trust.

That Forsyth would need help seemed probable. White-haired and goateed, the fifty-five-year-old Ohioan had amassed an enviable military record that included several citations for gallantry during the Civil War and two decades of duty as Phil Sheridan's aide-de-camp and military secretary before assuming command of the Seventh Cavalry in 1886, long after the fighting on the plains had ended.

Brooke's spoken orders to Forsyth were crisp and harsh. He was to "disarm Big Foot's band, prevent the escape of any; [and] if they fought to destroy them." Unbeknownst to the Miniconjous, they were not destined for Pine Ridge. Once disarmed, the Miniconjous would be hustled to the nearest railroad station for transport to Omaha and then eventual return to the Cheyenne River Reservation. Miles and Brooke wanted them out of the Oglala country.[13]

Forsyth reached Whitside's bivouac at 8:30 p.m. Finding "everything in perfect condition," he attacked a keg of whiskey. The "officers of the 7th Cavalry had a jolly time that night, celebrating the capture of Big Foot," averred a newspaperman who strolled awhile with Forsyth. Some time after midnight the two men shook hands and parted "to lay down to pleasant dreams."

Nothing remotely pleasant transpired in the Miniconjou camp. Ill at ease, most of the Lakotas passed a sleepless night, contemplating what dawn might bring. Dewey Beard dozed off only briefly. Fear for what might befall the children kept Dewey Beard awake and robbed him of his appetite. Before daybreak, Dewey Beard's father came from Big Foot's tent to counsel his sons. "They say it is peace, but I am sure there is going to be fighting today. I have been in war all my life, and I know when my heart is growing bitter that there is going to be a fight . . . My dear sons, stand together and if you die at once, among your relations defending them, I will be satisfied."[14]

*

Reveille sounded at 5:15 a.m. on December 29, 1890. The sun rose two hours later. Emerging from their tipis into the bright light of a clear, chill morning, the Indians saw their worst fears confirmed. Eight troops of cavalry surrounded the village. Four Hotchkiss guns, loaded and zeroed in on the village, frowned from atop a low knoll. The soldiers and scouts outnumbered the Lakota warriors nearly five to one. Including the artillerymen, there were 36 officers, 436 enlisted men, and 110 Indian scouts confronting 120 men of fighting age and 250 women, children, and elderly Miniconjous and Hunkpapas.

Few men on either side had ever seen a fight. Most of the warriors had been boys at the time of the Little Bighorn. Twenty percent of the Seventh Cavalry were raw recruits and had never even fired a weapon. Combat experience was limited to the handful of sergeants and six troop commanders who had served under Custer. The weaponry had not improved since then; enlisted men still carried single-shot carbines and revolvers. Big Foot's warriors were better armed with repeating rifles. But if Colonel Forsyth had his way, the Indians and their weapons would soon be parted.[15]

At 8:00 a.m., the interpreters summoned the Lakota men to an open tract between Whitside's bivouac and the Indian encampment. Some came with faces painted; nearly all wore Ghost Shirts. Colonel Forsyth, with John Shangrau interpreting, spoke "kindly and pleasantly" to the warriors. Forsyth said he regretted the need to disarm them, but the Lakotas were prisoners and as such must surrender all weapons—for which, the colonel promised, they would be compensated. He implored them not to compel him to search for guns, "but to have confidence in him and bring them themselves." Father Craft was guardedly optimistic of the outcome, but Forsyth's adjutant braced for the worst. He'd never known an Indian to give up a rifle—his most precious and costly possession—without a struggle. On this occasion, the Indians opted for passive resistance, simply turning their backs on Forsyth.[16]

At a loss what to do, the befuddled colonel bade Major Whitside take charge. Fed up with the Indians' stalling, Whitside told Shangrau to assemble the warriors. He wanted their rifles—now. Dutifully, the interpreter delivered the message to the bedridden Big Foot. The chief, however, had had enough. He had tried to live at peace among the whites, to follow the often capricious dictates of Indian agents and imperious demands of army officers. He had assured Whitside that his people would surrender their arms as soon as they reached the agency; why would the major doubt his word? Why the urgent need to remove their means of self-defense? He would turn over a handful of broken rifles but keep the good ones until his people reached Pine Ridge. Shangrau begged Big Foot to reconsider, but the dying chief was obdurate.

Philip Wells, also a bilingual mixed blood, took over interpreting duty. Shangrau walked off, apparently without telling Whitside what Big Foot had said, because the major counted off twenty Indians and ordered them to fetch their rifles. They returned with a handful of broken muzzle-loaders. Forsyth and Whitside were unamused. Having recovered from his momentary funk, Forsyth told the hospital stewards to bring Big Foot out of the tent on a blanket; perhaps the chief could talk sense into his men. But it was no use. Big Foot insisted he had no more guns, that Sumner's troop had burned them. The warriors watched their dissembling chief with concern. Blood flowed freely from his nose. He tried to sit up to tell his followers to keep calm but fell back on his cot, unable to speak further.[17]

Forsyth lost his composure. "You are lying to me in return for all my kindness to you," he snapped at the dying chief. At Whitside's suggestion, the colonel called forward Troops B and K, numbering approximately fifty-five men each, to cordon off the council area. Troop B lined up on foot on the warriors' flank, facing east. Troop K deployed between the Lakota men and their village, fronting north. Soldiers and warriors confronted each other at five yards. Raw recruits fidgeted; young Lakotas grumbled. Several tried to shove past the soldiers. Philip Wells upbraided the Indians for their "faithlessness"; they responded, said the regimental adjutant, "with the sullen defiance so often displayed by strikers during labor troubles."[18]

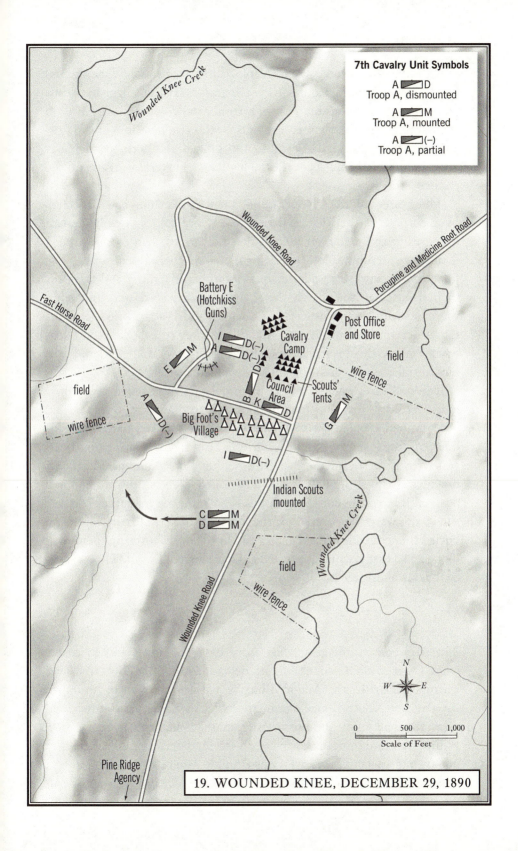

7th Cavalry Unit Symbols

A ▰ D
Troop A, dismounted

A ▰ M
Troop A, mounted

A ▰ (–)
Troop A, partial

Wounded Knee Creek

Wounded Knee Road

Porcupine and Medicine Root Road

Fast Horse Road

Battery E
(Hotchkiss
Guns)

Post Office
and Store

field

wire fence

I ▰ D(–)

A ▰ D(–)

E ▰ M

Cavalry
Camp

D

Council
Area

Scouts'
Tents

B K ▰ D

G ▰ M

field

wire fence

A ▰ D(–)

Big Foot's
Village

I ▰ D(–)

Indian Scouts
mounted

C ▰ M

D ▰ M

Wounded Knee Creek

field

wire fence

Wounded Knee Road

N
W ✦ E
S

0   500   1,000
Scale of Feet

Pine Ridge
Agency

19. WOUNDED KNEE, DECEMBER 29, 1890

The mood darkened. Forsyth told Captains Charles Varnum and George Wallace to take one squad each and search the village for weapons. Struggling to muster a bit of aplomb, the colonel spoke softly to the warriors, apparently unaware of the explosive potential of the situation. Certainly Captain Varnum recognized the peril, particularly after he glimpsed rifles beneath the blankets of several warriors on the council ground.

The search of the village went about as Varnum had expected. Women greeted the soldiers with screams and curses. The lieutenant found everything so well hidden that he "almost had to dig it out." The women employed various stratagems to conceal weapons. "The first rifle I found was under a squaw who was moaning and who was so indisposed to the search that I had her displaced, and under her was a beautiful Winchester rifle." Varnum and Wallace tried to maintain order, but the troops grew impatient. They rolled over recumbent women, yanked rifles from beneath the skirts of seated girls, and ransacked tipis, seizing anything that resembled a weapon.

Dewey Beard listened to the commotion from inside the family lodge. Waiting for an opportune moment to crawl into a wagon and hide, he had avoided the council. "But when I looked out, I saw soldiers coming loaded with guns, knives, axes, crowbars, war clubs, bows and arrows," he recalled. Hurriedly, he dug a hole and buried his carbine, barely finishing before a soldier poked his head into the tipi and ordered him to the council ground. Remembering his father's words, the young warrior prepared for the worst. "I took some cartridges and buried them outside my lodge, in front of the door, covering them with manure, so that if while at council trouble started, I would know where to find ammunition."[19]

＊

The Miniconjou village yielded forty old and mostly unserviceable rifles. Once again, Colonel Forsyth demanded that Big Foot hand over the repeating rifles that Major Whitside had seen the warriors brandish the day before. And once again, the chief insisted that Sumner had taken them all. Only one alternative remained: pat down every warrior. Philip Wells announced the protocol—the Lakotas were to pass one by one through a gap between Troops B and K, where Whitside, Wallace, and Varnum would search their persons. The older men consented, but the younger warriors held back. Garbed in his black cassock, Father Craft moved through the crowd distributing cigarettes and trying to reassure them.[20]

Few warriors listened to him. They had turned their attention to a medicine man named Sits Straight. Adorned in an elaborate Ghost Shirt and flowing warbonnet, his face painted green, he had begun a boisterous one-man Ghost Dance on the edge of the council ground. Sits Straight twisted and gyrated, reminding the warriors of the power of their Ghost Shirts. Twice Colonel Forsyth told the medicine man to desist and, as befitted his name, sit down. "He will sit down when he gets around the circle," retorted Big Foot's brother-in-law. The medicine man completed the circle and then squatted in silence. For the moment at least, a crisis had been averted.[21] But then a deaf warrior— some Indians said he was also demented or "a good-for-nothing" or both—took up where Sits Straight had left off. Thrusting his rifle overhead, he proclaimed that it had cost him a great deal; if anyone wanted the weapon, they would have to pay him for it. Three cavalry sergeants approached the man from behind. Two grabbed his arms while the third tried to wrest away the rifle. And then the gun went off. As if on cue with the crack of the rifle, Sits Straight leaped to his feet, scooped up a handful of dirt, and threw it in the air. Six warriors pulled Winchester rifles from beneath their blankets. To one startled lieutenant on the line, it seemed as if they hesitated an eternity. "I thought, the pity of it! What can they be thinking?" The Miniconjou Long Bull could have answered him. "Indians much like white man. They get mad when a man hurts them and tears their clothes and pulls their guns away. That made us fight."

"Fast, like a prairie fire, came the response to an accidental shot," lamented First Sergeant Theodore Ragnar of Troop K. Father Craft had no doubt who fired first: "The Indians, excited by the shot, poured volley after volley into the lines of B and K troops, their fire also mowing down like grass the crowd of their own women and children who stood in the camp looking on behind the soldiers."[22]

Mayhem ensued. Warriors grabbed dead soldiers' carbines and cartridge belts or retrieved surrendered weapons. Firing their fifteen-round Winchesters as fast as they could pump the levers, the Lakotas devastated the ranks of Troops B and K. No one bothered to reload. When the chambers were empty, warriors and soldiers fought hand to hand with revolvers, clubbed rifles, knives, and war clubs. Captain

Wallace shot four warriors with his revolver before a bullet took off the top of his head. Apparently unable to recognize Father Craft's black cassock through the smoke, a warrior drove a knife into the priest's back, puncturing his right lung. Craft ministered to wounded soldiers until he collapsed. A warrior charged Philip Wells. Dropping down on one knee, the interpreter used his empty rifle as a shield to ward off the Indian's upraised butcher knife. The Indian's wrist struck the gun, but the blade nearly severed Wells's nose, which flopped down over his mouth, sustained by a shred of skin. Wells shot the warrior in the side. A corporal rushed up and fired his rifle point-blank into the Lakota's prostrate body. An instant later the corporal was shot dead.

When the shooting began, Chief Big Foot had tried to lift himself up from his stretcher to watch the bloody fracas; as he did so, an officer and an enlisted man shot him in the back. At first, no one noticed. "The smoke was so dense I couldn't see anything," a warrior recalled. "So I didn't make a move, just stood there. When it cleared a little I saw Big Foot lying down with blood on his forehead and his head to the right side." Big Foot's wife writhed beside him with a shattered left thigh.[23]

Dewey Beard, who carried only a knife, saw nothing through the murk save the glint of soldiers' buttons. A cavalry carbine cracked beside his ear. In need of a rifle, Dewey Beard lunged for it, sinking his knife in the soldier's side. The wounded man grabbed Dewey Beard's neck, and Dewey Beard again plunged his knife into him. The soldier fell, and Dewey Beard straddled him. Holding down the man's head with one hand, he stabbed him to death in the kidney with the other. Another soldier fired at Dewey Beard but missed, killing a fellow trooper instead. Dewey Beard had had enough close combat. Dashing through the village, he made for the ravine. Behind him, beneath the smoke, lay twenty-six dead or wounded troopers and, by Colonel Forsyth's count, sixty-two dead warriors. The struggle on the council ground had lasted less than ten minutes.[24]

The first phase of the clash—the melee on the council ground—was over. The second phase—the running fight through the village—began when the Lakota warriors breached the ranks of Troops B and K and the troopers spun around and fired at them. The Indians withdrew slowly, facing front and shooting as they went. Sergeant Ragnar leveled his carbine at "one redskin who walked backwards in fleeing, all the time coolly aiming until I at last put a bullet through his brain."

Gun smoke rolled from the council ground to the village. It was "awful thick," said a Miniconjou woman, so dense that troopers could not distinguish warriors from noncombatants. Any moving form became a target. Above the din, officers shouted, "Cease Fire!" Some troopers, too agitated to heed orders, kept shooting. "In that strange silence were ejaculations from all sides," confessed a lieutenant, "giving voice to horror at what had happened—the killing of women with papooses on their backs."[25]

The third phase of the Wounded Knee tragedy—the slaughter of Lakota noncombatants—had only begun. After the opening volley on the council ground, the village had boiled over in three directions with panic-stricken women, children, and elders. Some piled into wagons and bounded up a road leading to the northwest, the soldiers nearest them holding their fire while the Indians passed. Others started east toward Wounded Knee Creek. They were less fortunate, because soldiers from another troop coldly gunned down several of them, including five girls who tried to outrun the mounted troopers. Moments before the soldiers overtook them, the girls sat down and faced their killers. The troopers raised their rifles, the girls covered their faces with blankets, and in a muzzle flash they were dead.

By far the greatest number of noncombatants, intermingled with dozens of warriors, either ran or drove wagons headlong into the broad ravine south of the village. The ravine became the killing field of Wounded Knee, artillery the indiscriminate executioner.

The crews of the Hotchkiss guns had had a panoramic view of the opening of the struggle. As long as the soldiers were commingled with the Indians, they could do nothing. But once the survivors of Troops B and K had withdrawn to seek shelter beneath the knoll, Captain Allyn Capron ordered his battery to commence firing, opening the fourth phase of the carnage—the promiscuous shelling of the intermingled Lakota warriors and noncombatants. Several percussion shells were directed at Indians twenty-five hundred yards away who posed no conceivable threat to anyone. But most of the rounds, which came at the rate of thirty per minute, were concentrated on the village in the form of canister-encased shot that resembled a coffee can containing layers of metal balls packed in sawdust. At close range, its effect was devastating, shredding tipis and mangling humans and animals. One woman received fourteen wounds but lived. Another woman dragged her torn body to the nearest wounded soldier and drove a knife into his breast before his comrade shot her in the head.

Captain Capron later defended his actions on the grounds that it had been impossible to distinguish warriors from women, "all of whom seemed to be firing." Given the nearly impenetrable smoke and rapidly unfolding and wildly confused situation, Captain Capron probably told the truth. Father Craft, as unbiased a participant as could be found, absolved Capron of criminal intent. Indirectly blaming the warriors for the shelling of the village, the priest later testified that several Lakotas were shooting from inside the tipis when the Hotchkiss guns opened up. Be that as it may, the artillery raked the village, now crackling with burning tipis, from one end to the other for nearly thirty minutes before their crews turned the barrels toward the ravine.[26]

Colonel Forsyth had run up the knoll after the opening volleys. He not only interposed no objections to Capron's actions but, beyond scribbling a brief report to General Brooke from beside the battery, also did nothing of consequence. The colonel, it seems, was little more than a mute observer to the incomprehensible butchery unfolding in front of him. Major Whitside later claimed to his wife that he himself had "managed the whole business." In point of fact, no one exercised overall control, and few officers were able to restrain their men.

After the Hotchkiss guns blasted apart the village, enough warriors continued to resist to keep the fury of the Seventh Cavalry troopers—who believed themselves to have been the victims of Indian treachery—at a fever pitch, which only prolonged the slaughter. A newspaperman caught up in the fray called it "a war of extermination. About the only tactic was to kill while it could be done whenever an Indian could be seen." Sergeant Ragnar blamed most of the killing of women and children on the regiment's raw recruits: they behaved, he said, in a manner "not worthy of the uniform."[27]

In the ravine, wounded women clawed holes in which to hide their children. Dewey Beard lay among them. He had been shot twice, first in the arm and then in "the lap." Faint from loss of blood, Dewey Beard watched soldiers at the top of the ravine shoot every woman and child in sight. "Now when I saw all those little infants lying there dead in their blood, I felt that even if I ate one of the soldiers it would not appease my anger." Struggling to his feet, Dewey Beard followed the course of the ravine west. As he rounded a bend, he ran into his grievously wounded mother. She beseeched him not to stop. Another bullet struck her, and she slumped to the ground, dead.

Gradually, the shelling and rifle fire subsided, and the ravine grew silent. Sergeant Ragnar and his men climbed down the bank with orders to mop up, the fifth and final act of violence. Bodies lay in heaps. A family writhed in agony beneath an overturned cart, their legs crushed. "And here rests the beautiful young squaw whom yesterday I offered a cigarette—dying, with both her legs shot off. She lies there without wailing and greets me with a faint smile on her pale lips."

Suddenly shooting broke out beyond the west end of the ravine. Thirty women and perhaps a dozen warriors, including Dewey Beard, had sheltered themselves in a heavily wooded gulch separated from the ravine by a narrow trench. Dewey Beard was too weak to fire his Winchester, but other warriors drove off Sergeant Ragnar and his dismounted detail. Captain Capron responded by rolling a Hotchkiss gun up to the entrance of the gulch. Then came a perfect "storm of thunder and hail." A shell tore a six-inch-wide hole in the stomach of a man near Dewey Beard. Another struck a woman between the shoulder blades. Dewey Beard said she laughed, unconscious of her wound. "And then there went up from [my] dying people, a medley of death songs that would make the hardest heart weep." To remain in the gulch meant death. "Even if there was no more shooting, the smoke was so thick that the wounded could not live for it; it was suffocating."[28]

The slaughter in the gulch lasted twenty minutes. As Indian fire weakened, the troopers cautiously advanced. The mixed-blood Philip Wells, his partially severed nose still dangling above his mouth, yelled into the smoky pit, "All of you that are still alive get up and come on over, you will not be molested or shot anymore." A handful of Indians came forth. Dewey Beard, however, was gone. Somehow he had worked his way onto the prairie, where he met five Oglala warriors from the Pine Ridge Agency who carried him to a place of safety.

What had been the Miniconjou village was now a smoldering abattoir. Blackened and splintered lodge poles, broken wagons, mangled ponies, and the detritus of a devastated Indian camp littered the plain. One newspaperman found forty-five dead warriors "with their impregnable ghost shirts on" crumpled on the council ground; another journalist counted forty-eight dead Indians in a half-acre square.[29]

Stumbling about in shock, "bleeding profusely, my senses having almost left me," Philip Wells berated the Lakotas. "These white people came to save you and you have brought death on yourselves. Still white people are merciful to save the wounded enemy when he is harmless; so if some of you are alive, raise your hands; a man of your own blood is talking to you." A dozen hands went up. One wounded warrior propped himself on his elbow and asked Wells if he knew the identity of a seared Lakota corpse lying near the wreckage of an army tent. Wells said he supposed that it was Sits Straight. Pointing at the medicine man's body, the warrior shot out his fingers—a Lakota insult—and snarled, "If I could be taken to you, I would stab you!" Then, to Wells, he said, "He is our murderer! Only for him inciting our other young men we would have been alive and happy!"

The search for survivors began. Combing the field, a humane private came across a dead woman and her baby, who was sucking on a piece of hardtack. He picked up the child and cradled it in his arms. Continuing on, he found another dead woman with a baby still alive beside her. He carried both infants to the hospital tent, where a number of Indian women had gathered. As he neared the tent, the private encountered a burly sergeant, who suggested he smash the babies against a tree; otherwise, the sergeant said, "someday they'll be fighting us." The soldier recoiled in disgust. "I told him I would rather smash him than those little innocent children. The Indian women were so glad that I saved the papooses that they almost kissed me."[30]

While the dead were counted and the wounded collected, a wagon train laden with rations and forage for Big Foot's band appeared. Dumping the supplies on the ground, the wagoners placed sacks of oats in the wagon beds and then spread a thick layer of hay over them. It was the only comfort enjoyed by the wounded soldiers and the surviving Indians, nearly all of whom were women and children. At sunset, the sad procession started for Pine Ridge. With no room in the wagons for the Lakota dead, they were left where they had fallen—like so many dark blotches beneath the winter moon. Sergeant Ragnar observed, "Their sign of peace—the white flag, moved gently in the wind."

Forsyth reached the Pine Ridge Agency at 9:30 p.m. He had lost one officer and twenty-four enlisted men killed and another four officers, thirty-three enlisted men, and two civilians (Wells and Father Craft) wounded. A close count of Indian casualties would have to wait, but clearly they were staggering. As Forsyth told General Brooke, "Big Foot's party has practically ceased to exist."

So too had much of the Lakota population of Pine Ridge. The muffled rumble of the Hotchkiss guns that morning had been audible at the agency. Recognizing the sound for what it was, several warriors had ridden toward the place where the "wagon-guns were going off." They included Dewey Beard's rescuers, as well as the Oglala medicine man Black Elk, who had taken his first white scalp at the Little Bighorn when only a boy. At about noon, he and his comrades reached a hill overlooking the valley, "and then we saw all that they had done there." The heaped and mangled bodies evoked a raging grief in Black Elk. "When I saw this I wished that I had died too, but I was not sorry for the women and children. It was better for them to be happy in the other world, and I wanted to be there too. But before I went there I wanted to have revenge."[31]

The return of Black Elk and his friends set off a general panic. Short Bull's and Kicking Bear's bands, which had approached to within four miles of the agency the night before, turned back toward White Clay Creek, about seventeen miles from the agency. The recently surrendered Brulé bands of Two Strike and Crow Dog also decamped, after which Two Strike led two hundred warriors to the Wounded Knee battlefield. They skirmished briefly with Forsyth's troops at long range and then doubled back to burn several cabins and fire into the agency in reprisal, wounding several soldiers. Having made their point, Two Strike's men drew off before sunset and also headed for White Clay Creek.

Red Cloud's people vacillated until mid-afternoon before joining the general stampede. When Red Cloud refused to leave, agitated young men kidnapped him from his cabin. "I had to go with them and follow my family. Some would shoot their guns around me and make me go faster." To such depths of humiliation had the once mighty chief of the Oglalas fallen in his old age. By nightfall on December 29, nearly four thousand Lakotas had assembled on White Clay Creek. It was to their angry camp that the wounded Dewey Beard was taken.[32]

*

The night of December 29 was intensely cold. Inside the Episcopal Chapel of the Holy Cross at Pine Ridge, the lights burned brightly, creating the illusion of warmth. Green holiday garlands festooned the walls and windows. Above the pulpit, a huge banner mockingly proclaimed, "Peace on earth, good will to men." Lying on quilts and disassembled pews, the wounded Lakotas bore their agony in silence. The most audible sound was that of a three-year-old girl intoning, "Min-nie, min-nie, min-nie [water]." A newspaperman brought her a cupful. It did her no good. No sooner had she swallowed it than it gushed in a bloody stream from a hole in her neck. The horror was too much even for those accustomed to gore. Entering the chapel, the post surgeon nearly fainted. "This is the first time I've seen a lot of women and children shot to pieces," he mumbled to no one in particular. "I can't stand it." After the surgeon steadied himself and set to work, an elderly Miniconjou woman offhandedly asked him when the soldiers intended to kill them.[33]

The next morning, a blizzard struck the reservation, heralding a whiteout that lasted for three days. When the skies cleared on January 2, 1891, the agency physician, Dr. Charles Eastman, a Dakota Sioux graduate of Boston University Medical School, and several Indian scouts went to Wounded Knee to look for survivors. Not that they expected to find any. Three days of subzero temperatures and ravening winds had contorted the corpses hideously. "It took all of my nerve to keep my composure in the face of this spectacle, and of the excitement and grief of my Indian companions, nearly every one of whom was crying aloud or singing his death song," recalled Eastman. "All this was a severe ordeal for me who had so lately put all his faith in the Christian love and lofty ideals of the white man."

His mercy mission, however, was successful, rescuing eleven wounded Lakotas, including two infants swaddled beside their mothers' corpses and an old blind woman huddled beneath a wagon. The frozen dead remained where they had fallen. Mournful Lakotas called the ground "the Place of the Big Killings."[34]

Three days later, an army detail and a party of hired civilians interred the Indian dead. The inevitable corps of newspapermen and photographers accompanied them. One reporter wrote of "a placid-looking corpse of a pretty Indian girl, her hands clasped and face upturned, and her blanket blown back to disclose a cruel wound in the breast, from which the blood had flowed to stiffen her clothing to the frozen body." No less compelling were the "children just of an age to play tag [lying] half-buried under the snow." Even the dead warriors evoked his sympathy. One corpse, however, utterly repelled the reporter. "The face was painted a horrible green. Blood had mingled with the paint and washed red rivers in the coating . . . His hands were clinched, his teeth were clinched. One hand was raised in the air. The arm had frozen in that position." An army officer told the reporter it was the body of Sits

Straight. In contrast to the medicine man, Chief Big Foot "lay in a sort of solitary dignity" until a wandering photographer propped up the stiff corpse for a photograph.[35]

A mixed-blood scout had contracted to bury the dead at two dollars a corpse. His workers tossed the bodies into a long trench hacked on the frozen knoll from whence the Hotchkiss guns had dealt death. Then came the counting of Indian casualties. The army reported that 146 Lakotas—82 men and 64 women and children—were deposited in the mass grave. There were undoubtedly other dead, either carried off by Lakotas or obscured beneath the snow out of sight of the Place of the Big Killings. Of the fifty-one wounded Indians in the Episcopal chapel, seven died. Another thirty-three wounded were in the Lakota camp on White Clay Creek. Although it remains impossible to arrive at a precise casualty total, it is clear very few of Big Foot's band emerged from Wounded Knee unscathed.[36]

*

General Miles was furious and apparently unaware that his wrong-headed orders had precipitated the bloodbath at Wounded Knee. Instead of the pacific resolution to the Ghost Dance he had expected, the general now faced a genuine outbreak of four thousand understandably vengeful Indians. On New Year's Eve, Miles hastened to Pine Ridge to try to broker a peace.[37]

Miles's first order of business was to ring the agency with trenches and artillery emplacements. He did not plan to attack unless absolutely necessary. With the thirty-five hundred troops at his disposal, Miles intended to encircle the Indians and then contract his lines, hoping gradually to press the Lakotas toward the agency. Assigning General Brooke to command the field operations, while he opened negotiations with the Lakotas, on New Year's Day 1891, Miles sent the first of several conciliatory messages to Red Cloud and the chiefs, assuring them that he understood the wrongs that had been done the Indians and that no further harm would come to them if they obeyed his orders. Red Cloud was pleased with Miles's note, as were the other Oglala chiefs, who regretted their decision to leave Pine Ridge. Like the Miniconjou chief Hump, many of them had surrendered to Miles during the Great Sioux War. They knew Bear Coat spoke with a straight tongue. He had made good on his promise of just and humane treatment then, and they had no doubt he would do so now. The Oglalas were ready to talk terms.

Not so the Brulés. Miles was a stranger to them. Moreover, they refused to recognize the hopelessness of their situation. Contentious councils between Oglala and Brulé leaders were a daily occurrence; Short Bull and Kicking Bear threatened that no man would leave camp alive. Brulé *akicitas* policed the village, and at least two Indians were killed in altercations between the tribes. On January 4, Red Cloud threatened to muscle his way out. But nobody took him seriously, and he went nowhere.

Red Cloud's resolve returned three days later, when the young Brulé Plenty Horses murdered Edward W. Casey, an officer of great promise who had a deep affection for the Lakotas, while the lieutenant was reconnoitering the Oglala village.[38] The bullet that killed Lieutenant Casey was fired in despair by a cultural orphan—Plenty Horses was a graduate of the Carlisle Indian Industrial School who had returned to the reservation to find himself an outcast. The aspiring warrior said that he shot Casey to make a place for himself among his people. "They will be proud of me," he later told a federal grand jury.[39]

The Brulés might have been proud of the act, but the Oglalas deplored the murder. For many, it was the last straw. After dark on January 7, Red Cloud stole away from the village with his son Jack (the coward of the Rosebud) and two hundred followers. They traveled all night in arctic cold, reaching the camp of an Oglala scout company the next morning. The commanding officer brought the chief, who was "all in a tremble, cold, wet, exhausted, hardly able to articulate . . . a poor, down-and-out old man," into his tent and helped him to a bench beside the warming flames of a conical stove. Miles hastened to widen the wedge between the Oglalas and the Brulés, sending a respected Oglala progressive leader to exert his influence on behalf of peace.

The Oglalas needed little convincing. Many had returned to the agency after Red Cloud, and the rest pledged to come in soon. Unsettled by the Oglala defections, which had become too numerous to halt, the Brulés reluctantly conceded to move the village closer to the agency. Miles instructed Brooke to follow the Indians—but not so closely as to precipitate either a clash or a "stampede." Brooke understood the "delicacy of the situation," assuring Miles that he had been "exceedingly cautious and at the same time [was] watching them closely."[40]

Miles reeled in the Brulés so adroitly that they found themselves crawling toward their appointed place of capitulation on the west bank of White Clay Creek, opposite the agency and under army guns, even as they debated the advisability of moving at all. As an inducement to surrender, Bear Coat delegated to the chiefs the task of disarming their warriors—a concession that the general probably now realized he should have made to Big Foot. Miles also obtained authority to temporarily supplant the agents on the Lakota reservations with army officers.[41]

On January 12, the Brulé and Oglala holdouts reached the Holy Rosary Mission, a short four-mile march from Pine Ridge. There the Jesuits did everything possible to reassure the warriors, who remained a turbulent lot, discharging rifles in the air and galloping about menacingly. A frantic few attacked their own ponies and dogs, shooting them down in a pathetic burlesque of a massacre. As Brooke's column neared the mission, a Brulé subchief "came charging back waving a white sheet and excitedly pleaded for the soldiers not to come so fast because it was frightening and annoying the Indians." Sunset found the soldiers and the Indian village less than two miles apart.

A palpable tension pervaded Pine Ridge that night. "The greatest difficulty is now to restore confidence," Miles wired General Schofield. "The Indians have great fear that arms will be taken away, and then all treated like those who were on Wounded Knee." There was no room for error. As the Brulés searched their souls for the courage to make the last march, the progressive chief Young Man Afraid of His Horses shuttled between the hostile village and the agency as a proxy for General Miles. On January 13, the Indian village remained stationary, and the army completed its envelopment. Five regiments sealed off all possible avenues of escape. Still the chiefs temporized. The old scout Frank Grouard came to their camp at Miles's behest to remind them that Bear Coat's patience had its limits.

The next day, the chiefs agreed on surrender terms: Warriors would turn over their rifles to their leaders, who in turn would load them in wagons for delivery to Miles. The general would ensure that every man was reimbursed. After disarming their warriors, the chiefs would move their people to designated locations at the agency and send their children forthwith back to school, where they would become potential hostages of the army, in case any were needed.

Disquieting rumors reached Miles that evening. The Brulés, it was said, intended to break away from the Oglalas at midnight and force their way through the army cordon. Spies told of "vicious and noisy" arguments in the hostile camp. Still, Miles was hopeful. His daily press bulletin promised that "expectations will be realized and the Indians will not give further trouble." To General Schofield, he wrote, "Everything indicates that the military will have control. Nothing but a mistake or accident can now prevent a most desirable result." Also emanating from headquarters that night, however, was a "strictly confidential" note to General Brooke. There must be no gaps in the lines, Miles told Brooke. "Between eight and nine hundred men are in the hostile camp and, should they endeavor to escape, the commands should be so placed as to be all effective at the same time." In other words, in the event of a misstep the Indians were to be crushed with overwhelming force.[42]

*

Thursday, January 15, 1891, broke chill and misty. A light frost coated the 742 tipis of the combined Brulé and Oglala village. Oglala women were up early, dismantling lodges and loading farm wagons and travois with family possessions. "With the Oglalas who were in the hostile band there was no difficulty," a journalist recorded. "They went to work with a will—that is, they encouraged their squaws to work and were ready to move before 8:00 a.m." But the Brulés balked. "They believed that as soon as the two tribes became separated the soldiers would attack and utterly destroy [them], for they realized that they alone were responsible for the outbreak and had no confidence in the promises of the military." The impasse was brief. Oglalas mingled with the Brulés in the interest of peace. In a little while, the two bands were mixed together so thoroughly that the Brulés had all the protection they thought necessary.[43]

Neither the Brulé nor the Oglala chiefs were taking any chances, however. They deployed parties of dismounted warriors on the flanks of the moving village of thirty-five hundred Indians. The main body rode in front on their finest war ponies, traversing the rolling, treeless plain in a long, winding column of twos. Most had been mere boys during the days of war with the whites, but they daubed their faces with war paint as if they had done many deeds of glory. This was the final display of Plains Indian might, and they knew it.

The sun shone brightly. The day grew mild, melting the last traces of snow. General Brooke's command followed close behind the Lakotas, almost pushing them out of camp. In the entrenchments around Pine Ridge, infantrymen and artillery pieces stood ready for action. Miles and his staff gathered on a rise squarely in the Indians' path. The general had grayed considerably and gained weight since 1877, when he last accepted a Lakota surrender. Missing was the cocky dash, the bear coat, the buffalo cape, and the fur cap of those earlier campaigns. Miles now wore a simple army overcoat and regulation campaign hat. Perhaps as a hopeful gesture of peace, he had shaved off the handlebar mustache he had worn since the Civil War. On January 15, 1891, Miles looked more like a stern middle-aged schoolmaster than one of the most nakedly ambitious generals the army had ever known.

Over the ridge past Miles came the Lakotas, pale reflections of the once mighty Plains nation. Wagons and carts loaded with children and the elderly rolled by. Young women burdened with babies walked alongside the wagons. Middle-aged Oglalas jogged along seemingly pleased that something besides fighting was going on. Suspicious Brulé warriors guarded the flanks, glaring hard at the soldiers gathered across the narrow creek.

By mid-afternoon, the Indians had reassembled their village in a two-mile-long cantonment near the Pine Ridge Agency. Rations of coffee, sugar, and bread awaited them. As General Brooke's forces arrived, Miles deployed them in three strong camps, occupying, as he put it, "the tree points of a triangle, with the Indian camp in the center in close proximity to the troops." The Brulés feigned nonchalance. "They threw out pickets just as though there were no soldiers in sight," said a white eyewitness, "and one of the last features of their camp that was visible before the sun went down was the silhouette of a mounted Brulé warrior perched on the summit of one of the hills which form the western portion of the Pine Ridge horizon."

Then came sounds ominous to untutored whites. From the village arose the voices of hundreds of women, joined in a repetitive mantra, accompanied by the rapid and steady pounding of drums. But there was no danger. It was not the Ghost Dance. The Lakotas were merely trying to ease the trauma of the day with the familiar strains of the Omaha Dance, a social festivity reminiscent of happier times.[44]

Those times seemed but a distant memory. In fact, the transformation of the Lakota world, and of the Indian West, had come in the blink of an eye. Less than a generation had passed since Red Cloud had won his war on the Bozeman Trail forts but then gradually lost the peace. The Lakotas had held the Crow lands they had conquered for less than a decade. It had been just fifteen years since the great but ultimately Pyrrhic Indian victory at the Little Bighorn. Now nothing remained. The Lakotas, the Cheyennes, the Arapahos, the Nez Perces, the Utes, the Modocs, the Apaches, and even some Texan-hating Kiowas and Comanches had tried to coexist amicably with the white man, but he would not be peaceably contained. Tribes had divided bitterly over the issue of war or peace. The Indians who had gone to war against the government had usually done so reluctantly, and they had lost their land and their way of life anyway.

Accommodation had failed. War had failed. And the bullet-riven Ghost Shirts buried with their wearers in the mass grave on the lone knoll above Wounded Knee Creek were ample proof that religion too had failed the Indians. There was no room left for the Indians in the West but what the government saw fit to permit them. One elderly Lakota chief who had witnessed the march of events from the Treaty of Fort Laramie in 1851 to the tragedy at Wounded Knee four decades later saw nothing remarkable in what had transpired. "The [government] made us many promises," he told a white friend, "more than I can remember, but they never kept but one; they promised to take our land, and they took it."[45]

*

There was no formal Lakota capitulation, not on January 15, 1891, or afterward. Warriors arriving at Pine Ridge were to hand over their rifles to their chiefs for delivery to army clerks, who would issue receipts for payment. That, at least, had been the plan. The execution, however, was uncomfortably reminiscent of Wounded Knee. One progressive Oglala chief with a large following turned in just nine rifles. By day's end, no more than seventy-five guns, many of them antiquated or broken, had passed into army hands. Miles wisely declined to order a search, confident the weapons would come with time and with a measured application of pressure on the chiefs. They did.[46]

Kicking Bear refused to hand over his rifle to a clerk. The proud Oglala was only one man. But because he was both the co-architect and the high priest of the Lakota Ghost Dance, his actions were watched closely by all. Before a single warrior relinquished his weapon, Kicking Bear sought out General Miles. Dismounting, he strode toward the general clutching his carbine. For a moment, the two stared at each other. Then Kicking Bear laid his weapon at Miles's feet.[47]

The Indian Wars for the American West were over.

ACKNOWLEDGMENTS

I would like to express my sincere gratitude to the historians S. C. Gwynne, James Donovan, Edwin R. Sweeney, and Mark Bradley and to the filmmaker Daniel Ostroff for their careful reading of the manuscript and their many and invaluable suggestions for improving it.

I wish to thank Peter Brown, formerly the owner of History America Tours, for organizing and leading me on a five-day personal tour of the Indian Wars sites of the Texas Panhandle and southwestern Oklahoma. It was an adventure I shall not soon forget. Peter also introduced me to Ken and Cheri Graves, whose Red Fork Ranch lies on the site of the Dull Knife Fight. Cheri generously shared her deep knowledge of the battle and gave me a remarkable tour of the ground. I would also like to thank Keith Herrin of the U.S. Cavalry School, who invited me on a staff ride of the Little Bighorn battlefield that greatly contributed to my understanding of the battle.

I am deeply grateful to my literary agent, Deborah Grosvenor, for her support of this project from the beginning and for her ideas and critiques along the way. I learned a great deal from her. My editor at Knopf, Andrew J. Miller, provided inestimable assistance. He kept me on track and focused in my writing, making this a far better book than it would otherwise have been. I am also most grateful to Ingrid Sterner, a marvelous copyeditor whose diligence saved me from a great many errors. My deepest debt is to my wife, Antonia. She believed in me whenever I doubted myself, and she supported me unfailingly during the four years I spent writing this book.

NOTES

EPIGRAPHS

1. 40th Cong., *Report of the Indian Peace Commissioners*, 28.
2. DeMallie, *Sixth Grandfather*, 106.
3. Britton Davis, *Truth About Geronimo*, 167.

PROLOGUE: OUR CHILDREN SOMETIMES BEHAVE BADLY

1. *New York Times*, April 11, 1863.
2. *New York Times*, April 8 and 11, 1863; Hoig, *Peace Chiefs*, 74.
3. *Washington Evening Star*, March 27, 1863.
4. *Washington Daily Intelligencer*, March 27, 1863.
5. Basler, *Collected Works of Abraham Lincoln*, 6:151–53; *Washington Daily Intelligencer*, March 27, 1863: Powell, *People of the Sacred Mountain*, 1:244.
6. *New York Times*, April 7, 13, and 17, 1863.
7. Berthrong, *Southern Cheyennes*, 168–86; Powell, *People of the Sacred Mountain*, 1:257, 263; Hoig, *Sand Creek Massacre*, 47–50.
8. Powell, *People of the Sacred Mountain*, 1:263–64; Grinnell, *Fighting Cheyennes*, 145; Hoig, *Peace Chiefs*, 75–76; *War of the Rebellion: Official Records*, vol. 34, pt. 1, 931.
9. "Bannock Troubles," 756.
10. Quoted in Powers, *Killing of Crazy Horse*, 36.

CHAPTER I: THE PLAINS AFLAME

1. Prucha, *American Indian Treaties*, 18, 21, 22, 65, 72, 100–101.
2. Calculations of Indian populations in the West represent rough approximations at best. About 75,000 Indians ranged the Great Plains from Texas to British Canada. Texas was home to 25,000 Indians, the Mexican Cession (present-day California and New Mexico) contained 150,000 Indians, and the Oregon Country, comprising the future states of Washington, Oregon, and Idaho, had an Indian population of 25,000. Utley, *Indian Frontier*, 4.
3. 31st Cong., *Annual Report of the Commissioner of Indian Affairs* (1849), 7.
4. Koster, "Smallpox in the Blankets," 36; Powell, *People of the Sacred Mountain*, 1:93–97.

5. Hassrick, *Sioux*, 3–7, 65–67; Berthrong, *Fighting Cheyennes*, 15–18; 39th Cong., *Condition of the Indian Tribes*, app., 12; Ewers, "Intertribal Warfare," 397, 406; Richard White, "Winning of the West," 336–37.

6. Gwynne, *Empire of the Summer Moon*, 32, 35, 45, 49, 57, 59; Berthrong, *Southern Cheyennes*, 17–26; Mayhall, *Kiowas*, 170–72.

7. Prucha, *American Indian Treaties*, 239; 33rd Cong., *Annual Report of the Office of Indian Affairs* (1853), 368–70; Utley, *Indian Frontier*, 61.

8. Utley, *Frontiersmen in Blue*, 118–20; Hyde, *Spotted Tail's Folk*, 92–93.

9. Berthrong, *Southern Cheyennes*, 10–12; Utley, *Indian Frontier*, 53–55.

10. The classification of Apaches within the two divisions has been the subject of considerable difference of opinion. The Western Apaches occupied much of present-day eastern Arizona and are generally agreed to have consisted of the White Mountain, Cibecue, San Carlos, Southern Tonto, and Northern Tonto groups, each with its component bands.

    Ethnologists normally divide the Chiricahuas into three bands: the Central Chiricahuas, or Chokonens, who inhabited the Chiricahua and Dragoon Mountains of southeastern Arizona; the Southern Chiricahuas, or Nednhis, who roamed the northern reaches of Sonora and Chihuahua, Mexico, and made the Sierra Madre their stronghold; and the Eastern Chiricahuas, or Chihennes, who occupied the country from the Arizona–New Mexico border to the Rio Grande. A fourth and smaller band, the Bedonkohes, looked to Mangas Coloradas for leadership. After his death, the Bedonkohes were absorbed by the three larger bands. The Chihennes are sometimes divided further into the Mogollons, who dwelled near the mountains of the same name, and the Mimbres, also known as the Warm Springs or Ojo Caliente Apaches. The Western Apaches and Chiricahuas numbered approximately six thousand. Cozzens, *Struggle for Apacheria*, xvi–xvii.

11. Cremony, *Life Among the Apaches*, 172–73; Sweeney, *Cochise*, 142–45; Utley, *Frontiersmen in Blue*, 239–47.

12. Hoig, *Sand Creek Massacre*, 74–90; Grinnell, *Fighting Cheyennes*, 145–62, 151–59; 39th Cong., *Condition of the Indian Tribes*, app., 81. Colonel Chivington and the Third Colorado Cavalry mustered out of federal service before the army was able to bring charges against them. But the Sand Creek Massacre dashed Chivington's political aspirations. Coloradans cooled on him, and a congressional committee investigating the massacre found that Chivington had "deliberately planned and executed a foul and dastardly massacre which would have disgraced the veriest savage among those who were the victims of his cruelty." Utley, *Frontiersmen in Blue*, 297.

13. Cozzens, *General John Pope*, 252–67; 39th Cong., *Suppression of Indian Hostilities*, 1.

14. 39th Cong., *Annual Report of the Commissioner of Indian Affairs*, 701–2, 704; Prucha, *American Indian Treaties*, 271.

15. Sherman to Benjamin H. Grierson, Aug. 16, 1865, in Marszalek, *Sherman*, 378; Sherman to John A. Rawlins, Aug. 31, 1866, in 39th Cong., *Protection Across the Continent*, 10–11; *Addresses to the Graduating Class*, 36–37.

16. Athearn, *Sherman and the Settlement of the West*, 29, 37; Sherman to Rawlins, Aug. 17 and 31, 1866, in 40th Cong., *Protection Across the Continent*, 1–4, 6, 10; 39th Cong., *Military Posts*, 3; Crawford, *Kansas in the Sixties*, 226–27.

CHAPTER 2: RED CLOUD'S WAR

1. Larson, *Red Cloud*, 34–73; Paul, *Autobiography of Red Cloud*, 68–69.
2. 40th Cong., *Indian Hostilities*, 62; Olson, *Red Cloud and the Sioux Problem*, 32–33.
3. McDermott, *Red Cloud's War*, 1:53; Olson, *Red Cloud and the Sioux Problem*, 34–39; Frances C. Carrington, *My Army Life*, 291–92.
4. Margaret I. Carrington, *Absaraka*, 39–40, 90; McDermott, *Red Cloud's War*, 1:48, 69, 72.
5. Murphy, "Forgotten Battalion," 4:65–67; Margaret I. Carrington, *Absaraka*, 101–110; McDermott, *Red Cloud's War*, 1:47, 88, 99–100, 116–17, 136–38, 184; 50th Cong., *Indian Operations*, 10; Bridger, "Indian Affairs"; 40th Cong., *Indian Hostilities*, 63; Powell, *People of the Sacred Mountain*, 1:443.
6. Murray, "Hazen Inspections," 28; 39th Cong., *Fort Phil Kearney* [sic] *Massacre*, 8; Murphy, "Forgotten Battalion," 4:73; Fetterman to Charles Terry, Nov. 26, 1866, Graff Collection, Newberry Library; Margaret I. Carrington, *Absaraka*, 198; Frances C. Carrington, *My Army Life*, 119.
7. McDermott, *Red Cloud's War*, 1:184–97; Monnett, *Where a Hundred Soldiers Were Killed*, 118.
8. Larson, *Red Cloud*, 99; Vestal, *Warpath*, 54; Stands in Timber and Liberty, *Cheyenne Memories*, 103.
9. McDermott, *Red Cloud's War*, 1:208–24; Monnett, *Where a Hundred Soldiers Were Killed*, 123–34, 280–81n; Frances C. Carrington, *My Army Life*, 144; *Army and Navy Journal*, March 9, 1867.
10. Belish, "American Horse," 56–57; Jensen, *Voices of the American West*, 1:280–81; Private Horace Vankirk to his father, Jan. 30, 1867, Fort Kearny, in *Cleveland Plain Dealer*, Feb. 5, 1867; Stands in Timber and Liberty, *Cheyenne Memories*, 103–4; Vestal, *Warpath*, 60, 64–65; McDermott, *Red Cloud's War*, 1:207n, 223–24.
11. Vankirk to his father, Jan. 30, 1867; 39th Cong., *Fort Phil Kearney* [sic] *Massacre*, 10; Murphy, "Forgotten Battalion," 4:71–72; Guthrie, "Detail of the Fetterman Massacre," 8; Vestal, *Warpath*, 68. The Indians suffered casualties of twenty warriors killed and an indeterminate number of warriors wounded.
12. 39th Cong., *Indian Hostilities*, 27; McDermott, *Red Cloud's War*, 2:317, 403; Larson, *Red Cloud*, 111.
13. McDermott, *Red Cloud's War*, 2:381–82, 391–401; Greene, "Hayfield Fight," 40; David, *Finn Burnett*, 166–67; J. B. Burrowes to George M. Templeton, Aug. 3, 1867, George M. Templeton Papers.
14. Vestal, *Warpath*, 71–73, 76; Gibson, "Wagon Box Fight," 2:52–54, 63–67; Littman, "Wagon Box Fight," 2:76, 79–80; McDermott, *Red Cloud's War*, 2:436.
15. Bradley to Ione Dewey, Sept. 5, 1867, Bradley Papers, U.S. Army Military History Institute; Grenville M. Dodge, *How We Built the Union Pacific*, 28–29.
16. Olson, *Red Cloud and the Sioux Problem*, 72–82, 341–49.

CHAPTER 3: WARRIOR AND SOLDIER

1. Richard I. Dodge, *Our Wild Indians*, 426–27.
2. Mails, *Mystic Warriors*, 520; Grinnell, *Story of the Indian*, 111.
3. Grinnell, "Coup and Scalp," 296–307; Marian W. Smith, "War Complex," 452; Linderman, *Plenty-Coups*, 106–8; Mails, *Mystic Warriors*, 43–44; Nabokov, *Two Leggings*, 49.

4. Linderman, *Plenty-Coups*, 49, 106–7.
5. Parker, *Old Army*, 273–76; Clark, *Indian Sign Language*, 77–78; Richard I. Dodge, *Our Wild Indians*, 416–20, 422; Powell, *People of the Sacred Mountain*, 1:120.
6. Marquis, *Wooden Leg*, 140; DeMallie, *Sixth Grandfather*, 107.
7. Richard I. Dodge, *Our Wild Indians*, 430; de Trobriand, *Military Life*, 62; Grinnell, *Story of the Indian*, 100–108; Linderman, *Plenty-Coups*, 104.
8. Richard I. Dodge, *Our Wild Indians*, 434; Stands in Timber and Liberty, *Cheyenne Memories*, 60–61.
9. Rickey, *Forty Miles a Day*, 18, 22–24; "Army Abuses," 80; Sherman, "We Do Our Duty," 85.
10. Rickey, *Forty Miles a Day*, 339–42; Rideing, "Life at a Frontier Post," 564–65; Kurz, "Reminiscences," 11; "Causes of Desertion," 322; 45th Cong., *Reorganization of the Army*, 122; Henry, "Cavalry Life in Arizona," 8; Brackett, "Our Cavalry," 384.
11. Sherman to Rawlins, Aug. 24, 1866, 39th Cong., *Protection Across the Continent*, 5–6, 9.
12. Rickey, *Forty Miles a Day*, 122–24; Forbes, "United States Army," 146; Harry L. Bailey to Lucullus V. McWhorter, Dec. 7, 1930, McWhorter Papers, Washington State Libraries.
13. Rickey, *Forty Miles a Day*, 116–21, 131, 141, 159, 168–69; "Life in Arizona," 223; Forsyth, *Story of the Soldier*, 140–41; Elizabeth B. Custer, "'Where the Heart Is,'" 309.
14. Forsyth, *Story of the Soldier*, 131–32; Rickey, *Forty Miles a Day*, 180–82, 190; Mazzanovich, "Life in Arizona," 1; Parker, *Old Army*, 18.
15. 40th Cong., *Army Organization*, 4; Utley, *Frontier Regulars*, 21.
16. Jacob, "Military Reminiscences," 34; Forsyth, *Story of the Soldier*, 140–41; *Montana Post*, Oct. 27, 1866; Sibbald, "Inebriates with Epaulets," 50–57.
17. "Army Abuses," 630–31; Godfrey, "Some Reminiscences," 417; Rickey, *Forty Miles a Day*, 143, 147, 152; Forbes, "United States Army," 133; Mulford, *Fighting Indians*, 56.
18. Schubert, *Voices of the Buffalo Soldier*, 47, 49, 85–86, 114–28; Parker, *Old Army*, 92–93; Leckie, *Buffalo Soldiers*, 26, 164; Theodore A. Davis, "Summer on the Plains," 304; lyrics quoted in Emmitt, *Last War Trail*, 220.
19. Utley, *Frontier Regulars*, 46; Baird, "Miles' Indian Campaigns," 351; de Trobriand, *Military Life*, 63.
20. 45th Cong., *Reorganization of the Army*, 237; Dunlay, *Wolves for the Blue Soldiers*, 36–38; Utley, *Frontier Regulars*, 49, 56.

CHAPTER 4: HANCOCK'S WAR

1. Crawford, *Kansas in the Sixties*, 226–27; 41st Cong., *Difficulties with Indian Tribes*, 18; Hancock, "Indians," 43; 39th Cong., *Protection Across the Continent*, 17; 40th Cong., *Expeditions Against the Indians*, 2.
2. Powell, *People of the Sacred Mountain*, 1:465–68; 41st Cong., *Difficulties with Indian Tribes*, 54–56, 80; *New York Herald*, April 28, 1867; Kennedy, "On the Plains with Custer and Hancock," 58.
3. 41st Cong., *Difficulties with Indian Tribes*, 27–28, 51–52, 82–83; Chalfant, *Hancock's War*, 156–60; Kenny, "Roman Nose," 10–20; Hyde, *Life of George Bent*,

259–61, 307–8; Powell, *People of the Sacred Mountain*, 1:468–73; Grinnell, *Fighting Cheyennes*, 253.

4. Utley, *Cavalier in Buckskin*, 19, 33; Wert, *Custer*, 200.

5. George A. Custer, *My Life on the Plains*, 78–85.

6. Chalfant, *Hancock's War*, 204; 41st Cong., *Difficulties with Indian Tribes*, 69–71, 75, 87.

7. Morris F. Taylor, "Kicking Bird," 295–309; Chalfant, *Hancock's War*, 245; 41st Cong., *Difficulties with Indian Tribes*, 101–7, 119–23; Stanley, *My Early Travels*, 1:61, 82–83.

8. Kennedy, *On the Plains*, 87; George A. Custer, *My Life on the Plains*, 109–11; Nye, *Plains Indian Raiders*, 79–80.

9. Powell, *People of the Sacred Mountain*, 1:479–84; Stanley, *My Early Travels*, 1:119–20.

10. Wert, *Custer*, 256–57; Utley, *Life in Custer's Cavalry*, 51, and *Cavalier in Buckskin*, 52; Nye, *Plains Indian Raiders*, 89–91.

11. Powell, *People of the Sacred Mountain*, 1:487; George A. Custer, *My Life on the Plains*, 198; Voigt, "Death of Lyman S. Kidder," 15, 21, 23.

12. Chalfant, *Hancock's War*, 409–10; Hutton, "Libbie Custer," 28.

13. Utley, *Life in Custer's Cavalry*, 87, 93; Wert, *Custer*, 259–64; Chalfant, *Hancock's War*, 409–21.

14. Danker, *Man of the Plains*, 58–59; Chalfant, *Hancock's War*, 450; Powell, *People of the Sacred Mountain*, 1:506.

CHAPTER 5: THE LAST TREATY

1. Cong. Globe, July 16 and 18, 1867, 667–68, 701–15; 40th Cong., *Indian Peace Commissioners*, 1–2, and *Indian Hostilities*, 121.

2. Simon, *Papers of Grant*, 17:241–42; Athearn, *Sherman and the Settlement of the West*, 174, 178–83; 40th Cong., *Indian Peace Commissioners*, 4.

3. Hyde, *Life of George Bent*, 282; Jones, *Treaty of Medicine Lodge*, 51–53; Isern, "Stanley's Frontier Apprenticeship," 26–27; *Daily Missouri Democrat*, Oct. 19 and 23, 1867; *Cincinnati Daily Gazette*, Oct. 28, 1867.

4. Satanta quoted in Proceedings of the Indian Peace Commission, 1:98–101; Jones, *Treaty of Medicine Lodge*, 51–53; Isern, "Stanley's Frontier Apprenticeship," 26–27; Omen, "Beginning of the End," 38–39; *Daily Missouri Democrat*, Oct. 23 and 25, 1867.

5. Proceedings of the Indian Peace Commission, 1:105–12; *Daily Missouri Democrat*, Oct. 25 and 28, 1867; Kappler, *Indian Affairs*, 2:984–89; Gwynn, *Empire of the Summer Moon*, 230; Jones, *Treaty of Medicine Lodge*, 127–30, 134.

6. Powell, *People of the Sacred Mountain*, 1:521–22, 524–25; *Daily Missouri Democrat*, Oct. 28 and Nov. 2, 1867; Godfrey, "Medicine Lodge Treaty," 8; Jones, *Treaty of Medicine Lodge*, 164–67; Omen, "Beginning of the End," 40.

7. Proceedings of the Indian Peace Commission, 1:116–23; Powell, *People of the Sacred Mountain*, 1:527–29.

8. *Daily Missouri Democrat*, Nov. 2, 1867; Jones, *Treaty of Medicine Lodge*, 176–78; Powell, *People of the Sacred Mountain*, 1:530–31; *New York Evening Post*, Jan. 9, 1868; Utley, *Life in Custer's Cavalry*, 116–17; Hyde, *Life of George Bent*, 284.

9. Hutton, *Sheridan and His Army*, 2, 34.

10. Powell, *People of the Sacred Mountain*, 1:532–33; Nye, *Plains Indian Raiders*, 111–

15; *Annual Report of the Secretary of War, 1868*, 3; Sheridan to Sherman, Sept. 26, 1868, Sheridan Papers, Library of Congress.

11. Sheridan, *Personal Memoirs*, 2:286–88; Sheridan to Sherman, Sept. 26, 1868, and Beecher to Sheridan, May 22, June 5, 13, 21, and 22, 1868, Sheridan Papers.

12. *Annual Report of the Secretary of War, 1868*, 64; 40th Cong., *Report of the Commissioner of Indian Affairs*, 1868, 534; Sheridan to Sherman, Sept. 26, 1868.

13. Quoted in Athearn, *Sherman and the Settlement of the West*, 219.

14. Forsyth, "Frontier Fight," 42–44, and "Report of the Organization and Operations of a Body of Scouts, March 21, 1869," 45, Sheridan Papers; Whitney, "Beecher Island Diary," 297; Zigler, "Beecher Island Battle," 176; Schlesinger, "Scout Schlesinger's Story," 196; Monnett, *Beecher Island*, 126.

15. Grinnell, *Fighting Cheyennes*, 282–83; Hyde, *Life of George Bent*, 298–99; Forsyth, "Frontier Fight," 47–48; Walter M. Camp, interview with John Hurst, Camp Papers, Brigham Young University; Murphy, "Battle of the Arikaree"; Monnett, *Beecher Island*, 133.

16. Forsyth, "Report" and "Frontier Fight," 48–54; Whitney, "Beecher Island Diary," 297–98; Vilott, "Withstood the Siege"; Grinnell, *Fighting Cheyennes*, 161, 286–88.

17. Whitney, "Beecher Island Diary," 298–99; Louis A. Carpenter, "Story of a Rescue," 6–7; Schubert, *Voices of the Buffalo Soldier*, 25; Hyde, *Life of George Bent*, 305.

18. Sheridan, *Personal Memoirs*, 2:294, and "Annual Report," Oct. 15, 1868, Sheridan Papers; Godfrey, "Some Reminiscences," 419–22; Elliott to "My Dear Davis," Oct. 31, 1868, Miscellaneous Collection, Kansas State Historical Society.

19. Sherman quoted in Athearn, *Sherman and the Settlement of the West*, 223, 227.

20. 40th Cong., *Report of the Commissioner of Indian Affairs*, 1868, 536–39; Hazen, "Some Corrections," 303.

21. Powell, *People of the Sacred Mountain*, 1:573.

CHAPTER 6: OF GARRYOWEN IN GLORY

1. Sheridan to Chauncey McKeever, Nov. 22, 1868, Sheridan Papers; Sheridan, *Personal Memoirs*, 2:308–10; 41st Cong., *Difficulties with Indian Tribes*, 169–70; Greene, *Washita*, 78–79.

2. Greene, *Washita*, 86; Hoig, *Battle of the Washita*, 82; Sheridan to McKeever, Nov. 22, 1868; George A. Custer, *My Life on the Plains*, 280–83.

3. Greene, *Washita*, 102–4; Berthrong, *Southern Cheyennes*, 323–24; 40th Cong., *Indian Battle*, 22–23. Two Lakota and two Arapaho lodges, whose occupants had family members in Black Kettle's band, were also present in the village.

4. Hardorff, *Washita Memories*, 133; 40th Cong., *Indian Battle*, 27; George A. Custer, *My Life on the Plains*, 285–87, 296–97, 319–20; Greene, *Washita*, 99–100.

5. 40th Cong., *Indian Battle*, 27; Utley, *Life in Custer's Cavalry*, 219; Hoig, *Battle of the Washita*, 124.

6. Powell, *People of the Sacred Mountain*, 1: 599–600; Hardorff, *Washita Memories*, 191, 207, 306, 325; 40th Cong., *Indian Battle*, 33.

7. Powell, *People of the Sacred Mountain*, 1:603; Hardorff, *Washita Memories*, 307, 309; Hoig, *Battle of the Washita*, 131–32, 198–99; *New-York Tribune*, Dec. 24, 1868.

8. Hardorff, *Washita Memories*, 21, 209, 309, 333, 338; Mathey, "Washita Campaign," Brigham Young University; 40th Cong., *Indian Battle*, 28.

9. Hardorff, *Washita Memories*, 140–42, 193, 208, 213, 326, 359; George A. Custer, *My Life on the Plains*, 346; Powell, *People of the Sacred Mountain*, 1:605, 608–10, 614–15; *Daily Missouri Democrat*, Feb. 3, 1869; Greene, *Washita*, 123.

10. George A. Custer, *My Life on the Plains*, 346–48; Gibson, "Our Washita Battle," 388; Hardorff, *Washita Memories*, 143–44, 210–12, 236; Greene, *Washita*, 127–28, 136; 40th Cong., *Indian Battle*, 28, 30.

11. George A. Custer, *My Life on the Plains*, 391–94; Utley, *Cavalier in Buckskin*, 70; Mathey, "Washita Campaign"; Hutton, *Sheridan and His Army*, 70, 72; *Daily Missouri Democrat*, Feb. 8, 1869; *New York Times*, Feb. 15, 1869. I agree with the historian James Donovan's conclusion that the tactical situation as Custer understood it was such that there was little he could have done to save Elliott without endangering the regiment. The surrounding hills swarmed with Indians in great numbers, darkness was approaching, and Elliott had been gone for several hours when Custer decided to leave the battlefield. There was certainly no malicious intent on Custer's part; he liked and respected the young major. Donovan, *Terrible Glory*, 67.

12. Captain Miles Keogh quoted in Hutton, *Sheridan and His Army*, 389–90; Powell, *People of the Sacred Mountain*, 2:696.

13. Samuel F. Tappan to Nathaniel G. Taylor, Dec. 4, 1868, Tappan Papers, History Colorado Center; Hutton, *Sheridan and His Army*, 95–96; 40th Cong., *Battle on the Washita*, 36, 26, 32, 38; 40th Cong., *Indians Killed*, 3; Greene, *Washita*, 164–65, 168.

14. Powell, *People of the Sacred Mountain*, 2:693–94; 40th Cong., *Indian Battle*, 35–39; Hazen, "Some Corrections," 296.

15. Hoig, *Battle of the Washita*, 149, 152; 40th Cong., *Battle on the Washita*, 39; George A. Custer, *My Life on the Plains*, 414–19.

16. Hardorff, *Washita Memories*, 41–43; Keim, *Sheridan's Troopers*, 150; *Lawrence Bulletin*, Dec. 22, 1868; Sheridan, *Personal Memoirs*, 331; Hutton, *Sheridan and His Army*, 81; 40th Cong., *Difficulties with Indian Tribes*, 160; 40th Cong., *Indian Affairs*, 1.

17. Hoig, *Battle of the Washita*, 163–64; Sheridan, *Personal Memoirs*, 2:334–35; 40th Cong., *Indian Battle*, 40; Sheridan to McKeever, Dec. 19, 1868, Sheridan Papers; Hazen, "Some Corrections," 302, 305–6, 309–10, 315, 318.

18. Moore, "Indian Campaign," 274–75; Sheridan, *Personal Memoirs*, 2:336.

19. Rister, "Evans' Fight," 292–98; Sheridan to McKeever, Jan. 20, 1869, Sheridan Papers; 40th Cong., *Further Information*, 1.

20. Powell, *People of the Sacred Mountain*, 2:701–2; Greene, *Washita*, 179; 40th Cong., *Further Information*, 1–2; Hoig, *Peace Chiefs*, 145–46.

21. Moore, "Indian Campaign," 275; Powell, *People of the Sacred Mountain*, 2:707–8; Custer to Sheridan, March 21, 1869, Sheridan Papers.

22. George A. Custer, *My Life on the Plains*, 557–60; Powell, *People of the Sacred Mountain*, 2:708–11, 720; Rodgers, "Few Years' Experience."

23. Custer to Sheridan, March 21, 1869; George A. Custer, *My Life on the Plains*, 560–65; Rodgers, "Few Years' Experience"; Broome, *Dog Soldier Justice*, 141–45; Powell, *People of the Sacred Mountain*, 2:711–21; Cheyenne chief quoted in Hoig, *Washita*, 180.

24. Grierson to John Kirk, April 6, 1869, Grierson Papers, Newberry Library;

Berthrong, *Southern Cheyennes*, 339–40; Utley, *Frontier Regulars*, 156; Henry Jackson to Chauncey McKeever, June 6, 1869, Sheridan Papers.

25. *Record of Engagements*, 22; Carr, "Reminiscences of Indian Wars," 12, Carr Papers, U.S. Army Education and Heritage Center.

26. Carr, "Reminiscences of Indian Wars," 3, 22, and Carr to Cody, July 2, 1906, Carr Papers; Lonnie J. White, "Indian Raids," 374–83; "Capture of a Cheyenne Village"; Hyde, *Life of George Bent*, 332–34; Grinnell, *Two Great Scouts*, 199; Broome, *Dog Soldier Justice*, 174–75, 181–82; *Record of Engagements*, 24.

CHAPTER 7: THE BLOODY POLICY OF PEACE

1. Sherman quoted in *Cincinnati Daily Gazette*, Jan. 3, 1868; Richard I. Dodge, *Plains of the Great West*, 436; "The Army and the Indian."

2. Slattery, *Felix Brunot*, 145; Board of Indian Commissioners, *Fourth Annual Report*, 4; 40th Cong., *Indian Tribes*, 1–2; *New York Evening Post*, Jan. 9, 1868; 40th Cong., *Department of Indian Affairs*, 1–3.

3. Prucha, *American Indian Policy*, 47–51; Utley, "Celebrated Peace Policy," 125–26; 41st Cong., *Report of the Commissioner of Indian Affairs 1869*, 5, 485–87; Simon, *Papers of Grant*, 20:38; Fritz, "Grant's Peace Policy," 430.

4. Dunn, *Massacres of the Mountains*, 522–24, 532; Hutton, "Sheridan's Pyrrhic Victory," 36–38; 41st Cong., *Piegan Indians*, 37–39, 45–46; *Philadelphia Inquirer*, March 13, 1870.

5. Hutton, "Sheridan's Pyrrhic Victory," 39–42; Sherman, *Memoirs*, 2:437; Prucha, *American Indian Policy*, 51–53.

6. 41st Cong., *Report of the Commissioner of Indian Affairs 1869*, 6.

7. *New York Herald*, June 8 and 9, 1870; *New York Times*, June 9, 1870.

8. Genetin-Pilawa, "Parker and the Peace Policy," 213–14; Armstrong, *Warrior in Two Camps*, 151–60; Prucha, *American Indian Policy*, 69–70; Grant quoted in *Philadelphia Inquirer*, June 9, 1871.

9. *Portland Daily Press*, March 6, 1871; *Philadelphia Post*, March 17, 1871; *New York Herald Tribune*, Aug. 6, 1871.

10. *Dallas Weekly Herald*, June 3, 1871; Richardson, *Comanche Barrier*, 158–61; *Outrages Committed by Indians*, 1–4; Tatum, *Our Red Brothers*, 29–30.

11. Hutton, *Sheridan and His Army*, 227–34; Nye, *Carbine and Lance*, 107–14, 124, 126; *Galveston Tri-weekly News*, Aug. 1, 1870; Morris F. Taylor, "Kicking Bird," 309–10.

12. Dorst, "Ranald Slidell Mackenzie," 367–75; Robert G. Carter, *On the Border with Mackenzie*, 81–82, 184, 255.

13. Robert G. Carter, *On the Border with Mackenzie*, 81–82.

14. Tatum, *Our Red Brothers*, 116–17; Nye, *Carbine and Lance*, 134–43; Marriott, *Ten Grandmothers*, 112–20; Sherman to Mackenzie, May 28, 1871, Records of Edmund Jackson Davis, Texas State Library and Archives Commission.

15. Robert G. Carter, *On the Border with Mackenzie*, 92–94; Nye, *Carbine and Lance*, 113–14, 144–45.

16. Tatum, *Our Red Brothers*, 122; Rister, "Jacksboro Indian Affair," 193–94.

17. Nye, *Carbine and Lance*, 148; Jacob, "Reminiscences," 27–28; Robert G. Carter, *On the Border with Mackenzie*, 125–47; Morris F. Taylor, "Kicking Bird," 313.

18. Gwynn, *Empire of the Summer Moon*, 7–8, 199–200; Neeley, *Last Comanche War Chief*, 208.

19. Gwynn, *Empire of the Summer Moon*, 9–10, 242–43, 247–48; Robert G. Carter, *On the Border with Mackenzie*, 165–67, 193–94; Wallace, *Mackenzie on the Texas Frontier*, 49–50.

20. Robinson, *Bad Hand*, 116; Mayhall, *Kiowas*, 277–78, 280; Tatum, *Our Red Brothers*, 126, 132–33. Tatum resigned effective March 31, 1873.

21. Robinson, *Bad Hand*, 53–54, 113–18, 192–96; Wallace, *Mackenzie on the Texas Frontier*, 64–69.

22. Wallace, *Mackenzie on the Texas Frontier*, 77–79, 80–83; Robert G. Carter, *Old Sergeant's Story*, 84–86; Thompson, "Scouting with Mackenzie," 162.

23. Richardson, *Comanche Barrier*, 186–87.

24. Quoted in Rister, "Jacksboro Indian Affair," 196.

25. Nye, *Carbine and Lance*, 170, 180, 181, 183; Mayhall, *Kiowas*, 285–86.

CHAPTER 8: TRAGEDY IN THE LAVA BEDS

1. Meacham, *Wigwam and War-Path*, 355; 43rd Cong., *Modoc War*, 154–56; Riddle, *Indian History of the Modoc War*, 69–70; Dillon, *Burnt-Out Fires*, 213–14.

2. Murray, *Modocs and Their War*, 8–32; Bancroft, *History of Oregon*, 2:555–56; Powers, "California Indians," 542–43.

3. Riddle, *Indian History of the Modoc War*, 26, 35, 104, 130, 191, 235; Meacham, *Wigwam and War-Path*, 295, 302, 316–20, 326–27, 348, 425.

4. Riddle, *Indian History of the Modoc War*, 32, 36–37, 201–23; Meacham, *Wigwam and War-Path*, 297, 304–7, 312–23; 42nd Cong., *Modoc Indians*, 2; Murray, *Modocs and Their War*, 44–53.

5. Heyman, *Prudent Soldier*, 38, 349–50; Schofield, *Forty-Six Years in the Army*, 436.

6. Odeneal, *Modoc War*, 7–8, 23, 26, 32, 44; Schofield, *Forty-Six Years in the Army*, 435–36.

7. Boutelle, "Major Boutelle's Account," 264–65, 268–69; James Jackson, "Modoc War," 74–77; *Klamath Express*, Jan. 10, 1895; Riddle, *Indian History of the Modoc War*, 45, 47; *Report of Governor Grover*, 7–8; 43rd Cong., *Modoc War*, 177.

8. Fitzgerald, "Modoc War," 516; Murray, *Modocs and Their War*, 8–10, 97–99; 43rd Cong., *Modoc War*, 181.

9. Thompson, *Modoc War*, 28–29, 34; Boyle, "Personal Observations," Bancroft Collection, University of California; Trimble, "Reminiscences," 280–81.

10. Meacham, *Wigwam and War-Path*, 386–87, and *Wi-ne-ma*, 129–30; Thompson, *Modoc War*, 31.

11. Perry, "First and Second Battles," 295, 297; *New York Herald*, Feb. 16, 1873; Boyle, "Personal Observations."

12. 43rd Cong., *Modoc War*, 169–70; Murray, *Modocs and Their War*, 123; Boyle, "Personal Observations"; *Report of Governor Grover*, 38–39.

13. *New York Herald*, March 6, 8, 17, 20, 26, and April 7, 1873; Meacham, *Wigwam and War-Path*, 430–32; *Oregonian*, March 13 and 20, 1873; Riddle, *Indian History of the Modoc War*, 64, 231–34, 274–75.

14. Heyman, *Prudent Soldier*, 370–74; *Trenton Evening Times*, Nov. 2, 1887; Meacham, *Wigwam and War-Path*, 440–43, 464–65; *New York Herald*, March 2 and April 9, 1873; Riddle, *Indian History of the Modoc War*, 70–71.

15. Heyman, *Prudent Soldier*, 375–77; Meacham, *Wigwam and War-Path*, 470, 474–75, 478–90; *Oregonian*, April 14, 1873; 43rd Cong., *Modoc War*, 139, 142, 161–66; Annual Report, *Indian Affairs 1873*, 77–78.

16. Heyman, *Prudent Soldier,* 379.
17. Boyle, "Personal Observations"; Boutelle, "Disaster to Thomas' Command," 306–11; Thompson, *Modoc War,* 83–86.
18. Boyle, "Personal Observations"; Hardin, "'Gosh Dash It, Let's Charge,'" 4; Hasbrouck, "Last Fight," 320–22; Riddle, *Indian History of the Modoc War,* 124–25.
19. Thompson, *Modoc War,* 115; Perry, "First and Second Battles," 303–4.
20. *Army and Navy Journal,* June 21, 1873, 714; Riddle, *Indian History of the Modoc War,* 188–89.
21. Dunn, *Massacres of the Mountains,* 380–82; Murray, *Modocs and Their War,* 303; Landrum, *Guardhouse,* 76. Gathering Indian skulls for the Army Medical Museum was official policy, the stated purpose, as articulated by the Surgeon General, being to "aid in the progress of anthropological science by obtaining measurements of a large number of skulls of aboriginal races of North America." Quoted in Simpson, *Making Representations,* 175.

CHAPTER 9: THE BUFFALO WAR

1. Kicking Bird quoted in Neeley, *Last Comanche Chief,* 81; Haley, *Buffalo War,* 21–22, 25; Mooar, "Buffalo Days," 470, 473; Hyde, *Life of George Bent,* 353–55.
2. Quoted in Haley, *Buffalo War,* 49; Hyde, *Life of George Bent,* 355; Berthrong, *Southern Cheyennes,* 380–82.
3. Haley, *Buffalo War,* 43; Powell, *People of the Sacred Mountain,* 2:862.
4. Gwynn, *Empire of the Summer Moon,* 263–67; Haley, *Buffalo War,* 52–54; Hyde, *Life of George Bent,* 358.
5. Neeley, *Last Comanche Chief,* 92–93; Nye, *Carbine and Lance,* 189–91; Mooar, "Buffalo Days," 476–77.
6. Quoted in Haley, *Buffalo War,* 75; Gwynn, *Empire of the Summer Moon,* 270–72.
7. Haley, *Buffalo War,* 76–77; Richardson, *Comanche Barrier,* 194, 246n; Morris F. Taylor, "Kicking Bird," 318–19; Nye, *Carbine and Lance,* 192–200.
8. Joe F. Taylor, *Indian Campaign,* 1:11–13.
9. Cozzens, *General John Pope,* 316–17; Hutton, *Soldiers West,* 212–16.
10. Miles, *Personal Recollections,* 1:164–65; 44th Cong., *Report of the Secretary of War* (1875), 78.
11. Joe F. Taylor, *Indian Campaign,* 1:21–23; Miles, *Personal Recollections,* 1:166–70; Frank D. Baldwin to his wife, Sept. 14, 1874, Brown Papers, University of Colorado; *Pampa Daily News,* Oct. 1, 1933.
12. Powell, *People of the Sacred Mountain,* 2:836–37; Meredith, *Girl Captives of the Cheyennes,* v–vi; Jauken, *Moccasin Speaks,* 97–98.
13. Haley, *Buffalo War,* 108–9, 111–23; Joe F. Taylor, *Indian Campaign,* 1:31–33.
14. Nye, *Bad Medicine and Good,* 192–94.
15. Brininstool, "Billy Dixon," 15–17; Joe F. Taylor, *Indian Campaign,* 1:34–35, 89–100; Nye, *Carbine and Lance,* 219; Powell, *People of the Sacred Mountain,* 2:874; Utley, *Frontier Regulars,* 225.
16. *New York Herald,* Oct. 16, 1874; Robert G. Carter, *On the Border with Mackenzie,* 485–89; Powell, *People of the Sacred Mountain,* 2:868; Charlton, "Battle at Palo Duro Canyon," 257–58.
17. Haley, *Buffalo War,* 187–88.
18. Joe F. Taylor, *Indian Campaign,* 1:105–6; Steinbach, *Long March,* 93; Meredith, *Girl Captives of the Cheyennes,* x–xi.

19. Henely, "Sappa Creek Fight," 6–7; West, "Battle of Sappa Creek," 160–72.
20. Joe F. Taylor, *Indian Campaign*, 91; Miles, *Personal Recollections*, 1:183; Hyde, *Life of George Bent*, 365; Haley, *Buffalo War*, 213–14; Morris F. Taylor, "Kicking Bird," 319.
21. Gwynn, *Empire of the Summer Moon*, 284–91; Haley, *Buffalo War*, 206, 208–9.
22. Quoted in Cozzens, *Conquering the Southern Plains*, xliii.

CHAPTER 10: NO REST, NO PEACE

1. Whitman to J. G. C. Lee, May 17, 1871, in Colyer, *Peace with the Apaches*, 31; Eskiminzin quoted in Cargill, "Camp Grant Massacre," 74.
2. Hastings, "Tragedy at Camp Grant," 155–56, 78; Jacoby, *Shadows at Dawn*, 82–90, 185–88; Altshuler, *Chains of Command*, 191; *Tucson Daily Star*, July 1, 1879; *Prescott Weekly Journal*, May 13 and 27, 1871.
3. Crook, "Resume of Operations," 571; Bourke, *Apache Campaign*, 50–51.
4. Carr, "Days of Empire," 14; Gressley, "Soldier with Crook," 36–39; *Tucson Daily Citizen*, May 30, 1874; *Chicago Daily Inter Ocean*, July 10, 1874. Sweeney, *Cochise*, 261–305, 395, attributes Cochise's death to one of two causes—dyspepsia or stomach cancer. Because the former, unless it presages a peptic ulcer, is seldom fatal, I have elected to attribute his death to cancer.
5. Altshuler, *Chains of Command*, 188–96; *Chicago Daily Inter Ocean*, July 5, 1883; *Memorial and Affidavits Showing Outrages Perpetrated by the Apache Indians*, 10, 30.
6. Schmitt, *General George Crook*, 160–62; Robinson, *General Crook*, 106–7; Thrapp, *Conquest of Apacheria*, 92.
7. Schmitt, *General George Crook*, 144; Azor H. Nickerson, "Major General George Crook," 4, Crook-Kennon Papers, U.S. Army Heritage and Education Center. The interminable succession of small clashes that characterized what became known as the Snake War is exhaustively described in the only serious study of the conflict, Michno's *Deadliest Indian War in the West*.
8. James T. King, "George Crook," 334–35; Bourke, *On the Border with Crook*, 112–13; Nickerson, "Major General Crook," 4; Goldin, "Terry and Crook," 38.
9. Bourke, *On the Border with Crook*, 108–9; Schmitt, *General George Crook*, 170–71. John G. Bourke (1846–1896) enlisted in the Union army at age sixteen, winning a Medal of Honor at the Battle of Stones River. After the Civil War, he attended West Point and was commissioned in the Third U.S. Cavalry. A dedicated ethnologist, meticulous observer, and superb writer, Bourke published widely on the Indian tribes that he came to know. He also kept a remarkably full diary, 124 volumes of which are preserved in the U.S. Military Academy Library. Bourke's diary entries from 1872 to 1881 have been published in five volumes as Robinson, *Diaries of Bourke*.
10. Crook to Adjutant General, U.S. Army, July 10, 1871, Crook Letter Book 1, Hayes Library Center. Unless otherwise noted, all Crook correspondence cited here is from the Crook Letter Book; Schmitt, *General George Crook*, 163–66.
11. Crook to Adjutant General, Sept. 8, 1871; *Chicago Daily Inter Ocean*, July 5, 1885.
12. The White Mountain Indian Reservation encompassed some six thousand square miles in east-central Arizona. It was bounded on the north by the Mogollon Rim and stretched south below the Gila River. The southern half of the reservation was commonly and erroneously called the San Carlos Res-

ervation. The San Carlos Agency at the conjunction of the San Carlos and the Gila Rivers administrated the White Mountain Indian Reservation. In 1896, the reservation was divided into the Fort Apache and the San Carlos Reservations. See explanatory notes to the White Mountain Indian Reservation map in Utley, *Geronimo*.

13. Crook to Rutherford B. Hayes, Nov. 28, 1871; Crook to Schofield, Sept. 1, 1871, quoted in James T. King, "George Crook," 339.

14. Schmitt, *General George Crook*, 169–70; Howard, "Major General George Crook," 326–27.

15. "General Howard's Treaties," 622–24; Sweeney, *Cochise*, 342, 352, 356–66; *Tucson Arizona Citizen*, Dec. 7, 1872; Safford to Howard, Nov. 16, 1872, Howard Papers, Bowdoin College; Crook to Henry M. Teller, March 27, 1883.

16. Crook to the Assistant Adjutant General, Military Division of the Pacific, Sept. 21, 1872, and Jan. 24, 1873, to the Adjutant General of the Army, Dec. 13, 1872; Bourke, *On the Border with Crook*, 182; Schmitt, *General George Crook*, 175.

17. Robinson, *Diaries of Bourke*, 1:44–49; "Early Days in Arizona," 3.

18. Schmitt, *General George Crook*, 178; Thrapp, *Conquest of Apacheria*, 136–38; the Yavapai chief Cha-lipun quoted in Nickerson, "Major General Crook," 233; Bourke, *On the Border with Crook*, 212–14.

19. Robinson, *General Crook*, 141; Thrapp, *Conquest of Apacheria*, 143, 146–54; Crook to Assistant Adjutant General, Military Division of the Pacific, July 3, 1873.

20. Nickerson, "Major General Crook," 233; Thrapp, *Conquest of Apacheria*, 156–61; Schmidt, *General George Crook*, 156–57.

21. Crook to Assistant Adjutant General, Military Division of the Pacific, Feb. 11, 1873; Bourke, "Conference with Cochise," 152–54.

22. Account of an unidentified army officer at Fort Bowie printed in the *Chicago Daily Inter Ocean*, July 10, 1874; Sweeney, *Cochise*, 395; *Arizona Republic*, April 10, 1935.

23. Thrapp, *Conquest of Apacheria*, 165–71; Sweeney, *From Cochise to Geronimo*, 37–66; Schmitt, *General George Crook*, 184; Daklugie quoted in Ball, *Indeh*, 37.

CHAPTER 11: SITTING BULL AND CRAZY HORSE

1. Sitting Bull quoted in *New York Herald*, Nov. 22, 1877.

2. LaPointe, *Sitting Bull*, 19–31, 46–47; Higheagle, "Memories of Sitting Bull"; Valentine McGillycuddy to Walter S. Campbell, April 16, 1929, Aaron M. Beede to Campbell, Sept. 27 and Dec. 23, 1929, and One Bull interview, all in Campbell Collection, Western History Collection, University of Oklahoma; Utley, *Lance and Shield*, 31–37.

3. McGillycuddy to Campbell, April 16, 1929; *Annual Report of the Secretary of War, 1867*, 32, 51–52; *New York Post*, April 11 and May 15, 1867; Larpenteur, *Forty Years*, 358–60; White Bull interview, Campbell Collection.

4. Lakota numbers cited here are drawn from Bray, "Teton Sioux." Cheyenne and Northern Arapaho numbers are extrapolated from inflated figures given by Red Cloud Agency officials in 44th Cong., *Report of the Commissioner of Indian Affairs* (1875), 608.

5. Proceedings of the Indian Peace Commission, 2:151–52, Record Group 48, National Archives; *St. Paul Daily Press*, Sept. 12, 1868; *Helena Weekly Herald*, Oct. 1, 1868; Utley, *Lance and Shield*, 91.

6. Utley, *Lance and Shield*, 85–86; Higheagle, "How Sitting Bull Was Made a Chief," and One Bull, "Information in Sioux and English with Regard to Sitting Bull," both in Campbell Collection.

7. McMurtry, *Crazy Horse*, 7–8, 16–17; Bray, *Crazy Horse*, 71; Chips interview in Jensen, *Voices of the American West*, 1:73; Powers, *Killing of Crazy Horse*, 32–34; He Dog interview in Paul, *Nebraska Reader*, 186–92; John M. Marshall, *Journey of Crazy Horse*, 77–162.

8. White Bull interview, 29, Campbell Collection; McGinnis, *Counting Coups*, 119–25.

9. *Daily Nebraska Press*, Aug. 13, 1873; *Sioux City Journal*, Aug. 12, 1873; Hyde, *Red Cloud's Folk*, 208; McGinnis, *Counting Coups*, 125–26; *Dakota Republican*, Aug. 21, 1873.

10. Cox quoted in 41st Cong., *Report of the Secretary of War, 1869*, 7.

11. One Bull and White Bull interviews, Campbell Collection; 41st Cong., *Report of the Secretary of War, 1869*, 7; Lubetkin, "Forgotten Yellowstone Surveying Expeditions," 34–35, and *Jay Cooke's Gamble*, 53; Robertson, "Big Sioux War," 4.

12. Lubetkin, "No Fighting," 30, and *Custer and the 1873 Yellowstone Survey*, 33; Howe, "Expedition to the Yellowstone," 526.

13. Spotted Eagle quoted in Powers, *Killing of Crazy Horse*, 64; *Sioux City Journal*, April 23, 1872; Lubetkin, *Jay Cooke's Gamble*, 135–39; Vestal, *Warpath*, 136–38.

14. LaPointe, *Sitting Bull*, 55–57; Vestal, *Warpath*, 139–43; Lubetkin, "No Fighting," 38, and *Custer and the 1873 Yellowstone Survey*, 33.

15. Sherman to Sheridan, Oct. 7, 1872, quoted in Athearn, *Sherman and the Settlement of the West*, 327; Utley, *Lance and Shield*, 111; 42nd Cong., *Report of the Secretary of War*, 40.

16. Utley, *Cavalier in Buckskin*, 103–10; Howe, "Expedition to the Yellowstone River," 523–24, 526; *Sioux City Daily Journal*, Aug. 9, 1873; Wert, *Custer*, 304; Colonel Stanley's report of the Yellowstone Expedition in *Rockford Daily Register*, Sept. 3, 1873; Lubetkin, *Custer and the 1873 Yellowstone Survey*, 219–20.

17. Utley, *Lance and Shield*, 112.

18. George A. Custer, "Battling with the Sioux," 95; Howe, "Expedition to the Yellowstone River," 532; Lubetkin, *Jay Cooke's Gamble*, 245–46.

19. Lubetkin, *Jay Cooke's Gamble*, 246–47; George A. Custer, "Battling with the Sioux," 101–2; Howe, "Expedition to the Yellowstone River," 532–33; Utley, *Cavalier in Buckskin*, 121–22, and *Lance and Shield*, 112–13.

20. *Annual Report of the Commissioner of Indian Affairs, 1873*, 5; Hutton, *Sheridan and His Army*, 287.

21. Utley, *Cavalier in Buckskin*, 123; Lubetkin, *Custer and the 1873 Yellowstone Survey*, 247–48; Stanley's Report in *Rockford Daily Register*, Sept. 3, 1873.

22. *New York Times*, Sept. 11, 1873.

CHAPTER 12: THE THIEVES' ROAD

1. Olson, *Red Cloud and the Sioux Problem*, 145–65.

2. 43rd Cong., *Report of the Secretary of War*, 23–24; Hutton, *Sheridan and His Army*, 290–91; Powers, *Killing of Crazy Horse*, 78–79; Utley, *Lance and Shield*, 115.

3. Custer quoted in Calhoun, *With Custer in '74*, 103, and Danker, *Man of the Plains*, 187–88; Headquarters Black Hills Expedition, June 30, 1874, General Order No. 3, quoted in Krause, *Custer's Prelude to Glory*, 165; Ewert quoted in Donald Jackson, *Custer's Gold*, 28.

4. DeMallie, *Sixth Grandfather*, 158–60; John M. Marshall, *Journey of Crazy Horse*, 167–68; McMurtry, *Crazy Horse*, 79.

5. Wert, *Custer*, 315–16; Custer to Assistant Adjutant General, Department of Dakota, Aug. 2, 1874, in *New York World*, Aug. 16, 1874; Krause, *Custer's Prelude to Glory*, 268; Donald Jackson, *Custer's Gold*, 87.

6. *Chicago Daily Inter Ocean*, Aug. 27, 1874; *Boston Journal*, Aug. 10, 1874; *Virginia City Territorial Enterprise*, Sept. 2, 1874; *Yankton Press and Dakotan*, Sept. 3, 1874; Donald Jackson, *Custer's Gold*, 102–3.

7. Stiles, *Custer's Trials*, 402–3; *Bismarck Tribune*, Sept. 10, 1874; 43rd Cong., *Report of the Secretary of War*, 24; *Cincinnati Enquirer*, Sept. 18, 1874; Sheridan to Terry, Sept. 3 and 4, 1874, in 44th Cong., *Black Hills*; *Chicago Daily Tribune*, Sept. 4 and 25, 1874; Sheridan to Sherman, March 25, 1875, in *Washington Reporter*, March 31, 1875; 44th Cong., *Report of the Commissioner of Indian Affairs*, 683.

8. Billy Garnett interview in Jensen, *Voices of the American West*, 2:83–84; Olson, *Red Cloud and the Sioux Problem*, 175–85.

9. *New-York Tribune*, June 6, 1875; Gray, *Centennial Campaign*, 20; Crook to Assistant Adjutant General, Military Division of the Missouri, Aug. 16 and Sept. 15, 1875; Crook quoted in *New York Herald*, Aug. 16, 1875.

10. Powell, *People of the Sacred Mountain*, 1:xvii–xviii and 2:928–29; Hebard, *Washakie*, 209; Utley, *Lance and Shield*, 122–23.

11. "Report of the Commission Appointed to Treat with the Sioux Indians for the Relinquishment of the Black Hills," in 44th Cong., *Report of the Commissioner of Indian Affairs*, 686–701; DeBarthe, *Life and Adventures of Frank Grouard*, 174–75; Powers, *Killing of Crazy Horse*, 93.

12. "Report of the Commission," 686–701; *Cincinnati Daily Enquirer*, Nov. 18, 1875; Gray, *Centennial Campaign*, 20–21, 23–27; *Cheyenne Leader*, Jan. 15, 1876; *Omaha Republican*, Jan. 16, 1876; Hutton, *Sheridan and His Army*, 298–99; Sheridan to Terry, Nov. 9, 1875, Sheridan Papers, Library of Congress.

13. E. C. Watkins to Edward P. Smith, Nov. 9, 1875, in 44th Cong., *Military Expedition*, 8–9; *Chicago Daily Inter Ocean*, Nov. 17, 1875; Sheridan quoted in Gray, *Centennial Campaign*, 33.

CHAPTER 13: GUARD US AGAINST ALL MISFORTUNE

1. Gibbon, "Indian Department," 388.

2. Gray, *Centennial Campaign*, 36–37, 41–42; 44th Cong., *Military Expedition*, 17, 22, 26, and *Report of the Secretary of War, 1876*, 443.

3. Crook to Assistant Adjutant General, Military Division of the Missouri, Dec. 22, 1875, and Crook to Hayes, March 1, 1876, Hayes Papers, both in Hayes Library; *Rocky Mountain News*, March 23, April 4 and 6, 1876.

4. DeBarthe, *Life and Adventures of Frank Grouard*, 188; Robinson, *Diaries of Bourke*, 1:246–47; *Rocky Mountain News*, April 7, 1876.

5. Powell, *People of the Sacred Mountain*, 2:938–45; Robinson, *Diaries of Bourke*, 1:249–58, and *General Crook*, 169–70.

6. Two Moons interview in Hardorff, *Lakota Recollections*, 133; Utley, *Lance and Shield*, 134–36; Marquis, *Wooden Leg*, 173.

7. Terry to Sheridan, Feb. 21, 1876; Sheridan to Sherman, May 29, 1876; and Sherman to Sheridan, April 1, 1876; all in Sheridan Papers, Library of Congress.

8. For excellent treatments of Custer's flirtation with ruin, see Utley, *Cavalier in Buckskin*, 156–64, and Hutton, *Sheridan and His Army*, 305–11.

9. Mangum, *Battle of the Rosebud*, 23–27.

10. Marquis, *Wooden Leg*, 177–79, 185; Utley, *Lance and Shield*, 134–35; Powell, *People of the Sacred Mountain*, 2:950. Rounding out the village in early June 1876, according to methodical calculations in Gray, *Centennial Campaign*, 324, were 70 Oglala lodges, 55 Miniconjou lodges, 55 Sans Arc lodges, 12 Blackfoot Lakota lodges, and 15 lodges of Yanktonai exiles, who had come down from Canada to join the great assemblage. Forcibly displaced from Minnesota after the 1862 uprising and hounded by the army in the Dakota Territory in 1863–1864, the Yanktonais were poor in material possessions but strong in their hatred of the whites.

11. One Bull, "Prophecy of Sitting Bull of Complete Annihilation of Custer and His Soldiers" and "Sitting Bull's Sun Dance Vision," and White Bull, "Sitting Bull and the Sundance," all in Campbell Collection; Utley, *Lance and Shield*, 137–38.

12. *Chicago Tribune*, July 5, 1876; Robinson, *Diaries of Bourke*, 1:306–12; Hebard, *Washakie*, 199.

13. Mills, "Battle of the Rosebud," 7; Robinson, *Diaries of Bourke*, 1:325.

14. Marquis, *Wooden Leg*, 197–99; Powell, *People of the Sacred Mountain*, 2:955–57; Eastman, "Indian Version of Custer's Last Battle," 354.

15. Mills, "Battle of the Rosebud," 7–8; *Chicago Tribune*, July 5, 1876; *New York Herald*, July 6, 1876; Lemly, "Fight on the Rosebud," 14; Marquis, *Wooden Leg*, 198–200.

16. Grinnell, *Fighting Cheyennes*, 336; Powell, *People of the Sacred Mountain*, 2:336.

17. Lemly, "Fight on the Rosebud," 14; Mills, "Battle of the Rosebud," 8–9; Daniel C. Pearson, "Military Notes," 301; Crook quoted in Mangum, *Battle of the Rosebud*, 75.

18. *Chicago Tribune*, July 5, 1876; *New York Herald*, July 6, 1876; Lemly, "Fight on the Rosebud," 15.

19. Quoted in Utley, *Lance and Shield*, 141; Grinnell, *Fighting Cheyennes*, 343; Eastman, "Indian Version of Custer's Last Battle," 357.

20. Mills, *My Story*, 398, 408; Mangum, *Battle of the Rosebud*, 85–87; Lemly, "Fight on the Rosebud," 16–17; "Report of Killed, Wounded, and Missing . . . on Rosebud River," Crook Letter Book 1:393; Linderman, *Plenty-Coups*, 170; *Helena Daily Independent*, June 30, 1876.

21. Crook to Sheridan, June 19, 1876, Crook Letter Book 1:390–91, Hayes Library; Robinson, *Diaries of Bourke* 1:356.

22. Utley, *Cavalier in Buckskin*, 165; Wert, *Custer*, 247–48; Donovan, *Terrible Glory*, 56, 93, 120–25, 139–40, 365; Graham, *Custer Myth*, 189; Charles A. Varnum interview in Hammer, *Custer in '76*, 63.

23. William O. Taylor, *With Custer on the Little Bighorn*, 18; Elizabeth B. Custer, *Boots and Saddles*, 217.

24. Gaff, *Adventures on the Western Frontier*, 121–23; Bradley, "Sioux Campaign," 184, 189–94, 203–6.

25. Godfrey, "Custer's Last Battle," 362; Custer quoted in Gray, *Centennial Campaign*, 127.

26. Quoted in Donovan, *Terrible Glory*, 168.

27. Quoted in Gray, *Centennial Campaign*, 140.

28. Donovan, *Terrible Glory*, 175–76; Godfrey, "Custer's Last Battle," 364–65; Gibbon, "Last Summer's Campaign," 130; Gray, *Centennial Campaign*, 141–43; James S. Brisbin to Edward S. Godfrey, Jan. 1, 1892, Ayer Manuscript Collection, Newberry Library.
29. Bradley, "Sioux Campaign," 215.
30. Merington, *Custer Story*, 307–8; Gibbon, "Last Summer's Expedition," 131.
31. Donovan, *Terrible Glory*, 190–91.
32. Godfrey, "Custer's Last Battle," 365.
33. Marquis, *Wooden Leg*, 214–15; Graham, *Custer Myth*, 102; Sitting Bull quoted in Utley, *Lance and Shield*, 144.

CHAPTER 14: LAST STAND

1. William O. Taylor, *With Custer on the Little Bighorn*, 27, 30; Donovan, *Terrible Glory*, 196–98, 201; Godfrey, "Custer's Last Battle," 366.
2. Myles Moylan to Edward S. Godfrey, Jan. 17, 1892, Godfrey Papers, Library of Congress; Marquis, *Wooden Leg*, 250; Luther Hare interview in Hammer, *Custer in '76*, 64; Frederick W. Benteen to Theodore Goldin, Feb. 24, 1892, in Graham, *Custer Myth*, 194.
3. Donovan, *Terrible Glory*, 212–13; Godfrey, "Custer's Last Battle," 368; Linderman, *Plenty-Coups*, 175.
4. Donovan, *Terrible Glory*, 215; Wert, *Custer*, 343.
5. Lieutenant Charles DeRudio and Private Thomas F. O'Neill interviews, both in Hammer, *Custer in '76*, 84, 106–7; William O. Taylor, *With Custer on the Little Bighorn*, 36–37; Donovan, *Terrible Glory*, 230; Stewart, *Custer's Luck*, 349–52.
6. Marquis, *Wooden Leg*, 218–19; DeMallie, *Sixth Grandfather*, 180–81; Moving Robe Woman interview in Hardorff, *Lakota Recollections*, 93; Gall quoted in Graham, *Custer Myth*, 89; White Bull interview, Campbell Collection.
7. Iron Hawk interview in Hardorff, *Lakota Recollections*, 64; Marquis, *Wooden Leg*, 220; Donovan, *Terrible Glory*, 443–44n; Silverstein, "Reminiscences of the Reno Fight," 579.
8. Stewart, *Custer's Luck*, 363; Donovan, *Terrible Glory*, 240–41; *Hardin Tribune*, June 22, 1923; Greene, *Lakota and Cheyenne*, 49; Marquis, *Wooden Leg*, 220–21.
9. Standing Bear interview in Hammer, *Custer in '76*, 215; Hardorff, *Lakota Recollections*, 64–65, and *Indian Views*, 166; Graham, *Custer Myth*, 102; DeMallie, *Sixth Grandfather*, 183.
10. Gray, *Centennial Campaign*, 294–95; William O. Taylor, *With Custer on the Little Bighorn*, 44–47; Brininstool, *Troopers with Custer*, 53; Graham, *Custer Myth*, 27; *Hardin Tribune*, June 22, 1923.
11. Utley, *Lance and Shield*, 153; Hardorff, *Lakota Recollections*, 199; Sitting Bull interview in *New York Herald*, Nov. 22, 1877.
12. Custer quoted in Stewart, *Custer's Luck*, 330; Kanipe, "New Story of Custer's Last Battle," 280; Graham, *Custer Myth*, 290; John Martin interview in Hammer, *Custer in '76*, 101.
13. See especially Donovan, *Terrible Glory*; Gray, *Custer's Last Campaign*; Hutton, "Could Custer Have Won?"; and Hardorff, *Lakota Recollections* and *Cheyenne Memories*.
14. Donovan, *Terrible Glory*, 266–67; Utley, *Cavalier in Buckskin*, 187; Sitting Bull interview in *New York Herald*, Nov. 22, 1877; Marquis, *Wooden Leg*, 231, 234.

15. Hutton, "Could Custer Have Won?," 36–37; Graham, *Custer Myth*, 77; Donovan, *Terrible Glory*, 272; Hardorff, *Indian Views*, 166; He Dog interview in Hammer, *Custer in '76*, 207; Greene, *Lakota and Cheyenne*, 37.

16. "Personal Story of Rain-in-the-Face," in Brady, *Indian Fights*, 288; DeMallie, *Sixth Grandfather*, 192.

17. Donovan, *Terrible Glory*, 275, and Hutton, "Could Custer Have Won?," 39, estimate the number of troopers on Last Stand Hill as fifty. I have added forty to that total to account for a group that broke down the hill in the last moments of the battle.

18. Hardorff, *Lakota Recollections*, 66, 86; Marquis, *Wooden Leg*, 237; Donovan, *Terrible Glory*, 276; Kanipe, "New Story of Custer's Last Battle," 95; Brininstool, *Troopers with Custer*, 61.

19. DeMallie, *Sixth Grandfather*, 193; Hardorff, *Lakota Recollections*, 32; Donovan, *Terrible Glory*, 276; Marquis, *Wooden Leg*, 247. The man whom Wooden Leg scalped was Lieutenant William W. Cooke.

20. Donovan, *Terrible Glory*, 253; Godfrey, "Custer's Last Battle," 372.

21. John Martin quoted in Graham, *Custer Myth*, 291. In an interview with Walter Camp, Martin gave Reno's words as "Well, I have lost about half of my men, and I could do no better than I have done." Hammer, *Custer in '76*, 105.

22. Stewart, *Custer's Luck*, 179, 180; Brininstool, *Troopers with Custer*, 81, 102, 121; Donovan, *Terrible Glory*, 460–62n.

23. Donovan, *Terrible Glory*, 280–86, 462n; Godfrey, "Custer's Last Battle," 375; Marquis, *Wooden Leg*, 256.

24. Gray, *Centennial Campaign*, 181, 294–96; William O. Taylor, *With Custer on the Little Bighorn*, 57, 59, 63; Stanislas Roy interview in Graham, *Custer Myth*, 182; Godfrey, *Field Diary*, 17; Marquis, *Wooden Leg*, 269–70.

25. Thomas, "Indian Casualties," http://www.littlebighorn.info/articles/indiancasualties.pdf; Garland, "Custer's Last Fight"; Gray, *Centennial Campaign*, 296.

26. Quoted in Utley, *Lance and Shield*, 161.

CHAPTER 15: THE GREAT FATHER'S FURY

1. Hanson, *Conquest of the Missouri*, 298; *Philadelphia Inquirer*, July 7, 1876; *Cleveland Plain Dealer*, July 8, 1876; Hutton, *Sheridan and His Army*, 316.

2. 44th Cong., *Hostile Demonstrations*, 1–4.

3. Sheridan to Sherman, July 7, 1876, in *Cleveland Plain Dealer*, July 8, 1876; Gray, *Centennial Campaign*, 255–59; Robinson, *Good Year to Die*, 224–25.

4. Robinson, *Diaries of Bourke*, 1:362–63, 369; Crook to Sheridan, July 23, 1876, Crook Letter Book 1:395, Hayes Library.

5. Robinson, *Good Year to Die*, 232–33; Powell, *People of the Sacred Mountain*, 2:1049.

6. Robinson, *Diaries of Bourke*, 2:35, and *Good Year to Die*, 238–39; Goldin, "Terry and Crook," 73; Finerty, *War-Path and Bivouac*, 223; Miles quoted in Hutton, *Sheridan and His Army*, 320.

7. *Chicago Times*, Sept. 22, 1876; Daniel C. Pearson, "Military Notes," 300.

8. Terry to Crook, Aug. 25, 1876, in Robinson, *Diaries of Bourke* 2: 88–89; Crook to Terry, Aug. 25, 1876, Crook Letter Book 1:399–400, Hayes Library.

9. *Cincinnati Daily Tribune*, Sept. 1, 1876; Powell, *People of the Sacred Mountain*, 2:1047; Neihardt, *Black Elk Speaks*, 137.

10. Bourke, *On the Border with Crook*, 367–68, 372–73; Finerty, *War-Path and Bivouac*, 244–46; Greene, *Slim Buttes*, 77, 115, and *Lakota and Cheyenne*, 86–88; Eugene A. Carr to his wife, Sept. 8, 1876, Carr Papers; Robinson, "Horse Meat March," 47, and *General Crook*, 194–95; Daniel C. Pearson, "Military Notes," 312.

11. Olson, *Red Cloud and the Sioux Problem*, 224.

12. Quoted in Hyde, *Spotted Tail's Folk*, 255.

13. Quoted in Olson, *Red Cloud and the Sioux Problem*, 322.

14. Robinson, *Bad Hand*, 322–23, and *Good Year to Die*, 264; *New York Herald*, Sept. 23, 1876; Crook to Merritt, Sept. 25, 1876, Crook Letter Book 1:424–25, Hayes Library.

15. Olson, *Red Cloud and the Sioux Problem*, 231–33; William Garnett interview in Jensen, *Voices of the American West*, 1:13; Crook to Sheridan, Oct. 23 and 27, 1876, Crook Letter Book 1:403–6, Hayes Library; Manypenny, *Our Indian Wards*, 300; Robinson, *Good Year to Die*, 266; Hutton, *Sheridan and His Army*, 325.

16. Miles quoted in Robinson, *Good Year to Die*, 268; Sheridan to Crook, Sept. 8, 1876, in Robinson, *Diaries of Bourke* 2:124–25; *Chicago Times*, Sept. 16, 1876.

17. Robinson, *Good Year to Die*, 270–71; Miles, *Personal Recollections*, 2:217–18, 225–26; Greene, *Battles and Skirmishes*, 134–35, and *Lakota and Cheyenne*, 106–7; Utley, *Lance and Shield*, 172.

18. Vestal, *Warpath*, 222–23; Greene, *Battles and Skirmishes*, 138–42.

19. Marquis, *Wooden Leg*, 281–82.

20. Robinson, *Diaries of Bourke*, 2:172.

21. *New York Herald*, Dec. 11, 1876; Greene, *Morning Star Dawn*, 40; Greene, *Lakota and Cheyenne*, 113–14; Powell, *People of the Sacred Mountain*, 2:1054–56.

22. Danker, *Man of the Plains*, 211–12; Powell, *People of the Sacred Mountain*, 2:1058–64, 1069; Greene, *Morning Star Dawn*, 122–23, 135–36, and *Battles and Skirmishes*, 180; *New York Herald*, Dec. 11, 1876.

23. Greene, *Morning Star Dawn*, 139–40; Robinson, *Diaries of Bourke*, 2:187.

24. Sherry L. Smith, *Sagebrush Soldier*, 88; Kime, *Powder River Journals*, 98.

25. Crook to Assistant Adjutant General, Military Division of the Missouri, Jan. 8, 1877, with endorsement by Sheridan to Sherman dated Jan. 27, 1877, Hayes Papers, Hayes Library; Crook interview with the *Chicago Tribune*, reprinted in *Army and Navy Journal*, Dec. 30, 1876.

26. Powell, *People of the Sacred Mountain*, 2:1069–78; Greene, *Lakota and Cheyenne*, 119–21; Stands in Timber and Liberty, *Cheyenne Memories*, 216–18; Robinson, *Diaries of Bourke*, 2:275, 278.

27. Marquis, *Wooden Leg*, 308–9; 46th Cong., *Removal of the Northern Cheyenne Indians*, 9, 14, 111, 224–25.

28. Miles quoted in Grinnell, *Fighting Cheyennes*, 398; Wild Hog Testimony in 46th Cong., *Removal of the Northern Cheyenne Indians*, 5–6.

29. 46th Cong., *Removal of the Northern Cheyenne Indians*, 267–68, 271–72; Bronson, "Little Wolf's Escape," 208.

30. Grinnell, *Fighting Cheyennes*, 401–2; Wild Hog Testimony in 46th Cong., *Removal of the Northern Cheyenne Indians*, 7.

31. Quoted in Grinnell, *Fighting Cheyennes*, 403.

32. Monnett, *Tell Them We Are Going Home*, 43, 52; Marquis, *Wooden Leg*, 321.

33. Little Wolf quoted in Grinnell, *Fighting Cheyennes*, 413; Jordan, "Soldier's

Life," 148; Monnett, *Tell Them We Are Going Home*, 53–57, 66–72, 74; Wild Hog Testimony in 46th Cong., *Removal of the Northern Cheyenne Indians*, 21.

34. Dull Knife quoted in Grinnell, *Fighting Cheyennes*, 414; Monnett, *Tell Them We Are Going Home*, 109–11.

35. 46th Cong., *Removal of the Northern Cheyenne Indians*, 214; Red Cloud quoted in Powell, *People of the Sacred Mountain*, 2:1189; Wild Hog quoted in Monnett, *Tell Them We Are Going Home*, 118; Dull Knife quoted in Powell, *People of the Sacred Mountain*, 2:1191.

36. 46th Cong., *Removal of the Northern Cheyenne Indians*, 244; Monnett, *Tell Them We Are Going Home*, 118–22.

37. Powell, *People of the Sacred Mountain*, 2:1197–98, 1225–27; Grinnell, *Fighting Cheyennes*, 421–22; Monnett, *Tell Them We Are Going Home*, 123–34, 143–61.

38. Quoted in 46th Cong., *Removal of the Northern Cheyenne Indians*, 249.

39. Monnett, *Tell Them We Are Going Home*, 147, 159, 161, 202, and "Little Wolf," 54–55.

CHAPTER 16: A WARRIOR I HAVE BEEN

1. Greene, *Yellowstone Command*, 115; Miles, *Personal Recollections*, 1:217–19, 231; Baldwin, "Winter Campaigning," 2.

2. Baldwin, "Winter Campaigning," 2–3; Utley, *Lance and Shield*, 176–77; Greene, *Yellowstone Command*, 150–52.

3. Major Alfred L. Hough quoted in Greene, *Yellowstone Command*, 158.

4. Bray, "Crazy Horse and the End of the Sioux War," 97; Greene, *Battles and Skirmishes*, 196.

5. Greene, *Lakota and Cheyenne*, 130–31, 133; Power, *Killing of Crazy Horse*, 249; Neihardt, *Black Elk Speaks*; Miles, *Personal Recollections*, 1:238–39.

6. Quoted in Utley, *Lance and Shield*, 181–82.

7. DeMallie, *Sixth Grandfather*, 202; Bray, "Crazy Horse and the End of the Sioux War," 101–6, 108–9; Neihardt, *Black Elk Speaks*, 142; Hyde, *Spotted Tail's Folk*, 266–68.

8. Olson, *Red Cloud and the Sioux Problem*, 237–39; Jeffrey V. Pearson, "Tragedy at Red Cloud Agency," 16; Bray, "Crazy Horse and the End of the Sioux War," 112; Robinson, *Diaries of Bourke*, 2:297, 299; Powers, *Killing of Crazy Horse*, 262.

9. On May 7, 1877, Miles defeated the band of Chief Lame Deer near the present-day Montana town of the same name. Lame Deer had had no particular vision for the future; he had wavered between defiance and a nostalgic desire for one last buffalo hunt before coming in. He was inadvertently killed when a white scout interrupted a parley between the chief and Colonel Miles. See Miles, "Rounding Up the Red Men," 113–14.

10. Quoted in Hutton, *Phil Sheridan and His Army*, 320.

11. Jeffrey V. Pearson, "Tragedy at Red Cloud Agency," 17–18; Powers, *Killing of Crazy Horse*, 331; Lee, "Capture and Death," 327.

12. Jeffrey V. Pearson, "Tragedy at Red Cloud Agency," 20; Powers, *Killing of Crazy Horse*, 361–62; Hardorff, *Surrender and Death of Crazy Horse*, 104–5, 173.

13. Jeffrey V. Pearson, "Tragedy at Red Cloud Agency," 21–22; Hardorff, *Surrender and Death of Crazy Horse*, 183–84.

14. Crazy Horse quoted in Lee, "Capture and Death," 333, and Powers, *Killing of Crazy Horse*, 395.

15. Jeffrey V. Pearson, "Tragedy at Red Cloud Agency," 24–25; Lee, "Capture and Death," 337–38; Lemly, "Murder of Chief Crazy Horse," 7; Sheridan to James Gillis, Sept. 5, 1877, in Robinson, *Diaries of Bourke*, 3:508.

16. Powers, *Killing of Crazy Horse*, 411–12, 424, 426; Valentine T. McGillycuddy to Elmo S. Watson, April 13, 1922, Watson Papers, Newberry Library; Lemly, "Murder of Crazy Horse," 10.

17. My accounts of Sitting Bull's time in Canada and his subsequent surrender are drawn largely from Utley, *Lance and Shield*, 164–233. See also Neihardt, *Black Elk Speaks*, 150–59.

CHAPTER 17: I WILL FIGHT NO MORE FOREVER

1. West, *Last Indian War*, 21, 23, 35–74.

2. Joseph, "Indian's View of Indian Affairs," 417–20; McWhorter, *Yellow Wolf*, 35, 125–29; West, *Last Indian War*, 81–84.

3. Howard, "True Story of the Wallowa Campaign," 318–20; Joseph and commissioners quoted in Greene, *Nez Perce Summer*, 16–18; Josephy, *Nez Perce*, 483–92; West, *Last Indian War*, 117–19; McWhorter, *Yellow Wolf*, 40.

4. Howard, *Nez Perce Joseph*, 69–70; Joseph, "Indian's View of Indian Affairs," 306–7.

5. Josephy, *Nez Perce*, 499; Beall, "*I Will Fight No More Forever*," 280–82; McWhorter, *Yellow Wolf*, 36–45; Joseph, "Indian's View of Indian Affairs," 424–25.

6. McDonald, "Nez Perce War," 466–67; Joseph, "Indian's View of Indian Affairs," 309; McWhorter, *Hear Me, My Chiefs!*, 246–47; Greene, *Nez Perce Summer*, 40, 130, 359–60, 372.

7. 45th Cong., *Report of the Secretary of War*, 120; McWhorter, *Hear Me, My Chiefs!*, 264–70; Howard, *Nez Perce Joseph*, 149.

8. *New York Herald*, July 2, 1877; *Indianapolis Sentinel*, July 3, 1877; *New York Herald*, July 5, 1877; Josephy, *Nez Perce*, 528, 542; 45th Cong., *Report of the Secretary of War*, 120–21.

9. McCarthy Journal, 24, Library of Congress; McWhorter, *Hear Me, My Chiefs!*, 298, 306, and *Yellow Wolf*, 85–88; Bailey to McWhorter, Dec. 7, 1930, McWhorter Papers; Greene, *Nez Perce Summer*, 86; 45th Cong., *Report of the Secretary of War*, 11–23.

10. Trimble, "Battle of the Clearwater," 145; McWhorter, *Hear Me, My Chiefs!*, 314; 45th Cong., *Report of the Secretary of War*, 123.

11. McWhorter, *Hear Me, My Chiefs!*, 316–20, and *Yellow Wolf*, 96–97.

12. Army casualties during the two-day Battle of the Clearwater were thirteen killed, two mortally wounded, and twenty-five wounded. Nine of the casualties were officers or noncommissioned officers. The Nez Perces lost four warriors killed and six wounded. Greene, *Nez Perce Summer*, 361–62, 373.

13. McWhorter, *Hear Me, My Chiefs!*, 334–35, 349–56; Josephy, *Nez Perce*, 568–73; Buck, "Nez Perce Campaign," 508–10.

14. Josephy, *Nez Perce*, 576–77; McDonald, "Nez Perce War," 484–85; McWhorter, *Yellow Wolf*, 108–10, 134; Woodruff, "Battle of the Big Hole," 427.

15. Sherman quoted in Greene, *Nez Perce Summer*, 124; John A. Carpenter, "General Howard," 135.

16. Gaff, *Adventures on the Western Frontier*, 207–11; Woodruff, "Battle of the Big Hole," 326; Caitlin, "Battle of the Big Hole," 444; Greene, *Nez Perce Summer*, 128–29.

17. Gibbon to Daniel S. Tuttle, Sept. 7, 1877, Ayer Manuscript Collection, Newberry Library.

18. Coon, "Outbreak," Coon Collection, Yale University; Gaff, *Adventures on the Western Frontier*, 212; Woodruff, "Battle of the Big Hole," 427–28; Greene, *Nez Perce Summer*, 131.

19. McWhorter, *Hear Me, My Chiefs!*, 375–77, and *Yellow Wolf*, 117, 120, 133, 135, 145; Woodruff, "Battle of the Big Hole," 428.

20. Gaff, *Adventures on the Western Frontier*, 212–14; Caitlin, "Battle of the Big Hole," 12–13.

21. McDonald, "Nez Perce War," 486–87; Greene, *Nez Perce Summer*, 136–37, 164–65; Joseph, "Indian's View of Indian Affairs," 427.

22. Josephy, *Nez Perce*, 575, 590; Greene, *Nez Perce Summer*, 153; Sutherland, "Howard's Campaign," 393; McWhorter, *Yellow Wolf*, 168.

23. 45th Cong., *Report of the Secretary of War*, 13.

24. *Harper's Weekly*, Sept. 1, 1877; Sherman to Sheridan, Aug. 31, 1877, quoted in Greene, *Nez Perce Summer*, 168.

25. Greene, *Nez Perce Summer*, 201–5, 229; Goldin, "A Bit of the Nez Perce Campaign," Special Collections, Newberry Library; McWhorter, *Hear Me, My Chiefs!*, 460–65.

26. McWhorter, *Yellow Wolf*, 187; Josephy, *Nez Perce*, 611–12; Greene, *Nez Perce Summer*, 242.

27. Miles, *Personal Recollections*, 261–62; Sturgis and Howard quoted in Wooster, *Miles*, 100–101.

28. McDonald, "Nez Perce War," 490; Yellow Bull interview, Camp Collection, Little Bighorn National Monument.

29. Luther S. Kelly account of Bear Paw Mountain, Camp Collection; Romeyn, "Capture of Chief Joseph," 563; McWhorter, *Hear Me, My Chiefs!*, 479, and *Yellow Wolf*, 205.

30. Tilton, "After the Nez Perces," 403; Myles Moylan's report of the Battle of Bear Paw Mountain, transcript in Ayer Manuscript Collection; Miles, *Personal Recollections*, 1:268.

31. Young Two Moon interview, Camp Collection; Josephy, *Nez Perce*, 617–19; McWhorter, *Yellow Wolf*, 205; Joseph, "Indian's View of Indian Affairs," 428–29.

32. Moylan report; Tilton, "After the Nez Perce," 403; Josephy, *Nez Perce*, 619; Joseph, "Indian's View of Indian Affairs," 429; *New York Herald*, Oct. 11 and 30, 1877; Noyes, *In the Land of Chinook*, 77; McWhorter, *Yellow Bull*, 209. For the definitive account of the first day's fighting, see Greene, *Nez Perce Summer*, 271–91.

33. Miles, *Personal Recollections*, 1:273; Wooster, *Miles*, 104; McWhorter, *Hear Me, My Chiefs!*, 485.

34. Tilton, "After the Nez Perce," 404; Miles, *Personal Recollections*, 1:273–75. Sitting Bull knew of the Nez Perce predicament. He and his subchiefs held at least one council on the question of going to their aid. But Sitting Bull's friend and protector, Major James M. Walsh of the North-West Mounted Police, made it clear that the Lakotas would lose their Canadian sanctuary if they staged an armed foray south of the international border. Utley, *Lance and Shield*, 193.

35. Josephy, *Nez Perce*, 623–25; Tilton, "After the Nez Perce," 404; Greene, *Nez Perce Summer*, 297; *New York Herald*, Oct. 11, 1877.

36. McWhorter, *Hear Me, My Chiefs!*, 494–95; Joseph, "Indian's View of Indian Affairs," 312.

37. Wood's account as published in *Harper's Weekly*, Nov. 17, 1877; Greene, *Nez Perce Summer*, 309; Hampton, *Children of Grace*, 307.

38. *Harper's Weekly*, Nov. 17, 1877; Greene, *Nez Perce Summer*, 310–13; McWhorter, *Hear Me, My Chiefs!*, 498–99; Miles to Alfred H. Terry, Oct. 17, 1877, Godfrey Papers.

39. The conclusion of the Nez Perce War did not bring a permanent peace to the Pacific Northwest. While the nation fixed its gaze on the Nez Perce bid for freedom in 1877, the familiar combination of Indian Bureau mismanagement and white encroachment on Indian hunting grounds was driving two other friendly Rocky Mountain tribes, the Northern Paiutes and the Bannocks, toward war. The Northern Paiutes had fought a decade-long guerrilla conflict called the Snake War against Oregonians until George Crook crushed them in 1868. Since their defeat, they had progressed rapidly as farmers at the Malheur Reservation. But in 1876, a sadistic, politically connected local bootlegger became agent. As punishment for petty infractions, he withheld rations, beat children, and shot Indian ponies. Remarkably, the Paiutes refrained from dealing him a well-merited death. Instead, when the hunger and the humiliation became more than they could bear, the Paiutes fled to their southeastern Oregon homeland and fell under the influence of an incendiary shaman.

On the Fort Hall Reservation two hundred miles to the east, the Bannocks also were hungry. They had signed a treaty during the Civil War according them "absolute and undisturbed use" of their beloved Camas Prairie in southern Idaho, but a clerical error omitted the Camas Prairie guarantee from the ratified treaty, and whites overran the land. A fragile peace obtained until May 1878, when a Bannock shot two cowboys in a quarrel over a buffalo robe. Concluding that all would suffer for the crime, the Bannocks went on the warpath, burning ranches and ambushing stagecoaches. Thundering into the Northern Paiute village, by threats and cajolery they compelled their erstwhile allies to join them. The Bannocks had carried their war into General Howard's department; the distasteful duty of subduing them fell upon him. Howard was still recovering from the public abuse he had endured during the Nez Perce Campaign. It was with great reluctance, therefore, that he took the field in June 1878 for what he feared would be "another summer amid the horrors of savage warfare" over terrain even more rugged than the Nez Perce country.

Fortunately, the horrors proved minimal, largely because Howard conducted the campaign expertly. He pursued the hostiles relentlessly until the coalition collapsed. The Paiutes scattered throughout southeastern Oregon, and the Bannocks dispersed into mountainous central Idaho. Howard left the Indians nowhere to hide, and in mid-August the Paiutes surrendered. The last Bannocks were rounded up a month later, ending what the army called the Bannock War. It had not been a particularly sanguinary contest. The Indians had killed nine soldiers and thirty-one civilians (mostly settlers slain by the Bannocks in the opening days of their breakout). The army reported seventy-eight Indians killed, most certainly an exaggerated body count. Perhaps half of the surviving Bannocks surrendered or were captured.

General Howard's victory over the Bannock-Paiute alliance partially redeemed his reputation. He took small satisfaction from the campaign, however. "There is little doubt," the Christian General reflected, "but that many frontier people who have suffered extremely from Indian outrages entertain a feeling of soreness toward us army officers, who seem so much to sympathize with the Indians. We would judge them to be wholly right, did we not know from long experience that primarily nine-tenths of our Indian outbreaks had been occasioned by the misconduct of wicked white men." So it was with the Bannock War.

The Bannock War did not quite draw the curtain on Indian conflict in the Pacific Northwest. There remained a final, largely forgotten campaign. The victims were the Sheepeaters, a small band of pitiable outcasts from the Bannock and Shoshone tribes who eked out a subsistence living by hunting mountain sheep and fishing deep in the Salmon River Mountains, a forbidding country of precipitous cliffs, profound ravines, and towering peaks. Trails were few, and snow fell year-round.

The Sheepeaters bothered no one. They got along well with neighboring gold prospectors, bartering hides for food and gratefully accepting gifts of old clothing and camp refuse. When the diggings were exhausted in the late 1870s, Chinese prospectors replaced the whites. They spurned the Sheepeaters, who accepted the rebuke until Bannock fugitives joined them in the winter of 1877–1878. Several weeks later, a group of Chinese miners were murdered and their camp plundered, probably by renegade Bannocks or marauding white horse thieves. White miners had been poised to return to the Salmon River Mountains, but the killings dissuaded them.

It took three months for the news to reach General Howard, who sent a seasoned Indian-fighting subordinate to find the perpetrators. His army detachment spent 101 days in the field without seeing a single Indian, and Howard recalled him in favor of a company of Umatilla Indians, who, braving frigid high-mountain nights and pounding snowstorms, located an abandoned Sheepeater camp and seized the band's winter cache of meat. As the weather worsened, the woebegone Sheepeaters straggled into the Umatilla camp and surrendered.

With the sorry culmination of the 1878 Sheepeater Campaign, the wars for the Pacific Northwest were over, and the "troublesome" Indians were tucked safely away on reservations for good. New and larger mines were carved out of the Idaho wilderness, and farms and ranches soon blanketed the fertile Salmon River valley and Camas Prairie. Brimlow, *Bannock Indian War,* 150–52, 189–99; Howard, "Close of the Paiute and Bannock War," 106, and "Results of the Paiute and Bannock War," 197; Quinn, "Mountain Charade," 21, 26; Reuben F. Bernard to Commanding Officer, Boise Barracks, June 14, 1878, Brown Collection, University of Colorado; Hardin, "Sheepeater Campaign," 32–40.

40. Josephy, *Nez Perce,* 636–43.

CHAPTER 18: THE UTES MUST GO!

1. Emmitt, *Last War Trail,* 21; Dunn, *Massacres of the Mountains,* 675.
2. Decker, *Utes Must Go!,* 58; Sprague, *Massacre,* 92.
3. Quoted in Decker, *Utes Must Go!,* 59.
4. Sprague, *Massacre,* 39–50; Decker, *Utes Must Go!,* 59, 61–62, 68, 82–92; 45th

Cong., *Report of the Secretary of Interior, 1877*, x–xi; *Springfield Republican*, Nov. 22, 1877.

5. *Springfield Republican*, Nov. 22, 1877; Josephine Meeker Testimony in 46th Cong., *Ute Outbreak*, 75; Vickers, *History of Denver*, 129; Nathan C. Meeker to Teller, May 27, 1878, Teller Letters, Colorado Historical Museum.

6. Meeker to Thornburgh, March 17, 1879; George McCrary to Schurz, April 9, 1879; E. A. Pratt to Edward Hatch, May 2, 1879, with endorsements by Sheridan, May 9, 1879, Sherman, May 14, 1879, E. J. Brooks to George McCrary, Sept. 1, 1879, all in "Ute War," Record Group 98, Records of the Office of the Adjutant General, National Archives.

7. Pitkin quoted in Emmitt, *Last War Trail*, 87; Meeker to Edward A. Hayt, July 7, 1879; Thornburgh to the Assistant Adjutant General, Department of the Platte, July 27, 1879, both in "Ute War."

8. Meeker to Edward A. Hayt, Aug. 11, 1879, "Ute War"; Meeker to Hayt, Sept. 8, 1879, and Jack, Johnson, Douglass, and Josephine Meeker testimony in 46th Cong., *White River Commission*, 3, 53–54, 83; Sprague, *Massacre*, 175, 176.

9. Jack's testimony in 45th Cong., *White River Commission*, 69, and in *Ute Outbreak*, 199; Meeker to Hayt, Sept. 10, 1879; Crook to Commanding Officer, Fort Fred Steele, Wyoming, Sept. 16, 1879, both in "Ute War."

10. Payne, "Incidents of the Recent Campaign," 116; Miller, *Hollow Victory*, 16–32; Thornburgh to Meeker, Sept. 25, 1879, in 45th Cong., *White River Commission*, 37; Thornburgh to Adjutant General, Department of the Platte, Sept. 26, 1879, in "Ute War."

11. Testimony of Jack, Payne, and Samuel A. Cherry in 45th Cong., *Ute Outbreak*, 63, 171, 172–73, 194–95; Meeker to Thornburgh, Sept. 27, 1879, in 45th Cong., *White River Commission*, 38; Green, "White River Campaign," 3, Order of Indian Wars Collection, U.S. Army Educational and Heritage Center.

12. Payne, "Incidents of the Recent Campaign," 119.

13. Jack quoted in Utley, *Frontier Regulars*, 356; Colorow testimony in 45th Cong., *White River Commission*, 64; Robinson, *Diaries of Bourke*, 3:314–15.

14. Payne, "Incidents of the Recent Campaign," 123–24; Miller, *Hollow Victory*, 66–84; Payne and Cherry testimony, in 45th Cong., *Ute Outbreak*, 65–66, 174, 196–97; Colorow testimony in 45th Cong., *White River Commission*, 64.

15. Arvilla Meeker, Josephine Meeker, and Mrs. S. F. Price statements in 45th Cong., *White River Commission*, 21–23.

16. Colorow quoted in Emmitt, *Last War Trail*, 218; Payne, "Incidents of the Recent Campaign," 127.

17. Sumner, "Besieged by the Utes," 843; Kimball, *Soldier-Doctor*, 99, 101–2; Merritt to Adjutant General, Department of the Platte, Oct. 5, 1879, in *Rocky Mountain News*, Oct. 11, 1879; Merritt, "Marching Cavalry."

18. 45th Cong., *White River Commission*, 28; Cherry testimony in 45th Cong., *Ute Outbreak*, 67.

19. Decker, *Utes Must Go!*, 146–48, 149; Sheridan to Sherman, Oct. 3, 8, and 15, 1879, Sherman to Sheridan, Oct. 8, 1879, and Sherman to Schurz, Oct. 17, 1879, all in "Ute War"; Sherman's "Atlantic coast" remark quoted in Decker, *Utes Must Go!*, 149.

20. Wilson Stanley and Ouray to the Interior Department, Oct. 12, 1879, Sherman to Schurz, Oct. 17, 1879, Sheridan to Sherman, Oct. 17, 1879, Schurz to Sherman, Oct. 18, 1879, all in "Ute War."

21. 45th Cong, *White River Commission*, 17, 20, 26, 44, 51, 76, 82.
22. Decker, *Utes Must Go!*, 158, 162; 46th Cong., *Agreement with Ute Indians*, 6–8. Congress appropriated an additional $350,000 to purchase homes, mills, schoolhouses, wagons, cattle, and other trappings of white civilization for the Utes.
23. P. David Smith, *Ouray*, 175–82.
24. Quoted in Emmitt, *Last War Trail*, 295.
25. Miller, *Hollow Victory*, 198.

CHAPTER 19: RETURN TO APACHERIA

1. Chamberlain, *Victorio*, 6–10; Sweeney, *Making Peace with Cochise*, 114–15; Kemble, "Victorio and His Young Men," 209; Ball, *In the Days of Victorio*, 57.
2. Thrapp, *Victorio*, 148–49; Sweeney, *Making Peace with Cochise*, 114–18.
3. Thrapp, *Conquest of Apacheria*, 172–75, and *Victorio*, 186.
4. Thrapp, *Victorio*, 187–200; Betzinez, *I Fought with Geronimo*, 50, 54; *Tucson Weekly Citizen*, April 1, 1880; Sweeney, *From Cochise to Geronimo*, 47–48.
5. Thrapp, *Victorio*, 206–11; Betzinez, *I Fought with Geronimo*, 50; Cozzens, *Struggle for Apacheria*, xxv; *Tucson Weekly Star*, April 8, 1880; Sweeney, *Cochise to Geronimo*, 125–26.
6. Thrapp, *Conquest of Apacheria*, 180–81; *Report of the Secretary of War, 1880*, 86; *Las Cruces Thirty-Four*, April 28, 1880; Leckie, *Buffalo Soldiers*, 211–12. Leckie places the number of civilians killed at nine.
7. Leckie, *Buffalo Soldiers*, 212; Ball, *In the Days of Victorio*, 72. The Mimbres Mountains, located fifty miles southwest of Ojo Caliente, were one range in a chain of ranges—the others being the Black Range, the Sierra Negretta, and the San Mateo Mountains—that constituted the sixty-mile-long Chihenne stronghold.
8. Gatewood, "Campaigning Against Victorio," 102–3; *Annual Report of the Secretary of War, 1880*, 89, 105–6; Thrapp, *Victorio*, 248–50; Morrow quoted in Thrapp, *Encyclopedia*, 2:1019.
9. Rockwell, *Indian Affairs*, 250; Grossman, *Political Corruption*, 158; Sweeney, *From Cochise to Geronimo*, 149–50; Thrapp, *Victorio*, 261–62.
10. *Annual Report of the Secretary of War, 1880*, 86, 89, 94; Thrapp, *Victorio*, 267–71; Cruse, *Apache Days*, 76–77.
11. Ball, *In the Days of Victorio*, 84–85; Cruse, *Apache Days*, 76–77.
12. Thrapp, *Conquest of Apacheria*, 196, 202–3, and *Victorio*, 277–78; Robinson, *Apache Voices*, 145.
13. Quoted in Hutton, *Soldiers West*, 164.
14. *Annual Report of the Secretary of War, 1880*, 159.
15. Ibid., 159–60.
16. Leckie, *Buffalo Soldiers*, 203–4; Thrapp, *Victorio*, 286–87; Grierson, "Journal," 14–17, Fort Davis National Historic Site. Colonel Grierson reported seven Apaches killed at a loss of one man killed and one man wounded. *Annual Report of the Secretary of War, 1880*, 160.
17. *Annual Report of the Secretary of War, 1880*, 160–63; Trapp, *Victorio*, 288–89; Hutton, *Soldiers West*, 166.
18. *Annual Report of the Secretary of War, 1880*, 88.
19. Thrapp, *Conquest of Apacheria*, 209, and *Victorio*, 301–5, 308–11; Chamberlain,

Victorio, 200; Sweeney, *From Cochise to Geronimo*, 165–66; Robinson, *Apache Voices*, 18.

20. *Las Cruces Thirty-Four*, Oct. 20, 1880; President Hayes quoted in *Las Vegas Weekly Optic*, Oct. 30, 1880.

21. Ogle, *Federal Control*, 179–96; 45th Cong., *Report of the Secretary of War*, 144.

22. Sweeney, *From Cochise to Geronimo*, 132; Britton Davis, *Truth About Geronimo*, 49.

23. Ogle, *Federal Control*, 189–90, 201–3; Elliott, "Indian Reservation," 98; Carr, "Report of Operations," 3, Record Group 94, National Archives; Thrapp, *Conquest of Apacheria*, 217; Cruse, *Apache Days*, 93–94; Loring, "Report on Coyotero Apaches," 200.

24. Charles Collins, *Apache Nightmare*, 18; Statement of Thomas Cruse in the Trial of Dead Shot, 23, Court-Martial Case Files, QQ2821, Record Group 153, National Archives; Carr, "Report of Operations," 5–6; Cruse to My Dear Abbott, May 25, 1883, Gatewood Papers, Arizona Historical Society; "Apache Story of the Cibecue," 300–301.

25. Charles Collins, *Apache Nightmare*, 21–23, 27–28; Carr, "Report of Operations," 3; Cruse to My Dear Abbott, May 25, 1883.

26. Carr, "Report of Operations," 6; "Apache Story of the Cibecue," 298–99; Thrapp, *Conquest of Apacheria*, 221. Including civilian personnel, Carr's force numbered 117 men.

27. Cruse, *Apache Days*, 106; Farish, *History of Arizona*, 3:337.

28. Carr, "Report of Operations," 11–12.

29. Cruse, *Apache Days*, 107–8.

30. William H. Carter, *Yorktown to Santiago*, 215; "Apache Story of the Cibecue," 298, 300, 301; Cruse, *Apache Days*, 110–11; Carr, "Report of Operations," 14; Charles Collins, *Apache Nightmare*, 56, 240n.

31. Statement of Sergeant No. 4, alias Dead Shot, "Trial of Dead Shot," 112; "Apache Story of the Cibecue," 298, 300–301; Charles Collins, *Apache Nightmare*, 52; Cruse, *Apache Days*, 139.

32. Finerty, "On Campaign," 248.

33. Charles Collins, *Apache Nightmare*, 54; Carr, "Report of Operations," 14–16; William H. Carter, *Yorktown to Santiago*, 219.

34. Charles Collins, *Apache Nightmare*, 70–81; "Apache Story of the Cibecue," 297; Finerty, "On Campaign," 245.

35. Charles Collins, *Apache Nightmare*, 88–134.

36. McDowell to Robert Todd Lincoln, Dec. 26, 1881, quoted in ibid., 192; Cruse, *Apache Days*, 139.

CHAPTER 20: LIKE SO MANY VULTURES, GREEDY FOR BLOOD

1. Utley, *Geronimo*, 105; Betzinez, *I Fought with Geronimo*, 47; Robinson, *Apache Voices*, 57.

2. 51st Cong., *Apache Indians*, 52; Britton Davis, *Truth About Geronimo*, 206.

3. Utley, *Geronimo*, 21; Sweeney, "Geronimo, Apache Shaman," 30–32.

4. Barrett, *Geronimo, His Own Story*, 110; Utley, *Geronimo*, 15–16.

5. Sweeney, *From Cochise to Geronimo*, 16.

6. Debo, *Geronimo*, 101–2; Opler, "Chiricahua Apache's Account," 369; Robinson, *Apache Voices*, 57–58; Miles, *Personal Recollections*, 525.

7. Hugh L. Scott, *Some Memories*, 347, 374; Sweeney, *From Cochise to Geronimo*, 183.

8. Sweeney, *From Cochise to Geronimo*, 181–95.

9. Shapard, *Chief Loco*, 139–46; Robinson, *Apache Voices*, 39, 146–50; Forsyth, *Thrilling Days in Army Life*, 79; Betzinez, *I Fought with Geronimo*, 56; Sweeney, *From Cochise to Geronimo*, 211.

10. Rafferty, "Rafferty's Trail," 286–87; Sieber, "Military and Indians," 292–94; Betzinez, *I Fought with Geronimo*, 67–76; Shapard, *Chief Loco*, 166, 179, 181.

11. Thrapp, *Crook and the Sierra Madre*, 97–101; Cruse, *Apache Days*, 159.

12. Crook to Henry M. Teller, March 27, 1883, Hayes Papers, Hayes Library.

13. Bourke, *On the Border*, 433–34; "Apache Story of the Cibecue," 295.

14. Crook's 1883 Annual Report, 2, Hayes Papers; Crook, "Resume of Operations Against Apache Indians," 570; "Apache Troubles," 311.

15. Crook's 1883 Annual Report, 2–3, 21–23; Masterson, "General Crook's Return," 316; Britton Davis, *Truth About Geronimo*, 63.

16. Davis, *Truth About Geronimo*, 48; Sweeney, *From Cochise to Geronimo*, 320–21; Opler, "Chiricahua's Account of Geronimo"; *Denver Tribune*, Nov. 2, 1882; Crook to Teller, March 27, 1883, Hayes Papers.

17. Crook's 1883 Annual Report, 4; Bourke, *Apache Campaign*, 31; Sweeney, *From Cochise to Geronimo*, 300.

18. Sweeney, *From Cochise to Geronimo*, 290–98; Britton Davis, *Truth About Geronimo*, 87–90. Jason Betzinez said Peaches left for San Carlos with the permission of the war party, which respected his right to rejoin his remaining family members. Betzinez, *I Fought with Geronimo*, 116–18.

19. Bourke, "With Crook in the Sierra Madre," 346; *Chicago Times*, May 24, 1883.

20. *El Paso Times*, May 20, 1883; Bourke, "With Crook in the Sierra Madre," 347, 353, 356; Account of White Mountain scout John Rope in Basso, *Western Apache Warfare and Raiding*, 154–56.

21. Bourke, "With Crook in the Sierra Madre," 358–61, 362, 368–69; Sweeney, *From Cochise to Geronimo*, 306; John Rope's account in Basso, *Western Apache Warfare and Raiding*, 162.

22. Betzinez, *I Fought with Geronimo*, 113.

23. Bourke, "With Crook in the Sierra Madre," 377–78; Fiebeger, "General Crook's Campaign," 200; Sherman Curley interview, Goodwin Papers, Arizona State Museum; Utley, *Geronimo*, 140.

24. Sweeney, *From Cochise to Geronimo*, 288–89, 331–32.

25. Sweeney, *From Cochise to Geronimo*, 317, 325; Thrapp, *Conquest of Apacheria*, 295–302.

26. Utley, *Frontier Regulars*, 381, and *Geronimo*, 143–47; Sweeney, *From Cochise to Geronimo*, 329–60.

27. *San Francisco Bulletin*, June 26, 1886; Sweeney, *From Cochise to Geronimo*, 414–15; Britton Davis, *Truth About Geronimo*, 155–56, 202–14, and "Difficulties of Indian Warfare," 488–90.

28. Unbeknownst to Davis, Crook did not learn of the telegram's existence until two months later. Had he been aware of the difficulties, Crook believed that he could have prevented a breakout. Crook, "Resume of Operations," 572.

29. Davis, "Difficulty of Indian Warfare," 489–90, and *Truth About Geronimo*, 215–17; Sweeney, *From Cochise to Geronimo*, 423; *Resolution Regarding Outbreak of Indians*, 20–21.

30. Sweeney, *From Cochise to Geronimo*, 444–45; Crook, "Resume of Operations," 573; Britton Davis, *Truth About Geronimo*, 218.

31. 49th Cong., *Report of the Secretary of War*, 151; Sweeney, *From Cochise to Geronimo*, 479–83, 507–11.

32. Sweeney, *From Cochise to Geronimo*, 489–91; Utley, *Geronimo*, 175–76.

CHAPTER 21: ONCE I MOVED LIKE THE WIND

1. Shipp, "Crawford's Last Expedition," 348; Daly, "Geronimo Campaign," 458.

2. Shipp, "Crawford's Last Expedition," 353–55; Sweeney, *From Cochise to Geronimo*, 496–99.

3. Shipp, "Crawford's Last Expedition," 355–59; Thrapp, *Dateline Fort Bowie*, 181–82; Opler, "Chiricahua's Account," 373–74.

4. Daly, "Geronimo Campaign," 460; Utley, *Geronimo*, 180–82.

5. 49th Cong., *Report of the Secretary of War, 1886*, 153; Sweeney, *From Cochise to Geronimo*, 515–21.

6. Britton Davis, *Truth About Geronimo*, 287–88; Sweeney, *From Cochise to Geronimo*, 522; Crook, "Resume of Operations," 576.

7. Thrapp, *Dateline Fort Bowie*, 61–62.

8. Sweeney, *From Cochise to Geronimo*, 525–27; 51st Cong., *Apache Indians*, 33; Crook, "Resume of Operations," 583–84.

9. *Tombstone Daily Epitaph*, April 4 and 6, 1886; Thrapp, *Dateline Fort Bowie*, 60; Miles, *Personal Recollections*, 2:476.

10. Miles, *Personal Recollections*, 2:476; Britton Davis, *Truth About Geronimo*, 313.

11. Miles, *Personal Recollections*, 2:481–85; Neifert, "Trailing Geronimo by Heliograph," 1.

12. Sweeney, *From Cochise to Geronimo*, 535–44; 51st Cong., *Apache Indians*, 33.

13. Daly, "Geronimo Campaign," 479; Miles, *Personal Recollections*, 2:487; Lane, *Chasing Geronimo*, 25.

14. Lane, *Chasing Geronimo*, 69–78; Miles, *Personal Recollections*, 2:509, 517; Vinton, "Geronimo Campaign," 28.

15. Miles, *Personal Recollections*, 2:497, 504; 51st Cong., *Apache Indians*, 3–4, 34; Sweeney, *From Cochise to Geronimo*, 566.

16. Sweeney, *From Cochise to Geronimo*, 556–57; Robinson, *Apache Voices*, 49; Ball, *Indeh*, 107.

17. Kraft, *Gatewood*, 121–52; Lane, *Chasing Geronimo*, 87–88, 92, 96–100; Ball, *Indeh*, 110.

18. 51st Cong., *Apache Indians*, 83, 7–10, 18–19.

19. 51st Cong., *Apache Indians*, 83, 7–10, 18–19, 35; Kraft, *Gatewood*, 152–53; 49th Cong., *Surrender of Geronimo*, 10–11.

20. Sweeney, *From Cochise to Geronimo*, 573–74. On October 18, Mangas surrendered his small band of three men and eight women and children at Fort Apache. He and his people were also exiled to Florida.

21. 51st Cong., *Apache Indians*, 32.

22. Debo, *Geronimo*, 366–440.

CHAPTER 22: A CLASH OF VISIONS

1. Hedren, *After Custer*, 46, 101.

2. Prucha, *American Indian Policy in Crisis*, 139, 149, 169, 180.

3. Pope, *Indian Question*, 5, 12; Terry, "Indian Management," 214; Miles, "Indian Problem," 307.
4. Henry B. Carrington, *Indian Question*, 4–6.
5. Utley, *Last Days of the Sioux Nation*, 20–33, and *Indian Frontier*, 241–43.
6. Utley, *Lance and Shield*, 249–50; McGillycuddy to Walter S. Campbell, Dec. 15, 1928, and April 16, 1929, Campbell Collection; Hyde, *Sioux Chronicle*, 63–65, and *Spotted Tail's Folk*, 335.
7. Prucha, *American Indian Policy in Crisis*, 254–55.
8. Red Cloud quoted in Greene, "Sioux Land Commission," 53–54; Lone Man, "Sitting Bull's Address to the Silent Eaters Protesting the Treaty of 1889," Campbell Collection; Crook quoted in Utley, *Last Days of the Sioux Nation*, 68.
9. McLaughlin, *My Friend the Indian*, 281–93; Neihardt, *Black Elk Speaks*, 235; "General Crook on Indians," 179; Mooney, *Ghost Dance*, 201–2; *Washington Evening Star*, Jan. 20, 1891.
10. Aaron M. Beede to Walter S. Campbell, n.d., 1929, Campbell Collection; Neihardt, *Black Elk Speaks*, 217–18.
11. Mooney, *Ghost Dance*, 203; Greene, "Sioux Commission," 66; Craft, "Indian Troubles," *Roman Catholic Weekly*, Jan. 4, 1891.
12. Boyd, *Recent Indian Wars*, 190–91; Mooney, *Ghost Dance*, 149–50; Sword, "Story of the Ghost Dance," 28–30.
13. Mooney, *Ghost Dance*, 126–43, 181–82; Utley, *Last Days of the Sioux Nation*, 72–73.
14. Quoted in Utley, *Last Days of the Sioux Nation*, 84.
15. McGillycuddy quoted in *Omaha Bee*, Jan. 19, 1891; Big Road interview in *Washington Evening Star*, Jan. 28, 1891.
16. Greene, *American Carnage*, 88–89; Hump interview in *Washington Evening Star*, Jan. 28, 1891; Utley, *Last Days of the Sioux Nation*, 112; Moody, *Ghost Dance*, 207–8.
17. Sword, "Story of the Ghost Dance," 30–31; *Omaha World Herald*, Nov. 17 and 21, 1890; *Grand Forks Daily Herald*, Nov. 29, 1890; *Aberdeen Daily News*, Nov. 30, 1890; Utley, *Last Days of the Sioux Nation*, 95.
18. *Aberdeen Daily News*, Nov. 22, 1890; Moody, *Ghost Dance*, 211.
19. Utley, *Last Days of the Sioux Nation*, 104–5; Coleman, *Voices of Wounded Knee*, 63; McGillycuddy to Campbell, n.d., Campbell Collection.
20. Greene, *American Carnage*, 97–99, 133–34; Utley, *Last Days of the Sioux Nation*, 108, 110–11; Coleman, *Voices of Wounded Knee*, 85–87; *Omaha World Herald*, Nov. 21, 1890; Tibbles, *Buckskin and Blanket Days*, 393–94.
21. *Chicago Tribune*, Nov. 22, 1890; Olson, *Red Cloud and the Sioux Problem*, 329.
22. Utley, *Last Days of the Sioux Nation*, 112; Greene, *American Carnage*, 135, 149–56; 52nd Cong., *Report of the Commissioner of Indian Affairs, 1891*, 33; Kelley, "Indian Troubles," 583.
23. Quoted in Greene, *American Carnage*, 143.
24. 52nd Cong., *Report of the Secretary of War*, 149; Greene, *American Carnage*, 195.
25. McLaughlin to T. J. Morgan, Oct. 17, 1890, Campbell Collection; Utley, *Lance and Shield*, 264–65; Aaron McGaffey Beede to Walter S. Campbell, n.d. [1929], Campbell Collection.
26. Utley, *Lance and Shield*, 254–55; One Bull interview in Carroll, *Arrest and Killing of Sitting Bull*, 71; McLaughlin to Morgan, Oct. 17, 1890, and Feb. 16, 1891, Campbell Collection.

27. Fechet, "True Story of the Death of Sitting Bull," 599–600; Utley, *Lance and Shield*, 297–98; McLaughlin, *My Friend the Indian*, 215–18.
28. John Lone Man, "Arrest and Killing of Sitting Bull," 1–2, Campbell Collection.
29. McLaughlin to Morgan, Dec. 16, 1890, in Carroll, *Arrest and Killing of Sitting Bull*, 114–15; Little Eagle to McLaughlin, Dec. 31, 1890, and John M. Carignan to McLaughlin, Jan. 6, 1891, Campbell Collection; LaPointe, *Sitting Bull*, 94–95.
30. John Lone Man, "Arrest and Killing of Sitting Bull," 3, and A. L. Bloome to Walter S. Campbell, Dec. 26, 1929, Campbell Collection.
31. John Lone Man, "Arrest and Killing of Sitting Bull," 6–7; Shoots Walking interview in Carroll, *Arrest and Death of Sitting Bull*, 89; Utley, *Lance and Shield*, 300–301.
32. John Lone Man, "Arrest and Killing of Sitting Bull," 7; Fechet, "True Story of the Death of Sitting Bull," 603; Shoots Walking interview in Carroll, *Arrest and Death of Sitting Bull*, 88; Utley, *Lance and Shield*, 165, 304–5; Greene, *Indian War Veterans*, 177.
33. Lone Man, "Arrest and Killing of Sitting Bull," 8; McLaughlin, *My Friend the Indian*, 21–22; Greene, *American Carnage*, 187.

CHAPTER 23: THE PLACE OF THE BIG KILLINGS

1. *Philadelphia Inquirer*, Dec. 17, 1890; McLaughlin to Morgan, Dec. 16, 1890; McLaughlin to Herbert Welsh, Jan. 19, 1891, Campbell Collection; *Omaha World Herald*, Dec. 21, 1890; Boyd, *Recent Indian Wars*, 207–9.
2. Greene, *American Carnage*, 169–70; Sumner to the Assistant Adjutant General, Feb. 3, 1891, in 52nd Cong., *Report of the Secretary of War*, 223–24; McLaughlin to William F. Drum, Feb. 10, 1891, box 114, folder 6, Campbell Collection; Joseph Horn Cloud interview in Jensen, *Voices of the American West*, 1:192–93.
3. Dewey Beard interview in Jensen, *Voices of the American West*, 1:210; Utley, *Last Days of the Sioux Nation*, 177–78; Sumner to the Assistant Adjutant General, Feb. 3, 1891, 224, 229.
4. Joseph Horn Cloud and Dewey Beard interviews in Jensen, *Voices of the American West*, 1:194–95, 213; Utley, *Last Days of the Sioux Nation*, 180–81; Long Bull interview in *Washington Evening Star*, Jan. 28, 1891.
5. Sumner to the Assistant Adjutant General, Feb. 3, 1891, 226–27; Marion Maus to Sumner, Dec. 23, 1890, in Utley, *Last Days of the Sioux Nation*, 185.
6. Greene, *American Carnage*, 193, 201; *Omaha World Herald*, Dec. 13, 1890.
7. Big Foot quoted in Greene, *American Carnage*, 206; *Chicago Daily Inter Ocean*, Jan. 7, 1891; Dewey Beard interview, 1:215.
8. Greene, *American Carnage*, 207; Tibbles, *Buckskin and Blanket Days*, 405–6; Utley, *Last Days of the Sioux Nation*, 193.
9. Lindberg, "Foreigners in Action," 171, 174; Dewey Beard interview, 1:215–16.
10. Shangrau, Dewey Beard, and Joseph Horn Cloud interviews in Jensen, *Voices of the American West*, 1:197, 216, 259–60.
11. Lindberg, "Foreigners in Action," 174.
12. Utley, *Last Days of the Sioux Nation*, 197; Dewey Beard interview, 1:216.
13. Greene, *American Carnage*, 212–15; Utley, *Last Days of the Sioux Nation*, 197–98; 52nd Cong., *Report of the Secretary of War*, 150.
14. Utley, *Last Days of the Sioux Nation*, 199; Allen, *From Fort Laramie to Wounded Knee*, 190; Dewey Beard interview, 1:217.

15. Greene, *American Carnage*, 221; Charles W. Taylor, "Surrender of Red Cloud," 4.

16. Foley, *At Standing Rock and Wounded Knee*, 300; McCormick, "Wounded Knee and Drexel Mission Fights," 566; Russell, "Major Whitside's Campaign Letters," Army at Wounded Knee, http://armyatwoundedknee.com/2014/08/01/major-samuel-marmaduke-whitsides-campaign-letters; John Shangrau interview in Jensen, *Voices of the American West*, 1:261–62.

17. Lindberg, "Foreigners in Action," 175; McCormick, "Wounded Knee and Drexel Mission Fights," 567; Joseph Horn Cloud and John Shangrau interview, 1:200–201, 261–62.

18. McCormick, "Wounded Knee and Drexel Mission Fights," 567; Greene, *American Carnage*, 225.

19. Varnum quoted in Utley, *Last Days of the Sioux Nation*, 209; Foley, *At Standing Rock and Wounded Knee*, 330; Allen interview, 2:13; Greene, *American Carnage*, 225–26; Dewey Beard interview, 1:218.

20. McCormick, "Wounded Knee and Drexel Mission Fights," 568.

21. Jensen, *Eyewitnesses at Wounded Knee*, 110, 201; Long Bull interview in *Washington Evening Star*, Jan. 28, 1891; Lindberg, "Foreigners in Action," 175–76; Wells, "Ninety-Six Years Among the Indians," 285–86.

22. Joseph Horn Cloud interview, 1:200; McCormick, "Wounded Knee and Drexel Mission Fights," 568–69; Utley, *Last Days of the Sioux Nation*, 212; Lindberg, "Foreigners in Action," 176.

23. Joseph Horn Cloud interview, 1:201; Lindberg, "Foreigners in Action," 272, 281; *Omaha Weekly Herald*, Jan. 6, 1891; Foley, *At Standing Rock and Wounded Knee*, 310; Neihardt, *Black Elk Speaks*, 252; Wells interview, 2:157; Greene, *American Carnage*, 232, 280. Father Craft not only survived his wound but also enjoyed a remarkably quick recovery.

24. Dewey Beard and Joseph Horn Cloud interviews, 1:197, 220; Greene, *American Carnage*, 232, 243.

25. Medicine Woman Statement in McGregor, *Wounded Knee Massacre*, 105; Lindberg, "Foreigners in Action," 176; Officer quoted in Greene, *American Carnage*, 234.

26. Utley, *Last Days of the Sioux Nation*, 216; George A. Bartlett interview in Jensen, *Voices of the American West*, 2:33.

27. Foley, *At Standing Rock and Wounded Knee*, 302, 235; Whitside to his wife, Jan. 5, 1891, in Sam Russell, "Army at Wounded Knee"; *Omaha Bee*, Dec. 30, 1890; Lindberg, "Foreigners in Action," 181.

28. Dewey Beard interview, 1:221–23; Lindberg, "Foreigners in Action," 176–77.

29. Lindberg, "Foreigners in Action," 177; Rough Feather statement in McGregor, *Wounded Knee Massacre*, 100; *Chadron Democrat*, Jan. 1, 1891; *Chicago Daily Inter Ocean*, Jan. 7, 1891.

30. Wells, "Ninety-Six Years Among the Indians," 276; Flynn, "Looking Back," 6.

31. Lindberg, "Foreigners in Action," 178; Greene, *American Carnage*, 243; Neihardt, *Black Elk Speaks*, 266.

32. Red Cloud quoted in Utley, *Last Days of the Sioux Nation*, 233; Miles's 1891 Annual Report in Pohanka, *Miles*, 220.

33. Tibbles, *Buckskin and Blanket Days*, 424–29; Elaine Goodale Eastman, *Sister to the Sioux*, 161–62; Charles Eastman, *From Deep Woods to Civilization*, 233–34.

34. Eastman, *From Deep Woods to Civilization*, 237–39; Greene, *American Carnage*, 288.

35. *Omaha World Herald*, Jan. 4, 1891.
36. Greene, *American Carnage*, 288, 301–2; Utley, *Last Days of the Sioux Nation*, 227–28.
37. Miles's 1891 Annual Report, 219.
38. Utley, *Last Days of the Sioux Nation*, 255–56; Greene, *American Carnage*, 326, 512.
39. Quoted in McGillycuddy, *McGillycuddy, Agent*, 272. Plenty Horses was arraigned before a federal grand jury in Deadwood, South Dakota, in March 1891. Valentine T. McGillycuddy served as foreman. Plenty Horses's poignant confession left the grand jury no alternative but to indict him. Despite his confession, Plenty Horses's trial in federal district court in Sioux Falls resulted in a hung jury, because jurors were unable to agree on whether the offense constituted manslaughter or murder. In a subsequent trial, the judge ruled that Plenty Horses had acted as a wartime combatant and was therefore not subject to criminal penalty. Plenty Horses returned to Rosebud a free man.

    Plenty Horses did not come home a hero as he had expected. He lived for four decades in a one-room log cabin, "quite unloved" by his neighbors and acquaintances. Plenty Horses died on June 15, 1933, a year after the deaths of his wife and son. Utley, "Ordeal of Plenty Horses," 1–13.
40. Charles W. Taylor, "Surrender of Red Cloud," [undated typescript], Order of the Indian Wars Collection; Brooke quoted in Utley, *Last Days of the Sioux Nation*, 259.
41. Miles's 1891 Annual Report, 219; *Omaha World Herald*, Jan. 12, 1891.
42. Greene, *American Carnage*, 328–31; Northrop, *Indian Horrors*, 599–600; *Aberdeen Weekly News*, Jan. 12 and 16, 1891; *Omaha Weekly Herald*, Jan. 14 and 15, 1891; *Washington Evening Star*, Jan. 20, 1891.
43. *Washington Evening Star*, Jan. 20, 1891; Green, *After Wounded Knee*, 67.
44. *Omaha World Herald*, Jan. 16, 1891; Greene, *American Carnage*, 331; *Washington Evening Star*, Jan. 20, 1891; Thiel, "Omaha Dance," 5.
45. Lakota chief quoted in Utley, *Last Days of the Sioux Nation*, 59.
46. Green, *After Wounded Knee*, 67–68; *Washington Evening Star*, Jan. 16, 1891; *Omaha World Herald*, Jan. 17, 1891.
47. Kelley, "Indian Troubles," 594; Boyd, *Recent Indian Wars*, 276; "As Narrated by Short Bull," 19, Buffalo Bill Museum and Grave Archives; *Omaha Weekly Herald*, Jan. 16, 1891.

BIBLIOGRAPHY

BOOKS

Allred, B. W. *Great Western Indian Fights*. Garden City, N.Y.: Doubleday, 1960.

Altshuler, Constance W. *Chains of Command: Arizona and the Army, 1856–1875*. Tucson: Arizona Historical Society, 1981.

Armstrong, William H. *Warrior in Two Camps: Ely S. Parker, Union General and Seneca Indian Chief*. Syracuse, N.Y.: Syracuse University Press, 1978.

Athearn, Robert G. *William Tecumseh Sherman and the Settlement of the West*. Norman: University of Oklahoma Press, 1956.

Ball, Eve. *In the Days of Victorio: Recollections of a Warm Springs Apache*. Tucson: University of Arizona Press, 1972.

———. *Indeh: An Apache Odyssey*. Provo, Utah: Brigham Young University Press, 1980.

Barrett, S. M., ed. *Geronimo's Story of His Life*. New York: Duffield, 1906. Reprint, 1999.

Basler, Roy. *The Collected Works of Abraham Lincoln*. 10 vols. New Brunswick, N.J.: Rutgers University Press, 1953.

Basso, Keith H., ed. *Western Apache Warfare and Raiding*. Tucson: University of Arizona Press, 1973.

Battey, Thomas C. *The Life and Adventures of a Quaker Among the Indians*. Boston: Lee and Shepard, 1875.

Beall, Merrill D. *"I Will Fight No More Forever": Chief Joseph and the Nez Perce War*. Seattle: University of Washington Press, 1963.

Berthrong, Donald J. *The Southern Cheyennes*. Norman: University of Oklahoma Press, 1963.

Betzinez, Jason. *I Fought with Geronimo*. Harrisburg, Pa.: Stackpole Books, 1960.

Bland, T. A. *The Life of Albert B. Meacham*. Washington, D.C.: T. A. & M. C. Bland, 1883.

Bourke, John G. *An Apache Campaign in the Sierra Madre*. New York: Charles Scribner's Sons, 1886. Reprint, 1958.

———. *On the Border with Crook*. New York: Charles Scribner's Sons, 1891.

Boyd, James P. *Recent Indian Wars, Under the Lead of Sitting Bull, and Other Chiefs*. Publishers Union, 1891.

Bray, Kingsley M. *Crazy Horse: A Lakota Life*. Norman: University of Oklahoma Press, 2006.

Brimlow, George F. *The Bannock War of 1878*. Caldwell, Idaho: Caxton Printers, 1938.

Brininstool, E. A. *Troopers with Custer*. Harrisburg, Pa.: Stackpole, 1952.

Broome, Jeff. *Dog Soldier Justice: The Ordeal of Susan Alerdice in the Kansas Indian War.* Lincoln, Kans.: Lincoln County Historical Society, 2003.

Calhoun, James. *With Custer in '74: James Calhoun's Diary of the Black Hills Expedition.* Provo, Utah: Brigham Young University Press, 1979.

Canfield, Gale W. *Sarah Winnemucca of the Northern Paiutes.* Norman: University of Oklahoma Press, 1983.

Carrington, Frances C. *My Army Life and the Fort Phil. Kearney Massacre.* Philadelphia: J. B. Lippincott, 1910.

Carrington, Margaret I. *Absaraka, Home of the Crows.* Chicago: Lakeside Press, 1950.

Carter, Robert G. *The Old Sergeant's Story, Winning the West from Indians and Bad Men, 1870–1876.* New York: Frederick H. Hitchcock, 1926.

———. *On the Border with Mackenzie; or, Winning West Texas from the Comanches.* Washington, D.C.: Eynon Printing, 1933. Reprint, 2013.

Carter, William H. *From Yorktown to Santiago with the 6th U.S. Cavalry.* Baltimore: Lord Baltimore Press, 1900. Reprint, 1989.

Chalfant, William Y. *Hancock's War: Conflict on the Southern Plains.* Norman, Okla.: Arthur H. Clark, 2010.

Chamberlain, Kathleen P. *Victorio, Apache Warrior and Chief.* Norman: University of Oklahoma Press, 2010.

Clark, Philo. *Indian Sign Language.* Philadelphia: L. R. Hamersly, 1885.

Clavin, Tom, and Bob Drury. *The Heart of Everything That Is: The Untold Story of Red Cloud, an American Legend.* New York: Simon and Schuster, 2013.

Collins, Charles. *Apache Nightmare: The Battle of Cibecue Creek.* Norman: University of Oklahoma Press, 1999.

Collins, Charles D., Jr. *Atlas of the Sioux Wars.* Fort Leavenworth, Kans.: Combat Studies Institute, 2006.

Cozzens, Peter. *The Army and the Indian.* Vol. 5 of *Eyewitnesses to the Indian Wars, 1865–1890.* Mechanicsburg, Pa.: Stackpole Books, 2005.

———. *Conquering the Southern Plains.* Vol. 3 of *Eyewitnesses to the Indian Wars, 1865–1890.* Mechanicsburg, Pa.: Stackpole Books, 2003.

———. *General John Pope: A Life for the Nation.* Urbana: University of Illinois Press, 2000.

———. *The Long War for the Northern Plains.* Vol. 4 of *Eyewitnesses to the Indian Wars, 1865–1890.* Mechanicsburg, Pa.: Stackpole Books, 2004.

———. *The Shipwreck of Their Hopes: The Battles for Chattanooga.* Urbana: University of Illinois Press, 1994.

———. *The Struggle for Apacheria.* Vol. 1 of *Eyewitnesses to the Indian Wars, 1865–1890.* Mechanicsburg, Pa.: Stackpole Books, 2000.

———. *The Wars for the Pacific Northwest.* Vol. 2 of *Eyewitnesses to the Indian Wars, 1865–1890.* Mechanicsburg, Pa.: Stackpole Books. 2002.

Crawford, Samuel J. *Kansas in the Sixties.* Chicago: A. C. McClurg, 1911.

Cremony, John C. *Life Among the Apaches.* San Francisco: A. Roman, 1868.

Cruse, Thomas A. *Apache Days and After.* Caldwell, Idaho: Caxton Printers, 1941.

Custer, Elizabeth B. *Boots and Saddles, or Life in Dakota with General Custer.* New York: Harper & Brothers, 1885.

———. *Following the Guidon.* New York: Harper & Brothers, 1890.

Custer, George A. *My Life on the Plains; or, Personal Experiences with the Indians.* New York: Sheldon, 1874. Reprint, 1952.

Danker, Donald. *Man of the Plains: Recollections of Luther North, 1856–1882.* Lincoln: University of Nebraska Press, 1961.

David, Robert B. *Finn Burnett Frontiersman*. Glendale, Calif.: Arthur H. Clarke, 1937.

Davis, Britton. *The Truth About Geronimo*. New Haven, Conn.: Yale University Press, 1929. Reprint, 1932.

De Trobriand, Phillipe Regis. *Military Life in Dakota: The Journal of Phillipe Regis de Trobriand*. St. Paul: Alvord Memorial Commission, 1951.

DeBarthe, Joe. *The Life and Adventures of Frank Grouard, Indian Scout*. Norman: University of Oklahoma Press, 1958.

Debo, Angie. *Geronimo: The Man, His Time, His Place*. Norman: University of Oklahoma Press, 1982.

Decker, Peter R. *The Utes Must Go! American Expansion and the Removal of a People*. Golden, Colo.: Fulcrum, 2004.

DeMallie, Raymond J., ed. *The Sixth Grandfather: Black Elk's Teachings Given to John G. Neihardt*. Lincoln: University of Nebraska Press, 1984.

Dillon, Richard. *Burnt-Out Fires: California's Modoc Indian War*. New York: Prentice-Hall, 1973.

Dodge, Grenville M. *How We Built the Union Pacific Railway*. Council Bluffs, Iowa: Monarch, n.d.

Dodge, Richard I. *Our Wild Indians: Thirty-Three Years' Experience Among the Red Men of the Great West*. Hartford: A. D. Worthington, 1883.

———. *The Plains of the Great West and Their Inhabitants*. New York: Putnam, 1877.

Donovan, James. *A Terrible Glory: Custer and the Little Bighorn, the Last Great Battle of the American West*. New York: Little, Brown, 2008.

Dunlay, Thomas W. *Wolves for the Blue Soldiers: Indian Scouts and Auxiliaries with the United States Army, 1860-1890*. Lincoln: University of Nebraska Press, 1982.

Eastman, Charles A. *From Deep Woods to Civilization: Chapters in the Autobiography of an Indian*. Boston: Little, Brown, 1917. Reprint, 2001.

Eastman, Elaine Goodale. *Sister to the Sioux: The Memoirs of Elaine Goodale Eastman*. Lincoln: University of Nebraska Press, 1985.

Ege, Robert J. *"Tell Baker to Strike Them Hard!": Incident on the Marias, 23 Jan. 1870*. Bellevue, Neb.: Old Army Press, 1970.

Emmitt, Robert. *The Last War Trail: The Utes and the Settlement of Colorado*. Norman: University of Oklahoma Press, 1954.

Farish, Thomas E. *History of Arizona*. 8 vols. Phoenix: State of Arizona, 1915.

Finerty, John F. *War-Path and Bivouac; or, The Conquest of the Sioux*. Chicago: Donohue and Henneberry, 1890.

Forsyth, George A. *The Story of the Soldier*. New York: D. Appleton, 1900.

———. *Thrilling Days in Army Life*. New York: Harper & Brothers, 1900.

Gaff, Alan D., and Maureen Gaff, eds. *Adventures on the Western Frontier: Major General John Gibbon*. Bloomington: Indiana University Press, 1994.

Graham, W. A. *The Custer Myth: A Source Book of Custeriana*. Harrisburg, Pa.: Stackpole, 1953.

Grant, Ulysses S. *Personal Memoirs of U. S. Grant*. 2 vols. New York: Charles L. Webster, 1885 and 1886.

Gray, John S. *Centennial Campaign: The Sioux War of 1876*. Fort Collins, Colo.: Old Army Press, 1976.

———. *Custer's Last Campaign: Mitch Boyer and the Little Bighorn Reconstructed*. Lincoln: University of Nebraska Press, 1991.

Green, Jerry, ed. *After Wounded Knee: Correspondence of Major and Surgeon John Vance*

Lauderdale While Serving with the Army Occupying the Pine Ridge Indian Reservation, 1890–1891. East Lansing: Michigan State University Press, 1996.

Greene, Jerome A. *American Carnage: Wounded Knee, 1890*. Norman: University of Oklahoma Press, 2014.

———, ed. *Battles and Skirmishes of the Great Sioux War, 1876–1877: The Military View*. Norman: University of Oklahoma Press, 1996.

———. *Indian War Veterans: Memories of Army Life and Campaigns in the West, 1864–1898*. El Dorado Hills, Calif.: Savas Beattie, 2007.

———. *Lakota and Cheyenne: Indian Views of the Great Sioux War, 1876–1877*. Norman: University of Oklahoma Press, 1998.

———. *Morning Star Dawn: The Powder River Expedition and the Northern Cheyennes, 1876*. Norman: University of Oklahoma Press, 2003.

———. *Nez Perce Summer, 1877: The U.S. Army and the Nee-Me-Poo Crisis*. Helena: Montana Historical Society Press, 2000.

———. *Slim Buttes, 1876: An Episode of the Great Sioux War*. Norman: University of Oklahoma Press, 1982.

———. *Washita: The U.S. Army and the Southern Cheyennes, 1867–1869*. Norman: University of Oklahoma Press, 1999.

———. *Yellowstone Command: Colonel Nelson A. Miles and the Great Sioux War, 1876–1877*. Norman: University of Oklahoma Press, 1994.

Grinnell, George B. *The Fighting Cheyennes*. New York: Charles Scribner's Sons, 1915.

———. *The Story of the Indian*. New York: D. Appleton, 1895.

———. *Two Great Scouts and Their Pawnee Battalion: The Experiences of Frank J. and Luther H. North, Pioneers of the Great West, 1856–1862, and Their Defence of the Building of the Union Pacific Railroad*. Cleveland: Arthur H. Clark, 1928.

Grossman, Mark. *Political Corruption in America: An Encyclopedia of Scandals, Power, and Greed*. Santa Barbara, Calif.: ABC-CLIO, 2003.

Gwynne, S. C. *Empire of the Summer Moon: Quanah Parker and the Rise and Fall of the Comanche Nation, the Most Powerful Indian Tribe in American History*. New York: Scribner, 2011.

Hagan, Barry J. *"Exactly in the Right Place": A History of Fort C. F. Smith, Montana Territory, 1866–1868*. El Segundo, Calif.: Upton and Sons, 1999.

Haley, James L. *The Buffalo War*. Garden City, N.Y.: Doubleday, 1976.

Hammer, Kenneth, ed. *Custer in '76: Walter Camp's Notes on the Custer Fight*. Provo, Utah: Brigham Young University Press, 1976.

Hampton, Bruce. *Children of Grace: The Nez Perce War of 1877*. New York: Henry Holt, 1994.

Hanson, Joseph M. *The Conquest of the Missouri*. Chicago: A. C. McClurg, 1909.

Hardorff, Richard G. *Hokahey! A Good Day to Die! The Indian Casualties of the Custer Fight*. Spokane: Arthur H. Clark, 1993.

———. *Indian Views of the Custer Fight*. Spokane: Arthur H. Clark, 2004.

———. *Lakota Recollections of the Custer Fight*. Spokane: Arthur H. Clark, 1991.

———. *The Surrender and Death of Crazy Horse*. Spokane: Arthur H. Clark, 1998.

———. *Washita Memories: Eyewitness Accounts of Custer's Attack on Black Kettle's Village*. Norman: University of Oklahoma Press, 2008.

Hassrick, Royal B. *The Sioux*. Norman: University of Oklahoma Press, 1964.

Hebard, Grace R. *Washakie: An Account of Indian Resistance*. Cleveland: Arthur H. Clark, 1930.

Hebard, Grace R., and E. A. Brininstool. *The Bozeman Trail*. 2 vols. Cleveland: Arthur H. Clark, 1922.

Hedren, Paul L. *After Custer: Loss and Transformation in Sioux Country.* Norman: University of Oklahoma Press, 2011.

Heyman, Max L., Jr. *Prudent Soldier: A Biography of Major General E. R. S. Canby.* Glendale, Calif.: Arthur H. Clark, 1959.

Hoig, Stan. *The Battle of the Washita: The Sheridan-Custer Indian Campaign of 1867–1869.* Garden City, N.Y.: Doubleday, 1976.

———. *The Peace Chiefs of the Cheyennes.* Norman: University of Oklahoma Press, 1980.

———. *The Sand Creek Massacre.* Norman: University of Oklahoma Press, 1961.

Howard, Oliver O. *Famous Indian Chiefs I Have Known.* New York: Century, 1908.

———. *My Life and Experiences Among Our Hostile Indians.* Hartford: A. D. Worthington, 1907.

———. *Nez Perce Joseph.* Boston: Lee and Shepard, 1881.

Hutton, Paul A. *Phil Sheridan and His Army.* Norman: University of Oklahoma Press, 1999.

———, ed. *Soldiers West: Biographies from the Military Frontier.* Lincoln: University of Nebraska Press, 1987.

Hyde, George F. *Life of George Bent, Written from His Letters.* Norman: University of Oklahoma Press, 1968.

———. *Red Cloud's Folk: A History of the Oglala Sioux Indians.* Norman: University of Oklahoma Press, 1937.

———. *Spotted Tail's Folk: A History of the Brulé Sioux.* Norman: University of Oklahoma Press, 1961.

Jackson, Donald. *Custer's Gold: The United States Cavalry Expedition of 1874.* New Haven, Conn.: Yale University Press, 1966.

Jacoby, Karl. *Shadows at Dawn: A Borderlands Massacre and the Violence of History.* New York: Penguin, 2008.

Jauken, Arlene F. *The Moccasin Speaks: Living as Captives of the Dog Soldier Warriors.* Lincoln, Neb.: Dageford, 1998.

Jensen, Richard E., ed. *The Indian Interviews of Eli S. Ricker, 1903–1919.* Vol. 1 of *Voices of the American West.* Lincoln: University of Nebraska Press, 2005.

———. *The Settler and Soldier Interviews of Eli S. Ricker, 1903–1919.* Vol. 2 of *Voices of the American West.* Lincoln: University of Nebraska Press, 2005.

Jones, Douglas C. *The Treaty of Medicine Lodge: The Story of the Great Treaty Council as Told by Eyewitnesses.* Norman: University of Oklahoma Press, 1966.

Josephy, Alvin M., Jr. *The Nez Perce Indians and the Opening of the Northwest.* New Haven, Conn.: Yale University Press, 1965. Reprint, 1979.

Kappler, Charles J., ed. *Indian Affairs: Laws and Treaties.* 5 vols. Washington D.C.: Government Printing Office, 1904–1941.

Keenan, Jerry. *The Wagon Box Fight.* Boulder, Colo.: Lightning Tree Press, 1992.

Keim, De B. Randolph. *Sheridan's Troopers on the Borders: A Winter Campaign on the Plains.* Philadelphia: Claxton, Remsen, and Haffelfinger, 1870.

Kennedy, William J., ed. *On the Plains with Custer and Hancock: The Journal of Isaac Coates, Army Surgeon.* Boulder, Colo.: Johnson Books, 1997.

Kimball, Maria B. *A Soldier-Doctor of Our Army, James P. Kimball.* Boston: Houghton Mifflin, 1917.

Kime, Wayne R., ed. *The Powder River Journals of Colonel Richard Irving Dodge.* Norman: University of Oklahoma Press, 1989.

Kraft, Louis. *Lt. Charles Gatewood and His Apache War Memoir.* Lincoln: University of Nebraska Press, 2005.

Krause, Herbert, and Harry D. Olson, eds. *Custer's Prelude to Glory: A Newspaper Accounting of Custer's 1874 Expedition to the Black Hills.* Sioux Falls, S.D.: Brevet Press, 1974.

Lane, Jack C., ed. *Chasing Geronimo: The Journal of Leonard Wood, May–September 1886.* Lincoln: University of Nebraska Press, 1970.

LaPointe, Ernie. *Sitting Bull: His Life and Legacy.* Layton, Utah: Gibbs Smith, 2009.

Larpenteur, Charles. *Forty Years a Fur Trader on the Upper Missouri: The Personal Narrative of Charles Larpenteur.* New York: Francis P. Harper, 1898.

Larson, Robert W. *Red Cloud: Warrior Statesman of the Lakota Sioux.* Norman: University of Oklahoma Press, 1973.

Leckie, William H. *The Buffalo Soldiers: A Narrative of the Negro Cavalry in the West.* Norman: University of Oklahoma Press, 1967.

———. *The Military Conquest of the Southern Plains.* Norman: University of Oklahoma Press, 1963.

Leonard, Elizabeth D. *Men of Color to Arms! Black Soldiers, Indian Wars, and the Quest for Equality.* New York: W. W. Norton, 2010.

Linderman, Frank B. *Plenty-Coups, Chief of the Crows.* Lincoln: University of Nebraska Press, 1962.

Lockwood, Frank C. *The Apache Indians.* New York: Macmillan, 1938. Reprint, 1987.

Lubetkin, M. John. *Custer and the 1873 Yellowstone Survey: A Documentary History.* Norman: Arthur H. Clark, 2013.

———. *Jay Cooke's Gamble: The Northern Pacific Railroad, the Sioux, and the Panic of 1873.* Norman: University of Oklahoma Press, 2006.

McConnell, William J. *Early History of Idaho.* Caldwell, Idaho: Caxton Printers, 1913.

McGillycuddy, Julia B. *McGillycuddy, Indian Agent.* Palo Alto, Calif.: Stanford University Press, 1941.

McGinnis, Anthony. *Counting Coup and Cutting Horses: Intertribal Warfare on the Northern Plains, 1738–1889.* Lincoln: University of Nebraska Press, 2010.

McGregor, James H. *The Wounded Knee Massacre from the Viewpoint of the Sioux.* Minneapolis: Lund Press, 1950.

McMurtry, Larry. *Crazy Horse.* New York: Viking, 1999.

McWhorter, Lucullus V. *Hear Me, My Chiefs! Nez Perce Legend and History.* Caldwell, Idaho: Caxton Press, 1952. Reprint, 2001.

———. *Yellow Wolf: His Own Story.* Caldwell, Idaho: Caxton Printers, 1940. Reprint, 1984.

Madsen, Brigham D. *The Bannock of Idaho.* Caldwell, Idaho: Caxton Printers, 1958.

Mails, Thomas E. *The Mystic Warriors of the Plains.* Garden City, N.Y.: Doubleday, 1972.

Malone, Dumas, ed. *The Dictionary of American Biography.* 21 vols. New York: Charles Scribner's Sons, 1937.

Marquis, Thomas B. *Wooden Leg: A Warrior Who Fought Custer.* Minneapolis: Midwest Company, 1931. Reprint, 1962.

Marriott, Alice. *The Ten Grandmothers.* Norman: University of Oklahoma Press, 1957.

Marshall, John M. *The Journey of Crazy Horse: A Lakota History.* New York: Viking Press, 2004.

Marshall, J. T. *The Miles Expedition of 1874–1875: An Eyewitness Account of the Red River War.* Austin, Tex.: Encino Press, 1971.

Marszalek, John F. *Sherman: A Soldier's Passion for Order.* New York: Free Press, 1993.

Mayhall, Mildred P. *The Kiowas.* Norman: University of Oklahoma Press, 1962. Reprint, 1971.

Meacham, Alfred B. *Wigwam and War-Path.* Boston: John P. Dale, 1875.

Meredith, Grace E. *Girl Captives of the Cheyennes.* Los Angeles: Gem, 1927. Reprint, 2004.

Merington, Marguerite. *The Custer Story: The Intimate Letters of General George A. Custer and His Wife Elizabeth.* New York: Devon-Adair, 1950.

Michno, Gregory F. *The Deadliest Indian War in the West: The Snake Conflict, 1864–1868.* Caldwell, Idaho: Caxton Press, 2007.

———. *Encyclopedia of Indian Wars: Western Battles and Skirmishes, 1850–1890.* Missoula, Mont.: Mountain Press, 2003.

Michno, Gregory F., and Susan Michno. *A Fate Worse Than Death: Indian Captivities in the West, 1830–1895.* Caldwell, Idaho: Caxton Press, 2007.

Miles, Nelson A. *Personal Recollections and Observations of General Nelson A. Miles.* Chicago: Werner, 1896. Reprint, 2 vols., 1992.

Miller, Mark E. *Hollow Victory: The White River Expedition of 1879 and the Battle of Milk Creek.* Niwot: University of Colorado Press, 1997.

Mills, Anson. *My Story.* Washington, D.C.: Press of Byron S. Adams, 1918.

Monnett, John H. *The Battle of Beecher Island and the Indian War of 1867–1869.* Niwot: University of Colorado Press, 1992.

———. *Red Cloud's War: The Bozeman Trail.* 2 vols. Norman: Arthur H. Clark, 2010.

———. *Tell Them We Are Going Home: The Odyssey of the Northern Cheyennes.* Norman: University of Oklahoma Press, 2001.

———. *Where a Hundred Soldiers Were Killed: The Struggle for the Powder River Country in 1866 and the Making of the Fetterman Myth.* Albuquerque: University of New Mexico Press, 2006.

Mooney, James. *The Ghost Dance Religion and the Sioux Outbreak of 1890.* Chicago: University of Chicago Press, 1965.

Murray, Keith A. *The Modocs and Their War.* Norman: University of Oklahoma Press, 1959.

Nabokov, Peter. *Two Leggings: The Making of a Crow Warrior.* New York: Thomas Y. Crowell, 1967.

Neeley, Bill. *The Last Comanche Chief: The Life and Times of Quanah Parker.* New York: Wiley, 1995.

Neihardt, John G. *Black Elk Speaks: Being the Life Story of a Holy Man of the Oglala Sioux.* New York: William Morrow, 1932. Reprint, 1988.

Northrop, Henry D. *Indian Horrors; or, Massacres by the Red Men.* Chicago: L. P. Miller, 1891.

Noyes, Alva. *In the Land of Chinook; or, The Story of Blaine County.* Helena, Mont.: State Publishing, 1917.

Nye, Wilbur S. *Bad Medicine and Good: Tales of the Kiowa.* Norman: University of Oklahoma Press, 1962.

———. *Carbine and Lance: The Story of Old Fort Sill.* Norman: University of Oklahoma Press, 1937.

———. *Plains Indian Raiders: The Final Phases of Warfare from the Arkansas to the Red River.* Norman: University of Oklahoma Press, 1968.

Odeneal, Thomas B. *The Modoc War: Statement of Its Origin and Causes.* Portland, Ore.: "Bulletin" Steam Book and Job Print Office, 1873.

Ogle, Ralph H. *Federal Control of the Western Apaches, 1848–1886*. Albuquerque: University of New Mexico Press, 1970.

Olson, James C. *Red Cloud and the Sioux Problem*. Lincoln: University of Nebraska Press, 1965.

Parker, James. *The Old Army: Memories, 1872–1918*. Philadelphia: Dorrance, 1929. Reprint, 2003.

Paul, R. Eli, ed. *Autobiography of Red Cloud, War Leader of the Oglalas*. Helena: Montana Historical Society Press, 1997.

———. *The Nebraska Indian Wars Reader*. Lincoln: University of Nebraska Press, 1998.

Philbrick, Nathaniel. *The Last Stand: Custer, Sitting Bull, and the Battle of the Little Bighorn*. New York: Viking Penguin, 2010.

Pohanka, Brian, ed. *Nelson A. Miles: A Documentary Biography of His Military Career*. Glendale, Calif.: Arthur H. Clark, 1985.

Powell, Peter J. *People of the Sacred Mountain: A History of the Northern Cheyenne Chiefs and Warrior Societies, 1830–1879*. 2 vols. New York: Harper & Row, 1981.

Powers, Thomas. *The Killing of Crazy Horse*. New York: Alfred A. Knopf, 2011.

Prucha, Francis P. *American Indian Policy in Crisis: Christian Reformers and the Indian, 1865–1890*. Norman: University of Oklahoma Press, 1964.

———. *American Indian Treaties: The History of a Political Anomaly*. Berkeley: University of California Press, 1994.

Record of Engagements with Hostile Indians Within the Military Division of the Missouri from 1868 to 1882, Lieutenant General P. H. Sheridan, Commanding. Chicago: Headquarters Military District of the Missouri, 1882.

Richardson, Rupert N. *The Comanche Barrier to South Plains Settlement*. Cleveland: Arthur H. Clark, 1933. Reprint, 1991.

Rickey, Don. *Forty Miles a Day on Beans and Hay: The Enlisted Soldier Fighting the Indian Wars*. Norman: University of Oklahoma Press, 1963.

Riddle, Jeff C. *The Indian History of the Modoc War*. San Francisco: privately printed, 1914.

Robinson, Charles M., III. *Bad Hand: A Biography of General Ranald S. Mackenzie*. Austin, Tex.: State House Press, 1993.

———, ed. *The Diaries of John Gregory Bourke*. 5 vols. Denton: University of North Texas Press, 2003–2013.

———. *General Crook and the Western Frontier*. Norman: University of Oklahoma Press, 2001.

———. *A Good Year to Die: The Story of the Great Sioux War*. New York: Random House, 1995.

Rockwell, Stephen J. *Indian Affairs and the Administrative State in the Nineteenth Century*. Cambridge, U.K.: Cambridge University Press, 2010.

Roe, Francis M. A. *Army Letters from an Officer's Wife, 1871–1888*. New York: Appleton, 1909.

Russell, Don. *One Hundred and Three Fights and Scrimmages: The Story of General Reuben F. Bernard*. Washington, D.C.: United States Cavalry Association, 1936. Reprint, 2003.

Sandoz, Mari. *Crazy Horse, the Strange Man of the Oglalas*. New York: Alfred A. Knopf, 1942.

Schmitt, Martin F., ed. *General George Crook, His Autobiography*. Norman: University of Oklahoma Press, 1946.

Schofield, John M. *Forty-Six Years in the Army.* New York: Century, 1897.

Schubert, Frank N. *Voices of the Buffalo Soldiers: Records, Reports, and Recollections of Military Service in the West.* Albuquerque: University of New Mexico Press, 2003.

Schultz, James W. *Blackfeet and Buffalo: Memories of Life Among the Indians.* Norman: University of Oklahoma Press, 1962.

Scott, Hugh L. *Some Memories of a Soldier.* New York: Century, 1928.

Scott, Kim A. *Yellowstone Denied: The Life of Gustave Cheyney Doane.* Norman: University of Oklahoma Press, 2007.

Shapard, Bud. *Chief Loco: Apache Peacemaker.* Norman: University of Oklahoma Press, 2010.

Sheridan, Philip H. *Personal Memoirs of General P. H. Sheridan.* 2 vols. New York: Charles L. Webster, 1888.

Simon, John Y., ed. *The Papers of Ulysses S. Grant.* 31 vols. Carbondale: Southern Illinois University Press, 1967–2009.

Simpson, Moira G. *Making Representations: Museums in the Post-Colonial Era.* London: Taylor and Francis, 2001.

Slattery, Charles L. *Felix Reville Brunot, 1820–1898.* New York: Longmans, Green, 1901.

Smith, P. David. *Ouray: Chief of the Utes.* Ridgeway, Colo.: Wayfinder Press, 1980.

Smith, Sherry L. *Sagebrush Soldier: Private William Earl Smith's View of the Sioux War of 1876.* Norman: University of Oklahoma Press, 1989.

Sprague, Marshall. *Massacre: The Tragedy at White River.* Boston: Little, Brown, 1957.

Stands in Timber, John, and Margot Liberty. *Cheyenne Memories.* New Haven, Conn.: Yale University Press, 1967.

Stanley, Henry M. *My Early Travels and Adventures in America and Asia.* 2 vols. London: Sampson Low, Marston, 1895.

Steinbach, Robert H. *A Long March: The Lives of Frank A. and Alice Baldwin.* Austin: University of Texas Press, 1990.

Stewart, Edgar I. *Custer's Luck.* Norman: University of Oklahoma Press, 1955.

Stiles, T. J. *Custer's Trials: A Life on the Frontier of a New America.* New York: Alfred A. Knopf, 2015.

Sweeney, Edwin R. *Cochise, Chiricahua Apache Chief.* Norman: University of Oklahoma Press, 1991.

———. *From Cochise to Geronimo: The Chiricahua Apaches, 1874–1886.* Norman: University of Oklahoma Press, 2010.

———. *Making Peace with Cochise: The 1872 Journal of Captain Joseph Alton Sladen.* Norman: University of Oklahoma Press, 1997.

Tatum, Lawrie. *Our Red Brothers and the Peace Policy of President Ulysses S. Grant.* Philadelphia: John C. Winston, 1899. Reprint, 1970.

Taylor, Joe F., ed. *The Indian Campaign on the Staked Plains, 1874–1875.* 2 vols. Canyon, Tex.: Panhandle-Plains Historical Society, 1961–1962.

Taylor, William O. *With Custer on the Little Bighorn.* New York: Viking, 1996.

Thompson, Erwin N. *Modoc War, Its Military History and Topography.* Sacramento, Calif.: Argus Books, 1971.

Thrapp, Dan L. *The Conquest of Apacheria.* Norman: University of Oklahoma Press, 1967.

———. *Dateline Fort Bowie: Charles Fletcher Lummis Reports on an Apache War.* Norman: University of Oklahoma Press, 1979.

————. *Encyclopedia of Frontier Biography*. 4 vols. Spokane: Arthur H. Clark, 1988, 1994.

————. *Victorio and the Mimbres Apaches*. Norman: University of Oklahoma Press, 1974.

Tibbles, Thomas Henry. *Buckskin and Blanket Days: Memoirs of a Friend of the Indians*. Garden City, N.Y.: Doubleday, 1957.

Utley, Robert M. *Cavalier in Buckskin: George Armstrong Custer and the Western Military Frontier*. Norman: University of Oklahoma Press, 1988.

————. *Frontier Regulars: The United States Army and the Indian, 1866–1891*. New York: Macmillan, 1973.

————. *Frontiersmen in Blue: The United States Army and the Indian, 1848–1865*. New York: Macmillan, 1967.

————. *Geronimo*. New Haven, Conn.: Yale University Press, 2013.

————. *The Indian Frontier of the American West*. Albuquerque: University of New Mexico Press, 1984.

————. *Indian Wars*. Boston: Houghton Mifflin, 2002.

————. *The Lance and the Shield: The Life and Times of Sitting Bull*. New York: Henry Holt, 1993.

————. *The Last Days of the Sioux Nation*. New Haven, Conn.: Yale University Press, 1963.

————, ed. *Life in Custer's Cavalry: Diaries and Letters of Albert and Jennie Barnitz, 1867–1869*. New Haven, Conn.: Yale University Press, 1977.

Vestal, Stanley. *Warpath: The True Story of the Fighting Sioux Told in the Biography of Chief White Bull*. Boston: Houghton Mifflin, 1932.

Vickers, W. B. *The History of Denver, Arapahoe County, and Colorado*. Chicago: O. L. Baskin, 1880.

Wallace, Ernest. *Ranald S. Mackenzie on the Texas Frontier*. Lubbock: West Texas Museum Association, 1965. Reprint, 1993.

Webb, William P. *The Great Plains*. Boston: Ginn, 1931.

Wert, Jeffry D. *Custer: The Controversial Life of George Armstrong Custer*. New York: Simon and Schuster, 1996.

West, Elliott. *The Last Indian War: The Nez Perce Story*. Oxford: Oxford University Press, 2000.

Wharfield, H. B. *Cooley: Army Scout, Arizona Pioneer, Wayside Host, Apache Friend*. El Cajon, Calif.: H. B. Wharfield, 1966.

White, Lonnie J., ed. *Hostiles and Horse Soldiers*. Boulder, Colo.: Pruett, 1972.

Wooster, Robert. *Nelson A. Miles and the Twilight of the Frontier*. Lincoln: University of Nebraska Press, 1993.

ARTICLES, ESSAYS, AND ADDRESSES

Addresses to the Graduating Class of the U.S. Military Academy at West Point, N.Y., June 14th, 1876. New York: D. Van Nostrand, 1876.

"The Apache Story of the Cibecue." In Cozzens, *Struggle for Apacheria*.

"Army Abuses—Our Recruiting System." *Army and Navy Journal*, April 29, 1876.

"The Army and the Indian." *Army and Navy Journal*, March 14, 1874.

Army Officer's Wife. "The Beauties of Indian Frontier Life." *Army and Navy Journal*, Aug. 24, 1867.

"The Bannock Troubles." *Army and Navy Journal*, June 29, 1878.

Belish, Elbert D. "American Horse (Wasechun-Tashunka): The Man Who Killed Fetterman." *Annals of Wyoming* 33, no. 1 (Spring 1961).

Bourke, John G. "With Crook in the Sierra Madre." In Cozzens, *Struggle for Apacheria*.

Boutelle, Frazier A. "The Disaster to Thomas' Command." In *Northwestern Fights and Fighters*, by Cyrus T. Brady. New York: McClure, 1907.

———. "Major Boutelle's Account of His Duel with Scar-Faced Charley in the First Engagement." In *Northwestern Fights and Fighters*, by Cyrus T. Brady. New York: McClure, 1907.

Braden, Charles G. "The Yellowstone Expedition of 1873." In Cozzens, *Long War for the Northern Plains*.

Bradley, James H. "The Sioux Campaign of 1876 Under General John Gibbon." *Contributions to the Historical Society of Montana* 2 (1896).

Bray, Kingsley M. "Crazy Horse and the End of the Great Sioux War." *Nebraska History* 79 (1998).

———. "Teton Sioux: Population History, 1655–1881." *Nebraska History* 75 (1994).

Brewster, Charles. "Battle of Washita." *National Tribune*, Sept. 18, 1899.

Bridger, James. "Indian Affairs in the Powder River Country." *Army and Navy Journal*, June 29, 1867.

Bronson, Edgar B. "Little Wolf's Escape and Dull Knife's Capture." *Pearson's Magazine*, Feb. 1909.

———. "Soldier Creek Ambuscades." *Pearson's Magazine*, March 1909.

Buck, Henry. "The Story of the Nez Perce Campaign During the Summer of 1877." In Cozzens, *Wars for the Pacific Northwest*.

Caitlin, John B. "The Battle of the Big Hole." In *Society of Montana Pioneers, Forty-Fourth Annual Convention, Missoula, Montana, August 4, 5, and 6, 1927, Historian's Annual Report*. Missoula: Montana Bureau of Printing, 1927.

"Capture of a Cheyenne Village." *Army and Navy Journal*, July 31, 1869.

Cargill, Andrew H. "The Camp Grant Massacre." *Arizona Historical Review* 7, no. 3 (July 1936).

Carpenter, John A. "General Howard and the Nez Perce War of 1877." *Pacific Northwest Quarterly* 49, no. 4 (Oct. 1958).

Carpenter, Louis A. "The Story of a Rescue." *Winners of the West*, Feb. 1925.

Carr, Camilo C. C. "The Days of Empire—Arizona, 1865–1890." *Journal of the United States Cavalry Association* 2, no. 4 (March 1889).

Carrington, Henry B. *The Indian Question: An Address Before the Geographical and Biological Sections of the British Association for the Advancement of Science, at Their Forty-Fifth Meeting, at Bristol, 1875*. Boston: Charles H. Whiting, 1884.

"Causes of Desertion." *Army and Navy Journal*, Jan. 14, 1871.

[Chief Joseph]. "An Indian's Views of Indian Affairs." *North American Review* 128 (April 1879).

Clum, John P. "Apache Misrule." *New Mexico Historical Review* 5 (1930).

Craft, Francis M. J. "Indian Troubles." *Roman Catholic Weekly*, Jan. 4, 1891.

Cremony, John C. "Some Savages." *Overland Monthly* 8, no. 3 (March 1871).

Crook, George. "The Apache Troubles." In Cozzens, *Struggle for Apacheria*.

———. "The Bannock Troubles." *Army and Navy Journal*, June 29, 1878.

———. "Resume of Operations Against Apache Indians, 1882–1886." In Cozzens, *Struggle for Apacheria*.

Custer, Elizabeth B. "'Where the Heart Is': A Sketch of Woman's Life on the Frontier." *Lippincott's Magazine*, Feb. 1900.

Custer, George A. "Battling with the Sioux on the Yellowstone." *Galaxy* 22, no. 1 (July 1876).

Daly, Henry W. "The Capture of Geronimo." *Winners of the West*, Dec. 1933.

———. "The Geronimo Campaign." In Cozzens, *Struggle for Apacheria*.

Davis, Britton. "The Difficulty of Indian Warfare." In Cozzens, *Struggle for Apacheria*.

Davis, Theodore R. "A Summer on the Plains." *Harper's New Monthly Magazine*, Feb. 1868.

Dorst, Joseph H. "Ranald Slidell Mackenzie." In Cozzens, *Army and the Indian*.

Dougherty, William E. "Personal Experiences Among the Indians of North America and the Wounded Knee Fight." *Overland Monthly*, April 1892.

Eastman, Charles A. "The Indian Version of Custer's Last Battle." *Chautauquan* 31 (July 1900).

Ewers, James C. "Intertribal Warfare as the Precursor of Indian-White Warfare on the Northern Great Plains." *Western Historical Quarterly* 6, no. 4 (Oct. 1973).

Fechet, Edmond G. "The True Story of the Death of Sitting Bull." *Cosmopolitan*, March 1896.

Fiebeger, Gustav J. "General Crook's Campaign in the Sierra Madre." In *The Papers of the Order of Indian Wars*, by John M. Carroll. Fort Collins, Colo.: Old Army Press, 1975.

Finerty, John F. "On Campaign After Cibecue Creek." In Cozzens, *Struggle for Apacheria*.

Fitzgerald, Maurice. "The Modoc War." *Americana Illustrated*, Oct. 1927.

Flynn, Andrew M. "Looking Back over Forty-Nine Years: A 7th Cavalryman Remembers." *Winners of the West*, Nov. 1939 and Dec. 1939.

Forbes, Archibald. "The United States Army." *North American Review* 135, no. 309 (Aug. 1882).

Forsyth, George A. "A Frontier Fight." *Harper's New Monthly Magazine*, June 1895.

Fritz, Henry E. "The Making of Grant's Peace Policy." *Chronicles of Oklahoma* 37 (1959).

Garfield, James A. "The Army of the United States." *North American Review* 126, no. 261 (March–April 1878).

Garfield, Marvin H. "Defense of the Kansas Frontier, 1866–1867." *Kansas Historical Quarterly* 1, no. 4 (Aug. 1932).

Garland, Hamlin. "Custer's Last Fight as Seen by Two Moon." *McClure's Magazine*, Sept. 1898.

"Garryowen, Regimental Battle Song of the Seventh U.S. Cavalry." *Cavalry Journal*, July–Aug. 1942.

Gashuntz. "Candid Opinion of Arizona." *Army and Navy Journal*, March 25, 1871.

Gatewood, Charles B. "Campaigning Against Geronimo in 1879." *Great Divide*, April 1894.

"General Crook on Indians." *Council Fire* 2, no. 12 (Dec. 1889).

"General Howard's Treaties." *Old and New* 6 (Nov. 1872).

Genetin-Pilawa, C. Joseph. "Ely Parker and the Contentious Peace Policy." *Montana: The Magazine of Western History* 41, no. 2 (Summer 2010).

Gibbon, John. "The Indian Department." *Army and Navy Journal*, Jan. 1, 1876.

———. "Last Summer's Expedition against the Sioux and Its Great Catastrophe." *American Catholic Quarterly* 2 (October 1877).

Gibson, Frank M. "Our Washita Battle." In Cozzens, *Conquering the Southern Plains*.

Godfrey, Edward S. "Custer's Last Battle." *Century Magazine*, Jan. 1892.

——. "The Medicine Lodge Treaty, Sixty Years Ago." *Winners of the West*, March 1929.

——. "Some Reminiscences, Including an Account of General Sully's Campaign Against the Southern Plains Indians, 1868." *Cavalry Journal* 36 (July 1927).

Goldin, Theodore W. "Terry and Crook." *Ours, a Military Magazine*, March 1888.

Greene, Jerome A. "The Hayfield Fight: A Reappraisal of a Neglected Action." *Montana: The Magazine of History* 22, no. 4 (Autumn 1972).

Gressley, Gene M. "A Soldier with Crook: The Letters of Henry R. Porter." *Montana: The Magazine of Western History* 8 (July 1958).

Grinnell, George B. "Coup and Scalp Among the Plains Indians." *American Anthropologist* 12, no. 2 (April–June 1910).

——. "An Indian Perspective on the Wagon Box Fight." *Midwest Review* 9, no. 3 (March 1926).

Guthrie, John. "A Detail of the Fetterman Massacre." *Winners of the West*, Sept. 1939.

Hamalainem, Pekka. *The Comanche Empire*. New Haven, Conn.: Yale University Press.

Hancock, Winfield S. "The Indians." *Army and Navy Journal*, Sept. 7, 1867.

Hardin, Charles B. "The Sheepeater Campaign." *Journal of the Military Service Institution of the United States* 47 (1910).

Hasbrouck, H. C. "The Last Fight of the Campaign." In *Northwestern Fights and Fighters*, by Cyrus T. Brady. New York: McClure, 1907.

Hastings, James H. "The Tragedy at Camp Grant in 1871." *Arizona and the West* 1, no. 2 (Summer 1959).

Hazen, William B. "Some Corrections of 'Life on the Plains.'" *Chronicles of Oklahoma* 3, no. 4 (Dec. 1935).

Henely, Austin. "The Sappa Creek Fight." *Winners of the West*, Dec. 20, 1929.

[Henry, Guy V.]. "Cavalry Life in Arizona." *Army and Navy Journal*, June 10, 1871.

Howard, Oliver Otis. "Close of the Paiute and Bannock War." *Overland Monthly*, Jan. 1888.

——. "Major General George A. Crook." *Chautauquan* 11 (June 1890).

——. "Results of the Paiute and Bannock War." *Overland Monthly*, Feb. 1888.

——. "The True History of the Wallowa Campaign." *North American Review* 128 (July 1879).

Howe, George F. "Expedition to the Yellowstone River in 1873: Letters of a Young Cavalry Officer." *Mississippi Valley Historical Review* 39, no. 3 (Dec. 1952).

Hutton, Paul A. "Could Custer Have Won?" *MHQ: The Quarterly Journal of Military History* 25, no. 2 (Winter 2013).

——. "Libbie Custer." *Wild West* 25, no. 1 (June 2012).

——. "Phil Sheridan's Pyrrhic Victory: The Piegan Massacre, Army Politics, and the Transfer Debate." *Montana: The Magazine of Western History* 32, no. 2 (Spring 1982).

Isern, Thomas D. "Henry M. Stanley's Frontier Apprenticeship." *Montana: The Magazine of Western History* 28, no. 4 (Autumn 1978).

Jackson, James. "The Modoc War: A Personal Reminiscence." *Public Service Review* 1, no. 5 (June 1887).

Jacob, Richard T. "Military Reminiscences of Captain Richard T. Jacob." *Chronicles of Oklahoma* 2, no. 1 (March 1924).

Jenness, George B. "The Battle on Beaver Creek." *Collections of the Kansas State Historical Society* 9 (1904–6).

Jordan, Weymouth T., Jr. "A Soldier's Life on the Frontier, 1876–1878: Letters of 2Lt. C. D. Cowles." *Kansas Historical Quarterly* 38, no. 2 (Summer 1972).

Kanipe, Daniel A. "A New Story of Custer's Last Battle; Told by a Messenger Boy Who Survived." *Contributions to the Historical Society of Montana* 4 (1903).

Keenan, Jerry. "The Wagon Box Fight: Its Meaning and Place in History." *Montana: The Magazine of Western History* 42, no. 2 (Spring 1992).

Kelley, William F. "The Indian Troubles and the Battle of Wounded Knee." In Cozzens, *Long War for the Northern Plains.*

Kemble, E. C. "Victorio and His Young Men." In Cozzens, *Struggle for Apacheria.*

Kenny, Maurice. "Roman Nose, Cheyenne: A Brief Biography." *Wicazo Sa Review* 5, no. 1 (Spring 1989).

King, Charles. "My Friend, Buffalo Bill." *Winners of the West*, Dec. 1932.

King, James T. "George Crook, Indian Fighter and Humanitarian." *Arizona and the West* 9, no. 4 (Winter 1967).

Koster, John. "Smallpox in the Blankets." *Wild West* 25, no. 3 (Aug. 2012).

Kurz, Frederick C. "Reminiscences of an Old 8th U.S. Cavalryman." *Winners of the West*, March and April 1931.

Lee, Jesse M. "The Capture and Death of an Indian Chieftain." *Journal of the Military Service Institution of the United States* 54, no. 189 (May–June 1914).

Lemly, Henry R. "The Fight on the Rosebud." In *The Papers of the Order of the Indian Wars*, by John M. Carroll. Fort Collins, Colo.: Old Army Press, 1975.

———. "The Murder of Chief Crazy Horse." *Hunter-Trader-Trapper*, May 1933.

"Life in Arizona." *Army and Navy Journal*, Jan. 14, 1871.

Lindberg, Christer, ed. "Foreigners in Action at Wounded Knee." *Nebraska History* 71 (Fall 1990).

Littman, Max. "The Wagon Box Fight as I Saw It." In *The Bozeman Trail*, by Grace R. Hebard and E. A. Brininstool.

Loring, L. Y. "Report on [the] Coyotero Apaches." In Cozzens, *Struggle for Apacheria.*

Lubetkin, M. John. "The Forgotten Yellowstone Surveying Expeditions of 1871: W. Milnor Roberts and the Northern Pacific Railroad in Montana." *Montana: The Magazine of Western History* 52, no. 4 (Winter 2002).

———. " 'No Fighting Is to Be Apprehended': Major Eugene Baker, Sitting Bull, and the Northern Railroad's 1872 Western Yellowstone Surveying Expedition." *Montana: The Magazine of Western History* 56, no. 2 (Summer 2006).

McCormick, Lloyd S. "The Wounded Knee and Drexel Mission Fights." In Cozzens, *Wars for the Northern Plains.*

McDonald, Duncan. "The Nez Perce War of 1877—the Inside History from Indian Sources." In Cozzens, *Wars for the Pacific Northwest.*

Masterson, Murat. "General Crook's Return." In Cozzens, *Struggle for Apacheria.*

Mazzanovich, Anton. "Life in Arizona Army Posts During the 1880s." *Arizona Daily Star, Fiftieth Anniversary Edition*, 1927.

Merritt, Wesley. "Marching Cavalry." *Journal of the United States Cavalry Association* 1, no. 1 (March 1888).

Miles, Nelson A. "The Indian Problem." *North American Review* 128, no. 268 (March 1879).

———. "Rounding Up the Red Men." *Cosmopolitan*, June 1911.

Mills, Anson. "The Battle of the Rosebud." In *The Papers of the Order of the Indian Wars*, by John M. Carroll. Fort Collins, Colo.: Old Army Press, 1975.

Monnett, John H. "Indian Wars Letter Resurfaces." *Wild West* 27, no. 5 (Feb. 2015).

———. "Little Wolf: Sweet Medicine Chief." *Wild West* 25, no. 3 (Aug. 2012).

Mooar, J. Wright. "Buffalo Days." In Cozzens, *Conquering the Southern Plains.*

Moore, Horace L. "An Indian Campaign." In Cozzens, *Conquering the Southern Plains.*

Murphy, William. "The Forgotten Battalion." In Cozzens, *Long War for the Northern Plains.*

Murray, Robert A. "The Hazen Inspections." *Montana: The Magazine of History* 18, no. 1 (Winter 1968).

Myres, Sandra L. "Romance and Reality on the American Frontier: Views of Army Wives." *Western Historical Quarterly* 13, no. 4 (Oct. 1982).

Neifert, William W. "Trailing Geronimo by Heliograph." *Winners of the West*, Oct. 1935.

Omen, Kerry R. "The Beginning of the End: The Indian Peace Commission of 1867–1868." *Great Plains Quarterly* 22 (Winter 2002).

Opler, Morris E. "A Chiricahua Apache's Account of the Geronimo Outbreak of 1886." *New Mexico Historical Review* 13, no. 4 (Oct. 1938).

Payne, J. Scott. "Incidents of the Recent Campaign Against the Utes." *United Service* 2, no. 1 (1880).

Pearson, Daniel C. "Military Notes, 1876." *Journal of the United States Cavalry Association* 12, no. 63 (Sept. 1899).

Pearson, Jeffrey V. "Tragedy at Red Cloud Agency: The Surrender, Confinement, and Death of Crazy Horse." *Montana: The Magazine of Western History* 55, no. 2 (Summer 2005).

Perry, David. "The First and Second Battles in the Lava-Beds and the Capture of Captain Jack." In *Northwestern Fights and Fighters*, by Cyrus T. Brady. New York: McClure, 1907.

"Personal Story of Rain-in-the-Face." In *Indian Fights and Fighters*, by Cyrus T. Brady. Garden City, N.Y.: Doubleday, Page, 1904.

Peters, S. S. "A Military Tragedy." *National Tribune*, Oct. 4, 1894.

Pope, John. *The Indian Question: Address by General Pope, Before the Social Science Association, at Cincinnati, Ohio, May 24, 1878.* Cincinnati, n.p., 1878.

Powers, Stephan. "The California Indians: The Modocs." *Overland Monthly*, June 1873.

Quinn, Joan C. "A Mountain Charade: The Sheepeater Campaign, 1879." *Montana: The Magazine of Western History* 28, no. 1 (Winter 1978).

Rafferty, William A. "Rafferty's Trail." In Cozzens, *Struggle for Apacheria.*

Rideing, William H. "Life at a Frontier Post." *Appleton's Journal*, April 29, 1876.

Rister, C. C. "Colonel A. W. Evans' Christmas Day Indian Fight (1868)." *Chronicles of Oklahoma* 16, no. 3 (Sept. 1938).

———. "The Significance of the Jacksboro Indian Affairs in 1871." *Southwestern Historical Quarterly* 29, no. 3 (Jan. 1926).

Robertson, Francis B. "'We Are Going to Have a Big Sioux War': David S. Stanley's Yellowstone Expedition." *Montana: The Magazine of History* 34, no. 4 (Autumn 1984).

Romeyn, Henry. "The Capture of Chief Joseph and the Nez Perce Indians." In Cozzens, *Wars for the Pacific Northwest.*

Schlesinger, Sigmund. "Scout Schlesinger's Story." In Cozzens, *Conquering the Southern Plains.*

Sheridan, Philip H. "The Black Hills." *Army and Navy Journal*, April 3, 1875.

Sherman, William T. "We Do Our Duty According to Our Means." *Army and Navy Journal*, Sept. 26, 1868.

Shipp, William E. "Captain Crawford's Last Expedition." In Cozzens, *Struggle for Apacheria.*

Sibbald, John R. "Inebriates with Epaulets." *Montana: The Magazine of Western History* 19, no. 3 (Summer 1969).

Sieber, Al. "Military and Indians." In Cozzens, *Struggle for Apacheria.*

Silverstein, John. "Reminiscences of the Reno Fight." *Teepee Book* 2, no. 6 (June 1916).

Smith, Marian W. "The War Complex of the Plains Indians." *Proceedings of the American Philosophical Society* 78, no. 3 (Jan. 31, 1938).

Sumner, Edwin V. "Besieged by the Utes." *Century Illustrated Monthly*, Oct. 1891.

Sutherland, Thomas A. "Howard's Campaign Against the Nez Perce Indians, 1877." In Cozzens, *Wars for the Pacific Northwest.*

Taylor, Morris F. "Kicking Bird." *Kansas Historical Quarterly* 38, no. 3 (Autumn 1972).

Terry, Alfred H. "Indian Management." *Army and Navy Journal*, Nov. 11, 1876.

Thiel, Mark G. "The Omaha Dance in Oglala and Sicangu Sioux History." *Whispering Wind* 23, no. 5 (Fall/Winter 1990).

Thompson, William A. "Scouting with Mackenzie." *Journal of the United States Cavalry Association* 10 (1897).

Tilton, Henry R. "After the Nez Perces." *Forest and Stream and Rod and Gun*, Dec. 1877.

Trimble, Joel G. "Battle of the Clearwater." In *Northwestern Fights and Fighters*, by Cyrus T. Brady. New York: McClure, 1907.

———. "Reminiscences of Major J. G. Trimble." In *Northwestern Fights and Fighters*, by Cyrus T. Brady. New York: McClure, 1907.

Upham, Frank K. "Incidents of Regular Army Life in Time of Peace." *Overland Monthly*, April 1885.

Utley, Robert M. "The Celebrated Peace Policy of General Grant." *North Dakota History* 20, no. 3 (July 1953).

———. "The Ordeal of Plenty Horses." *American Heritage* 26, no. 1 (Dec. 1974).

Vilott, Fletcher. "Withstood the Siege: The Story of Col. George A. Forsyth's Brave Defense at Arikaree Fork." *National Tribune*, Nov. 5 and 12, 1896.

Vinton, Lawrence. "The Geronimo Campaign." In *Hostiles and Horse Soldiers*, edited by Lonnie J. White.

Voigt, Barton R. "The Death of Lyman S. Kidder." *South Dakota History* 6, no. 1 (Spring 1975).

Wells, Philip F. "Ninety-Six Years Among the Indians of the North West." *North Dakota History* 15 (Oct. 1948).

West, G. Derk. "The Battle of Sappa Creek." *Kansas Historical Quarterly* 34, no. 2 (Summer 1968).

White, Lonnie J. "Indian Raids on the Kansas Frontier, 1869." *Kansas Historical Quarterly* 38, no. 4 (1972).

White, Richard. "The Winning of the West: The Expansion of the Western Sioux in the Eighteenth and Nineteenth Centuries." *Journal of American History* 65, no. 2 (Sept. 1978).

Whitney, Chauncey B. "Beecher Island Diary." *Collections of the Kansas State Historical Society* 12 (1911–1912).

Wilkinson, Melville C. "Origins of the Difficulties with the Nez Perces." *Army and Navy Journal*, Aug. 18, 1877.

Wilmot, Luther P. "Narratives of the Nez Perce War." In Cozzens, *Wars for the Pacific Northwest.*

Woodruff, Charles A. "The Battle of the Big Hole." In Cozzens, *Wars for the Pacific Northwest.*

Zigler, Eli. "The Story of the Beecher Island Battle." In Cozzens, *Conquering the Southern Plains.*

GOVERNMENT DOCUMENTS

Annual Report of the Board of Indian Commissioners to the President of the United States. Washington, D.C.: Government Printing Office, 1873.

Annual Report of the Commissioner of Indian Affairs, 1873. Washington, D.C.: Government Printing Office, 1874.

Annual Report of the Secretary of the Interior, 1873. Washington, D.C.: Government Printing Office, 1874.

Annual Report of the Secretary of War, 1867. Washington, D.C.: Government Printing Office, 1868.

Annual Report of the Secretary of War, 1868. Washington, D.C.: Government Printing Office, 1869.

Annual Report of the Secretary of War, 1873. Washington, D.C.: Government Printing Office, 1874.

Annual Report of the Secretary of War, 1876. Washington D.C.: Government Printing Office, 1877.

Annual Report of the Secretary of War, 1880. Washington, D.C.: Government Printing Office, 1881.

31st Cong., 2nd sess. House Executive Doc. 1, Pt. 5. *Report of the Commissioner of Indian Affairs, 1850.*

33rd Cong., 1st sess. Senate Executive Doc. 1, Pt. 5. *Report of the Commissioner of Indian Affairs, 1853.*

39th Cong., 1st sess. House Executive Doc. 1, Pt. 5. *Report of the Commissioner of Indian Affairs, 1865.*

39th Cong., 1st sess. House Executive Doc. 23. *Protection Across the Continent.*

39th Cong., 2nd sess. House Executive Doc. 15. *Fort Phil Kearney* [sic] *Massacre.*

39th Cong., 2nd sess. House Executive Doc. 20. *Inspection of Military Posts.*

39th Cong., 2nd sess. Senate Executive Doc. 13. *Suppression of Indian Hostilities on the Frontier.*

39th Cong., 2nd sess. Senate Report 156. *Condition of the Indian Tribes.*

40th Cong., 1st sess. Senate Executive Doc. 2. *Protection of Trains on the Overland Route.*

40th Cong., 1st sess. Senate Executive Doc. 7. *Expeditions Against the Indians.*

40th Cong., 1st sess. House Executive Doc. 13. *Origin and Progress of Indian Hostilities on the Frontier.*

40th Cong., 2nd sess. House Executive Doc. 1, Pt. 1. *Report of the Commissioner of Indian Affairs, 1867.*

40th Cong., 1st sess. House Executive Doc. 1, Pt. 7. *Report of the Commissioner of Indian Affairs, 1868.*

40th Cong., 2nd sess. House Executive Doc. 97. *Department of Indian Affairs.*

40th Cong., 2nd sess. House Executive Doc. 97. *Report of the Indian Peace Commissioners.*

40th Cong., 2nd sess. House Miscellaneous Doc. 165. *Indian Tribes: Memorial on Behalf of the Indians, by the United States Indian Commission.*

40th Cong., 3rd sess. House Report 33. *Army Organization.*

40th Cong., 3rd sess. Senate Executive Doc. 13. *Battle of the Washita River.*

40th Cong., 3rd sess. Senate Executive Doc. 18. *Indian Battle on the Washita River.*

40th Cong., 3rd sess. Senate Executive Doc. 18, Pt. 2. *Further Information in Relation to the Late Indian Battle on the Washita River.*

40th Cong., 3rd sess. Senate Executive Doc. 36. *Indians Killed by General Custer.*

41st Cong., 2nd sess. House Executive Doc. 1, Pt. 1. *Report of the Secretary of the Interior, 1869.*

41st Cong., 2nd sess. House Executive Doc. 195. *Expedition Against Piegan Indians.*

41st Cong., 2nd sess. House Executive Doc. 246. *Difficulties with Indian Tribes.*

42nd Cong., 3rd sess. House Executive Doc. 1, Pt. 2. *Report of the Secretary of War, 1872.*

42nd Cong., 3rd sess. House Executive Doc. 201. *Modoc Indians.*

43rd Cong., 2nd sess. House Executive Doc. 1, Pt. 2. *Report of the Secretary of War, 1874.*

44th Cong., 1st sess. House Executive Doc. 1, Pt. 2. *Report of the Secretary of War, 1875.*

44th Cong., 1st sess. House Executive Doc. 1, Pt. 16. *Report of the Commissioner of Indian Affairs, 1875.*

44th Cong., 1st sess. House Executive Doc. 184. *Military Expedition Against the Sioux Indians.*

44th Cong., 1st sess. Senate Executive Doc. 81. *Hostile Demonstrations of Sioux Indians.*

44th Cong., special sess. Senate Executive Doc. 2. *Information in Relation to the Black Hills Country in the Sioux Reservation.*

45th Cong. 1st sess. House Executive Doc. 1, Pt. 5. *Report of the Secretary of the Interior, 1877.*

45th Cong., 2nd sess. House Miscellaneous Doc. 56. *Reorganization of the Army.*

45th Cong., 3rd sess. House Executive Doc. 1, Pt. 2. *Report of the Secretary of War, 1877.*

45th Cong., 3rd sess. House Executive Doc. 1, Pt. 5. *Report of the Secretary of the Interior, 1878.*

46th Cong., 2nd sess. House Executive Doc. 1, Pt. 2. *Report of the Secretary of War, 1879.*

46th Cong., 2nd sess. House Executive Doc. 38. *Ute Indian Outbreak.*

46th Cong., 2nd sess. House Executive Doc. 83. *White River Utes Investigation.*

46th Cong., 2nd sess. Senate Report 708. *Removal of the Northern Cheyenne Indians.*

49th Cong., 2nd sess. House Executive Doc. 1, Pt. 2. *Report of the Secretary of War, 1886.*

49th Cong., 2nd sess. Senate Executive Doc. 117. *Correspondence with General Miles Relative to the Surrender of Geronimo.*

50th Cong., 1st sess. Senate Executive Doc. 33. *Indian Operations.*

51st Cong., 1st sess. Senate Executive Doc. 83. *Treatment of Certain Apache Indians.*

52nd Cong., 1st sess. House Executive Doc. 1, Pt. 2. *Report of the Secretary of War, 1891.*

52nd Cong., 1st sess. House Executive Doc. 1, Pt. 15. *Report of the Commissioner of Indian Affairs, 1891.*

Memorial and Affidavits Showing Outrages Perpetrated by the Apache Indians in the Ter-

ritory of Arizona During the Years 1869 and 1870. San Francisco: Francis & Valentine Printers, 1871.

Report of Governor Grover to General Schofield on the Modoc War. Salem, Ore., n.p., 1874.

War of the Rebellion, A Compilation of the Official Records of the Union and Confederate Armies. Washington, D.C.: Government Printing Office, 1880–1901.

MANUSCRIPTS

Arizona Historical Society, Tucson
  Charles B. Gatewood Papers

Arizona State Museum, Tucson
  Charles E. Goodwin Papers

Bowdoin College, Brunswick, Maine
  Oliver Otis Howard Papers

Brigham Young University, Harold B. Lee Library, Provost, Utah
  Walter M. Camp Papers
  Edward G. Mathey, "The Washita Campaign and the Battle of the Washita"

Buffalo Bill Museum and Grave Archives, Golden, Colo.
  "As Narrated by Short Bull"

Fort Davis National Historic Site, Fort Davis, Tex.
  Robert K. Grierson Journal

History Colorado Center, Denver
  Samuel F. Tappan Papers
  Henry M. Teller Papers

Kansas Historical Society, Topeka
  Kansas History Collection: Thomas B. Murphy, "The Battle of the Arikaree"
  Miscellaneous Collections:
    Joel H. Elliott Letter, Oct. 31, 1868
    Joseph P. Rodgers, "A Few Years' Experience on the Western Frontier"

Library of Congress, Washington, D.C.
  Edward S. Godfrey Papers
  Michael McCarthy Journal
  Philip H. Sheridan Papers

Little Bighorn National Monument, Crow Agency, Mont.
  Walter M. Camp Collection:
    Luther S. Kelly Account
    Young Two Moon Interview

National Archives and Records Administration, Washington, D.C.
  Record Group 48: Records of the Office of the Secretary of the Interior, Indian Division

General Records Entry 665: Proceedings of the Indian Peace Commission, 1867–1868
Record Group 94: Adjutant General's Office, Letters Received, 1805–1889
    Eugene A. Carr, "Report of Operations August to September 3, 1881"
Record Group 94: Records of the Office of the Adjutant General
Record Group 98: Records of the Office of the Adjutant General
    Correspondence Pertaining to the Ute War
Record Group 153, Records of the Judge Advocate General's Office
    Court-Martial Case Files, QQ2821 (Noch-ay-det-klinne Affair)

Newberry Library, Chicago
Edward E. Ayer Manuscript Collection:
    James S. Brisbin to Edward S. Godfrey, Jan. 1, 1892
    Myles Moylan, "Report of the Battle of Bear Paw Mountain"
Edward D. Graff Collection:
    William J. Fetterman Letter, Nov. 26, 1866
Benjamin H. Grierson Papers
Special Collections: Theodore W. Goldin, "A Bit of the Nez Perce Campaign"
George M. Templeton Papers

Rutherford B. Hayes Presidential Center Library, Spiegel Grove, Fremont, Ohio
George Crook Letter Book
Rutherford B. Hayes Papers

Texas State Library and Archives, Austin
Records of Edmund Jackson Davis, Texas Office of the Governor

U.S. Army Heritage and Education Center, Carlisle, Pa.
Eugene A. Carr Papers
Crook-Kennon Papers
Azor H. Nickerson, "Major General George Crook and the Indians"
Order of the Indian Wars Collection:
    Lewis D. Greene, "The White River Campaign"
    Edward E. Hardin, "Early Service in the Army"
    Charles W. Taylor, "The Surrender of Red Cloud"

University of California, Bancroft Library, Berkeley
Hubert Howes Bancroft Collection
    William H. Boyle, "Personal Observations on the Conduct of the Modoc War"

University of Colorado, Boulder
William Carey Brown Papers

University of Oklahoma, Walter S. Campbell Collection Western History Collection, Norman
Aaron M. Beede Correspondence
Robert P. Higheagle, "How Sitting Bull Was Made a Chief"
———. "Memories of Sitting Bull"

Valentine T. McGillycuddy Correspondence
One Bull, "Information in Sioux and English with Regard to Sitting Bull"
———. "Prophecy of Sitting Bull of Complete Annihilation of Custer and His Soldiers"
———. "Sitting Bull's Sun Dance Vision"
White Bull, "Sitting Bull and the Sun Dance"

Washington State Libraries, Pullman
  Lucullus V. McWhorter Papers

NEWSPAPERS

Aberdeen (S.D.) Daily News
Aberdeen (S.D.) Weekly News
Arizona Republic (Phoenix)
Bismarck Tribune
Boston Journal
Chadron (Neb.) Democrat
Cheyenne Leader
Chicago Daily Inter Ocean
Chicago Times
Chicago Tribune
Cincinnati Daily Enquirer
Cincinnati Daily Gazette
Cincinnati Enquirer
Cleveland Plain Dealer
Daily Missouri Democrat (St. Louis)
Daily Nebraska Press (Nebraska City)
Dakota Republican (Vermillion, S.D.)
Dallas Weekly Herald
Denver Tribune
Galveston Tri-weekly News
Grand Forks (N.D.) Daily Herald
Greeley Tribune
Hardin (Mont.) Tribune
Harper's Weekly
Helena Daily Independent
Helena Weekly Herald
Idaho Statesman (Boise)
Indianapolis Sentinel
Kansas Weekly Champion and Press (Atchison)
Klamath (Ore.) Express
Las Cruces (N.M.) Thirty-Four
Las Vegas (N.M.) Weekly Optic
Lawrence (Kans.) Bulletin
Leavenworth Bulletin
Missouri Democrat (St. Louis)
Montana Post (Virginia City)
New York Evening Post

New York Herald
New York Herald Tribune
New York Post
New York Times
New-York Tribune
New York World
Omaha Republican
Omaha Weekly Herald
Oregonian (Portland, Ore.)
Owyhee Avalanche (Silver City, Idaho)
Pampa (Tex.) Daily News
Philadelphia Inquirer
Philadelphia Post
Portland (Ore.) Daily Press
Prescott (Ariz.) Weekly Journal
Rockford Daily Register
Rocky Mountain News (Denver)
San Francisco Bulletin
Sioux City (Iowa) Journal
Springfield (Mass.) Republican
St. Paul Daily Press
Topeka State Record
Trenton Evening Times
Tucson Arizona Citizen
Tucson Daily Star
Tucson Weekly Star
Virginia City Territorial Enterprise
Washington (D.C.) Daily Intelligencer
Washington (D.C.) Evening Star
Washington (Pa.) Reporter
Yankton (S.D.) Press and Dakotan

INTERNET SOURCES

Russell, Samuel L. "Major Samuel Marmaduke Whitside's Campaign Letters," Army at Wounded Knee. http://armyatwoundedknee.com/2014/08/01/major-samuel-marmaduke-whitsides-campaign-letters/.

Taylor, Rodney G. "Indian Casualties of the Little Bighorn." http://www.littlebighorn.info/.

INDEX

ILLUSTRATION CREDITS

William T. Sherman: National Archives and Records Administration

Red Cloud: Library of Congress, LC-USZ62-91032

Captain William J. Fetterman: Courtesy of First Division Museum at Cantigny

A Plains Indian village in winter: Nelson A. Miles, *Personal Recollections and Observations of General Nelson A. Miles*. Chicago: Werner Publishing Company, 1896

"Buffalo Soldiers": *Century Illustrated Monthly Magazine*, October 1891

On a winter campaign: Richard I. Dodge. *Our Wild Indians: Thirty-Three Years' Personal Experience among the Red Men of the Great West*. Hartford: A. D. Worthington and Company, 1882

"The Fight for the Pony Herd": Nelson A. Miles, *Personal Recollections and Observations of General Nelson A. Miles*. Chicago: Werner Publishing Company, 1896

Winfield S. Hancock: National Archives and Records Administration

Kiowa Chief Satanta: National Anthropological Archives, Smithsonian Institution, SPC BAE 3912-B Vol. 1 01158200

George and Elizabeth Custer: Library of Congress, LC-DIG-cwpbh-03129

Custer discovers corpses: Richard I. Dodge. *Our Wild Indians: Thirty-Three Years' Personal Experience among the Red Men of the Great West*. Hartford: A. D. Worthington and Company, 1882

Philip H. Sheridan: National Archives and Records Administration

The Battle of Beecher Island: *Harper's New Monthly Magazine*, June 1895

Custer leads at the Battle of the Washita: Richard I. Dodge. *Our Wild Indians: Thirty-Three Years' Personal Experience among the Red Men of the Great West*. Hartford: A. D. Worthington and Company, 1882

Ranald S. Mackenzie: National Archives and Records Administration

Chief Quanah: National Anthropological Archives, Smithsonian Institution BAE GN 01746A2 06299100

Kicking Bird: National Archives and Records Administration

Chief Lone Wolf: National Anthropological Archives, Smithsonian Institution SPC BAE 3912-B Vol 1 01159200

Nelson A. Miles: National Anthropological Archives, Smithsonian Institution SPC BAE 4605 01605206

Red River War: Nelson A. Miles, *Personal Recollections and Observations of General Nelson A. Miles*. Chicago: Werner Publishing Company, 1896

Palo Duro Canyon: Photograph by author

Captain Jack: National Anthropological Archives, Smithsonian Institution, SPC BAE 4605 01604204

Edward R. S. Canby: Library of Congress, LC-B813-6574

Toby Riddle: National Anthropological Archives, Smithsonian Institution

George Crook: National Anthropological Archives, Smithsonian Institution, SPC BAE 4605 01604805

Sitting Bull: Library of Congress, LC-USZ-62-111147

Custer's expedition into the Black Hills: National Archives and Records Administration

Chief Washakie: National Anthropological Archives, Smithsonian Institution, BAE GN 01666 06287300

Alfred H. Terry: Library of Congress, LC-BH83-2231

John Gibbon: Library of Congress, LC-BH83- 2231

The Custer Fight: Library of Congress, LC-USZCN4-268

The killing of Crazy Horse: Thomas Powers, *The Killing of Crazy Horse.* New York: Knopf, 2010

Dull Knife and Little Wolf: National Anthropological Archives, Smithsonian Institution, BAE GN 00270B 06108800

Slaughter of Chief Dull Knife's band: *Harper's New Monthly Magazine,* August 1897

Oliver Otis Howard: Library of Congress, LC-USZ62-100786

Chief Joseph: National Archives and Records Administration

Ollokot: Cyrus T. Brady, *Northwestern Fights and Fighters.* New York: The McClure Company, 1907

Chief Looking Glass: National Archives and Records Administration

Nathan C. Meeker: A1-4233, City of Greely Museums, Greeley, Colorado

Ute Jack: National Anthropological Archives, Smithsonian Institution, SPC BAE 4605 01603607

Battle of Milk Creek: *Century Illustrated Monthly Magazine,* October 1891

Chief Victorio: National Anthropological Archives, Smithsonian Institution, SPC Sw Apache NM ACC 20263 Cat 129781 #9–49 02040900

Geronimo: Library of Congress, LC-USZ62-36613

Chihenne Chief Loco: National Anthropological Archives, Smithsonian Institution, Negative 2519 B

Geronimo and General Crook: National Anthropological Archives, Smithsonian Institution, SPC Sw Apache No # Group Portraits 02089200

Chiricahua prisoners of war: National Archives and Records Administration

Sitting Bull's cabin: National Anthropological Archives, Smithsonian Institution, Photo Lot 89-8

The Opening of the Fight at Wounded Knee: Harper's Weekly, January 24, 1891

Chief Big Foot: National Archives and Records Administration